Warfare in History

THE NORWEGIAN INVASION
OF ENGLAND IN 1066

Warfare in History

General Editor: Matthew Bennett
ISSN 1358–779X

THE NORWEGIAN INVASION
OF ENGLAND IN 1066

Kelly DeVries

THE BOYDELL PRESS

First published 1999
The Boydell Press, Woodbridge

ISBN 0 85115 763 7

The Boydell Press is an imprint of Boydell and Brewer Ltd
PO Box 9, Woodbridge, Suffolk IP12 3DF, UK
and of Boydell and Brewer Inc.
PO Box 41026, Rochester, NY 14604–4126, USA
website: http://www.boydell.co.uk

A catalogue record for this book is available
from the British Library

Library of Congress Cataloging-in-Publication Data
DeVries, Kelly, 1956–
    The Norwegian invasion of England in 1066 / Kelly DeVries.
        p.   cm. – (Warfare in history, ISSN 1358–779X)
    Includes bibliographical references and index.
    ISBN 0–85115–763–7 (hardback : alk. paper)
    1. Harold, King of England, 1022?–1066.   2. Harald III Harðráði,
King of Norway, 1015–1066.   3. Great Britain – History, Military –
449–1066.   4. Stamford Bridge, Battle of, 1066.   5. Great
Britain – History – Invasions.   6. Norway – History, Military.
I. Title. II. Series.
DA161.D48   1999
942.02'1 – dc21   99–37405

This publication is printed on acid-free paper

Printed in Great Britain by
St Edmundsbury Press Ltd, Bury St Edmunds, Suffolk

CONTENTS

MAPS AND GENEALOGIES

To the Midgley Family:

Michael, Elizabeth, Edward, Emma, Matthew, Eleanor, and William

and to their extended family
in the Wharfe Valley Branch and Leeds 1st Ward
who have proven that the people of Yorkshire in the 1990s
are much more friendly to foreigners
than their ancestors were in 1066

GENERAL EDITOR'S PREFACE

The Norwegian invasion of England in 1066 only lasted a few days and ended in disaster. It might seem a difficult task then to write such a substantial book as this on the subject. Yet although the history of Haraldr Harðráði's last campaign was brief, bloody and terminal for the great warrior, the context in which his bid for the English throne lay has bever been explored in such detail before. Kelly DeVries is able to lay bare the personal, dynastic and military history of all the main participants on that fateful day at Stamford Bridge, just outside York.

Haraldr's own career had taken him as far as Constantinople and Sicily, via the kingdom of Kiev where he had acquired a bride. His acquisition of the Norwegian throne in 1047 provided the incentive for his daring bid for the far greater prize of England two decades later. In his entourage, and also dead by the end of the day, was Tostig, the younger brother of the English king Harold Godwinson. The opposition of the two brothers bears testimony to the tangled events that preceded the crisis year of 1066, which witnessed two coronations and the triumph of a French-speaking Norman rather than a Scandinavian. Fifty years earlier, of course, a Scandinavian king had come to power. Knútr the Great and his successors had ruled for a quarter of a century, drawing England into a North Sea orbit which the events of 1066 were decisively and permanently to change.

Yet this is not apparent even by the end of 1066, for another Scandinavian ruler, Sveinn Estriðson, king of Denmark, had a claim to the English throne. Long after the defeat of the Norwegians the Danes were to play a significant if eventually unsuccessful role in English military affairs in the late 1060s and early 1070s. In 1085, the preparations of Sveinn's son Knútr the Good to invade England forced William I into hugely expensive defensive measures. Their cost directly influenced the organization of the survey known as Domesday Book, by which the Conqueror sought to calculate his kingdom's resources. As late as 1098, another Norwegian king, Magnús 'Barelegs', could sail in the Irish Sea, land at Chester and defeat and kill its Norman earl.

So Scandinavian influence in English affairs did not cease after Stamford Bridge, nor did Scandinavian and Icelandic historians lose interest in events there. Professor DeVries' love for saga material comes over well in this volume. He is able to draw upon an enormously wide range of source materials and proudly demonstrates his knowledge of Old Norse. He is able to supplement Latin narrative and documentary references with the richly evocative descriptions of Snorri Sturluson and the Norwegian Kings Sagas, together with pithy translations of skaldic poetry. Anyone interested in the late Viking era will find fascinating insights from the materials upon which the author has drawn.

Many aspects of the book read like a detective story, too, as Professor

DeVries attempts to untangle the skein of events in England prior to 1066. He explores the role of Godwin, who rose to be earl of Wessex, and his sons, as military legitimate rulers – warlords – who were too important even for a king to dismiss for long. Godwin returned triumphant from a brief exile in 1051–52 to drive out Edward the Confessor's Norman favourites and create the circumstances which eventfully enabled Harold Godwinson to take the throne on 6 January 1066. His military career is studied in some detail as is the military organisation of Anglo-Saxon (really Anglo-Scandinavian) England. There is plenty in this volume to excite the interest of military historians together with a challenging reassessment of what Professor Warren Hollister called *Anglo-Saxon Military Institutions on the Eve of the Conquest* (Oxford, 1962). That title may be taken to sum up older, more stereotyped views of the changes which came about in the kingdom of England after 1066, which imply that somehow its inhabitants were hanging around waiting for William, duke of Normandy, to come and take over. This may seem obvious with hindsight; but as the author explains, it could all have been very different but for the Norwegian invasion of 1066.

Matthew Bennett
Royal Military Academy Sandhurst
1999

ACKNOWLEDGMENTS

This book began nearly twenty years ago when I entered my final year as an undergraduate student at Brigham Young University. As an Honors Program student, I had the option of doing an undergraduate thesis, known at Brigham Young University as a University Scholar's Project. As I was the only student in a Medieval Studies program developed for me by the Department of Humanities there, I had the freedom to write my thesis on almost any subject and under any of a number of professors on campus. I had read about this obscure Norwegian invasion of England which preceded by less than a month the Norman invasion of that same kingdom in 1066, and I thought that it would be fun to write about it. As I had already taken several Latin courses and was then enrolled in an Old English course, I figured that the primary source material would not be difficult to work with which it proved not to be (I was given approval to use Snorri Sturluson's *King Harald's Saga* in translation for the Old Norse material). The resulting 150-page manuscript passed without difficulty, but the thought that I had not completely researched the story bothered me throughout my graduate and professorial careers. I did not choose to work on the subject for my Ph.D. dissertation, at the University of Toronto's Centre for Medieval Studies, nor for my first two books, although I did publish an article derived from my University Scholar's Project in the first issue of *Scintilla*, the Centre for Medieval Studies' graduate student journal. However, as I was suffering through a small amount of writers' block in writing my last book, I took out the old thesis and began to read through and rework what I had previously written. The result eventually became this book. What had begun as a 150-page manuscript has grown into more than a 700-page one. It has also delved far more into the subject than I ever thought that I would or could, and it has come a lot closer to answering the questions which have bothered me about the subject for nearly twenty years.

Many wonderful teachers and scholars have assisted me with this book. I would like to thank those individuals at Brigham Young University who helped me with the initial project: Professors Paul Pixton of the History Department (who served as my advisor at the time), George Tate of the Humanities Department, Larry Best of the English Department, Thomas Mackay of the Classics Department, and Eugene England of the Honors Program. I would also like to thank my colleagues and teachers at the Centre for Medieval Studies, especially Dr Harry Roe, who in my first year there taught me Old Norse. His method of teaching is considered by many to be a bit unorthodox, but it worked for me, although I am sure that Harry never thought that my language skills would amount to anything. Finally, I would like to thank my colleagues and students at Loyola College in Maryland. They continue to be very supportive of my work. Among the latter, I would like to extend a special thanks to Ashley Loper. As an student in love with medieval Scandinavia, Ashley approached me as a sophomore and asked if I might help him in studying the history and literature of the subject. By the end, he had taken all of my history courses, as well as two directed reading courses in Old Norse language and literature. This, above all, helped me to reawaken my Old Norse linguistic skills, and I cannot thank him enough for the help that he gave me. Indeed, some of the translations which I have used were those which he and I worked through in his final Old Norse course when we focused on the Norwegian Kings' Sagas of Haraldr Harðráði.

In addition, I cannot thank my wife, Barbara Middleton, and children, Elisabeth, Michael, and Catherine, enough for their love, patience, and tolerance. Hey Catie, here's another book I've written! (That's an in-family joke which I will be glad to divulge to anyone who should ask.)

I dedicated my first book to my family; of course, all my books are dedicated to them. However, my special dedication for *The Norwegian Invasion of England in 1066* goes to a family who has also made itself my family: the Midgleys. In 1994 I went to the first International Medieval Congress in Leeds, England. Staying on after the conference, the Midgleys met me at church and 'adopted' me. I hope in some small way that this dedication will help repay their kindness and hospitality. After all, this book is set practically in their backyard.

CHAPTER ONE

INTRODUCTION

THE BATTLEFIELD OF Hastings has always been a location regarded with respect and honor. William the Conqueror set aside his place of victory by establishing a monastery, fittingly called Battle Abbey, less than five years after having defeated King Harold II (Godwinson) there. It is owned by English Heritage, having purchased the site from the Webster family in 1976 using a sizeable grant from American donors. Today, while scurrying rabbits might have replaced the Norman horses, one can still see a battlefield at which the course of English history was changed.

At Stamford Bridge, several hundred miles to the north of Hastings, none of the same honor or prestige can be found. There is no abbey, nor is there a commemorative cross or even a modern historical plaque evident near the battlefield. The bridge itself is also modern and probably does not cross the river at the place where its eleventh-century predecessor once did. In fact, no one can really be sure where it was that, not four weeks prior to Hastings, on 25 September, 1066, another battle was fought, this one won by Harold II against a large invading Norwegian army led by its king, Haraldr Harðráði.

So it seems that the battle of Stamford Bridge is a conflict which has been forgotten or, at best, played down in modern English memory. William's army at Hastings put him on the throne of England and, as military history has always established, it is the victors who write the history of warfare, leaving others only to ask questions which begin with 'what if.' What if William the Conqueror had landed before Haraldr Harðráði, as the Norman duke had initially planned to do? Would the English language now have more of a Scandinavian quality? Of course, all of this presupposes that Harold Godwinson had only one victory in 1066, and that in this case it would have been over the Normans, while his loss would have been to the Norwegians. Alternatively, William might have had to face Haraldr Harðráði; could he have had only one victory in 1066, thus perhaps losing to the Norwegians himself? Would he have been able to succeed against them as Harold Godwinson did? Had he defeated Haraldr Harðráði, might his policy against the north of England have been different, less a 'harrying' and more an alliance?

Questions like these are not popular among academic historians, and this book will not delve into them itself. Let the reader do that, for this is a book not interested in the Norman Conquest of England in 1066. In fact, William the Conqueror, while certainly an important figure in forming the history of mid-eleventh-century England, is actually a minor character in this story, one far less important than Harold Godwinson or Haraldr Harðráði, and even less important than Edward the Confessor, Tostig Godwinson, Eadgyða (Edith) Godwinson, Gruffydd ap Llywelyn, or Baldwin V of Flanders. This is a book about the first two important battles of 1066, those fought at Fulford Gate on 20 September 1066 and at Stamford Bridge five days later.

Why were there three important battles fought between defending and invading forces of England in 1066, and why is the battle at Stamford Bridge so important? The answer is simple, but not well understood by the myriad of historians who have written only about the war between Harold Godwinson and William the Conqueror. The eleventh century was a century completely dominated by warlords. They threatened and frightened their neighbors with their warlike actions, a violence which they used to gain power, land, and wealth, not entirely unlike our modern concept of warlords as African, South American, or Middle Eastern dictators who control and manipulate their neighbors by threats of bellicosity. They lived by a law of military legitimacy, the idea that they could not guarantee their own security among their numerous lords and nobles who were suspicious of their political ascension without showing these same individuals military victory. Once victory was achieved, these warlords could rest in the assurance that for someone to try and remove them from their throne, he would have to defeat an experienced and victorious general. How better to ally with him, and thereby profit from that general's military legitimacy, than to attack him and risk the wrath and might of those who had been wise enough to attach themselves to his entourage, to become his companion and not his enemy.

We need not look far to find a military legitimate warlord in the eleventh century. William the Conqueror certainly was one, first in northern France and then in England; so too was William's Norman cousin, Robert Guiscard, in Sicily and southern Italy. Emperor Henry III was one, determining his power in the Holy Roman Empire, Italy, and the Low Countries by domestic repudiation and foreign conquest. Baldwin V of Flanders was also one, fighting against both the Holy Roman Empire and France, and, although losing for the most part in these conflicts, winning enough military respect and/or fear that he eventually could control and manipulate most of northern Europe. Later in the century, we might also be able to call the leaders of the First Crusade military legitimate warlords, for they too, in the personages of Godfried and Baldwin of Bouillon, Bohemond of Antioch, Tancred, and others, were able to rise far above their more hierarchical noble counterparts to control not only the actions of the Crusaders, but also the lands won from their conquests.

Two of those not mentioned very often when discussing successful military leaders of the eleventh century are Haraldr Harðráði and Harold Godwinson. Few have defined them as military legitimate warlords, and none, in my research, since Edward August Freeman, and then only Harold Godwinson. For the legacy of both is that of a loser. Yet they were not!

Haraldr Harðráði was a successful warlord. Although beginning his rise to fame by being spirited from the battlefield of Stiklarstaðir, wounded in the vain attempt to restore his brother, Óláfr (later Saint Óláfr), to the throne of Norway, Haraldr later fought victoriously first as a leader of the Kievan Russian troops of Grand Prince Iaroslav, then as a member and later captain of the Byzantine Varangian Guard in the Mediterranean and Constantinople, and finally as co-king and then king of Norway against Denmark and England. That he lost at the battle of Stamford Bridge to Harold Godwinson does not diminish these activities.

The victor in that battle, Harold Godwinson, was also a successful warlord. Even before coming to the English throne on 6 January 1066, he had won great military victories, primarily against the Welsh, and had become regarded as military legitimate to those in his kingdom. Undoubtedly, this is the reason why he was given the throne of England by Edward the Confessor, who was not himself a warlord, but was wise enough to protect himself first with the very powerful warlord, Godwin, and then with his equally powerful son, Harold Godwinson (Edward's attempt to rule without these warlords, in 1051–52, proved disastrous enough to convince him of renewing these alliances). This is also why he was confirmed in this conferral by the witenagemot, despite their promises of rule to William the Conqueror. Once on the throne, Harold Godwinson won another great victory, over Haraldr Harðráði, at Stamford Bridge. That he lost at Hastings does not seem so demeaning, historically, in view of these victorious adventures.

This is the purpose of this book: to reacquaint those interested in the history of eleventh-century England with the events leading up to the battle of Hastings, to detail what happened *before* William became the Conqueror and changed the history of Europe. It is a military history, one which will show not only that Haraldr Harðráði and Harold Godwinson were military legitimate warlords equal to others in the eleventh century, but also that they were able either to work with and gain respect from other warlords of their time, or to contend against them, still retaining the respect and honor of an impressed ally or an enemy who recognized that war was won less from brilliance than it was lost from stupidity or 'bad luck.' When they faced each other, it was a clash resembling few others in the Middle Ages, one which, if we follow through with the argument, guaranteed the result at the battle of Hastings. But that is a conclusion which will not be dwelt on here. This is more of an old-fashioned war story, a narrative giving the details of the first 1066 invasion and not conjecturing on what it might have meant to the second one.

This book will give both sides of the Norwegian Invasion of England, although, as neither side comes out victoriously by the end of 1066, sometimes this is difficult to do with the sources available. It will begin by briefly discussing the Anglo-Scandinavian atmosphere of eleventh-century England, especially in the earldom of Northumbria. It will then introduce the major players in the story: Haraldr Harðráði, Godwin and his family, and Harold Godwinson. A chapter will focus on the conflict between Harold and his rebellious brother, Tostig, who joined forces with Haraldr Harðráði in his invasion of England. Then it will move on to a brief description of what constituted the Norwegian and English armies, their strategy, technology and tactics. Finally, the book will end with a two-chapter chronological description of the Norwegian invasion: Haraldr Harðráði's and Tostig's campaign along the coast of Northumbria, the battle of Fulford Gate, Harold Godwinson's march to the north, and, ultimately, the battle of Stamford Bridge.

Before going on, it is necessary to briefly discuss the original sources on which this book is based. As this history is a narrative, almost all of these sources, those addressing the history from an English perspective, from a Norwegian perspective, and from a 'foreign' perspective, are narrative in nature: chronicles, saints' lives, sagas, narrative poems, etc. Few non-narrative sources for this history exist, although from an English perspective, at least, the Domesday Book does help in analyzing ownership, and hence power, patterns among the Godwin family.

The English, that is the Anglo-Saxon/Anglo-Norman, sources are well known and analyzed in great detail elsewhere,[1] so it is not my intention to dwell on them. For this study, these sources basically fall into three categories: those which were written in England close to the time of the events which they discuss; those written (or, in the case of the Bayeux Tapestry, embroidered) in England or Normandy after the conquest of William the Conqueror but before the turn of the twelfth century; and those written in England or Normandy during the early part of the twelfth century by historically astute writers compiling their histories from other earlier sources and eye-witnesses.

The first category contains only the *Anglo-Saxon Chronicle* (in most of its versions) and the *Vita Ædwardi regis*. To historians of pre-conquest England, the *Anglo-Saxon Chronicle* really needs no introduction. It is by far the most extensive and most trustworthy source, or more properly group of sources, which exists from the period. Composed in Old English at no fewer than five monastic sites, it was begun during the ninth century – some say during the reign and at the behest of Ælfred the Great – and continued in at least one form until 1154. (One Latin version was also written.) During the middle of the eleventh century, anonymous monastic authors were still writing three versions of the *Anglo-Saxon Chronicle*, identified as C, D, and E. Of these, only E's place of composition is known, Peterborough Abbey, with D thought also to be a northern composition, possibly from York, Worcester, or Evesham. C was probably finished at Abingdon, although where it was started is unknown. These provenances are based on biases evident within the various versions of the chronicle, as all of the versions of the work have their 'favored' and their 'not-so-favored' individuals and factions. Let the reader be cautious, however, as these biases have been identified by modern historians and are anything but certain. For example, although the *Anglo-Saxon Chronicle* (D and E) are gener-

---

[1] See, for example, Antonia Gransden, *Historical Writing in England, c.550 to c.1307* (Ithaca, 1974) and A.G. Rigg, *A History of Anglo-Latin Literature 1066–1422* (Cambridge, 1992).

ally accorded northern composition, it is C which best reports the events of the Norwegian invasion into Northumbria, including, although added by a later hand, being the only one of these three versions to report the story of the lone Norwegian defending the bridge over the Ouse River during the battle of Stamford Bridge. Its narrative also stops at this battle without recording the battle of Hastings or William the Conqueror's invasion, although it is generally assumed that this part of the chronicle has been lost as the single manuscript of C is incomplete. Because there are frequent problems with the recorded dates in this source, I have chosen to cite any footnote references with the version's identification letter and then the date under which the author of the chronicles placed the referred-to passage before identifying the page number where the reference will be found; in the text, I will only identify the letter of the version being cited.[2]

The second contemporary source written in England before (or more probably during the year of) the conquest was the *Vita Ædwardi regis qui apud Westmonasterium requiescit*. This very valuable historical work was discovered only last century and is extremely important as a source of what was going on in and around Edward the Confessor's court, especially concerning the eldest of Godwin's children: Eadgyða (Edith), Edward's queen, Harold, Edward's chief earl, and Tostig, the earl of Northumbria. It is thought to have been composed by a Flemish monk from St Omer residing at court and under the patronage of Eadgyða, and the anonymous author of this work was not only an astute witness to the events of his time, but also a poetic psychologist of the individuals whom he was chronicling. Written in Latin, it avoids any description of the Norwegian or the Norman invasions, while the battle of Stamford Bridge is referred to only in metaphoric verse, and the battle of Hastings is not mentioned at all. Generally it is believed that this was because of the pain which these events caused to the author's patron, as she lost four of her brothers in these battles. Finally, while not being a saint's life in the truest sense, meaning that it does not record any miracles or divinations of Edward the Confessor, it does record Edward's life as one of spirituality, chastity, and concern for his kingdom, issues which would be developed into the miraculous by later hagiographers. Frank Barlow made an excellent edition and translation of this source, now published in a second edition in the Oxford Medieval Text Series.[3]

---

2 The edition which I have used is *Anglo-Saxon Chronicle* in *Two of the Saxon Chronicles Parallel*, 2 vols., ed. Charles Plummer and John Earle (Oxford, 1892). Although a number of fine translations of this work exist, I have chosen to make my own translation of all passages taken from this work. For a study of this source see Gransden, pp. 32–41.

3 *Vita Ædwardi regis qui apud Westmonasterium requiescit*, ed. and trans. F. Barlow, 2nd edn (London, 1992). For a discussion of this work see Gransden, pp. 63–66 and Rigg, pp. 12–13. I have used other lives of Edward sparingly. Those include: Osbert of Clare, *La vie de S. Édouard le Confesseur par Osbert de Clare*, ed. M. Bloch, *Analecta Bollandiana* 41 (1923), 5–131; Aelred of Rielvaux, *Vita sancti Aedwardi regis*, ed. J.P. Migne, *Patriologia latina*, 195 (Rome, 1855); and *L'Estoire de Seint Aedward le Rei*, ed. and trans. H.R. Luard, in *Lives of Edward the Confessor* (London, 1858).

One other narrative source should also perhaps be placed in this category, *The Waltham Chronicle*. Although undoubtedly written at Waltham Abbey after the conquest, because this was a monastery established and patronized by Harold Godwinson, it contains some very valuable information about him not contained elsewhere, including details on the identification of his corpse. A fine edition and translation of it, by L. Watkiss and Marjorie Chibnall, also appears in the Oxford Medieval Text Series.[4]

There are four important sources written (or woven) in England or Normandy after Duke William's conquest but before 1100 which contain historical details of importance for a history of the Norwegian Invasion of England. Two of these were written by monastic chroniclers who were adherents to the Conqueror and never write anything of him that is negative – consequently, they never write anything that is positive about Harold Godwinson or any of the other members of the Godwin family. William of Poitiers' *Gesta Guillelmi* was written sometime in the middle 1070s by a former soldier turned clerical writer of noble background who served as chaplain to William's invasion army and was thus probably an eyewitness to the conquest of England and the battle of Hastings.[5] William of Jumièges' *Gesta Normannorum ducum* was probably written even earlier, in the early 1070s, than the *Gesta Guillelmi* of William of Poitiers, but it is believed that it was composed in Normandy, and most probably at the abbey of Jumièges. Yet its writer, a monk at the abbey of Jumièges, knew quite a lot about the invasion of England by William the Conqueror which had taken place less than a decade earlier, and some of the events leading up to it, which he may have derived from eyewitness testimony. The *Gesta normannorum ducum*, a history of all the dukes of Normandy, as its title indicates, was reworked and added to later in the century by Orderic Vitalis and Robert of Torigni.[6]

A third source, the *Carmen de hastingae proelio*, has been much discussed of late by historians. Called into question are its credibility and date. A rambling but extraordinarily detailed poem on the battle of Hastings, the *Carmen de hastingae proelio* also contains a few details about events leading up to this battle which cannot be found elsewhere. More than likely it is this narrative poem was composed around 1100; the author was a great fan of the Conqueror and vehemently opposed to Harold Godwinson's right to rule in England, although

---

4 *The Waltham Chronicle: An Account of the Discovery of Our Holy Cross at Montacute and Its Conveyance to Waltham*, ed. and trans. L. Watkiss and M. Chibnall (Oxford, 1994). See also Gransden, p. 271.

5 William of Poitiers, *The Gesta Guillelmi of William of Poitiers*, ed. and trans. R.H.C. Davis and M. Chibnall (Oxford, 1998). See also Gransden, pp. 98–103, and R.H.C. Davis, 'William of Poitiers and his History of William the Conqueror,' in *The Writing of History in the Middle Ages: Essays Presented to Richard William Southern*, ed. R.H.C. Davis and J.M. Wallace-Hadrill (Oxford, 1981), pp. 71–100.

6 William of Jumièges, *The Gesta Normannorum ducum of William of Jumièges, Orderic Vitalis, and Robert of Torigni*, ed. and trans. E.M.C. van Houts, 2 vols. (Oxford, 1995). See also Gransden, pp. 94–99.

perhaps not the eyewitness to the battle that scholars once thought.[7] All of these works appear well edited with good facing page translations in the Oxford Medieval Text Series. A final work to be included in this group is the Bayeux Tapestry. This unprecedented and unequaled narrative tapestry actually adds very little to the narrative of the Norwegian Invasion of England, except that it does describe the visit of Harold Godwinson to Normandy in the mid-1060s and his pledges to William the Conqueror at that time. It is also an excellent source for the study of arms and armor of the period, weaponry which was also used by the Norwegians in their invasion of England as well as the Anglo-Saxons and Normans, as portrayed in this almost cinematic work of art.[8]

Of far more importance to the subject of this book than those works just mentioned are narrative histories of six Anglo-Norman authors writing in the early twelfth century. Not needing to praise a living conqueror, these authors, John of Worcester, Symeon of Durham, Henry of Huntingdon, William of Malmesbury, Orderic Vitalis, and Geoffrey Gaimar, all wrote histories which they derived from other historical works as well as the memories of their elders. As such, they seem to have written histories which do not carry the historiographical baggage of those works written during the life of William the Conqueror. They were all of at least partial English parentage, except probably for Geoffrey Gaimar.

Of these works, undoubtedly the most important for the history of the events leading up to the battle of Stamford Bridge is that of John of Worcester. His chronicle was once thought to have been written by two individuals, the earliest of whom was named 'Florence,' but recent research undertaken primarily by the work's latest editor-translators, R.R. Darlington and P. McGurk, has determined it to be the work of one author named John. Little is known about John of Worcester, who wrote his chronicle from c.1118 to 1140. He appears to have been born in England, was a monk at Worcester, was learned in Old English and Latin, and had an ability to seek out historical minutiae which brought him

---

[7] *Carmen de hastingae proelio*, ed. C. Morton and A. Muntz (Oxford, 1972). This work has generated quite a lot of discussion lately. See Gransden, pp. 97–99; Rigg, pp. 15–17; Frank Barlow, 'The *Carmen de hastingae proelio*,' *The Norman Conquest and Beyond* (London, 1983), pp. 189–222; R.H.C. Davis, 'The *Carmen de hastingae proelio*,' *English Historical Review* 93 (1978), 231–61; and Elisabeth M.C. van Houts, 'Latin Poetry and the Anglo-Norman Court, 1066–1135: The *Carmen de Hastingae proelio*,' *Journal of Medieval History* 15 (1989), 39–62.

[8] The best source for the *Bayeux Tapestry* illustrations is *The Bayeux Tapestry: A Comprehensive Survey*, ed. by Frank M. Stenton, 2nd edn (London, 1957). There are a number of recent works on the historical use of the *Bayeux Tapestry*. Some of these include: N.P. Brooks and H.E. Walker, 'The Authority and Interpretation of the Bayeux Tapestry,' *Proceedings of the Battle Conference* 1 (1978), 1–34; Shirley Ann Brown, 'The Bayeux Tapestry: History or Propaganda?' in *The Anglo-Saxons: Synthesis and Achievement*, ed. J.D. Woods and D.A.E. Pelteret (Waterloo, 1985), pp. 11–25, 153–54; H.E.J. Cowdrey, 'Towards an Interpretation of Bayeux Tapestry,' *Anglo-Norman Studies* 10 (1987), 49–65; and David S. Spear, 'Recent Scholarship on the Bayeux Tapestry,' *Annales de Normandie* 42 (1992), 221–26. See also the collected articles in Richard Gameson, ed., *The Study of the Bayeux Tapestry* (Woodbridge, 1997).

respect from some, including Orderic Vitalis, and plagiarism from others, namely Symeon of Durham. Finally, he displayed an inordinate amount of English patriotism which shows itself in an attentive partiality to the Godwin family when the political atmosphere of his time spoke against it.[9]

Sometime before John of Worcester finished his *Chronicle*, a copy of what he had written up to 1118 was delivered to the monastery at Durham where it came into the hands of a monk possibly named Symeon. Using this book, this monk, whose identity is disputed, composed his own history of Anglo-Saxon and early Anglo-Norman history which he titled *Historia regum*. Although primarily a rewriting of John of Worcester's narrative, Symeon of Durham does add a few interesting and original facts, mostly dealing with northern England issues; he is, for example, the only source which identifies the location of the first battle fought in the Norwegian Invasion as Fulford Gate. Symeon of Durham is also credited with writing a religious history of Durham, which has been used in a couple of places.[10]

Another important twelfth-century Anglo-Norman chronicler is Henry of Huntingdon. Henry was born in 1080 either in Cambridgeshire or Huntingdonshire, and was educated more than likely while serving as a young man in the episcopal court of Lincoln. Rising to the office of archdeacon, he began composing his *Historia Anglorum* before 1133 and would continue to write until 1154, when he is presumed to have died. His knowledge of and love for the English people is evident in his entire chronicle, which was especially popular after its completion, and his work adds much to our knowledge of late Anglo-Saxon history.[11]

The most prolific and perhaps most famous of all twelfth-century Anglo-Norman historians is undoubtedly William of Malmesbury. Born in 1095, or slightly earlier, William was the offspring of a Norman father and an English mother. He was learned in many fields, and collected and studied classical as well as more contemporary histories, all of which aided him in his composition of a history of the English kings, the *Gesta regum Anglorum*, and another of the English archbishops and bishops, the *De Gestis pontificum Anglorum*, as well as a history of more recent events, a history of Glastonbury, especially of its ecclesiastic affairs, and several saints' lives. All of these were accorded high honors

---

[9] John of Worcester, *The Chronicle of John of Worcester*, ed. R.R. Darlington and P. McGurk, trans. J. Bray and P. McGurk, 2 vols. (Oxford, 1995, 1999). See also Gransden, pp. 143–48 and R.R. Darlington and P. McGurk, 'The "Chronicon ex chronicis" of "Florence" of Worcester and Its Use of Sources for English History Before 1066,' *Anglo-Norman Studies* 5 (1982), 185–96.

[10] Symeon of Durham, *Historia regum*, ed. T. Arnold, 2 vols. (London, 1882–85), and *Historia ecclesiae Dunhelmensis*, ed. T. Arnold (London, 1882). See also Gransden, pp. 115–16, 148–51.

[11] Henry, archdeacon of Huntingdon, *Historia Anglorum: The History of the English People*, ed. and trans. D. Greenway (Oxford, 1996). See also Gransden, pp. 193–200 and Rigg, pp. 36–40.

in his day, and they have continued to be praised today.[12] Antonia Gransden writes: 'As a historian William deserves his reputation for two reasons: he occupies an important place in the development of historical method, and his works are repositories of information and views of value to the historian today.'[13]

Orderic Vitalis' *Ecclesiastical History* was probably begun and its history of the 1066 invasions of England written in the early twelfth century. Born in Shrewsbury in 1075, Orderic Vitalis was, like William of Malmesbury, the product of a Norman father and an English mother. However, Orderic's father was a priest, and he sent the later historian to St. Évroul in Normandy while Orderic was still a child, probably around the age of ten. From then until the end of his life, probably 1141/42, he lived away from his homeland. During thirty of those years, he wrote an ecclesiastical history which focused to a large part on Normandy and William the Conqueror and his sons. It is a lengthy work, which has been partly reworked and edited. It is also extremely valuable for any historical research of the period.[14]

A final twelfth-century Anglo-Norman historical writer to introduce briefly is Geoffrey Gaimar. Far less is known or can be discerned about Gaimar than his colleagues. It is not known who he was, although there is an indication in his *Lestoire des Engles* that he had some connection with the important founder of monasteries, Walter Espec. He also displays a special knowledge of the history of Hampshire, Lincolnshire, and the north of England, which may indicate a background from there, while at the same time he writes in vernacular (Anglo-Norman) octosyllabic rhyming couplets, which may indicate a Norman background. The latter is generally ruled out, however, as he shows a favoritism to the English over the Normans in most matters, the Godwin family's concerns excluded. It is believed that he finished his narrative poem in England sometime before 1140.[15]

The above works, with the exception of Gaimar, Symeon of Durham, and William of Malmesbury's *De gestis pontificum Anglorum*, have all recently appeared in the Oxford Medieval Text Series.

The Norwegian sources are much less well known, and far less used by historians writing on the history of Norway, let alone England, during this period. Part of the reason for this is the dating of most of these sources, with only one contemporary chronicle, not written in Norway, detailing any of the history of

12 The works which are of most use to this study are: William of Malmesbury, *Gesta regum Anglorum: The History of the English Kings*, ed. and trans. R.A.B. Mynors, R.M. Thomson, and M. Winterbottom, 2 vols. (Oxford, 1998) and William of Malmesbury, *De gestis pontificum Anglorum*, ed. N.E.S.A. Hamilton (London, 1870). See also Gransden, pp. 166–85 and Rodney Thomson, *William of Malmesbury* (Woodbridge, 1987).

13 Gransden, p. 167.

14 Orderic Vitalis, *The Ecclesiastical History of Orderic Vitalis*, ed. and trans. M. Chibnall, 6 vols. (Oxford, 1969–80). See also Gransden, pp. 151–65 and Marjorie Chibnall, *The World of Orderic Vitalis* (Oxford, 1984).

15 Geoffrey Gaimar, *Lestoire des Engles*, ed. T.D. Hardy and C.T. Martin, 2 vols. (London, 1888–89). See also Gransden, pp. 209–12.

Haraldr Harðráði, and most others, dating from the late twelfth or early thirteenth century, primarily the Norwegian Kings' Sagas. Part of the reason is also linguistic, with only one of the Norwegian Kings' Sagas translated from Old Norse to English.

The single contemporary narrative source for eleventh-century Scandinavian history, *Gesta Hammaburgensis ecclesiae pontificum*, was not even written in Scandinavia but in Hamburg. Its author, Adam of Bremen, wrote this work, completed in 1075, at the behest of the archbishop of Hamburg–Bremen, Adalbert, in an effort to demonstrate his claim to ecclesiastical dominion over all of Scandinavia. As such, Adam not only describes the history of that region, through which he seems to have traveled extensively, but also highlights its paganism and lack of civilization in order to show that the inhabitants were incapable of ecclesiastically governing themselves. He failed to do so – this governance responsibility went to a new see in Lund – but his work was nevertheless very popular among later Scandinavian writers. Not to be missed in his criticism is Haraldr Harðráði, although Adam of Bremen does positively report some of the king's activities which not even the highly favorable Norwegian Kings' Sagas record.[16]

A later chronicle which borrows from Adam of Bremen is Saxo Grammaticus' *Gesta Danorum*. Written between 1170 and 1200 in a difficult Latin style, giving its Danish author his cognomen, this work is far less critical of the Scandinavians and their history than Adam was, although it too is more favorable to the church than it is to the secular powers. This has indicated to some scholars that Saxo was patronized by Archbishop Absalon of Lund, a church reform archbishop who frequently ran up against royal hindrances in his efforts to extend his ecclesiastical goals. Critical of kings this chronicle may be, but when it comes to defending the Danish king, Sveinn Estriðson, against the bellicosity of King Haraldr Harðráði of Norway, there is no question where this Danish author's loyalty lies.[17]

Neither of these sources was written in Norway, but it was there that the strongest of the late Viking kings ruled. By the end of the twelfth century this began to be recognized, resulting in a large number of works written over the next half-century devoted to the history of these strong rulers. Generically known as the Norwegian Kings' Sagas because of their stylistic similarities to those literary works also being composed at the time, most of them were written in the vernacular Old Norse and were highly favorable to the Norwegian kings,

---

[16] Adam of Bremen, *Gesta Hammaburgensis ecclesiae pontificum*, ed. B. Schmeidler, 3rd edn (Hanover, 1917). For a discussion of Adam's work, see the Introduction in Adam of Bremen, *History of the Archbishops of Hamburg–Bremen*, trans. F.J. Tschan (New York, 1959), and Birgit Sawyer and Peter Sawyer, *Medieval Scandinavia: From Conversion to Reformation, circa 800–1500* (Minneapolis, 1993), pp. 222–24.

[17] Saxo Grammaticus, *Historia Danica*, ed. P.E. Müller and J.M. Velschow, 2 vols. (Hannover, 1839). (Although its nineteenth-century editor has chosen to call the work *Historia Danica*, it is better known by the title *Gesta Danorum*.) See also Sawyer and Sawyer, pp. 2, 221–26.

particularly to the man who ruled Norway from 1046 until he was killed invading England in 1066, Haraldr Harðráði.

The only exception to both of those characteristics is the *Monumenta historica Norvegiæ* written by a man known only as Theodoricus. Composed c.1180, although the work ends in 1130, Theodoricus wrote in Latin and probably at the instigation of the exiled archbishop of Niðaróss, Øysteinn, who was staying in England from 1180 to 1183 at the command of the king of Norway, Sverri, with whom he differed on church reform issues. This may make Theodoricus English, although his historical work in no way confirms this suspicion, especially in its rather abbreviated account of the Norwegian invasion of England.[18]

Perhaps written in opposition to Theodoricus' *Monumenta historica Norvegiæ* was the *Ágrip af Nóregs konunga sögum*. Composed in Norway within a decade of Theodoricus' history and perhaps under the patronage of King Sverri, who judged the former work to be too critical of his royal ancestors, this also very brief saga actually repeats almost verbatim the short remarks of Theodoricus about King Haraldr and his invasion of England. However, its Old Norse language indicates that it may have had a more popular audience than its predecessor.[19]

Following the *Ágrip*'s vernacular precedent, but adding a great deal more detail, were the three early thirteenth-century Norwegian Kings' Sagas on which much of the history of Haraldr Harðráði and his invasion of England in 1066 must needs be based. The *Morkinskinna*, *Fagrskinna*, and Snorri Sturluson's *Heimskringla* were all written in Iceland about the same time, 1220–1230. Which came first is almost pure conjecture – most scholars claim that *Morkinskinna* was written first, with *Fagrskinna* following it by only a couple of years, followed by Snorri Sturluson's *Heimskringla* – and, while ties between *Morkinskinna* and *Fagrskinna* seem to have been established, and perhaps between *Fagrskinna* and *Heimskringla*, these too are speculative at best. The authors of *Morkinskinna*, which literally means 'rotten skin,' perhaps an indication of the material on which it was originally written, and *Fagrskinna*, which means 'fine skin', are now unknown and little about them can be determined from the texts themselves,[20] but Snorri Sturluson, the author of *Heimskringla*, meaning 'the orb of the world,' is justifiably considered to be the most famous composer of sagas. Not only was he perhaps the most prolific author of these works, but he

---

[18] Theodoricus, *Monumenta historica Norvegiæ: Latinske kildeskrifter til Norges historie I middelalderen*, ed. G. Storm (Christiana (Oslo), 1880). See also Sawyer and Sawyer, pp. 226–27.

[19] *Ágrip af Nóregs konunga sögum*, ed. F. Jónsson (Halle, 1929). See also Sawyer and Sawyer, pp. 226–27 and R.G. Poole, *Viking Poems on War and Peace: A Study in Skaldic Narrative* (Toronto, 1991), pp. 7–10.

[20] *Morkinskinna: Pergamentsbog fra første halvdel af det trettende aarhundrede*, ed. C.R. Unger (Christiania (Oslo), 1867) and *Fagrskinna: Kortfattet Norsk Konge-Saga*, ed. P.A. Munch and C.R. Unger (Christiania (Oslo), 1847). See also Sawyer and Sawyer, pp. 219–20 and Poole, pp. 7–17.

was also adept in writing poetic works as well as prose. Additionally, Snorri Sturluson was a great diffuser of early Scandinavian myths, with many of these known only because of his recording of them. Of course, this has led some scholars to denounce Snorri's historical sagas, found principally in the lengthy *Heimskringla*, also as fiction. But this charge is simply unfounded, for Snorri does nothing more than any other narrative historical writer of his age does. Indeed, one might say that he is more conscious of his role as a historian than many other medieval writers, and in some instances he seems more cautious too in what he writes. For example, in describing some of Haraldr Harðráði's deeds, he pauses and remarks (in the first person plural):

> And although many more of his famous deeds are not written, these came not as history and thus were not included, because we will not put unsubstantiated stories into this book. Although we have heard more stories and have obtained more parts of stories, it seemed to us better that the work should be enlarged later than be required to have things removed from it.[21]

Furthermore, Snorri Sturluson acknowledges the problems that all historians face when assembling their histories from various sources: some details are from better sources than others, but some must be believed simply because it would be a break from learned tradition not to believe them. Thus he begins the *Heimskringla*:

> In this book I let be written old narratives about rulers who have had king-doms in Scandinavia and have spoken in the Danish language which I have heard from well-informed men, also certain histories of previous generations as they were taught to me. Some of this is found in genealogies of kings or other well-descended men who have traced their families, and some is written from old declarations or narrative poems which men have had to entertain themselves. And although we do not know the truth of these, we know that old, learned men have judged such to be true.[22]

A further vernacular Norwegian Kings' Saga, the *Flateyjarbók*, a fifteenth-century compilation of the *Morkinskinna*, *Fagrskinna*, *Heimskringla*, and other

---

[21] Snorri Sturluson, *Heimskringla*, ed. B. Aðalbjarnarson, 3 vols. (Reykjavik, 1941–51), III:118–19:

En þó er miklu fleira óritat hans frægðarverka. Kømr til þess ófrœði vár ok þat annat, at vér viljum eigi setja á bœkr vitnislausar sǫgur. Þótt vér heyrt rœður eða getit fleiri hluta þá þykkir oss heðan í frá betra, at við sé aukit, en þetta sama þurfi Ñr at taka.

[22] Snorri Sturluson, *Heimskringla*, I:3–4:

Á bók þessi lét ek rita fornar frásagnir um hǫfðingja þá, er riki hafa haft á Norðrlöndum ok á danska tungu hafa mælt, svá sem ek hefi heyrt fróða menn segja, svá ok nǫkkurar kynslóðir þeira sum þat, er finnsk í langfeðgatali, þar er konungar eða aðrir stórættaðir menn hafa rakit kyn sitt, en sumt er ritat eptir fornum kvæðum eða söguljóðum, er menn hafa haft til skemmtanar sér. En þótt vér vitim eigi sannendi á því, þá vitum vér dœmi til, at gamlir frœðimenn hafi slíkt fyrir satt haft.

For an assessment of the *Heimskringla* as history see Sawyer and Sawyer, pp. 219–20 and Poole, pp. 7–18, 167.

works now lost, will also be used, although primarily for information not included in the other Norwegian Kings' Sagas.[23]

As Snorri Sturluson has rightly observed, discerning what actually happened is always a difficult matter for the historian, but it is his or her chief responsibility. In this work, the sagas will be used as historical sources, despite their dates and reputations, although always in conjunction with other, 'more trustworthy' original sources.

In translating passages from all of these sources, with the exception only of those included in the Oxford Medieval Text Series, I have used my own translations. As in the quotations above, the translation will appear in the body of the text with the quotations in their original languages appearing in the footnotes. Also, on the frequent occasions when I have disagreed with the translators of the Oxford Medieval Text Series, and have retranslated a passage, or part of a passage, a reason why I have done so will also appear in the footnotes.

Finally, I wish to say something briefly about the spellings of the many names which occur throughout this book. In keeping with one of the themes of this book, that England in 1066 was very much an Anglo-Scandinavian realm, I have retained the original spellings of names. This means that names of individuals born in Scandinavia, primarily in Norway and Denmark, retain their Old Norse spellings, and those born in England retain their Old English spellings. This may confuse some readers who are accustomed to reading a modern English 'normalization' of these names, but it is certainly a more accurate representation of their eleventh-century identity. Thus, Knútr = Cnut (or Canute), Harðaknútr = Hathacnut, Sveinn Estriðson = Swein Estrithson, Óláfr = Olaf, Gyða = Gytha, Eadgyða = Edith, Gyrð = Gyrth, and, in particular, Haraldr Sigurðson 'Harðráði' = Harald (or Harold) Sigurdson 'Hardrada.' Pronunciation of these names is sometimes made more difficult than it needs to be. Two fast rules to remember are: all 'ð' or 'þ,' either capitalized or in lower-case, are most easily pronounced as 'th'; and the nominative 'r' at the end of Scandinavian names is silent.

While Scandinavian and English names retain their Old Norse and Old English spellings, for ease of transmission, Byzantine and Russian names are spelled using Roman letters.

---

23 *Flateyjarbók: En samling af Norske Konge-Sagaer*, ed. G. Vigfusson and C.R. Unger, 3 vols. (Christiania (Oslo), 1860–68).

CHAPTER TWO

ANGLO-SCANDINAVIAN ENGLAND

WHEN THE mid-eleventh-century English worried about foreign invaders, they looked east and north, toward Scandinavia, before they looked south and west, toward Normandy.

In 789, when the event occurred which the *Anglo-Saxon Chronicle* (E) later recorded as

> Here, King Breohtric took the daughter of Offa, Eadburge, to wife. And in his days there came for the first time three ships of Northmen from Hörthaland. And then the reeve rode there, and he wanted to take them to the king's town, for he did not know what they were. And these men killed him. That was the first time that ships of the Danes had sought the land of the English,[1]

there was probably no indication that a new, extremely formidable enemy had set its sights on England. By 793, that blissful ignorance had been completely erased. Again, it is recorded in the *Anglo-Saxon Chronicle* (E):

> Here, terrible portents were come over the Northumbrian land, which miserably frightened the people; there were huge flashes of lightning, and fiery dragons were seen flying in the air. Much hunger soon followed these signs, and a little after that in the same year, on January 8, the raiding of heathen men miserably destroyed God's church on Lindisfarne Island by looting and the killing of men.[2]

---

[1] *Anglo-Saxon Chronicle*, in *Two of the Saxon Chronicles Parallel*, 2 vols., ed. Charles Plummer and John Earle (Oxford, 1892), E 787, I:55:
> Her nam Breohtric cining Offan dohter Eadburge. ⁊ on his dagum comon ærest .iii. scipu Norðmanna of Hereða lande. ⁊ þa se ge refa þær to rad. ⁊ he wolde drifan to ðes cininges tune þy he nyste hwæt hi wæron. ⁊ hine man ofsloh þa. Ðæt wæron þa erestan scipu Deniscra manna þe Angel cynnes land gesohton.

See also *Anglo-Saxon Chronicle* (A and F) 787, I:54; Frank M. Stenton, *Anglo-Saxon England*, 3rd edn (London, 1971), p. 239; Henry R. Loyn, *The Vikings in Britain* (Oxford, 1994), pp. 38–39; F. Donald. Logan, *The Vikings in History*, 2nd edn (London, 1991), pp. 37–38; Else Rosedahl, *The Vikings*, trans. S.M. Margeson and K. Williams (Harmondsworth, 1992), p. 233

[2] *Anglo-Saxon Chronicle* (E) 793, I:55–57:
> Her wæron reðe forebecna cumene ofer Norðanhymbra land. ⁊ þ folc earmlice bregdon; þ wæron ormete ligræscas, ⁊ wæron gescowene fyrene dracan on þam lyfte fleogende. þam tacnum sona fyligde mycel hunger. ⁊ litel æfter þam þæs ilcan geares

England was not the first target nor the only target of the Scandinavian Vikings, for that is the name which modern scholarship calls all of these raiders, whether from Sweden, Denmark, Norway, or, later, Iceland, and the British Isles. Nor did England offer any more resistance against the Vikings than did any other target, at least among the British Isles,[3] but England's proximity to Norway and Denmark, as well as its large number of unfortified, and virtually undefended, monasteries, villages and towns made it a land which probably saw more than its fair share of early raids.

For a while, these Scandinavian raiders, carried onto the English shores in their dragon-prowed ships, were content to feast on the easy monastic and small urban pickings which were spread throughout the countryside. These were fairly rich locations waiting, it seems, for someone to attack them. The fact that they were filled with unarmed ecclesiastics and farmers meant nothing to the raiders whose plunder and booty, for it was in a sense a military operation, would be returned to their homelands, giving purpose to their journeys away from their families and fields, while at the same time inspiring new Viking raiding voyages.[4] Eventually, the Vikings even wintered in England, establishing base camps from which they could raid longer and farther inland than ever before.[5]

Naturally, the English did not succumb to these attacks without defending themselves. Many local kings and chieftains tried to oppose these early to mid-eighth-century expeditions, but they were largely unsuccessful, although their lack of success has more often been blamed on their disunity and disorganization than on the Vikings' military capabilities. Often these brave but unsuccessful defenders of their lands met their own ends at the hands of the invaders, adding more plunder to the Viking coffers and another saint to the heavens.[6]

Finally, one of these local kings, Æðelred, king of the West Saxons, put together an army which began to successfully oppose the Scandinavian invaders. He, and, after his death in April 871, his successor, Ælfred, defeated the Vikings in battles fought at Englefield and Ashdown. Then, although previously having

on .vi. idus Iañr earmlice heðenra manna hergung adiligode Godes cyrican in Lindisfarena ee. þurh reaflac. ꝺ man sleht.
See also *Anglo-Saxon Chronicle* (A and F) 793, I:54–56; Stenton, *Anglo-Saxon England*, p. 239; Loyn, *Vikings in Britain*, p. 39; Logan, pp. 38–40; and Gwyn Jones, *A History of the Vikings* (London, 1968), pp. 194–96. This idea was also confirmed in 794 when the Vikings burned the monastery at Jarrow.
3 For these attacks on the British Isles outside of England see Loyn, *The Vikings in Britain*, pp. 30–38; Logan, pp. 40–56; and Rosedahl, *The Vikings*, pp. 210–32.
4 Stenton, pp. 240–45; Loyn, *Vikings in Britain*, pp. 39–41; Logan, pp. 141–58; Rosedahl, *The Vikings*, pp. 234–39; and Peter Sawyer, *The Age of the Vikings* (New York, 1962), pp. 120–24.
5 Logan, pp. 151–54 and Sawyer, *Age of Vikings*, pp. 126–29. On the wintering of the Vikings in England see Rosedahl, *The Vikings*, pp. 237–39, and Martin Biddle and Birth Kjølbye-Biddle, 'Repton and the Vikings,' *Antiquity* 66 (1992), 36–51.
6 The perfect example of this is the East Anglian king, Edmund (later known as Saint Edmund the Martyr) who was killed defending his lands against the Vikings in 869. See Loyn, *Vikings in Britain*, pp. 40–41.

suffered a number of small defeats against the Vikings, in 878 Ælfred won a major, although hardly decisive victory against the 'Danish great army' at Edington.[7] Ælfred also devised a system of fortifications, earth-and-wood ramparts, known as *burhs* which surrounded many of the larger and previously unfortified towns in his kingdom.[8] All of this led to peace treaties being signed, a diminishing of Viking activity, and Ælfred's assumption of the kingship over the entirety of England. Ælfred became 'the Great.'[9]

In reality, of course, the Vikings never left England. Indeed, none of the peace treaties signed by Ælfred and his opponents even required this. The reason was quite simple. The Scandinavians, for a very long time, had ceased being simply foreign raiders. They had begun to settle parts of England, especially in the north and east. No one knows when the first of these settlements had been founded, or even why some Scandinavians, especially from Norway and Denmark, had decided to leave their rural existences in their homelands to take up equally rural existences in the British Isles. (It was not only England which gained a large number of settlers, but also Scotland, the Orkney, Shetland, and Faroe Islands, Wales, and Ireland.) Some historians, especially those who wish to diminish the historical weight of the raiding activities of the Vikings, wish to place the initial date of settlement early in the eighth century; they contend that this in fact was the premise for raiding in the first place, to scout out and 'prepare' these lands for settlement. Others place the date later in the century. Whatever the answer, by the time of Ælfred's victories in the south, an extremely large number of Scandinavian settlements had been founded in what would later be the earldoms of Northumbria, Mercia, and East Anglia.[10]

---

[7] On the battle of Edington see Richard P. Abels, *Alfred the Great: War, Kingship and Culture in Anglo-Saxon England* (London, 1998), pp. 161–62.

[8] On the *burhs* built by Ælfred and his successors, Eadward (the Elder), his son, and Æðelflæd, his daughter, see Logan, pp. 154–58; Abels, *Alfred the Great*, pp. 194–207; Kelly DeVries, *Medieval Military Technology* (Peterborough, 1992), pp. 194–97; Richard P. Abels, *Lordship and Military Obligation in Anglo-Saxon England* (Berkeley and Los Angeles, 1988), pp. 58–78; David Hill and Alexander R. Rumble, eds., *The Defence of Wessex: The Burghal Hidage and Anglo-Saxon Fortifications* (Manchester, 1996); Edward J. Schoenfeld, 'Anglo-Saxon *Burhs* and Continental *Burgen*: Early Medieval Fortifications in Constitutional Perspective,' *Haskins Society Journal* 6 (1994), 49–66; and Bernard Bachrach and Rutherford Aris, 'Military Technology and Garrison Organization: Some Observations on Anglo-Saxon Military Thinking in Light of the Burghal Hidage,' *Technology and Culture* 31 (1990), 1–17.

[9] Stenton, *Anglo-Saxon England*, pp. 245–76; Loyn, *Vikings in Britain*, pp. 41–46; Jones, pp. 220–29, 877–78, 892–96; and Logan, pp. 144–51. Abels, *Alfred the Great*, readjusts some of Ælfred's history while not demeaning his achievements.

[10] On the Scandinavian settlements in England see Loyn, *Vikings in Britain*, pp. 77–117; Logan, pp. 165–72, Rosedahl, pp. 239–50; Sawyer, *Age of the Vikings*, pp. 45–66; Peter Sawyer, *Kings and Vikings: Scandinavia and Europe, AD 700–1100* (London, 1982), pp. 102–08; Neils Lund, *De Danske vikinger i England* (Copenhagen, 1967); Neils Lund, *De Hærger og de brænder: Danmark og England i vikingtiden* (Copenhagen, 1993); David Hey, *Yorkshire from AD 1000* (London, 1986), pp. 11–23; Dawn M. Hadley, ' "And They Proceeded to Plough and to Support Themselves": The Scandinavian Settlement of England,' *Anglo-Norman Studies* 19 (1996), 69–96; and, for a case-study, Christine Mahaney and David

Even more importantly, these Scandinavian settlers had done more than simply move into the neighborhood. They had integrated themselves into the institutions and the culture, and among the people. In doing so, they had become Christian, and they had begun to write using a Latin script, but they in turn, had their own influences. They began to affect the language, changing it from an Germano-Celtic to a Anglo-Scandinavian mixture. Place names became Scandinavian, and governing nobles took on Scandinavian titles. York, that once great seat of Roman power, especially became Scandinavianized, with the settlements of Vikings far surpassing those of the non-Vikings in size, and the rulership over the community as a whole falling to men carrying names such as Óláfr Guðríðson, Óláfr Sigtryygson, and Eiríkr Blóðøx (Bloodaxe). Most importantly for later history, these settlements adopted the Scandinavian legal system, an adoption which to a great extent gave a reason to the name which this Scandinavian-settled area was known as, the Danelaw.[11] By 878, when Ælfred began to sign peace treaties with his Viking opponents, it would have been impossible to demand the removal of all Scandinavians from Anglo-Saxon England, for, in reality, Anglo-Saxon England had become Anglo-Scandinavian England.

For more than a century, from 878 to 980, England was largely at peace with its Scandinavian neighbors, both those living across the seas and those living in the Danelaw. There had been a few raids, it is true, but almost all of these were made into the Anglo-Scandinavian north by Viking chieftains mostly wishing to extend their political control over more than their own British Isle regions.[12] Most, too, had failed in these endeavors. In the south of England, away from most Anglo-Scandinavian influence, the royal descendants of Ælfred had prospered. Eadward (or Eadweard) 'the Elder' (899–924), followed by Æðelstan (924–39) and Eadgar (959–75), were strong and powerful rulers who even managed to reconquer much of the Anglo-Scandinavian English lands, while at the same time retaining peaceful relationships with the Scandinavians abroad.[13] Æðelstan even raised Hákon, the son of the Norwegian king, Haraldr Hárfagri (Finehair), as his own 'foster-son' in his English court.[14] Even poorer kings, Eadmund (939–46), Eadred (946–55), and Eadwig (955–59) did not encourage a breakdown in peaceful relations with either the English or foreign Scandinavians.

However after the death of Eadgar, and the murder of his son, Eadward, in

Roffe, 'Stamford: The Development of an Anglo-Scandinavian Borough,' *Anglo-Norman Studies* 5 (1982), 197–219. Many more works could be cited. For an excellent survey of the literature on this subject up to 1976 see Inge Skovgaard-Petersen, 'Vikingerne I den nyere forskning,' *Historisk tidsskrift* (Copenhagen) (12) 5 (1971), 651–721.

11 On the changes brought about by the influence on and from the Scandinavians in this part of England see Stenton, *Anglo-Saxon England*, pp. 502–25; Loyn, *Vikings in Britain*, pp. 89–101; and Logan, pp. 158–65.

12 Logan, pp. 161–62.

13 Stenton, *Anglo-Saxon England*, pp. 319–63 and Loyn, *Vikings in Britain*, pp. 46–51.

14 Loyn, *Vikings in Britain*, p. 50.

975, England fell into a period of political unrest and instability.[15] Perhaps this is the reason for the renewed Viking attacks from 980 on, although most historians seem to believe that this instability, while certainly destructive to the English defensive capabilities, was only coincidental to a renewed drive by Scandinavian political powerhouses, principally the kings of Norway and Denmark, as well as other, lesser chieftains, to increase their non-Scandinavian holdings. Raids were undertaken in 980 against Southampton, the Isle of Thanet, Cheshire, and the southwest. This was followed by the looting of London and other key southern English locations, places which had once seemed quite safe from these invaders. In 991, the battle of Maldon was fought and lost; celebrated in the famous Old English vernacular poem, this defeat led to the first payment of a ransom known as 'Danegeld.'[16] In 994, the Norwegian chieftain, Óláfr Tryggvason, who had fought at Maldon and profited from the Danegeld, returned to England in the company of the Danish king, Sveinn Haraldsson, known to history as 'Fork-beard' because of his uniquely shaped beard. Despite being driven back from London, the two gained much Danegeld from their other bellicose activities. Óláfr was converted to Christianity and did not return, but Sveinn's appetite for conquest had only been whetted. His return would become almost annual. Peace disappeared, as can be seen in a selection of passages from the *Anglo-Saxon Chronicle* (E):

> 994 . . . And they . . . wrought the most evil which any army might do, in burning and raiding and slaughter of men, both along the sea coast in Essex and in the land of Kent and Sussex and in Hampshire.
> 997. Here in this year the army traveled throughout Devonshire into the mouth of the Severn, and there they raided, both in Cornwall and in North Wales and in Devon; then they went up at Watchet, and there wrought much evil by burning and by the slaughtering of men, and after that traveled back through-out Penwith Tail to the south side, and traveled then into the mouth of the Tamar, and then went up until they came to Lydford, and burned and killed everything that they met, and burned down Ordwulf's monastery in Tavistock, and brought incredible war-booty with them to the ships.
> 1001. Here the army came to the mouth of the Exe and then went up to the stronghold, and were determinedly fighting there, and the men determinedly and ardently withstood them, then they traveled through the countryside, and did what they were accustomed: killing and burning. Then there was gathered an immense army of Devon people and Somerseters, and then they came together at Pinhoe; and as soon as they joined battle the English army gave way and many were slaughtered there, and then rode over the countryside; and

---

15 Stenton, *Anglo-Saxon England*, pp. 370–74.
16 On the renewal of Scandinavian attacks during this period see Stenton, *Anglo-Saxon England*, pp. 375–79; Loyn, *Vikings in Britain*, pp. 64–65; Logan, 172–78; and Rosedahl, *The Vikings*, pp. 250–55. On the battle of Maldon see Eric John, 'War and Society in the Tenth Century: The Maldon Campaign,' *Transactions of the Royal Historical Society* (5) 27 (1977), 173–91 and the various articles in D. Scragg, ed. *The Battle of Maldon, AD 991* (London, 1991).

each following occasion was always worse than the one before; and they brought much war-booty with them to the ships, and traveled from there into the Isle of Wight, and there traveled wherever they wished, and nothing withstood them. No navy on sea nor army on land dared approach them, however far inland they went. In every way it was a heavy time, because they never left off their evil.

1004. Here Sveinn came with his fleet to Norwich, and raided and burned down all the town.

1010. Here in this year after Easter the aforesaid army came to East Anglia, and traveled to Ipswich, and went straight to where they had heard that Ulfcytel was with his army . . . And then the East Anglians immediately fled; then Cambridgeshire firmly stood against them. There was killed Æðelstan, the king's son-in-law, and Oswy and his son, and Wulfric, Leofwine's son, and Eadwig, Ælfic's brother, and many other good thegns and countless people . . . and the Danes had possession of the place of slaughter, and then became horsed and afterwards took over East Anglia, and for three months raided and burned that land; they even traveled into the wild fens, and they killed men and cattle, and burned throughout the fens, and burned down Thetford and Cambridge, and afterwards traveled southwards onto the Thames; and the horsed men rode towards the ships, and afterwards quickly traveled westwards into Oxfordshire, and from there into Buckinghamshire, and so along the Ouse until they came to Bedford, and so on until Tempsford; and always burned as they traveled. Then they traveled back to their ships with their war-booty . . . Then before the feast of St. Andrew [November 30], the army came to Northampton and immediately burned down the market-town and round about there seized for themselves as much as they wanted, and from there traveled over the Thames into Wessex, and so on towards Cannings Marsh, and burned it all. Then, when they had gone as far as they wanted, they came to their ships in midwinter.[17]

---

[17] *Anglo-Saxon Chronicle* (E), I:129–41:

994 . . . hi ahredde wið heora feondum. ⁊ hi þanon ferdon. ⁊ wrohton þ mæste yfel þe æfre ænig here don mihte on bærnette ⁊ hergunge ⁊ on manslihtum ægðer be ðam særiman on EastSeaxum, ⁊ on Centlande. ⁊ on SuðSeaxum.

997. Her on þisum geare ferde se here abutan Defnan scire in to Sæfernmuðon. ⁊ þær gehergodon ægðer on Cornwealum ge on Norðwalum. ⁊ on Defenan. ⁊ eodon him þa úp æt Wecedport. ⁊ þær mycel yfel wrohton on bærnette. ⁊ on manslihtum. ⁊ æfter þam wendon eft abutan Penwihtsteort on ða suðhealfe. and wendon þa in to Tamermuðan. & eodo'n' þa up oð þa hi comon to Hlidaforda. ⁊ ælcþing bærndon ⁊ slogon þ hi gemetton. ⁊ Ordulfes mynster æt Tefingstoce forbærndon. ⁊ un ascgendlice here huðe mid him to scipa brohtan.

1001. Her com se here to Exanmuðan. ⁊ úp ða eodan to ðere byrig. ⁊ þær fæstlice feohtende wæron. Ac him man swyðe fæstlice wiðstod. ⁊ heardlice. Ða gewendon hi geond þ land. ⁊ dydon eall swa hi bewuna wæron. Slogon ⁊ beorndon. Þa gesomnode man þær ormæte fyrde of De'fe'nisces folces. ⁊ Sumorsætisces. ⁊ hi ða tosomne comon æt Peonnho. ⁊ sona swa hi togædere fengon. þa beah seo Englisce fyrd. ⁊ hi þær mycel wæl ofslogon. ⁊ ridan þa ofer þ land. ⁊ wæs æfre heora æftra syð wyrse þonne se ærra. ⁊ mid him þa mycele herehuðe to scipon brohtan. ⁊ þanon wendon in Wiht land. ⁊ þær him ferdon onbuton swa swa hi sylf woldon. ⁊ him nanþing ne wiðstod. ne him to ne

Many more selections of this type could be included. All give the same impression: England had become a kingdom completely overrun by the violent incursions of Scandinavian invaders. The king, Æðelred II, sometimes called 'the Unready' because of his inability to defend his kingdom against these attacks, was completely impotent in facing the Scandinavians.[18] Even when an army of his countrymen could be raised, it fled or was quickly and violently defeated, as witnessed by the *Anglo-Saxon Chronicle* above. Paying the Danegeld to the raiders was also not a solution; while it might keep the attackers from one's territory for a season, the following year the Vikings would return and, finding that the coffers had run dry, would ravage the area with even greater ferocity.

Ultimately, the English people found that they could no longer endure the continual violence. They chose to submit to Sveinn. Exiling the fairly useless Æðelred, they wished to crown Sveinn, whose military activities had given him the legitimacy to rule (a theme which would be repeated frequently in the next century) as king of England as well as Denmark,[19] but Sveinn died in February 1014, and for two years the violent times once again returned to England. Finally, in 1016, with Æðelred and his son/successor, Edmund Ironside, dead, Knútr, Sveinn's able son took over the kingdom. He would rule until 1035, bringing renewed prosperity to England; above all, his reign ended the Scandinavian attacks on the island.[20]

dorste sciphere on sæ. ne landfyrd. ne eodon hi swa feor úp. Wæs hit þa on ælce wisan hefig tyma. forðam þe hi næfre heora yfeles geswicon.
1004. Her com Swegen mid his flotan to Norðwic. ⁊ þa burh ealle gehergade. ⁊ forbærndon.
1010. Her on ðissum geare com se foresprecenda here ofer Eastron to [East]Englum. ⁊ wendon up æt Gipeswic. ⁊ eodon anreces þær hi geaxodon Ulfcytel mid his fyrde . . . þa sona flugon EastEngla. þa stod Grantabrycgscir fæstlice ongean. þær wæs ofslægen Æðelstan þes cynges aðum. ⁊ Oswi ⁊ his sunu. ⁊ Wulfric Leofwines sunu. ⁊ Eadwig Ælfrices broðor. ⁊ feala oðra godra þegna. ⁊ folces ungerim . . . þa Dæniscan ahton East- Engle géweald. ⁊ þone eard .iii. monþas hergodon ⁊ bærndon. Gefurðon on þa wildan fennas hi ferdon. ⁊ menn ⁊ yrfe hi slogon. ⁊ bærndon geond þa feonnas. ⁊ Þeodford forbærndon. ⁊ Grantabrycge. ⁊ syððon wendon eft suðweard into Temese. ⁊ ridon þa gehorsedan menn ongean þa scipo. ⁊ syððon hrædlice wendon westweard on Oxnafordscire. ⁊ þanon to Bucinghamscire. ⁊ swa andlang Usan. oð hi comon to Bedanforda ⁊ swa forð oð Temesanford. ⁊ a bærndon swa hi geferdon. wendon þa eft toscipon mid heora herehuðe . . . Þa ætforan sanctus Andreas mæssan. ða com sehere to Hamtune. ⁊ þone port sona forbærndon. ⁊ þær namon abuton swa mycel swa hi woldon sylfe. ⁊ þanon wendon ofer Temese in to WestSeaxum. ⁊ swa wið Caningan mærsces. ⁊ þ eall forbærndon. Þa hi swa feor gegan hæfdon swa hi þa woldon. þa comon hi to ðam mid-danwintra to scipon.

18 Stenton, *Anglo-Saxon England*, pp. 372–90, 394–95; Loyn, *Vikings in Britain*, pp. 65–66; and the articles in David Hill, *Ethelred the Unready: Papers from the Millenary Conference* (Oxford, 1978).
19 Stenton, *Anglo-Saxon England*, pp. 378–86 and Loyn, *Vikings in Britain*, pp. 65–66.
20 On Knútr's reign see Stenton, *Anglo-Saxon England*, pp. 386–410; Loyn, *Vikings in Britain*, 66–67; D.J.V. Fisher, *The Anglo-Saxon England, c.400–1042* (London, 1976), pp. 319–41; M.K. Lawson, *Cnut: The Danes in England in the Early Eleventh Century* (London, 1993); and the articles in Alexander R. Rumble, ed., *The Reign of Cnut* (London, 1994).

Throughout this late tenth-/early eleventh-century turmoil, the Anglo-Scandinavian parts of England above the Danelaw had been left alone. Perhaps wishing not to attack his 'cousins,' or perhaps knowing that they would readily accept him as king, Sveinn stayed away from the north of England. When he became king, and, later, when Knútr became king, the north did support them. This meant that by 1016 all of England had become Anglo-Scandinavian.[21]

At Knútr's death, his sons, Harold and Harðaknútr, would vie for control of the vacant English throne. Both would occupy it, but for only a short time before meeting their own deaths (discussed below). In their place was crowned Edward (who would later become known as 'the Confessor'), the exiled son of Sveinn's and Knútr's enemy, Æðelred II. With this crowning, some historians claim that Knútr's Anglo-Scandinavian legacy had died. His empire certainly had dissolved, broken into three parts – England, Denmark, and Norway – ruled over by three separate individuals, but his Anglo-Scandinavian institutions, laws, language, military organization, and governing bodies thrived; and in 1066, at the death of Edward, one of the individuals ruling over a part of Knútr's dissolved empire decided that he had the right to put that empire back together – Haraldr Harðráði, king of Norway.

[21] On this see Susan Reynolds, 'What Do We Mean by "Anglo-Saxon" and "Anglo-Saxons"?' *Journal of British Studies* 24 (1985), 395–414 and Ann Williams, ' "Cockles Amongst the Wheat": Danes and English in the Western Midlands in the First Half of the Eleventh Century,' *Midland History* 11 (1986), 1–22.

Haraldr Hardráði's Travels

CHAPTER THREE

HARALDR HARÐRÁÐI

SOME HISTORIANS regard 1066 as the last year of the Viking conquests, and Haraldr Sigurðarson (known more often as Haraldr Harðráði) as the last Viking 'hero.'[1] To the modern writer, Haraldr was not a hero; for us this appellation depends largely on our perspective of victory and defeat, with the defeated rarely described in heroic terms, and before 1066 was finished, after setting out to conquer England as other Vikings before him had, Haraldr Harðráði was defeated at the battle of Stamford Bridge.

Of all eleventh-century warlords, perhaps none displayed the traits which characterized those individuals better than Haraldr Harðráði. This is Gwyn Jones' description:

> With every allowance made for the subsequent growth of his legend, he showed himself . . . fierce, resourceful, cunning, resilient and enduring, and when occasion called for it, double-dealing, vengeful, and cruel. In brief, the epitome of a viking who lived by rapine and war, believed in fame, riches, and power, and employed fair means and foul to obtain them.[2]

Snorri Sturluson's portrayal is somewhat kinder:

> It is true that all men said that King Haraldr was above other men in wisdom and eloquent counsel, whether he was performing his duties quickly or making long-term plans for himself or others. He was very skilled with weapons. He was also fortunate in gaining victory . . . King Haraldr was a handsome and noble man, white-haired with a white beard and long mustache; one of his eyebrows was somewhat higher than the other. He had large and well developed hands and feet. He was five ells tall. He was merciless to his enemies and punished all grievances . . . King Haraldr was greedy for power and possessions.[3]

---

[1] See, for example, Gwyn Jones, *A History of the Vikings*, 1st edn (London, 1968), p. 392. On the name 'Harðráði,' see Gabriel Turville-Petre, *Haraldr the Hardruler and His Poets* (London, 1966), p. 3.

[2] Jones, pp. 405–06.

[3] Snorri Sturluson, *Heimskringla*, ed. B. Aðalbjarnarson (Reykjavik, 1941–51), III:198–99: Var þat allra manna mál, at Haraldr konungr hafði verit um fram aðra menn at speki ok ráðsnilld, hvárt er hann skyldi til taka skjótt eða gera long rað fyrir sér eða oðrum. Hann var allra manna vápndjarfastr. Hann var ok sigrsæll . . . Haraldr konungr var fríðr maðr ok tíguligr, bleikhárr ok bleikt skegg ok langa kanpa, nokkuru brúnin onnur ofar

Above all, Haraldr seemed to love warfare. One of his favorite poets, Þjóðólfr, calls him the 'promoter of battle' (*dolgstærandi*), 'the storm of spears' (*odda skúrar herðir*), 'feeder of the raven/battle-starling' (*folkstara feitir*), 'one who overcomes the sorrow of the wolf' (*eyðir heiðingja sútar*).[4] He served almost his entire life as a soldier, and most of that time as a military leader. Forced from his home by defeat in battle, Haraldr honed his skills as a mercenary, fighting for whomever he could learn the military arts from as much as for whomever would pay him. His travels took him first to Russia and then to Constantinople, Sicily, and the Holy Land, where he became a soldier in and then the leader of the Varangian Guard, before he returned to Scandinavia. As a leader, of the Varangian Guard or of Norway, he had a reputation of strength and firmness in his decision making; his cognomen Harðráði meant 'Hard-Ruler,' one who demanded allegiance and love from his comrades and subjects, whether soldiers, Norwegians, Danes, or Varangians.[5] This generally brought praise from the Norwegian and Icelandic historians and saga writers, most of whom seem to have had a fondness for absolute rulers, but from the more southern European clerics, Adam of Bremen and Saxo Grammaticus, the 'Hard-Ruler' brought disdain. Saxo remarks that Haraldr's cognomen should instead be *malus*,[6] while Adam portrays him as the 'thunder-bolt of the north, a fatal evil,' and writes that Haraldr 'exceeded with cruelty all the madness of tyrants.'[7]

On the other hand, Haraldr Harðráði seemed to appreciate poetry and surrounded himself with poetic storytellers. He even composed some poetry himself. As Gabriel Turville-Petre has expressed, 'No king of Norway was himself a better poet, and none showed a deeper appreciation of the art than

en ǫnnur, miklar hendr ok fœtr ok vel vaxit hvárt tveggja. Fimm alna er hátt mál hans. Hann var grimmr óvinum ok refsingasamr um allar mótgørðir . . . Haraldr konungr var inn ágjarnasti til ríkis ok til allra farsælligra eigna.

As pointed out by Magnus Magnusson and Hermann Pálsson, in their translation of the *King Harald's Saga* portion of the *Heimskringla* (*King Harald's Saga*, trans. M. Magnusson and H. Pálsson (Harmondsworth, 1966), p. 161), the Icelandic ell was eighteen inches long, which would make Haraldr Harðráði more than seven feet tall. They surmise that Snorri's measurement might be based on an earlier, shorter Danish ell. See also H.R. Ellis Davidson, *The Viking Road to Byzantium* (London, 1976), p. 212.

4 *Sexstefja* in *Den norske-islandske Skjaldedigtning*, ed. F. Jónsson (Oslo, 1912), B, I, 339–46. See also Turville-Petre, pp. 15–16.

5 While 'hard-ruler' is the accepted translation of the Harðráði, R.I. Page (*Chronicles of the Vikings: Records, Memorials and Myths* (Toronto, 1995), p. 23) has suggested that 'savage in counsel, tough, tyrannical' is a more fitting translation.

6 Saxo Grammaticus, *Historia Danica*, ed. P.E. Müller and J.M. Velschow (Hannover, 1839), II:556. See also Peter G. Foote and David M. Wilson, *The Viking Achievement* (New York, 1970), p. 45.

7 Adam of Bremen, *Gesta Hammaburgensis ecclesiae pontificum*, ed. B. Schmeidler, 3rd edn (Hanover, 1917), p. 159: 'rex Haraldrus crudelitate sua omnes tyrannorum excessit furores.' Later on the same page, Adam of Bremen calls Haraldr 'fulmen septentrionis, fatale malum.' See also Jones, p. 404.

Haraldr did.'[8] These poems and those by the poets whom he patronized left an oral legacy of this royal Norwegian warlord. Of course, for Theodoricus the Monk, Snorri Sturluson, and the anonymous authors of the Norwegian Kings' Sagas, who used these poems to write their histories, this too was evidence of Haraldr's 'heroism.' It is from these poems which the sagas also gain much historical credibility.

It is believed that Haraldr was born in 1015, for although there is no record of his birth in any contemporary source, the later Norwegian sagas record his age as fifteen at the battle of Stiklarstaðir[9] (fought 29 July 1030 near Þrándheimr (Trondheim)) where Haraldr fought in an attempt to restore his half-brother, Óláfr (later St Óláfr), to the throne of Norway, which had been seized two years previously by Knútr, then king of Denmark and England as well as Norway.[10] In this battle Haraldr showed considerable military talent as he led some of his brother's forces, despite his young age, but the brothers could not defeat the Norwegians who supported Knútr; Haraldr Harðráði was wounded, and Óláfr was killed.[11] Helped from the battlefield by an ally, Rǫgnvaldr Brúsason, the earl of Orkney, and secretly nursed in a 'farmhouse in a forest far from other men,'[12] Haraldr was forced to flee from Norway. He escaped east through Sweden to Russia.

Grand Prince Iaroslav of Kievan Russia welcomed the fugitive prince. Although there is no record of this, the two may have met previously. At least it seems that they knew of each other, through kinship and intermarriage, as Scan-

8 Turville-Petre, p. 5; see also pp. 19–20. For a selection of some of these poems see Page, *Chronicles of the Vikings*, pp. 23–24. See also Snorri Sturluson, *Heimskringla*, III:119.

9 The name of this battle is spelled in many ways, i.e. Stikkelstad, Stiklestad, Stiklestadir, etc. I have used the Old Norse spelling.

10 See Theodoricus, *Monumenta historica Norvegiæ: Latinske kildeskrifter til Norges historie I middelalderen*, ed. G. Storm (Christania (Oslo), 1880), p. 35; *Ágrip af Nóregs konunga sögum*, ed. F. Jónsson (Halle, 1929), pp. 31–32; and Snorri Sturluson, *Heimskringla*, III:68.

11 For original sources on the battle of Stiklarstaðir see Saxo Grammaticus, I:520–21; Theodoricus, pp. 34–36; *Ágrip*, pp. 31–32; Snorri Sturluson, *Heimskringla*, III:68–69; and *Flateyjarbók: En samling af Norske Konge-Sagaer*, ed. G. Vigfusson and C.R. Unger, 3 vols. (Christiania (Oslo), 1860–68), II:357–58, 408. Secondary sources include: Jones, pp. 383–84; Edward August Freeman, *The History of the Norman Conquest*, 2nd edn (Oxford, 1869–75), II:75; Johannes Brønsted, *The Vikings*, trans. K. Skov (Harmondsworth, 1965), pp. 104–05; M.K. Lawson, *Cnut: The Danes in England in the Early Eleventh Century* (London, 1993), p. 101; Peter Sawyer, 'Cnut's Scandinavian Empire,' in *The Reign of Cnut: King of England, Denmark and Norway*, ed. A.R. Rumble (London, 1994), p. 21; Paddy Griffith, *The Viking Art of War* (London, 1995), p. 191; and Knut Berg, 'Haralds dronning Ellisiv,' in *Harald Hardråde*, ed. A. Berg (Oslo, 1966), p. 28. On Knútr's conquest of Norway in 1028 see the *Anglo-Saxon Chronicle*, in *Two of the Saxon Chronicles Parallel*, 2 vols, ed. Charles Plummer and John Earle (Oxford, 1892), C, D, and E (1028), I:156–57; Adam of Bremen, pp. 118–20; Lawson, p. 100; and Sawyer, 'Cnut's Scandinavian Empire,' pp. 20–21.

12 Theodoricus (pp. 35–36), the *Ágrip* (p. 32), Snorri Sturluson (*Heimskringla*, III:68–69), and *Flateyjarbók* (II:357–58, 408) all contain the story of Rǫgnavaldr Brusáson's aid to Haraldr. Only Snorri contains the details that he was nursed in a 'bjó í skógi langt frá ǫðrum mǫnnum.' See also Davidson, *Viking Road to Byzantium*, pp. 209–10.

dinavian royal families throughout Europe remained close, and through reputa-
tion. Iaroslav had been the ruler of this part of Russia since 1019, although until
1036 he shared control of his father, Vladimir's, lands with his half-brother,
Mstislav. Iaroslav's wife, Ingigerd, was the daughter of King Óláfr Eiriksson of
Sweden, and it is perhaps through this marriage that Haraldr was known to this
Russian Grand Prince. Whatever their earlier relationship may have been, it is
certain that the young Grand Prince, his own family relatively new to the rule of
Russia, quickly recognized in his even younger counterpart a potential for leadership, especially for military leadership, which he badly needed to assist him in
keeping domestic peace and in protecting his borders against outside invasion.[13]

Before his reign was finished in 1054, Iaroslav would bring growth and pros-
perity to Kievan Russia. In an attempt to make Kiev the capital of Christianity in
the east, this ruler, who would come to be known as Iaroslav the Wise, tied the
Christianity established at his father's behest in the region to Constantinople.
Importing religious artisans and teachers from Byzantium, he built the Sancta
Sophia Cathedral, several other churches and monasteries, and a large library.
He also had a number of religious books translated from Greek into Slavic and
used them to create Russia's first educational institute and to form the land's
first codified legal system.[14]

What role, if any, Haraldr Harðráði played in this growth and prosperity is not
known, for not much is mentioned about his Russian stay in Scandinavian
sources and nothing in Russian ones.[15] What we do know is that for Iaroslav the
building of a strong Christian capital was tied directly to its military strength;
peace yielded prosperity. Consequently, he supported a strong army, and he built

---

[13] This need for military leadership is understandable when the history of Iaroslav's acquisition of his throne is recounted. At the death of Vladimir, a polygamist who had sired numerous offspring, sibling warfare broke out among most of his sons, all of whom had received a
portion of their father's realm. Most aggressive among these was Sviatopolk who, after
putting to death brothers Boris, Gleb, and Sviatoslav, turned against Iaroslav. An initial
victory in 1015 put Iaroslav on the throne, but in 1018, Sviatopolk, whose army consisted of
Poles, Germans, Hungarians, and Pechnegs, defeated Iaroslav and conquered Kiev. A year
later and once Sviatopolk's western allies had deserted him, Iaroslav recaptured Kiev. Still,
peace was to elude the future Grand Prince; in 1021, his nephew, Briacheslav, rose up against
him, and, in 1023, his half-brother, Mstislav, attacked Kiev. Iaroslav won the first war, but lost
the second. Despite this defeat, Mstislav allowed Iaroslav to rule Kiev and Novgorod until
1036 when, upon Mstislav's death and after imprisoning another sibling threat, his brother
Sudislav, Iaroslav gained the entire Kievan Russian kingdom. See Simon Franklin and Jonathan Shepard, *The Emergence of Rus, 750–1200* (London, 1996), pp. 184–88; B. Grekov, *Kiev
Rus*, trans. Y. Sdobnikov, ed. D. Ogden (Moscow, 1959), pp. 645–49; and G. Vernadsky,
Kievan Russia (New Haven, 1942), pp. 74–76.
[14] On the accomplishment of Iaroslav's reign in Russia, see Franklin and Shepard, pp. 183,
208–44, 303–04; Grekov, pp. 649–52; Berg, pp. 28–40; Vernadsky, *Kievan Russia*, pp. 79–83,
277; G. Vernadsky, *The Origins of Russia* (Oxford, 1959), pp. 305–06; and Janet Martin,
Medieval Russia, 980–1584 (Cambridge, 1995), p. 8.
[15] Theodoricus and the *Ágrip* contain nothing about Haraldr's stay with Iaroslav, while the
Morkinskinna manuscript is damaged at this point.

numerous fortifications, the Golden Gate of Kiev being the most prominent extant example. To this end, he welcomed the fugitive Norwegians.

This was not the first time Iaroslav had welcomed his Scandinavian cousins to Kievan Russia. He had used Scandinavians, or Varangians as most historians call them, as mercenaries in his warfare against his brothers, Sviatopolk and Mstislav,[16] and he quickly employed these new warriors as independent military units in his *druzhina*, or army. According to the *Fagrskinna* and the *Heimskringla*, Haraldr was made one of their captains.[17] The *Fagrskinna* also indicates that Haraldr fought often during his stay in Russia,[18] but against whom did he fight? It is certain that Haraldr and his Norwegians participated in Iaroslav's war against the Poles in 1031, as Snorri Sturluson makes reference to these as enemies, and he may also have fought against the Chudians in Estonia and the Pechnegs, Byzantines, and Steppe nomads, all of whom contended against the southern and eastern borders of Kiev during the 1030s, although no contemporary work refers to them as Haraldr's opponents.[19] (Snorri Sturluson also mentions the 'Austr-Vinðum' as Haraldr's enemy during his stay in Russia, but who these might have been is not known.[20]) Haraldr may also have assisted Iaroslav to extend his defenses south along the Ros' River in 1032.[21]

According to the author of the *Fagrskinna* and Snorri Sturluson, Haraldr Harðráði learned much about military and political affairs in Russia. While serving in the army, he continued to master his fighting skills and gain military prominence. It seems that Haraldr also developed a particular relationship with Iaroslav, and by extension with his family, in particular his daughter, Elizaveta. Eventually the two would be married. However, there is some confusion as to

---

[16] Franklin and Shepard, pp. 195–204; Vernadsky, *Kievan Russia*, pp. 74–76; Davidson, *Viking Road to Byzantium*, pp. 158–73; and F. Donald Logan, *The Vikings in History*, 2nd edn (London, 1991), p. 204. The *Fagrskinna* (*Fagrskinna: Kortfattet Norsk Konge-Saga*, ed. P.A. Munch and C.R. Unger (Christiania (Oslo), 1847), p. 106) also makes reference to Iaroslav's previous employment of Scandinavians in his military forces, although the author of this work is not specific as to where these forces were used.

[17] *Fagrskinna*, p. 106 and Snorri Sturluson, *Heimskringla*, III:69–70. The *Fagrskinna* seems to indicate that Haraldr Harðráði was placed as a commander over only the Varangians, while Snorri Sturluson claims that Haraldr was made leader over the 'lanvarnarǫmnnum konungs,' the 'king's defensive forces.' Sigfus Blöndal (*The Varangians of Byzantium*, trans. B.S. Benedikz (Cambridge, 1978), p. 54) believes that Snorri's claim here is 'so obvious an exaggeration as to be nonsensical,' but does admit that Haraldr would have been a welcome addition to Iaroslav's *druzhina* and that he undoubtedly would have gained 'some kind of subordinate officer's rank.'

[18] *Fagrskinna*, pp. 106–07.

[19] Snorri Sturluson, *Heimskringla*, III:70. See also Franklin and Shephard, p. 203; Vernadsky, *Kievan Russia*, pp. 76–77, 79; Janet Martin, *Medieval Russia, 980–1584* (Cambridge, 1995), p. 45; Davidson, *Viking Road to Byzantium*, p. 210; and Blöndel, p. 55. Snorri puts this detail into the verses of the poet, Þjóðólfr, one of his favorite Icelandic sources; that he specifically names the Poles as one of Haraldr's enemies enhances his credibility.

[20] Magnusson and Pálsson's translation of these as 'Slavs' is not accurate, nor does it assist the historian to answer this question.

[21] See Martin, p. 47.

whether this was the plan when Haraldr was in Russia, or whether it developed during his time in Byzantium. On the one hand, the sagas report that whatever treasure Haraldr gained on his Mediterranean adventures was sent for safe-keeping to Iaroslav, perhaps indicating that he and the Grand Prince had previously agreed on the marriage.[22] On the other hand, the *Morkinskinna* claims that, on his return to Kiev, Haraldr had to remind Iaroslav of the promised marriage,[23] while Snorri Sturluson includes in one of Haraldr's own poems the verse, 'Yet the goddess in Russia/ will not accept my gold rings,' which, the Icelandic historian maintains, is a reference to Elizaveta.[24]

Haraldr Harðráði's next stop in his youthful adventures – he was still not yet twenty years old – was at Constantinople. Here too he sought to gain in military skills and leadership training. He would get lots of practice. Edward August Freeman's description of the Byzantine Empire at the time of Haraldr's arrival, while somewhat flamboyant, is nevertheless accurate:

> He found the Eastern Empire in one of those periods of decay which so strangely alternate its history with periods of regeneration at home and victory abroad. The great Macedonian dynasty was still on the throne; but the mighty Basil was in his grave, and the steel-clad lancers of New Rome were no longer the terror of Saracen, Bulgarian, and Russian. The Empire which he saved, and which he had raised to the highest pitch of glory, had now become the plaything of a worthless woman [Zoe], and the diadem of the Caesars was passed on at every caprice of her fancy from one husband or lover to another.[25]

Byzantine enemies could be found both abroad and at home, and, it seems, that Haraldr faced all of them. During the eight years he spent in Byzantium, he fought on the Mediterranean Sea, in Asia Minor, in Sicily, in the Holy Land, in Bulgaria, and in Constantinople. As the author of *Fagrskinna* records in typical saga-writer understatment: 'Haraldr stayed there for a long time and fought in many battles.'[26]

---

[22] *Fagrskinna*, p. 112 and Snorri Sturluson, *Heimskringla*, III:89–90.

[23] *Morkinskinna: Pergamentsbog fra første halvdel af det trettende aarhundrede*, ed. C.R. Unger (Christiania (Oslo), 1867), p. 16.

[24] Snorri Sturluson, *Heimskringla*, III:89: 'Þó lætr Gerðr í Gǫrum / gollhrings við mér skolla.' See Davidson, *Viking Road to Byzantium*, p. 210, and Blöndal, pp. 55, 67. Blöndal believes that such a marriage would not have been contracted as Elizaveta was only ten years old, but this is hardly a defensible criticism when it comes to royal marriage contracts. On Elizaveta, see Berg.

[25] Freeman, *Norman Conquest*, III:75. It interesting to note that while modern Byzantine historians do not use Freeman's flamboyant words, they agree with their sentiment. See Warren Treadgold, *A History of the Byzantine State and Society* (Stanford, 1997), pp. 583–90; Romilly Jenkins, *Byzantium: The Imperial Centuries, AD 610–1071* (1966; rpt. Toronto, 1987), pp. 333–47; and Michael Angold, *The Byzantine Empire, 1025–1204: A Political History* (London, 1984), p. 5.

[26] *Fagrskinna*, p. 106: 'Nú dvaldisk Haraldr þar langa hrið ok átti margar orostur.' See also the *Sexstefja*, B, I, 339–46.

In arriving at Constantinople, sometime in 1034 it is thought,[27] Haraldr Harðráði joined the Varangian Guard. According to the later *Flateyjarbók*, Haraldr initially kept his royal identity secret, wishing to avoid the Byzantine tradition of not allowing men of nobility to serve as mercenaries among their forces,[28] but the *Fagrskinna* and *Heimskringla* argue against this by having Haraldr arrive with his company of men intact, and requesting that they remain together as a separate unit under his command in the Varangian Guard.[29] As the reputation of Haraldr and his Scandinavians seems to have been well known throughout the east by this time, as confirmed by the anonymous Byzantine *Book of Advice for an Emperor*, written c.1070, undoubtedly this is what occurred.[30]

At the time that Haraldr and his cadre joined the Varangian Guard, it had been in existence as a part of the Byzantine army since its institution by Emperor Basil II in 988, although Scandinavians had been serving as mercenaries with the Byzantines for more than a century before that. Initially, the men who made up the Varangian Guard were mostly Rus from Kiev and Novgorod, but by the time of Haraldr Harðráði's association with this elite unit, more northern Scandinavians had begun to fill out the ranks, with a few Normans and Anglo-Saxon English serving as well.[31] Eventually, the Varangian Guard would become known primarily as the emperor's bodyguards, but Haraldr at first did not serve as such; instead, until his last year, he fought on nearly every frontier of the still large Empire.

These adventures began with naval service in the eastern Mediterranean against Arab pirates. Not much is recorded about these expeditions, except that the Varangian *galeiðir* (literally galleys) destroyed many opposing *kussurum* (literally corsairs).[32] Also recorded on these adventures is the experienced Byzantine general, Georgios Maniaces, a man who would come to be associated

---

[27] Only Freeman (*Norman Conquest*, II:581–82) believes that Haraldr Harðráði arrived in Constantinople later than 1034, in 1038. All other historians accept the 1034 date.

[28] *Flateyjarbók*, III:290–304. See also Blöndal, pp. 58–59.

[29] *Fagrskinna*, pp. 106–07 and Snorri Sturluson, *Heimskringla*, III:71–72.

[30] *Book of Advice for an Emperor*, edited with the *Strategicon of Cecaumenos*, ed. V.G. Vasilievsky and V. Jernstedt (St Petersburg, 1896), pp. 95–97.

[31] The best histories of the Varangian Guard are Blöndal (pp. 54–60 are specifically about Haraldr Harðráði's experiences there); Davidson, *Viking Road to Byzantium*, pp. 177–229 (pp. 207–29 are about Haraldr); Warren Treadgold, *Byzantium and Its Army, 284–1081* (Stanford, 1995), pp. 37, 79, 84, 115–16; B.S. Benedikz, 'The Evolution of the Varangian Regiment in the Byzantine Army,' *Byzantinische Zeitschrift* 62 (1969), 20–25; and, to a lesser extent, Emily Albu Hanawalt, 'Scandinavians in Byzantium and Normandy,' in *Peace and War in Byzantium. Essays in Honor of George T. Dennis, S.J.*, ed. T.S. Miller and J. Nesbitt (Washington, 1995), pp. 114–22. See also Jones, p. 266; Logan, p. 196; and Dimitri Obolensky, *The Byzantine Commonwealth: Eastern Europe, 500–1453* (London, 1971), pp. 302–04.

[32] The *Fagrskinna* (p. 107) records the Varangian ships as *galeiðir*; Snorri Sturluson (*Heimskringla*, III:72) records the opposing ships as *kussurum*. See also Davidson, *Viking Road to Byzantium*, p. 211 and Blöndal, pp. 59–60.

with most of the Varangians' early successes, and with some of Haraldr's problems as well.[33]

This naval campaign eventually turned inland against those towns and villages in Asia Minor which had supported the pirates hunted by Haraldr and his Varangians; they were his, because by this time, according to Snorri Sturluson, Haraldr Harðráði had become the 'leader over all the Varangians.'[34] In this war Haraldr once again showed his military skill, achieving distinction with his heroic exploits. By 1035 the Byzantines had pushed the Arabs out of Asia Minor and their campaign shifted to the east, as far as the Euphrates, where the Norwegian Kings' Sagas record that Haraldr participated in the capture of eighty Arab strongholds there.[35]

The sagas follow this by having Haraldr and his force turn south from Asia Minor towards Jerusalem. In these sources there is no doubt that this was a military expedition, with the *Fagrskinna*, *Morkinskinna*, and *Heimskringla* all reporting the fall of the Holy City, as well as several other nearby 'towns and castles,' to the Varangians.[36] However, there are problems with this story. Not only do these sagas all place the trip to Jerusalem chronologically after Haraldr's Sicilian wars rather than before, when it more than likely occurred, if at all, but more trustworthy Byzantine and Arabic sources confirm that in 1036 the Byzantine Emperor, Michael IV, and the Caliph of Baghdad, Moustansir-Billah, signed a thirty-year peace treaty which guaranteed Christian access to the holy places in Jerusalem.[37] Thus no military action was needed, nor was any taken in that region by the Byzantines until the battle of Manzikert in 1071.

Nevertheless, there is no need to completely dismiss the notion that Haraldr Harðráði traveled to Jerusalem during his stay in the Byzantine Empire. Probably after his adventures in Asia Minor and before those in Sicily, it seems likely that Haraldr did pay a visit to the Holy Land. Perhaps this was in conjunction

---

33 Snorri Sturluson, *Heimskringla*, III:72. See also Davidson, *Viking Road to Byzantium*, pp. 211–12. Georgios Maniaces had captured Edessa in 1032 and thus had gained prominence in Byzantine military leadership. See Treadgold, *Byzantium and its Army*, p. 215; Angold, p. 9; and A.A. Vasiliev, *The History of the Byzantine Empire, 324–1453*, 2nd edn (Madison, 1964), I:312.

34 Snorri Sturluson, *Heimskringla*, III:72: 'Kom þá svá, at Haraldr gerðisk hǫfðingi yfir ǫllum Væringjum.' Blöndal (p. 62) contends that Haraldr never had this leadership role, serving only in a subordinate position as one of the many Varangian lieutenants under Georgios Maniaces, but this contention seems to conflict with the *Book of Advice for an Emperor* which identifies the Norwegian prince as the leader of the Varangian Guard.

35 *Fagrskinna*, p. 108 and Snorri Sturluson, *Heimskringla*, III:74. Both of these sources place these cities in Africa, but this is obviously an error, as there was no Byzantine conflict in Africa during this time, while there was fighting in Asia Minor with the Varangians taking part. The *Sexstefja* (B, I, 339–46) claims that Haraldr was the origin of this tale. See also Davidson, *Viking Road to Byzantium*, p. 219; Blöndal, pp. 61–63; and Turville-Petre, p. 13.

36 *Fagrskinna*, p. 110; *Morkinskinna*, pp. 11–12; and Snorri Sturluson, *Heimskringla*, III:83–84. The quote is from Snorri Sturluson, who mentions 'allar borgir ok kastalar' surrendering to Haraldr Harðráði.

37 On this peace treaty see Blöndal, p. 65; Davidson, *Viking Road to Byzantium*, pp. 219–20; and T.D. Kendrick, *A History of the Vikings* (New York, 1930), p. 172.

with a party of masons and other artisans who traveled from Constantinople to Jerusalem to rebuild the Church of the Holy Sepulchre there; one of the provisions of the 1036 peace treaty was that such a rebuilding would be undertaken. Alternatively perhaps Haraldr accompanied a number of high-ranking Byzantine citizens who it is thought made a pilgrimage to the Holy City to celebrate the peace treaty. This latter party may also have included members of the Imperial family, possibly even Empress Zoe and her cloistered sister, Theodora. In both of these situations a bodyguard would have been needed to ensure the safety of the non-military travelers. Why not a company of the Varangian Guard?[38] In such a case it would not be difficult to believe that while there Haraldr did the rest of what Snorri Sturluson and the anonymous authors of the *Fagrskinna* and *Morkinskinna* attribute to his visit: bathing in the Jordan River, giving money to the churches, and removing bandits from nearby regions.[39]

Haraldr's next military adventure was in Sicily as the Byzantines attempted to recapture the strategic Mediterranean island from the Muslims. During these engagements, Haraldr's command seems to have included not only the Varangian Guard, but also a group of Norman mercenaries. Before too long, many of the important Sicilian towns had fallen to the Byzantine army; even Messina came under Imperial control. However, the island as a whole remained in Muslim hands, as the capable Byzantine general-in-chief, Georgios Maniaces, was removed because of a controversy with the emperor, Michael IV, and was replaced by an inept imperial favorite. Morale plummeted. Even Haraldr's highly disciplined force suffered: the Normans deserted to the Italian mainland where they began to prey on Byzantine lands there, and Haraldr and the Varangian Guard were called back to Constantinople.

All of this, as recorded in the Norwegian Kings' Sagas, seems to be accurate.[40] Other sources confirm that from 1038 to 1041 the Byzantine army, led by Georgios Maniaces, did fight a campaign in Sicily, and that it was quite successful, at least until Maniaces was removed from command and imprisoned by the emperor. Thereafter, despite no recorded fondness for this leader among his soldiers, especially the Varangians, Byzantine military matters on the Mediterranean island disintegrated, perhaps due to the mutiny of the Normans[41] and perhaps due to a removal of Byzantine forces to other frontiers of the Empire – both the Pechnegs and Bulgarians were threatening Imperial borders at

---

38 See Davidson, *Viking Road to Byzantium*, pp. 219–20 and Blöndal, pp. 64–65. The first journey is known to have occurred, the second one is merely a conjecture, primarily made by Blöndal.

39 *Fagrskinna*, p. 110; *Morkinskinna*, p. 11; and Snorri Sturluson, *Heimskringla*, III:84.

40 Found in *Fagrskinna*, pp. 109–10; *Morkinskinna*, pp. 7–11; and Snorri Sturluson, *Heimskringla*, III:76–81. The *Morkinskinna* manuscript is complete again during the first part of these adventures.

41 On the Italian mainland, there was a revolt in Bari in 1038 and another one in Mottola in 1040, but whether the Normans who had been with Haraldr were responsible for either or both of these is not known. See Blöndal, p. 70 and Treadgold, *Byzantium and its Army*, p. 215.

the time. Among those eventually removed from Sicily were the Varangian Guard.[42]

The sagas enliven their accounts of Haraldr's Sicilian adventures with 'heroic' anecdotes that stretch historical credibility. For example, outside one targeted town which had refused to surrender to the Byzantines, Haraldr had his men tie firebrands to birds who in returning to their nests inside the town set it ablaze.[43] Another town was captured by the Varangians tunneling under its walls and emerging in a hall where most of the inhabitants were dining. The surprise was effective, many were killed, and the town surrendered.[44] A third town was captured when its Byzantine attackers appeared to be taking a break from their siege to enjoy sports. These athletic displays, foreign as they were to southern Europeans, lulled the townspeople into a false security which changed into terror as the Varangians turned from their games, took up hidden weapons, and charged into the town.[45] Finally, a fourth was captured when the Varangian Guard was able to convince the inhabitants that their leader, Haraldr Harðráði, had died and needed to have a Christian funeral within the walls of the besieged town. Much smaller than the Trojan Horse, the funeral procession accomplished the same thing, when the Byzantine mercenaries attacked through gates opened to receive their leader's coffin.[46] All of these ruses were well known to ancient and medieval storytellers, and while that does not mean that they did not occur in Sicily at the instigation of Haraldr – certainly military leaders are known to have repeated successful tactics – most modern commentators doubt their validity.[47]

One final ruse of Haraldr's should also be noted: this one was made not against his enemies, but against his leader, Georgios Maniaces. Snorri Sturluson and the *Fagrskinna* report that one night during their campaigns (probably in Asia Minor, although this is not specified in these sources) the Varangian Guard did not wish to camp in the marshlands where Maniaces customarily placed them. Arriving first, they took the high ground instead, a campsite which was contested by the Byzantine general when he arrived later. In an effort to resolve the issue, the two leaders ultimately decided to draw lots. The lots were to be marked and then they were to be thrown onto a piece of cloth where a third party would secretly select one. This was to be an extremely important selection. Not only were these lots to determine who would take the favored campsite on this occasion, but they were also to decide which unit would have priority in all decisions: in riding or rowing, in putting in at a harbor, and in selecting future camp-

---

[42] See Blöndal, pp. 66–71; Davidson, *Viking Road to Byzantium*, pp. 213–19; Jenkins, pp. 345–46; Treadgold, *Byzantium and its Army*, p. 215; Treadgold, *History of the Byzantine State*, pp. 587–88; Angold, p. 9; and Vasiliev, I:312, 329.

[43] *Fagrskinna*, p. 108; *Morkinskinna*, pp. 7–8; and Snorri Sturluson, *Heimskringla*, III: 76–77.

[44] *Morkinskinna*, pp. 8–9, and Snorri Sturluson, *Heimskringla*, III:77–78.

[45] *Morkinskinna*, pp. 9–10, and Snorri Sturluson, *Heimskringla*, III:78–80.

[46] *Fagrskinna*, p. 109; *Morkinskinna*, p. 10; and Snorri Sturluson, *Heimskringla*, III:80–81.

[47] See especially Blöndal, pp. 65–74 and Davidson, *Viking Road to Byzantium*, pp. 213–19.

sites. Before choosing one of these lots, Haraldr asked to observe how Georgios Maniaces marked his lot. Copying his general's mark, Haraldr then added his own lot to the piece of cloth. Once a lot was selected, Haraldr grabbed the chosen lot, laughed, and threw it into the sea, declaring that this was his lot. When the general disagreed, Haraldr justified his action with the words: 'Look then at the one left behind. You will recognize your mark there.' After that, the sagas declare, the Varangians were given their way in all disputed matters.[48]

While not having a folkloric legacy like the anecdotes of the Sicilian campaign (at least Sigfús Blöndal, the most ardent critic of these stories, has not located one),[49] the presence of this ruse in the sagas at least suggests an animosity which had developed between the mercenary Varangians and their commander-in-chief. Thus when Georgios Maniaces was removed from command, the scandal did not infect Haraldr and his Guard. Instead, on his return to Constantinople he and his troops were presented with honors and regarded with distinction. According to *The Book of Advice for an Emperor*, Michael IV even made Haraldr a *manglavites*, an official of the imperial court,[50] but, again the Norwegian prince's stay in Constantinople was brief as he was again called to war, this time in the north of the Empire against the Bulgarians. Here too Haraldr Harðráði served with distinction, gaining many victories,[51] and, once again recorded in the *Book of Advice for an Emperor*, on his return to Constantinople a few months later he was promoted to the rank of *spatharocandidate*, an even higher rank in the imperial court (perhaps the third highest rank).[52]

All of these adventures occurred before 1041. After that year everything changed, and the honor and imperial favoritism which Haraldr had received previously quickly declined, for on 10 December 1041, Emperor Michael IV the Paphlagonian, Haraldr's chief imperial patron, died and was replaced by his nephew and adopted son, Michael V Calaphates.[53] Actually, it would be more

---

[48] *Fagrskinna*, pp. 108–09 and Snorri Sturluson, *Heimskringla*, III:72–74. The quote comes from the *Heimskringla*: ' "Sé nú," segir Haraldr, "þann, er eptir er. Muntu þar kenna þitt mark".'

[49] Blöndal, pp. 68–69. Blöndal's acceptance of this as a possible historical occurrence is justified by a belief that Maniaces might have given into the Varangians' demands because he did not want them to risk malaria from marshy campsite. See also Davidson, *Viking Road to Byzantium*, p. 213.

[50] *Book of Advice for an Emperor*, p. 97. Blöndal's claim (p. 75) that this was not a very important position is not convincing.

[51] Haraldr's campaign in Bulgaria is not recorded in the Norwegian Kings' Sagas. It is mentioned without details in the *Book of Advice for an Emperor* (p. 97) and *Sexstefja* (B,I,339), however, it has been accepted by almost all modern commentators. See Blöndal, pp. 74–75; Davidson, *Viking Road to Byzantium*, pp. 220–21; Jenkins, pp. 343–44; Treadgold, *History of the Byzantine State*, pp. 588–89; and Angold, p. 9.

[52] *Book of Advice for an Emperor*, p. 97. Again, Blöndal's contention (p. 75) that this was not a very important achievement is not convincing. Davidson (*Viking Road to Byzantium*, pp. 220–21) believes that these were very important awards, granting Haraldr Harðráði leadership positions unprecedented for a Varangian.

[53] On Michael IV's death and the rise of Michael V see Jenkins, p. 344.

accurate to say that both of these emperors, as well as their predecessor, Romanus III Argyrus, came to a throne which was under the control of Empress Zoe. Romanus III and Michael IV had been married to her; indeed, it is through her lineage that they retained the imperial title,[54] but Zoe had no marriage ties to Michael V, and within a year he had become determined to remove her influence over him. Complaining to the Senate that she had attempted to poison him, he sent her to a nunnery on the Prinkipo Islands. Michael V also ordered the popular Patriarch of Constantinople, Alexius, into retirement, and he freed the unpopular Georgios Maniaces from prison.[55]

Where was Haraldr Harðráði during all of this? As leader of the palace guard, it would seem that he either should have been carrying out the arrests or, more likely due to his attachment to the former emperor, trying to prohibit them. Instead, he was languishing in his own imprisonment, having been arrested together with two of his Scandinavian lieutenants, Halldor Snorrason and Ulf Ospaksson.[56] Why had he been arrested? That is difficult to determine from the sources which report this 'adventure'; in this case there are not too few, but too many, and it seems that each source has its own opinion as to why Haraldr and his comrades had been jailed.

According to the sagas, a short time prior to these actions, Haraldr received word that Knútr, usurper of his brother's throne in Norway, had died, and that a succession crisis had followed (between Knútr's sons, Harold and Harðaknútr), which left Haraldr's nephew, Magnús, in charge of the kingdom. It was Haraldr's desire to return to Scandinavia to 'aid' Magnús in governing his homeland, a land which he had not seen since he was fifteen years old, but it was not so easy for the Norwegian to leave Constantinople, and his attempt to do so landed him in prison. Still, even after writing this, the saga writers seem somewhat unclear as to whether this was the exact reason for Haraldr's imprisonment. They claim that the Byzantine court had charged Haraldr with defrauding the emperor of his treasure, a charge which even the saga writers admit might well have been true. Haraldr, it seems, resented the lack of favor granted him by the Byzantine government and may have been keeping more than his promised share of booty. However, these writers also insist that there was an added cause of Haraldr's imprisonment: it appears that the empress had a niece, Maria, who Haraldr had asked for in marriage. Zoe turned him down, the empress herself,

---

[54] Because of Zoe's advanced age at the time of her marriage to these emperors, no children had been born to whom she could pass the throne.

[55] The best source for these actions of Michael V and their consequences is Michael Psellus, a Constantinoplitan intellectual who was present during much of what occurred and who later wrote it down in his *Chronographia*. The most accessible version of this work is Michael Psellus, *Fourteen Byzantine Rulers*, trans. E.R.A. Sewter (Harmondsworth, 1966). He covers the short reign of Michael V on pp. 121–51. On his rise to power see also Davidson, *Viking Road to Byzantium*, pp. 221–22; Blöndal, pp. 76–77; Treadgold, *History of the Byzantine State*, pp. 587–89; and Jenkins, p. 344.

[56] *Fagrskinna* (p. 111) reports that Zoe allowed Haraldr to take two of his lieutenants into prison with him.

now close to seventy years old, desiring to marry Haraldr, the sagas claim, and thus the leader of the Varangian Guard had ended up in prison.[57]

Other near contemporary northern European sources which also tell of Haraldr's confinement, namely the Anglo-Norman William of Malmesbury and the Danish Saxo Grammaticus, have their own reasons for Haraldr's imprisonment. According to William of Malmesbury, the future Norwegian king had been arrested for defiling an *illustra femina* (a distinguished/noble woman),[58] while Saxo Grammaticus blames Haraldr's incarceration on a *crimen homicidii* (a crime of murder).[59]

It should come as no surprise that modern historians have tended to discount all but the most rudimentary elements of Haraldr's imprisonment as recounted in these sources, and as this incident is not recorded in any Byzantine chronicle or document, these later northern European sources are all that are available. They admit that Haraldr Harðráði was probably imprisoned, and that it was more than likely as a result of monetary impropriety. As evidence they recall that the *Morkinskinna* even contains an account of a dispute between Haraldr and Georgios Maniaces over shares of booty which the Varangian leader had illegally kept for himself.[60] It is possible that this information was delivered to Michael V by Maniaces when he was released from prison;[61] perhaps it was even the information which he used to purchase his freedom.

Sigfús Blöndal goes one step further. He argues that Snorri Sturluson's statement that Haraldr Harðráði's great wealth had come from customary palace plunder (a statement which will be addressed in its context below) actually means that Haraldr had been given the right to collect taxes. Therefore, it was likely that this is where the Norwegian prince had embezzled the emperor's funds.[62]

Of course, the answer simply may be that Michael V knew of Haraldr's loyalty to the previous emperor, that he feared that the Varangian leader would not approve of his treatment of Zoe, among others, and that it would be better for him to have Haraldr away from his leadership post at the time of his administrative changes. Any charges that needed to be trumped up to ensure the imprisonment of Haraldr Harðráði would be.

Some of the northern European sources also report that Haraldr shared his prison cell with more than Halldor and Ulf. According to the *Morkinskinna* and Saxo Grammaticus, Haraldr's companion was a large serpent/dragon,[63] accord-

---

[57] *Fagrskinna*, pp. 110–11; *Morkinskinna*, pp. 12–13; and Snorri Sturluson, *Heimskringla*, III:85–87.

[58] William of Malmesbury, *Gesta regum Anglorum: The History of the English Kings*, ed. and trans. R.A.B. Mynors, R.M. Thomson, and M. Winterbottom (Oxford, 1998), I:480–81.

[59] Saxo Grammaticus, II:549–50.

[60] *Morkinskinna*, pp. 8–9.

[61] See Davidson, *Viking Road to Byzantium*, p. 222.

[62] Blöndal, pp. 77–87.

[63] *Morkinskinna*, pp. 12–13 and Saxo Grammaticus, II:549–51. Modern commentators include Davidson, *Viking Road to Byzantium*, pp. 222–24 and Blöndal, pp. 87–88.

ing to William of Malmesbury it was a lion.[64] The *Morkinskinna*'s account is the most extensive. It states that when the Norwegians were thrown into their prison – actually it was little more than an oubliette – they discovered a large sleeping snake surrounded by the bones of its previous victims. When Haraldr did not know where to turn, his brother, St Óláfr, appeared to the prisoners and revealed where a knife was hidden in their cell. Wielding this, Haraldr slew the serpent. Saxo Grammaticus adds that the knife which Haraldr used to dispatch the snake was later owned by King Valdemar the Great of Denmark who a century after the event was still showing the weapon to guests.[65] (William of Malmesbury has Haraldr strangle the lion with his own hands. There is no vision of Óláfr or knife mentioned in his account.)

Neither the *Fagrskinna* nor Snorri Sturuluson mention the serpent, but both include the vision of Óláfr.[66] The saint's message was of course different from that recorded in the *Morkinskinna*: he would simply assist them to escape from their prison. St Óláfr then appeared to a 'powerful woman' whom 'he had once healed' and instructed her to free his brother, which she did, according to the *Fagrskinna*, by having her servants pull Haraldr and his lieutenants up from the oubliette with a rope.[67] (*Morkinskinna* also relates the story of Óláfr's visit to the 'powerful woman,' but names her as Maria, Haraldr's love interest.[68])

Strangely, the latter part of this story may have an inkling of truth: Haraldr and his companions might well have been freed by a 'powerful woman' or even a group of powerful Byzantine citizens, for, in response to the changes that Michael V had made, the Constantinopolitans had begun to revolt. They even attacked the imperial palace, only being driven off at the last moment by the emperor's archers and ballistae. Michael V tried to pacify the situation by recalling Zoe, but the citizens, led by the freed Patriarch Alexius and, it seems, the freed Haraldr Harðráði, kept up their attacks. Soon Zoe returned and was joined by her sister, Theodora, who had been convinced that it was to the best interest of the state for her to come out of her monastic seclusion, both were crowned co-empresses. Ultimately, the palace fell, the Varangians guarding the emperor being defeated by the Varangians, revolting against him, led by Haraldr. The palace was vandalized, and Michael V, who sought sanctuary in the Studion chapel, was dragged to the square where he was blinded and exiled to a mon-

---

[64] William of Malmesbury, *Gesta regum Anglorum*, I:480–81.
[65] Strangely, it is Saxo's mention of King Valdemar's ownership of this knife which gives credibility to the account, according to Blöndal (pp. 87–88), otherwise an extremely harsh critic of all of the folkloric aspects of the life of King Haraldr.
[66] *Fagrskinna*, p. 111 and Snorri Sturluson, *Heimskringla*, III:85–86.
[67] The phrase Snorri uses is 'rík kona.' *Fagrskinna* (p. 111) is alone in noting how the prisoners were freed.
[68] *Morkinskinna*, pp. 13–14.

astery.[69] The sagas report that it was Haraldr Harðráði who gouged out the emperor's eyes.[70]

Haraldr may have been one of the heroes of the rebellion against Michael V, but that distinction did not keep him long from offending the new Imperial powers. Soon after the restoration of Zoe to her throne, on 11 June 1042, she married Constantine IX Monomachus and made him emperor.[71] Almost at the same time, Haraldr Harðráði asked to be allowed to return to Norway. This request was refused. Why Zoe would do this, and it is Zoe who the sagas blame for the decision in this matter,[72] is not revealed in these sources or in the *Book of Advice for an Emperor*, which also recounts Haraldr's request.[73] There may have been a general ban against travel in the wake of the recent Imperial crisis which could have prohibited the Norwegians from leaving the city, but more than likely Zoe's refusal originated possibly from the need to have Haraldr and his Varangians on guard in Constantinople against the rebellion of Haraldr's former adversary, Georgios Maniaces, who had gone to Italy after Michael V freed him, raised an army, and was marching towards the Byzantine capital. (He would not reach there, dying at the battle of Ostrovo on the Greek mainland early in 1043.) Alternatively, Zoe may have feared that, should the Norwegians return to their homeland through Kiev, the logical route, especially if Haraldr still intended to marry Elizaveta, they might reveal to a potential enemy the political and military weakness of the Byzantine state. While this latter fear admittedly might have seemed remote in 1042, at the end of 1043 the Russians did in fact attack the Empire, and one must wonder if this was not based on the intelligence passed to Iaroslav by Haraldr Harðráði or one of his companions[74] as Haraldr did indeed escape, although it was 'difficult for him' and was only accomplished 'by stealth,' to use the words of the *Book of Advice for an Emperor*.[75] The

---

[69] On the revolt against Michael V see Michael Psellus, pp. 138–51. Psellus does not mention Haraldr Harðráði in this revolt. See also Blöndal, pp. 88–96; Davidson, *Viking Road to Byzantium*, pp. 224–25; Treadgold, *History of the Byzantine State*, pp. 589–90; and Jenkins, p. 344.

[70] All of the Norwegian Kings' Sagas which mention the revolt record that it was Haraldr who blinded Michael V: *Fagrskinna*, 111; *Morkinskinna*, pp. 13–14; and Snorri Sturluson, *Heimskringla*, III:86–87. The *Sexstefja* (B, I, 339–46) claims that it was Haraldr Harðráði himself who reported that he blinded the emperor. See also Turville-Petre, p. 13.

[71] On this marriage and the future rule of Constantine IX see Jenkins, pp. 344–47; Treadgold, *History of the Byzantine State*, pp. 590–96; and Angold, pp. 36–37.

[72] Blöndal (p. 97) believes that this was not Zoe's decision, however, giving it instead to Constantine IX.

[73] The original sources which relate the story of Haraldr's escape are: *Fagrskinna*, p. 112; *Morkinskinna*, pp. 14–15; Snorri Sturluson, *Heimskringla*, III:88–89; and the *Book of Advice for an Emperor*, p. 97.

[74] On the escape see Davidson, *Viking Road to Byzantium*, pp. 226–27 and Blöndal, pp. 96–97. On the Russo-Byzantine war of 1043 see Angold, pp. 12–14 and Treadgold, *History of the Byzantine State*, p. 592. The Russian attack failed when its accompanying fleet was destroyed in the Bosporus by Greek fire and the army was unable to breach Byzantine fortifications along the Danube River.

[75] *Book of Advice for an Emperor*, p. 97.

Norwegian Kings' Sagas fill in the story.[76] One night after having been refused permission to leave, Haraldr and his men broke into the lodgings of Zoe's niece and, at one time, Haraldr's intended marriage partner, Maria, and took her to their ships (Varangian 'galleys,' according to Snorri Sturluson). Taking two of these ships, they rowed into the Bosporus, only to encounter the famous chains which the Byzantines spread across the Strait. Knowing of this impediment, Haraldr was prepared for the situation and shouted to his men to row as hard as they were able. Those who were not rowing he instructed to run to the stern of the ships. In response to this maneuver, the bows of both ships rose out of the water so that they drove on top of the chains. At that moment, Haraldr shouted to his men to run forward into the bows. The galleys also moved forward over the metal barrier. Haraldr's ship slid safely off, but the second vessel became stuck on the chains. Its keel broke, and many of the crew drowned. The remaining ship sailed into the Black Sea, but, before continuing on to Russia, Haraldr put Maria ashore and returned her to Constantinople. He did this, Snorri Sturluson remarks, to show the empress 'how little power she had on Haraldr for in no way could her imperial might keep him from taking her niece.'[77] More importantly, a marriage to Maria could not benefit this Norwegian prince, while a marriage to Elizaveta would.

At the time that he left Byzantium, Haraldr Harðráði was only twenty-seven years old. He had much of his life, at least the remaining twenty-four years, ahead of him, yet it could be said that some of the greatest adventures for this young prince had passed – the greatest adventures and the greatest learning experiences. In Russia he had begun to develop his military skills, and he gained some military experience; in observing Iaroslav, his future father-in-law, he had also learned how a successful warlord operated. In Byzantium he continued this training, learning strategy and tactics from one of the best generals which the Empire could provide as a teacher, Georgios Maniaces. Eventually, as so often happens, the pupil surpassed the teacher. In Sicily, and then again later in Constantinople, Haraldr showed that he had become the model of a brilliant tactician and strategist. Even if the stories recounted in the sagas are not true, the fact that there are so many of them indicates a military reputation that far exceeded his time and his eventual defeats. Also, by observing in close proximity the failures of Zoe and her cadre of enthroned husbands, Haraldr was presented with a negative example of political leadership which, together with the positive one of Iaroslav, would later enable him to develop his own political, economic, and military royal character.

---

[76] *Fagrskinna*, p. 112; *Morkinskinna*, pp. 14–15; and Snorri Sturluson, *Heimskringla*, III:88–89. Blöndal's speculation (pp. 99–100) that Haraldr's escape was connected to the performance of garrison duty is not convincing.

[77] Snorri Sturluson, *Heimskringla*, III:88–89:

> Ok áðr en hann sigldi henni gott fǫruneyti aptr til Miklagarðs, bað hana þá segja Zóe, frændkonu sinni, hversu mikit vald hon hafði á Haraldi eða hvárt nǫkkut dróttningar ríki fyrir staðit, at hann mætti fá jungfrúna.

See also *Fagrskinna*, p. 112 and *Morkinskinna*, pp. 14–15.

While in the east, Haraldr also became extremely rich. Snorri Sturluson reports that when the future Norwegian king arrived in Russia and stayed the winter in Novgorod with Iaroslav, 'he took into his possession all the gold that he had previously sent there from Constantinople, also a very large treasure.' It seems that during his stay in Byzantium, whether he was supposed to or not, Haraldr Harðráði had sent a huge amount of riches to Russia for safe-keeping. Snorri describes it further: 'There was so much wealth that no man in this northern land had ever seen its like in one man's possession.' This was acquired, the Icelandic historian rationalizes, because as leader of the Varangian Guard, Haraldr had three times been able to participate in *pólútasvarf*, a term loosely translated as 'palace-plunder,' which was traditionally allowed to the Varangians after the death of an emperor: 'they are able to go into all of the emperor's palaces, where his treasures are, and there they are able to take freely whatever they can put their hands on.'[78] Of course, there is no such thing as permissible palace-plunder recorded in Byzantine laws or annals, so, as mentioned above, perhaps Sigfús Blöndal is correct in wondering if this was the crime which landed Haraldr in prison.[79]

While in Novgorod over the winter, Haraldr also married Elizaveta.[80]

When weather conditions allowed it, early in 1046, Haraldr Harðráði returned to Scandinavia. No source mentions what he was thinking of doing once he arrived in Norway, although it seems apparent that he was desirous of ruling the kingdom that had been lost by his brother.[81] By his future actions, it can be seen that Haraldr expected to seize the throne by whatever means was necessary, and military force was undoubtedly an option.

What Haraldr could not have known was how his nephew, Magnús, would react. There is of course no doubt as to Magnús' ruling legitimacy. He was Óláfr's son and as such was the obvious heir to his father's crown.[82] Once

---

[78] Snorri Sturluson, *Heimskringla*, III:89–90:

En er Haraldr kom til Hólmgarðs, fagnaði Jarizleifr konungr honum forkunnar vel. Dvalðisk hann þar um vetrinn, tók þá í sína varðveizlu gull þat allt, er hann hafði áðr sent þannug útan af Miklagarði, ok margs konar dýrgripi. Var þat svá mikit fé, at engi maðr norðr í lǫnd hafði sét slíkt í eins manns eigu. Haraldr hafði þrim sinnum komit í pólútasvarf, meðan hann var í Miklagarði. Þat eru þar lǫg, at hvert sinn, er Grikkjakonungr deyr, þá skulu Væringjar hafa pólútasvarf. Þeir skulu þá ganga um allar pólútir konungs, þar sem féhirzlur hans eru, ok skal hverr þá eignask at frjálsu, er hǫndum kømr á.

See also Davidson, *Viking Road to Byzantium*, pp. 226–28. Interestingly, neither *Fagrskinna* nor *Morkinskinna* mention this accumulation of wealth.

[79] See n. 62 above. On the other hand, many Scandinavians did make large fortunes while serving in the Varangian Guard. See Obolensky, pp. 305–06.

[80] On the marriage see *Fagrskinna*, pp. 112–13; *Morkinskinna*, pp. 15–16; Snorri Sturluson, *Heimskringla*, III:90–91; and Per Sveaas Andersen, *Samlingen av Norge og kristningen av landet, 800–1300* (Bergen, 1977), 147.

[81] *Morkinskinna*'s claim (p. 16) that Haraldr was convinced by his father-in-law, Iaroslav, to return to Norway is not supported by the other sagas.

[82] Adam of Bremen (p. 135) claims that Magnús was illegitimate, born to Óláfr's concubine, but he is the sole author to maintain this.

Knútr's sons chose to abandon Norway and fight over England, Magnús was able to assume the throne, and since both Harold Harefoot and Harðaknútr died early in their English reigns, even before Haraldr Harðráði returned to Scandinavia, their threat to Magnús' royal security was removed. There also seems to have been no question as to Magnús' support among the Norwegian people.[83] By the time of Haraldr's return, Magnús had sat on Óláfr's throne for almost eleven years and during that time there appears to have been no major domestic insurrection against him, at least none are recorded in the contemporary or near contemporary sources.[84] His rule, more than that of a wandering uncle, was surely the 'legitimate' one.

However, during the High Middle Ages, royal inheritance in northern Europe was not guaranteed to the obvious candidate, even if he was the eldest son of the former occupant of the throne. As Harðaknútr discovered in 1040, and as Robert II of Normandy and Baldwin VI of Flanders would discover later in the eleventh century, being the eldest son but weaker in military strength than a younger brother usually meant that the younger would take the throne from the elder. Such was the nature of military legitimacy, and this was the problem which presented itself to Magnús. He was not a warlord; he had not acquired his throne, despite his father's loss of it, by military action. In contrast, Haraldr Harðráði was a famous military leader, and his legendary exploits in Russia and Byzantium were well known, and probably embellished, throughout Scandinavia. Snorri Sturluson writes:

> It was also said that Haraldr was larger than other men and stronger, and so wise that there was nothing which he was unable to do, and that he was always victorious wherever he fought. He was also so rich with gold that no man could count it.[85]

Perhaps it was this lack of military legitimacy which led Magnús to wage war in Denmark against his cousin, Sveinn Estriðson. According to Adam of Bremen and Saxo Grammaticus, the best sources for Danish history at this time, when Harðaknútr died in England, leaving his Danish throne vacant, the Danes selected Magnús as their king, thus again uniting the two Scandinavian kingdoms, although on this occasion under Norwegian and not Danish leadership.[86]

---

[83] Saxo Grammaticus (I:538) claims that the Norwegians selected Magnús as their king because 'his father's sanctity brought him the favor of the people' (quippe spectata patris sanctitas popularium ei favorem conciliaverat). See also Adam of Bremen, pp. 135–36 and Andersen, *Samlingen av Norge og kristningen*, p. 147.

[84] On Magnús' rule before Haraldr's arrival in Scandinavia see Theodoricus, pp. 46–50, and *Ágrip*, pp. 34–36. *Fagrskinna*, *Morkinskinna*, Snorri Sturluson, and *Flateyjarbók* do not mention Magnús' reign without Haraldr.

[85] Snorri Sturluson, *Heimskringla*, III:95:
Þat var ok sagt með, at Haraldr væri meiri en aðrir menn ok sterkari ok svá vitr, at honum var ekki ófœrt ok hann hafði ávallt sigr, er hann barðisk – hann var ok svá auðigr at gulli, at engi maðr vissi dœmi til.

[86] Saxo Grammaticus, I:540–41. See also *Fagrskinna*, p. 104; Snorri Sturluson, *Heimskringla*, III:35–39; and *Flateyjarbók*, III:273–74. Saxo Grammaticus (I:539–40), Theodoricus

Sveinn, who these sources claim was in England with Harðaknútr at the latter's death, although his presence is not noted in any contemporary Anglo-Saxon source, was understandably irritated by the Danes' choice of Magnús as their king. Indeed, Sveinn, who was related to Harðaknútr, according to Adam of Bremen and the *Ágrip*,[87] believed that he himself should have been elevated to the throne instead of his Norwegian cousin. Thus despite possibly being appointed as earl of Denmark by Magnús,[88] it was not long before Sveinn wanted complete control of and title to the kingdom. In response, Magnús led an army from Norway to Denmark and defeated Sveinn in battle. His plans checked for the moment, Sveinn fled to the safety of his mother's lands in Sweden, leaving Magnús in control of both Norway and Denmark.[89]

(Adam of Bremen and Saxo Grammaticus insist that this was not long a peaceful reign, as Magnús was forced to defend his Danish subjects against a Slavic invasion that followed his ouster of Sveinn. Magnús was victorious against them, too, earning the following from Saxo Grammaticus:

> Thus Magnús began to be held dear by the Danes for having defended their borders, so that by the consent of all, it was proposed that he be given the cognomen 'the Good,' and although it was traditionally awarded to others for their morals, he achieved it from the praises of fortune.[90]

(pp. 46, 48), *Ágrip* (p. 36) and the *Chronicon Rokskildense* (*Chronicon Roskildense et Chronicon Lethrense*, in *Scriptores minores historiae Danicae medii aevi*, ed. C. Gertz (Copenhagen, 1917–18), I:22) all contain a confusing story of a pact made between Harðaknútr and Magnús which promised Magnús Denmark if Harðaknútr was to precede him in death. See also Sten Körner (*The Battle of Hastings, England, and Europe, 1035–1066* (Lund, 1964), pp. 147–48).
[87] Adam of Bremen (p. 135) and *Ágrip* (p. 36) are the only sources for this relationship; however, it is probable based on what followed between Sveinn and Magnús. What is not probable is that Sveinn was Knútr's son, as averred by *Ágrip*. Saxo Grammaticus seems to be confused on this issue. On the one hand, he claims that Sveinn was of 'Canuti familia' (I:540), while at the same time arguing that he had no right to the throne 'by blood' (I:540).
[88] This is according to *Fagrskinna* (p. 104), Snorri Sturluson (*Heimskringla*, III:40), and *Flateyjarbók* (III:274–75) only. Other sources – Adam of Bremen (p. 136), Saxo Grammaticus (I:541–42), Theodoricus (pp. 46–48), *Ágrip* (pp. 36–37), and the *Chronicon Roskildense* (I:22) – all claim an immediate attack by Sveinn on Magnús in Denmark without an intervening agreement between the two cousins.
[89] Saxo Grammaticus (I:544) contends that Magnús defeated Sveinn both on sea and then on land, in Jutland. Snorri Sturluson (*Heimskringla*, III:40–64) claim that the two fought three battles, with the last of the three fought at Helganess on the cost of Jutland. All of the other sources of this event mention only the defeat of Sveinn, without more details. See Adam of Bremen, p. 135 (Adam's chronology is faulty here, having this defeat occur before Harðaknútr's death); *Chronicon Rokskildense*, p. 22; Theodoricus, pp. 48, 50; *Ágrip*, p. 36–37; *Fagrskinna*, pp. 104–05; and *Flateyjarbók*, III:275, 283–84. See also Turville-Petre, pp. 8–9.
[90] Saxo Grammaticus, I:545:
> Adeo autem Magnús ob vindictam finium suis carus haberi coeptus est, ut omnium consensu Boni cognomine censeretur, quodque aliorum moribus tribui assolet, fortunae laudibus impetraret.
Some contemporary poems also discuss an attack, but from the Wends and not the Slavs. See

However, as Adam and Saxo confuse most of the details – for example, Adam claims that the Slavs were led by eight brothers who attacked the Danes and were killed by them in an attempt to avenge the death of their father, Ratibor, while Saxo claims that the Slavic attack was made because an unnamed noble was seeking revenge for the deaths of his twelve sons previously killed in Denmark[91] – and as no other contemporary source records a Slavic assault on Denmark, such an invasion might not have occurred.

Thus it was, as Haraldr Harðráði proceeded through Scandinavia on his way to meet his nephew in 1046, that he gained an ally in the defeated Sveinn. Almost all of the Norwegian Kings' Sagas report that Haraldr had learned of Sveinn's loss in Denmark while in the east and that he therefore traveled to Sweden to seek the aid of his fellow exile, also his nephew.[92] The two swore fealty to each other and joined forces, thus uniting a army of Scandinavians from Norway, Sweden, Denmark, Russia, and perhaps even Byzantium.[93]

Haraldr and Sveinn's first combined military adventure was a raid along the coast of Denmark. Their reason for doing this, seemingly a poor choice of conflict for two who wished to conquer lands and not simply pillage them, was actually quite simple: their effort was to impress upon the natives of the lands which they raided that Magnús offered them no protection. Intimidation in medieval warfare was often more important and always quicker than conquest, as it frequently led to the capitulation of places not even attacked. Haraldr Harðráði and Sveinn Estriðson undoubtedly hoped that such a raid would lead the Danes to surrender to them and later to join them against a more powerful Norwegian army. That this was successful can be seen in Snorri Sturluson's statement that 'the Danes were submitting to them everywhere'.[94]

How could Magnús react to such an attack? The sagas report that he quickly learned of the success of Haraldr and Sveinn in Denmark, and that he also knew that their next target was to be Norway.[95] What could he do but prepare for war? Þjóðólfr's poem expresses such an attitude:

> Now the seafaring warriors
> Have little hope of peace;
> Fear stirs in men's hearts,
> Warships lie off the beaches.

Den norske-islandske Skjaldedigtning, ed. F. Jónsson (Oslo, 1912), B, I, strophe 11–13 and Turville-Petre, pp. 8–9.

[91] Adam of Bremen, p. 137, and Saxo Grammaticus, I:543.

[92] Sveinn was the son of Haraldr's half-sister. For his genealogy see Magnusson and Pálsson, pp. 65–66.

[93] Theodoricus, p. 50; Fagrskinna, p. 113; Morkinskinna, pp. 17–18; Snorri Sturluson, Heimskringla, III:91–92; and Flateyjarbók, III:306–07. Morkinskinna claims that it was Sveinn who asked for Haraldr's assistance and not the other way around.

[94] Snorri Sturluson, Heimskringla, III:95: 'en landsfólk gekk víða undir þá.' See also Andersen, Samlingen av Norge og kristningen, p. 148.

[95] Morkinskinna, p. 18; Snorri Sturluson, Heimskringla, III:94–95; and Flateyjarbók, III: 307.

Death-dealing King Magnús
Will sail his vessels southwards,
While Haraldr's ocean-dragons
Are pointing to the north.[96]

Such a war would have brought ruin to the kingdoms of Norway and Denmark, and Magnús' councillors who realized this asked the king to seek a reconciliation with his uncle instead of war. Magnús agreed to do this and, the Norwegian Kings' Sagas report, secretly sent a fast ship to Haraldr to petition for peace; the king, holding two reeds before him, representing the two halfs of Norway, offered to split his kingdom with his uncle who in turn would share his wealth with his nephew.[97]

The offer was a decent one, but acceptance of it did not come without consequences. For Haraldr to accept one nephew's petition was to break his agreement with his other nephew. On the other hand, it was an opportunity too good to refuse. By Magnús' showing weakness in the face of military conflict, Haraldr knew that he would undoubtedly be able to control the co-ruled kingdom of Norway, while, at the same time, as Sveinn had shown no particular strength in Denmark without Haraldr's participation, that kingdom too looked vulnerable. Besides, oath breaking, as will be seen in the case of Harold Godwinson with William the Conqueror, was not an uncommon trait of eleventh-century warlords, who nearly always recognized their own profit above what would later be called chivalric.

Snorri Sturluson records no immediate answer from Haraldr Harðráði, although Haraldr did keep open clandestine contact with his nephew. While the lack of chivalry in Haraldr's acceptance of Magnús' proposal may not have affected the eleventh-century warlord, it is clear that Snorri has some problem with it, so he produces an incident which 'justifies' Haraldr's disloyalty to Sveinn. The incident has to do with a banner owned by Sveinn but believed magical by Haraldr. Sveinn, who does not hold the same belief in the powers of

---

[96] As found in Snorri Sturluson, *Heimskringla*, III:95:

> Nú es valmeiðum víðis,
> veit drótt mikinn ótta,
> skeiðr hefr herr fyr hauðri,
> hætt góðs friðar vætta.
> Mildr vill Magnús halda
> morðs hlunngotum norðan,
> ítr, en ǫnnur skreytir
> unnvigg Haraldr sunnan.

(I have used Magnusson and Pálsson's translation of this poem (p. 68).)

[97] Theodoricus, pp. 54–55; *Ágrip*, pp. 38–39; *Morkinskinna*, pp. 18–19; Snorri Sturluson, *Heimskringla*, III:95–96; and *Flateyjarbók*, III:307–08. Both the *Morkinskinna* and *Flateyjarbók* have Haraldr Harðráði take the initiative in asking Magnús for half of his kingdom, which the king initially refuses to do, only to reconsider the proposal later. I feel that Snorri's account of this, which is recounted above, is the more probable. *Morkinskinna* and *Flateyjarbók* are alone in mentioning the reeds.

the banner, taunts his uncle by challenging him to fight and win three battles against Magnús to prove the banner's magic. This leads to an argument between the two leaders over Haraldr's loyalty which only ends when they retire to their beds for the night. Haraldr, suspicious of his nephew's words, decides not to sleep in his bed, placing a log in it instead. Sure enough, during the night an assassin attacks Haraldr's bed, sinking his axe deep into the log placed where Haraldr should have been. This treachery, which Haraldr blams on Sveinn, convinces the Norwegian to flee with his men to Magnús and to agree with the latter's proposition for co-rule.[98]

Did this incident of betrayal really occur, and, if so, was Sveinn to blame, something which Snorri does not actually say? Probably not. All of the other sources record Haraldr's quick acceptance of Magnús' proposal without mentioning his argument with Sveinn or the attack on his life.[99] Yet, to Snorri it rationalizes Haraldr's own disloyalty to Sveinn while at the same time explains why there was such an enmity between these two erstwhile allies.

So the agreement was made. While the kingdom was not physically split, all of the economic gains were divided equally (*skyldum ok skǫttum* in Old Norse), and both were to carry the same royal title, although Magnús was to have seniority when they both were together. On his part, Haraldr shared his own immense wealth with Magnús and his retainers, equally, Snorri Sturluson insists, a gesture which caused Magnús to exclaim, 'you are much more generous than I.'[100]

At the best of times co-rule over any political entity breeds jealousy and discontentment, especially when that political entity is one as large as the kingdom of Norway, especially when it is in the eleventh century, and especially when the two rulers have been brought together by the threat of war, with neither trusting the other. Indeed, in this instance, the fact that the two kings had separate courts and were rarely together after their dividing of the kingdom, should indicate that their co-rule was anything but peaceful. Snorri Sturluson says as much when he writes: 'Soon, differences arose between the two kings, and there were many people so eager to do evil, that they encouraged evil between them.'[101]

One incident in particular pushed their union to the very brink of failure. Less than a year later and at the only meeting of the two kings after their division of the kingdom recorded in the medieval sources, Haraldr Harðráði moored his ships in the royal berths reserved for Magnús, something he had been strictly

---

[98] Snorri Sturluson, *Heimskringla*, III:96–98.

[99] Theodoricus, pp. 50–51; *Ágrip*, pp. 38–39; *Fagrskinna*, pp. 113–15; *Morkinskinna*, pp. 18–19; and *Flateyjarbók*, III:308–09. See also Freeman, *Norman Conquest*, II:90; Davidson, *Viking Road to Byzantium*, pp. 226–27; and Henry R. Loyn, *The Vikings in Britain* (Oxford, 1994), p. 57.

[100] Snorri Sturluson (*Heimskringla*, III:98–102) is the most detailed source in his description of the dividing of Norway between Magnús and Haraldr. The original of Magnús' exclamation, as written by Snorri (III:100), is: 'Ertu maðr miklu ǫrvari en ek.' See also Davidson, *Viking Road to Byzantium*, p. 227.

[101] Snorri Sturluson, *Heimskringla*, III:102: 'Brátt gerðusk greinir í um samþykki konunganna, ok váru margir svá illgjarnir, at þeira gengu svá illa í milli.'

forbidden from doing. This absolutely enraged Magnús who prepared to attack Haraldr until the elder but lesser king cut his moorings and removed his ships from Magnús' docks. The two exchanged angry words and insults but the matter ended without bloodshed. To Snorri Sturluson, Haraldr's wisdom had conquered Magnús' 'youthful excitement' and peace had been preserved, while the anonymous author of the *Fagrskinna* is more circumspect in his judgement of the affair and Haraldr's role in it, claiming that witnesses to what occurred were split on their verdict over the older king's actions. One thing that the two authors seem to agree on, however, is that it was obvious that the co-rule of Norway was floundering.[102]

It was perhaps fortuitous then that King Magnús the Good passed away the next year. Yet, as suspicious as the timing of this may seem, Haraldr did not have anything to do with his nephew's demise, at least not according to the original sources; even Adam of Bremen and Saxo Grammaticus, no friends to the Norwegian king, do not try to tie him to his co-ruler's death.[103] According to the Norwegian Kings' Sagas, Magnús simply fell ill and died; of course, a dream from Óláfr to Magnús prophesying his death preceded it, but Haraldr played no part.[104]

All of the original sources praise the dead king. Theodoricus writes:

> This Magnús, son of Saint Óláfr the Martyr, was a man conspicuous in goodness, prodigious in generosity, strong in military affairs, experienced with a remarkable genious in the administration of government, at which he also appeared almost always to be the victor in debates. Towards all of his subjects, he was especially gracious, charming, and liberal.[105]

---

[102] Snorri Sturluson, *Heimskringla*, III:103–04 (the phrase is 'bernska er bráðgeð') and *Fagrskinna*, pp. 118–19. *Morkinskinna* (pp. 19–46) and, following that source, *Flateyjarbók* (III:308–28) record much of what occurred during the two kings' rule together in Norway, none of which is recorded in any of the other Scandinavian sources, but neither contain this incident. While interesting as a study of how Magnús and Haraldr ruled separately, it should be noted that none of this material discusses issues which concerned the two kings together and thus it does not assist in understanding the faltering political situation of Norway.

[103] Theodoricus, p. 55; *Ágrip*, pp. 39–40; *Fagrskinna*, p. 120; *Morkinskinna*, p. 46 (the manuscript is damaged at this point, although the *Flateyjarbók* probably carries the story written in the *Morkinskinna*); Snorri Sturluson, *Heimskringla*, III:104–06; and *Flateyjarbók*, III:328–30. Saxo Grammaticus (II:551) writes only that on his return from Byzantium, Haraldr 'occupied' the Norwegian throne (which was rightfully Sveinn's, Saxo insists), while Adam of Bremen says nothing about how Haraldr came to rule Norway.

[104] Theodoricus, p. 55; *Ágrip*, pp. 39–40; *Fagrskinna*, p. 120; *Morkinskinna*, p. 46; Snorri Sturluson, *Heimskringla*, III:104–06; and *Flateyjarbók*, III:328–30. Brønsted (p. 99) claims that Magnús died when he fell from his horse, but he does not state the source of that information.

[105] Theodoricus, p. 55:

> Iste Magnús filius beati Olavi martyris vir fuit bonitate conspicuus, lenitate praeditus, in re militari strenuus, in rerum publicarum administratione miro callebat ingenio, unde et in congressionibus paene semper victor extitit; morum suavitate et liberalitate subjectis omnibus gratissimus fuit.

Snorri uses similar honorific words:

> King Magnús had been a man of average height, with regular features, a fair complexion, and fair hair. He was eloquent and quick thinking, noble in temperament, very generous with his possessions, a great warrior, and brave in warfare. He was the most popular of all the kings, praised by both his friends and his enemies.[106]

And everyone throughout Norway mourned the dead king, all, it seemed, except for Haraldr Harðráði. He was quick to react to the news by gathering all of the Norwegian local leaders together, declaring himself king not only of Norway but of Denmark – Magnús had specified that Denmark was to be ruled over by Sveinn after his death – and announcing that he intended to muster an army to oust Sveinn from that southern Scandinavian land. He did not even accompany the corpse of his co-ruler to its resting place beside St Óláfr in Þrándheimr. This task was performed instead by Magnús' most trusted advisor, Einarr Þambarskelfir (Paunch-Shaker), a man who would later oppose the new sole king, Haraldr Harðráði.[107]

Haraldr Harðráði began to rule Norway alone in 1047, and he would continue to do so until 1066, when he was killed at the battle of Stamford Bridge while attacking England. For almost twenty years then this king influenced Norwegian economic, ecclesiastical, social, and political affairs, and yet there is very little known about his domestic policies. The Norwegian Kings' Sagas simply do not spend much time discussing this part of Haraldr's life. In these sagas, there is far more space devoted to his lengthy war with Sveinn in Denmark and to his short and final attack of England than to his governance of Norway. Undoubtedly this is proof of the large amount of interest in warfare that modern commentators have all too frequently accused the authors of these sagas of having, but it may also indicate that Haraldr's Norwegian administration was one of peace and progress, one that benefitted his Scandinavian kingdom as much as its absolutism may have substantiated his nickname, 'Hard-Ruler.'

Such a conclusion is in fact the case, as evidenced by archaeological and other non-narrative sources, as well as what little can be found in the sagas. First, Haraldr seems to have instituted several sound economic policies. Coin hoards and other numismatic evidence have shown that he had a large number of mints throughout Norway, so many that he became the first Scandinavian king who required all of his coins to carry the name of their mint and some to carry the name of their mint-master. These mints in turn issued so many coins that, in

---

[106] Snorri Sturluson, *Heimskringla*, III:107:
Magnús konungr hafði verit meðalmaðr á vǫxt, réttleitr ok ljósleitr, ljóss á hár, snjallmælt ok skjótráðr, skǫrungglyndr, inn mildasti af fé, hermaðr mikill ok inn vápndjarfasti. Allra konunga var hann vinsælstr, bæði lofuðu hann vinir ok óvinir.
[107] See Snorri Sturluson, *Heimskringla*, III:106–07, and *Flateyjarbók*, III:328–30, who are alone in these details. (NB. The *Morkinskinna* manuscript continues to be damaged at this point.)

the words of Else Rosedahl, 'a viable coin economy came into being.'[108] Gwyn Jones adds:

> Harald Hardradi, as befitted a strong, ambitious king who had seen the civilization of the Byzantine, Muslim, and Mediterranean worlds, did much to develop a Norwegian currency, manage it in his own interest, and give it permanence.[109]

This coin economy was needed to support Norway's participation in international trade. Haraldr, who had traveled widely throughout much of the known world and had grown wealthy on its riches, understood the importance of a vibrant trade, and, because of the connections which he had made in Russia and Byzantium, Norway sent exports to and received imports from those faraway places.[110] Trade was also carried out with the more nearby lands of Scotland and Ireland.[111]

Additionally, Haraldr Harðráði proved to share with his brother, St Óláfr, an interest in advancing Christianity in Norway. Archaeological excavations have shown that he continued to build and improve churches throughout the kingdom. These included especially the Church of St Mary in Niðaróss, where it appears that Haraldr was responsible for most of the construction of the church and its associated ecclesiastical buildings, St Gregory's Church at the mouth of the Nið, which he built as part of his palace, and St Óláfr's Church in Þránd- heimr, which he completed in order to house his saintly brother's body and relics.[112]

To improve the ceremonial and theological practices of his people, Haraldr imported priests and monks from outside Scandinavia. Most of these, it should be said, came from Russia and Byzantium, thus presenting a different form of Christianity from elsewhere in northern Europe.[113] Of course this is logical, as Haraldr knew very little Christianity other than that of the places where he had spent the majority of his life. Yet, as this occurred before the schism between

---

108 Else Rosedahl, *The Vikings*, trans. S.M. Margeson and K. Williams (Harmondsworth, 1992), p. 114.

109 Jones, p. 6. See also Kolbjørn Skaare ('Harald Hardråde som myntherre,' in *Harald Hardråde*, ed. A. Berg *et al.* (Oslo, 1966), pp. 41–67), who reproduces Haraldr's coins and details the mints which produced them.

110 See Davidson, *Viking Road to Byzantium*, p. 228 and Blöndal, pp. 100–101.

111 As evidenced by Haraldr's later connections with King Malcolm of Scotland and the presence of Norwegian ships traveling from Ireland to Wales in 1058. Both incidents will be discussed at length below.

112 Snorri Sturluson, *Heimskringla*, III:121, mentions the construction of all of these churches; archaeological evidence confirms the building of St Mary's and St Óláfr's during this part of the eleventh century. *Fagrskinna* (p. 127) highlights the construction of St Mary's, but does not mention the others. See also Andersen, *Samlingen av Norge og kristningen*, p. 153 and Håkon Christie, 'Haralds Oslo,' in *Harald Hardråde*, ed. A. Berg *et al.* (Oslo, 1966), pp. 69–89.

113 Foote and Wilson, p. 46; Davidson, *Viking Road to Byzantium*, p. 228; and Blöndal, pp. 100–101.

eastern and western Christianity had taken place, what these priests and monks delivered to the Norwegian people probably did not alter their ecclesiastical bearing, at least there appears to have been no lingering 'orientalism' in the Christianity of later times.[114] However, the presence of Orthodox ecclesiastics does seem to have created a controversy when papal legates visited Haraldr and chastised him for his behavior toward his people, especially the Catholic clergy. In response, Haraldr Harðráði promptly threw them out of his court. This brought the following invective from Adam of Bremen:

> The tyrant, moved to anger by their mandates, ordered the hated papal legates to leave, exclaiming that he did not know that there was any archbishop or power in Norway except for Haraldr himself.[115]

Adam, as a Catholic monastic chronicler, can be forgiven for his criticism of Haraldr's action in dealing with the legates, but even he had to accept Haraldr's religious inclination towards Christianity when he recounts that the Norwegian king gave a large gift of money to Bishop Adalward of Sweden to purchase the freedom of Christian slaves; because of this, more than 300 were liberated.[116]

Finally, while Haraldr Harðráði was publically close to the Christian Church, his personal morality appears not to have matched the Christian ideal. Married to Elizaveta and having produced several children by her, although the correct number cannot be known from the sources available (Snorri Sturluson indicates that it was two daughters, María and Ingigerðr), he also had at least two sons, Magnús and Óláfr, from Þóru, the daughter of Þorbergs Árnasonar.[117] (Her son, Óláfr, would succeed his father as king in 1066.) Although the Norwegian Kings' Sagas insist that Þóru was also Haraldr's wife, Elizaveta was alive throughout Haraldr's life and no divorce is known nor likely to have been granted. Nor would the Norwegian church officials, western or eastern, have accepted a polygamous relationship of their king. One can only imagine the denunciation of Adam of Bremen and Saxo Grammaticus had such a relationship existed! It should also be noted that kings having illegitimate children by adulterous companionships was not novel nor does it appear to have been criticized in the eleventh century as it would be later. After all, Haraldr's previous

---

[114] As can be seen in Birgit Sawyer and Peter Sawyer, *Medieval Scandinavia: From Conversion to Reformation, circa 800–1500* (Minneapolis, 1993), pp. 100–28.

[115] Adam of Bremen, p. 160:
Ad haec mandata commotus ad iram tyrannus legatos pontificis spretos abire precepit, clamitans se nescire, quis sit archiepiscopus aut potens in Norvegia, nisi solus Haroldus.
Adam of Bremen also writes that Alexander II rebuked Haraldr personally for this action. Adam does not connect the clash with the papal legates, which is not mentioned in any of the Norwegian Kings' Sagas, with the presence of eastern ecclesiastics in Norway. However, Foote and Wilson (p. 46) believe that this was in fact the reason for Haraldr's problems with the papacy.

[116] Adam of Bremen, p. 254. See also Foote and Wilson, p. 67.

[117] Snorri Sturluson, *Heimskringla*, III:112. See also *Morkinskinna*, p. 54 and *Flateyjarbók*, III:335–37.

co-ruler, Magnús, was St Óláfr's illegitimate son from an adulterous union, and this in no way kept the saint from becoming the holy man that medieval Scandinavian society saw him as, even as early as the mid-eleventh century. Nor does Harold Godwinson appear to have been stigmatized by the continual presence of his mistress and the mother of his children, Eadgyð Swanneshals, at his court, even after his marriage to Ealdyð.[118]

Haraldr Harðráði, again as befits someone who had traveled widely throughout the world, was also interested in exploring both his own realm, which the *Morkinskinna* recounts was done in person,[119] and outside its borders, which trips he seems to have sponsored. He may even have known of and sought out the legendary land called Vinland which Viking sailors had discovered only a short time before, but which, according to Adam of Bremen, was widely reported in Denmark and Norway. Adam writes:

> The most enterprising Prince Haraldr of the Norwegians lately attempted this [sea]. Who, having searched thoroughly the length of the northern ocean in ships, finally had before his eyes the dark failing boundaries of the savage world, and, by retracing his steps, with difficulty barely escaped the deep abyss in safety.[120]

Snorri Sturluson adds that Haraldr had many connections with Icelanders and that ships from his kingdom frequently sailed between Norway and Iceland bearing trade goods, on which he controlled the price, and gifts, including a bell for a church built at the Alðing from timber sent to the island earlier by St Óláfr.[121]

Finally, as already mentioned, Haraldr Harðráði was a great admirer of poetry and even skilled in the art himself. The sagas dedicated to his life, especially that written by Snorri Sturluson, are filled with poems delivered by many diverse poets which praise his heroism and stature. Snorri writes that the reason for his including so many poems in his saga, mostly delivered by Icelandic poets, was that 'many stories about King Haraldr were spoken in the poems which Icelandic men gave to him and his sons.'[122]

---

118 This will be discussed below in the chapter on Harold Godwinson.

119 See, for example, Haraldr's trip to Uppland as recounted in *Morkinskinna*, pp. 42–44.

120 Adam of Bremen, pp. 275–76:

Temptavit hoc nuper experientissimus Nordmannorum princeps Haraldus. Qui latitudinem septentrionalis oceani perscrutatus navibus tandem caligantibus ante ora deficientis mundi finibus inmane baratum abyssi retroactis vestigiis pene vix salvus evasit.

Adam takes the last part of this quote from Virgil's *Aeneid* VIII:245. None of the Norwegian Kings' Sagas record such a trip.

121 Snorri Sturluson, *Heimskringla*, III:119.

122 Snorri Sturluson, *Heimskringla*, III:119: 'Er saga mikil frá Haraldi konungi sett í kvæði, þau er íslenzkir menn fœrðu honum sjálfum eða sonum hans. Var hann fyrir þá sǫk vinr þeira mikill.' See also *Fagrskinna*, p. 126. On Haraldr's love for and patronage of poetry see Turville-Petre.

One story found in the *Morkinskinna* and the *Flateyjarbók* confirms Haraldr's love for poetry. One day when Haraldr was sailing with his fleet, he
encountered a man fishing alone. The king asked him: 'Can you by any chance
make verses, my man?' 'No, sir,' replied the fisherman. 'Oh yes,' said the king,
'just make a verse for me.' The fisherman agreed, but only if the king made a
verse for him in return. The fisherman's verse went like this:

> I pulled up a haddock.
> It took long: it wasn't pleased.
> I bashed its head in.
> That was just now.
> Quite different, I remember,
> I had a sword, gold-wired.
> As I lad I splashed spears in blood.
> That was long ago.

The king congratulated the fisherman on his poem and asked, 'Have you been
among men of authority or in battles?' The poetic fisherman replied: 'Sir, maybe
I have been among men quite as powerful as you are, though now everything
seems lowly compared with you.' He then requested that Haraldr fulfill his
promise. The king's poem was:

> My bloody bold retainers
> Chopped down sturdy Danes,
> Chased the fleeing enemy
> Onwards – that was just now.
> Another time, earlier,
> Far from my homeland
> I reddened swords in Serkland.
> That was long ago.

Haraldr then required his court poet (his *skald*), Þjóðólfr, to compose a poem:

> Our gracious king was reddened
> In the spear-river: a tough encounter.
> The Danes had angered the god.
> That was just now.
> The prince set his standard
> Down in flat Serkland.
> Its staff stood at the king's bidding.
> That was long ago.

Neither Haraldr nor the fisherman were pleased by the *skald*'s poem and criticized it on technical grounds. Then a second round of poems commenced
which, when completed, again proved that the king and the fisherman were
better poets than Þjóðólfr. This left the king puzzled, not at the poor quality
of the poems of his court-poet, but at the good quality of those composed by
the fisherman. The solution to the puzzle came when the fisherman revealed

that he was not a poor laborer of Haraldr's realm but 'a very valiant man' in disguise.[123]

With seemingly so many positive features of Haraldr's governance of Norway, it seems odd then that he was given his cognomen, 'Hard-Ruler,' or that modern historians the quality of Peter Foote and David M. Wilson would write:

> Haraldr's aggressive maintenance of Norwegian independence was matched by his consolidation of the king's sovereignity at home. The dynasty of the earls of Lade disappeared in his day and the title of earl fell into disuse for a century. He tightened the monarchy's hold on the settlements of the Uplands, using force on occasion to make his authority clear and increasing royal property in the region by subsequent forfeitures.[124]

It is true that Adam of Bremen writes similar lines,[125] but these can be excused because of his general dislike of Haraldr, and, besides, they alone are unlikely to have swayed Foote and Wilson, nor could they be responsible for what was a contemporary, Norwegian cognomen. Instead, perhaps the anonymous author of the *Fagrskinna* and Snorri Sturluson are correct when they assert that as Haraldr grew in power and stability, his absolutism became so egotistic that no one would argue or even differ with him. Þjóðólfr composed this poem about Haraldr's requirements during this time:

> Subjects of King Haraldr
> Must show their subjection
> By standing up or sitting
> Just as the king wishes.
> All the people humbly
> Bow before this warrior;
> The king demands obedience
> To all his royal orders.[126]

---

123 *Flateyjarbók*, III:377–78. It is also found in similar language in *Morkinskinna*, pp. 101–103. I have used the translation of this episode, with its difficult-to-translate poems, found in Page, *Chronicles of the Vikings*, pp. 23–24. Consequently, I have not included a transcription of the lengthy Old Norse original. See also Turville-Petre, pp. 12–13. Another poetic game was played between Haraldr and Þjóðólfr as they passed the houses of a tanner and a blacksmith. Again, Haraldr bests his court poet. See *Den norske-islandske Skjaldedigtning*, B, I, str. 350 and Turville-Petre, pp. 10–12.

124 Foote and Wilson, p. 46.

125 Adam of Bremen, especially pp. 159–62.

126 Þjóðólfr's poem is recorded only in Snorri Sturluson, *Heimskringla*, III:123:
Haraldr konungr var ríklundaðr, ok óx þar, sem hann festisk í landinu, ok kom svá, at flestum mǫnnum dugði illa at mæla í móti honum eða draga fram annat mál en þat, er hann vildi vera láta. Svá segir Þjóðólfr skáld:
> Gegn skyli herr sem hugnar
> hjaldrvitjaðar sitja
> dolgstœranda dýrum
> dróttinvandr ok standa.
> Lýtr folkstara feiti,

In such conditions, it is not difficult to imagine that, as alluded to in the quote from Foote and Wilson above, Haraldr Harðráði began to suffer some domestic problems. The principal opponents to Haraldr's rule in Norway were the descendants of Earl Hákon Sigurðsson. Earl Hákon Sigurðsson, also known as 'the Powerful,' had ruled Norway from 975 to 995 when he was overthrown by and killed in an invasion of the kingdom by Óláfr Tryggvason.[127] His progeny, who seem to have been quite numerous during the mid-eleventh century, lived throughout the more northern Norwegian region of Trondelag and the remoteness of this land had given them quite a bit of sovereignty over the area and the many farmers who resided there. They may even have felt that the Norwegian throne belonged rightfully to them, although it seems that they put no specific claim forward for this at the death of either Knútr or Magnús. Power in the north may have been all that they wished for.

The leader of this family was Einarr Þambarskelfir (Paunch-Shaker), who was married to Hákon the Powerful's daughter. Einarr had been close to King Magnús who undoubtedly had profited from this friendship in keeping the northern regions loyal to him. In turn, Magnús awarded Einarr with power, title, and wealth; Einarr Paunch-Shaker was extremely wealthy, and certainly did not fear Haraldr Harðráði. He had shown this at Magnús' death when he took the body of his friend to be buried, as seen above, and he would continue to oppose Haraldr throughout the early part of his reign.[128]

Snorri Sturluson writes with some understatement that during the time that Haraldr was king relations between himself and Einarr 'were rather distant,'[129] but as long as Einarr remained in the north and Haraldr in the south there was no confrontation between them. Only when Haraldr traveled to his northern court, at Þrándheimr, was there possible confrontation. On one particular occasion, the Norwegian Kings' Sagas report that Einarr made a show of force at the Þrándheimr court, arriving with 'eight or nine longships and almost five hundred men.'[130] In doing this, he was obviously looking for a confrontation with Haraldr, but the king was not provoked by the incident.

There are two different versions of what happened next. According to the *Fagrskinna* and Snorri Sturluson, Einarr would not allow his yearning to confront the king to subside. Thus he tried another tactic. At court one day, a thief

---

fátt es til nema játta
þat, sem þá vill gotnum,
þjóð ǫll, konungr bjóða.

I have used Magnusson and Pálsson's translation of Þjóðólfr's poem (p. 91). See also *Fagrskinna*, pp. 126–27.

[127] On Earl Hákon the Powerful's rule, see Jones, pp. 124–33.

[128] On Einarr Þambarskelfir's position in Norway, see *Morkinskinna*, pp. 29–31; Snorri Sturluson, *Heimskringla*, III:122; and *Flateyjarbók*, III:319–21.

[129] Snorri Sturluson, *Heimskringla*, III:122. The phrase in Old Norse is 'heldr var fátt.'

[130] *Fagrskinna*, p. 127 and Snorri Sturluson, *Heimskringla*, III:123–24. *Fagrskinna* uses the phrase 'húskarla lið' to describe these troops. Haraldr, fearing what was to occur between the two of them, composed a poem found in Snorri Sturluson, *Heimskringla*, III:124.

was presented to the king for judgement and punishment. This unnamed thief had previously been a favored servant to Einarr, and, fearing for his safety, Einarr took him forcibly from the court. Haraldr was livid at this affront to his authority, but he was persuaded to seek reconciliation and called Einarr to court. Einarr went, but only because his son, Eindriði, who was married to Haraldr's niece and close to the king, promised him security in the king's presence. However, such kinship and promise mattered little to Haraldr Harðráði at this point in his rule, and, as soon as Einarr entered the meeting place, the king's men attacked and slew the powerful northern chieftain. When Eindriði tried to intervene, he too was killed.[131]

The second version of what occurred at Þrándheimr between Haraldr and Einarr is found in the *Morkinskinna* and *Flateyjarbók*. In this version Haraldr had invited Einarr to a feast. As the two lay full of food and inebriated, Einarr fell asleep during the telling of some of Haraldr's exploits. Haraldr then asked one of his kinsmen, Grjótgarðr, to take some straw, weave it together, and place it in Einarr's hands (*Flateyjarbók* has it placed under Einarr's nose). Grjótgarðr then woke Einarr with the words, 'Let's get ready, Einarr.' The northern leader woke, became disoriented by the straw, and embarrassed himself by passing wind. On the following morning Einarr killed Grjótgarðr for his offense, and a few days later Einarr and Eindriði were killed in revenge.[132]

Whatever actually happened, the problem with Hákon the Powerful's descendants was solved for the moment; the bodies of Einarr and Eindriði were buried in St Óláfr's Church near the tombs of St Óláfr himself and his son, Magnús. The family of Einarr was stunned and angered by what had occurred, but they could do little about it. Snorri Sturluson writes:

> After Einarr's death King Haraldr was so very much hated for this deed that only the lack of a leader to raise the standard for the farmers kept the landed men and farmers from going to battle with him.[133]

---

131 *Fagrskinna*, pp. 127–28 and Snorri Sturluson, *Heimskringla*, III:125–26. These works leave open the possibility that Haraldr knew of the relationship between the accused and Einarr. If so, then perhaps Haraldr was trying to provoke Einarr to do what in fact occurred. On the death of Einarr see Andersen, *Samlingen av Norge og kristningen*, pp. 150–51.

132 *Morkinskinna*, pp. 59–60 and *Flateyjarbók*, III:344–50. Kari Ellen Gade ('Einarr þambarskelfir's Last Shot,' *Scandinavian Studies* 67 (1995), 153–62) attempts to decipher the confusing element of this story, the straw and its result on Einarr; her conclusion is acceptable, but not altogether convincing: 'In Haraldr's opinion, Einarr is a feeble old man, unfit for fighting, and the only þomb (belly) he is able to cause trembling in, is his own intestines' (p. 160).

133 Snorri Sturluson, *Heimskringla*, III:126:
Eptir fall Einars var Haraldr konungr svá mjǫk óþokkaðr af verki þessu, at þat einu skorti á, er lendir menn ok bœndr veittu eigi atferð ok heldu bardaga við hann, at engi varð forgǫgumaðr til at reisa merki fyrir bóandaherinum.
Fagrskinna (p. 127) contains a poem written about the hatred held by this family for Haraldr Harðráði.

To prevent such a leader from rising, Haraldr sent his trusted aide, Finnr Árnason, to quiet feelings in the north. Finnr was an ideal diplomat to send to the descendants of Hákon the Powerful. He was related to Haraldr Harðráði – he was married to the king's niece while his own niece was Haraldr's mistress and mother to his sons – while also a close friend of Hákon Ívarsson, the most powerful nobleman remaining in Einarr's family and destined to be the new leader of Hákon Sigurðsson's descendants. Finnr and Hákon Ívarsson had 'spent some summers as Vikings traveling to the west,' writes Snorri Sturluson.[134] Finnr was not pleased with Haraldr's assignment, for the death of Einarr and Eindriði put Norway in a civil war situation. Snorri reports that Finnr scolded the king: 'You have become the worst person of all. You do every evil, and afterwards are so frightened because you do not know what you must do.'[135] Haraldr allowed this rebuke to stand without punishment, partly because it was certainly true, but mostly because he needed Finnr Árnason to bring peace to his kingdom. Finnr finally agreed to perform Haraldr's task and he set off to the north to meet with Hákon Ívarsson.[136]

In meeting with Finnr, Hákon initially was not willing to make peace with Haraldr Harðráði. The honor of his position in the family leadership necessitated his vengeance for the deaths of Einarr and Eindriði. The rest of Hákon the Powerful's descendants also seemed ready to support such a vengeance, even to the point of rebelling against the crown,[137] but Finnr appealed to his old Viking partner's greed: Hákon Ívarsson would gain honors and wealth from the king, while rebellion would lead only to the forfeiture of property, title, and life. Even if he did succeed in removing Haraldr Harðráði from his throne, Finnr reckoned that Hákon's legacy would be that only of a traitor.[138] Finally, Hákon Ívarsson agreed to accept Haraldr's offer, but only if a marriage could be arranged between himself and Ragnhildar, King Magnús' daughter and Haraldr Harðráði's niece.[139]

Such a lengthy story of murder and reconciliation indeed shows how the ruthless absolutism which Haraldr had come to acquire led him to exceed the boundaries of good governance, just as the *Fagrskinna* and Snorri Sturluson had charged. For a time it appeared that Norway was on the brink of civil war. Yet, in the end everything Haraldr had done turned out to profit him and him alone. Finnr Árnason was upset by the king's actions and yet Haraldr bought his par-

---

[134] Snorri Sturluson, *Heimskringla*, III:126: 'Finnr Árnason hafði verit nǫkkur sumur í vestrviking. Hǫfðu þeir þá verit allir saman í hernaði Finnr ok Guthormr Gunnhildarson ok Hákon Ívarsson.' The translators of Snorri Sturluson, Magnusson and Pálsson, translate 'vestr' as the British Isles, but there is no indication in this saga or elsewhere that this was in fact the place of Finnr and Hákon's 'viking'.

[135] Snorri Sturluson, *Heimskringla*, III:126–27: 'Þér er verst farit at hvívetna. Þú gerir hvatvetna illt, en síðan ertu svá hræddr, at þú veizt eigi, hvar þú hefir þik.'

[136] Snorri Sturluson, *Heimskringla*, III:127.

[137] On this assertion see Snorri Sturluson, *Heimskringla*, III:128–29.

[138] Snorri Sturluson, *Heimskringla*, III:128–29.

[139] Snorri Sturluson, *Heimskringla*, III:129.

ticipation for a fairly inexpensive promise of restoring Finnr's brother, Kálfr, to his Norwegian lands and citizenship – Kálfr had fought against Óláfr and Haraldr at the battle of Stiklarstaðir and was later exiled for this by Magnús.[140] Finnr Árnason, in turn, was able to convince Hákon Ívarsson to pacify his family's anger by also surrendering only a relatively small promise, marriage into the royal family.

At the time, both of these promises may have seemed significant to those gaining them, but ultimately they both turned against the recipients. Ragnhildar initially spurned Hákon's advances, and Haraldr refused to force her into this obviously unwanted marriage.[141] Haraldr also refused to grant Hákon the title of earl when the latter asked for it in place of his desired union with Haraldr's niece.[142] Hákon's weakness revealed and the king's promises unfulfilled, the erstwhile leader of the north fled to Denmark only to return later, humbled by Haraldr's mastery at manipulating the political situation in Norway. Only then was Hákon Ívarsson rewarded with marriage to Ragnhildar and the title of earl.[143] Hákon the Powerful's descendants never again threatened rebellion against King Haraldr Harðráði. (Hákon Ívarsson, after siding with Haraldr during most of the wars against Denmark, which will be discussed below, would once again turn against him, only to discover that without the support of the northerners who felt that he had betrayed them, he could no longer stay in Norway. With Haraldr in pursuit, Hákon escaped to Sweden where he was made earl of Västergötland.[144] His own saga, *Hákonar Saga Ivarssonar*, has him return to Norway in 1066 where he is reconciled to the king, Haraldr's son, Óláfr, Haraldr having died at Stamford Bridge earlier that year.[145])

Even Finnr Árnason's scolding of and disagreement with Haraldr Harðráði would ultimately turn in the king's favor. Purchasing the return of his brother, Kálfr, to Norway, Finnr could not prevent Haraldr from sending him on a 'suicide' mission into Denmark. Kálfr was killed,[146] and Finnr, in anger at the king's treachery, fled to Sveinn Estriðson and offered his services to him.

---

140 Snorri Sturluson, *Heimskringla*, III:127.
141 Snorri Sturluson, *Heimskringla*, III:129–30.
142 *Morkinskinna*, pp. 76–77; Snorri Sturluson, *Heimskringla*, III:129–30; and *Flateyjarbók*, III:360–61. *Fagrskinna* (p. 132) has Haraldr refuse the title to Hákon after his treachery in freeing Sveinn Estriðson after the battle of Niså. The chronology of the other Norwegian Kings' Sagas is more logical.
143 *Morkinskinna*, pp. 82–87; Snorri Sturluson, *Heimskringla*, III:132; and *Flateyjabók*, III:365–71.
144 *Fagrskinna* (pp. 131–32), *Morkinskinna* (pp. 88–93), Snorri Sturluson (*Heimskringla*, III:145–47), and *Flateyjarbók* (III:372–74) have Hákon standing with Haraldr at the battle of Niså, where he saves Sveinn Estriðson's life and allows him to escape, thus earning the accusation of treason against the Norwegian king. *Morkinskinna* (pp. 91–93), Snorri Sturluson (*Heimskringla*, III:130–33), and *Flateyjarbók* (III:375–77) tell of Hákon's problems with Haraldr that result from this treason and his flight to Sweden.
145 *Hákonar Saga Ivarssonar*, ed. J. Helgason and J. Benediktsen (Copenhagen, 1952).
146 Snorri Sturluson, *Heimskringla*, III:133. See also Andersen, *Samlingen av Norge og kristningen*, pp. 151–52.

Sveinn immediately elevated the Norwegian deserter to an earldom (of Halland) and military leadership.[147] Finnr Árnason would oppose Haraldr Harðráði at the battle of Niså and be captured there.[148] To make matters worse for Finnr, after his capture, Haraldr refused to kill his kinsman, keeping him in camp as a kind of jester for a number of days until the earl had lost all dignity. Finnr was a defeated man; again Haraldr had won. Finally, freed, Finnr returned to his earldom in Denmark and never again ventured out of that kingdom against the hated Norwegian ruler.[149]

Thus there seems little doubt that Haraldr Harðráði was a ruthless, egotistical, absolute ruler, a 'tyrant' is the appellation Adam of Bremen uses, well deserving of his more generally accepted nickname 'Hard-Ruler.' Yet this warlord's strong leadership brought prosperity and domestic peace to Norway for his entire reign. At very little cost to himself, his problems with the descendants of Hákon the Powerful had in fact strengthened his control over the kingdom and its people.

As undoubtedly surmised, the above incidents took place within an extended war fought between King Haraldr Harðráði of Norway and King Sveinn Estriðson of Denmark. The difficulty in not examining Haraldr's reign chronologically is that certain domestic events overlap ones not yet discussed because they more properly address Haraldr's foreign policies, his dealings with non-Norwegian entities, first Denmark and then England. The fact is that as the warlord that he was, Haraldr carried on constant warfare with his old ally, Sveinn. His purpose was to wrest Denmark from Sveinn's grasp, but, despite being victorious in nearly every engagement, Haraldr was never able to occupy that southern Scandinavian kingdom.

Adam of Bremen writes:

> But as soon as he came to the Norwegians and perceived that they were faithful to him, he was easily persuaded to rebel [against the promise he made to Magnús that Sveinn should be king of Denmark] and he devastated all the shores of Denmark with iron and fire . . . Between Haraldr and Sveinn there was war all of the days of their lives.[150]

As wrong as Adam of Bremen is about other things, he could not have been more accurate about this one. As soon as Haraldr became sole king of Norway,

---

[147] *Fagrskinna*, p. 128; *Morkinskinna*, pp. 78–79; Snorri Sturluson, *Heimskringla*, III:134–35; and *Flateyjarbók*, III:377–78.

[148] Snorri Sturluson, *Heimskringla*, III:147–52.

[149] *Fagrskinna*, p. 273 and Snorri Sturluson, *Heimskringla*, III:147–48. The *Ágrip* (p. 41) has Finnr return to Haraldr's service after the battle of Niså, but this makes little sense.

[150] Adam of Bremen, p. 154:
> Sed mox ut ad suos venit et Nortmannos sibi fideles esse persensit, facile ad rebellandum persuasus omnia Danorum maritima ferro vastavit et igne . . . Inter Haroldum et Suein prelium fuit omnibus diebus vitae eorum.

See also Andersen, *Samlingen av Norge og kristningen*, pp. 158–68. Jones' idea (p. 407) that there were actually two periods of war between Haraldr and Sveinn punctuated by a Norwegian civil war, I believe, is incorrect. The war seems to have been much more constant from 1048 to 1064.

he called for an attack on Denmark. The plan was thwarted, although for this time only, by Magnús' funeral and the fact that so many in the Norwegian army followed Einarr Þambarskelfir to Þrándheimr and the burial of their beloved king.[151] Not yet powerful enough to enforce his will on this occasion, it was to be the only time when Haraldr's call for war with Denmark was not heeded. From then almost yearly until 1064, Norway attacked Denmark.

Adam of Bremen is also accurate in his description of how this warfare was carried out. For with the exception of only two battles, one large and one small, most of the combat was confined to swift and violent raids along the coasts of Denmark. These might be called traditional Viking raids, except that Haraldr's principle concern was not to capture booty; his overall strategy was to prove to the Danish people that Sveinn could not protect them from outside incursion. As such he hoped to terrorize the inhabitants until they sought his protection over that of the Danish king. In this strategy, of course, Haraldr was mimicking that used by himself and Sveinn against Magnús' Denmark in 1046–47; it had worked then, as Magnús had acquiesced to Haraldr's wishes to rule Norway, or at least to co-rule Norway, so Haraldr undoubtedly thought that it would work in Denmark again.

Often these raids were small, fairly local in focus, and quickly concluded.[152] Snorri Sturluson even claims that Haraldr never took along a large force of men on most of his raids.[153] Other raids were large, well planned, campaign-length affairs which, with their large amount of violence and terror, were meant to intimidate all Danes, both those who were attacked and those who would inevitably hear of the attacks. Such was the case, for example, in the very first of these raids, undertaken in 1048, the year after Magnús' death. On this occasion, the Norwegian Kings' Sagas report, Haraldr Harðráði 'sent for troops out of the entire land,' half of which were mobilized for war. With these soldiers he attacked the Jutland peninsula and 'plundered and burned widely that summer.' The poet Bǫlverkr composed these lines in honor of Haraldr's action:

> Next year you raised a levy
> In the fair land of Norway;
> Waves caressed the gunwales
> As your fleet ploughed the ocean.
> A host of splendid vessels
> Lay on the blue billows,
> Laden with hardy warriors;
> The Danes watched in terror.[154]

---

151 Snorri Sturluson, *Heimskringla*, III:106–07.
152 This appears to have been the case in the raid which cost Kálfr his life. See Snorri Sturluson, *Heimskringla*, III:147–48. Another example can be found in Snorri Sturluson, *Heimskringla*, III:156.
153 Snorri Sturluson, *Heimskringla*, III:139.
154 The quotes come from *Fagrskinna* (p. 21); *Morkinskinna* (p. 51); Snorri Sturluson

This raid was successful: meeting no resistance, much booty was taken and much terror given out.[155]

In 1049, Haraldr Harðráði set out again with a large force to raid Denmark. After encountering and dispersing the Danish fleet with little difficulty, Haraldr divided his army, sending home his 'farmer army' (the term Snorri Sturluson uses is *bóndaherinn*, undoubtedly denoting the non-professional levy of the Norwegian force). With his 'landed men and select soldiers' (*lendum mǫnnum ok vildarliðinu*), he sailed further south and attacked one of the most populous, best protected towns in Scandinavia, Hedeby, which he pillaged and burned. The Norwegian Kings' Sagas record the following poem, claiming that it was written by one of Haraldr's raiders:

> All Hedeby was blazing,
> Fired by Haraldr's fury;
> There's no limit to the courage
> Of Norway's warrior sea king.
> Sveinn now feels the havoc
> Of Haraldr's deadly vengeance.
> At dawn in Hedeby's outskirts
> I saw the tall fires raging.[156]

(*Heimskringla*, III:109–10); and *Flateyjarbók* (III:335). Bǫlverkr's poem can be found on the same pages in those sources:

> Leiðangr bjóttu af láði,
> lǫgr gekk of skip, fǫgru,
> gjalfrstóðum reistu grœði
> glæstum, ár et næsta.
> Skokkr lá dýrr á døkkri,
> Danir vóru þá, bóru,
> skeiðr sá herr fyr hauðri
> hlaðnar, illa staðnir.

(There are some variant spellings between the two sources of this poem; I have used that in Snorri's saga.) The translation of this poem has been taken from Magnusson and Pálsson, p. 80.

155 The story of the raid can be found in *Fagrskinna*, pp. 21–22; *Morkinskinna*, pp. 51–54; Snorri Sturluson, *Heimskringla*, III:108–11; and *Flateyjarbók*, III:335–37. Before this raid was undertaken, Sveinn asked King Edward the Confessor for assistance, but was given none. As will be seen in the following chapter, Earl Godwin wished to send fifty ships in aid of the Danes, but this was denied him by Edward.

156 *Fagrskinna*, p. 124; *Morkinskinna*, pp. 54–56; Snorri Sturluson, *Heimskringla*, III:114–15; and *Flateyjarbók*, III:338–40:

> Brenndr vas upp með endum
> allr, en þat má kalla
> hraustligt bragð, es hugðak,
> Heiðabœr af reiði.
> Vón es, at vinnim Sveini,
> vask í nótt fyr óttu,
> gaus hór logi ór húsum,
> harm, á borgar armi.

(Again, there are some variations in the spelling of words between the two sources, and I have

Rarely did these raids encounter any resistance. Perhaps this was because their fierceness and violence frightened off any would-be opponents, although certainly the example of Kálfr's raid ending in his death and the quick defeat of the Norwegians with him argues against this.[157] More than likely Haraldr sought to avoid direct encounters with the Danish forces, his strategy not requiring this type of military action. One summer Haraldr set out against Denmark with only 'some light ships' (*nǫkkurum léttiskipum*) and 'not many men' (*ekki mikit lið*), according to Snorri Sturluson. Obviously not planning a major engagement, Haraldr's raiding was hindered because 'everywhere he went the Danes had an army in front of him.'[158] Trapped on an uninhabited island in need of water, the Norwegians were forced to use a small stratagem to replenish their supply: they captured a snake, made it dehydrated, and, using a string tied to its tail, followed the snake to its water source. Then, trapped in a fjord by Sveinn Estriðson and a large Danish fleet, the Norwegians were forced to use a larger strategem to escape: they traveled down a nearby creek to where only a narrow isthmus separated their ships and the North Sea; that night, under the cover of darkness, they dragged their ships over the small amount of land and sailed on to Norway.[159]

On only two occasions were more major engagements fought between the two kings and their armies. The first battle was fought in 1049, probably on the Djurså River.[160] Saxo Grammaticus tells the story. Sveinn Estriðson had been trying to raise an army to oppose Haraldr ever since the Norwegians had first raided the Jutland peninsula, but he had been somewhat unsuccessful. Despite the Danes' acceptance of Sveinn as king, they were reluctant to join him in defending his kingship, which may indicate that Haraldr's strategy was working. (Snorri Sturluson reports that the two kings had actually planned to fight on the Gota River before, but that Sveinn had not appeared because of lack of troops, leaving Haraldr alone to plunder the nearby lands.[161]) Sveinn had finally raised his army, but they were smaller in number than the Norwegians; they were also inexperienced, while Haraldr's force at least had participated in raids before. Saxo writes that as the Norwegians approached the Danes, the latter became so frightened that they tried to jump into the water and escape. Most drowned:

---

used Snorri's.) The translation of this poem is from Magnusson and Pálsson, p. 83. This incident more than any others in the wars between Haraldr and Sveinn has excited the most secondary comment: Jones, pp. 407–08; Brønsted, pp. 106, 153–54; Logan, p. 21; and Per Sveaas Andersen, 'Harald Hardråde, Danmark og England,' in *Harald Hardråde*, ed. A. Berg (Oslo, 1966), pp. 116–17. Archaeological excavations of Hedeby have shown that the Norwegian Kings' Sagas are correct in their accounts of the burning of this town. See Else Rosedahl, *Viking Age Denmark*, trans. S. Margeson and K. Williams (London, 1982), pp. 70–76, and Rudolf Poertner, *The Vikings: Rise and Fall of the Norse Sea Kings* (London, 1975), pp. 198–208.

157 Snorri Sturluson, *Heimskringla*, III:133.
158 Snorri Sturluson, *Heimskringla*, III:139: 'en Danir hǫfðu hvarvetna samnað fyrir.'
159 Snorri Sturluson, *Heimskringla*, III:139–40.
160 Saxo Grammaticus (II:551) is the only source which identifies the location of this battle.
161 Snorri Sturluson, *Heimskringla*, III:112–13.

The largest number of the Jutlanders, afraid of swords, jumped into the river, doing the work of the enemy. They took their own life by drowning rather than be killed by a stranger. Thus, because they feared the enemy, and given a choice of two fates, they decided that they preferred to perish by water than by arms. Therefore, while they declined one kind of death out of fear, they took the other kind eagerly, and while they sought refuge against the adversary, they exercised their cruel hostility on themselves, as if by fleeing they might be restored by the placid spirit of the water rather than in the air to die by the more violent sword. So, one does not know if they sought death more manfully or effeminately, and it is uncertain which of the fates appeared to be cowardice or courage, since so rash was the heat of their emotions, that it is difficult to judge, they being the robbers of their spirit, whether they were strong or fearful.[162]

The Norwegian Kings' Sagas relate the story somewhat differently. They write that as Haraldr Harðráði was returning to Norway from his Hedeby excursion, Sveinn Estriðson, with a large army, called to the Norwegians to come ashore and fight a battle. This Haraldr refused to do, as his army was 'less than half the size of [Sveinn's] army.' So Haraldr challenged Sveinn to a naval battle, which the Danish king accepted. In this battle, the larger number of Danish vessels, which were also faster than the booty-laden Norwegian ships, tried to run down Haraldr's fleet. Thus Haraldr decided that it was wiser to try and flee the confrontation than to fight it. Still, the Danish ships grew closer. In desperation, the Norwegian king ordered planks thrown overboard with some of the Danish booty on them. The Danish fleet stopped to pick up this cargo, and Haraldr was able to put more distance between himself and his enemies, but it was not enough. Again the Danish ships began to catch up with their Norwegian opponents. This time Haraldr ordered all of the other cargo and even the Danish prisoners to be cast overboard. This worked: as Sveinn stopped to retrieve his people, Haraldr and the Norwegians escaped. In the end, only seven small vessels were captured, manned Snorri Sturluson asserts, 'only with the levy and farmers.'[163]

---

[162] Saxo Grammaticus, II:551–52:

Maxima Jutorum pars ferri metu flumen insiluit, praereptoque hostis officio, sua vi quam aliena consumi tutius duxit. Itaque, quod ab hoste timebat, sibi ipsa conscivit, inque gemino fati delectu, unda quam armis perire maluit. Igitur dum alterum mortis genus timide declinavit, alterum cupide comprehendit, dumque adversarium refugit, hostilem in se ipsa crudelitatem exercuit, tanquam spiritum placidus aquis quam aeri redditura ac violentiorem exitum ferro quam fluctibus expertura. Ita nescias, viriliter mortem an effoeminate petiverint, incertumque, utrum fati cupidis ignavia an virtus incesserit, quoniam tam vehemens animi aestus, fortesne an timidi spiritus sui raptores extiterint, ambiguae existimationis esse fecit.

Saxo's repetition is rather emphatic.

[163] Snorri Sturluson, *Heimskringla*, III:115–18. See also *Morkinskinna*, pp. 56–59 and *Flateyjarbók*, III:340–43. It is possible that these are not the same engagement, but two separate incidents in the long war fought between the Norwegians and Danes from 1048 to 1064. Griffith (p. 202), not knowing of Saxo Grammaticus' account, accepts only Snorri's.

The second battle, a more significant military encounter, with a clear-cut victor, Haraldr Harðráði, and a clear-cut loser, Sveinn Estriðson, was fought on the sea at Niså on 9 August 1062. Obviously unhappy about being unable to conquer Denmark despite his successful annual raids, Haraldr decided to push for one large, decisive victory over Sveinn. The Norwegian king 'requested an army (*leiðangri*) from all the men of Norway,' writes Snorri Sturluson,[164] and placed them on board ships, some three hundred in total. He led this armada from his own large ship, called a *drekanum* (dragon) in the *Fagrskinna* because of its dragon ornamentation. It was an impressive sight. Rarely had a ship of this size set sail – it was powered by seventy oars – at least no others are referred to in other Viking sagas. In honor of the vessel and its important voyage, Þjóðólfr composed this descriptive verse:

> I watched the ship, my lady,
> Launched down river to ocean;
> See where the great longship
> Proudly lies at anchor.
> Above the prow, the dragon
> Rears its glowing head;
> The bows were bound with gold
> After the hull was launched.[165]

To Haraldr, this was the battle which would decide the fate of Denmark.

Sveinn Estriðson had also been preparing for a final onslaught. He had his fleet outfitted and ready to do battle. Snorri Sturluson also indicates, although without giving more details, that a preassigned time and place for the battle had been set,[166] but if this was the case, Sveinn did not meet his obligations, as this saga writer declares that Sveinn was not at the appointed spot for the engagement when Haraldr arrived there. Haraldr must have thought that it was to be just another year of raiding, as this had happened before, and, also as before, he dismissed his non-professional soldiers (his *bóndaherrin*), half of his army, and

---

164 Snorri Sturluson, *Heimskringla*, III:141: 'Þann vetr bauð Haraldr konungr út leiðangri, almenning ór Nóregi.' See also *Fagrskinna*, p. 128; *Morkinskinna*, p. 75; and *Flateyjarbók*, III:359.
165 This poem is found only in Snorri Sturluson, *Heimskringla*, III:141–42:
> Skeið sák framm at flœði,
> fagrt sprund, ór ó hrundit.
> Kenndu, hvar liggr fyr landi
> lǫng súð dreka ens prúða.
> Orms glóar fax of farmi
> fráns, síz ýtt vas hónum,
> bóru búnir svírar
> brunnit gull, af hlunni.
The translation is from Magnusson and Pálsson, p. 108. On this ship see *Fagrskinna*, pp. 129–30 and Snorri Sturluson, *Heimskringla*, III:141–45.
166 Snorri Sturluson, *Heimskringla*, III:145. See also *Morkinskinna*, p. 77 and *Flateyjarbók*, III:361.

proceeded on with only his professional troops, veterans of these kinds of raids.[167]

This may have been what Sveinn was waiting for, as a short time later, after Haraldr's dismissed ships had rowed out of sight, the Danish fleet with three hundred ships of its own approached the Norwegians.[168] (Saxo Grammaticus charges otherwise, that Haraldr's fleet was always the larger in the conflict.[169]) Counseled to flee this larger force, Haraldr is said to have replied, 'we have a such a large and fair army that no one would choose to flee; we would rather be cast down in a heap than flee.'[170] He ordered his ships in a line, with his large *drekanum* placed in the middle. He tied the ships together to prevent gaps in the line. On his wings floated the unfettered ships of Hákon Ívarsson and the men of Trondelag.[171] Aboard the Norwegian vessels were the finest soldiers. Most were veterans of many Danish raids, and some may even have fought with Haraldr since his days in Russia and Byzantium. Þjóðólfr describes their preparations for battle:

> Battle-eager Haraldr
> Bade his crew be steadfast;
> Warriors made a bulwark
> Of shields along the gunwales.
> The doughty king of Norway
> Lined his dragon longship
> With a wall of living shields;
> No foe could find a gap there.[172]

Sveinn Estriðson's battle array mirrored Haraldr's, with his own ship in the center, facing that of the Norwegian king, but unlike Haraldr, Sveinn's lieuten-

---

[167] *Fagrskinna*, p. 128; *Morkinskinna*, p. 77; Snorri Sturluson, *Heimskringla*, III:145; and *Flateyjarbók*, III:361.

[168] *Fagrskinna*, p. 128; *Morkinskinna*, pp. 77–78; Snorri Sturluson, *Heimskringla*, III:145–46; and *Flateyjarbók*, III:361–62.

[169] Saxo Grammaticus, II:552.

[170] *Fagrskinna*, p. 128: 'Þá svaraði Haraldr konungr: "... en vér hǫfum lið svá mikit ok fritt, at engum kosti viljum vér flýja, ok heldr skal hverr várr liggja um þveran annan." ' See also *Morkinskinna*, p. 77; Snorri Sturluson, *Heimskringla*, III:145; and *Flateyjarbók*, III:361.

[171] *Fagrskinna*, p. 130; *Morkinskinna*, pp. 77–78; Snorri Sturluson, *Heimskringla*, III: 145–46; and *Flateyjarbók*, III:361–62.

[172] This poem is found only in Snorri Sturluson, *Heimskringla*, III:146:
> Fast bað fylking hrausta
> friðvandr jǫfurr standa.
> Hamalt sýndisk mér hǫmlur
> hildings vinir skilda.
> Ramsyndan lauk rǫndum
> ráðandi manndáða
> nýtr fyr Nizi útan
> naðr, svát hver tók aðra.

The translation is from Magnusson and Pálsson, p. 111.

ant, Finnr Árnason, placed his ship next to the king's. The Danish fleet was also roped together.[173]

The Norwegian Kings' Sagas claim that the Danes made the first charge in the battle, aroused by their larger numbers.[174] Not agreeing that the Danish fleet was larger than the Norwegian one, Saxo Grammaticus, however, does agree that the Danes took the initiative in the battle.[175] In response, the Norwegian fleet rowed out to meet its oncoming opponents, and the battle commenced. It was already late in the evening.

Naval battles were rare in the Middle Ages precisely because it seems that no one knew how to fight one. Without a ram, medieval ships could not duplicate the maneuvers of the ancients, and they were left without an option except to try to close on an opposing vessel, grapple the two ships together, and then wage a mock land battle until one side was defeated, its ship taken or, if damaged, scuttled. The only defensive tactic of any efficiency was to tie one's own ships together. Saxo Grammaticus gives the reason for this:

> Having ordered the ships in a line, they joined them together with grapples, so that being bound together the fleet might easily ride down any enemy in its path. And when they all were brought together for this purpose, they were joined together solidly, for flight or victory, as it would also not be possible for anyone to break free from his colleagues. Thus they planned to make their weakness strong by this tactic.[176]

Before and even during these mock land battles, bows became the principle weapons, as was the case at Niså. Even Haraldr Harðráði used his bow, wielding it 'for a long time,' writes Snorri Sturluson, who adds Þjóðólfr's emphatic poem:

> Norway's king was bending
> His bow throughout that night,
> Raining a shower of arrows
> On the white shields of Denmark,
> Bloody spear-points opened
> Holes in iron armor;

---

173 Saxo Grammaticus, II:552; *Morkinskinna*, p. 78; Snorri Sturluson, *Heimskringla*, III:147–48; and *Flateyjarbók*, III:362.

174 *Fagrskinna*, pp. 129–30; *Morkinskinna*, pp. 78–79; Snorri Sturluson, *Heimskringla*, III:147–48; and *Flateyjarbók*, III:362. The *Morkinskinna* and *Flateyjarbók* switch some of the details of the story around here, but the changes do not significantly alter the narrative.

175 Saxo Grammaticus, II:553.

176 Saxo Grammaticus, II:552:
digesta in ordinem navigia tenaculis sociare caeperunt, quatenus continenti nexu cohaerens classis expeditus opi invicem ferendae iter sterneret, cunctisque hac necessitate duratis, tam fugae quam victoriae indissolubilis communio foret, nec cuiquam a tanta collegii firmitate dilabendi fas esset. Adeo imbecillitatem necessitate roborandum duxerunt.

Shields were pierced by arrows
From Haraldr's deadly dragon.[177]

The grappling of ships on both sides, the attempted mock land battle, and, especially, the use of bows as the principle weapons, meant that medieval naval battles also tended to drag out far longer than engagements fought on land. According to the sources, the battle of Niså lasted into and throughout the night.[178]

For much of the conflict the two sides were evenly matched, and no one bettered the other. Finally, Earl Hákon Ívarsson sailed into the fray. As mentioned, he had kept back his flanking ships free from the rest of the grappled Norwegian line, and while the two main forces had been locked together for nearly the entire conflict, Hákon had sailed around the main battle group, encountering smaller and weakened Danish vessels which his own larger fleet had no trouble in defeating. After several hours, a small Norwegian boat approached the earl with the message that one side of their line was collapsing and needed assistance. Like the reserve force that he was obviously meant to be, Hákon swept down on the failing flank and forced the Danes back.[179] Sveinn, who seems not to have kept a similar reserve force, could do nothing to counter Hákon's tactic, and by dawn the Danish fleet was defeated. The ships of Sveinn Estriðson and Finnr Árnason were the last boarded, and Haraldr Harðráði gave no quarter; all aboard jumped overboard or were killed. Finnr fought until he was captured. Sveinn jumped into the water.[180] This 'cowardly' means of escape brought derision from at least one of the poets present, Arnórr Jarlaskáld (Earl's-poet):

Brave King Sveinn of Denmark
I am sure had every reason
To leave his stricken longship;
Steel bit hard on helmets.
The royal ship lay empty
When Denmark's quick-tongued leader

---

[177] Snorri Sturluson, *Heimskringla*, III:149–50:
Alm dró uppllenzkr hilmir
alla nótt, enn snjalli.
Hremsur lét á hvítar
hlífr landreki drífa.
Brynmǫnnum smó benjar
blóðugr oddr, þars stóðu,
flugr óx Fáfnis vigra,
Finna gjǫld í skjǫldum.
The version of this poem in *Fagrskinna* (p. 129), *Morkinskinna* (p. 78), and *Flateyjarbók* (III:362) is shorter. The translation is found in Magnusson and Pálsson, pp. 113–14.
[178] Saxo Grammaticus, II:551–54; *Ágrip*, pp. 40–41; *Fagrskinna*, pp. 128–32; *Morkinskinna*, pp. 75–81; Snorri Sturluson, *Heimskringla*, III:145–52; and *Flateyjarbók*, III:359–65. Secondary sources which discuss this battle include: Jones, p. 407 and Griffith, p. 202.
[179] Snorri Sturluson, *Heimskringla*, III:148–52.
[180] *Fagrskinna*, pp. 131–32 and Snorri Sturluson, *Heimskringla*, III:150–51.

Leapt from the bloodied gunwales,
Leaving his fallen comrades.[181]

Sveinn made for Hákon Ívarsson's ship, hoping that he might receive mercy from his old ally and friend. (As mentioned, Hákon had sought and received succor from Sveinn during his earlier dispute with Haraldr.) Sveinn had also taken the precaution of disguising himself with a 'wide hood.'[182] Wearing this disguise and calling himself, 'Vandráðr,'[183] Sveinn was led to shore by Hákon's order, where he escaped back to the safety of Denmark. The earl is never reported to have known who the disguised individual was.[184]

Everyone recognized Hákon Ívarsson as the hero of the engagment, even King Haraldr, but this recognition was short-lived as Haraldr discovered that Sveinn had been led to safety at Hákon's order. The king did not believe that his earl could not have known who his prisoner was. Thus Hákon's unwillingness to reveal to Haraldr that he held the Danish king and his eventual complicity in Sveinn's escape was seen as greater treachery than his actions in the battle of Nisá were seen as heroic. Hákon's time remaining in Norway would be brief.[185]

Snorri Sturluson concludes his account of the battle of Nisá: 'There was a very great slaughter. And where the kings themselves had fought and most of the ships had been roped together, there lay empty more than seventy of Sveinn's ships.'[186] Haraldr had won a great victory, but it was not the decisive victory which he had sought. Danish ships and Danish men had escaped,[187] and on one

---

181 Snorri Sturluson, *Heimskringla*, III:150–51:
    Gekkat Sveinn af snekkju
    saklaust enn forhrausti,
    malmr kom harðr við hjalma,
    hugi minn es þat, sinni.
    Farskostr hlaut at fljóta
    fljótmælts vinar Jóta,
    áðr an qðlingr flœði,
    auðr, frá verðung dauðri.
Versions of this poem are also found in *Morkinskinna*, p. 80 and *Flateyjarbók*, III:363–64. The translation used is from Magnusson and Pálsson, p. 114.

182 Snorri Sturluson, *Heimskringla*, III:152. The words used are 'víðan hǫtt.'

183 According to Magnusson and Pálsson (p. 116), 'Vandráðr' means 'one who is in trouble.'

184 This episode is recorded in *Fagrskinna*, pp. 131–32; *Morkinskinna*, pp. 88–93; Snorri Sturluson, *Heimskringla*, III:145–47; and *Flateyjarbók*, III:372–74. None of these authors write that Hákon knew who this prisoner was, although none explicitly removes his guilt in the escape either.

185 *Morkinskinna*, pp. 82–93; Snorri Sturluson, *Heimskringla*, III:152–54; *Flateyjarbók*, III:365–77. Saxo Grammaticus also gives credit to Hákon Ívarsson for the victory (II:553–54), but the *Fagrskinna* does not assign Hákon the same honor (pp. 130–32). On Hákon's need to flee Norway see Andersen, *Samlingen av Norge og kristningen*, pp. 151–52.

186 Snorri Sturluson, *Heimskringla*, III:151: 'Þar varð allmikit mannfall. En þar er konungarnir sjálfir hǫfðu barzk ok tengð váru flest skipin, þar lágu eptir auð skip Sveins konungs meirr en sjau tigir.' See also *Morkinskinna*, p. 80 and *Flateyjarbók*, III:364.

187 *Fagrskinna* (p. 131), *Morkinskinna* (p. 80), Snorri Sturluson (*Heimskringla*, III:151), and *Flateyjarbók* (III:364) all indicate that Haraldr tried to pursue the fleeing Danes, but that the

of them, Haraldr presumed, sailed his opponent, King Sveinn Estriðson, whose continued resilience in the face of the constant defeats would mean to Haraldr that the war would have to continue. Or must it? The constant raiding of and war in Denmark had absolutely destroyed its economic and social fabric. Numerous coin hoards determined to be from this extended period of war provide evidence that the people lived in constant fear of the Norwegians.[188] Yet, politically and militarily Haraldr had not defeated the Danes. Warfare being a seasonal activity in the eleventh century, whatever the Norwegians had gained in the summer was then lost by them during the winter. Each year Sveinn always returned as king of Denmark, and he always returned with an army, recruited from those inhabitants who were not intimidated by Haraldr's strategy to conquer their land.[189]

Fatigue, especially in the wake of the non-decisive, extremely costly battle of Niså, also certainly had set in, even for the seemingly indefatigably bellicose Haraldr Harðráði. After all, he was also nearing fifty years of age, and thirty-five of those years had been devoted to warfare. Additionally, despite never facing his own invasion by Sveinn – although it is clear that on at least one occasion the Danish king is said to have been planning such an invasion[190] – Norway had suffered its own losses, especially economic losses. Evidence for this can be seen in Snorri's reporting of Haraldr's problems in collecting taxes from the Upplanders, and probably from others also, after the battle of Niså.[191]

Thus in 1064 (the *Morkinskinna* dates it to 1065) Haraldr Harðráði decided to seek peace, unconditional and without reparations or loss of land. Initially, Sveinn was suspicious of Haraldr's petition, the Norwegian king being renowned for his stratagems, but the Norwegians were sincere and eventually convinced Sveinn of this. Even loud arguments given by zealots on both sides and meant to interrupt the peace process could not do so. Ultimately, the two kings exchanged prisoners and concluded a peace that would never again be broken, at least not by the two of them.[192]

Besides, there was a new target for Haraldr Harðráði, just over the horizon to the west: England. It is probably doubtful that Haraldr was thinking of England as his next conquest when agreeing to peace with Sveinn Estriðson. Certainly his lack of victory over Denmark could not have encouraged his military confi-

fjord was so crowded with derelict vessels that no successful pursuit could be made. See also Saxo Grammaticus, II:554.

188   See Peter Sawyer, *The Age of the Vikings* (New York, 1962), p. 103.

189   See Foote and Wilson, p. 46; Brønsted, p. 99; and Loyn, *Vikings in Britain*, pp. 57–58.

190   Snorri Sturluson, *Heimskringla*, III:112.

191   Snorri Sturluson, *Heimskringla*, III:158.

192   Snorri Sturluson, *Heimskringla*, III:159–62. See also Page, pp. 164–66 and Poole, pp. 73–85. Saxo Grammaticus (II:554) has no peace treaty made between Haraldr and Sveinn. Instead, following the battle of Niså, he has Sveinn prepare for the further defense of his 'injured country' (*lacessita patria*), but Haraldr turned toward England instead of Denmark. For secondary sources on the peace agreement, see Jones, p. 408 and Brønsted, p. 99. It is interesting to note that none of the other Norwegian Kings' Sagas contain this account of the peace-making procedure.

dence. Also, in 1064 there seemed no reason to think of England as vulnerable to conquest. On the other hand, maybe England *did* appear to be an easy military goal to Haraldr. There is also the incident in 1058 when a Norwegian fleet, commanded by Haraldr's son, Magnús, involved itself in Gruffydd ap Llywelyn's war against Harold Godwinson.[193] It is hard not to see this as a possible 'reconnaissance', a test of the situation in England, even though there was no further 'testing' done until eight years later, with the 1066 invasion. This may indicate that, if Haraldr was responsible for the 1058 intervention in English affairs, he was convinced by the Anglo-Saxon military operations carried out at that time, and perhaps subsequently, especially in 1063 in Wales, that an invasion before peace could be made with Sveinn Estriðson would be militarily unwise.

Of course, in 1064, while making peace with Sveinn, Haraldr Harðráði could also not have envisioned the invitation which he would receive late in 1065 or early in 1066 by Earl Tostig Godwinson, brother of the new king of England (king after 6 January 1066). If it was dormant, Tostig seemed to re-awaken the military fire within the Norwegian royal warlord. He seemed to convince Haraldr that England could easily be his. He could follow in the footsteps of Knútr, the man who had taken Norway from him at the battle of Stiklarstaðir, the man who had made his brother a martyr and a saint. What better revenge than to take over the land which Knútr valued so highly, but which his own progeny could not hold. It would be an unfulfilled, fatal dream.

What kind of man was Haraldr? Much is written condemning his soul because of the injustices which were caused by him. He seemed to fear neither man nor God. By our modern standards, Haraldr Harðráði was certainly a despot, but by the standards of the Scandinavian lands of the eleventh century he was a strong and perhaps even a good warrior-king. He also seems to have been a vicious man. Haraldr loved warfare – Johannes Brønsted calls him 'the most feared warrior of his time'[194] – and the killing that such an occupation brought with it. He even composed a poem to that effect:

> Now I have caused the deaths
> Of thirteen of my enemies;
> I kill without compunction,
> And remember all my killings.[195]

---

[193] This is recorded in *Anglo-Saxon Chronicle* (D) 1058, I:188 and John of Worcester, *The Chronicle of John of Worcester*, ed. R.R. Darlington and P. McGurk, trans. J. Bray and P. McGurk (Oxford, 1995), II:584–85. It will be discussed at greater length in the chapter on Harold Godwinson below.

[194] Brønsted, p. 106.

[195] Snorri Sturluson, *Heimskringla*, III:134:
> Nú emk ellifu allra,
> eggjumsk vigs, ok tveggja,
> þau eru, enn svát mank, manna
> morð, ráðbani orðinn.

The translation is from Magnusson and Pálsson, p. 102. This poem is written after Haraldr had put down a rebellion.

However, one thing does seem certain about Haraldr's character. He was respected by friends and enemies alike for his strength and power. Even Harold Godwinson, his foe at Stamford Bridge, is reported to have held such an admiration for the Norwegian king. Before encountering Haraldr Harðráði in battle, the king of England is recorded as saying: 'He is a large and powerful man. Here it is likely that we have come to the end of our luck.'[196]

It was Haraldr Harðráði whose luck had run out though. He died at Stamford Bridge, and with him died an era. Many obituaries have been written about this king and the end of his kind, but perhaps the best one was penned by Peter Sawyer:

> With the defeat and death of Haraldr Hardrada, king of Norway, by Harold of England at Stamford Bridge in 1066 . . . the period of effective Scandinavian interference in Western Europe came to an end.[197]

---

[196] Snorri Sturluson, *Heimskringla*, III:186: 'Englakonugr segir: "Mikill maðr ok ríkmann-ligr, ok er vænna, at farinn sé at hamingju." ' This quote, with only a few variations, is also found in *Fagrskinna*, p. 138.
[197] Sawyer, *Age of Vikings*, p. 4.

CHAPTER FOUR

GODWIN AND HIS FAMILY

INVOLVED ON BOTH SIDES of the conflict which ended at Stamford Bridge were two English warlords, brothers, Harold and Tostig Godwinson, second and third sons of another English warlord, the famous Earl Godwin of Wessex, whose own military legitimacy had made him the most powerful individual in eleventh-century England. His power spanned the reign of four kings beginning with Knútr the Great, followed by Harold I (Harefoot) and Harðaknútr, and ending with Edward the Confessor. He was also related to two of these kings: he married Knútr's sister-in-law, Gyða, in 1019, and his daughter, Eadgyða, married Edward the Confessor. Also, although dead by this time, he was the father of a third, King Harold Godwinson, and five of his sons held earldoms as well.

Such power has caused modern assessors to describe him as a 'kingmaker,'[1] while at the same time a 'problematical figure.'[2] Edward August Freeman, perhaps his greatest modern admirer, uses these words:

> One who rose to power by the favour of strangers, only to become the champion of our land against strangers of every race; one who never himself a King, was to be the maker, the kinsman, the father of Kings.[3]

His is a description which we might think only a Victorian historian capable of, but it does no less than echo a similar, although negative, description assigned Godwin by the near contemporary William of Jumièges:

> At that time the fierce and unscrupulous Godwin was the most powerful earl in England and strenuously held sway over the great part of the English realm,

---

[1]   Miles W. Campbell, 'The Rise of an Anglo-Saxon "Kingmaker": Earl Godwin of Wessex,' *Canadian Journal of History* 13 (1978), 17–33.
[2]   David G.J. Raraty, 'Earl Godwine of Wessex: The Origins of his Power and his Political Loyalties,' *History* 74 (1989), 3.
[3]   Edward August Freeman, *The History of the Norman Conquest*, 2nd edn (Oxford, 1869–75), I:405. See also John Gillingham, 'Thegns and Knights in Eleventh-Century England: Who Was Then the Gentleman?' *Transactions of the Royal Historical Society*, 6th ser., 5 (1995), 149.

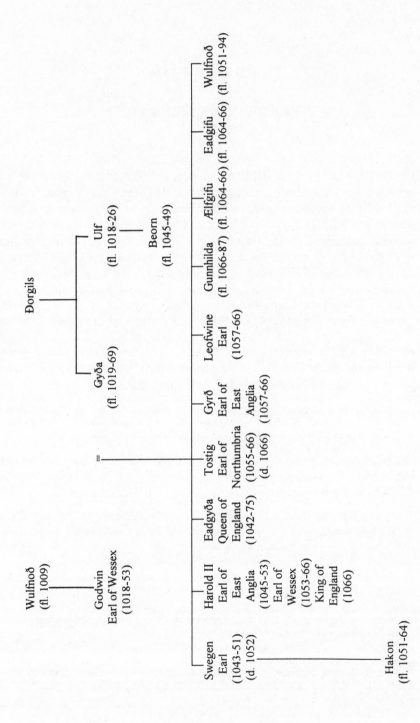

The Godwin Family

Wulfnoð
(fl. 1009)

Godwin
Earl of Wessex
(1018-53)   =

Þorgils

Gyða
(fl. 1019-69)

Ulf
(fl. 1018-26)

Beorn
(fl. 1045-49)

Swegen
Earl
(1043-51)
(d. 1052)

Harold II
Earl of
East
Anglia
(1045-53)
Earl of
Wessex
(1053-66)
King of
England
(1066)

Eadgyða
Queen of
England
(1042-75)

Tostig
Earl of
Northumbria
(1055-66)
(d. 1066)

Gyrð
Earl of
East
Anglia
(1057-66)

Leofwine
Earl
(1057-66)

Gunnhilda
(fl. 1066-87)

Ælfgifu
(fl. 1064-66)

Eadgifu
(fl. 1064-66)

Wulfnoð
(fl. 1051-94)

Hakon
(fl. 1051-64)

which he had obtained either from his noble ancestors or by violence and corruption.[4]

Whether one might find that he was 'the champion of our land against strangers of every race' or 'fierce and unscrupulous,' Godwin possessed three attributes which must be considered to understand how he rose and attained power in England and then how, or perhaps whether, he passed that power on to his sons. First, Godwin seems to possess an ability to adapt to whatever political situation arose and, no matter how dire it initially looked to his governing status, by the end of the crisis he was able to survive and indeed to prosper from it. Such people seem to be described only with clichés – 'teflon-coated' is the modern one. Second, from what can be determined by filtering through the Norman propaganda, such as that given by William of Jumièges above, Godwin remained loyal to all of the kings whom he served, although his presence nearly caused two civil wars among other ruling parties in the kingdom, and on one occasion he was exiled from England for nearly a year. Third, despite his powerful political position in England, Godwin also seems to have been extremely well liked among the people of the island kingdom. All of these traits can be explained only by recognizing Godwin's military legitimacy; he was a successful military leader when one king, Knútr, valued it, and three others, Harold I, Harðaknútr, and Edward the Confessor, depended on it.

No record exists of Godwin's birth, and no date is certain for it. Moreover, there seems to be little record of his family, and then only of his father, a man named Wulfnoð. While once in much dispute, it now seems certain that the man, Wulfnoð, identified in the *Anglo-Saxon Chronicle* (version F) as 'Godwines fæder (Godwin's father)'[5] was the same Wulfnoð described as Wulfnoð 'Cild' by the *Anglo-Saxon Chronicle* (versions C, D, and E) and repeated later in Henry of Huntingdon's *Historia Anglorum*. This Wulfnoð's fame, according to these sources, comes from his rebellion against King Æðelred the Unready in 1009. Wulfnoð, 'the South Saxon', after being accused of an unknown crime before

---

[4] William of Jumièges, *The Gesta Normannorum ducum of William of Jumièges, Orderic Vitalis, and Robert of Torigni*, ed. and trans. E.M.C. van Houts (Oxford, 1995), II:106–09:
Ferox dolique commentor Goduinus eo tempore comes in Anglia potentissimus erat, et magnam regni Anglorum partem fortiter tenebat, quam ex parentum nobilitate seu ui uel fraduulentia uendicauerat.
Similar negative depictions can be found in William of Poitiers, *The Gesta Guillelmi of William of Poitiers*, ed. and trans. R.H.C. Davis and M. Chibnall (Oxford, 1998), pp. 4–7 and Wace, *Le Roman de Rou*, ed. A.J. Holden (Paris, 1971), II:87–89. The existence of such universal animosity toward Godwin among the Norman writers of the time perhaps gives an indication of just how powerful this lord was. For a different contemporary view of Godwin, see the *Vita Ædwardi regis qui apud Westmonasterium requiescit*, ed. and trans. F. Barlow, 2nd edn (Oxford, 1992), pp. 6–9; William of Malmesbury, *Gesta regum Anglorum: The History of the English Kings*, ed. R.A.B. Mynors, R.M. Thomson, and M. Winterbottom (Oxford, 1998), I:322–25; and Eadmer, *Historia novorum in Anglia*, ed. M. Rule (London, 1884), p. 5.
[5] *Anglo-Saxon Chronicle* (F) 1009, in *Two of the Saxon Chronicles Parallel*, ed. Charles Plummer and John Earle (Oxford, 1892), I:138 n. 6: 'Godwines faeder eorles quendam nobilem virum nomine Wulfnoð.'

Æðelred by a lesser noble, Brihtric (the brother of one of the earldom's adminis-
trators, the ealdorman of Mercia, Eadric Streona), gathered a force of twenty
ships, ravaged the south coast of England, and destroyed a larger pursuing fleet
before disappearing from contemporary record. The following is from Henry of
Huntingdon:

> The king [Æðelred] had banished Wulfnoð 'Cild', a nobleman of Sussex, who
> began to ravage along the sea-coast with twenty ships. So Brihtric, brother of
> Ealdorman Eadric, wishing to win praise for himself, took with him eighty
> vessels of the said fleet, and promised to bring the enemy to the king, alive or
> dead. But while he was on the journey, a fearful and extraordinary wind drove
> all his ships ashore and destroyed them. Wulfnoð, falling on them, immediate-
> ly burnt them. Troubled by the bad news, the remaining ships returned to
> London.[6]

If this was Godwin's father, being his son seems as if it should not have been
an auspicious beginning for someone who would eventually rise to such power
in England. Thus, some historians have questioned the validity of this parental
line. Even as early as the writing of the *Knytlinga Saga*, in the mid-twelfth
century, Godwin's parentage had changed to a rich yeoman, with Godwin
himself rising to the recognition of the attacker of England, Knútr, because he
helped Knútr's lieutenant, Earl Ulf, after he became lost in the woods while
fleeing from the English.[7]

However most recent historians of the period seem to argue against such a
fanciful origin. When the ætheling Æðelstan, Æðelred's eldest son, in his will of
June 1014 granted to Godwin, 'Wulfnoð's son' an estate 'at Compton, which his
father possessed,' it seems that some of the land which the king had confiscated
from Wulfnoð 'Cild' was being returned to his son. Moreover, as there is an
estate at Compton in West Sussex identified in the *Domesday Book* as that of
Godwin's, there seems to be little doubt that the rebel of 1009 was the father of
the man who would become the most powerful individual in England less than
half a century later.[8]

---

[6] Henry, Archdeacon of Huntingdon, *Historia Anglorum: The History of the English People*,
ed. and trans. D. Greenway (Oxford, 1996), pp. 346–47:
Siquidem rex exulauerat Wlnod puerum nobilem Sudsexe. Ille uero cum uiginti
nauibus cepit perdari iuxta littora maris. Igitur Brictric, frater ducis Edrici, laudem sibi
uolens adquirerer, octoginta ex puppibus oredictis secum duxit, et hostem uiuum uel
defunctum se regi allaturum promisit. Sed intereundum uentus ultra modum horribilis
naues eius omnes ad terram pernitiose iactauit. Wlnod uero superueniens, statim eas
combussit. Sinistris angariate nuntiis, puppes relique Lundoniam redierunt.
See also *Anglo-Saxon Chronicle* (C, D, E) 1009, I:138–39 and John of Worcester, *The Chronicle of John of Worcester*, ed. R.R. Darlington and P. McGurk, trans. J. Bray and P. McGurk
(Oxford, 1995), II:460–63.
[7] See Freeman, *Norman Conquest*, I:706–11.
[8] Recent acceptance of Wulfnoð 'Cild' as Godwin's father can be found in Raraty, pp. 4–5;
Simon Keynes, 'Cnut's Earls,' in *The Reign of Cnut: King of England, Denmark and Norway*,
ed. A.R. Ramble (London, 1994), pp. 70–71; M.K. Lawson, *Cnut: The Danes in England in
the Early Eleventh Century* (London, 1993), pp. 176–77; Ian W. Walker, *Harold: The Last*

Obviously, this is the most limited of evidence to link the two names together, and naturally it would be nice if there was a more substantial basis on which to develop the parental lineage, but whether one accepts Wulfnoð 'Cild' as Godwin's father or not, the question of how Godwin later rose to prominence in the eyes of Knútr, once he became king in 1017, must still be answered.

Although Wulfnoð's rebellion was before Knútr's time and was against Knútr's enemy, it seems somewhat illogical for the new king even to acknowledge Godwin let alone to select the son of a rebel as his chief earl. On the other hand, it does appear that Godwin did something to earn back the land confiscated from his father, an act of faithfulness to the king, or to the king's son, which outweighed any treason by his father. This aspect of Godwin's character is shown in many later examples.

Perhaps it was this loyalty which Knútr recognized and which he valued. It is known that Knútr killed all those who overthrew Æðelred, although this had allowed the Danish king's ascension to the throne.[9] Most have seen this as a sign that Knútr valued loyalty over anything else. There also might have been a special relationship between Knútr and Wulfnoð, now lost from the sources, which kept the new king from exacting the same harsh punishment on him and his family. He may have been the Danish advocate in England during Æðelred's reign. At the very least, if this was Godwin's father, it could indicate that he had a noble background and possibly even some military leadership training by the time of his service to Knútr. It might also indicate how Godwin was able to come to Knútr's attention so quickly.

Whatever the reason for his prominence, in 1017, when Knútr became king, Godwin seems to have been one of his most noble retainers and an extremely valuable military asset. Indeed, within a year of Knútr's conquest, Godwin signed a charter of the new king's with the title *dux*.[10] Undoubtedly this title was a political one, denoting the office of earl. Yet, the title is also a strange one, and how Godwin gained it has confused many historians. It should be remembered that in Classical Latin a *dux* was not a political but a military leader, and depriving the word of this military definition confuses what may be an easy answer to

Anglo-Saxon King (Stroud, 1997), pp. 1–6; and Pauline Stafford, *Queen Emma and Queen Edith: Queenship and Women's Power in Eleventh-Century England* (Oxford, 1997), p. 255. Campbell ('Anglo-Saxon "Kingmaker",' p. 18) is less convinced of the patriarchical connection. Edward August Freeman's own doubts about this parentage are expressed in *Norman Conquest*, I:406, 701–11 and 'On the Life and Death of Earl Godwine,' *The Archaeological Journal* 11 (1854), 237–45.

9   On these executions see Freeman, *Norman Conquest*, I:411–15.

10 F.E. Harmer, *Anglo-Saxon Writs* (Manchester, 1952), p. 561. See also Keynes, 'Cnut's Earls,' p. 71; Campbell, 'Anglo-Saxon "Kingmaker",' p. 18; and I. Walker, p. 8. All three of these authors read *dux* as 'earl.' Godwin's military skill can be seen in Eadmer's statement (p. 5): 'At this time, Godwin the earl of Kent [Wessex] was held throughout England to be a great man on both land and sea' (Qua tempestate Godwinus Cantiae comes magnus per Angliam terra marique habebatur).

the question of Godwin's ascension. Godwin must have been one of Knútr's military leaders.

Once his military leadership has been recognized as one of the reasons for Knútr's favoritism toward Godwin – in other words, once Godwin's military legitimacy for power has been acknowledged – contemporary stories of his military expertise abroad begin to make sense. There are in early chronicles three separate accounts affirming Godwin's leadership in Knútr's army. The earliest, and perhaps the most credible account of Godwin's military legitimacy can be found both in the *Vita Ædwardi* and in John of Worcester's *Chronicle*. These works assert that Knútr gave Godwin power, wealth, and favor because, after Knútr had conquered England, Godwin accompanied him to Denmark to put down a rebellion there. The anonymous author of the *Vita Ædwardi* writes:

> When, however, some fitting business of the kingdom called Knútr to his own people [Denmark] – for in his absence some unbridled men, putting off his authority from their necks, had prepared to rebel – Godwin was his inseparable companion on the whole journey. Here the king tested more closely his wisdom, here his perseverance, here his courage in war, and here the strength of the nobleman.[11]

In Henry of Huntingdon's *Historia Anglorum*, written c.1130, can be found the second account of Godwin's military leadership abroad for Knútr. In this instance Godwin leads an English contingent against the Wends trying to occupy Denmark while Knútr was away:

> In the third year of his reign [1019] Knútr went to Denmark, leading an army of English and Danes against the Wends. When he had moved close to the enemy in readiness to attack the following day, Godwin, the English earl, led the army in a night attack on the enemy without the king's knowledge. So he fell upon them, unawares, slaughtered, and routed them, but when dawn broke, the king thought that the English had fled or faithlessly gone over to the enemy, so he directed his army, in battle formation, against the enemy, but found only blood, corpses, and spoils in the enemy camp. Because of this, he henceforth esteemed the English as highly as the Danes.[12]

---

[11] *Vita Ædwardi*, pp. 8–11:
Vocantibus autem quibusdam regni competentibus negotiis regem in gentem suam – absenti enim rebellare parauerant collo effreni eius abicientes potentiam – adhesit comes [Godwinus] indiuiduus per omnium uiam. His eius prudentiam, hic laborum constantiam, hic uirtutiis militiam, hic attentius expertus est idem rex tanti principis ualentiam.
On this trip see also John of Worcester, II:182. Modern commentators include Keynes, 'Cnut's Earls,' pp. 71–72 and Stafford, *Queen Emma and Queen Edith*, pp. 255–56.
[12] Henry of Huntingdon, pp. 362–65:
Cnut, tercio anno regni sui, iuit in Daciam, ducens exercitum Anglorum et Dacorum in Wandalos. Cum autem hostibus crastina die conflicturus appropinquasset, Godwinus consul Anglorum ducens exercitum, rege inscio, nocte profectus est in hostes. Igitur improuidos invasit, occidit, fugauit. Rex uero summo mane cum Anglos fugisse uel ad hostes perfide transisse putaret, acies ordinatas in hostem dirigens, non inuenit in

Finally, a third account of Godwin's military leadership, found in the writings of William of Malmesbury, c.1124, is that Godwin led an English force in Knútr's attempted conquest of Sweden in 1026–27:

For his [Knútr's] was 'the valour that knows not how to stand still', and not content with Denmark which he held by inheritance and England which was his by right of war, he set upon the Swedes . . . The greatest readiness in this battle was shown by the English, who were encouraged by Earl Godwine to remember their former glory and display their courage before the eyes of their new lord: they owed it to fortune, he said, that they had once been beaten by Knútr; they would owe it to their own valour that they were too much for those who had beaten him. The English therefore exerted all their strength, and by completing their victory secured an earldom for their leader and renown for themselves.[13]

Most historians have tried to discount the validity of all but the first of these accounts, and in doing so to lessen Godwin's military leadership during Knútr's reign.[14] They contend that both Henry of Huntingdon's and William of Malmesbury's data are incorrect, and that in both cases no such battles between the Danes and their foes, either the Wends or the Swedes, took place.[15] Yet, if we realize that Henry of Huntingdon may be writing about the same Danish rebellion as was the author of the *Vita Ædwardi* and John of Worcester, with only a few facts wrong, like the enemy Knútr's army was facing, at least the relevance of his account can be justified. Also, while there is no strong evidence to support William of Malmesbury's description of the Swedish engagement, there is no strong evidence to dismiss it either. Indeed, as Simon Keynes and Miles W. Campbell have pointed out, there were military engagements in which English forces participated both in Denmark in 1022–23 and in Norway in 1025–27 or

castris nisi sanguinem, et cadauera, et predam. Quamobrem summo honore deinceps Anglos habuit, nec minori quam Dacos.

13 William of Malmesbury, *Gesta regum Anglorum*, I:322–25:

Nam nescia uirtus eius stare loco, nec contenta Danemarkia quam auito, et Anglia quam bellico iure obtinebat, martem in Sweuos transtulit . . . promptissimis ea pugna Anglis, hortante Goduino comite ut pristinae gloriae memores robur suum oculis noui domini assererent: illud fuisse fortunae quod ab eo quondam uicti fuissent, istud uirtutis quod illos premerent qui eum uicissent. Incubuere igitur uiribus Angli et uictoriam consummantes commitatum duci, sibi laudem pararunt.

The internal quote comes from Lucan I:144–45.

14 While agreeing with Godwin's military capabilities, few historians are able to link the rise of Godwin's power to his military leadership. See, for example, Keynes, 'Cnut's Earls,' pp. 70–74, who believes that

In the absence of any better evidence suggesting that Godwine went overseas with the king, we are left free to imagine that he remained all the while in England, doing the things which came most naturally to him: accumulating land at the expense of others, extending the network of men dependent upon him and generally increasing his power. (p. 74)

15 See, for example, Charles Plummer and John Earle's commentary in their edition of the *Anglo-Saxon Chronicle* (*Two of the Saxon Chronicles Parallel*, II:203, 205).

1028–29; William's account easily could refer to either of these expeditions, again with a few facts in error.[16] Discounting the validity of these accounts or not, one thing is for certain: Godwin's military abilities impressed these contemporary authors, allowing them to consider this as legitimacy for his power during Knútr's reign and later.

Other evidence of Godwin's military service and leadership under Knútr might be seen in his association with the *huscarls*. According to two historians, Miles W. Campbell and Tryggvi J. Oleson, somewhere along the line, or perhaps from the very outset of his rise to power, Godwin became a member or maybe even the leader of this special group of elite soldiers. The huscarls formed the core of the English military force, serving both as bodyguard to the king and leaders for the army as a whole. They may also have controlled the *witenagemot*, Anglo-Saxon England's 'parliamentary' body. While based on very limited evidence, mostly surrounding his later rebellion in 1051, Campbell and Oleson insist that Godwin's standing among the *huscarls* may also explain why he was favored by Knútr.[17]

By 1018 then Godwin had become a powerful individual in the kingdom of England. In 1019 he was married to Knútr's sister-in-law, Gyða (although this may have taken place as late as 1023),[18] and in 1020 he became earl of Wessex, the largest and most powerful earldom in Anglo-Saxon England.[19] With these events, it appears that Knútr wished to bind Godwin firmly to him. He must

---

[16] Keynes, 'Cnut's Earls,' pp. 172–74 and Campbell, 'Anglo-Saxon "Kingmaker",' pp. 20–24. See also Lawson, p. 189 and Freeman, *Norman Conquest*, I:419–21, 450, 722–23. However, that Godwin is not mentioned in any of the contemporary narrative accounts of Knútr's 1028–29 invasion of Norway may tend to eliminate this engagement as the one which William of Malmesbury was referring to. See Henry of Huntingdon, p. 365; Adam of Bremen, *Gesta Hammaburgensis ecclesiae pontificum*, ed. B. Schmeidler, 3rd edn, Monumenta Germaniae historica (Hanover, 1917), pp. 125–32; and Symeon of Durham, *Historia regum*, ed. T. Arnold (London, 1882–85), II:157.

[17] Campbell, 'Anglo-Saxon "Kingmaker",' pp. 19, 25; and Tryggvi J. Oleson, *The Witenagemot in the Reign of Edward the Confessor: A Study in the Constitutional History of Eleventh-Century England* (Toronto, 1955), pp. 1–5, 26–29, 48–49, 53–54, 63–65, 105–09. On the huscarls see Freeman, *Norman Conquest*, I:733–37; L.M. Larson, *The King's Household in England before the Norman Conquest* (Madison, 1904), pp. 152–171; C. Warren Hollister, *Anglo-Saxon Military Institutions* (Oxford, 1962), pp. 12–15; and Nicholas Hooper, 'The Housecarls in England in the Eleventh Century,' *Anglo-Norman Studies* 7 (1984), 161–76.

[18] *Vita Ædwardi*, pp. 10–11; Adam of Bremen, *History of the Archbishops*, p. 92; Saxo Grammaticus, *Historia Danica*, ed. P.E. Müller and J.M. Velschow (Hannover, 1839), I:522; Freeman, *Norman Conquest*, I:420–21, 722–25; Freeman, 'On the Life and Death of Earl Godwine,' pp. 246–50; Campbell, 'Anglo-Saxon "Kingmaker",' pp. 18–19; Keynes, 'Cnut's Earls,' pp. 72–73; I. Walker, pp. 9–10; and Stafford, *Queen Emma and Queen Edith*, p. 256. Ann Williams, ' "Cockles Amongst the Wheat": Danes and English in the Western Midlands in the First Half of the Eleventh Century,' *Midland History* 11 (1986), 4, contains a genealogical chart of earls and kings in early eleventh-century England which shows how Godwin's marriage to Gyða tied him to Knútr. Campbell, Keynes, and I. Walker all contend that Godwin's marriage could have been as late as 1022 or 1023.

[19] Freeman, *Norman Conquest*, I:422–23; Keynes, 'Cnut's Earls,' p. 72; and Williams, ' "Cockles Amongst the Wheat",' p. 2.

have been extremely impressed by the young English earl. This the *Vita Ædwardi* reports:

> He [the king] also found out how profound he [Godwin] was in eloquence, and what advantage it would be to him in his newly acquired kingdom if he were to bind him more closely to him by means of some fitting reward. Consequently he admitted the man, whom he had tested in this way for so long, to his counsel and gave him his sister as wife. And when Godwin returned home [from Denmark], having performed all things well, he was appointed by him earl and office-bearer of almost all the kingdom.[20]

Throughout the rest of Knútr's reign, as earl and office-bearer of the kingdom, Godwin prospered. He respected the king, and Knútr returned this respect with land and favor.[21] Godwin governed Knútr's army and, when the king was away, for example on his pilgrimages to Rome in 1027 and 1035, Godwin governed his kingdom as well.[22] Indeed, this earl of Wessex may have performed the same 'subregulus' duties that his son, Harold, who would succeed him as earl of Wessex, would provide during the latter part of the reign of Edward the Confessor. Such at least seems to be the estimation of the author of the *Vita Ædwardi*:

> In the reign of this King Knútr, Godwin flourished in the royal palace, having the first place among the highest nobles of the kingdom; and as was just, what he wrote all decreed should be written, and what he erased, erased.[23]

---

20 *Vita Ædwardi*, pp. 10–11:
    . . . hic attentius expertus est idem rex . . . quam profundus eloquio, et si sum sibi artius astringeret quouis decenti beneficio, quante commoditatis sibi foret in mouiter acquisito Anglorum regno. Taliter ergo diutius probatum, ponit eum sibi a seuretis, dans illi in coniugem sororem suam. Unde cum repatriaret in Angliam, feliciter actis omnibus totius pene regni ab ipso constituitur dux et baiulus.

21 Although there can be no certainty of how much land was acquired by Godwin during the reign of Knútr, some of his estates in Hampshire and Sussex can be traced to this time, given to him, according to Robin Fleming, to improve south-coast defenses. See Robin Fleming, 'Domesday Estates of the King and the Godwines: A Study in Late Saxon Politics,' *Speculum* 58 (1983), 996–999; Robin Fleming, *Kings and Lords in Conquest England* (Cambridge, 1991), pp. 92–96; Peter A. Clarke, *The English Nobility under Edward the Confessor* (Oxford, 1994), pp. 16–17, 24–25, 146–47, 164–69 (pp. 164–69 list all of Godwin's land holdings recorded in the *Domesday Book*); Freeman, *Norman Conquest*, pp. 422–23; Campbell, 'Anglo-Saxon "Kingmaker",' p. 20; Raraty, pp. 6–9; Lawson, p. 188; and I. Walker, pp. 11–12. However, most of these authors believe that the bulk of Godwin's land was acquired during the reign of Edward the Confessor (so much so that Godwin actually held more land in most English counties than did the king). Against this are Freeman and I. Walker.

22 Campbell, 'Anglo-Saxon 'Kingmaker',' pp. 24–25. On the dates and purpose of these pilgrimages see Frank Barlow, 'Two Notes: Cnut's Second Pilgrimage and Queen Emma's Disgrace in 1043,' in *The Norman Conquest and Beyond* (London, 1983), pp. 49–51.

23 *Vita Ædwardi*, pp. 10–11:
    Regnante supradicto Cnuto rege, floruit hic in eius aula primus inter summos regni proceres, et agente equitatis ratione quod scribebat scriptum, quod delebat omnes delendum.

Against this is Campbell, 'Anglo-Saxon "Kingmaker",' p. 23 and Lawson, pp. 188–89, 216.

Knútr died in 1035, but Godwin continued in power. This was not as easy task, however. Knútr seems to have left no specific instructions as to his succession, and thus two men claimed the English throne. One, Harold Harefoot, asserted his claim as a son of Knútr, albeit an illegitimate son by Knútr's mistress, a Northampton woman named Ælfgifu; he was favored by the northern English earldoms. The other claimant, favored by the southern earldoms, Harðaknútr, was the legitimate son of Knútr, born to his wife, Ælfgifu Emma, and thus the more 'legitimate' heir to his father's holdings. However Harðaknútr was ruling Denmark at the time of Knútr's death – his father had given him this kingdom to rule before he died[24] – while his half-brother was in England. This not only gave the throne to Harold practically by default, but also made it dangerous for Harðaknútr to approach England without sufficient strength to force Harold's dethronement, a strength which he was unable to acquire. At least initially, Harðaknútr decided to remain in Denmark, waiting for the opportunity to more forcefully assert his claim to his 'lost' throne.[25]

Godwin's position in this controversy was somewhat troublesome. If he supported the wrong party, his life and position could be lost. Together with most other southern English nobles, he supported Harðaknútr for as long as it was possible. He even housed Harðaknútr's mother, Emma, who had remained in England, and kept Wessex in support of the 'exiled' son of Knútr for a considerable amount of time, lasting even after the witenagemot met and chose Harold as king. The *Anglo-Saxon Chronicle* (E) recalls Godwin's actions:

> And Earl Godwin and all the leading men of Wessex opposed it [the kingship of Harold] for as long as they could, but they could not do anything against it. It was then agreed that Ælfgifu, Harðaknútr's mother, would stay in Winchester with the king's, her son's, huscarls, and that they should keep Wessex all in his position. Earl Godwin was their most loyal man.[26]

Lawson, although believing that Godwin owed much to Knútr, plays down Godwin's power under the king, stating: '. . . given Cnut's readiness to destroy over-mighty subjects such as Eadric Streona and Thorkell it seems improbable that he saw Godwin in this light' (p. 188).
[24] John of Worcester. II:520–21.
[25] John of Worcester, II:520–21, 524–25 and Lawson, pp. 113–15. On the problems with Knútr's wishes for his succession see Lawson, pp. 113–14. There is some dispute among original sources as to who was to rule after Knútr. Adam of Bremen (p. 134) claims that Knútr wished Swegen, probably his eldest son (by Ælfgifu of Northampton), to rule Norway – something he had done since 1030 – Harðaknútr to rule Denmark, and Harold to rule England. Symeon of Durham (*Historia regum*, II:158) also makes Harold the successor to Knútr in England, but the *Encomium Emmae Reginae* (ed. A. Campbell (London, 1949), pp. 38–39) reports that Knútr pledged all of his holdings to his legitimate son, Harðaknútr. The *Encomium Emmae* then professes the illegitimacy of Harold. On the mothers of the two heirs see Miles W. Campbell, 'Queen Emma and Ælfgifu of Northampton: Canute the Great's Women,' *Mediaeval Scandinavia* 4 (1971), 66–79. On the situation of Emma see Stafford, *Queen Emma and Queen Edith*, pp. 233–37 and Miles W. Campbell, 'Emma, reine d'Angleterre, mère dénaturée ou femme vincidative?' *Annales de Normandie* 23 (1973), 106–08.
[26] *Anglo-Saxon Chronicle* (E) 1036, I:159–61:
ꓶ Godwine eorl. ꓶ ealle þa yldestan menn on West Seaxon. lagon ongean swa hi lengost

For a while the kingdom of England was divided. Harold ruled north of the River Thames, while Wessex was held by Godwin and Emma for the absent Harðaknútr, but eventually even the powerful Godwin could not keep Harold from ruling all of England. When Godwin finally did submit to and accept the reign of Harold, it was, as William of Malmesbury asserts, because he was overwhelmed 'in power and in numbers.'[27]

Despite his initial opposition to Harold Harefoot's rule, after submitting to him Godwin remained earl of Wessex and, according to Henry of Huntingdon, Harold's 'leader in military affairs.'[28] Once he began to support Harold, he was loyal to him. Harold ruled for only four or five years, and Godwin never failed him in his duty as earl. Perhaps his greatest test of loyalty to this king came in 1036 when the æthelings, Edward and Alfred, came to England. Edward and Alfred were the sons of Knútr's predecessor, Æðelred the Unready. Their mother was Ælfgifu Emma, later wife to Knútr,[29] and thus they were Knútr's stepsons and half-brothers to Harðaknútr, all reasons for Harold Harefoot to be curious as to why they were in England.

Exactly why the æthelings returned to England during Harold's reign is not known – they had been in exile in Normandy since 1013.[30] They may have been trying to assert their claim to the throne, as William of Poitiers insists,[31] but

---

mihton. ac hi ne mihton nan þing ongean wealcan. ⁊ man gerædde þa þ Ælfgifu Hardacnutes modor sæte on Winceastre mid þæs cynges huscarlum hyra suna. ⁊ heoldan ealle West Seaxen him to handa. ⁊ Godwine eorl wæs heora healdest mann.
See also *Anglo-Saxon Chronicle* (C, D, F) 1036, I:158–59; Henry of Huntingdon, pp. 368–69; William of Malmesbury, *Gesta regum Anglorum*, I:334–35; Freeman, *Norman Conquest*, I:477–84, 752–55; Campbell, 'Queen Emma and Ælfgifu of Northampton,' pp. 76–77; Campbell, 'Anglo-Saxon 'Kingmaker',' pp. 25–26; Raraty, p. 13; Lawson, pp. 114–15; I. Walker, pp. 12–13; Stafford, *Queen Emma and Queen Edith*, pp. 236–46; Frank Barlow, *Edward the Confessor* (Berkeley and Los Angeles, 1970), pp. 44–45; and Pauline Stafford, *Unification and Conquest: A Political and Social History of England in the Tenth and Eleventh Centuries* (London, 1989), pp. 77–79. Numismatic evidence suggests that the kingdom was divided for some time between the two half-brothers. See T. Talvio, 'Harold I and Harthacnut's *Jewel Cross* Type Reconsidered,' in *Anglo-Saxon Monetary History*, ed. M.A.S. Blackburn (Leicester, 1986), pp. 273–90. John of Worcester (II:520–25), William of Malmesbury (*Gesta regum Anglorum*, I:334–35), and Symeon of Durham (*Historia regum*, II:158) contend that the first act of Harold was to deprive Emma of her belongings, although she was not forced from England until after the death of her son, Alfred.

27 William of Malmesbury, *Gesta regum Anglorum*, I:334–35: 'sed tandem, ui et numero impar, cessit uiolentiae.' Campbell contends that Godwin switched his allegiance to Harold 'in part motivated by a desire for personal gain' and in part because, as a member of the huscarls, he was required to be loyal to the king, in this instance the newly crowned Harold I ('Anglo-Saxon "Kingmaker",' pp. 26–27). See also Frank Barlow, *The English Church, 1000–1066: A Constitutional History* (London, 1963), pp. 73–74.

28 Henry of Huntingdon, pp. 368–69: 'Godwinus uero consul dux eis esset in re militari.'

29 On the marriage of Knútr and Emma see Freeman, *Norman Conquest*, I:407–10, 713–17 and Campbell, 'Queen Emma and Ælfgifu of Northampton.'

30 On the æthelings in exile see Simon Keynes, 'The Æthelings in Normandy,' *Anglo-Norman Studies* 13 (1990), 173–205.

31 William of Poitiers, pp. 2–5.

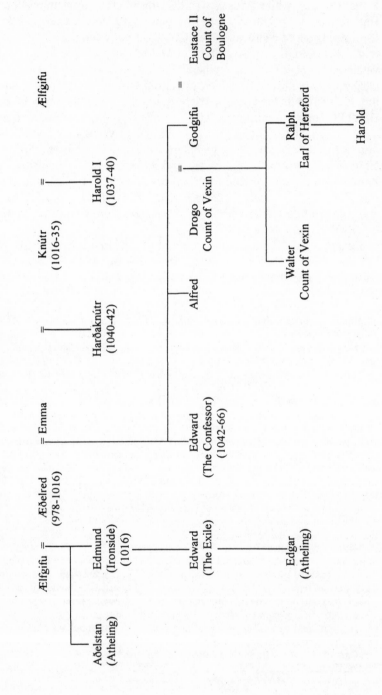

Kings of England and Their Descendants, 1016-1066

(Dates signify rule as king of England)

Frank Barlow lays the blame on their mother, Emma. Having seen her son Harðaknútr's claim to the throne fail, with even Godwin changing sides to support Harold Harefoot, Emma's hatred of the king had grown. She began spreading a rumor that Harold was not the son of Knútr, but the child of a servant smuggled into Ælfgifu of Northampton's bed.[32] Whatever the reason was for their return, once in England, it is certain that their 'visit' presented a problem to King Harold.[33] Yet, by this time most of the earls felt a strong devotion to the current king, and they sought to expel the æthelings and their supporters.

There may have been two separate visits of the ætheling brothers in 1036. The first, made by Edward, was a successful raid of Southampton, according to Norman chroniclers William of Jumièges and William of Poitiers. William of Jumièges writes:

> When King Edward, who at that time lived in the duke [of Normandy]'s household, heard of his [Knútr's] long-desired death, he immediately sailed with forty ships full of soldiers to Southampton, where he met an innumerable multitude of Englishmen ready to join battle with him. He started to fight against them the minute he came on land and swiftly sent a considerable part of their number to their death. As a victor he and his men then returned to their ships.

However it was a victory which accomplished more in convincing Edward that an armed attempt to take over the throne could not be achieved without a larger army. William of Jumièges concludes: 'Seeing, however, that he could not possibly obtain the kingdom of the English without a larger army, he turned the fleet about and, richly laden with booty, sailed back to Normandy.'[34]

---

[32] Barlow (*Edward the Confessor*, p. 44) uses the *Encomium Emmae* (pp. 40–43) for this claim. According to that source, Emma was also to have asserted that Harold forged a letter allegedly from her and sent it to her sons, telling them of his behavior toward their mother and bidding them to come and protect her. This, she claimed, brought them to England and caused the death of Alfred. See also Campbell, 'Anglo-Saxon "Kingmaker",' p. 77; I. Walker, pp. 13–14; Stafford, *Queen Emma and Queen Edith*, pp. 239–40; and Stafford, *Unification and Conquest*, pp. 79–80. William of Poitiers (pp. 2–3) has Emma already in exile when the æthelings travel to England. This is an obvious error, as all of other contemporary chronicles have her in England with her exile to Flanders following Alfred's death.

[33] William of Poitiers, pp. 2–5.

[34] William of Jumièges, II:104–07:

> Cuius diu cupitam mortem Ewardus rex audiens, adhuc cum duce degens, quamtotius cum quadraginta nauibus milite plenis, superato mari, Hantonam appulit, ubi innumerabilem Anglorum multitudinem ad sui perniciem se operientem offendit. Qui protinus congressus cum eis non minimam partem ex illis ocius orcho transmisit. Ipse uero uictor existens ad naues est regressus cum suis. Videns autem non absque plurimo numero militum se posse regnum obtinere Anglorum, regiratis nauium proris, Normanniam cum maxima preda repetiit.

See also William of Poitiers, pp. 2–5; Freeman, *Norman Conquest*, I:485–86; Stafford, *Queen Emma and Queen Edith*, p. 239; Frank Barlow, 'Edward the Confessor's Early Life, Character and Attitudes,' in *The Norman Conquest and Beyond* (London, 1983), pp. 65–66; Barlow,

Perhaps following his older brother's example, Alfred crossed over the Channel a short time later. Although he seems to have had a force equal in size to Edward's, Alfred's result was less successful, leading eventually to his capture, blinding, and murder. As leader of troops sent to contest Alfred's 'invasion,' Godwin played a role in the affair, which eventually led to the ætheling's mutilation and death. John of Worcester reports what occurred:

> He [Godwin] detained Alfred, when he was hastening towards London to confer with King Harold as he had commanded, and placed him in strait custody. Indeed, he disposed of some of his companions, some of whom he put in chains and afterwards blinded. He tortured several by scalping and punished them by cutting off their hands and feet; he also ordered many to be sold and he put 600 men to pitiable deaths at Guilford. Yet it is to be believed that the souls of those whose blameless bodies were so cruelly destroyed on earth now rejoice in paradise with the saints. . . . Then at the command of Godwin and certain others, the ætheling Alfred was led most tightly bound in chains to the island of Ely, but as soon as the ship touched land his eyes were most bloodily plucked out, and he was thus led to the monastery, and handed over to the custody of the monks. When shortly afterwards he departed this light . . . his body was buried with due honour . . .[35]

Edward the Confessor, pp. 44–45; and I. Walker, p. 14. John of Worcester (II:522–23), Symeon of Durham (*Historia regum*, II:158–59), and the *Liber Elienses* (ed. E.O. Blake (London, 1962), pp. 158–59) claim that Edward's and Alfred's journeys to England came at the same time.

[35] John of Worcester, II:522–25:

Hic [Godwinus] quidem Alfredum, cum uersus Lundoniam, ad regis Haroldi colloquium ut mandarat properaret, retinuit, et artam in custodiam posuit. Sociorum ueroillius quosdam disturbauit, quosdam catenauit, et postea cecauit. Nonullos cute capitis abstracta cruciauit, et, manibus ac pedibus amputatis, multauit, multos etiam uendere iussit, et mortibus uariis ac miserabilibus, apud Gyldefordam sexcentos uiros occidit. Sed illorum nunc animas in paradiso creditur gaudere cum sanctis, quorum corpora tam crudeliter sine culpa perempta sunt in aruis . . . Deinde Goduuini et quorundam aliorum iussione, ad insulam Elig clito Alfredus strictissime uinctus dicitur, sed ut ad terram nauis applicuit in ipsa mox eruti sunt oculi eius cruentissime, et sic ad monasterium ductus, monachis traditur custodienus. Vbi breui post tempore, de hac migrauit luce . . . corpus eius sepelitur debito cum honore . . .

See also *Anglo-Saxon Chronicle* (C and D) 1036, I:158–59; *Vita Ædwardi*, pp. 32–35; *Encomium Emmae*, pp. 40–47; William of Malmesbury, *Gesta regum Anglorum*, I:336–39; William of Jumièges, II:106–07; William of Poitiers, pp. 4–5; Symeon of Durham, *Historia regum*, II:158–59; *Liber Elienses*, pp. 158–60; Freeman, *Norman Conquest*, I:486–97, 755–64; Freeman, 'On the Life and Death of Earl Godwine,' pp. 330–38; Campbell, 'Anglo-Saxon "Kingmaker",' p. 26; Stafford, *Queen Emma and Queen Edith*, pp. 239–40; Campbell, 'Queen Emma and Ælfgifu of Northampton,' pp. 77–78; Raraty, p. 14; Keynes, 'Æthelings in Normandy,' pp. 195–96; Barlow, *Edward the Confessor*, pp. 45–46; I. Walker, pp. 13–15; and Philip Grierson, 'The Relations between England and Flanders before the Norman Conquest,' *Transactions of the Royal Historical Society* 23 (1941), 96. Henry of Huntingdon (p. 373) and Geoffrey Gaimar, *Lestoire des Engles*, ed. T.D. Hardy and C.T. Martin (London, 1888), I:203–05 incorrectly date the murder of Alfred to after the death of Harðaknútr. According to John of Worcester (II:524–25) and the *Encomium Emmae* (pp. 46–47), after Alfred's death,

His part in this plan would come back to haunt Godwin on several later occasions.[36]

Harold died in 1039 or 1040,[37] and Harðaknútr, his earlier opponent, with an ostentatious show of force came to England to take the throne – John of Worcester claims that Harðaknútr sailed across the Channel from Bruges with 'sixty ships which he manned with Danish troops.'[38] Worcester also claims that he 'was joyfully received by all,'[39] all that is except for Godwin. Godwin, by this time, had completely changed his allegiance to King Harold, probably believing

and fearing for the life of her other ætheling son, Emma sent Edward back to Normandy 'in great haste.'

[36] William of Poitiers, pp. 4–7; William of Jumièges, II:107; and Gillingham, pp. 149–50. Henry of Huntingdon (pp. 384–85, 392–93) twice reports that William the Conqueror uses this death as a provocation for the conquest of England in 1066, although obviously not against Godwin, but against his son, Harold. Freeman (*Norman Conquest*, I:492–97), never willing to see Godwin as anything other than the 'perfect' earl, attempts to remove any guilt which he might have had in the murder of Alfred:

> On the whole then I incline to the belief that the great Earl, every other recorded action of whose life is the action of an English patriot, who on every other occasion appears as conciliatory and law-abiding, who is always as strongly opposed to everything like wrong or violence as the rude age in which he lived would let him be, did not, on this one occasion, act in a manner so contrary to his whole character as to resort to fraud or needless violence to compass the destruction of a man of English birth and royal descent. The innocence of Godwin seems to me to be most probable in itself, most inconsistent with the circumstances of the time, and not inconsistent with such parts of our evidence as seem most trustworthy. But in any case, even if, while rejecting the palpable fables and contradictions, we take the evidence, so far as it is of, at the worst, even then it seems to me that the great Earl is at least entitled to a verdict of Not Proven, if not Not Guilty. (I:497)

See also I. Walker, p. 15.

[37] The *Anglo-Saxon Chronicle* (A, C, and D) (I:160–61) and John of Worcester (II:528–29) all agree that the date of Harold's death was 1040, but the *Anglo-Saxon Chronicle* (E and F) (I:161) record it as 1039, with Harðaknútr taking the throne in 1040. Almost all modern historians use March 17, 1040 as the date of this death, following Freeman (*Norman Conquest*, I:504).

[38] John of Worcester, II:528–29: 'Qui nauibus xl. paratis et Danicis militibus instructis, ante mediam estatem Angliam aduehitur.' See also *Anglo-Saxon Chronicle* (C) 1040 and (E) 1039, I:160–62; *Encomium Emmae*, pp. 48–53; William of Poitiers, pp. 6–7; *Chronicon abbatiae de Evesham*, ed. W.D. Macray (London, 1863), pp. 36–37; Freeman, *Norman Conquest*, I:507–08; Barlow, *Edward the Confessor*, p. 48; Stafford, *Queen Emma and Queen Edith*, pp. 246–47; and Grierson, 'The Relations between England and Flanders,' pp. 96–97. Symeon of Durham (*Historia regum*, II:160) claims that the fleet contained only forty ships, and Adam of Bremen (p. 134) reports that the fleet was assembled for an invasion of England which became unnecessary once Harold had died. Freeman (*Norman Conquest*, I:505–06) discounts this choosing to side with the anonymous author of the *Encomium Emmae*'s assertion that an embassy had been made by the bishop of London and the abbot of Evesham to Harðaknútr announcing Harold's death and asking Harðaknútr to take the throne. The Danish sailors were paid for by a tax levied on the English people. See *Anglo-Saxon Chronicle* (C and E) 1040; John of Worcester, II:530–31; I. Walker, p. 16; and Stafford, *Unification and Conquest*, pp. 80–81.

[39] John of Worcester, II:528–29: 'et gaudenter ab omnibus suscipitur.'

that the young king was due for a long rule. Naturally, Harðaknútr was not pleased with the earl of Wessex who had not only shifted his support to Harold but had also participated at least in the torture and imprisonment of his half-brother. Initially, it seems that Harðaknútr blamed Godwin for Alfred's death, and one of his first acts as king was to put the once powerful earl on trial for murder.[40] In order to free himself from the responsibility of this crime, Godwin made an oath to Harðaknútr, claiming that what was done to Alfred was all done at the command of Harold;[41] as a good soldier he was merely following orders. Godwin, true to his military character, also presented Harðaknútr with a beautiful ship, manned by a number of richly armed men, a description of which John of Worcester records:

> However, Godwin to regain his friendship, gave the king a skillfully made galley, with a gilded prow or beak, furnished with the best tackle, well-equipped with suitable arms and picked soldiers. Each one of them had two golden armlets on his arms weighing sixteen ounces, was clad in a triple mail corselet, with a helmet on his head, was girt about the loins with a sword with gilded hilts; a Danish axe bound with gold and silver hung from his left shoulder; in his left hand was a shield with gilded boss and studs, in his right a spear, called an *ætgar* in English.[42]

Such a beautiful ship naturally appealed to Harðaknútr's vanity and greed. The oath of allegiance was undoubtedly also important, but Godwin knew of the new king's weaknesses. Godwin was an extremely valuable man. As his gift had shown, he was of great military importance in England. Besides, Harðaknútr had probably never even met Alfred, and the loss of Anglo-Saxon military leadership by punishing Godwin with death or exile might cost the king more than he could gain by vengeance, so the gift of the ship was gratefully accepted by

---

[40] William of Malmesbury, *Gesta regum Anglorum*, I:338–39; Freeman, *Norman Conquest*, I:766–67; and Campbell, 'Anglo-Saxon "Kingmaker",' p. 27. This may not have been a formal trial, as none of the more contemporary sources identify it as such, although it is clear that Godwin was forced to account for his behavior. Also, John of Worcester (II:530–31) claims that the king 'burnt with great anger' against Godwin for this crime. If so, however, he seems quickly mollified by the earl's oath and gift.

[41] John of Worcester, II:530–33; Campbell, 'Anglo-Saxon "Kingmaker",' p. 27; and I. Walker, p. 16.

[42] John of Worcester, II:530–33:

> Goduuinus autem regi pro sua amicitia dedit trierem fabrefactam, uel rostrum caput deauratum habentem, armamentis optimis instructam, decoris armis electisque octoginta militibus decoratam, quorum unusquisque habebat duas in suis brachiis aureas armillas, sedecim uncias pendentes, loricam trilicem indutam, in capite cassidem ex parte deauratam, gladium deauratis capulis renibus accinctum, Danicam securim auro argentoque redimitam in sinistro humero pendentem, in manu sinistra clipeum, cuius umbo clauique erant deaurati, in dextra lanceam, que lingua Anglorum ategar appellatur.

See also William of Malmesbury, *Gesta regum Anglorum*, I:338–39; Symeon of Durham, *Historia regum*, II:161 (who is obviously using John of Worcester's account to write his chronicle); Campbell, 'Anglo-Saxon "Kingmaker",' p. 27; Raraty, p. 15; and I. Walker, p. 16.

him. Godwin's punishment was more symbolic than it was punitive: he, with several other supporters of Harold's reign, were ordered to disinter the former king's body and throw it into a marsh and then into the Thames River.[43] (John of Worcester assures us, however, that 'a short time later, it [Harold's body] was taken by a certain fisherman, borne in haste to the Danes, and was honourably buried in a cemetery they had in London.'[44]) With this minor act of fealty to Harðaknútr, Godwin was once again the most powerful earl of England.[45]

Harðaknútr was not a popular king. During the first year of his reign, he excised a severe tax from the inhabitants of the kingdom. Many of the English rebelled at this tax, but none so relentlessly as the citizens of Worcester. In an open rebellion against Harðaknútr's tax, two of the king's huscarls, who had been sent to the town to collect the tax, were slain by the townspeople. In order to put down the rebellion and to teach the inhabitants of Worcester a lesson, the king sent an army of his nobles and huscarls to ravage the town. Godwin was among them and may have led them. Fortunately, the citizens of Worcester had been warned of the oncoming raid and had fled the town. Few were killed, but the town was sacked and burned, thus satisfying the king's lust for revenge. The incident also showed that Godwin had once more conformed to his sovereign's wishes.[46] More importantly, it seems to have solidified Harðaknútr's legacy as, in the words of Edward Freeman, 'a rapacious, brutal, and bloodthirsty tyrant.'[47]

One act of Harðaknútr's which had positive consequences was his invitation to his half-brother, Edward, to return to England and to administer in some governance responsibilities. This was perhaps at the instigation of their mother, Emma, who wanted her remaining sons together. Although it may be too much

---

43 *Anglo-Saxon Chronicle* (C) 1040, I:160–52; John of Worcester, II:530–31; Symeon of Durham, *Historia regum*, II:160; Freeman, *Norman Conquest*, I:508–09, 764–66; Freeman, 'On the Life and Death of Earl Godwine,' p. 337; Barlow, *Edward the Confessor*, p. 48; I. Walker, p. 16; and Stafford, *Unification and Conquest*, p. 81. William of Malmesbury (*Gesta regum Anglorum*, I:336–37) adds that the body was also beheaded. Others who participated in this included Ælfric, archbishop of York (who had probably crowned Harold), Stor, master of Harold's household, Eadric, his steward, Thrond, his executioner, and other great men of London.

44 John of Worcester, II:530–31: 'Breui autem post tempore, a quodam captum est piscatore, et ad Danos allatum sub festinatione, in cimiterio, quod habuerunt Lundonie, sepultum est ab ipsis cum honore.' See also Symeon of Durham, *Historia regum*, II:160 and Freeman, *Norman Conquest*, I:508–09, 765.

45 Lawson (p. 216) suggests rather too freely that Harðaknútr 'had Godwin well under control.' In fact, the opposite seems to have been the case.

46 *Anglo-Saxon Chronicle* (C and D) 1041, I:162–63; John of Worcester, II:532–33; William of Malmesbury, *Gesta regum Anglorum*, I:338–39; Symeon of Durham, *Historia regum*, II:161; Freeman, *Norman Conquest*, I:513–17; Raraty, p. 15; Lawson, p. 31; I. Walker, p. 16; and Stafford, *Unification and Conquest*, p. 81. The names of the huscarls killed were Feader and Thurstan. Those named in the attacking party included Earls Godwin of Wessex, Siward of Northumbria, Leofric of Mercia, and Hrani of the *Magonsæte*, as well as all of the English ealdormen and almost all of Harðaknútr's remaining huscarls.

47 Freeman, *Norman Conquest*, I:507. This is not, however, the conclusion of Anglo-Norman chroniclers, Henry of Huntingdon (pp. 370–71) and William of Poitiers (pp. 6–7).

to say that Edward operated with his brother as co-ruler at this time, as the *Encomium Emmae* contends, it did make succession to the throne easier for the Confessor after Harðaknútr's death than it had been for the last two kings. It also gave Edward and Godwin a chance to become acquainted with each other, and for Edward to begin to value Godwin's leadership.[48]

Harðaknútr's reign was even shorter than his predecessor's. He died suddenly in 1042.[49] Edward heard immediately of his half-brother's death, and he ascended the throne with little contention.[50] Godwin supported Edward's taking of the crown, and the new king from the very beginning of his reign seemed to ask the earl of Wessex for his advice and fealty. William of Malmesbury describes the transfer of the crown in England and Godwin's role in it:

> When Edward received the sad news of Harðaknútr's death, he was in a quandary, and did not know what to do or which way to turn. After deep thought, it seemed the best plan to assess his future with help from the advice of Godwine. Invited by emissaries to a conference, under a prior agreement to keep the peace, Godwine hesitated and thought it over for a long time, but at length agreed. When Edward came to him and attempted to throw himself at his feet, he raised him; and when he told the story of Harthacnut's death, and begged for assistance in returning to Normandy, Godwine loaded him with

---

[48] *Anglo-Saxon Chronicle* (D and E) 1040, I:161–63; John of Worcester, II:532–33; William of Malmesbury, *Gesta regum Anglorum*, I:336–37; Henry of Huntingdon, pp. 370–71; Saxo Grammaticus, I:538–40; Freeman, *Norman Conquest*, I:518–19; Raraty, pp. 15–16; Barlow, *Edward the Confessor*, pp. 48–53; Barlow, 'Edward the Confessor's Early Life,' p. 67; Keynes, 'Æthelings in Normandy,' pp. 198–200; Stafford, *Queen Emma and Queen Edith*, pp. 247–48; Campbell, 'Emma, reine d'Angleterre,' pp. 107–09; Stafford, *Unification and Conquest*, pp. 81–82. The *Encomium Emmae* (pp. 52–53) holds that this was Emma's decision and that once it occurred, all three, Emma and her two sons, ruled England together. On this see Barlow, *Edward the Confessor*, pp. 48–49 and Stafford, *Unification and Conquest*, p. 82.

[49] According to John of Worcester (II:534–35), Harðaknútr's death was unexpected:

Harðaknútr, king of the English, merry, in good health, and in great heart, was standing drinking with the aforementioned bride [Gyða, daughter of Osgod Clapa, one of the king's retainers] and certain men when he suddenly crashed to the ground in a wretched fall while drinking. He remained speechless until his death on Tuesday, 8 June.

(Rex Anglorum Heardecanutus . . . letus, sospes et hilaris, cum sponsa predicta et quibusdam uiris bibens staret, repente inter bibendum miserabili casu ad terram corruit et sic mutus permanens, .vi. idus Iunii, feria .iii., expiravit.)

See also the *Anglo-Saxon Chronicle* (C and D) 1042, I:162–63 and Symeon of Durham, *Historia regum*, II:162. Adam of Bremen (p. 136) reports that when Harðaknútr died he was on the verge of attacking Magnús, the king of Norway, who had recently attacked Denmark. On this see Freeman, *Norman Conquest*, I:523. David C. Douglas (*William the Conqueror* (Berkeley and Los Angeles, 1964), pp. 411–12) suggests the possibility of Harðaknútr having been poisoned, although by whom or for what purpose is not mentioned.

[50] Freeman's idea (*Norman Conquest*, II:9–12) that the election of Edward was contested seems to be an exaggeration of what was undoubtedly conventional practice of engendering favor by gift-giving and homage-exchange when newly assuming the throne.

copious promises: he would do better to live in glory on his throne than to die in obscurity in exile.[51]

William of Malmesbury obviously has some facts wrong here. Edward, according to all of the versions of the *Anglo-Saxon Chronicle*, was in London at the death of his brother and was thus not worried about 'dying in exile.' Still, the working relationship between Godwin and Edward portrayed here by Malmesbury was certainly a reality.[52]

Godwin did help and advise Edward, and Edward in turn sought the help and advice of his chief earl, seemingly forgiving his participation in the death of his ætheling brother, Alfred; however, this would become an issue for the king and earl later. Yet Godwin himself must have been wary of his role in Edward's brother's death, and thus he sought to secure his relationship with the new king further. This was accomplished by marrying his daughter, Eadgyða, to Edward in 1045. There was at least fifteen years difference in their ages,[53] but the match was successful, and the working relationship between earl and king was sealed.[54]

---

51 William of Malmesbury, *Gesta regum Anglorum*, I:350–51:
Hardecnuto mortuo, Eduardus tam tristi nuntio accepto, incertumque fluctans quid ageret, quo se uerteret nesciebat. Multa uoluenti potior sententia uisa ut Goduini consilio fortunas suas trutinaret. Conuentus ille per legatarios ut pace prefata colloquerentur, diu hesitabundus et cogitans tandem annuit; uenientem ad se et conantem ad genua procumbere alleuat; Hardecnuti mortem exponentem orantemque in Normanniam reditus auxilium ingentibus promissis onorat. Melius esse ut uiuat gloriosus in imperio quam ignominiosus moriatur in exilio.
Also recording Godwin's assistance to Edward are the *Vita Ædwardi*, pp. 14–15; John of Worcester, II:534–35; Symeon of Durham, *Historia regum*, II:162; Freeman, *Norman Conquest*, II:7–8, 513–21; Freeman, 'On the Life and Death of Earl Godwine,' pp. 339–41; and Stafford, *Unification and Conquest*, pp. 86–87. The *Vita Ædwardi* (pp. 20–21) mentions a gift of a ship from Godwin to Edward similar to the one which the *Anglo-Saxon Chronicle* and John of Worcester contends that he gave to Harðaknútr. While Freeman (*Norman Conquest*, II:19–20), Barlow (*Vita Ædwardi*, p. 20 n. 46 and *Edward the Confessor*, pp. 50, 57), and Stafford (*Unification and Conquest*, p. 80) accept this, believing that this exchange had become a custom with the earl of Wessex, I find that it is easier to believe that there was only one ship, that given to Harðaknútr, and that author of the *Vita Ædwardi*, who mentions nothing of the first ship, is confused on this matter. See also *Lives of Edward the Confessor*, ed. Henry Richards Luard (London, 1858), p. 397 n. 2 and Richard Southern, 'The First Life of Edward the Confessor,' *English Historical Review* 58 (1943), 395. Also, Barlow (*Edward the Confessor*, pp. 55–57) finds Godwin's support of Edward 'surprising' based on his closeness to Knútr, the enemy and eventual usurper of Edward's father's throne. Yet, as a military leader supporting his king, I find Godwin's fealty fairly standard.
52 Because William of Malmesbury has Edward in Normandy at the death of Harðaknútr, Freeman (*Norman Chronicle*, II:7–9, 517–18) holds that he had returned to Normandy before his brother's death. I think that there is a greater likelihood for Malmesbury's error, especially as the more contemporary *Anglo-Saxon Chronicles* declare that Edward was in England, than for his unsubstantiated return to Normandy. See also Barlow, *Edward the Confessor*, p. 53 n. 5.
53 *Vita Ædwardi*, p. lxxv. See Kenneth E. Cutler, 'Edith, Queen of England,' *Mediaeval Studies* 38 (1976), 223–24 for a discussion on the age difference between the two.
54 The marriage of Edward and Eadgyða will be examined below.

For the next nine years, there was peace between Godwin and Edward. Despite later claims by Norman chroniclers that there was constant discord between the king and the earl of Wessex,[55] Edward seemed to prize Godwin's friendship, and Godwin in turn counseled Edward and protected him from elements in the kingdom which sought conflict with the king. In this first part of his reign, Edward rarely proceeded without Godwin's assistance and advice.

Among matters decided with Godwin's counsel was Edward's dispossession of his mother, Emma. Although she was seemingly responsible for her son's return during Harðaknútr's reign, Edward could not forgive his mother's marrying Knútr after the Danish conqueror had dethroned her husband and Edward's father, Æðelred. He may also have believed that she had disowned him and his brother, Alfred, whom she also had with Æðelred, in support of their younger half-brother, Harðaknútr, who was Knútr's son. Finally, Edward may also have blamed Emma for Alfred's death, as he was in England at the time presumably to assist his mother against the abusive King Harold. For any or all of these reasons, in 1043 the Confessor denounced his mother and deprived her of her possessions. The *Anglo-Saxon Chronicle* (D) insists that it was Godwin among other earls who accompanied and supported Edward in this procedure.[56]

Another royal affair assisted by the earl of Wessex was the temporary resignation of Eadsige as archbishop of Canterbury and the secret consecration of Siward, abbot of Abingdon, in his place, which, again recorded in the *Anglo-Saxon Chronicle*, was done with the permission of Edward's chief earl as well as the king.[57] For these and other services, two of Godwin's sons, Swegen and Harold, were raised to the position of earl in 1043 and 1044 respectively.[58]

---

55 See, for example, Wace, II:88–89.

56 *Anglo-Saxon Chronicle* (D and E) 1043, I:163–65. See also John of Worcester, II:534–35 and Symeon of Durham, *Historia regum*, II:162. The best discussion of this is Barlow, 'Two Notes,' pp. 51–56. Barlow also reprints a portion of the *Miracle of St. Mildred* which discusses Emma's dispossession. In that work, the anonymous hagiographer claims that Edward was angry at his mother for supporting Magnús, King of Norway, for king of England in 1042 instead of himself. It also claims that Emma was eventually exonerated from this crime and that she also regained her son's favor. While the fact that she remained in England does give some credibility to this story, that she brought Edward to England before Harðaknútr's death certainly does not give credence to her later support of Magnús for the throne. The full edition of the *Miracle* can be found in *Descriptive Catalogue of Materials Relating to the History of Great Britain and Ireland*, ed. T. Hardy (London, 1862–71), II:381. See also Freeman, *Norman Conquest*, II:59–63; Campbell, 'Anglo-Saxon "Kingmaker",' p. 28; Stafford, *Queen Emma and Queen Edith*, pp. 248–51; Campbell, 'Emma, reine d'Angleterre,' pp. 109–14; Campbell, 'Queen Emma and Ælfgifu of Northampton,' p. 79; Barlow, *Edward the Confessor*, pp. 76–78; Barlow, 'Edward the Confessor's Early Life,' pp. 67, 69; and Stafford, *Unification and Conquest*, pp. 86–87.

57 *Anglo-Saxon Chronicle* (C) 1044, I:162–64 and William of Malmesbury, *De gestis pontificum Anglorum*, ed. N.E.S.A. Hamilton (London, 1870), p. 34. See also Freeman, *Norman Conquest*, II:67–68 and Barlow, *Edward the Confessor*, p. 78.

58 See Harmer, p. 535; Freeman, *Norman Conquest*, II:79, 555–68; Campbell, 'Anglo-Saxon "Kingmaker",' pp. 27–28; *Vita Ædwardi*, p. 8 n. 11; and Henry R. Loyn, 'Harold, Son of Godwin,' in *Society and Peoples: Studies in the History of England and Wales, c. 600–1200*

However it would be a misunderstanding to think that Godwin and Edward agreed on all issues and that Godwin's choices in these disagreements always succeeded; indeed on most of these occasions of disagreement, the king's wishes prevailed over those of the earl of Wessex. Most of these disagreements were also on military matters, in which Godwin played the 'hawk' and Edward the 'dove.' For example, in 1047, Sveinn Estriðson, king of Denmark, asked the English for assistance in defending Denmark against invading Norwegians led by their king, Magnús. John of Worcester writes that Godwin suggested sending a fleet of 'at least fifty ships with their complement of soldiers,' but that the king refused to send any. Without this assistance, Sveinn's army was soundly defeated by the Norwegians, and Denmark became a kingdom ruled over by Magnús.[59] Magnús' rule of Denmark was to be short, however; a little while after this conquest he died, and in 1048 Sveinn retook Denmark, but there was to be no peace between Norway and Denmark. Magnús' uncle and heir, Haraldr Harðráði, after sending envoys to make peace with Edward, made plans to regain Denmark. Once again, Sveinn petitioned the English for assistance, and, once again, according to John of Worcester, Godwin wished to send fifty ships to him, but as before Edward refused to do so.[60] It should also be noted that John of Worcester on both of these occasions identifies Leofric, the earl of Mercia, as the chief opponent of Godwin, indicating what had become a rivalry which would be passed on to both earls' sons.

One might conclude that Godwin's desire to assist the Danes in their defense against Norway was nothing more that this earl's wish to aid some of those who had been his allies during the reign of Knútr and their youthful military activities. Others say that this support was due to Sveinn Estriðson's kinship to the

---

(London, 1992), p. 303. The editor of this *Vita Ædwardi*, Frank Barlow, has estimated the dates of Swegen's and Harold's appointments based on the earliest charters and writs which they signed as 'earls.' The *Anglo-Saxon Chronicle* does not mention either appointment, but rather refers *post-facto* to the earls in their positions. Both of these Godwinsons will be examined separately below.

59 John of Worcester, II:544–45 and Symeon of Durham, *Historia regum*, II:164. The *Anglo-Saxon Chronicle* (D) 1048, I:167 indicates that it was Sveinn and not Godwin who asked for the fifty ships and that no one, including the earl of Wessex, supported this request. See also Freeman, *Norman Conquest*, II:90–92; Barlow, *Edward the Confessor*, pp. 92–93; I. Walker, pp. 22–23; and Miles W. Campbell, 'Earl Godwin of Wessex and Edward the Confessor's Promise of the Throne to William of Normandy,' *Traditio* 28 (1972), 146. Some modern historians see this and Edward's refusal to support the Danes again a year later as evidence of an anti-Danish policy of Edward taking place which would eventually lead to the ouster of Godwin and his family. See Campbell, 'Anglo-Saxon "Kingmaker",' pp. 29–30 and Barlow, 'Edward the Confessor's Early Life,' pp. 70–72. It should be noted that there is some problem with the dating of this request. Magnus was not sole king of Norway in 1047, and no such invasion of Denmark seems to have taken place during Magnus and Haraldr Harðráði's co-reign of 1046–47. This probably refers to Magnus' earlier attack of Denmark in 1045.

60 John of Worcester, II:544–45. The *Anglo-Saxon Chronicle* (D) 1049 (I:167) again makes no mention of Godwin's desire to assist Denmark. See also Freeman, *Norman Conquest*, II:92–93 and Barlow, 'Edward the Confessor's Early Life,' p. 71.

earl; the Danish king was his nephew by marriage. Instead, it seems to indicate the attitude of a warlord, a general, whose belief in military power as a means of delivering diplomacy and intimidation to one's friends and enemies was opposed by a king who had never tasted success in a military arena and who believed on the other hand in remaining outside affairs which did not directly affect his kingdom.[61] That said, however, Edward did support the Holy Roman Emperor, Henry III, in his request for assistance in his 1049 attack of the county of Flanders. In particular, Henry asked Edward to keep Baldwin V, the count of Flanders, on whom the emperor blamed the war between the Empire and Flanders, from retreating into the Channel and fleeing to France by sea. Consequently, Edward moved his fleet into the port of Sandwich where it remained until this war had ended. There is no record of what the Godwin family, whose close relationship to Baldwin V of Flanders will be examined below, thought of Edward's reaction to the emperor's request, although it is believed that at least his son, Harold, was with the fleet in Sandwich if not the earl of Wessex himself.[62]

Also in 1049, Ireland and Wales began to create problems for England. In late July or early August of that year, a large Irish piratical fleet, numbering thirty-six ships according to John of Worcester, with the help of Gruffydd ap Rhydderch, king of Deheubarth (in South Wales), raided up the Severn and Wye rivers. With its earl, Swegen Godwinson, in exile, as will be discussed below, Bishop Ealdred of Worcester was in charge of the earldom; he and a small

---

[61] I am here discounting Edward's participation in the naval defense of England in 1045 as mentioned in the *Anglo-Saxon Chronicle* (C) 1045 and (D) 1046 (I:164–65), John of Worcester (II:542–43), and Symeon of Durham (*Historia regum*, II:163). Although a fleet may have been assembled at Edward's behest, at least that is what John of Worcester reports, it did not engage in military action as there was no attack by Magnús. It is also curious that if Magnús seriously was threatening an invasion against England in 1045, why did Edward refuse to support a request by Sveinn Estriðson to help fight against the Norwegian king? See Freeman, *Norman Conquest*, II:72–74, 78 and Barlow, *Edward the Confessor*, p. 92.

[62] *Anglo-Saxon Chronicle* (C) 1049 and D (1050), I:166–67; John of Worcester, II:548–49; Symeon of Durham, *Historia regum*, II:164; Freeman, *Norman Conquest*, II:97–98; Barlow, *Edward the Confessor*, pp. 98–99; Barlow, 'Edward the Confessor's Early Life,' p. 79; Campbell, 'Earl Godwin of Wessex and Edward the Confessor's Promise,' p. 147; I. Walker, p. 24; and Grierson, 'The Relations between England and Flanders,' pp. 98–99. Godwin does not set sail with Beorn into the Channel until after the war between Flanders and the Holy Roman Empire was concluded and this may indicate that he was a part of the English fleet in Sandwich at this time. Why Edward the Confessor supported Henry III against Baldwin V at this time cannot be known. Edward had been a friend of the Flemish count early in the century, when in 1016 he spent Christmas in Ghent at the invitation of the Flemish count. At that time he promised to restore all of the English possessions of St Peter's should he become king, a promise which Edward fulfilled in 1044. See A. van Lokeren, *Chartes et documents de l'abbaye de Saint-Pierre au Mont-Blandin* (Ghent, 1898), nos. 96 and 124, pp. 72–73, 88–90 and Grierson, 'The Relations between England and Flanders,' pp. 95, 101. Grierson's idea that the enmity between Edward and Baldwin had resulted from Harðaknútr's and Emma's 'prejudicing' the count against the future king during their stay in Flanders in the winter of 1039–40 ('The Relations between England and Flanders,' pp. 97–98) assumes far too much from the slim sources available.

number of Gloucestershire and Herefordshire men put up a vain fight against them, but most were killed. The Irish and Welsh raiders retreated before winter, and before further military operations by Godwin or others could be undertaken against them, but this forecast the problem with Wales which would necessitate military action in the future.[63]

Godwin seems not to have been the only advisor to Edward the Confessor. After being forced from England as a child, Edward had gone to the European continent, primarily to Normandy, where he had been raised; after the murder of Alfred by Harold I, he again stayed in Normandy. During these sojourns, he had made many contacts with Norman nobles, and several of these began to join Edward's court in England after 1045. By 1051 there seems to have been a fairly large number of Norman advisors in England, although perhaps the most prominent and most listened to by Edward was Robert of Jumièges (also known as Robert Champart), bishop of London until 1050 when, over Godwin's objection, he became archbishop of Canterbury. Soon Robert and the others in this non-English congress began to exert significant influence on the king's councils, and Godwin and his sons' power began to wane as the Norman presence in the kingdom continued.[64] Still, at least initially, Godwin's family remained loyal to the throne despite an obvious dislike for the shrinking of their political power. William of Malmesbury writes:

> Godwine and his sons, they say, were men of noble spirit and great energy, founders and pillars of Edward's reign as king; it was not surprising if they were indignant when they saw new men and foreigners promoted over their heads, but they had never so much as spoken a harsh word against the king, whom they had raised to his high position once and for all.[65]

---

63 The bishop was only barely able to escape. *Anglo-Saxon Chronicle* (D) 1050, I:167; John of Worcester, II:550–53; Freeman, *Norman Conquest*, II:109–10, 595–98; Barlow, *Edward the Confessor*, pp. 99, 204–05; Barlow, *English Church*, p. 87; Stafford, *Unification and Conquest*, p. 88; K.L. Maund, *Ireland, Wales, and England in the Eleventh Century* (Woodbridge, 1991), p. 124; and Vanessa King, 'Ealdred, Archbishop of York: The Worcester Years,' *Anglo-Norman Studies* 18 (1995), 126–27. John of Worcester blames the defeat of the English on Welsh traitors in their midst. The confusion in dating results from the *Anglo-Saxon Chronicle*'s date of 29 July and John of Worcester's date of August.

64 On the Normans in England before 1051 see *Vita Ædwardi*, pp. 28–31; John of Worcester, II:552–53; William of Malmesbury, *Gesta regum Anglorum*, I:354–55; William of Malmesbury, *De gestis pontificum*, p. 35; Symeon of Durham, *Historia regum*, II:166; Freeman, *Norman Conquest*, II:69–70; Barlow, *Edward the Confessor*, pp. 104–08; Barlow, *English Church*, 46–49; Stafford, *Unification and Conquest*, pp. 90–91; Miles W. Campbell, 'A Pre-Conquest Norman Occupation of England?' *Speculum* 46 (1971), 21–31; and C.P. Lewis, 'The French in England before the Norman Conquest,' *Anglo-Norman Studies* 17 (1994), 123–44. Normans in England were not something introduced by Edward. There seems to have been a long-term connection between Anglo-Saxon England and Normandy. See R.L. Graeme Ritchie, *The Normans in England before Edward the Confessor* (London, 1948).

65 William of Malmesbury, *Gesta regum Anglorum*, I:354–55:
  Goduinum et natos magnanimos uiros et industrios, auctores et tutores regni Eduardi;
  non mirum si succensuerint quod nouos homines et aduenas sibi preferri uiderent;

Peace between the factions would not last long. Finally, the influence of the Normans became unbearable to Godwin. In 1051 he opposed the king and was banished from England with his family. Two versions of the story are reported. The first and most popular account of the banishment of Godwin is found in two versions of the *Anglo-Saxon Chronicle* (D and E), John of Worcester's *Chronicle*, and William of Malmesbury's *Gesta regum Anglorum*. It begins with the tale of Eustace, the count of Boulogne, who was married to Edward the Confessor's sister and who was traveling from London after a visit with his brother-in-law. The following is taken from the *Anglo-Saxon Chronicle* (E):

> Then Eustace . . . gathered his company and traveled to Dover. When they had arrived there they wished to lodge in a place which was suitably comfortable. Then came one of his men to him, and wished to stay at a house against the owner's will. He wounded the householder, and the householder killed him. Then Eustace mounted his horse, and his companions mounted theirs, and they rode to the householder and killed him on his own hearth. Afterwards, they went into the town and killed within and without more than twenty men. And the townspeople killed nineteen of their men, and they wounded they did not know how many. Eustace escaped with a few men and went to the king, where he gave him a prejudiced account of how they fared. And the king grew very angry with the townspeople.[66]

numquam tamen contra regem, quem semel fastigauerint, asperum etiam uerbum locutos.

See also *Vita Ædwardi*, pp. 28–33 and Barlow, *English Church*, p. 47. However, Godwin had been objecting to the power of newly arrived Norman priests since at least 1049. See Barlow, *English Church*, p. 47.

[66] *Anglo-Saxon Chronicle* (E) 1048, I:172–73:

Ða dyde he [Eustatius] on his byrnan. ⁊ his gefaren ealle. ⁊ foran to Dorfan. Þa hi þider comon. þa woldon hi innian hi þær heom sylfan gelicode. þa com an his manna. ⁊ wolde wician æt anes bundan huse his unðances. ⁊ gewundode þone husbondon. ⁊ se husbunda ofsloh þone oðerne. Ða wearð Eustatius uppon his horse. ⁊ his gefeoran uppon heora. ⁊ ferdon to þam husbundon. ⁊ ofslogon hine binnan his agenan heorðæ. ⁊ wendon him þa up to ðære burgeweard. ⁊ ofslogon ægðer ge wiðinnan ge wið utan. ma þanne .xx. manna. ⁊ þa burhmen ofslogon .xix. menn on oðre healfe. ⁊ gewundoden þ hi nystan hu fela. ⁊ Eustatius æt bærst mid feawum mannum. ⁊ gewende ongean to þam cynge. ⁊ cydde be dæle hu hi gefaren hæfdon. ⁊ wearð se cyng swiþe gram wið þa burhware.

See also the *Anglo-Saxon Chronicle* (D) 1052, I:173–75; John of Worcester, II:558–61; William of Malmesbury, *Gesta regum Anglorum*, I:356–59; Symeon of Durham, *Historia regum*, II:166; Freeman, *Norman Conquest*, II:129–32; Frank Stenton, *Anglo-Saxon England*, 3rd edn, Oxford History of England (London, 1971), pp. 562–63; Stafford, *Unification and Conquest*, pp. 90–91; Barlow, *Edward the Confessor*, pp. 109–10; Barlow, *English Church*, p. 49; I. Walker, p. 30; Campbell, 'Earl Godwin of Wessex and Edward the Confessor's Promise,' p. 155; Douglas, *William the Conqueror*, p. 168; Sten Körner, *The Battle of Hastings, England, and Europe, 1035–1066* (Lund, 1964), pp. 31–43; Eric John, 'Edward the Confessor and the Norman Succession,' *English Historical Review* 94 (1979), 252–53; and Heather J. Tanner, 'The Expansion of the Power and Influence of the Counts of Boulogne under Eustace II,' *Anglo-Norman Studies* 14 (1991), 265. Miles W. Campbell, in his article, 'A Pre-Norman Occupation of England?', suggests that the immediate cause of Godwin's

Edward ordered Godwin, his military leader, to 'carry war' into the area to seek revenge on the townspeople who killed Eustace's men. Despite having responded in a similar way against Worcester during the reign of Harðaknútr, Godwin refused to do what Edward ordered. Giving a stirring and emotional speech, the earl of Wessex explained that he did not believe Eustace's account of the battle, a foreigner's story, preferring to hear that of his townspeople, for Dover was in his earldom.[67] William of Malmesbury credits this course of action to Godwin's intelligent perception of the case at hand: 'Godwin, however, being a more clear-headed man, perceived that one ought not to pronounce a verdict after hearing the charges of one side only.'[68]

Godwin also perceived that by disobeying a royal order, he put his life in danger, and so, riding first to Beverstone, he raised an army from his earldom and marched to Gloucester, where the king was in residence. He was accompanied in this endeavor by his sons, Earls Swegen and Harold, who also had raised armies from their respective earldoms. Letting it to be known that they had assembled their armies to fight the Welsh, Godwin, Swegen, and Harold marched instead towards the king. All might have been lost for Edward, except that Earls Leofric of Mercia and Siward of Northumbria, who had constantly opposed the Godwin family's power in England, learned of the situation and marched with their own armies to Gloucester in support of Edward.[69] This created a potential civil war, except that English soldiers hesitated to fight with other Englishmen. The earls met with the witenagemot and agreed not to fight,

---

rebellion was William the Conqueror's attempts to put Norman garrisons in southern England, principally in Dover (pp. 21–31). This suggestion requires that the attack made by the citizens of Dover against Eustace of Boulogne was in actuality an attack made against a Norman garrison of the town, a speculation which, in my estimation, stretches the evidence farther than it should.

67 *Anglo-Saxon Chronicle* (E) 1048, I:173; John of Worcester, II:558–61; William of Malmesbury, *Gesta regum Anglorum*, I:356–57; Symeon of Durham, *Historia regum*, II:166–67; Freeman, *Norman Conquest*, II:132–35; Stenton, *Anglo-Saxon England*, p. 563; Barlow, *Edward the Confessor*, pp. 110–11; I. Walker, p. 32; and Campbell, 'Earl Godwin of Wessex and Edward the Confessor's Promise,' pp. 155–56. William of Malmesbury is the only author who records the text of Godwin's speech.

68 William of Malmesbury, *Gesta regum Anglorum*, I:356–57: 'intellexit uir [Goduinus] acrioris ingenii unius tantum partis auditis allegationibus non debere proferri sententiam.' See also *Anglo-Saxon Chronicle* (E) 1048, I:173 and John of Worcester, II:559.

69 *Anglo-Saxon Chronicle* (D) 1052 and (E) 1048, I:174–75; John of Worcester, II:560–61; William of Malmesbury, *Gesta regum Anglorum*, I:358–59; Symeon of Durham, *Historia regum*, II:167; Freeman, *Norman Conquest*, II:135–36, 139–41, 155–56; Stenton, *Anglo-Saxon England*, pp. 563–64; Barlow, *Edward the Confessor*, pp. 111–12; I. Walker, pp. 32–33; and R. Allen Brown, *The Normans and the Norman Conquest*, 2nd edn (Woodbridge, 1985), pp. 107–08. It is William of Malmesbury (*Gesta regum Anglorum*, I:358–59) who reports that Godwin and his sons tried to mislead the king by declaring that they were assembling their army to fight the Welsh. Freeman (*Norman Conquest*, II:155–56) disagrees with the timing and reasons for Leofric's and Siward's march to oppose Godwin and his sons. A discussion of possible military obligation and relationships in the 1051 crisis can be found in Clarke, pp. 93–94.

and the king responded by granting peace to all.[70] Another conference was also set for London later that year.

Before the second meeting could be held, however, Edward raised his own protective army. Marching at the head of a military force for perhaps the first and only time in his reign, Edward convened the witenagemot with the charge that they make an end to the growing threat to the kingdom. Driven by royal authority and undoubtedly influenced by the Normans in their midst, the witenagemot then declared Godwin's son, Swegen, an outlaw, exiling him, and ordered Godwin and Harold to come quickly to a royal meeting. The *Anglo-Saxon Chronicle* (E) describes what happened next:

> When they had arrived, they were summoned to the meeting. Then he [Godwin] asked for safe-conduct and hostages so that he might be able to come to the meeting and leave it, without being betrayed . . . Then the earl again asked for safe-conduct and hostages so that he might be able to exonerate himself of all those things which had been said against him. But he was refused hostages and granted five days of safe-conduct to leave the country.[71]

William of Poitiers' account of this incident differs from the *Anglo-Saxon Chronicle* only in claiming that Godwin was forced to give hostages, a son, Wulfnoð, and a grandson, Hakon, Swegen's son, to Edward in order to guarantee the rest of his family's safe passage to the coast.[72]

---

[70] *Anglo-Saxon Chronicle* (D) 1052 and (E) 1048, I:174–75; John of Worcester, II:560–61; William of Malmesbury, *Gesta regum Anglorum*, I:358–59; Symeon of Durham, *Historia regum*, II:167; Freeman, *Norman Conquest*, II:141–42; Stenton, *Anglo-Saxon England*, p. 564; Barlow, *Edward the Confessor*, p. 111; I. Walker, pp. 32–33; Douglas, *William the Conqueror*, p. 168; Oleson, *Witenagemot*, pp. 4–5, 26–28, 63, 105–09; and Campbell, 'Earl Godwin of Wessex and Edward the Confessor's Promise,' p. 156. This agreement not to fight leads Barlow (*English Church*, p. 49) to describe Godwin's effort as a 'half-hearted rebellion.'
[71] *Anglo-Saxon Chronicle* (E) 1048, I:174–76:

Þa hi þider ut comon. Þa stefnede heom man to gemote. þa gyrnde he griðes ¬ gisla. þet he moste unswican into gemote cuman. & ut of gemote . . . Þa geornde se eorl eft griðes ¬ gisla. þ he moste hine betellan æt ælc þære þinga þe him man on lede. Þa wyrnde him mann ðera gisla. ¬ sceawede him mann .v. nihta grið ut of lande to farenne.

See also *Anglo-Saxon Chronicle* (D) 1052, 175–76; *Vita Ædwardi*, pp. 32–37; John of Worcester, II:560–63; William of Malmesbury, *Gesta regum Anglorum*, I:358–59; Symeon of Durham, *Historia regum*, II:167; Freeman, *Norman Conquest*, II:144–48; Stenton, *Anglo-Saxon England*, pp. 564–65; Barlow, *Edward the Confessor*, pp. 113–14; I. Walker, p. 34; Douglas, *William the Conqueror*, p. 168; Oleson, *Witenagemot*, pp. 4–5, 26–28, 63, 105–09; and Campbell, 'Earl Godwin of Wessex and Edward the Confessor's Promise,' p. 157.
[72] William of Poitiers, pp. 20–21, 76–77, 120–21. William is agreed with by Eadmer (pp. 5–6) and Symeon of Durham (II:183), who supply the names, and Wace (II:88–89). John of Worcester (II:560–61) mentions the surrender of some hostages 'by both parties,' and William of Malmesbury (*Gesta regum Anglorum*, I:362–63) names Wulfnoð as a hostage, but does not mention when or for what reason he was such. Because of its importance in the later story, with these hostages in the hands of William the Conqueror, several modern historians accept these Anglo-Norman claims. See Barlow, *Edward the Confessor*, pp. 301–06; Barlow, *English Church*, p. 48; Brown, *The Normans and the Norman Conquest*, p. 107; Körner, pp. 126–31; Loyn, 'Harold, Son of Godwin,' p. 305; Campbell, 'Earl Godwin of Wessex and

In a treasure-laden ship, Godwin and most of his family fled to Flanders, the home of his daughter-in-law, Judith, Tostig's wife; Harold and another son, Leofwine, went to Ireland. Godwin's daughter, Queen Eadgyða, was also driven from the palace and sent to an abbey at Wherwell, placed under the control of the abbess, Edward's sister.[73]

A second version of the exile story appears in the *Vita Ædwardi regis*. This version omits any reference to Eustace and his problems at Dover. Instead, the anonymous author of this work, certainly influenced by the queen's patronage, brings up the old issue of Alfred's death and Godwin's role in it as the origin of the problems between the earl of Wessex and the king. Edward was also swayed by the counsel of the 'evil' Norman nobles. The primary 'evil' counselor was Archbishop Robert of Jumièges:

> And so Archbishop Robert asserted to King Edward . . . that the crime of his brother's death and of the massacre of his men was perpetrated on the advice of the glorious earl, since at that time also, as in the previous reign, he was the king's chief counsellor; and he persuaded him as much as he could that Godwin was now planning in the same way the ruin of even Edward himself.[74]

Edward the Confessor's Promise,' pp. 152–53; Campbell, 'A Pre-Conquest Norman Occupation,' pp. 22, 26; Stafford, *Unification and Conquest*, pp. 91–92; Brian Golding, *Conquest and Colonisation: The Normans in Britain, 1066–1100* (New York, 1994), pp. 17–18; Kenneth E. Cutler, 'The Godwinist Hostages: The Case for 1051,' *Annuale medievali* 12 (1971), 70–77; and Tryggvi J. Oleson, 'Edward the Confessor's Promise of the Throne to Duke William of Normandy,' *English Historical Review* 72 (1957), 221–28. Why Hakon, the son of Swegen, was included in this giving of hostages is not known. Körner (p. 130 n. 17) claims that such a hostage would have little political value, while Campbell ('Earl Godwin of Wessex and Edward the Confessor's Promise,' pp. 152–53) contends that, as Godwin wished to name one of his 'Danish' grandsons to the throne, Hakon was very much a hostage of great worth.

[73] See also *Anglo-Saxon Chronicle* (C) 1050, (D) 1052, and (E) 1048, I:171, 174–77; John of Worcester, II:560–63; William of Malmesbury, *Gesta regum Anglorum*, I:360–61; Symeon of Durham, *Historia regum*, II:167–68; Henry of Huntingdon, pp. 376–77; and Eadmer, p. 5. Geoffrey Gaimer (*Lestoire des Engles*, ed. T.D. Hardy and C.T. Martin (London, 1888), I:205–06) misdates this event and has Godwin's entire family flee to Denmark. See also Freeman, *Norman Conquest*, II:149–54; Stenton, *Anglo-Saxon England*, pp. 564–65; Brown, *The Normans and the Norman Conquest*, pp. 107–08; Barlow, *Edward the Confessor*, pp. 114–16; Barlow, *English Church*, p. 49; Barlow, 'Edward the Confessor's Early Life,', p. 68; I. Walker, pp. 34–36; Grierson, 'The Relations between England and Flanders,' pp. 99–100; Campbell, 'Earl Godwin of Wessex and Edward the Confessor's Promise,' pp. 157–58; Stafford, *Queen Emma and Queen Edith*, pp. 262–66; and Cutler, 'Edith, Queen of England,' pp. 228–30. The marriage of Tostig and Judith will be discussed below. On Eadgyða's exile to Wherwell Abbey see n. 165 below.

[74] *Vita Ædwardi*, pp. 32–35:
> Intendebat itaque . . . Rodbertus archiepiscopus in aurem regis hoc scelus fraterne necis et totius cladis suorum consilio actum esse eiusdem gloriosi ducis, quod eo quoque tempore, ut superius, regalium consiliorum erat baiulus, persuadebatque in quantum poterat eum eodem modo etiam ipsius regis Ædwardi generi sui perniciem intendere.

See also Barlow, *English Church*, pp. 85–87. For the exile of Godwin and his family see *Vita*

Edward, it appears, had not been as forgiving about his brother's death as he seemed to have been when trying to assert his claim to the throne and feeling that he needed Godwin's help to secure it.

There is a good possibility that both versions of Godwin's banishment are correct, that it was a combination of Godwin's unwillingness to punish the inhabitants of Dover and the lingering feeling that justice had not been served in the death of Alfred which caused Edward to banish Godwin and his family.[75]

Thus the facts behind the 1051 ouster of the Godwin family are relatively easy to determine, but how are we to *interpret* what occurred? The most conventional way of interpreting the events of 1051 leading to the Godwin family's exile has been that this was a Norman takeover of governmental power and royal favoritism. Popularized by, if not originating with, Edward August Freeman's *History of the Norman Conquest*, initially published in the 1870s, this thesis has received continuing support in the more recent works of R. Allen Brown and Miles W. Campbell.[76] It asserts that the removal of the earl of Wessex and his family was carried out in order to replace them with relations and friends from the land where Edward had been raised and presumably still had contacts. Highlighting the roles of Robert of Jumièges and Eustace of Boulogne, Freeman *et al.* also add as evidence of a Norman 'occupation' of England in 1051 the building of the Norman-controlled castles on Godwin family lands in Herefordshire (Hereford built by, Ewias Harold, and primarily Richard's Castle, built by Richard, the son of Scrob, and his son, Osbern[77]), the influence of Norman voices before and at the meetings of the witenagemot,[78] and the awarding of the outlawed Swegen's Mercian lands to Edward's Norman nephew, Ralph (known as 'of Mantes' or 'the Timid'), and the bishopric of London to the king's Norman chaplain, William.[79] Campbell writes: 'in spite of the silence of the

---

Ædwardi, pp. 34–39. Freeman's reasons for the *Vita Ædwardi* not containing the Dover incident can be found in *Norman Conquest*, II:599–603. See also Bertie Wilkerson, 'Freeman and the Crisis of 1051,' *Bulletin of the John Rylands Library* 22 (1938), 5–7.

[75] Freeman agrees with this assertion (*Norman Conquest*, II:599–603).

[76] Freeman, *Norman Conquest*, II:124–59, 599–605; Brown, *The Normans and the Norman Conquest*, pp. 102–07; Campbell, 'A Pre-Conquest Norman Occupation of England?', pp. 21–31; Campbell, 'Earl Godwin of Wessex and Edward the Confessor's Promise,' pp. 141–58; and Campbell, 'Anglo-Saxon "Kingmaker",' pp. 30–32. See also Loyn, 'Harold, Son of Godwin,' pp. 304–05 and D.J.A. Matthew, *The Norman Conquest* (London, 1966), pp. 31–35.

[77] *Anglo-Saxon Chronicle* (D) 1052 and (E) 1048, I:173–75; Freeman, *Norman Conquest*, II:136–37; Brown, *The Normans and the Norman Conquest*, pp. 100–01; Golding, p. 14; Fleming, *Kings and Lords in Conquest England*, p. 99; Kelly DeVries, *Medieval Military Technology* (Peterborough, 1992), p. 205; R. Allen Brown, H.M. Colvin, and A.J. Taylor, *The History of the King's Works*, vols. 1 and 2: *The Middle Ages* (London, 1963), I:19; and R. Allen Brown, 'The Norman Conquest and the Genesis of English Castles,' in *Castles, Conquest and Charters: Collected Papers* (Woodbridge, 1989), p. 84.

[78] *Vita Ædwardi*, pp. 30–35; Freeman, *Norman Conquest*, II:136, 146; and Campbell, 'Pre-Conquest Norman Occupation,' p. 22.

[79] *Anglo-Saxon Chronicle* (C) 1052, (D) 1052, and (E) 1048, I:177, 182; John of Worcester,

chroniclers, there would appear to be strong circumstantial evidence suggesting that such a [Norman] 'occupation' was undertaken.'[80] Brown is more confident:

> That Edward's Norman sympathies and preferments lead into the crisis of 1051, both through the resentment which they caused in themselves and through the recognition of William of Normandy as heir to the English throne, in which they culminated in the same year, is as clear as anything can be in the haze which inadequate English sources draw over the politics of the reign.[81]

Freeman, true to form, is positively nationalistic:

> Stealthily, but surely, the foreign favorites of Eadward had eaten into the vitals of England, and they soon found the means of showing how bitter was the hatred which they bore towards the champions of English liberty. England, under a native King of her choice, felt, far more keenly than she had ever felt under her Danish conqueror, how great the evil is when a King and those who immediately surround him are estranged in feeling the mass of his people.[82]

The sudden fall of the influential Godwin family was only to replace its 'Danish' influence with that of the Normans.

What guarantees this thesis for its adherents is the visit of Duke William of Normandy to England during the Godwin family's absence, either late in 1051 or early in 1052. These authors affirm that William, whose family had housed Edward when he was raised in Normandy, but who himself was probably too young to have had much to do with his exiled cousin, came to England not only to show his support for the now Norman-controlled throne, but also to accept the inheritance of that throne when the childless, and now queen-less, king died. Recorded in the *Anglo-Saxon Chronicle* (D) only as,

> Then soon came Duke William from across the sea with a large band of Frenchmen, and the king received him and as many of his men as it pleased him, and then he let him go again,[83]

few more details are known about this later conqueror's first visit to England.[84]

II:562–63; I:Freeman, *Norman Conquest*, II:158–59 and Brown, *The Normans and the Norman Conquest*, pp. 99–100. For a look at the life and career of Ralph see Ann Williams, 'The King's Nephew: The Family and Career of Ralph, Earl of Hereford,' in *Studies in Medieval History Presented to R. Allen Brown*, ed. C. Harper-Bill, C.J. Holdsworth, and J. Nelson (Woodbridge, 1989), pp. 327–43.

[80] Campbell, 'Pre-Conquest Norman Occupation,' p. 31.

[81] Brown, *The Normans and the Norman Conquest*, p. 102.

[82] Freeman, *Norman Conquest*, II:125.

[83] *Anglo-Saxon Chronicle* (D) 1052, I:176:
Ða sone com Willelm eorl fram geondan sæ mid mycclum werode Frencis[c]ra manna, ⁊ se cyning hine under feng. ⁊ swa feola his geferan swa him toonhagode. ⁊ let hine eft ongean.
See also John of Worcester (II:562–63), who adds only that Edward sent William back to Normandy 'in receipt of many great gifts,' and Wace (II:87).

[84] On William's visit to England in 1051 see Freeman, *Norman Conquest*, II:302–04; Stenton, pp. 565–66; Brown, *The Normans and the Norman Conquest*, pp. 104–06; Stafford,

However, to Freeman and his successors, that it occurred at all confirms that a Norman occupation of England in 1051 had happened.

Critics of the 1051 Norman takeover thesis have been numerous. As early as 1938, in an article entitled appropriately 'Freeman and the Crisis of 1051,' Bertie Wilkerson complains that Edward Freeman's approach to the exile of Godwin and his family inadequately explained many of the features of the revolt:

> . . . it does not really explain Edward's sudden anger against Godwin, unreasonable even for an unreasonable king, or, on the other hand, Godwin's haste to gather an army at Beverstone, before any hostile measures had actually been taken against him. It does not fully explain the strong support which Edward received from the rest of the country in his unjust attack, or Godwin's failure to await his trial.

At the same time, Wilkerson believes that the thesis cannot fully define the characters of Godwin and Edward, nor does it sufficiently explain their relationship:

> If it was unlike Godwin to run away, when – for once – he was so much in the right, it was equally unlike Edward to take such energetic steps against the Earl, and even go to the extent of repudiating the Earl's daughter Edith, all for the sake of a quarrel at Dover.[85]

As an alternative, Wilkerson offers this opinion: 'Godwin and not Edward was the real aggressor.'[86] Arguing that Godwin's failed actions in raising an army at Beverstone and marching to meet the king at Gloucester can only be described as 'aggressive,' if not treasonous, he concludes: 'The triumph of Edward in 1051 was the triumph of the monarch and the nation over a powerful and rebellious earl – the most powerful which Anglo-Saxon England had as yet produced.'[87]

To several later historians, Wilkerson's complaints against Freeman are convincing; however, his description of Godwin as the aggressor in the 1051

Unification and Conquest, pp. 92–93; Körner, pp. 107–08, 158–63; Campbell, 'Anglo-Saxon "Kingmaker",' pp. 30–31; Campbell, 'A Pre-Conquest Norman Occupation,' pp. 28–29; and Oleson, 'Edward the Confessor's Promise,' pp. 221–28. However, most historians see William's visit as too late for the inheritance to be given to him at that time by Edward. Following the declarations of William of Poitiers (pp. 174–77) and William of Jumièges (II:158–59), they believe that this was done earlier in 1051, when Robert of Jumièges visited the duke on his way to Rome to receive his archiepiscopal pallium. See Brown, *The Normans and the Norman Conquest*, pp. 105–06; Stafford, *Unification and Conquest*, pp. 92–93; Körner, pp. 107–08; Golding, pp. 15–22; and Campbell, 'Anglo-Saxon "Kingmaker",' pp. 30–31. Some also believe that the Godwin family hostages were delivered to William on this visit. Cutler ('The Godwinist Hostages,' 70–77) is especially insistent on this point. See also Brown, *The Normans and the Norman Conquest*, p. 107; Campbell, 'Earl Godwin of Wessex and Edward the Confessor's Promise,' pp. 152–53; and Campbell, 'A Pre-Conquest Norman Occupation,' pp. 22, 26.

85 Wilkerson, 'Freeman and the Crisis of 1051,' p. 7.
86 Wilkerson, 'Freeman and the Crisis of 1051,' p. 9.
87 Wilkerson, 'Freeman and the Crisis of 1051,' p. 22.

conflict is not.[88] Led by Frank Barlow and David C. Douglas, biographers of Edward the Confessor and William the Conqueror respectively, these critics of the Norman takeover thesis have chosen to portray the 1051 events merely as a power struggle between king and earl. Godwin, in effect, was only responding to what had been a constant decline in his political power in the few years before 1051, as evidenced by his inability to gain support for Sveinn Estriðson's and Baldwin V's conflicts and by his inability to prevent the investiture of Robert of Jumièges as archbishop of Canterbury, and in so responding, Godwin failed almost completely. His refusal to punish Dover may have been justified, but his plan to assemble an army and, with his sons, Swegen and Harold, to march on the king at Gloucester instead worked against him, especially after the northern earls, Leofric and Siward, refused to join his side. He also seemed to miscalculate Edward's later determination and was unprepared to face his adversary at the head of a military force in London. This, and not the Norman faction in England, led to Godwin and his family's exile.[89]

While Godwin was failing in every endeavor in 1051, the king could do little wrong. Barlow writes:

> In 1051 all the affairs in which Edward was most concerned came to a head and severely tested his political skill. He solved each problem in turn, adroitly and economically; and although each solution may have increased the difficulty of the next problem, for twelve months he could not put a foot wrong.[90]

He may even have used the Dover situation to 'provoke' the banishment of his chief earl. According to Ian W. Walker, the king played *The Prince*:

> The fact that Eustace and his men put their armour on before entering Dover indicates preparedness for trouble, probably because they planned to cause it. In order to banish Godwine, Edward needed a very good cause if he was to ensure the backing in England necessary to do so effectively. It would seem that he planned this incident with his former brother-in-law hoping, in the

---

[88] In fact, it can be said that only Wilkerson's student, Tryggvi J. Oleson, showed any support for his mentor's thesis that Godwin was the aggressor in the 1051 crisis. Even that support is muted in Oleson's 'Edward the Confessor's Promise' and *The Witenagemot in the Reign of Edward the Confessor.*

[89] Barlow, *Edward the Confessor*, pp. 104–15; Barlow, *English Church*, pp. 108–09; I. Walker, pp. 29–36; Douglas, *William the Conqueror*, pp. 168–69; Campbell, 'Earl Godwin of Wessex and Edward the Confessor's Promise,' pp. 144–52; and Golding, pp. 12–15. Barlow (*English Church*, pp. 108–09) actually dates Godwin's decline to the period from 1045 to 1046 when, he asserts, the earl of Wessex began to lose influential contests over church appointments and other matters. Campbell, too, is adamant that Godwin's decline in the late 1040s aided in his exile in 1051, but Golding asserts that Godwin's only loss during that time was the archbishopric of Canterbury in 1050.

[90] Barlow, *Edward the Confessor*, p. 104. See also Barlow, *English Church*, p. 49 and Barlow, 'Edward the Confessor and the Norman Conquest,' in *The Norman Conquest and Beyond* (London, 1983), pp. 99–111 (originally this was a 1966 commemorative lecture for the Hastings and Bexhill Branch of the Historical Association and published by them as a pamphlet).

charged atmosphere of the time, to provoke Godwine into a reaction which he could exploit.[91]

Of course, the problem facing those who deny that it was a Norman takeover which occurred in 1051 is what to do with the visit of Duke William of Normandy during the winter of 1051–52. If the Normans were not in control of political and royal power in England, why would William have made a trip to the kingdom across the Channel? An answer to that question for at least one of the critics of a Norman 'occupation,' David C. Douglas, is to deny that the duke made such a trip during the Godwin family's exile. After all, the journey is only recorded in the D version of the *Anglo-Saxon Chronicle* and in John of Worcester's *Chronicle*, the latter source obviously based on the former. As such, while not denying that William had been named as Edward's heir, David C. Douglas writes:

> One authority even seems to suggest that in 1051 the duke came over to England to receive the grant [of inheritance] in person. But, this, although very generally believed, is most unlikely – if only for the fact that William was desperately concerned with affairs in Normandy throughout that year.[92]

A more popular answer to the question of William's visit while denying a Norman control over Edward and his kingdom is to accept the visit as fact – made easier after Sten Körner showed that the affairs in Normandy would have allowed William time to visit England[93] – but only as a recognition of the duke's personal inheritance and not of Norman control. Alternatively, he may have come to call on his ailing great-aunt, Emma, who died in March 1052.[94]

Although no one seems to have been wanting to do so before, it seems easy to reconcile these two theses concerning the events of 1051 if we think of them in terms of warlords vying for power. Although appearing at the head of an army in 1051, Edward, as has been well established, was not a warlord, but needed one or more allied warlords in order to remain comfortably on the throne of England. From the beginning of his reign until 1051 these warlords had been Godwin and, as they grew older, his sons. Yet, since at least 1047 Godwin had

---

[91] I. Walker, p. 30.

[92] Douglas, *William the Conqueror*, p. 169, building on an argument put forth in his earlier article, 'Edward the Confessor, Duke William of Normandy and the English Succession,' *English Historical Review* 68 (1953), 526–45. See also Campbell, 'Anti-Norman Reaction,' pp. 434–38, and Matthew, pp. 38–41. The 'affairs' which kept William in Normandy was the Domfort and Alençon military campaign, which Douglas dates to 1051–52. For a discussion of that campaign and other affairs which kept William in Normandy, see Douglas, *William the Conqueror*, pp. 55–69, 383–90.

[93] Körner, pp. 158–63.

[94] Barlow, *Edward the Confessor*, pp. 116–17; Barlow, *English Church*, p. 51; Barlow, 'Edward the Confessor's Early Life,' pp. 80–83; I. Walker, pp. 37–38; Stafford, *Queen Emma and Queen Edith*, pp. 253–54; and John, 'Edward the Confessor and the Norman Succession,' pp. 253–55. Barlow's argument in 'Edward the Confessor's Early Life' (pp. 80–83) that William's major concern with accepting the inheritance was what to do about the Godwin family, and that this is the reason for his coming to England in 1051–52 is compelling.

begun to lose favor with the king. In military matters, he was unable to convince Edward to assist either the Danes or the Flemings, while at the same time he had been too slow in providing a response to the Irish and Welsh raids in Gloucestershire and Herefordshire.

Early in 1051, younger, seemingly more capable warlords appeared to offer Edward an alternative to the Godwin family, while at the same time they also allowed him to pay back some of the hospitality accorded him during his youthful exile in Normandy. Perhaps then it was both an anti-Godwin backlash and a Norman occupation when Edward turned to the Normans for assistance against the Godwin family that year. After all, Godwin had remained comfortably situated in his homeland during the reigns of Knútr and his sons, while Edward was being raised away from his homeland with little prospect of returning. Additionally, it must have been readily apparent to Edward by this time that his marriage with Godwin's daughter, which *had not* provided an heir, *would not* provide one, leaving the question of inheritance open. Finally, the Godwin family was away, in Flanders, celebrating the marriage of Tostig to Judith of Flanders. (Indeed, much of what happened in 1051 seems to have occurred shortly after the Godwin family returned from Flanders and were thus seemingly unprepared for it.) Did Edward desire the recently 'weak' Godwin family to rule after he died, or ought he to turn elsewhere, to a candidate then proving his worth as a protector for his own realm – William, duke of Normandy?[95] Certainly the advice that his new favorite, Robert of Jumièges, was providing him did not point toward the Godwin family. One can only imagine the conferences that these two men had when the Godwins were away in Flanders.

This solution may seem to some to be too close to Edward Freeman's nationalistic image of the Godwin family or to rely on Ian Walker's image of Edward the Confessor conspiring with Eustace of Boulogne and Robert of Jumièges, but even if the king did not 'conspire' against Godwin prior to the incident at Dover, although that may be the only rationale for the recognition of William of Normandy as heir to the English throne, Edward knew how to take advantage of the situation to force the once powerful but now weak earl from his spot of prominence, especially after Earls Leofric and Siward seemed to betray their military leader to stand by the king at Gloucester, and after the witenagemot, filled with the military elite huscarls, also failed to side with the earl. This advantage was again recognized at London, when the witenagemot this time not only abandoned Godwin and his family, but actually allowed the outlawry of one of its own, Swegen, as well as the condemnation and exile of his father and brothers.[96]

---

[95] William had been active militarily since 1046 and had won numerous victories between then and 1052 in asserting his authority against rebellious Norman lords. Barlow (*English Church*, p. 47) sees William's success beginning in 1048, with the Norman duke having emerged as 'a European power' by the time of Godwin's exile.

[96] Oleson, *Witenagemot*, pp. 63–64, 105–07. On the witenagemot as a body filled with huscarls and other soldiers, see Oleson, *Witenagemot*, pp. 168–69. Norman tradition had the witenagemot demanding William the Conqueror to be named the heir to Edward's throne for quite a while before the exile of the Godwin family. See Barlow, *English Church*, p. 48.

The military control and the legitimacy this control had brought to Godwin and his sons had seemingly ceased.

However if Edward expected the Normans to replace the Godwin family as his warlords in protecting the kingdom, and that certainly seems to have been the reason for the construction of Norman motte-and-bailey castles along the Welsh marches, then he had significantly overestimated their military capabilities. For no sooner was the Godwin family away to their respective hideaways, than the Welsh renewed their raids across the borders into England, and the Normans had very little success in stopping them. John of Worcester reports what happened:

> . . . Gruffydd [ap Llywelyn] king of the Welsh, ravaged a great part of Herefordshire. The people of that area and very many Normans from the castle rose against him but, when he had killed many of them, he had the victory, and took great booty away with him.[97]

Furthermore, as the *Anglo-Saxon Chronicle* and John of Worcester attest, shortly after the Welsh raids began, the sons of Godwin who had fled to Ireland, Harold and Leofwine, returned to England and plundered the region around Devon and Somerset. Again a local army was raised, but, as John of Worcester records, 'Earl Harold defeated them, having slain more than thirty noble thegns with many others.'[98] Harold and Leofwine then loaded their ships and made their escape. This episode forced even Edward to enter the fray, the king sending a navy of forty ships under the command of Earls Odda of Deerhurst and Ralph of Mantes, the latter Edward's nephew and the former Edward's kinsman, to the

---

[97] John of Worcester, II:566–67:
  . . . Walensium rex Griffinus magnam partem Herefordensis prouince depopulatus est, contra quem prouinciales illi et de castello quamplures Nortmanni ascenderunt, sed multis ex illis occisis, ille uictoriam habuit et secum predam magnam abduxit.
See also *Anglo-Saxon Chronicle* (D) 1052, I:176; Symeon of Durham, *Historia regum*, II:168; Freeman, *Norman Conquest*, II:309–10; Barlow, *Edward the Confessor*, pp. 120, 126; Maund, *Ireland, Wales, and England*, pp. 124, 131–32; Miles W. Campbell, 'The Anti-Norman Reaction in England in 1052: Suggested Origins,' *Mediaeval Studies* 35 (1973), 438–39; K.L. Maund, 'The Welsh Alliances of Earl Ælfgar of Mercia and his Family in the Mid-Eleventh Century,' *Anglo-Norman Studies* 9 (1988), 184–86; and David Walker, 'A Note on Gruffydd ap Llywelyn (1039–63),' *Welsh Historical Review* 1 (1960–63), 88–89. Ian Walker (p. 43) claims that the Welsh raids occurred due to Ralph's absence with the fleet and not due to Godwin and his sons' exile.
[98] John of Worcester, II:566–69:
  . . . Haroldus comes et frater eius Leofuuinus, de Hibernia redeuntes, et ostium Sabrine nauibus multis intrantes, in confinio Sumersetanie et Dorsetanie applicuerunt, et illis in partibus uillas Sumersetania quamplures congregatiascenderunt, sed eos uicit Haroldus, cesis ex illis plusquam triginta nobilibus ministris cum aliis multis. Dein ad naues cum preda rediit, et mox Penuuithsteort circumnauigauit.
See also *Anglo-Saxon Chronicle* (C, D, and E) 1052, I:178–80; *Vita Ædwardi*, pp. 40–43; Freeman, *Norman Conquest*, II:313–17, 623–25; Barlow, *Edward the Confessor*, pp. 120–21; and I. Walker, pp. 44–45. In this I am following the chronology of the *Anglo-Saxon Chronicle* and John of Worcester.

port of Sandwich, ordering them to defend the southern coast of England against further raids.[99]

Godwin, too, made a journey to England early in 1052. If the *Vita Ædwardi* is to be believed, many of his former countrymen, 'almost all the natives of the country,' had 'sent messages that they were ready, should he want to return, to receive him forcibly in the country, to fight for him, and, if need be, they were willing to die for him as well.'[100] If such messages were received, they were undoubtedly welcome; yet Godwin surely needed no such prodding, as his return must have been planned almost from the time of his departure.

Initially, Godwin's return to England met with some difficulty. There are two versions of this story: the *Anglo-Saxon Chronicle* (E) reports that Godwin sailed to Dungeness, where he encountered both the royal fleet and a storm, the latter allowing him to elude the former in returning to the continent, while John of Worcester has Godwin land at Kent, acquire a following, and then be chased back to Flanders by the royal fleet. The difference in these stories is not important. What is important is that in neither version of the story is Godwin discouraged from making another attempt to return to England. Indeed, if we are to accept the *Anglo-Saxon Chronicle* account, once the fleet had failed to capture Godwin or his sons, it returned to London to acquire new leaders. Clearly, even without remaining in England, this was a victory for Godwin.[101]

Thus far the Normans had proven themselves ineffective as replacement warlords for the protection of Edward and England, nor would that change when Godwin and his family decided to regain their lands and positions by force late in the summer of 1052. Godwin began his armed return at the Isle of Wight, a base frequently used by pirates and raiders as a shelter from which they could

[99] *Anglo-Saxon Chronicle* (C, D, and E) 1052, I:178–80 (D and E record the number of ships, with E also reporting the names of the commanders); John of Worcester, II: 566–69; William of Malmesbury, *Gesta regum Anglorum*, I:360–61; Symeon of Durham, *Historia regum*, II:168; Barlow, *Edward the Confessor*, p. 121; I. Walker, pp. 43–44; Williams, 'The King's Nephew,' p. 327; and Nicholas Hooper, 'Some Observations on the Navy in Late Anglo-Saxon England,' in *Studies in Medieval History for R. Allen Brown*, ed. C. Harper-Bill *et al.* (Woodbridge, 1989), p. 206. Freeman (*Norman Conquest*, II:308) dates the formation of the fleet to before Harold's raids and not as a result of them.

[100] *Vita Ædwardi*, pp. 40–41: '. quidam legationes mittunt, paratos se, si uelut reuerti, eum cum uiolentia in patria suscipere, pro eo pugnare, pro eo, si necesse sit, uelle se pariter occumbere et non modo a quibusdam sed pene ab omnibus indigenis patrie.' See also Freeman, *Norman Conquest*, II:307–08.

[101] The *Anglo-Saxon Chronicle* account is found in (E) 1052, I:177, the John of Worcester one in II:568–69. Symeon of Durham accepts John of Worcester's version of this event (II:168–69). See also Freeman, *Norman Conquest*, II:317–19; Stenton, *Anglo-Saxon England*, p. 566; Stafford, *Unification and Conquest*, p. 91; Barlow, *Edward the Confessor*, p. 122; and I. Walker, p. 44. The *Vita Ædwardi* (pp. 40–41) does not have Godwin make a first trip to England. According to this anonymous author, instead of Godwin making a trek to England to regain his and his sons' earldoms, legates from the king of France and the count of Flanders were sent to Edward to petition the king of England to restore the dismissed earl of Wessex. Edward refused. On this, which he accepts as valid, see Freeman, *Norman Conquest*, II:310–13.

plunder the English coast. He was met there by a ship from Ireland bearing his sons Harold and Leofwine.[102] From the Isle of Wight, Godwin sailed to Wessex and began to raise troops in his old earldom to gain by force the return of his lands and position. In this Godwin was incredibly successful. The *Vita Ædwardi* states: 'all came to meet him . . . like children their long-awaited father.'[103]

Taking to the sea again, and with increased numbers, Godwin then eluded the royal fleet at Sandwich and sailed up the Thames. Without further hindrance, he met with the king at Winchester, where Edward was staying for Easter. Edward, it seems, was completely surprised by this encounter, and just as completely unprotected except for a small band of soldiers at nearby London. His erstwhile Norman allies had deserted him, most having fled from England at the approach of Godwin and his soldiers. Edward resisted for a time, but abandoned by his warlords, pressured by the threat of bloodshed, and perhaps even recognizing the unwillingness of Englishmen to fight each other, he was soon forced to accept Godwin and his family back into England.[104]

Still, the *Vita Ædwardi* insists that Godwin was magnanimous in his first meeting with Edward after his return. Using the comparison of David returning to Saul after being wronged by him, the anonymous author of this work has Godwin approach the king with these words:

[102] *Anglo-Saxon Chronicle* (E) 1052, I:177–78; John of Worcester, II:568–69; Symeon of Durham, *Historia regum*, II:169; Freeman, *Norman Conquest*, II:319–20; Stenton, *Anglo-Saxon England*, pp. 566–67; Stafford, *Unification and Conquest*, p. 91; Barlow, *Edward the Confessor*, pp. 122–23; and I. Walker, pp. 44–45. Douglas (*William the Conqueror*, p. 169) is particularly impressed by this military endeavor, writing that this 'coordinated and brilliantly organized attack upon England was made by sea.'

[103] *Vita Ædwardi*, pp. 40–43: 'Occurrunt omnes ei, sicut filii suo diu exoptato patri.' See also the *Anglo-Saxon Chronicle* (C,D, and E) 1052, I:178–79; John of Worcester, II:568–69; Freeman, *Norman Conquest*, II:320–21; Campbell, 'Anti-Norman Reaction,' pp. 430–31, 434–38; Campbell, 'Anglo-Saxon "Kingmaker",' p. 32; and Oleson, *Witenagemot*, pp. 63–64. According to John of Worcester (II:568–69), Godwin returned this favor by refusing to take booty on his return to these regions.

[104] *Anglo-Saxon Chronicle* (C, D, and E) 1052, I:180–81; *Vita Ædwardi*, pp. 40–47; John of Worcester, II:568–71; William of Malmesbury, *Gesta regum Anglorum*, I:360–61; Henry of Huntingdon, pp. 376–77; Symeon of Durham, *Historia regum*, II:169–70; Freeman, *Norman Conquest*, II:320–36, 625–30; Brown, *The Normans and the Norman Conquest*, pp. 107–09; Körner, pp. 189–96; Stenton, *Anglo-Saxon England*, pp. 566–67; Stafford, *Unification and Conquest*, p. 91; Barlow, *English Church*, p. 50; Barlow, *Edward the Confessor*, pp. 120, 123–27; Douglas, *William the Conqueror*, pp. 169–71; I. Walker, pp. 46–49; Stafford, *Queen Emma and Queen Edith*, p. 265; Oleson, *Witenagemot*, pp. 63–64; Oleson, 'Edward the Confessor's Promise,' pp. 223–24; and Campbell, 'Anti-Norman Reaction,' pp. 428–29. On the flight of the Normans see Freeman, *Norman Conquest*, II:327–30, 344–46; Brown, *The Normans and the Norman Conquest*, pp. 107–09; Barlow, *Edward the Confessor*, pp. 123–27; Douglas, *William the Conqueror*, p. 170; I. Walker, p. 47; Campbell, 'Anti-Norman Reaction,' pp. 428–29; and Golding, pp. 14–15. It should be noted, however, that not all of the Normans in Edward's retinue fled. Edward's nephew, Ralph of Mantes, and William, the Norman Bishop of London, for two, remained. See Barlow, *English Church*, p. 50.

May I have . . . God in my heart today as a witness to its loyalty – that I would rather die than have done, or do, or, while I am alive, allow to be done, anything unseemly or unrighteous against my lord the king.

The earl then cast away his weapons, threw himself at Edward's feet, and begged in the name of Christ for forgiveness. Edward forgave Godwin, although the *Vita Ædwardi* notes, not only because of his need for mercy, but also because Godwin appeared 'much superior in arms, if he chose to use them' and because 'he had been deserted, especially by the flight of the archbishop and of many of his men who feared to face the earl since it was they who had been responsible for that storm of trouble.'[105] Edward also restored Godwin's and Harold's titles and possessions to them. The queen, Eadgyða, too was restored to her earlier station.

Godwin's return in 1052 can only be described as a military operation.[106] It was in some ways a foreign invasion, made from across the seas by exiled individuals, it is true, but probably on Flemish and Irish vessels with undoubtedly at least a few foreign sailors and soldiers, although the contemporary sources are silent on this. At the same time, it was a rebellion, with men from his own kingdom filling the majority of troops opposing Edward; the sources are secure on this.

However defined, it was a successful military venture, one which not only restored the Godwin family to their positions of power in the kingdom, but also to their roles as warlords protecting the kingdom (and the king) from 'destructive' influences. Although initially being chased off by the fleet, the later, nearly uninhibited landing of the Godwin, Harold, and Leofwine in Wessex, the declaring of London for the Godwins, the flight of the Normans, the inaction of the witenagemot and the northern earls, and finally the failure or perhaps the inability of the king to respond militarily on his own meant that, while Edward might have held the crown, the power and the people of England were held by the Godwin family.[107] Whatever doubts in Godwin's military leadership there

---

[105] *Vita Ædwardi*, pp. 42–47 (quotes are on pp. 40–43):
Verum fidelis et deo deuotus dux uerbis et nutu admodum abhorruit. 'Deum', inquid, 'fidelitatis sue in corde meo habeam hodie testem, me scilicet malle mortem, quam aliquid indecens et iniquum egerim uel agam, uel me uiuo agi permittam, in dominum meum regem.' Et ab huiusmodi conatu fortiter perturbatis omnibus, uiso rege protinus abiectis armis eius aduoluitur pedibus, orans suppliciter ut in Christi nomine, cuius signiferam regni coronam gestabat in capite, annueret ut sibi liceret purgare se de obiecto crimine, et purgato pacem concederet gratie sue. Rex itaque coactus tum misericordia et satisfactione ducis, quem utique uidebat sibi satis, si uti uellet, superiorem armis, tum uero destitutus imprimis fuga archipresulis et suorum multorum uerentium aspectum ducis, qui scilicet auctores fuerant illius concitati turbinis.
See also Freeman, *Norman Conquest*, II:346–47 and Barlow, *Edward the Confessor*, pp. 118–19.

[106] John of Worcester (II:568–71) certainly describes it as such.

[107] On the declaration of London for Godwin see John of Worcester, II:568–69 and Freeman, *Norman Conquest*, II:320–27. On the inactivity of the northern earls see Barlow, *Edward the Confessor*, p. 120.

might have been prior to 1051 were now erased, at least in the minds of the people, and certainly also in the mind of Edward, for the king settled into an almost sedentary, retired role for the rest of his life.

This return, and more importantly the manner in which it was made, was also undoubtedly the key to Godwin or one of his sons succeeding to the throne when the heirless Edward died. As Stenton writes:

> [The return of the Godwin family in 1052] established the house of Godwine so firmly in power that neither the king nor any rival family could ever dislodge it. It reduced the Normans in England to political insignificance, and thereby decided that if the duke of Normandy were ever to become the king of England it could only be through war.[108]

Yet it was Godwin who would die first. Less than a year after his return, on 15 April 1053, the earl of Wessex passed away at the royal court in Winchester. With him were his sons, Harold, Tostig, and Gyrð. John of Worcester records the earl's short, but painful end:

> In the same year, while Easter Monday was being celebrated in Winchester, the ultimate calamity befell Earl Godwin as he sat in his usual place at the table; struck down by a sudden and unexpected illness, he collapsed silent in his chair. Seeing this, his sons Earls Harold, Tostig and Gyrth, carried him into the king's chamber, hoping that he would recover a little later from his infirmity, but deprived of his strength, he departed this life the following thursday in wretched pain.[109]

---

[108] Stenton, *Anglo-Saxon England*, p. 568. See also Douglas, *William the Conqueror*, pp. 170–71 and Fleming, 'Domesday Estates of the King and the Godwines,' pp. 1006–07. Oleson ('Edward the Confessor's Promise,' pp. 223–24) disagrees with this, believing that his return was no triumph for Godwin or his family, in that he was forced to agree to William's inheritance. It was at this time, according to Oleson, when Godwin surrendered his son and grandson as hostages. In my estimation, the sources do not lead to this conclusion.

[109] John of Worcester, II:572–73:

> Eodem anno [1053], dum secunda pascalis festiuitatis celebrantur feria, Wintonie Goduuino comiti, solito regi ad mensam assidenti, suprema euenit calamitas graui etenim morbo ex improuiso percussus, mutus in ipsa sede declinauit. Quod filii eius, comes Haroldus, Tosti, et Gyrth uidentes, illum in regis cameram portabant sperantes eum post modicum de infirmitate conualescere, sed ille, expers uirium, quinta post hec feria, miserabili cruciatu uita decessit.

See also the *Anglo-Saxon Chronicle* (A, C, D, E) 1053, I:182–83; *Vita Ædwardi*, pp. 46–47; Symeon of Durham, *Historia regum*, II:170; Wace, II:89; Aelred of Rievaulx, *Vita sancti Aedwardi regis*, ed. J.P. Migne, *Patriologia latina*, 195 (Rome, 1855), cols 766–67; Freeman, *Norman Conquest*, II:346–50, 635–40; Stenton, *Anglo-Saxon England*, p. 569; Barlow, *English Church*, p. 51; Barlow, *Edward the Confessor*, pp. 125, 127; Douglas, *William the Conqueror*, pp. 412–13; I. Walker, pp. 52–53; Loyn, 'Harold, Son of Godwin,' p. 305; and Campbell, 'Anglo-Saxon "Kingmaker",' p. 33. In Aelred's saint's life, the miserable death of Godwin is 'divine judgement,' punishment delivered because of the 'crimes' committed by the earl against the king and his brother, Alfred. Trying to clear himself yet again from the murder of Alfred, Aelred reports that Godwin proposes a challenge to the king: should God make the morsel of food which Godwin is eating be caught in his throat, then he should be found divinely guilty of killing Edward's brother. The morsel of food becomes stuck, and the earl

So the patriarch of the most powerful family in eleventh-century England died. He was buried at the Old Minster in Winchester, in the heart of his county, Wessex, but his soul was not to remain in limbo for long. Gyða, Godwin's wife, initially escaped the conquest of William the Conqueror; but in 1068–69, she rose up against the new king in concert with her grandsons, the sons of Harold, and was forced to flee to Flanders.[110] A short while later, nearing her own death and rich in land ownership, in order to assure her and Godwin of eternal life, she founded a college of Priests at Hartland, Waltham. A copy of her grant is in the *Codex diplomaticus aevi saxonici*:

> I Countess Gyða, concede to the church of St. Olaf, king and martyr, my land at Scireford, which is from my dowry, for the souls of me and my lord, Count Godwin, so that same church would have it by perpetual law and hold it freely and silently from all earthly servitude.[111]

She was buried next to her husband.

Godwin and Gyða had a large and important family. Two of his sons, Tostig and Harold, will be dealt with at length in later chapters. The other members of his family were also quite powerful, but they did not play a significant role in the Norwegian invasion of 1066.

There is some evidence, although not substantial, that Godwin's first wife was not Gyða. William of Malmesbury mentions an earlier marriage, with a

---

dies. It is a story which Aelred may have acquired from Henry of Huntingdon (pp. 378–79) and then embellished for hagiographical purposes. On the creation of this story and its diffusion in later accounts, see Freeman, *Norman Conquest*, II:349–52, 637–40. It should be noted that Douglas (*William the Conqueror*, pp. 412–13) in commenting on Aelred of Rievaulx's tale, accepts the possibility of Godwin's death occurring as a result of poison, perhaps even administered at Edward's behest.

110 Plummer and Earle, eds., *Two of the Saxon Chronicles Parallel*, II:260; I. Walker, pp. 192–93; Grierson, 'The Relations between England and Flanders,' pp. 109–10; and Pauline Stafford, 'Women and the Norman Conquest,' *Transactions of the Royal Historical Society*, 6th ser., 4 (1994), 235. The uprising of Harold's sons will be dealt with in the following chapter.

111 Johannis M. Kemble, ed., *Codex diplomaticus aevi saxonici* (London, 1846), IV:264:
> Ego Gyða comitissa concedo aecclesiae sancti Olavi regis et martyris terram meam de Scireford, quae est de dote mea, pro anima mea et domini mei comitis Godwini; ut ipsa aecclesia eam perpetuo iure habeat et teneat liberam et quietam ab omni terreno servitio.

On Gyða's lands, which are valued at more than £500 in the *Domesday Book*, see Freeman, *Norman Conquest*, IV:752–54; Clarke, pp. 9, 204–05; and Marc A. Meyer, 'Women's Estates in Later Anglo-Saxon England: The Politics of Possession,' *Haskins Society Journal* 3 (1991), 122–23. For Gyða's gifts see *Annales de Wintonia*, in *Annales monastici*, ii, ed. H.R. Luard (London, 1865), p. 26. See also Freeman, *Norman Conquest*, II:350–51; Barlow, *Edward the Confessor*, p. 127; and Barlow, *English Church*, p. 58. Barlow (*English Church*, pp. 57–58) contends that Godwin himself made 'no pretense of an interest in religion' and was not pious, an element of the 'great depression in the religious life of the kingdom' during this time. According to the *Domesday Book*, he may even have robbed some churches of their possessions and lands. However, he did make gifts to the Old Minster in Winchester, where his body was eventually laid to rest.

daughter of King Knútr, in which Godwin had a son. However, both wife and son died horrible deaths:

> In his early years he was married to a sister of Knútr, by whom he had had a son. The child, when he had passed his early boyhood, was riding one day with boyish glee a horse given him by his grandfather, when the animal plunged with him into the Thames, and he sank into the eddying river and was drowned. His mother too was struck by lightning, and so paid the penalty for her cruel acts; she was said to buy parties of slaves in England and ship them to Denmark, young girls especially, whose beauty and youth would enhance their price, so that by this hideous traffic she could accumulate vast wealth.[112]

William of Malmesbury may be incorrect in this reference, for he is alone in making the assertion that Godwin had a prior marriage to that with Gyða. Also, while not positively denying the possibility of such an occurrence, there is no precedent for a marriage being granted by a king to his sister-in-law after the previous spouse, his daughter, had died. On the other hand, if his relationship to Godwin had been so important to Knútr as can be established, such a renewal of marriage ties would have kept the earl close to the king. Still, most historians doubt William of Malmesbury's claims concerning this marriage.[113]

Godwin's eldest son by Gyða was Swegen. Frank Barlow estimates that Swegen was born c.1023 and was raised to earl of Herefordshire in c.1043.[114] Being the eldest of Godwin's children, he was undoubtedly educated in the military arts and in generalship. He was a warlord's son – in fact, the eldest son –

---

112 William of Malmesbury, *Gesta regum Anglorum*, I:362–63:
Habuit primis annis uxorem Cnutonis sororem, ex qua puerum genuerat; qui primis pueritiae annis emensis, dum equo quem ab auo acceperat puerili iactantia superbiret, ab eodem in Tamensem portatus uoragine aquae suffocatus interiit. Mater quoque ictu fulminis exanimata seuitiae penas soluit, quod dicebatur agmina manicipiorum, in Anglia coempta Danemarkiam solere mittere, puellas presertim quas decus et aetas pretiosiores facerent, ut earum deformi commertio cumulos opum aggeraret.

113 See, for example, Freeman, *Norman Conquest*, I:722–25.

114 Barlow, *Edward the Confessor*, p. 74 and Barlow, ed., *Vita Ædwardi*, pp. 7–8 n. 10. See also Freeman, *Norman Conquest*, II:36. Swegen signs his first royal charter in 1044 (*Codex diplomaticus aevi saxonici*, IV:74). Ian Walker (p. 12) contends that Swegen was named such after Knútr's father; it is a compelling claim but without evidence. Indeed, there is some evidence that Swegen may have contended that he was a son of Knútr and not Godwin – see Hemming, *Hemingi Chartularium ecclesiae Wigornorniensis*, ed. T. Hearne (Oxford, 1723), I:275–76 – a claim which led Barlow (*English Church*, p. 58) to describe him as 'addicted to vainglory and pride.' Only when his mother called forth witnesses to his parentage was he convinced. Swegen also held land elsewhere throughout England, including, according to John of Worcester (II:558–59), perhaps all of Gloucestershire and Oxfordshire and parts of Somerset and Berkshire; he also held at least five hides of land in the southwest Midlands. See Douglas, *William the Conqueror*, p. 35. On the size of a hide see Stenton, *Anglo-Saxon England*, p. 279:
Despite the work of many great scholars, the hide of early English texts remains a term of elusive meaning. With hardly an exception, documents older than the Norman Conquest ignore the acreage of the hides with which they are dealing. . . . It points with reasonable clearness to the existence of a normal hide of 120 arable acres in

and as such trained to be a warlord. He surely would have inherited his father's power and titles and may even have been king instead of his brother, Harold, but Swegen ended up a disgrace to his family.

For the first three years, Swegen served with distinction as the earl of Herefordshire, attending to all the duties of his office, especially those of a military character. During the entirety of the Middle Ages the earls of Herefordshire had perhaps the most difficult responsibilities for ensuring the peace of England of any English baron. These lands, along the marches of Wales, provided a 'buffer zone' against raids from marauding bands of Welshmen. Some of these bands were supported by Welsh kings, others seem to have originated simply as groups of cattle rustlers, but all brought at least a disruption of society and economy if not death for those who dared to live along the marches. King Offa of Mercia (758–96) had tried to deter the Welsh with the construction of a large 'dyke,' a 192-kilometer long ditch dug across the marches between Wales and Mercia.[115] Later, after the conquest of William of Normandy, the largest concentration of castles in the kingdom would occupy the same territory,[116] but even with these fortifications, only one means of deterrence was a guarantee against Welsh incursions into England – a strong marcher lord or group of lords, individuals who could defend their territory with military strength and, if necessary, who could make their own avenging assaults into Wales.[117] For Edward the Confessor, there was no better individual to fill these responsibilities than Swegen Godwinson.

Swegen was effective. As the warlord over the marches, he was aggressive in his defense against the Welsh. No sooner had Swegen been raised to earl than he sought to make peace with the king of Gwynedd (in North Wales), Gruffydd ap Llywelyn, who had been raised to the throne himself only in 1039. This peace would work to the benefit of both magnates, as Gruffydd used his alliance with Swegen to gain power over the other primary Welsh lord, Gruffydd ap Rhydderch, king of Deheubarth, and Swegen was able to take advantage of the divisiveness of those same lords to keep them from attacking England. In 1046, Swegen even went so far as to join Gruffydd on an invasion of southern Wales. Although no details of this campaign are recorded, the *Anglo-Saxon Chronicle*

Cambridgeshire . . . But it is equally clear evidence that it amounted to 40 acres in Wiltshire . . .

See also James Tait, 'Large Hides and Small Hides,' *English Historical Review* 17 (1902), 280–82.

[115] Stenton, *Anglo-Saxon England*, pp. 212–15; DeVries, *Medieval Military Technology*, p. 195; Brown, Colvin, and Taylor, I:6–7; Richard P. Abels, *Lordship and Military Obligation in Anglo-Saxon England* (Berkeley and Los Angeles, 1988), pp. 68–69; and J. Forde-Johnston, *Castles and Fortifications of Britain and Ireland* (London, 1977), pp. 73–74.

[116] See, for example, Toby Scott Purser, 'Castles of Herefordshire, 1066–1135,' *Medieval History* 4 (1994), 72–90 and the large number of Herefordshire castles found in Adrian Pettifer, *English Castles: A Guide by Counties* (Woodbridge, 1995).

[117] On the problems of the Welsh in Herefordshire during the Anglo-Saxon period see n. 24 in the following chapter.

(C) does report that Swegen received hostages from those defeated by him and Gruffydd.[118]

However, according to contemporary sources, it is on returning from this campaign in Wales in 1046 that Swegen fell in love with and abducted the abbess of Leominster, Eadgifu, desiring in vain to marry her. Swegen kept the abbess for a year, only agreeing to release her after threats from Archbishop Eadsige of York and Bishop Lyfing of Wells compelled him to do so.[119] Why this was done cannot be explained from the few sources which discuss it, despite its severity as a crime. It could and would bring no good results. As a result of this offense, Swegen was banished from England.[120] He fled first to Flanders, and then to Denmark, where, according to the *Anglo-Saxon Chronicle*, he committed other unspecified crimes.[121]

In 1049, Swegen returned to England to beg for forgiveness from and

[118] *Anglo-Saxon Chronicle* (C) 1046, I:164. See also Freeman, *Norman Conquest*, II:87; Barlow, *Norman Conquest*, p. 91; I. Walker, p. 22; Maund, *Ireland, Wales, and England*, pp. 124, 128–29; Maund, 'Welsh Alliances of Earl Ælfgar,' p. 183; and D. Walker, pp. 85–86. Despite the lack of sources on this campaign, it seems to have been of limited success as Gruffydd ap Llywelyn was attacked the following year by men of the same region which he and Swegen had ravaged. Freeman has Gruffydd ap Llywelyn as the one giving hostages to Swegen; while this may have happened, there is no evidence of such found in the *Anglo-Saxon Chronicle* reference which Freeman cites.

[119] *Anglo-Saxon Chronicle* (C) 1046, I:164; John of Worcester, II:548–49; Symeon of Durham, *Historia regum*, II:164–65; and Hemming, I:275–76. John of Worcester, who does not mention the incident until 1049, in conjunction with the Beorn murder mentioned below, is the only source to give Eadgifu as the name of the abbess and that Swegen wished to marry her. See also Freeman, *Norman Conquest*, II:87–88, 592–93; Stenton, *Anglo-Saxon England*, p. 429; Barlow, *English Church*, p. 58; Barlow, *Edward the Confessor*, p. 91; I. Walker, p. 22; and Cutler, 'Edith, Queen of England,' pp. 226–27. The abbey of Leominster seems not to have survived this disgrace and was dissolved by the time of the *Domesday Book*.

[120] Henry of Huntingdon, pp. 374–75. The *Anglo-Saxon Chronicle* ((E) 1045, I:166) mentions that Swegen went to Flanders, but not that he had been sent there by Edward. John of Worcester (II:548–49) also mentions nothing about Edward's banishment of Swegen, nor about Flanders being the destination, only that the earl went to Denmark 'because he was not permitted to marry Eadgifu whom he had seduced.' Campbell's idea that Swegen could have been and was banished only by the huscarls ('Anglo-Saxon "Kingmaker",' p. 32) is compelling, but has no evidence to support it. On the other hand, Cutler's contention that 'the confrontation lasted so long without the king deposing Swegen as earl and depriving him of his earldom might be partially attributable to queen Edith's influence' ('Edith, Queen of England,' pp. 226–27) borders on a fantasy which even her patron, the anonymous author of the *Vita Ædwardi*, refused to make. Freeman (*Norman Conquest*, II:88), obviously not accepting Henry of Huntingdon's account, holds that Swegen left England 'out of disappointment' at not being able to marry Eadgifu, and that it is only after this abandonment that he was outlawed. See also Stenton, *Anglo-Saxon England*, p. 429; Barlow, *Edward the Confessor*, p. 91; Oleson, *Witenagemot*, p. 102; Campbell, 'Earl Godwin of Wessex and Edward the Confessor's Promise,' p. 145; and Bertie Wilkerson, 'Northumbrian Separatism in 1065 and 1066,' *Bulletin of the John Rylands Library* 23 (1939), 513–14.

[121] *Anglo-Saxon Chronicle* (D) 1050, p. 169. See also Raraty, p. 17 and Grierson, 'The Relations between England and Flanders,' p. 98. Oleson (*Witenagemot*, p. 102) wonders if

perform penance before the king,[122] but Swegen's return was not welcomed by his brother, Harold, or his cousin, Beorn, both of whom had profited from Swegen's absence and were reluctant to give up what they had acquired by his banishment. Beorn seems to have opposed the return of Swegen the most.[123] Eventually, however, Swegen was able to convince Beorn to support his return, but then something sudden and unexplained by any of the sources happened. Beorn met Swegen at Pevensey and agreed to join his own forces to those of his cousin and to travel together to meet the king at Sandwich and ask for Swegen's reinstatement. The two cousins disembarked near Bosham, one of the most important manors of the Godwin family, although why such a stop was made is unexplained. Near there Beorn was murdered. On discovering this murder, six of Beorn's eight ships deserted Swegen, and this Godwinson was forced once again to flee to Flanders, declared a *niðing* (a man without honor) at a military tribunal, a sentence later confirmed by Edward the Confessor and the witenagemot. The *Anglo-Saxon Chronicle* (C) claims that the murder was premeditated:

> Then came Earl Swegen with deceit, and he bid Earl Beorn to travel with him to the king at Sandwich, saying that he would swear oaths and would be loyal to him. Trusting his kinship with Swegen, Beorn and three others went with him. And they travelled to Bosham, as if they were sailing to Sandwich. Swegen's ships lay there. Then Beorn was bound and taken aboard a ship. And he was taken to Dartmouth, where he was slain and deeply buried.[124]

Swegen was sent to help Sveinn Estriðson against Magnús of Norway by Godwin after Edward had refused to assist.

[122] The best information concerning Swegen's return to England and the subsequent death of Earl Beorn is found in Earle and Plummer, eds., *Two of the Saxon Chronicles Parallel*, II:229–31. In tabular form, they show that there were various versions from three *Anglo-Saxon Chronicle* manuscripts (C, D, and E) and John of Worcester concerning this matter. On Swegen's return see Freeman, *Norman Conquest*, II:98–100 and I. Walker, pp. 23–24.

[123] At least Beorn was the first target of Swegen's revenge on his return to England. See *Anglo-Saxon Chronicle* (E) 1046, I:168 and Freeman, *Norman Conquest*, II:99–101.

[124] *Anglo-Saxon Chronicle* (C) 1049, I:168–71:

> Ða com Swegen eorl mid facne, ⁊ bæd Beorn eorl þ he his gefera wære to þam cinge to Sandwic. cwæð þ he him aþas swerigen wolde ⁊ him hold beon. Ða wende Beorn for þære sibbe þ he him swican nolde. nam ða .iii. geferan mid him. ⁊ ridon þa to Boshanham. eall swa hi sceoldon to Sandwic, þær Swegenes scypa lagon. ï hine man sona geband ⁊ to scype lædde. ⁊ ferdon þa to Dærentamuðan, ⁊ hine þar let ofslean. ⁊ deope bedelfan.

See also *Anglo-Saxon Chronicle* (C) 1049, (E) 1046, I:168–70; John of Worcester, II:548–51; Henry of Huntingdon, pp. 374–75; Symeon of Durham, *Historia regum*, II:165; and Adam of Bremen, pp. 154–55. It is clear that Bosham manor held some importance for the Godwin family; perhaps it was even their chief abode. It was also from Bosham that Godwin, Swegen, and Tostig fled in 1051, as seen above, while the *Bayeux Tapestry* shows Harold Godwinson feasting at the manor before setting sail for Normandy in 1064–65 (*The Bayeux Tapestry: A Comprehensive Survey*, Frank M. Stenton, 2nd edn (London, 1957), pl. 14). It is also known that the family held large amounts of land nearby, at Pevensey. See Ann Williams, 'Land and Power in the Eleventh-Century: the Estates of Harold Godwinson,' *Proceedings of the Battle Conference on Anglo-Norman Studies* 3 (1980), 185.

Why Swegen slew Beorn is a mystery. There seems to have been little logic to the murder. Indeed, the death of Beorn obviously weakened the political power of the Godwin family; with Beorn and Swegen in place, Godwin, his sons, and nephew held four of the six great English earldoms, with more, younger sons set to take other lands and earldoms. Yet all of the sources reporting the event are certain in their conviction of Swegen's guilt in the crime. So too are all modern commentators. As Frank Stenton writes: '. . . it was clear that he had been guilty of an act of atrocious treachery, and his condemnation took the form of a judgement by a military assembly that he had outraged its sense of honourable behaviour.'[125] What is more unusual, perhaps 'extraordinary', to use Frank Barlow's word, is that Swegen returned to England the following year and was reinstated as an earl by Edward. Henry of Huntingdon contends that it was done only 'on the surety of his father Godwine,' while John of Worcester claims that the influence in this matter was Bishop Ealdred of Worcester, who met with Swegen in Flanders on his way home from Rome and was touched by his repentant desire for a return to England.[126]

Swegen was not a peaceful man though, and his stay in England did not last long. In 1051, as discussed above, the Godwin family were all banished from England. At this time, Swegen's punishment, again inexplicably, was more severe than the others. He was outlawed at the outset of his father's rebellion; for while his father and brother Harold, were requested to come to a council with the king at the beginning of the rebellion, Swegen was exiled without recourse.[127] Once more, he fled to Flanders.

While there, he must have felt some remorse for his past crimes. Perhaps judging that it would be some time before he and his family were restored to their English lands and titles, if at all, he undertook a barefoot pilgrimage to Rome and Jerusalem. On his return journey to Flanders he was killed. However,

---

[125] Stenton, *Anglo-Saxon England*, p. 430. See also Freeman, *Norman Conquest*, II:101–06; Barlow, *Edward the Confessor*, pp. 99–101; I. Walker, p. 24–25; Oleson, *Witenagemot*, pp. 102–05; Campbell, 'Earl Godwin of Wessex and Edward the Confessor's Promise,' pp. 148–53; Wilkerson, 'Northumbrian Separatism in 1065 and 1066,' pp. 513–14; and Stafford, *Unification and Conquest*, p. 89. For a comparison of this tribunal with others in Icelandic sagas see Oleson, *Witenagemot*, p. 103 n. 1. Barlow (*Edward the Confessor*, p. 102) wonders if Beorn had not been the head of Edward's navy and if this was not the origin of the naval problems that would be apparent during the next few years.

[126] Henry of Huntingdon, pp. 374–75: 'Suein regi concordatus est cautela Godwini patris sui' and John of Worcester, II:550–51. See also Freeman, *Norman Conquest*, II:106–08, 113); Barlow, *Edward the Confessor*, pp. 101–03; *Anglo-Saxon Chronicle* (C and D) 1049, (E) 1046, I:170–71; Stafford, *Unification and Conquest*, pp. 89–90; Oleson, *Witenagemot*, p. 105; I. Walker, p. 25; and King, p. 127. All contemporary sources contain no further details on why Swegen was allowed to return to England. Freeman, Barlow, and King see no influence from Godwin in this matter, believing John of Worcester's account. Nor does Campbell ('Earl Godwin of Wessex and Edward the Confessor's Promise,' pp. 150–53) accept Godwin's role in the affair, contending instead that Swegen's return was linked both to the fall of the Godwin in 1051 and to the taking of Swegen's son, Hakon, as one of the Godwin hostages. All others see the return of Swegen as evidence of continued Godwinist control of the throne.

[127] See n. 71 above.

even with his death there is disagreement among the sources as to where Swegen died. John of Worcester records Swegen's death at Lycia in Asia Minor; William of Malmesbury reports that he was killed by Saracens in the Holy Land; and the *Anglo-Saxon Chronicle* (C) claims that it occurred at Constantinople. All, however, assure their readers that Swegen had already fulfilled his pilgrimage at his death and that his sins had been forgiven.[128]

What can be said about the character of such a man? Some historians have tried to minimize or rationalize Swegen's crimes, seeing his abduction of Eadgifu as a love tryst or as the desire for an alliance with a rich noble lady, and/or seeing the murder of his cousin, Beorn, as a play for power or as revenge,[129] but most have arrived at the conclusion that Swegen was somewhat of a psychopath, to use a modern definition of one who is not in full control of his violent behavior. Freeman's description is, if anything, generous:

> A youth, evidently of no common powers, but wayward, violent, and incapable of self-control, he was hurried first into flagrant violation of the sentiment of the age, and next into a still fouler breach of the eternal laws of right. His end may well arouse our pity, but his life, as a whole, is a dark blot on the otherwise chequered escutcheon of the house of Godwine.[130]

These conclusions are not new. Indeed, the *Vita Ædwardi* was probably describing Swegen when the anonymous author portrays one of Godwin's children as the 'gulping monster' who 'seeks the depths, attacks its root and mouths the parent trunk, and holds, until, as doomed, the breath of life creates a creature from a lifeless dam; and losing grip, pursues again its prey.'[131] Undoubtedly being the son of a powerful and bellicose lord gave license to tendencies which

---

128 John of Worcester, II:570–71; William of Malmesbury, *Gesta regum Anglorum*, I:362–65; and *Anglo-Saxon Chronicle* (C) 1052, I:182. See also Freeman, *Norman Conquest*, II:336–37, 630–32; Barlow, *English Church*, p. 88; Barlow, *Edward the Confessor*, pp. 120, 124; Douglas, *William the Conqueror*, p. 35; and I. Walker, p. 52. On why Freeman accepts Lycia, see *Norman Conquest*, II:630–32.

129 See, for example, Freeman (*Norman Conquest*, II:87–88) and I. Walker (pp. 22, 24–25) who are the most profound apologists for Godwin and his family. Yet even Freeman (*Norman Conquest*, II:105–06) cannot suspend his indignation for Swegen's action in the killing of his cousin.

130 Freeman, *Norman Conquest*, II:44–45. See also Stenton, *Anglo-Saxon England*, p. 430, and Barlow, *Edward the Confessor*, p. 101.

131 *Vita Ædwardi*, pp. 26–27:

> Illa pronfunda petit tranans inimica uoratrix, dampna sue stirpis faciens truncumque parentem pendit ab ore tenens, dum certo tempore uite flatus uiuificans animal de non animata matre creat; studet inde suis resoluta rapinis.

The *Vita Ædwardi*'s use of this poetic metaphor grows out of its description of Godwin's children as the four rivers flowing out of Paradise mentioned in Genesis II:10, with one (obviously Harold) which 'mounts the skies, to heaven twined, and tends its race's hope in tree-top nest' (Aera conscendit pars hec herendo supernis, spemque sui generis nido fouet arboris alte); his 'gulping monster' counterpart, most believe can only have been Swegen. See *Vita Ædwardi*, pp. 26–27 n. 57; Barlow, *Edward the Confessor*, p. 101; and Barlow, *English Church*, p. 58.

he may have thought permissible because of his wealth and station. Perhaps it was not until the army itself became involved and banished him as a 'man utterly and irreparably disgraced,' to use Barlow's definition of *niðing*,[132] that Swegen realized that he had exceeded all forms of behavior, even those made legitimate by his military occupation and station. Ultimately, this change of heart would lead to his death as a sinner repentant for his actions; it inevitably also led to his brother Harold's ascension to the throne after the death of Edward.

Only one child of Swegen's is known, Hakon, the boy offered as one of the hostages given to Edward in 1051 in exchange for the assurance of safe-passage to the coast for the rest of the Godwin family.[133] Nothing else is known about this child's life before the 1051 expulsion, not even who his mother was, although Edward Freeman wonders if it could not have been Eadgifu, the abbess of Leominster, abducted and seduced by Swegen in 1046, as she had been kept for over a year by this Godwinson.[134] After his return, and having broken the vow for which he had surrendered the hostages, Godwin was obviously not able to obtain the return of his son and grandson from Normandy. However, the Anglo-Norman chronicles of William of Poitiers and Eadmer both report that one of the purposes of Harold Godwinson's visit to Normandy in 1064, which will be discussed more fully in the following chapter, was to retrieve his brother and nephew, and that Hakon was sent back with Harold after the English earl had promised to support William the Conqueror in his bid to inherit the English throne.[135]

Besides Swegen, Harold and Tostig, Godwin had two other sons who fulfilled leadership roles, Gyrð and Leofwine. However, much less is written about their lives than about the rest of the Godwin family.[136] According to Frank Barlow, they were born c.1032 and c.1035 respectively.[137] Both spent large amounts of time at Edward's court with their royal sister;[138] both were granted earldoms between 1055 and 1057 – Gyrð received East Anglia, Cambridgeshire, and

---

[132] Barlow, *Edward the Confessor*, p. 101.

[133] On Hakon as a hostage see note 72 above.

[134] Freeman, *Norman Conquest*, II:88. Barlow (*Edward the Confessor*, p. 303) does not agree, as a 'five year old orphaned bastard would hardly be the most desired hostage.' Instead, he sees Hakon as the issue of a previous union with an Anglo-Scandinavian woman.

[135] William of Poitiers, p. 115, and Eadmer, pp. 6–8. Orderic Vitalis, in his emendation to William of Jumièges' *Gesta Normannorum ducum* (II:160–61), may have been meaning the same when said that only Harold's brother, Wulnoð, was left behind with William when Harold returned to England. See also Brown, *The Normans and Norman Conquest*, p. 113; Körner, pp. 126–131; I. Walker, pp. 99, 101; and Cutler, 'Godwinist Hostages,' pp. 74–75.

[136] The odd lack of information found in the *Vita Ædwardi* about these two Godwinsons is explained by Barlow as 'their unexpected importance in the story, either because Harold had taken the throne, or because they had been killed' (*Edward the Confessor*, pp. 292–95, quote is on p. 293).

[137] *Vita Ædwardi*, pp. 6–8 n. 10. See also Freeman, *Norman Conquest*, II:553–55 and Freeman, 'On the Life and Death of Earl Godwine,' pp. 248, 250–52.

[138] See Barlow, *Edward the Confessor*, p. 163.

Oxfordshire, and Leofwine received Kent, Essex, Middlesex, Hertford, Surrey, and probably Buckinghamshire;[139] both held large amounts of land throughout the kingdom;[140] both had their own 'clients,' men who were given land and favor by them and who, in turn, served under them in their military offices;[141] both served as Harold's lieutenants during his short reign;[142] and both led contingents of the army at Hastings in 1066 and were slain fighting next to their royal brother Harold.[143] For Leofwine, only one other reference to his life remains: it concerns his flight to Ireland with Harold in 1051 and his subsequent return the year following, as discussed above.[144]

Gyrð has a wider tradition. It is recorded that he fled to Flanders with the rest of his family in 1051, traveling on a ship with his brother, Swegen,[145] and that he returned there in 1061 when escorting his brother, Tostig, on a trip to Rome.[146] He was also present, according to John of Worcester, at his dying father's side.[147] (Leofwine's absence at this occasion is odd; he is the only prominent member of Godwin's children not mentioned at his father's deathbed.) There is also a tradition that Gyrð accompanied Harold to the battlefield at Stamford Bridge in 1066.[148]

A final Godwinson of note was the youngest, Wulfnoð, the offspring used by

---

[139] Freeman, *Norman Conquest*, II:418–19, 556, 560, 566–68; Stenton, *Anglo-Saxon England*, p. 574; Brown, *The Normans and Norman Conquest*, p. 71; Douglas, *William the Conqueror*, p. 172; I. Walker, p. 83, 206–07, 212; Fleming, *Kings and Lords in Conquest England*, p. 56; and Clarke, pp. 19–20. These earldoms were important because they gave control over the whole east of England to Harold and his brothers. Leofwine, although not an earl until 1055, was nevertheless witnessing royal charters from at least 1048–49. (See Barlow, *Edward the Confessor*, pp. 88–89, 332–33.) Also Barlow (*Vita Ædwardi*, pp. 50–51 n. 122) notes that although Gyrð received Norfolk in 1055, he may not have received the earldom of East Anglia until 1057, when Ælfgar inherited his father's earldom of Mercia. See also Barlow, *Edward the Confessor*, p. 193.

[140] See I. Walker, pp. 63–65; Fleming, *Kings and Lords in Conquest England*, pp. 70, 75–78, 102; Clarke, pp. 13–14, 19, 24–25, 101, 108, 205; and, for what this might have meant for the political structure of the kingdom, Fleming, 'Domesday Estates of the King and the Godwines,' pp. 987–1007. Clarke's appendix listing the lands held by each of the 'nobles' of England, as seen in the *Domesday Book*, is particularly detailed. For Gyrð see pp. 194–200 and for Leofwine see pp. 200–203.

[141] Fleming, *Kings and Lords in Conquest England*, pp. 75–78 and Clarke, p. 103.

[142] See Freeman, *Norman Conquest*, II:419–20; Barlow, *Edward the Confessor*, pp. 245–46; and I. Walker, pp. 113, 115–16.

[143] *Anglo-Saxon Chronicle* (D and E) 1066, I:198–99; *The Bayeux Tapestry*, pl. 64–65; Symeon of Durham, *Historia regum*, II:181; Stenton, *Anglo-Saxon England*, p. 574; Brown, *The Normans and Norman Conquest*, pp. 143–44, 150; Douglas, *William the Conqueror*, p. 200; and I. Walker, pp. 176, 180.

[144] See nn. 73, 98–99, and 102 above.

[145] *Anglo-Saxon Chronicle* (C) 1051 (D) 1052, I:172, 175 and John of Worcester, II:560–63.

[146] *Vita Ædwardi*, pp. 52–53. See also Plummer and Earle, eds., *Two of the Saxon Chronicles Parallel*, II:249; Barlow, *Edward the Confessor*, p. 210; and I. Walker, p. 87.

[147] John of Worcester, II:572–73.

[148] See *Vita Ædwardi*, pp. 89–90 nn. 217–18, which calls this a 'poor and confused tradition,' and I. Walker, pp. 159, 168–69. Should this have been so, Leofwine's absence again

his family as a hostage in 1052. Called a 'pulchrum adolescentem' by Orderic Vitalis, in his revision of William of Jumièges' *Gesta Normannorum ducum*, nothing is known about this boy outside of the use of him as a hostage and his later imprisonment.[149] There does appear to have been an attempt by Harold to gain his release when he visited Normandy in 1064, but, as mentioned, it was only Hakon who was released at that time.[150] Wulfnoð was destined to continue as a prisoner in William the Conqueror's hands, although according to William of Malmesbury, eventually he would be brought back to England:

> Wulfnoth, sent by King Edward into Normandy because his father had handed him over as a hostage, remained there, held in close custody, all Edward's time; under William's rule he was sent back to England and grew old in chains at Salisbury.[151]

However, whether Wulfnoð died in captivity cannot be known. He was to have been one of the prisoners freed at the death of the Conqueror, yet he stayed in prison for at least a part of the reign of King William Rufus. On the other hand, according to an epitaph written for him by Godfrey of Cambria, Wulfnoð may have died in 1094 as a free man at the priory attached to Winchester Cathedral. The epitaph speaks of a man who was every bit as strong a character as the rest of his family, but who, by fate of birth alone, was forced to spend his life as a prisoner to the political machinations of opposing warlords:

> The nobility of his forbears, his simple manners,
> His sound views and honourable judgements,
> The strength of his body and the fire of his intellect,
> All these glorify Earl Wulfnoth.
> Exile, prison, darkness, inclosure, chains
> Receive the boy and forsake the old man.
> Caught up in human bonds he bore them patiently,
> Bound even more closely in service to God.
> In spring while the Fishes were warmed by the February sun
> The ninth day under Hermes was the last for him.[152]

He was the last of Godwin's children known to have died.

---

would be curious and unexplained, although I. Walker's assumption that Leofwine was left in charge in the south is a possibility.

[149] William of Jumièges, pp. 160–61. On Wulfnoð as a hostage in 1051 see n. 72 above. I. Walker's claim (p. 196) that Wulfnoð was fifteen at the time of his captivity has no support from contemporary literature.

[150] See n. 134 above.

[151] William of Malmesbury, *Gesta regum Anglorum*, I:362–63:

> Wlnodus a rege Eduardo Normanniam missus, quod eum pater obsidem dederat, ibi toto tempore Eduardi inextricabili captione irretitus, regnante Willelmo in Angliam remissus, in uinculis Salesberiae consenuit.

[152] As translated in Frank Barlow, *William Rufus* (Berkeley and Los Angeles, 1983), pp. 65–66. The original is in *The Anglo-Satirical Poets and Epigrammatists of the Twelfth Century*, ed. T. Wright (London, 1872), II:148. Orderic Vitalis (III:178–79) has Wulfnoð

Orderic Vitalis records the name of one other son of Godwin and Gyða, Ælfgar, who fell in age between Gyrð and Leofwine, and who, he claims, lived and died as a monk in Rheims. However, most modern historians either ignore this reference or dispute its validity.[153]

The names of four daughters of Godwin and Gyða are found in contemporary records. The three youngest, Gunnhilda, Ælfgifu, and Eadgifu, have little written about them: Gunnhilda is found as the 'daughter of Earl Godwin' in the *Domesday Book*, Ælfgifu appears also in the same work as the 'sister of Earl Harold', and Eadgifu is found only in the *Liber Vitae* of Hyde Abbey as the 'daughter of Earl Godwin.' Ælfgifu may also be the sister claimed by Symeon of Durham to have been promised by Harold when he visited Normandy in 1064 as a wife for one of William the Conqueror's nobles.[154]

The eldest daughter, and perhaps even the eldest of Godwin's children, was Eadgyða. Unlike her sisters, much is written about Eadgyða in contemporary sources, especially in contemporary narrative sources. Most of these are extremely favorable to her, while the *Vita Ædwardi*, which was commissioned by and dedicated to Eadgyða, uses only superlatives in its portrayal of her.[155]

The date of Eadgyða's birth is not known. She may have been born sometime between 1020 and 1030, or even later, depending on when her parents were married and where in the order of Godwin's children she was born. Most modern historians assume that she was the eldest, but there is little contemporary evidence to support such an assumption.[156] Of course, her age at marriage may be the deciding factor in when Eadgyða was born; was she fifteen and thus

---

dying as a free man in Salisbury. See also Barlow, *Edward the Confessor*, p. 302; Brown, *The Normans and Norman Conquest*, pp. 174–75; and I. Walker, pp. 196–97.

[153] Orderic Vitalis, III:178–79. See, for example, Freeman, (*Norman Conquest*, II:553–54) who contends that there is little likelihood that a son of Godwin's would attend a French monastery.

[154] Symeon of Durham, *Historia regum*, II:183–84. See also *Liber Vitae: The Register and Martyrology of New Minister and Hyde Abbey*, ed. W. de G. Birch (London and Winchester, 1892), p. 71; Freeman, *Norman Conquest*, II:554–55; Meyer, 'Women's Estates in Later Anglo-Saxon England,' 119–20; and I. Walker, pp. 93–94, the last of whom also discusses whether she is the Aelfgyva of the *Bayeux Tapestry*. It does appear that Gunnhilda held some important, although relatively small tracts of land (see Clarke, pp. 13, 21, 25, 62). She also made several important religious bequests to the monasteries of St Bertin and St Donation, both of Bruges, in 1087. See I. Walker, pp. 192–93 and Grierson, 'The Relations between England and Flanders,' p. 109.

[155] *Vita Ædwardi*, pp. 22–27. For a less enthusiastic description of Eadgyða, see William of Malmesbury, *Gesta regum Anglorum*, I:352–53. On the *Vita Ædwardi* as a source written at Eadgyða's behest see Barlow, *Edward the Confessor*, pp. 291–300; Stafford, *Queen Emma and Queen Edith*, pp. 40–52; Stafford, *Unification and Conquest*, pp. 19, 94–95; I. Walker, pp. xxiv–xxv; and Joel T. Rosenthal, 'Edward the Confessor and Robert the Pious: 11th Century Kingship and Biography,' *Mediaeval Studies* 33 (1971), 16–19.

[156] See, for example, Freeman (*Norman Conquest*, II:555) who bases Eadgiða's eldest birth on a vague reading of a poem contained in the *Vita Ædwardi* (pp. 26–27). See also Barlow, *Edward the Confessor*, p. 80; Stafford, *Queen Emma and Queen Edith*, p. 257; and Cutler, 'Edith, Queen of England,' p. 222.

more appropriately aged for a royal marriage, or was she twenty-five and thus by medieval tradition seemingly too old for such a match? The answer is likely never to be known.

Where and how much she was educated can be determined. From the *Vita Ædwardi* and Goscelin of Saint-Bertin's *Life of St. Edith*, it can be established that Eadgyða was educated at Wilton Abbey.[157] One of the richest of Anglo-Saxon nunneries, Wilton had a royal foundation and was located in Godwin's earldom of Wessex, close to Winchester. Beautifully situated and luxuriously decorated, by the time Eadgyða attended, Wilton Abbey had long been the educational institution for noble and royal women, training them in all of the arts of court, as well as in reading, writing, painting, weaving, and spiritual devotion. It even contained a zoo, filled with animals not housed elsewhere in England. It was also a protected institution, walled against violence and visited frequently by kings and queens who gave prodigiously to its coffers. Its abbesses also wielded political power unknown to most other ecclesiastical leaders, male or female, during the tenth and eleventh centuries.[158] Therefore, it was the perfect place to educate Godwin's eldest daughter. (In fact, all of Godwin's daughters may have been taught there, although there is no contemporary evidence mentioning such.) Eadgyða was considered to be quite intelligent, known to have been well educated in numbers, music, grammar, and languages. Goscelin of Saint-Bertin agreed, describing her as 'a most learned' queen.[159]

Depending on her age, Eadgyða may have entered Wilton Abbey with a purpose other than marriage, let alone royal marriage, but by the time the spouseless Edward had returned from Normandy to take the English throne, in 1042, her destiny seems to have changed. A marriage between her and Edward the Confessor tied the most powerful warlord in England and his sons, two of whom, Swegen and Harold, were already earls, to a king who at the time needed their assistance to stay securely on the throne. They married on 23 January 1045.[160]

---

[157] *Vita Ædwardi*, pp. 22–23, 36–37, 70–73 and Goscelin of Saint-Bertin, *Life of St. Edith*, in 'La légende de Ste Édith en prose et vers par le moine Goscelin,' *Analecta Bollandiana* 56 (1938), 5–307.

[158] On Wilton Abbey, see Barlow, ed., *Vita Ædwardi*, pp. 134–39 and Stafford, *Queen Emma and Queen Edith*, pp. 257–59. King Edgar's daughter and Edward the Confessor's aunt, Saint Edith, had been a nun at Wilton, and her mother, Wulfðryð, who had been repudiated by her husband, had ended her days as the abbess there. As well, Eadgyða's niece, Gunnhilda, Harold's daughter, would be housed at Wilton after the conquest. Other royal women were also buried within its walls.

[159] As quoted in Stafford, *Queen Emma and Queen Edith*, pp. 258–59. See also the *Vita Ædwardi* (pp. 22–23) which describes her academic and artistic abilities.

[160] *Anglo-Saxon Chronicle* (C) 1044 and (E) 1043, I:164–65; Henry of Huntingdon, pp. 372–73; William of Malmesbury, *Gesta regum Anglorum*, I:352–53; William of Jumièges, pp. 108–09; Freeman, *Norman Conquest*, II:45–46; Stenton, *Anglo-Saxon England*, p. 425; Stafford, *Unification and Conquest*, pp. 86–87; Freeman, 'On the Life and Death of Earl Godwine,' pp. 342–43; Barlow, *Edward the Confessor*, pp. 65, 80–81; Barlow, 'Edward the Confessor's Early Life,' pp. 67–68; Douglas, *William the Conqueror*, p. 166; I. Walker, p. 18;

However the marriage between Edward and Eadgyða was to be a childless union. That Edward was more than forty years old when he married Eadgyða should not have mattered, nor should her age during the union, even if it started out at twenty-five. Was it simply a situation where the two for some unknown reason could not have children, or was there something more to it, a marital celibacy practiced? Certainly it seems that the latter notion would be foreign to the very idea of a union taking place between the king and his most powerful earl's daughter, although the fact that Edward had not been married before 1045 could point to a lack of sexual or procreative desire. Once king, however, Edward should have known that it was his duty to provide an heir for the throne and thus to keep the questions of inheritance from leading to the problems which had accompanied the ascension of Harold I and Harðaknútr.

Yet recent work by Dyan Elliott has shown that the notion of marital celibacy was not a foreign one during the Middle Ages, especially when the marriage was made for reasons other than love between the partners.[161] Even more important was the tradition which developed around Edward's sanctification that he and Eadgyða had never consummated their marriage, that they were so taken with a religious belief in purity that they remained completely chaste throughout their lives.[162] In fact, in later hagiographies of the king, his and his wife's marital celibacy becomes one of his 'miracles,' and promotes the determination of his sanctity.[163] One thing is certain: planned or not, that there was no offspring from this marriage when the king died in January 1066 led to an end not only of the Æðelred family dynasty but of the Godwin one as well.

As a political match, for its first six years, the marriage lived up to its acclaim. Although little is known about Eadgyða or her marriage with Edward from 1045 to 1051, both the king and the Godwin family seem to have benefitted from their now close kinship. Godwin and his family grew in power and wealth, and no significant threat was made against Edward or his throne.

As for Eadgyða, it seems that she did not take a pronounced role in politics or in matters of the court during this period, despite the *Vita Ædwardi*'s insistence

Raraty, p. 16; Stafford, *Queen Emma and Queen Edith*, pp. 259–60; and Cutler, 'Edith, Queen of England,' pp. 223–24. All of these accept the marriage as a political arrangement.

[161] Dyan Elliott, *Spiritual Marriage* (Princeton, 1993). Her discussion of Edward and Eadgyða's celibacy, which she accepts as accurate, is on pp. 120–23.

[162] See, for example, William of Malmesbury, *Gesta regum Anglorum*, I:352–55 (although he questions the veracity of this marital celibacy) and William of Jumièges, pp. 108–09. On the question of celibacy in the Edward-Eadgyða marriage see Freeman, *Norman Conquest*, II:46; Barlow, *Edward the Confessor*, pp. 81–85; I. Walker, p. 27; Stafford, *Queen Emma and Queen Edith*, pp. 260–61; and Elliott, pp. 120–22.

[163] For a general survey of the hagiographical sources which use Edward's celibacy as a sign of his sanctification see Freeman, *Norman Conquest*, II:526–31; Elliott, pp. 122–23; and Eric John, 'Edward the Confessor and the Celibate Life,' *Analecta Bollandiana* 97 (1979), 171–78. Hagiographical sources which make use of this include: Aelred of Rielvaux; Osbert of Clare, *La vie de S. Édouard le Confesseur par Osbert de Clare*, ed. M. Bloch, *Analecta Bollandiana* 41 (1923), 5–131; and Matthew Paris, *La estoire de Seint Aedward le rei attributed to Matthew Paris*, ed. K.Y. Wallace (London, 1983).

that she was present at every council and acted as 'a moderator and the fount of all goodness.'[164] Nevertheless, her standing as queen was immediately recognized after her marriage, especially in places where her father's position was respected and undoubtedly feared. Initially, at least, she seems not to have concerned herself with political matters better left in the hands of her husband and her father. Instead, her name appearing frequently in land grants and favors to ecclesiastical establishments may show that she saw her early royal role as one which could be better used to benefit the church in England.[165] There is, in particular, a story of her kindness to the poor at Abingdon Abbey. In visiting the abbey with her mother sometime between 1045 and 1048, Eadgyða noticed that poor children were being fed a lunch consisting only of bread. On being told that this was all that the abbey could afford to feed them, the queen requested that the king grant the abbey some revenue to improve their feeding of the poor. This Edward agreed to do as long as Eadgyða was willing to part with some of her wealth as well. Eadgyða quickly agreed, surrendering her newly acquired village of Lewknor for this purpose.[166]

Eadgyða again appears prominently during the 1051 banishment of her family. As mentioned, she was not chased to the continent or Ireland as was the rest of her family; she was sent instead to the monastery at Wherwell, placed there under the protection of Edward's sister, who was abbess. John of Worcester claims that Eadgyða was exiled 'because of his [Edward's] anger with her father Godwine' and that she was sent 'without ceremony' and with only 'one waiting-woman,' while the *Vita Ædwardi* has her exiled until the political troubles had ended. The *Vita Ædwardi* also notes that this banishment was wrong, 'contra ius religionis Christiane (against the law of Christian religion),' and that Eadgyða was deeply aggrieved at having been sent there.[167] Edward may even have entertained a suggestion of divorce from his 'infertile' wife made by Robert of Jumièges,[168] but there was little time to act on such a suggestion: her

---

164 *Vita Ædwardi*, pp. 36–39:
   Nec mirum, erat enim in omnibus regalibus consiliis, ut ita dicamus, moderatrix et quoddam principium totius honestatis, et quod regem deceret potissimum preferens []tibus et omnibus diuitiis.
I have chosen to translate 'moderatrix' as 'moderator' and not as 'governess' as Barlow has (p. 39). See also Barlow, *English Church*, p. 47.
165 See Stafford, *Queen Emma and Queen Edith*, pp. 261–62, 266.
166 *Chronicon monasterii de Abingdon*, ed. J. Stevenson (London, 1858), I:459–60.
167 *Vita Ædwardi*, pp. 36–39 and John of Worcester, II:563:
   Reginam uero Edgitham rex, propter iram quam aduersus patrem suum Goduuinum habuerat, repudiauit et cum una pedissequa ad Huuereuueallam eam sine honore misit, et abbatisse custodiendam commendauit.
See also the references found in n. 73 above. According to Freeman, the abbess, whose name has not been recorded, was 'no doubt one of the daughters of Æðelræd by his first wife' (*Norman Conquest*, II:153–54). Should this be true, and there is no evidence to support it, the abbess would have been quite old.
168 This according to the *Vita Ædwardi*, pp. 36–37. On the question of divorce in this matter see Stafford, *Queen Emma and Queen Edith*, pp. 264–65; Stafford, *Unification and Con-*

stay at Wherwell was brief, as she was returned to her position as queen at the reinstatement of her father to his position in England the following year. The *Vita Ædwardi* flamboyantly describes her return:

> A short time after [Godwin's return] a thegn was sent with royal pomp, as was right, to the monastery of Wilton. And, just as after the thick clouds of rain-storms or tempests have been driven away, clear sky and the jovial splendor of the sun are restored, so after all the kingdom's turmoil had abated, the queen, that earl's daughter, was brought back to the king's bed-chamber.[169]

There seems to have been a marked increase in Eadgyða's interest in political matters after she and her family returned to power in 1052, and especially after the death of her father the following year. She began to witness more charters, her name always appearing at the top of the witness lists, just below her husband's. As was the case before her banishment, she was interested principally in ecclesiastical matters, although not just in matters of land grants and other bene-fices as she had been previously, but also in ecclesiastical appointments; she seems to have influenced the episcopal appointments of Herman to Sherbourne in 1058, and Giso to Wells and Walter to Hereford in 1060.[170] Moreover, she had her favorites, such as Wilton Abbey, which she aided, while others which she did not favor, such as Peterborough Abbey, were treated poorly by her, even to the point of disputing land grants and wills benefitting such places.[171] There is also a curious account of her taking a bribe from Abbot Ælfwine of Ramsey Abbey to use her influence in a legal dispute concerning his abbey.[172] At the

---

quest, p. 92; Barlow, *Edward the Confessor*, pp. 114–15; Barlow, *English Church*, p. 49; Barlow, 'Edward the Confessor's Early Life,' p. 68; and Cutler, 'Edith, Queen of England,' pp. 228–29.

[169] *Vita Ædwardi*, pp. 44–45:

> Modico exinde interfluente tempore, mittitur eques regio, ut par erat, apparatu ad mon-asterium Wiltunense, et ut, fugatis ymbrium siue tempestatum condensis nubibus, red-ditur celi serentas uel iocundus splendor solis, sic ab omni motu sedato regno, reducitur regina, eiusdem ducis filia, ad thalamum regis.

The *Vita Ædwardi* has the queen at Wilton rather than Wherwell when he family returned to England. See also the references in n. 104 above.

[170] See William of Malmesbury, *De gestis pontificum*, p. 183; Barlow, *Edward the Confessor*, pp. 149, 189–90; Barlow, *English Church*, pp. 51–52, 82, 109 n. 4, 114; and Stafford, *Queen Emma and Queen Edith*, p. 267. She may have done so at a price; both Hermann and Giso 'lost' estates to her. See Barlow, *Edward the Confessor*, p. 149.

[171] See Barlow, *Edward the Confessor*, pp. 150, 232–33; Barlow, *English Church*, pp. 51–52, 81; Stafford, *Queen Emma and Queen Edith*, pp. 267–70; and Marc A. Meyer, 'The Queen's "Demesne", in Later Anglo-Saxon England,' in *The Culture of Christendom: Essays in Medi-eval History in Commemoration of Denis L.T. Bethell*, ed. M.A. Meyer (London, 1993), pp. 100–01. Among other things done for Wilton was the replacement of all its wooden structures by stone. Eadgyða also seems to have favored Bishop Giso of Wells, whose elevation she had initially supported. See Simon Keynes, 'Giso, Bishop of Wells (1061–88),' *Anglo-Norman Studies* 19 (1996), 203–71. On her attitude toward Peterborough Abbey see Hugh Candidus, *The Chronicle of Hugh Candidus, a Monk of Peterborough*, ed. W.T. Mellows (London, 1949), pp. 70, 73, and Barlow, *English Church*, pp. 51–52, 81, 136.

[172] *Chronicon abbatiae Rameseiensis*, ed. W.D. Macray (London, 1866), pp. 169–70.

same time, Eadgyða, grew wealthy, holding much more land in England than anyone else, except for her husband and her brother, Harold.[173] Still, none of this was out of the ordinary for a queen in the eleventh century, in England or elsewhere.

Above all, Eadgyða was extremely loyal to her brothers in all political matters. Among other things, her influence doubtless was felt in gaining earldoms for Tostig, Gyrð, and Leofwine, leaving only the earldom of Mercia outside of Godwin sibling control by 1057.[174] Only when there was a dispute between her brothers, such as that between Harold and Tostig in 1065, which will be investigated in a later chapter, did she break her absolute loyalty to them. Even this, however, was not unusual for a medieval queen.

With her husband's later canonization, Eadgyða's sanctity was also frequently mentioned, as indicated by the report of their mutual chastity. Only one incident appears to have marred Eadgyða's saintly life. Indeed, even the *Vita Ædwardi* has difficulty in discounting her guilt in the affair. She seemed to have had some part in the murder of Gospatric, a young Northumbrian noble, for her brother Tostig in 1065. Because of this murder, which will be discussed in more detail later, the Northumbrian people revolted against Tostig and expelled him.[175]

Eadgyða outlived most of the rest of her family. Being the wife of Edward the Confessor may have saved her the fate of her male siblings in 1066; nevertheless, when she received the news of her brothers' defeat at Hastings, she fled to the safety of Chester.[176] Later, and granted safe conduct by William the Conqueror, Eadgyða returned to her lands at Winchester and Wilton where she lived a comfortable life, continuing to donate land and benefices to ecclesiastical establishments, and even at times visiting William's court. In turn, she arranged for the town of Winchester to surrender itself to William. Nor did she involve herself in the 1068–69 rebellious adventures of her nephews, Godwin, Edmund, and Magnus, Harold's sons, which sent them, her mother, Gyða, and her sister, Gunnhilda, into permanent exile in Bruges. She died in England on 19 December 1075 and was buried next to her husband at Westminster.[177]

According to this work, Edward too received a bribe; in fact, his was four times more than Eadgyða's. Freeman (*Norman Conquest*, II:45–46), Barlow (*Edward the Confessor*, p. 154 n. 4), and Cutler ('Edith, Queen of England,' pp. 229–30) all accept this without question, despite the existence of such a claim only in the *Chronicle of Ramsey Abbey*.

[173] See Barlow, *Edward the Confessor*, p. 74; Cutler, 'Edith, Queen of England,' p. 222; Meyer, 'Women's Estates in Later Anglo-Saxon England,' p. 116; and Meyer, 'The Queen's "Demesne",' pp. 81–85, 88–90.

[174] See Stafford, *Queen Emma and Queen Edith*, pp. 267–74.

[175] See the chapter 'The Conflict between Harold and Tostig Godwinson' below. On Eadgyða's sanctity see Barlow, *Edward the Confessor*, pp. 284–85.

[176] John of Worcester, II:604–05.

[177] *Anglo-Saxon Chronicle* (D) 1076 and (E) 1075, I:212; William of Malmesbury, *Gesta regum Anglorum*, I:502–03; Barlow, *Edward the Confessor*, p. 267; I. Walker, p. 184; Stafford, *Queen Emma and Queen Edith*, pp. 274–79; Cutler, 'Edith, Queen of England,' p. 231;

Thus ended the saga of the Godwin family. By the end of the eleventh century, this most famous of late Anglo-Saxon warlord families had nearly died out, a daughter of Harold's in Kiev the only persistent, procreative descendant. They had risen to power under one foreign conqueror, Knútr, and were almost completely gone sixty years later under another foreign conqueror, William the Conqueror.

Meyer, 'The Queen's 'Demesne',' p. 83, 100–101; and J.J.N. Palmer, 'The Conqueror's Footprints in Domesday Book,' in *The Medieval Military Revolution: State, Society and Military Change in Medieval and Early Modern Europe*, ed. A. Ayton and J.L. Price (London, 1995), p. 31. Among other gifts were continued aid to Wilton Abbey and benefices to Bishop Giso of Wells and Walter the Deacon.

CHAPTER FIVE

HAROLD GODWINSON

ON JANUARY 6, 1066, the warlord Harold Godwinson ascended the throne of England. He succeeded King Edward the Confessor who had died after reigning for twenty-three years over the English people. Edward had left no direct descendant as successor, but Harold was his most powerful earl and also his brother-in-law. Additionally, Harold had proven himself to be an efficient military leader, capable of protecting the kingdom against foreign incursions and domestic uprisings. Having thus established himself as the militarily legitimate heir to the throne, Harold Godwinson 'naturally' followed Edward as king. He would reign, in the words of the *Anglo-Saxon Chronicle* (A), '.xl. wucena. ⁊ ænne dæg' (forty weeks and one day).[1]

Harold began his reign by showing kindness to his people. John of Worcester writes:

> He soon, when he had undertaken the government of the realm, destroyed iniquitous laws, and set about establishing just ones; becoming patron of churches and monasteries, cultivating and venerating at the same time bishops, abbots, monks, and clerks; showing himself pious, humble and affable to all good men; detesting malefactors, for he ordered the earls, ealdormen, sheriffs, and his own officers generally to seize thieves, robbers, and disturbers of the realm, and to exert themselves by land and sea for the defence of their country.[2]

---

[1] *Anglo-Saxon Chronicle* (A) 1066, in *Two of the Saxon Chronicles Parallel*, ed. Charles Plummer and John Earle (Oxford, 1892) I:194.

[2] John of Worcester, *The Chronicle of John of Worcester*, ed. R.R. Darlington and P. McGurk, trans. J. Bray and P. McGurk (Oxford, 1995), II:600–01:

> Qui mox ut regni gubernacula susceperat, leges iniquias destruere, equas cepit condere, ecclesiarum ac monasteriorum patronus fieri, episcopos, abbates, monachos, clericos colere simul ac uenerari, pium, humilem, affabilemque se bonis omnibus exhibere, malefactores exosos habere; nam ducibus, satrapis, uicecomitibus et suis in commune precepit ministris fures, raptores, regni disturbatores comprehendere, et pro patrie defensione ipsemet terra marique desudare.

Symeon of Durham (*Historia regum*, ed. T. Arnold (London, 1885), II:179) and *Liber Eliensis* (ed. E.O. Blake (London, 1962), p. 170) use these exact same words. See also William of Malmesbury, *Gesta regum Anglorum: The History of the English Kings*, ed. R.A.B. Mynors, R.M. Thomson, and M. Winterbottom (Oxford, 1998), I:418–21; Edward August Freeman, *The History of the Norman Conquest*, 2nd edn (Oxford, 1869–70), II:49–70 and III:627–35; Frank Barlow, *The English Church, 1000–1066: A Constitutional History* (London, 1963), pp. 58–59; and Ian W. Walker, *Harold: The Last Anglo-Saxon King* (Stroud, 1997), pp. 136–43.

However Harold was not able to continue to serve the people in this way, for his reign was soon be disrupted by other warlords who felt that they had a right to the throne. As there was no direct heir for Edward's kingdom when Harold Godwinson took over, other warlords, Duke William of Normandy, King Haraldr Harðraði of Norway, and King Sveinn Estriðson of Denmark, each put forth their legitimate claims to the English inheritance. They would all threaten Harold's security as king, and his entire reign was spent in trying to prohibit their conquests of England. Thus it was said with some understatement in two of the versions of the *Anglo-Saxon Chronicle* (C and D): 'there was little stillness in the realm while he ruled the kingdom.'[3]

No record exists of Harold's birth date, but from other sources it can be estimated. Using these Henry R. Loyn surmises: 'Harold was born in the early years of the 1020's, certainly not later than 1026 and probably in 1021 or 1022'; Frank Barlow chooses only the later date.[4]

Because of the power, wealth, and position of his father, Harold received the education and upbringing of a promising young noble. Although not Godwin and Gyða's eldest son – his brother, Swegen, was born first – it was the custom of important medieval European lords to prepare all of their male offspring to take over the duties and position of the lordship should tragedy strike their elder brothers, as it did in this case. Thus it was the practice of Godwin in eleventh-century England. The anonymous author of the *Vita Ædwardi* writes about the education provided the Godwin children: 'Attention was paid specially to those arts which would prepare them to be a strength and help to future rulers.'[5] Among other things, the sons of Godwin were taught the arts of war and the skills of military leadership: strategy, tactics, and logistics. In Harold these skills were especially recognized, as noted in *The Waltham Chronicle*:

> Harold was a fine soldier, tall of stature, incredibly strong, more handsome than all the leading men in the land, and the king's right-hand man. He was

---

[3] *Anglo-Saxon Chronicle* (C) 1065, I:194: 'ꝺ her wearð Harold eac to kynge gehalgod. ꝺ he lytle stillnesse þar on gebad. þa hwile þe he rices weold.' *Anglo-Saxon Chronicle* (D) 1065, I:195 differs with the above only by adding 'eorl' after 'Harold' and by using the spelling of 'cynge' for 'kynge.' See also R. Allen Brown, *The Normans and the Norman Conquest*, 2nd edn (Woodbridge, 1985), p. 93.

[4] Henry R. Loyn, 'Harold, Son of Godwin,' in *Society and Peoples: Studies in the History of England and Wales, c. 600–1200* (London, 1992), p. 303, and *Vita Ædwardi regis qui apud Westmonasterium requiescit*, 2nd edn, ed. Frank Barlow (London, 1992), pp. 6–8 n. 10. Freeman (*Norman Conquest*, II:555) believes that Harold could not 'have been born before 1021, perhaps not till 1022 or later.' I. Walker gives no date for Harold's birth.

[5] *Vita Ædwardi*, pp. 10–11:
Nati sunt ergo filii et filie tanto non degeneres, sed paterna et materna probitate insignes, in quibus nutriendis studiosius his artibus agitur, quibus futuro regno munimen pariter et iuuamen in his paratur.
See also Brown, *The Normans and Norman Conquest*, p. 93 and Barlow, *English Church*, pp. 31, 38, 59.

endowed with wisdom, skilled in all the military arts which became a soldier, and showed himself to be in all respects a man of distinction.[6]

As a result of his education and family ties, Harold became earl of East Anglia in 1044 or 1045.[7] He now held his own very prestigious and powerful position. This made three earls in the Godwin family; besides Harold's earldom, Godwin was earl of Wessex and Swegen was earl of Herefordshire. Such an arrangement, combined with other land holdings elsewhere, gave the family a solid hold on the southern half of the kingdom. Moreover, Harold, with his charismatic and conciliatory character, was poised to gain even more power in the English court. This became especially evident after the disappointing behavior of Swegen caused his first outlawry in 1046 (the abduction of the abbess of Leominster). With this action, Harold became not only the most powerful young earl in the kingdom, but he also became the immediate successor to the Godwin family wealth and political strength.

The first reference to Harold in the *Anglo-Saxon Chronicle* is from the year 1049. This was the year that Swegen returned to England to beg for the reinstatement of his lands and title from King Edward. As he had received a portion of Swegen's earldom and added power because of his brother's banishment, Harold was understandably interested in the outcome of this request for reinstatement and, at the same time, probably afraid of losing all that he had gained if Swegen was successful. He also must have recognized that there could be trouble between his brother and himself due to his quick profiting from Swegen's exile and forfeiture.

Thus it is obvious that Harold would oppose Swegen's reinstatement as earl; however, what resulted from Harold's opposition to his brother's return cannot be determined. Swegen's immediate target, as was seen in the previous chapter,

---

6   *The Waltham Chronicle: An Account of the Discovery of Our Holy Cross at Montacute and Its Conveyance to Waltham*, ed. and trans. L. Watkiss and M. Chibnall (Oxford, 1994), pp. 26–27:

> qui armis strenuus, procero corpore et inestimabili strenuitate, forma etiam pulchriudinis precellens cunctis primatibus terre, regis manus dextera, et sapientia preditus, et artium omnium que decent militem gnarus, se uirum agebat preclarum per omnia.

(The translators of this chronicle translated *militem gnarus* as 'knight'; I have chosen to translate it simply as 'soldier'.) As this chronicle was written more than a century after Harold's death and in a political climate not known for its support of the last Anglo-Saxon king, I find this passage to be quite remarkable.

7   Harold's holdings included East Anglia, Essex, Cambridgeshire, and Huntingdonshire. See Freeman, *Norman Conquest*, II:79; I. Walker, pp. 18–21; Loyn, 'Harold, Son of Godwin,' p. 303; Frank M. Stenton, *Anglo-Saxon England*, 3rd edn (London, 1971), p. 561; Pauline Stafford, *Unification and Conquest: A Political and Social History of England in the Tenth and Eleventh Centuries* (London, 1989), p. 93; Frank Barlow, *Edward the Confessor* (Berkeley and Los Angeles, 1970), p. 74; David C. Douglas, *William the Conqueror* (Berkeley and Los Angeles, 1964), p. 166; and Tryggvi J. Oleson, *The Witenagemot in the Reign of Edward the Confessor: A Study in the Constitutional History of Eleventh-Century England* (Toronto, 1955), p. 94. As it is not mentioned in the *Anglo-Saxon Chronicle*, Oleson wonders about the little fanfare given to this appointment.

was not his brother, but his cousin, Beorn. Harold had a close relationship to Beorn: after Beorn was killed by Swegen, the *Anglo-Saxon Chronicle* (C) has the future king travel to Dartmouth, dig up his cousin's body which had been 'deeply buried' by Swegen, and transport it to Winchester where it could be interred next to Knútr, Beorn's uncle.[8] Yet despite this kinship with his cousin, it seems apparent from later friendliness between the two estranged brothers, especially during the 1051 crisis – Harold escaped to Ireland on a ship anchored at Bristol which had been outfitted for Swegen's escape[9] – that whatever enmity had once existed between Harold and Swegen was settled and settled quickly, no doubt through the intercession of their father, Godwin.[10] What future problems that the two might have had were eliminated when Swegen died the following year on his pilgrimage.

Any setbacks which had resulted from Swegen's return were temporary, as Harold continued his growth in political strength and power as earl to Edward the Confessor. Early in their relationship, Edward seems to have been especially enamored by the young earl. A later Scandinavian author concerned with this period in English history, Snorri Sturluson, puts it best when he recounts that Edward loved Harold 'as if he were his own son,'[11] while the *Anglo-Saxon Chronicle* (C) reports that this Godwinson returned the king's affection with like affection, describing Harold as: 'the noble earl who in every instance faithfully obeyed his lord in words and deeds, with nothing neglected that the king was in need of.'[12] Perhaps Harold was the son that the queen had not been able to provide Edward; if nothing else, he certainly seems to have been a close friend, if not an extremely loyal ally to the king.

Yet, as much love as Edward might have had for Harold, with the rising influence of the Normans at the royal court coupled with the declining influence of Harold's father, Godwin, before and after refusing to ravage Dover, the young earl perhaps was forced to make a difficult choice: should he support the king or his family? If so, in this instance, kinship proved stronger than loyalty to the king. Later, in 1065, when forced to make the same decision between his brother, Tostig, and the king, Harold came to a different conclusion. But in 1051 Harold did not hesitate; he also raised an army from his province to defend his father's position. Godwin, Swegen, and Harold marched towards the king only to encounter the armies of Earls Leofric and Siward. As discussed, both armies were disbanded without bloodshed.[13]

---

8   *Anglo-Saxon Chronicle* (C) 1049, I:168. For other sources on this murder see n. 124 in the preceding chapter.
9   *Anglo-Saxon Chronicle* (D) 1052, I:175–76.
10 *Anglo-Saxon Chronicle* (C) 1049 and (E) 1046, I:168.
11 Snorri Sturluson, *Heimskringla*, ed. B. Aðalbjarnarson (Reykjavik, 1941–51), III:168. See also the *Waltham Chronicle*, pp. 26–27 and Wace, *Le Roman de Rou*, ed. A.J. Holden (Paris, 1971), II:94.
12 *Anglo-Saxon Chronicle* (C) 1065, I:194: 'æþelum eorle se in ealle tid/ hyrde holdlice hærran sinum/ wordum ⁊ dædum wihte ne agælde/ þæs þe þearf wæs þæs þeod kyninges.'
13 For references to Harold's role in this incident see n. 69 in the preceding chapter.

Peace lasted only a few days, however, and Harold was forced to flee to Ireland in the company of his brother, Leofwine. Yet, unlike Godwin and the rest of the family, Edward did try to make a effort to catch these fleeing Godwinsons, by ordering Bishop Ealdred of London to follow Harold and Leofwine, but the bishop failed. The *Anglo-Saxon Chronicle* (D) reports: 'The king sent Ealdred, bishop of London, with an army to intercept them before they could reach their ship, but they could not or would not.'[14] Why they 'could not or would not' is not explained: perhaps there was little desire in the English soldiers to pursue their leaders, especially, if we are to believe the *Vita Ædwardi*, since this command came not from the king but from his Norman archbishop of Canterbury.[15] Harold and Leofwine escaped by ship to Ireland, which they reached safely, despite sailing through rough weather. In Ireland, King Diarmait mac Máel na mBó, king of Leinster and Ui Chennselaig, granted them asylum and protection.[16]

Less than a year later, in 1052, Harold and Leofwine returned to England, anticipating the joining of their forces with those of their father. Whereas Godwin did not plunder much on return, Harold and Leofwine lacked this reserve and allowed their forces to pillage heavily throughout Devonshire and Somersetshire before joining their father's army on the Isle of Wight. The *Anglo-Saxon Chronicle* (C) reports this plundering and the deaths caused by it:

> There came Earl Harold with a fleet from Ireland to the mouth of the Severn River, near the boundary of Somerset and Devonshire, and there they did much harm. And the inhabitants of both Somerset and Devonshire gathered against him, and [at Porlock] he put them to flight, killing more than thirty good thegns as well as other people. Soon thereafter, they went around Land's End . . . to Wight[17]

Certainly this was not the way that Godwin planned to operate his military cam-

---

[14] *Anglo-Saxon Chronicle* (D) 1051, I:176: '⁊ se cining sende Ealdred b of Lundene mid genge; ⁊ sceoldon hine of ridan ær he to scipe come. ac hi ne mihton. oððe hi noldon.
[15] *Vita Ædwardi*, p. 37. See p. 37 n. 82 for Barlow's suggestion that this, while able to be read as if these soldiers were to follow Godwin, could only have been referring to the chase by Bishop Ealdred of Harold and Leofwine.
[16] See *Vita Ædwardi*, pp. 40–41. He is called only King Dermodo in this text. This is the same king who would host Harold's sons after the defeat at Hastings. For the rough weather struggled against by Harold and Leofwine, see the *Anglo-Saxon Chronicle* (D) 1051, I:176.
[17] *Anglo-Saxon Chronicle* (C) 1052, I:178:
> Her com Harold eorl of Irlande mid scipum on Sæfern murðan. neh Sumersætan gemæran and Defenescire. ⁊ þær mycel gehergode. ⁊ þ landfolc him ongean gaderodan ægðer ge of Sumersæton ge of Defenescire. ⁊ he hig aflymde. ⁊ þær ofsloh ma þonne xxx godera ðegna buton oðran folce, ⁊ sona æfter þan for abutan Penwiðsteort . . . to Wiht.
See also John of Worcester (II:566–69) and Symeon of Durham (*Historia regum*, II:164–70) who alter nothing about the pillaging but do indicate a greater difference in time between when it occurred and when Harold and Leofwine joined forces with their father. See also Freeman, *Norman Conquest*, II:314–17, 623–25; Barlow, *Edward the Confessor*, pp. 121–22; and I. Walker, pp. 414–15.

paign, and it undoubtedly cost the family some favor among the locals in that region. Even Harold's cheerleader, Edward August Freeman, recognizes it as such:

> On such a character as his it is distinctly a stain to have resorted for one moment to needless violence, or to have shed one drop of English blood without good cause. The ravage and slaughter at Porlock distinctly throws a shade over the return of Godwine and over the fair fame of his son. It is a stain rather to be regretted than harshly to be condemned; but it is a stain nevertheless.[18]

On the other hand, this incident may have taught Harold a lesson. From this time on, he seems to have been very reluctant to cause any amount of bloodshed, being willing instead to pursue whatever diplomatic means of stopping violence he could until forced to resort to fighting. Such was the case when Harold dealt with the Welsh king, Gruffydd ap Llywelyn, on numerous occasions, and also in 1965 when he was drawn into the position of mediator between the Northumbrian rebels and his brother, Tostig. It was not the case, however, in 1066 when, as newly crowned king, he faced Tostig and Haraldr Harðraði at Stamford Bridge and William the Conqueror at Hastings.

In the end, this was the only blood spilled in 1052. After Harold and Leofwine joined their father, the two deposed earls gathered men from Wessex and journeyed to Winchester to meet with the king. Edward, faced with this sizable force, no longer under the influence of the Normans, and not wanting to cause further dismay, surrendered to his opponents. He returned Godwin's and Harold's titles to them as well as the rest of the family's possessions. Harold Godwinson was reinstated as earl of East Anglia.[19]

A year later Godwin died in the presence of the king and Harold. His powerful and important earldom of Wessex was in turn granted to his then eldest son. The *Anglo-Saxon Chronicle* (E) for the year 1053 makes a simple entry: 'In this year Earl Godwin died on April 15 . . . and Earl Harold, his son, succeeded to the earldom and to all that his father had possessed.'[20] With this appointment Harold had inherited his father's role as the most powerful earl in England.

---

[18] Freeman, *Norman Conquest*, II:317. Freeman rather bombastically does conclude, however, that Harold would make up for this by his later actions:
> It is a stain which was fully wiped out by later labours and triumphs in the cause of England. Still we may well believe that the blood of those thirty good Thegns and of those other folk was paid for in after years by prayers and watchings and fastings before the Holy Rood of Waltham; we may well believe that it still lay heavy on the hero's soul as he marched forth to victory at Stamfordbridge and to more glorious overthrow at Senlac.

[19] For references to the return of the Godwin family and Harold's role in it see nn. 102–05 in the preceding chapter.

[20] *Anglo-Saxon Chronicle* (E) 1053, I:183–185: 'Her on þisum geare forðferde Godwine eorl on xvii k Mai . . . ˥ feng Harold eorl his sunu to ðam eorldome ˥ to eallum þam þe his fæder ahte.' See also John of Worcester, II:572–73; Henry of Huntingdon, pp. 378–79; and Freeman, *Norman Conquest*, II:354–55.

After his ascension to the earldom of Wessex, which placed him constantly at the royal court, Harold began to further strengthen his power and to educate himself on the ruling of the English kingdom. Frank Barlow's contentions that with Godwin's death, 'Edward found himself not only free from long-standing restraints but also able to work with new and younger men' and that 'much of the frustration and tension had disappeared from the government'[21] initially may be correct, but within only a very short time, all of Godwin's power seems to have been appropriated by Harold. As Frank Stenton writes: 'The rise of Earl Harold to supremacy among the [great nobles] is the most important fact in the political history of England between 1053 and 1066.'[22] In particular during this period, Harold's influence with Edward personally increased; as a result of this influence, he gained much wealth and power. He was also able to secure earldoms for his brothers, for Tostig in 1055, and then for Gyrð and Leofwine between 1055 and 1057.[23] The sons of Godwin now held the island kingdom in their power.

Harold Godwinson also had accepted his father's military leadership responsibilities. Despite the later, Norman idea that he willingly accepted Duke William of Normandy's claim to the throne, Harold must have known that the barren royal family meant that, should he perform his military functions well, he could be acknowledged as the next king. As Frank Stenton has written:

> Harold's chance of obtaining the crown turned on the question of whether Englishmen would allow their respect for royal descent to outweigh the advantage of possessing a king who could defend the land.[24]

Yet, before 1055, Harold had few opportunities to gain military legitimacy and thereby prove to Edward and the people of England that he was fit to rule after the king's death. Indeed, when he previously led an army into a military situation, it had either backed down without entering into conflict, as had happened in facing the king at Gloucester and London in 1051, or, when it had fought, had seemingly caused unnecessary bloodshed, as had occurred at Porlock in 1052.

A new opportunity for Harold to display his leadership and skills in war came in fighting the Welsh between 1055 and 1063. The king in Wales whom Harold fought was Gruffydd ap Llywelyn. Although Welsh rulers seem to have always created problems for their Anglo-Saxon counterparts,[25] none provoked more

---

[21] Barlow, *English Church*, p. 51.

[22] Stenton, *Anglo-Saxon England*, p. 572. Recognizing Harold's growth in power during this period are Freeman, *Norman Conquest*, II:423–24; Stafford, *Unification and Conquest*, pp. 93–94; Brown, *The Normans and Norman Conquest*, pp. 67, 70–71, 109; I. Walker, pp. 74–75; and Oleson, *Witenagemot*, pp. 3–4.

[23] On Tostig's earldom see the *Anglo-Saxon Chronicle* (E) 1055, I:185–86. On the earldoms for Gyrð and Leofwine see n. 139 in the preceding chapter. See also Douglas, *William the Conqueror*, p. 172.

[24] Stenton, *Anglo-Saxon England*, p. 577. See also Freeman (*Norman Conquest*, II:420–21, 428–230) and Oleson (*Witenagemot*, pp. 3–4), who resolutely believes that Harold desired the throne as early as 1052; Freeman also concludes that he was the most likely heir.

[25] See Freeman, *Norman Conquest*, II:56; Stenton, *Anglo-Saxon England*, pp. 212–15, 340–42; Wendy Davies, *Wales in the Early Middle Ages* (Leicester, 1982), 102–16; Robin

conflict between these two neighboring areas than did Gruffydd ap Llywelyn. From the very beginning of his reign as king of Gwynedd in 1039, Gruffydd seemed to be determined to acquire power and lands by whatever bellicose and diplomatic means were possible, both elsewhere in Wales and across the march in England. (Upon Gruffydd's ascension to the throne, northern Wales was attacked by an army of Mercians, an attack which was turned back at a heavy cost to the Mercians, including Eadwine, the brother of the Mercian earl, Leofric. Such a futile incursion, meant probably as a test or a lesson for the new king, could very well have set his demeanor or perhaps given him the confidence to wage war continually throughout his life.[26]) He was in this sense every bit the warlord that Godwin, Harold Godwinson, Haraldr Harðraði, William the Conqueror, and others were in the eleventh century, and like so many of those other warlords, he would meet his end violently, and in direct relation to another warlord, in this case Harold Godwinson.

Contemporary English authors depict Gruffydd ap Llywelyn as little more than a thug, a border irritant who, according to the *Vita Ædwardi* constantly 'carried wrongful war across the Severn [River]' into England,[27] raids which brought such destructive turmoil that finally his actions could no longer be tolerated, and he was attacked by the full force of English military might, leading inevitably to his and his people's destruction. To contemporary Welsh authors, however he was the *rex Britanniae et totius Gualiae de fine ad finem* (the king of all Britain and Wales from end to end)[28] and the 'persecutor of the English and "gentiles".'[29] Today, Gruffydd ap Llywelyn is often portrayed as 'immensely energetic' . . . 'the most dramatically successful ruler of Wales'

Fleming, *Kings and Lords in Conquest England* (Cambridge, 1991), pp. 99–100; K.L. Maund, *Ireland, Wales, and England in the Eleventh Century* (Woodbridge, 1991), pp. 120–123, 141. Most of these actions were quick raids across the marches for cattle and other booty.

26 *Anglo-Saxon Chronicle* (C) 1039, I:160; John of Worcester, II:528–29; *Annales Cambriae*, ed. J. Williams ab Ithel (London, 1860), pp. 23–24; Stenton, *Anglo-Saxon England*, p. 572; Barlow, *Edward the Confessor*, p. 204; J.E. Lloyd, *A History of Wales*, 3rd edn (London, 1939), II:357–71; Maund, *Ireland, Wales, and England*, pp. 127–28; K.L. Maund, 'The Welsh Alliances of Earl Ælfgar of Mercia and his Family in the Mid-Eleventh Century,' *Anglo-Norman Studies* 9 (1988), 182–83; and Frederick C. Suppe, 'Who was Rhys Sais? Some Comments on Anglo-Welsh Relations before 1066,' *Haskins Society Journal* 7 (1995), 63.

27 *Vita Ædwardi*, pp. 86–87. See also the *Anglo-Saxon Chronicle* (C) 1055, (D) 1055, 1058, 1063, and (E) 1055, 1063, I:184–88, 190–91 and John of Worcester, II:576–79, 592–93. On these views see Benjiman T. Hudson, 'The Destruction of Gruffudd ap Llywelyn,' *Welsh Historical Review* 19 (1991), 331.

28 This appears in the *Book of Llandaff*, printed in *Council and Ecclesiastical Documents Relating to Great Britain and Ireland*, ed. A.W. Haddan and W. Stubbs (Oxford, 1869), I:294. See also Hudson, 'The Destruction of Gruffudd ap Llywelyn,' p. 331.

29 *Annales Cambriae*, p. 23: '1039 . . . Griffinus filius Lewelin in Nortwallia regnare inchoavit; qui dum regnavit Anglos et gentiles persecutus est.' On these views see Hudson, 'The Destruction of Gruffudd ap Llywelyn,' p. 331.

(Wendy Davies),[30] a 'dominating figure' (R.R. Davies),[31] a 'formidable enemy' (Edward Freeman),[32] and a 'national figure' (David Walker).[33] At the same time, he was the archetypical Welsh military leader who recognized that he had to lead his soldiers to fight with and against England to gain prestige, lands, and wealth. 'They were swift to shed blood,' writes Frank Barlow.[34] He also found that he could profit immensely from the discord among the English political leadership.

As early as the twelfth century, Gruffydd's characteristics and actions had become legendary; Walter Map even devotes a large section of his *De nugis curialium* to discuss his exploits. Map relates a story of a 'lazy and sluggish' young boy who, chastened by his sister for not carrying on the traditions of Welsh young men on New Year's Eve, that 'all young men should go out to raid and steal,' was 'awakened by this, as if his soul were roused form a heavy sleep,' to become one of the greatest but at the same time one of the most tyrannical of Welsh warrior monarchs.[35] In this Map compares Gruffydd with Alexander the Great and 'all others in whom covetous lust destroys self-control, liberal, vigilant, quick, bold, courteous, affable, extravagant, pertinacious, untrustworthy, cruel.'[36] Without confidence in his wife's or his people's loyalty and extremely protective of his position, he thought little of 'murdering or maiming' anyone, including family members, who might contend with him for affection or power in Wales. In excusing this, Map has Gruffydd respond: 'I kill no one; I only blunt the horns of Wales lest they wound their mother.'[37]

In his dealings with England, Map contends, Gruffydd ap Llywelyn was 'obnoxious and oppressive'. The Welsh to fight, and if they could not fight with each other, or if they were unified under one leader, as with Gruffydd, they would fight with their neighbors, the English. Map continues:

> The glory of the Welsh is in plunder and theft, and they are so fond of both that it is a reproach to a son that his father should have died without a wound.

---

30 W. Davies, pp. 103, 112.

31 R.R. Davies, *Conquest, Coexistence, and Change: Wales, 1063–1415* (Oxford, 1987), p. 24.

32 Freeman, *Norman Conquest*, II:55–56.

33 David Walker, 'A Note on Gruffydd ap Llywelyn (1039–63),' *Welsh Historical Review* 1 (1960–63), 83. See also Maund, *Ireland, Wales, and England*, pp. 126–27.

34 Barlow, *Edward the Confessor*, p. 204. See also K.L. Maund, 'The Welsh Alliances of Earl Ælfgar of Mercia,' pp. 182–83.

35 Walter Map, *De nugis curialium*, ed. and trans. M.R. James, revised edn C.N.L. Brooke and R.A.B. Mynors (Oxford, 1983), pp. 186–95. The quotes are on pp. 188–91. On Map's commentary on Gruffydd ap Llywelyn see Barlow, *Edward the Confessor*, pp. 204, 207–8 and Hudson, 'The Destruction of Gruffudd ap Llywelyn,' pp. 331–32.

36 Map, pp. 190–91:
   Similis enim erat Alexandri Macedonis, et omnium quos auara cupiditas fecit effrenos, largus, peruigil, inpiger, audax, facetus, affabilis, dapsilis, improbus, perfidus et crudelis.

37 Map, pp. 190–91: 'Neminem occido, sed obtundo cornua Wallie, ne possint ledere matrem.'

For which reason few grow grey. There is a proverb there, 'Dead youth or poor old man,' meaning that everyone should brave death early rather than beg when he is old.[38]

Yet, on one occasion, during a peace conference with Edward the Confessor present, Gruffydd was so impressed with the king that instead of contending against him, he embraced the saintly man, saying:

Wisest of kings, your modesty has vanquished my pride, your wisdom has triumphed over my foolishness. The neck which I foolishly stiffened against you shall mount and so enter the territory which your mildness has to-day made your own.[39]

Even then, Map acknowledges, the peace between England and Wales 'was only kept till they felt able to do mischief.'[40]

In so describing this adversary of Harold Godwinson, Walter Map seems to have difficulty deciding whether to despise Gruffydd or to praise him. Although there is little to be discovered in more contemporary sources about his life outside of his conflict with England, what can be learned about this Welsh king makes him neither more despicable nor more praiseworthy than Map would have it. He was merely someone with whom Harold had to contend and by whom Harold eventually proved his military leadership and legitimacy to rule.

Like most of his predecessors, Gruffydd ap Llywelyn had a desire to plunder the marches of England. During his reign, he had many opportunities to do so; and, it seems, he allowed none of these opportunities to go by without taking an army into England. His most frequent target was Herefordshire. This was undoubtedly the reason why Edward appointed Swegen Godwinson as earl of Herefordshire in c.1043, hoping that this warlord would put an end to Gruffydd's raids. As mentioned, Swegen chose to negotiate a pact with the Welsh king which led to peace in Herefordshire and a joint Gwynedd–English attack on Gruffydd's southern Welsh enemy.

Keeping the Welsh kings fighting among themselves was a successful policy for Swegen, and as long as he held the earldom, it was in peace.[41] Unsuccessful against Gruffydd were the Normans who replaced Swegen during his and then the family's exile. Most importantly, and despite the construction of several

---

[38] Map, pp. 196–97:
In rapina et furto gloria Walensium, et adeo eis utrumque placet, ut improperium sit filio si pater sine uulnere decesserit. Vnde fit ut pauci canescant. Prouerbium ibi est 'Iuuenis mortuus aut senex pauper', scilicet ut cito quisque in mortem irruat, ne senex mendicet.

[39] Map, pp. 194–95:
Sapientissime rex, tua humilitas meam uicit superbiam, et sapiencia triumphauit inepciam; collum quod contra te fatuus erexi ascendes, et sic intrabis terram quam tibi hodie tuam fecit benignitas.

[40] Map, pp. 194–95: 'Hoc inicium pacis egregium, sed more Walensium obseruatum est usque ad potestatem nocendi.'

[41] See n. 118 in the preceding chapter.

castles along the border marches, they were unable to stop Gruffydd's raids in 1052, a lack of success which, as explained in the preceeding chapter, aided the return of the Godwin family later that year.[42] For the next three years, the border was relatively quiet. (In 1053, according to the *Anglo-Saxon Chronicle* and John of Worcester, Edward the Confessor had Rhys, the brother of the king of Deheubarth, Gruffydd ap Rhydderch, assassinated and his head brought to him. In retaliation, some Welsh soldiers crossed the border and killed a few Englishmen at Westbury.[43] This was, however, a minor incident and completely unrelated to King Gruffydd ap Llywelyn of Gwynedd.)

In 1055, Harold, as earl of Wessex and chief earl of England, had his first opportunity to face Gruffydd ap Llywelyn and his Welsh raiders. In that year Ælfgar, earl of East Anglia, was found guilty of treason before the witenagemot, outlawed, and exiled from the kingdom. What his specific crime was cannot be determined from the contemporary sources, although almost all have a definite opinion as to whether he was guilty of the offense. Even the different versions of the *Anglo-Saxon Chronicle*, usually fairly uniform in their recording of events, have contrasting opinions as to the guilt of this earl. The *Anglo-Saxon Chronicle* (E) claims that Ælfgar confessed to all gathered at the tribunal that he was 'a traitor to the king and the whole nation,' although the anonymous author adds that this confession 'escaped him unawares.'[44] The *Anglo-Saxon Chronicle* (C) insists that he was innocent of the charge, 'without any guilt.'[45] And the *Anglo-Saxon Chronicle* (D) stands right in the middle, maintaining that he was '*almost not guilty*' (italics mine).[46] Most modern historians (Brown, Douglas, Oleson, Maund, and Green) maintain that Ælfgar's sentence of outlawry was connected

---

[42] See n. 97 in the preceding chapter.

[43] *Anglo-Saxon Chronicle* (C and D) 1053, I:182–85; John of Worcester, II:572–73; and Symeon of Durham, *Historia regum*, II:170. According to the *Anglo-Saxon Chronicle* (D), Rhys was put to death 'forðy he hearmes dyde' (on account of the crimes which he had committed), but these crimes are not defined. They do not seem to have been related to the raids of the previous year, as these were carried out by Gruffydd ap Llywelyn and not Gruffydd or Rhys ap Rhydderch. See also Freeman, *Norman Conquest*, II:347–48; Barlow, *Edward the Confessor*, p. 126; and Maund, *Ireland, Wales, and England*, p. 124. Freeman contends that Rhys was guilty of many raids into England.

[44] *Anglo-Saxon Chronicle* (E) 1055, I:185–86:

⁊ útlagode mann Ælfgar eorl. forðon him man wearp ón. þ he wæs þes cynges swica. ⁊ ealra landleoda. ⁊ he þæs geanwyrde wes ætforan eallum þam mannum þe þær gegaderode wæron. þeah him þ word ofscute his unnþances.

See also Henry of Huntingdon, pp. 380–81, who claims that Ælfgar was convicted of treason, and I. Walker, p. 77.

[45] *Anglo-Saxon Chronicle* (C) 1055, I:184: 'Ða ðæræfter binnan lyttlan fyrste wæs witenagemót on Lundene. ⁊ man geutlagode þa Ælfgar eorl. Leofrices sunu eorles butan ælcan gylte.' See also John of Worcester (II:576–77) and Symeon of Durham (*Historia regum*, II:171) who likewise agree that Ælfgar was entirely 'sine culpa.' R. Allen Brown (*The Normans and the Norman Conquest*, p. 71) agrees with this assessment.

[46] *Anglo-Saxon Chronicle* (D) 1055, I:185: '⁊ þæræfter sona man utlagode Ælfgar eorl Leofrices sunu eorles. forneh butan gylte.' Modern commentators who give no opinion of Ælfgar's guilt include: Stenton, *Anglo-Saxon England*, pp. 572–73; Stafford, *Unification and*

with the power of the Godwin family, especially Harold Godwinson, the power-ful chief earl of the kingdom: either Harold was directly responsible for the innocent earl's conviction, or, if Ælfgar was guilty of treason, he had committed this crime because he was 'increasingly isolated, surrounded, and threatened' by the Godwin family and their desired acquisition of more and greater power.[47] Yet, with only Harold in control of an earldom in 1055, such a fear would seem to have been rather prophetic on the part of the outlawed earl of Mercia.[48] Frank Barlow, to put forth an alternative theory, speculates that the relatively new, but highly ambitious earl (Ælfgar had received East Anglia in 1053 when Harold transferred to Wessex at the death of his father, Godwin[49]) might have had designs on the Northumbrian earldom of his father, Leofric, who was quite old at the time, and that in doing so he had 'perhaps intrigued both locally and nationally to achieve his aim.'[50] Still, there really is no evidence to support this or any other speculation on Ælfgar's crime and conviction.

Whatever the crime was, Ælfgar fled from England first to Ireland, where he picked up a fleet of eighteen 'pirate' ships,[51] and then to Wales. Perhaps appeal-ing to an old alliance or perhaps simply out of desperation, Ælfgar asked for Gruffydd ap Llywelyn's assistance in regaining his earldom.[52] With a small

Conquest, p. 87; Oleson, *Witenagemot*, p. 29; and D. Walker, p. 90. Oleson also points out that Ælfgar was outlawed by the witenagemot.

[47] The quote comes from Brown, *The Normans and Norman Conquest*, p. 71. See also Douglas, *William the Conqueror*, p. 172; Oleson, *Witenagemot*, p. 108; Oleson, 'Edward the Confessor's Promise of the Throne to Duke William of Normandy,' *English Historical Review* 72 (1957), 225; Maund, *Ireland, Wales, and England*, pp. 133–35; Maund, 'The Welsh Alli-ances of Earl Ælfgar,' pp. 181–82; and J.R. Green, *The Conquest of England*, 3rd edn (London, 1899), II:291–93.

[48] See Barlow, *Edward the Confessor*, p. 206 and I. Walker, p. 77.

[49] *Anglo-Saxon Chronicle* (C, D, and E) 1053, I:182–85; John of Worcester, II:572–73; and Henry of Huntingdon, pp. 378–39.

[50] Barlow, *Edward the Confessor*, p. 193. See also I. Walker (pp. 76–77) who agrees com-pletely with this theory.

[51] On the acquisition of the pirate fleet see the *Anglo-Saxon Chronicle* (C, D, and E) 1055, I:184–85, 187; John of Worcester, II:576–77; Symeon of Durham, *Historia regum*, II:171; Stenton, *Anglo-Saxon Chronicle*, p. 573; Barlow, *Edward the Confessor*, p. 206; and I. Walker, p. 78. In the original sources no reason is given for the employment of this fleet by Ælfgar, although I. Walker speculates that this might have come from a previous alliance between the earl of Mercia and these pirates. There was undoubtedly some connection between the Ælfgar and this force, as it seems to have been acquired quite easily; perhaps it was even prepared for Ælfgar's use. Could this fleet have been the basis of his treason charge?

[52] See the *Anglo-Saxon Chronicle* (C, D, and E) 1055, I:184–85, 187; John of Worcester, II:576–77; Symeon of Durham, *Historia regum*, II:171; Stenton, *Anglo-Saxon Chronicle*, p. 573; Barlow, *Edward the Confessor*, p. 206; Douglas, *William the Conqueror*, p. 172; I. Walker, p. 78; Lloyd, II:364; Maund, *Ireland, Wales, and England*, pp. 129–30; Maund, 'The Welsh Alliances of Earl Ælfgar,' pp. 182–86; D. Walker, p. 90; Hudson, 'The Destruction of Gruffudd ap Llywelyn,' p. 332; and Suppe, pp. 63–73. Lloyd, Stenton, Barlow, and Douglas maintain that this was an alliance made out of expediency only in 1055. Suppe agrees with Lloyd *et al.*, but sees the character of Rhys Sais as the intermediary between the two leaders. Against this, I. Walker and Maund contend that the connection between Ælfgar and Gruffydd

force, Gruffydd and Ælfgar entered Herefordshire, attacking and pillaging several towns and villages. In response, Earl Ralph of Mantes gathered a defensive army from the local inhabitants and 'rode out' of Hereford to meet the Welsh raiders approaching his earldom's chief town. The emphasis here should be on the cavalry, for both John of Worcester and Symeon of Durham insist that Ralph 'ordered the English, *contra morem* (contrary to tradition), to fight on horseback' next to the few French and Normans who remained with their Norman-born earl. It was a tactic which these authors contend led not to an English victory, but to the flight of those on horseback. The English infantry followed suit, losing many in the flight, and Gruffydd and Ælfgar had the victory. The Welsh then entered and looted the episcopal capital, Hereford, burning to the ground the cathedral which had been built by Æðelstan.[53]

Upon hearing of the devastation and Ralph's defeat, Edward sent his military leader, Harold, to the Welsh marches to stop these incursions. Harold did; but instead of attacking and destroying the Welsh army, who had fled from him, in a move similar to the one made earlier by his brother Swegen, Harold chose to make peace with them instead. John of Worcester details this event:

> When the king [Edward] was informed of this [the attacks on Herefordshire], he ordered an army to be mustered directly from the whole of England. It assembled in Gloucester, and the king put the vigorous Earl Harold in charge of it. Zealously obeying his orders, Harold energetically pursued Gruffydd and Ælfgar, and boldly invaded the Welsh borders. He encamped beyond Straddle, but they, because they knew him to be a strong and warlike man, not daring to

---

was the result of an older, pre-1055 alliance. The latter theory is perhaps the most logical and has the precedent of the earlier Swegen/Gruffydd alliance. On Ælfgar's exile, East Anglia was divided up, with part being given to Harold Godwinson and part to his brother, Gyrð.

53 John of Worcester, II:576–79:

> Ille [Griffinus] statim de toto regno suo copiosum exercitum congregans, Algaro precepit ut loco constituo sibi et exercitui cum suis copiis occurreret, quibus in unum conuenientibs fines Anglorum depopulaturi, Herefordensem prouiciam intrauerunt. Contra quos timidus dux Rauulfus, regis Eaduuardi sororis filius, exercitum congregans, et duobus miliariis a ciuitate Hereforda .ix. kalend. Nouembris [24 October] illis occurrens, Anglos contra morem in equis pugnare iussit, sed cum prelium essent commissuri comes cum suis Francis et Normannis fugam primitus capessit. Quod uidentes Angli, ducem suum fugiendo secuntur, quos aduersarii fere omnes insecuti .cccc. uel quingentos uiros ex eis peremerunt, multos uulnerauerunt.

Symeon of Durham (*Historia regum*, II:171–72) writes almost the same words, obviously using John of Worcester as the source for this story. See also *Anglo-Saxon Chronicle* (C, D, and E) 1055, I:184–87, with (C) the only version to record the use of cavalry by the English, and attributing the loss to this tactic; Henry of Huntingdon, pp. 380–81; *Annales Cambriae*, p. 25; *Brenhinedd y Saesson, or The Kings of the Saxons: BM Cotton MS. Cleopatra B.v and The Black Book of Basingwerk, NLW MS.7006*, ed. and trans. T. Jones (Cardiff, 1971), s.a. 1054; *Brut y Tywysogyon, Peniarth MS. 20*, ed. T. Jones (Cardiff, 1941), s.a. 1054; *Brut y Tywysogyon, or the Chronicle of the Princes: Red Book of Hergest Version*, ed. and trans. T. Jones, 2nd edn (Cardiff, 1973), s.a. 1056; Stenton, *Anglo-Saxon England*, p. 573; Barlow, *Edward the Confessor*, p. 206; I. Walker, pp. 78–79; Maund, *Ireland, Wales, and England*, pp. 124, 130–31; R. Davies, pp. 25–26; and D. Walker, pp. 90–91.

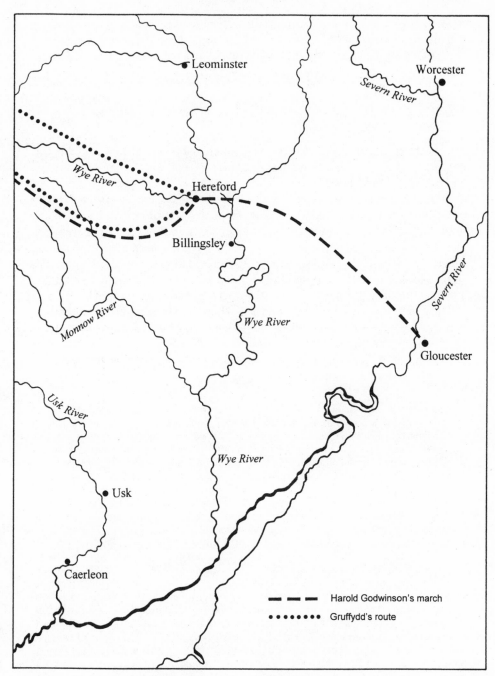

Gruffydd's raid on Hereford, 1055

embark on war with him, fled into South Wales. When this was known, he [Harold] dismissed the greater part of his army there, ordering the men to resist the enemy vigorously, if occasion should demand. On returning to Hereford with the rest of the host, he encircled it with a broad and deep ditch, and fortified it with gates and bars. Meanwhile, envoys were exchanged, and Gruffydd, Ælfgar, and Harold and those who were with him met at a place called Billingsley, and when peace had been given and received, they established a firm friendship among them.[54]

For his efforts at peace, and perhaps recognizing the potential danger of this earl aligned with Gruffydd, Edward restored Ælfgar's earldom to him 'and all that had been previously taken from him.'[55]

Harold's concern that his dismissed soldiers 'resist the enemy vigorously, if occasion should demand' and his efforts to encircle Hereford 'with a broad and deep ditch' and fortify 'it with gates and bars' must indicate the earl's suspicion that the Welsh might not keep the peace. In this the future king was correct; peace did not last. Only a few months after contracting the initial 'firm friendship,' and this time without his East Anglian ally, Gruffydd again rose up and attacked England, and again Harold was forced to put down the attack.

On this occasion, Gruffydd's raid was shorter than previous ones, both in time and distance away from Wales, but was no less bloody. Perhaps the citizens of Hereford and the surrounding shire should have remained behind their newly-built fortifications; instead, true to Harold's admonition to 'resist the

---

54 John of Worcester, II:578–79:

> Quod ubi regi innotuit, de tota mox Anglia exercitum congregari iussit, cui Glauuorne congregato strenuum ducem Haroldum prefecit, qui deuote iussis obtemperans, Griffinum et Algarum impigre insequitur ac fines Walanorum audacter ingressus, ultra Straddele castra metatus est, sed illi, quia uirum fortem et bellicosum ipsum sciebant, cum eo committere bellum non audentes, in Suthuualiam fugerunt. Quo comperto, maiorem exercitus partem ibi dimisit, mandans eis ut suis aduersariis, si res exposceret, uiriliter resisterent. Cum cetera uero multitudine Herefordam rediens, uallo lato et alto illam cincxit, portis et seris muniuit. Interea legatis intercurrentibus, Griffinus, Algarus et Haroldus et qui cum illis fuerant in loco, qui Bilgesleagea dicitur conuenerunt, et pace data et accepta, firmam amicitiam inter se pacti sunt.

See also *Anglo-Saxon Chronicle* (C, D, and E) 1055, I:184–87; Symeon of Durham, *Historia regum*, II:172; Stenton, *Anglo-Saxon England*, p. 573; Barlow, *Edward the Confessor*, p. 206; I. Walker, pp. 78–79; Maund, *Ireland, Wales, and England*, pp. 124, 130–31; R.R. Davies, p. 26; and D. Walker, p. 91. The *Anglo-Saxon Chronicle* (C) is the only version which mentions the building of an earthwork fortification around Hereford. For what fortifications may have existed at Hereford before Harold's reconstruction, see Barlow, *Edward the Confessor*, p. 205.

55 *Anglo-Saxon Chronicle* (C) 1055, I:186: '⁊ man geinlagode þa Ælfgar eorl, ⁊ man ageaf him eall þ him wæs ofgenumen.' See also John of Worcester, II:578–79; Symeon of Durham, *Historia regum*, p. 172; Stenton, *Anglo-Saxon England*, p. 573; Barlow, *Edward the Confessor*, pp. 206–07; I. Walker, pp. 79–80; Maund, *Ireland, Wales, and England*, pp. 130, 136–37; and D. Walker, p. 91. Maund sees this as a defeat for Harold, while D. Walker questions Harold's wisdom in the matter, now being faced 'with a potentially dangerous combination of Welsh and Mercian interests.' John of Worcester (II:578–79) also reports that Ælfgar's 'pirate' fleet sailed to Chester where they were paid for their services. See also Barlow, *Edward the Confessor*, pp. 206–07.

enemy vigorously,' on 16 June 1056, they went out to meet their attackers. Led by their newly crowned bishop, Leofgar, who had been Harold Godwinson's chaplain prior to his episcopal appointment, and Ælfnoð, their local governor, they met defeat at Glasbury on Wye, as many, including both leaders, were slaughtered by the Welsh. After that, and until Earls Harold and Leofric arrived with their armies, Herefordshire was defenseless against the destructive and violent assaults of the Welsh. The *Anglo-Saxon Chronicle* (C) reports:

> It is heartbreaking to tell of all the suffering, and all the travel and the fight-ing, and of all the struggles and the loss of men and horses, which all the English levy endured, until Earl Leofric came with Earl Harold and Bishop Ealdred to make peace between them [and the Welsh].[56]

By the time Harold arrived, it seems that Gruffydd's lust for blood, pillage, and booty had been satisfied, and the fighting had ceased. Once more the earl of Wessex resorted to diplomacy rather than warfare, preferring to make peace rather than to seek revenge. A treaty was signed between Kings Edward and Gruffydd in the presence of Harold, Leofric, and Ealdred of Worcester, who temporarily had been assigned to care for the see of Hereford. On his part, Gruffydd gained much by making peace with the English, principally the town and fortification of Rhuddlan (where Gruffydd would move his court) and the renders from the former English manor of Bishopstree (Bistre), which when added to his reacquired lands around Oswestry and from the Dee estuary in the north to the Severn River in the south, seems to indicate a strong victory for the Welsh king.[57]

---

[56] *Anglo-Saxon Chronicle* (C) 1056, I:186:

Earfoðlic is to atellanne seo gedrecednes ꝸ seo fare eall ꝸ seo fyrdung. ꝸ þ geswinc. ꝸ manna fyll ꝸ eac horsa. þe eall Engla here dreah. oððæt Leofric eorl com wið, ꝸ Harald eorl ꝸ Ealdred b, ꝸ macedan seht þær betweonan.

Ælfnoð is called a 'scirgerefa' in the *Anglo-Saxon Chronicle* and a 'vicecomes' by John of Worcester. Leofgar had gained the bishopric of Hereford at the death of Æðelstan a mere eleven weeks and four days prior to his own death. Neither of the versions of the *Anglo-Saxon Chronicle* which report this Welsh attack have much praise for Leofgar. The authors of both disdained the fact that Leofgar had continued to wear a moustache during his chaplaincy, although he had shaved it when he became bishop; and both also disliked the fact that he abandoned his 'spiritual weapons', his chrism and cross, to take up military weapons in defense of the town and shire. See also *Anglo-Saxon Chronicle* (D) 1056, I:187; John of Worcester, II:580–81; Symeon of Durham, *Historia regum*, II:172–73; *Annales Cambriae*, p. 25; Stenton, *Anglo-Saxon England*, pp. 573–74; Barlow, *Edward the Confessor*, pp. 207–08; I. Walker, pp. 80–81; Maund, *Ireland, Wales, and England*, pp. 125, 130–31, 146; and D. Walker, pp. 91–92. I. Walker contends that the reason behind this raid is that Gruffydd had been given a 'poor return' the 1055 peace and as such was attempting to reacquire his 'lost' lands.

[57] See *Anglo-Saxon Chronicle* (C and D) 1056, I:186–87; John of Worcester, II:580–81; Symeon of Durham, *Historia regum*, II:172–73; Stenton, *Anglo-Saxon England*, p. 574; Staf-ford, *Unification and Conquest*, p. 95; Barlow, *Edward the Confessor*, pp. 207–08; I. Walker, p. 81; Vanessa King, 'Ealdred, Archbishop of York: The Worcester Years,' *Anglo-Norman Studies* 18 (1995), pp. 128–29; R. Davies, p. 26; Maund, *Ireland, Wales, and England*, pp.

A year after the peace, when the king's nephew, Earl Ralph of Mantes, appropriately called 'the Timid' for his fainthearted defense of the earldom against the Welsh, had died, Harold Godwinson took over the responsibility for the protection of Herefordshire, adding the province to his earldom of Wessex.[58]

In 1058, Ælfgar, now earl of Mercia,[59] once again was banished from England by King Edward the Confessor. Once again his crime is not recorded in any contemporary source, only that he fled once again to Wales and the protective shelter of Gruffydd ap Llywelyn – by this time Gruffydd was married to Ælfgar's daughter, Ealdyð.[60] And, *once again*, his exile was short-lived, as he quickly returned to his governing position over Mercia. John of Worcester writes:

> Ælfgar, earl of the Mercians, was outlawed by King Edward a second time, but with the help of Gruffydd, king of the Welsh, and the support of the Norwegian fleet, which joined him unexpectedly, he quickly recovered his earldom by force.[61]

What the nature of this 'force' was, whether it was a military action or not, is not recorded in the sources, although the presence of a Norwegian fleet certainly leans to the conclusion that it was a bellicose act: in the *Anglo-Saxon Chronicle* (D), the fleet is called a 'scyp here' (naval army), while the *Annales Cambriae* records a devastation of England by the Norwegian prince, Magnús, son of Haraldr Harðráði, and Gruffydd ap Llywelyn; and, finally, the *Annals of Tigernach* reports it as an invasion with a large fleet drawn from Norway, the Orkneys, the Hebrides, and Dublin. On the other hand, there is no indication of the role played in this action by Harold Godwinson, although it is certain that if

---

136–37; Maund, 'The Welsh Alliances of Earl Ælfgar,' p. 184; D. Walker, pp. 91–92; and Suppe, p. 70. On the gains made by Gruffydd in this treaty see Barlow, *Edward the Confessor,* pp. 207–08; Maund, 'The Welsh Alliances of Earl Ælfgar,' p. 184; R. Davies, p. 26; and Suppe, p. 70. D. Walker connects this treaty signing with Walter Map's dramatic submission of Gruffydd to Edward that was mentioned above.

58 See Stenton, *Anglo-Saxon England*; I. Walker, pp. 83–85; and D. Walker, p. 92.

59 Ælfgar gained Mercia after the death of his father, Leofric, in 1057; but it was an earldom that had been diminished in size, with some lands being given to Harold, and some to his brothers, Gyrð (who gained East Anglia) and Leofwine. See John of Worcester, II:584–85; Douglas, *William the Conqueror,* p. 172; and I. Walker, p. 83.

60 This happened sometime around 1057. See Barlow, *Edward the Confessor,* p. 207; I. Walker, p. 85; Lloyd, II:369; and Maund, 'The Welsh Alliances of Earl Ælfgar,' pp. 186–87.

61 John of Worcester, II:584–85. See also *Anglo-Saxon Chronicle* (D) 1058, I:188; Freeman, *Norman Conquest,* II: 434–35; Stenton, *Anglo-Saxon England,* pp. 574–75; Stafford, *Unification and Conquest,* p. 87; Brown, *The Normans and Norman Conquest,* p. 71; Barlow, *Edward the Confessor,* pp. 208–09; I. Walker, p. 85; Maund, *Ireland, Wales, and England,* pp. 125, 130; Maund, 'The Welsh Alliances of Earl Ælfgar,' p. 184; D. Walker, p. 92; Hudson, 'The Destruction of Gruffudd ap Llywelyn,' p. 332; Henry R. Loyn, *The Vikings in Britain* (Oxford, 1994), p. 68; and Eric Linklater, *The Conquest of England: From the Viking Incursions of the Eighth Century to the Norman Victory at the Battle of Hastings* (New York, 1966), p. 3. Stenton holds that this rebellion was due to Ælfgar's fear of being surrounded by Godwinsons.

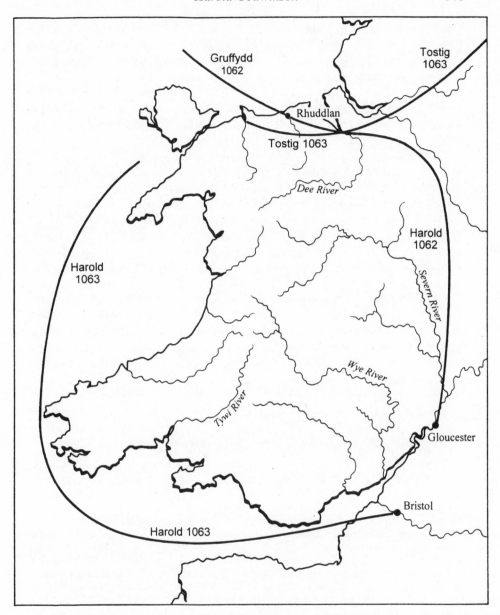

Harold and Tostig attack Wales, 1062–63

this was a military adventure into Herefordshire, an invasion or a raid, he surely would have been involved, and with the Norwegian fleet present and the seemingly easy return of Ælfgar to Mercia, it stands to reason that no attack of Herefordshire was made from Wales. Finally, why a Norwegian fleet joined in this obviously English domestic dispute is not known, although it does denote a growing Norwegian presence in northern European affairs, a presence which would continue to grow under their king, Haraldr Harðráði, until he would launch a major invasion of England in 1066.[62]

Thus without a major foray into England by Gruffydd ap Llywelyn in 1058, and then based only on evidence from the *Annales Cambriae*, it would seem that the peace of 1056 made between him and Edward the Confessor had been a fairly secure one. That would change in 1063 though, when Wales was invaded and Gruffydd was killed. While some assume that there was an attack of England by the Welsh king which prompted a brutal response by Harold Godwinson and his brother, Tostig,[63] no contemporary source actually reports such an attack. Instead, all merely record the two-fold invasion of Wales by Harold.

First, shortly after Christmas 1062, the earl of Wessex struck deep into the heart of Wales, campaigning northwest from Gloucester towards Gruffydd's fortified capital of Rhuddlan. Attacking early in the year, and traveling by horse and foot through the cold and snowy mountains, Harold's army took Gruffydd by surprise. They met little resistance in the endeavor: the troops sacked and burned Rhuddlan, destroying all of the ships which they found in the harbor, but Gruffydd was not captured or killed. He had successfully escaped from the town into the Irish Sea.[64]

Frustrated in his attempt to capture or kill Gruffydd, Harold Godwinson returned to Herefordshire and regrouped his forces. He also contacted his brother, Tostig, the earl of Northumbria, to unite with him in a joint campaign to

---

[62] On the Norwegian fleet participating in this event see *Anglo-Saxon Chronicle* (D) 1058, I:188–89; John of Worcester, II:584–85; *Annales Cambriae*, p. 25; 'The Annals of Tigernach: The Fourth Fragment A.D. 973–A.D. 1088,' ed. W. Stokes, *Revue celtique* 17 (1896), 399; Stenton, *Anglo-Saxon England*, pp. 574–75; Brown, *The Normans and the Norman Conquest*, p. 71; Barlow, *Edward the Confessor*, p. 209; Douglas, *William the Conqueror*, p. 172; I. Walker, pp. 85–86; W. Davies, p. 117; Maund, *Ireland, Wales, and England*, p. 130; D. Walker, p. 92; and Hudson, 'The Destruction of Gruffudd ap Llywelyn,' p. 332. Based on a *Domesday Book* reference to some devastated Northumbrian land of Tostig Godwinson, I. Walker suggests that these assaults may have been directed at Northumbria, and that this was the reason for his later participation in the 1063 attack of Wales. Sten Körner (*The Battle of Hastings, England, and Europe, 1035–1066* (Lund, 1964), pp. 152–53) rejects this story, but there seems to be too much contemporary evidence for the attack to be so dismissive of it.
[63] See, for example, Barlow, *Edward the Confessor*, pp. 210–11.
[64] See *Anglo-Saxon Chronicle* (D) 1063, I:191; John of Worcester, II:592–93; Symeon of Durham, *Historia regum*, II:177; Stenton, *Anglo-Saxon England*, p. 576; Barlow, *Edward the Confessor*, pp. 210–11; I. Walker, pp. 87–88; R. Davies, p. 26; Maund, *Ireland, Wales, and England*, p. 125; D. Walker, p. 92; and Hudson, 'The Destruction of Gruffudd ap Llywelyn,' pp. 332–33. Surprisingly, the *Vita Ædwardi* (pp. 64–65) records nothing about this expedition, preferring to 'deliberately reserve this story for a more faithful treatment in the future,' a treatment which, if written, has disappeared.

end Gruffydd's raids into England once and for all. It was to be a two-pronged attack, what might later be called a 'pincer maneuver.' At the end of May, Harold was to take a fleet from Bristol north around Wales, while Tostig was to take an army overland west from Northumbria. They would meet in Gwynedd, Gruffydd's home kingdom. In doing so, Harold hoped that they would conquer the Welsh and kill or capture their troublesome king.

The plan worked extremely well. John of Worcester writes:

> About Rogationtide he [Harold] set out from Bristol with a naval force, and sailed around a great part of Wales. His brother Earl Tostig met him with mounted troops, as the king commanded, and they at once joined forces, and began to lay waste that region. By that the Welsh were coerced, and gave hostages. They surrendered, and promised that they would pay him tribute, and they deposed and outlawed their King Gruffydd.[65]

Yet, Gruffydd still eluded Harold's grasp; 'deposed and outlawed,' Gruffydd was still alive and posed a potential threat to English-Welsh peace. Indeed, Gruffydd would try to return to Wales early in 1064 but, mindful of the destruction of the recent English campaign, the Welsh refused to allow their exiled king to re-establish his power over them: Gruffydd was captured and put to death. The Welsh then presented his head and the prow of his ship to Harold in keeping with their promise to and because of their veneration (or fear) of him.[66] As R.R. Davies writes: 'it was a stunning triumph [for Harold].'[67] Frank Barlow agrees:

---

[65] John of Worcester, II:592–93:
circa rogationes de Bryccstouue classica manu profectus, magna ex parte terram Walanorum circumnauigabat, cui frater suus comes Tostius, ut rex mandarat, cum equestri occurrit exercitu et uiribus simul iunctis, regionem illam depopulari coeperunt. Vnde Walani coacti, datis obsidibus, se dederunt et se tributum illi daturos promiserunt regemque suum Griffinum exlegantes abiecerunt.
Anglo-Saxon Chronicle (D and E) 1063, I:190–91; Harold of Huntingdon, pp. 382–83; Symeon of Durham, *Historia regum*, II:177; Geoffrey Gaimar, *Lestoire des Engles*, ed. T.D. Hardy and C.T. Martin (London, 1888), I:215; Stenton, *Anglo-Saxon Chronicle*, p. 576; Barlow, *Edward the Confessor*, p. 211; I. Walker, pp. 88–89; R. Davies, p. 26; Maund, *Ireland, Wales, and England*, p. 125; Maund, 'The Welsh Alliances of Earl Ælfgar,' p. 188; D. Walker, p. 92; and Hudson, 'The Destruction of Gruffudd ap Llywelyn,' pp. 333, 338–39.

[66] *Anglo-Saxon Chronicle* (D and E) 1063, I:190–91; *Vita Ædwardi*, pp. 64–65; John of Worcester, II:596–97; Henry of Huntingdon, pp. 382–83; Symeon of Durham, *Historia regum*, II:177; *Annales Cambriae*, p. 25; Freeman, *Norman Conquest*, II:683–86; Stenton, *Anglo-Saxon England*, p. 576; Barlow, *Edward the Confessor*, p. 211; I. Walker, p. 89; R. Davies, p. 24; D. Walker, p. 92; Hudson, 'The Destruction of Gruffudd ap Llywelyn,' pp. 333–50; K.L. Maund, 'Cynan ab Iago and the Killing of Gruffudd ap Llywelyn,' *Cambridge Medieval Celtic Studies* 10 (1985), 57–65; and J.W. James, 'Fresh Light on the Death of Gruffudd ap Llywelyn,' *Bulletin of the Board of Celtic Studies* 30 (1982–83), 147. James and Hudson contend that Gruffydd was killed by Cynan ab Iago, whose father had been killed by Gruffydd in 1039; Hudson adds the assertion that the murder was done in Ireland, where Gruffydd had sought refuge. (The latter suggestion goes against most contemporary English accounts of the murder.) Maund ('Cynan ab Iago') disputes Cynan's role in this affair, claiming instead that Gruffydd's death must 'be seen as the result of an internal Welsh power-struggle which exploited the crisis provoked by Harold's invasion' (p. 65).

Not since Agricola, and never again for many a year, was Wales so insolently invaded, so easily cowed by force of arms. Even if Gruffydd had been losing his countrymen's support, even if Welsh disunity facilitated the entry of a determined enemy, the English success in 1063 was in striking contrast to the earlier failures. It marks the rebirth of England as a military power.[68]

Did Gruffydd in some way induce this harsh English action, or was Harold solely responsible for what occurred in Wales in 1063 without justifiable provocation? Whatever may be the answer, the attack seems to have been related directly to the death of Earl Ælfgar of Mercia, whose kinship and alliance with Gruffydd ap Llywelyn for so many years had presented so many problems for Harold Godwinson. The exact date of Ælfgar's death cannot be known from the contemporary sources; his last mention in the *Anglo-Saxon Chronicle* or John of Worcester's *Chronicle* is in 1058, when he regained his earldom. There are also two charters from King Edward which mention Ælfgar and which might be dated to 1062.[69] Also, the *Vita Wulfstani* does indicate Ælfgar's support for Wulfstan's election as bishop of Worcester, which took place sometime on 8 September 1062, but the lateness of this source and its hagiographical re-arranging of historical events (see the following chapter) has caused some historians to doubt its validity, even on matters such as this which may be quite accurate.[70] Ælfgar's son and heir to Mercia, Edwin, is not named in contemporary sources as his father's replacement until 1065, although it is generally assumed that he must have succeeded to the earldom earlier, after his father had died.[71] Thus it is entirely possible that Ælfgar was dead by the time Harold launched his anti-Gruffydd action early in 1063.[72] It is equally possible that Edwin was either too young or disinclined to take his father's place in defending his sister's royal Welsh husband.[73]

Did this death prompt a reaction from Gruffydd or from Harold? Edward Freeman and Frank Barlow believe that the blame for what resulted must lie with King Gruffydd ap Llywelyn, and certainly there is some rationale for that conclusion: after all, Gruffydd had frequently raided the English marches almost since the very first year of his reign (1039), although not, it appears,

---

67 R. Davies, p. 26. See also Stafford, *Unification and Conquest*, p. 95; Brown, *The Normans and Norman Conquest*, p. 93; Barlow, *Edward the Confessor*, pp. 211–13; and I. Walker, p. 90
68 Barlow, *Edward the Confessor*, pp. 211–12.
69 See F.E. Harmer, ed., *Anglo-Saxon Writs* (Manchester, 1952), p. 457.
70 William of Malmesbury, *Vita Wulfstani*, ed. Reginald R. Darlington (London, 1928), p. 18. See also I. Walker, pp. 87–88 and Hudson, 'The Destruction of Gruffudd ap Llywelyn,' p. 339.
71 The earliest reference to Edwin as earl of Mercia comes in the 1065 account of the Northumbrian uprising found in the *Anglo-Saxon Chronicle* (D) 1065, I:191–93.
72 Freeman, *Norman Conquest*, II:465–66; Stenton, *Anglo-Saxon England*, p. 576; Brown, *The Normans and Norman Conquest*, p. 71; I. Walker, pp. 87–88; Maund, *Ireland, Wales, and England*, p. 138; Maund, 'The Welsh Alliances of Earl Ælfgar,' p. 188; and Hudson, 'The Destruction of Gruffudd ap Llywelyn,' p. 339.
73 See Stenton, *Anglo-Saxon England*, p. 576 and Barlow, *Edward the Confessor*, p. 210.

since 1056. Why should it be different in 1063? As Barlow writes of Gruffydd at this time: 'He regarded the death of his ally as bringing the peace to an end. Mercia could once more be raided, and, he may have mistakenly thought, with impunity. But the English nobles regarded the renewed Welsh hostilities as an insult not to be borne.'[74]

At the same time, it seems that few wish to blame Harold for something so heinous as an offensive war. So far in his dealings with the Welsh had he not endeavored to avoid bloodshed, especially behind the Welsh border? Besides, what could have been Harold's motive in waging such an offensive war? Peace between the kingdoms had endured quite nicely for the previous years, and there seems to have been no reason to think that Wales and England would ever again be anything but friends, at least while Gruffydd and Edward were still alive.

Could Harold Godwinson, however, have delivered such an unprovoked 'evil' blow? Yes, according to John of Worcester. Harold invaded Wales in 1063 not for any immediate reason, but 'because of the frequent and destructive raids which he [Gruffydd] often made within the English borders and the disgrace which he often brought upon his lord Edward.'[75] As some have suggested, in perpetrating this violence, Harold's purpose may have been to keep Ælfgar's sons from renewing their father's alliance with Gruffydd or to enhance the Godwin family and curb Mercian separatism,[76] but more likely his purpose was one of intimidation, to depose and kill Gruffydd and to conquer and subjugate the Welsh. In so doing, while not himself responsible for the capture and execution of Gruffydd, Harold was extremely successful, the terror of his military endeavor so affecting the Welsh that they became the means of their own king's execution, replacing Gruffydd with two of his half-brothers, Bleddyn and Rhiwallon who, according to the *Anglo-Saxon Chronicle* (D),

> swore oaths and gave hostages to the king and the earl, so that they would be bound to them in all things, would serve them everywhere on sea and on land, and would render to them such tribute of their country as had been paid to any other king.[77]

---

[74] Barlow, *Edward the Confessor*, pp. 210–11 and Freeman, *Norman Conquest*, II:465.

[75] John of Worcester, II:592–93:
> Strenuus dux Westsaxonum Haroldus, iussu regis Eduuardi post nauitatem Domini equitatu non multo secum assumpto de Glauuorna, ubi rex tunc morabatur, ad Rudelan multa cum festinatione profectus est, ut regem Walanorum Griffinum, propter frequentes depopulationes, quas in Anglorum finibus agebat, ac uerecundias, quas domino suo regi Eduuardo sepe faciebat, occideret.

See also Symeon of Durham, *Historia regum*, II:177; Stenton, *Anglo-Saxon England*, p. 576; I. Walker, pp. 88–89; R. Davies, p. 26; D. Walker, pp. 92–94; and Maund, 'Cynan ab Iago,' p. 64.

[76] The former reason is given by D. Walker (p. 93) and Maund ('Cynan ab Iago,' p. 64), the latter by R. Davies, p. 26.

[77] *Anglo-Saxon Chronicle* (D) 1064, I:191:
> Bleþgente ⁊ Rigwatlan, ⁊ hig aþas sworon ⁊ gislas saldan þæm cynge ⁊ þæm eorle þ heo

The terror which this invasion invoked would be remembered in England and Wales for a very long time, its details recalled and, to a certain extent embellished, by Gerald of Wales and John of Salisbury in the twelfth century. Recounting the legendary English conquerors of Wales, Gerald writes:

> Then last, but fully the greatest, Harold came, who on foot with his lightly clad infantry crossed through and around all of Wales, living off the land, so strongly that he 'left not one that pisseth against the wall' anywhere. In commemoration of his conquest, and to his perpetual memory, according to the ancient tradition, he erected inscribed stones in many places in Wales where he had won victories. On these stones you will discover many having the following insignia sculpted: HAROLD WAS THE VICTOR HERE.[78]

In fact, they were so effective, Gerald continues, that the three Norman kings of England who followed Harold had never had a problem with their western neighbors.[79]

John of Salisbury's account, in his *Policraticus*, is even more vivid in its praise of Harold's crushing of the Welsh:

> Recent history of the English tells that when the Britons had made an attack and were ravaging England, Duke Harold was sent by the most pious King Edward to fight against them. He was a strong warrior with a laudable record of praiseworthy achievements . . . Therefore, when he discovered the lightness of the people he had to deal with, he chose light-armed soldiers so that he might meet them on equal terms. He decided, in other words, to campaign with a light armament shod with boots, their chests protected with straps of very tough hide, carrying small round shields to ward off missiles, and using as offensive weapons javelins and a pointed sword. Thus he was able to cling to their heels as they fled and pressed them so hard that 'foot repulsed foot and spear repulsed spear,' and the boss of one shield that of another. And so he reached Snowdon, the Hill of Snow, and devastated the whole country. And prolonging the campaign to two years, he captured their chiefs and presented their heads to the king who had sent him; and slaying every male who could be

him on allum þingum unswicende beon woldon, ⁊ eig hwar him gearwe in wætere ⁊ on lande. ⁊ swylc of þam lande gelæstan swylc man dyde to foran ær oþrum kynge.
See also John of Worcester, II:596–97; Henry of Huntingdon, pp. 382–83; Symeon of Durham, *Historia regum*, II:177; Stenton, *Anglo-Saxon England*, p. 576; Stafford, *Unification and Conquest*, p. 95; Barlow, *Edward the Confessor*, p. 211; I. Walker, p. 89; R. Davies, p. 24; Maund, *Ireland, Wales, and England*, pp. 138–39; and Maund, 'The Welsh Alliances of Earl Ælfgar,' p. 188.
[78] Gerald of Wales, *Itinerarium Kambriae et descriptio Kambriae*, ed. J.F. Dimock (London, 1868), p. 217:
Et sicut longe plenius Haroldus ultimus: qui, pedes ipse, cumque pedestri turba, et levibus armis, victuque patriae conformi, tam valide totam Kambriam et circuivit, et transpenetravit, ut in eadem fere mingentem ad parietem non reliquerit.
In cujus victoriae signum, perpetuamque memoriam, lapides in Wallia more antiquo in titulum erectos, locis plerisque in quibus victor extiterat, literas hujusmodi insculptas habentes plurimos invenies, HIC FUIT VICTOR HAROLDUS.
The Biblical quote within the Gerald's text is from I Samuel 25:22 and I Kings 16:11.
[79] Gerald of Wales, pp. 217–18. See also R. Davies, p. 26.

found, even down to the pitiful boys, he thus pacified the province at the mouth of the sword. He established a law that any Briton who was found with a spear beyond a certain limit which he set for them, Offa's Dike, was to have his right hand cut off by the officials of the king. And thus by the valor of this duke the Britons were so broken that nearly the entire race seemed to disappear and by the indulgence of the aforesaid king, their women married to Englishmen.

Written as it is for a manual on statesmanship, Salisbury emphasizes the leadership, ending his discourse on Harold with this question: 'Do you not see then what follows from the election of a leader and from an army of youthful soldiers?'[80]

Harold was able use his victory against the Welsh in 1063 to secure his military legitimacy to what he perceived would soon be a vacant throne. His show of military courage, strength, and intelligence against Gruffydd ap Llywelyn and his people no doubt impressed King Edward the Confessor and his people. Harold was a warlord like his father, one who had proven capable of protecting the kingdom of England and its population from outside military forces. As Edward August Freeman writes:

In hunger and watchfulness, in the wearing labours of a campaign no less than in the passing excitement of the day of battle, he stood forth as the leader and the model of the English people. Alike ready and vigorous in action, he knew when to strike and how to strike; he knew how to measure himself against the enemies of every kind, and to adapt his tactics to every position in which the accidents of warfare might place him.[81]

He was fit to rule!

---

[80] John of Salisbury, *Policraticus sive nugis curialium et vestigiis philosophorum libri VIII*, ed. C.I. Webb (Oxford, 1909), II:19–20:
Anglorum recens narrat historia quod, cum Britones irruptione facta Angliam depopularentur, a piissimo rege Eadwardo ad eos expugnandos missus est dux Haroldus, uir quidem armis strenuus et laudabilium operum fulgens insignibus . . . Cum ergo gentis cognosceret leuitatem, quasi pari certamine militiam eligens expeditam, cum eis censuit congrediendum leuem exercens armaturam, peronatus incedens, fasciis pectus et praeduro tectus corio, missilibus eorum leua obiectans ancilia et in eos contorquens nunc spicula, nunc mucronem exercens, sic fugientium uestigiis inherebat ut premeretur
pede pes et cuspide cuspis
et umbo umbone repelleretur. Niuim itaque collem ingressus uastauit omnia, et expeditione in biennium prorogata reges cepit, et capita eorum regi, qui eum miserat, presentauit, et usque ad miserationem paruulorum omnem masculum qui inueniri potuit interficiens in ore gladii pacauit prouinciam; legem statuit ut quicumque Britonum exinde citra terminum quem eis praescripsit, fossam scilicet Offae, cum telo inueniretur, ei ab officialibus regni manus dextra praecideretur. Adeoque uirtute ducis tunc confecti sunt Britones ut fere gens tota deficere uideretur et ex indulgentia iam dicti regis mulieres eorum nupserint Anglis.
Videsne quantum electio ducis et exercitum iuuentutis militiae conferant?
[81] Freeman, *Norman Conquest*, II:38. See also Stenton, *Anglo-Saxon England*, p. 577; Stafford, *Unification and Conquest*, p. 95; Brown, *The Normans and Norman Conquest*, p. 93; Barlow, *Edward the Confessor*, pp. 211–13; and I. Walker, p. 90.

There are two interesting addenda to the 1063 invasion of Wales by Harold and Tostig Godwinson. The first is that according to the *Vita Haroldi*, Harold fell ill or was wounded on his campaign through Wales. That this illness or wound was one which paralyzed the earl of Wessex and one also which the doctors could not cure is all that is revealed by the author of this work. He does add however that Harold was eventually cured, by the intercession of God, and as thanks to God for delivering him from this ailment, that he refounded the collegiate church at Waltham.[82]

Second, although it would be a long time before Wales was to recover from the devastation caused by the armies of the Godwinsons, two years after his crushing attack on the Welsh, Harold decided to build a hunting lodge there at Portskewet, 'thinking,' according to the *Anglo-Saxon Chronicle* (D), 'to invite King Edward there for the sake of hunting,' but the plan was a bit too bold and the building was never completed. The lodge was attacked, robbed, and burned and the workmen killed by Caradog, the son of Gruffydd ap Rhydderch, the southern Welsh king whom Gruffydd ap Llywelyn had killed several years earlier. Thus old kinship differences were put aside as nationalism was discovered in a common enemy, the English. In making this gesture, Caradog gained a small measure of revenge for all Welshmen.[83]

Harold Godwinson also traveled much, both for himself and as an emissary of Edward. On one trip, in 1056, he may have visited Flanders, the Rhineland and Rome. The purpose of this journey is unknown; in fact it is not recorded in any contemporary narrative source, leading at least one historian, Sten Körner, to doubt that it occurred at all. However, it has been speculated by Philip Grierson, who discovered Harold's signature on a letter written at Saint Omer confirming the possessions of the abbey of St Peter's in Ghent, that this trip was used to negotiate the return of Edward's nephew, Edward Æðeling (also known as Edward the Exile), from Hungary.[84] (Edward did return in 1057, but almost

---

[82] *Vita Haroldi*, ed. W.D. Birch (London, 1885), pp. 17–21. See also Barlow, *English Church*, p. 59 and I. Walker, p. 72.

[83] *Anglo-Saxon Chronicle* (D) 1065, I:191:

> Her on þissum geare. foran to hlafmæssan het Harold eorl bytlian on Brytlande æt Portaschihð. þa þa 'he' hit gegan hefde, ⁊ þær mycel god to gegaderode. ⁊ þohte þonne cyng Eadward þær to habbane for huntoðes þingon. Ac þa hit eall wæs gearo. þa for Cradoc to Gryffines sunu mid eallon þam genge þe he begeotan mihte. ⁊ þ folc eall maest ofsloh þe þær timbrode. ⁊ þ god þe þær gegearcod wæs namon.

See also John of Worcester, II:596–97; Symeon of Durham, *Historia regum*, II:178; Freeman, *Norman Conquest*, II:474–76; Stafford, *Unification and Conquest*, p. 95; Barlow, *Edward the Confessor*, p. 233; R. Davies, p. 26; and Maund, *Ireland, Wales, and England*, pp. 125, 141.

[84] See Philip Grierson, 'A Visit of Earl Harold to Flanders in 1056,' *English Historical Review* 54 (1936), 90–97 and Philip Grierson, 'The Relations between England and Flanders before the Norman Conquest,' *Transactions of the Royal Historical Society* 23 (1941), 100–01. Almost all modern commentators accept Grierson's speculation. See, for example, Freeman, *Norman Conquest*, II:40–41, 430–31, 647–53, 665–67; Barlow, ed., *Vita Ædwardi*, p. 52 n. 125; Barlow, *Edward the Confessor*, pp. 226–27; Barlow, *English Church*, pp. 59, 291;

immediately died, unable to enjoy his relationship with the king and his expected inheritance of the English throne.[85]) This trip could also be the one on which Harold eventually visited Rome, declared to have occurred in the *Vita Ædwardi*. While on this journey, the author of this work reports, Harold took time to study the government of the leaders there:

> [Harold] studied the character, policy, and strength of the princes of Gaul not only through his servants but also personally; and adroitly and with natural cunning and at great length he observed most intently what he could get from them if he needed them in the management of any business.[86]

Even at this early date, Harold seems to have been preparing to rule the kingdom of England.

It also seems certain that Harold made a journey to Normandy during his reign as earl, although whether this was by accident or intentional is disputed. The most famous version of Harold's visit is depicted in the *Bayeux Tapestry*. Almost no one disputes the fact that this tapestry has a Norman bias, having been commissioned by Bishop Odo of Bayeux to commemorate his brother, William the Conqueror's, victory at Hastings,[87] but a sufficient number of other contemporary sources, also mostly Norman in origin it is true, confirm what is there depicted.[88] The Tapestry reports that Harold was sent to Normandy at

---

I. Walker, pp. 81–82; and King, pp. 130–31. Against the visit is Körner, pp. 205–06, 213–17. Diana Greenway, the editor of Henry of Huntingdon's *Historia Anglorum*, speculates that this trip may have led to the confusing statement by Henry that Harold was traveling to Flanders when he was blown off course to Normandy (pp. 380–83 and n. 145).

[85] See *Anglo-Saxon Chronicle* (D and E) 1057, I:187–88; John of Worcester, II:582–83; Symeon of Durham, *Historia regum*, II:173; William of Malmesbury, *Gesta regum*, I:416–17; Henry of Huntingdon, pp. 380–81; Freeman, *Norman Conquest*, II:369–71; Stenton, *Anglo-Saxon England*, pp. 570–71; Brown, *The Normans and Norman Conquest*, p. 109; Körner, pp. 196–205, 207–09; Barlow, *Edward the Confessor*, pp. 217–19; Douglas, *William the Conqueror*, pp. 171–72; I. Walker, pp. 82–83; and Nicholas Hooper, 'Edgar the Ætheling: Anglo-Saxon Prince, Rebel and Crusader,' *Anglo-Saxon England* 14 (1985), 196–205.

[86] *Vita Ædwardi*, pp. 50–51:

> At ille superior mores, consilia, et uires Gallicorum principium non tam per suos quam per se scrutatus, astutia et callido animi ingenio et diuturniori cum procrastinatione intentissime notauerat, quid in eis habiturus esset, si eis opus haberet in alicuius negotii administratione.

See the *Vita Ædwardi*, p. 52 n. 125. Freeman (*Norman Conquest*, II:666) had problems understanding this passage, but he did not have the benefit of Grierson's later discovery of the Saint Omer letter signed by Harold.

[87] The best source for the *Bayeux Tapestry* is Frank Stenton, *The Bayeux Tapestry: A Comprehensive Survey*, 2nd edn (London, 1957).

[88] See Symeon of Durham, *Historia regum*, II:182–84; William of Malmesbury, *Gesta regum Anglorum*, I:416–19; Henry of Huntingdon, pp. 380–83; Wace, II:94–98; *Carmen de hastingae proelio*, ed. C. Morton and A. Muntz (Oxford, 1972), pp. 68–72; William of Poitiers, *The Gesta Guillelmi of William of Poitiers*, ed. and trans. R.H.C. Davis and M. Chibnall (Oxford, 1998), pp. 68–79; William of Jumièges, *The Gesta Normanorum ducum of William of Jumièges, Orderic Vitalis, and Robert of Torigni*, ed. and trans. E.M.C. van Houts (Oxford, 1995), II:158–61; Eadmer, *Historia novorum in Anglia*, ed. M. Rule (London, 1884), pp. 6–8;

King Edward the Confessor's entreaty. Harold sailed from his manor at Bosham, but while crossing the Channel, his ship was blown off-course by fierce winds to St Valery on the French coast. There the earl of Wessex fell into the hands of Count Guy of Ponthieu, who imprisoned him and asked for ransom. Upon hearing of this, William, the duke of Normandy, marched to Count Guy's lands and demanded the release of the English nobleman. Count Guy released Harold immediately, and both William and Harold rode off to William's palace where Harold was entertained. From there the now good friends marched west to Brittany where they relieved William's castle of Dol, besieged by the rebellious Duke Conan II of Brittany. En route, Harold saved two Norman soldiers from certain death by courageously pulling them from quicksand. When they returned to Normandy, William rewarded Harold for his service with, among other things, the hand of his eldest daughter, Agatha (not depicted in the Tapestry), and Harold in turn pledged an oath of fealty to William. Then Harold sailed home to England.[89]

Beyond the question of whether the narrative of Harold Godwinson's trip and his oath to William is trustworthy, there are five issues to be resolved in this story. As it is, most historians do accept the Norman accounts of it – although the notion that some, like Frank Stenton, accept as proof the idea that 'the silence of those who wrote with native sympathies proves that there was an element of truth in the Norman story which they did not feel themselves at liberty to deny' is a bit troubling.[90]

The first of these may be the most easy: when was the date of this journey? As the date of the journey is not specified in any of the Norman sources, and as it is not mentioned in any of the English sources, a precise date cannot be determined. Most historians date the journey to between the defeat of Gruffydd in the summer of 1063, when Harold was known to be in Wales, and the summer of 1065 when it is known that he was trying to negotiate with the Northumbrian rebels at Oxford. Thus a date of 1064 seems most appropriate.[91]

Orderic Vitalis, *The Ecclesiastical History of Orderic Vitalis*, ed. and trans. M. Chibnall (Oxford, 1969–80), II:134–37; and Snorri Sturluson, *Heimskringla*, III:169–70. Of course, the absence of this incident in any of the versions of the more contemporary *Anglo-Saxon Chronicle*, in the *Vita Ædwardi*, or in John of Worcester's *Chronicle* has caused some to believe that the story of the voyage of Harold to Normandy is an Anglo-Norman 'fiction.' Modern historians who discuss this trip to Normandy include: Freeman, *Norman Conquest*, III:74, 215–17; 684–86; Stenton, *Anglo-Saxon England*, pp. 577–78; Brown, *The Normans and Norman Conquest*, pp. 83, 110–14; Körner, pp. 109–21; Barlow, *Edward the Confessor*, pp. 169, 220–29; Douglas, *William the Conqueror*, pp. 175–79; I. Walker, pp. 91–102; and Miles W. Campbell, 'Hypothèses sur les causes de l'ambassade de Harold en Normandie,' *Annales Normandie* 27 (1977), 243–65.

[89] William of Poitiers (pp. 70–77) reverses these last two events, placing Harold's taking of the oath of fealty to William before their combined attack on Conan.

[90] Frank M. Stenton, *William the Conqueror and the Rule of the Normans* (London, 1928), p. 154. See also Körner, p. 114.

[91] Agreeing with this date are: Freeman, *Norman Conquest*, III:315, 684–85; Stenton, *Anglo-Saxon England*, p. 578; Brown, *The Normans and Norman Conquest*, pp. 110–11;

The second issue is much more difficult to deal with. Indeed, the question 'why did Harold undertake this journey' is at the very center of this whole controversy and of that which would follow Harold's crowning in January 1066. By 1064, it seems evident that Harold must have known that he would ascend to the throne of England at the death of Edward, and, at the same time, he must have realized that Edward would not live much longer. What possible reason then would he have to want to journey to Normandy? Of contemporary or near-contemporary sources only William of Malmesbury contends that Harold did not intend to go to the continent, being driven there by a storm while on a fishing trip, but he is alone in this assertion.[92] All other original sources show a purpose in the voyage, with most having Edward direct his chief earl to visit Duke William.[93] (Wace insists that one version of the story which he had heard had Harold traveling to Normandy against Edward's wishes, but this version is discounted by him.[94])

This purpose, on the other hand, is difficult to ascertain. Some contemporary sources, all Norman in their authorship, contend that Harold was sent to William either to confirm Edward's promise of the throne or to have Harold give his support to William's inheritance of the throne.[95] Another purpose given in the original sources, primarily the Anglo-Norman ones, is that Harold was traveling to Normandy to try and free the hostages, his brother, Wulfnoð, and his nephew, Hakon, surrendered by his father in 1052. In this, as mentioned in the preceding chapter, he was at least partly successful, taking Hakon back to England with him at the end of his trip.[96]

However, neither of these contemporary explanations for why Harold traveled to Normandy in 1064 has appealed to too many modern historians. For one thing, the idea of Edward sending Harold to deliver confirmation of his inheritance to the throne of England to William, only to have the king of England revoke that confirmation by choosing Harold as his heir on his deathbed but a few months later, suggests a mendacity the likes of which a king who was known for his piety would be incapable of. At the same time, it is hard to believe that Harold would deliver his own fealty to William so soon after he was victorious against the Welsh, thereby gaining military legitimacy for rule, and so close

---

Douglas, *William the Conqueror*, pp. 175–76; and I. Walker, p. 91. Barlow (*Edward the Confessor*, pp. 169, 220–21) chooses a date of 1064 or early 1065, preceding the Northumbrian revolt, which is certainly possible; but Körner's (pp. 109–11) unwillingness to accept any date short of 'the 1060s' is a bit too skeptical.

92 William of Malmesbury, *Gesta regum Anglorum*, I:416–17. Against this is Körner, pp. 115–19 and I. Walker, p. 94.

93 For a listing of these see n. 88 above.

94 Wace, II:94–95.

95 William of Poitiers, pp. 68–69; William of Jumièges, II:158–59; Brown, *The Normans and Norman Conquest*, p. 113; Körner, p. 115; and Campbell, 'Hypothèses sur les causes de l'ambassade de Harold,' pp. 263–65.

96 Eadmer, pp. 6–7 and Symeon of Durham, *Historia regum*, II:183. See also Kenneth E. Cutler, 'The Godwinist Hostages: The Case for 1051,' *Annuale medievali* 12 (1971), 74–76.

to taking the throne himself from a king who figured to be near death.[97] Finally, if Harold was off to Normandy to free his brother and nephew, why had he waited for so long? Thirteen years had passed since they had left England, and it seems that Harold had had several opportunities to free the two before 1065, perhaps when he traveled to Flanders in 1056, to name but one instance. More than likely, the freeing of Hakon came as an afterthought, something which William could use to reward Harold's oath of fealty to him (while also keeping Wulfnoð behind as insurance of this fealty).[98]

Therefore, other theories of why Harold made this trip to Normandy have been introduced. For example, Miles W. Campbell argues that Edward's dispatching of the earl of Wessex to Normandy is a sign that the king's 1051 pro-Norman policies were being re-introduced.[99] David C. Douglas agrees that Edward wanted Harold to visit Normandy, a task which the earl did not want to undertake, but that once there, Harold realized that he could profit from the visit, acquiring freedom for his nephew and a strengthening of his own position at home.[100] Frank Stenton sees the voyage of Harold to Normandy as an opportunity to support the right man as king when his own inheritance possibilities seemed remote at the time, 'he may have doubted whether his following in England was strong enough to carry his election as king.'[101] If Harold had not gone to Normandy, then Tostig would have. So say R. Allen Brown and Tryggvi J. Oleson, who argue that had Tostig been the one making the journey to Normandy, Harold's position with the king might have been eroded, so much so, perhaps, that his own inheritance to the throne might have been compromised.[102] Sten Körner speculates that Harold's visit to Normandy was merely part of a larger diplomatic tour of the continent, not one to confirm William's inheritance of the English throne or to give Harold's fealty to the duke of Normandy: 'It is conceivable . . . that Harold planned to form some sort of alliance with William who was otherwise a potential enemy when the throne became vacant, as it must do sooner or later.'[103] It was a voyage to study the politics of French princes, writes Ian W. Walker.[104] Finally, if nothing else, Harold did acquire some badly needed military intelligence, information which would aid him, although in vain, to defend England against the Normans in 1066.[105]

This leads into the third issue which must be discussed concerning Harold's

---

[97] See, for example, Barlow, *Edward the Confessor*, p. 228 and I. Walker, p. 92.
[98] See Brown, *The Normans and Norman Conquest*, p. 113; Körner, pp. 115, 119–20; and I. Walker, p. 95.
[99] Campbell, 'Hypothèses sur les causes de l'ambassade de Harold,' pp. 263–64.
[100] Douglas, *William the Conqueror*, p. 176.
[101] Stenton, *Anglo-Saxon England*, p. 578. See also Körner, p. 121.
[102] Brown, *The Normans and the Norman Conquest*, p. 114 and Oleson, 'Edward the Confessor's Promise,' p. 226 n. 3.
[103] Körner, pp. 119–21. The quote is on p. 121.
[104] I. Walker, pp. 92–93, who takes this from a similar assertion made by the author of the *Vita Ædwardi* (p. 51) concerning Harold's 1056 visit to Flanders.
[105] See I. Walker, p. 102.

visit: once in Normandy, whatever the reason for going there, Harold seems to have willingly pledged his support of William's inheritance to the England throne. An oath was taken, on holy relics, which bound the earl to the duke; the violation of this oath would be used by most Norman sources to condemn Harold as treasonous, thereby justifying William the Conqueror's attack of England in 1066. However, there are some inconsistencies in the original accounts of this oath. Should William of Poitiers be believed, for example, this oath was detailed and demanding. Harold promised:

> That as long as he lived he would be the vicar of Duke William in the court of his lord King Edward; that he would strive to the utmost with his counsel and his wealth to ensure that the English monarchy should be pledged to him after Edward's death; that in the mean time the castle of Dover should be fortified in various places at his expense for William's soldiers; likewise that he would furnish with provisions and garrisons other castles to be fortified in various places chosen by the duke.[106]

Naturally, there must be some questioning of the source in this matter. Simply put, the idea of Harold building castles using his own funds and then immediately turning them over to William is fairly implausible.[107]

There is also some question as to where the oath was taken, the *Bayeux Tapestry* indicating Bayeux, William of Poitiers Bonneville-sur-Touques, and Orderic Vitalis Rouen.[108] This in itself is not important, although it has been used by some to cast doubt on what exactly occurred with this oath.[109]

A more important question is: why did Harold take the oath? Was it given in response to William's freeing him from Count Guy of Ponthieu?[110] Or was Harold simply taking the simplest way out of a difficult situation, one in which he could plead duress when breaking that same oath later, when Edward died?[111]

---

[106] William of Poitiers, pp. 70–71:
se in curia domini sui Edwardi regis quamdiu superesset ducis Guillelmi uicarium fore; enisurum quanto consilio ualeret aut opibus ut Anglica monarchia post Edwardi decessum in eius manu confirmaretur; traditurum interim ipsius militium custodiae castrum Doueram, studio atque sumptu suo communitum; item per diuersa loca illius terrae alia castra, ubi uoluntas ducis ea firmari iuberet, abunde quoque alimonias daturum custodibus.
(I think that the Davis and Chibnall's translation of *militium* as 'knights' in this passage is in error; a more accurate translation would be 'soldiers.') See also Brown, *The Normans and Norman Conquest*, p. 112 and Douglas, *William the Conqueror*, pp. 176–77.

[107] See, for example, Barlow, *Edward the Confessor*, p. 226.

[108] *Bayeux Tapestry*, pl. 29; William of Poitiers, pp. 70–71; and Orderic Vitalis, II:134. See also Brown, *The Normans and the Norman Conquest*, p. 111; Barlow, *Edward the Confessor*, p. 225; and Douglas, *William the Conqueror*, p. 176.

[109] See, for example, Brown, *The Normans and the Norman Conquest*, p. 111; Barlow, *Edward the Confessor*, p. 225; and Douglas, *William the Conqueror*, p. 176.

[110] As Brown (*The Normans and the Norman Conquest*, p. 114) suggests.

[111] As Stenton (*Anglo-Saxon England*, p. 578) and Douglas (*William the Conqueror*, p. 177) aver. Barlow (*Edward the Confessor*, p. 229) notes that 'Harold's own behaviour does not seem to have been affected by this incident.'

Was the oath taken only because William demanded that Harold take it?[112] Or, finally, was it done in trickery, Harold not knowing to what or on what he was pledging?[113] Or, did Harold take the oath of his own initiative, planning by this to give William the illusion that he supported the duke's right to the English throne and thereby buy himself time to secure his own inheritance?[114] No one may ever know the answers of any of those questions for sure. One thing seems certain, though: there seems to be sufficient evidence that Harold made such an oath. Even the pro-Harold *Vita Ædwardi* claims that Harold was 'rather too generous with oaths.'[115]

A fourth issue to be resolved in the tale of Harold's journey to Normandy is the betrothal of William's daughter to Harold. Did this in fact occur and, if so, why? Again, the narrative sources, while once again one-sided in their origin, seem to indicate a positive answer. In 1064, Harold was in the market for a wife after all, never having legitimized his long-term affair with Eadgyð Swanneshals. Eventually, in order to keep the peace with the northern earldoms after the Northumbrian revolt, he would be forced to marry Ealdyð, the widow of King Gruffydd ap Llywelyn and sister to Earls Edwin of Mercia and Morkere of Northumbria, but in 1064 the thought of securing a marriage alliance with Normandy, like that which his brother, Tostig, had with Flanders, must have been quite inviting.[116]

Finally, while all of the issues so far raised in the story of Harold's visit to Normandy have had to deal with Harold's role in the affair, the following question must also be asked: what did William hope to gain from Harold's visit? Was he a politically naive duke 'duped' by the astute treachery of his noble English visitor, as William of Poitiers underhandedly suggests,[117] or did he trap Harold into making an oath which he knew that the 'chief earl of England' could not keep, and thereby justify his planned invasion?[118] Perhaps all he did was to 'flex his muscles,' capitalizing on a situation which could have turned against him to show Harold 'how much Norman swords were superior to English axes,' to use William of Malmesbury's descriptive phrase.[119]

If he did make an oath of fealty to William, it was an unusual way for Harold

---

[112] As I. Walker (p. 99) claims.

[113] As Wace (II:97) would have us believe. See also Douglas, *William the Conqueror*, p. 177.

[114] Such, it seems, is the conclusion of William of Malmesbury (*Gesta regum Anglorum*, I:418–19). See also Douglas, *William the Conqueror*, p. 176.

[115] *Vita Ædwardi*, pp. 80–81. See also Körner, pp. 113–14 and Barlow, *English Church*, p. 59.

[116] The original sources recording this are Henry of Huntingdon, pp. 380–81; Wace, II:97; and Orderic Vitalis, III:112–13. See also Freeman, *Norman Conquest*, III:625–27; Brown, *The Normans and the Norman Conquest*, pp. 112–14; Körner, p. 116; Douglas, *William the Conqueror*, p. 394; I. Walker, pp. 93–94, 98; and Campbell, 'Hypothèses sur les causes de l'ambassade de Harold,' p. 243.

[117] William of Poitiers, pp. 70–71. Against this is Barlow, *Edward the Confessor*, p. 226.

[118] See I. Walker, p. 101.

[119] William of Malmesbury, *Gesta regum Anglorum*, I:440–41. See also Brown, *The Normans and the Norman Conquest*, p. 83, and Douglas, *William the Conqueror*, p. 176.

to acquire a friendship or alliance. Harold had two unmistakable means by which he solved such problems. The first was his wealth. By the time Harold ascended to the throne in 1066, he was undoubtedly the wealthiest man in England. From the *Domesday Book* it can be seen that his real estate holdings were extensive, certainly the greatest among all Englishmen,[120] and Harold was not afraid to use this wealth to buy friendship and to gain power.

He seems to have been interested especially in friendships with ecclesiastical establishments and persons, realizing perhaps better even than his father that ecclesiastical friendship ultimately led to political security.[121] Harold continued the family's friendship with Ealdred, the bishop of Worcester, who was later supported by the earl to become archbishop of York in 1060;[122] patronized Stigand as archbishop of Canterbury, even assisting him in stopping an ecclesiastical donation which went against the archbishop's wishes;[123] he sponsored his own chaplain, Leofgar, as bishop of Hereford in 1056 – Leofgar was killed in a Welsh raid a short time after taking over this position;[124] and he supported with lands and money Bishop (later Saint) Wulfstan of Worcester who in turn frequently advised the earl. According to William of Malmesbury's *Vita Wulfstani*, the saint even cured Harold's daughter of an eye complaint.[125]

In particular, Harold gave much to Waltham Abbey in East Anglia. Following King Edward's gift of the abbey to Harold sometime in the late 1040s, according to the later *Waltham Chronicle* (written c.1177), the then young earl began to

---

[120] Harold's wealth has been the subject of a number of recent studies, all of which come to the same general conclusion: he was a very wealthy man. See Ann Williams, 'Land and Power in the Eleventh-Century: the Estates of Harold Godwinson,' *Proceedings of the Battle Conference on Anglo-Norman Studies* 3 (1980), 171–87; Fleming, *Kings and Lords in Conquest England*; Robin Fleming, 'Domesday Estates of the King and the Godwines: A Study in Late Saxon Politics,' *Speculum* 58 (1983), 987–1007; Peter A. Clarke, *The English Nobility under Edward the Confessor* (Oxford, 1994); and I. Walker, pp. 54–73. See also Stafford, *Unification and Conquest*, p. 153, and Loyn, 'Harold, Son of Godwin,' p. 315.

[121] On the other hand, Barlow (*English Church*, pp. 52, 59) finds Harold 'not religiously inclined' and that he was 'secular in outlook and pagan in morals.' See also Brown, *The Normans and Norman Conquest*, p. 93. Freeman (*Norman Conquest*, II:428–30) believes the opposite, that Harold was actually quite attentive to church affairs, although not at the expense of his rule over Wessex or England. See also I. Walker, pp. 70–72. Against the allegations that Harold despoiled many churches and monasteries see Freeman, *Norman Conquest*, II:547–52 and I. Walker, pp. 67–68.

[122] I. Walker, pp. 132–33 and King, pp. 130–31.

[123] *Ecclesiastical Documents: A Brief History of the Bishopbrick of Somerset*, ed. J. Hunter (London, 1840), pp. 15–16; *Liber Elienses*, ed. E.O. Blake (London, 1962), p. 168; Freeman, *Norman Conquest*, II:432–33; Barlow, *Edward the Confessor*, p. 150; Barlow, *English Church*, pp. 75 n. 5 and 79 n. 1; and I. Walker, p. 127. The will in question was Bishop Dudec of Wells'. This may have led to Harold's quarrel with Dudec's successor, Bishop Giso of Wells. See Freeman, *Norman Conquest*, II:674–81.

[124] John of Worcester, II:580–81 and I. Walker, pp. 80–81.

[125] William of Malmesbury, *Vita Wulfstani*, pp. 13, 34, 49–50. See also Freeman, *Norman Conquest*, II:41; Barlow, *English Church*, pp. 59–60, 269; and I. Walker, p. 125.

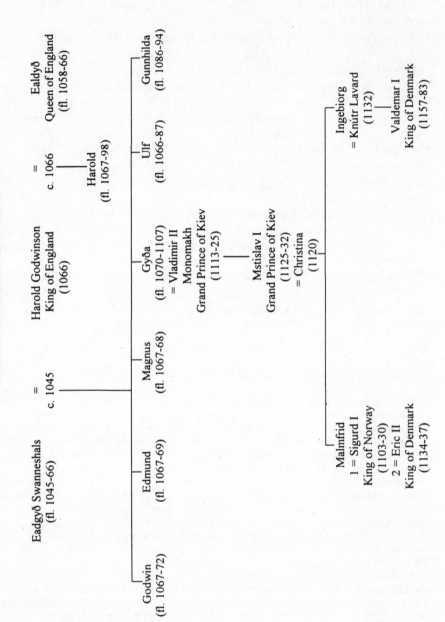

Harold Godwinson and His Descendants

enrich this establishment almost immediately, a practice which continued until his death:

> Throughout his whole life, like a true son of the Church, he occupied himself in making her rich in resources, heaping gifts upon her, and making her gleam with gold, silver and precious stones. He was particularly active in procuring as large a number of relics as he could from different part of the world, either by request or by purchase.[126]

He also added new clerics, 'wise and educated, selected by the community and chosen with care from among the best men in the land,' and a new dean, Wulwin, 'a devout man of high moral character, and distinguished for learning, a shining example of perfect chastity.'[127] He also rebuilt the collegiate church at Waltham, the Church of Waltham Holy Cross, which was consecrated by Cynesige, then archbishop of York, on 3 May 1060.[128] (Unfortunately, because of Harold's patronage, after the conquest, Waltham was not supported and eventually fell into ruin.[129])

Late in his life, and especially after he had ascended to the throne, what friendships Harold was not able to buy, he seems to have tried to acquire through marriage. This may be what happened in Normandy. As mentioned, William's reward for Harold's oath to him may have been marriage with his daughter, Agatha,[130] but no official marriage was ever made. Instead, Harold married Ealdyð, the widow of King Gruffydd ap Llywelyn of Wales, daughter of Ælfgar, earl of Mercia, and sister to later earls, Edwin and Morkere (of Mercia and Northumbria respectively). This marriage secured an alliance with the only rival family to the Godwins in England, and it seems also to have led to peace between the northern English earldoms and their new king.[131]

---

126 *Waltham Chronicle*, pp. 26–27:
Nam toto tempore uite ipsius, quasi uterinus filius ecclesie factus, opibus eam ditare, donariis augere, auro, argento, et gemmis prefulgentem exhibere sategit, presertim reliquiarum multiplicitate quatenus poterat prece uel precio, in diuersis terrarum partibus non segnis conquisitor fuit.
See also *Waltham Chronicle*, pp. 28–37. An inventory of some of these relics is found on pp. 30–33; a different list, taken from a more contemporary document, British Library Harley MS 3776, fols. 31–35, can be found in Nicholas Rogers, 'The Waltham Abbey Relic-List,' in *England in the Eleventh Century: Proceedings of the 1990 Harlaxton Symposium*, ed. C. Hicks (Stamford, 1992), pp. 157–81. See also Freeman, *Norman Conquest*, II:41–42, 438–45, 670–74 and I. Walker, pp. 72–73. Freeman holds that this was not a monastery with monks, but rather a college with canons.
127 *Waltham Chronicle*, pp. 26–29. On Harold's desire that this be an exceptional educational facility, see Freeman, *Norman Conquest*, II:443–44 and I. Walker, pp. 72–73.
128 Freeman, *Norman Conquest*, II:438–40, 444; Stenton, *Anglo-Saxon England*, p. 466; Barlow, *Edward the Confessor*, p. 199; and I. Walker, p. 72.
129 Brown, *The Normans and Norman Conquest*, pp. 89 (n. 190), 224.
130 See n. 115 above.
131 William of Jumièges, II:160–63; Orderic Vitalis, II:138–39; Freeman, *Norman Conquest*, III:625–27; Douglas, *William the Conqueror*, p. 183; I. Walker, pp. 129–31; Loyn, 'Harold, Son of Godwin,' p. 310; Maund, *Ireland, Wales, and England*, p. 137; Maund, 'The Welsh Alliances of Earl Ælfgar,' pp. 186–89; and Suppe, p. 63.

Yet Harold's great love always seems to have been Eadgyð Swanneshals, also known as 'the Fair.' In a way, this love for Eadgyð seems to have been a combination of that held for their women by his brothers, Swegen and Tostig. Although not the result of an abduction, like that of Swegen for Eadgifu, the abbess of Leominster, it too seems never to have been legitimized.[132] At the same time, it was also a devotion between a man and woman which seems to have existed for years, imitating that between Judith of Flanders and Tostig.

Little is known about Eadgyð, perhaps because of the illegitimate nature of the relationship. What her background or her station was cannot be known, although the lower German 'Swanneshals' (Swan's neck) could indicate an English or Flemish origin. She was also possibly a woman of status and prestige.[133] She must have been quite beautiful, however, as determined both by her anatomical name, which would have denoted a particularly attractive feature, as well as her cognomen 'the Fair,' by which she was known in the *Domesday Book* and other later sources.

Also not known is where and under what conditions Harold and Eadgyð met. They may have begun their relationship early in Harold's political career, as three of his sons assumed to have been born to Eadgyð were old enough to carry on campaigns against William the Conqueror in 1068 and 1069. Therefore, Ian Walker's estimate of a mid-1040s date for their 'marriage' is certainly reasonable.[134] She was also with him at the end of his life, despite his 'other' marriage to Ealdyð, as the *Waltham Chronicle* has her identifying Harold's body at Hastings because she 'knew the secret marks on the king's body better than others did.'[135] After his death, Eadgyð was far from the 'cast off,' impoverished ex-mistress. According to the *Domesday Book*, she held close to 280 hides of land, worth over £520, mostly in eastern England. More than twenty-nine men and three women were directly commended to her.[136]

Together, Harold and Eadgyð had at least six and perhaps seven children. Four were sons – Godwin, Edmund (or Edwin), Magnus, and Ulf (although some historians have suggested that Ulf was a son of Harold by Ealdyð) – and two were daughters – Gyða and Gunnhild – with one more, its gender unknown,

---

132 Some historians believe that Harold in fact was married, although perhaps *more Danico* (in the Danish manner) to Eadgyð. See, for example, I. Walker, pp. 20, 61, 127–28.
133 See Freeman, *Norman Conquest*, III:763–65 and I. Walker, pp. 128–29. I. Walker's assertion (pp. 128–29) that she was of East Anglian origin and of noble status is possible, but really has no evidence to support it, especially if it was not a legitimate relationship. Equally problematic is the statement by Frank Barlow (*English Church*, p. 59) that Harold's relationship with Eadgyð is evidence that the earl 'was secular in outlook and pagan in morals' or that 'the Danish side of his character was dominant.'
134 I. Walker, p. 128.
135 *Waltham Chronicle*, pp. 54–55. The complete quote will be transcribed below. See I. Walker, pp. 129–30 also.
136 I. Walker, pp. 61, 72, 128–29 and Clarke, pp. 57–58, 100–01, 273–79. On Clarke, pp. 273–79, is a list of these *Domesday Book* sites.

dying unbaptized in childbirth.[137] The eldest was undoubtedly Godwin, who appears to have been the only one of Harold's children to have been granted lands which are listed in the *Domesday Book*.[138] Although seemingly old enough to have joined his father at the battle of Hastings, Godwin was not there. Nevertheless, with his brothers, Edmund and Magnus, he rose up against his father's Hastings opponent in 1068 and 1069,[139] before all three fled from England, first to Ireland, then to Flanders, and finally to Denmark.[140] Whether they then settled in Denmark or traveled elsewhere is not known, although there is a possibility that they may have traveled to Russia, as it is there that their sister, Gyða, was married to Vladimir Monomakh, the Russian Prince of Smolensk. Why this union was made cannot be known. Undoubtedly it was a fortuitous marriage for an exiled daughter of a dead king, but what did Vladimir receive in exchange? Perhaps only a desired connection to royalty. Vladimir and Gyða had several children before she died in 1107; eight sons and three daughters are mentioned in the sources. In 1113, Vladimir became the Grand Prince of Kiev, a title which he passed on to his eldest son by Gyða, Mstislav.[141] Thus the Godwin family had appeared again as European royalty.

The other progeny of Harold were not so fortunate as Gyða. Ulf, his last possible son by Eadgyð, was imprisoned by William the Conqueror in Normandy until William's death, whereupon Duke Robert of Normandy released this Haroldson and knighted him.[142] Gunnhild, his second daughter, after being educated at Wilton Abbey, like her royal aunt, Eadgyða, joined the nuns living there, only to be 'abducted' in August 1093 by Alan the Red, the Breton earl of Richmond. For less than a year, she lived with Alan the Red, when he suddenly died, seemingly freeing her from his imprisonment. However, instead of returning to Wilton she took up with Alan the Black, the dead earl's brother and heir to

137 A general look at Harold's children can be found in Freeman, *Norman Conquest*, III:754–57; I. Walker, pp. 131, 187–97; and Benjamin T. Hudson, 'The Family of Harold Godwinsson and the Irish Sea Province,' *Journal of the Royal Society of Antiquaries of Ireland* 109 (1979), 92–100. Despite being unbaptized, the deceased child of Harold and Eadgyð was buried in consecrated ground, near St. Dunstan's tomb in Christ Church, Canterbury, a situation which offended some later writers. See Osbern, *Miracula S. Dunstani*, in *Memorials of St. Dunstan*, ed. W. Stubbs (London, 1874), pp. 141–42; Barlow, *English Church*, pp. 59, 210; and I. Walker, p. 131.
138 See Clarke, pp. 164–69, for a list of Godwin's land holdings mentioned in the *Domesday Book*.
139 See n. 174 below for references to these uprisings.
140 See Saxo Grammaticus, *Historia Danica*, ed. P.E. Müller and J.M. Velschow (Hannover, 1839), I:556; Freeman, *Norman Conquest*, IV:159; I. Walker, pp. 192–94; and Hudson, 'The Family of Harold Godwinsson,' pp. 92–94.
141 See *The Russian Primary Chronicle*, ed. S. H. Cross and O.B. Sherbowitz-Wetzor (Cambridge, 1973); Freeman, *Norman Conquest*, IV:159–60, 754–55; I. Walker, pp. 193–95; Hudson, 'The Family of Harold Godwinsson,' pp. 93, 97; and G. Vernadsky, *Kievan Rus* (New Haven, 1942), pp. 96–97, 336.
142 See 'Florence' of Worcester, *Chronicon ex chronicis*, ed. B. Thorpe (London, 1849), II:21; Freeman, *Norman Conquest*, IV:755–56; I. Walker, p. 197; and Hudson, 'The Family of Harold Godwinsson,' p. 93.

Richmond. Such a refusal to return to the abbey may show that these relation-ships, if not instigated, were welcomed by her. At least this is the indication of her correspondence with Anselm, the archbishop of Canterbury, who tries vainly to compel her to return to Wilton after the death of her first 'husband.' Nothing further is known about Gunnhild. She also appears to have had no children.[143]

A final son of Harold Godwinson, named after his father, was born to Queen Ealdyð at Chester after the death of his father at Hastings. Too young to partici-pate in the struggles of his elder step-brothers and uncles, Earls Edwin and Morkere, against William in the late 1060s, as the only legitimate son of King Harold Godwinson, Harold was still a threat to the new king. By 1071, he too had been forced to flee from England, traveling first to Ireland and then to Norway, where he was welcomed into the palace of King Olaf Haraldson, a gesture Snorri Sturluson affirms was made because of the kindness shown to him by Harold's father after the Norwegians had been defeated at Stamford Bridge. Harold Haroldson would appear one final time in the sources, fighting in 1098 off the Welsh island of Anglesey alongside the Norwegian king, Magnús Ólafsson, against the Norman earls of Shrewsbury and Chester.[144]

Edward the Confessor died on 5 January 1066; he was followed on the throne a day later by Harold Godwinson, consecrated as king by either Stigand, the archbishop of Canterbury, or Ealdred, the archbishop of York.[145] According to contemporary English chroniclers, Edward not only wished Harold to succeed to the throne after him, but the king also prepared his successor for this regal inheritance.[146] John of Worcester even uses the term 'subregulus' to describe Harold at the death of Edward, adding 'whom the king had chosen before his demise as successor to the kingdom.'[147] The *Anglo-Saxon Chronicle* (E) agrees with John of Worcester's assessment of Harold's preparation for the throne: 'Earl Harold ascended to the throne of England, just as the king had given it to

---

143 See Freeman, *Norman Conquest*, IV:756–57; Douglas, *William the Conqueror*, p. 268 n. 2; I. Walker, pp. 195–96; Richard W. Southern, *Saint Anselm and his Biographer* (Cambridge, 1963), pp. 183–95; Frank Barlow, *William Rufus* (Berkeley and Los Angeles, 1983), pp. 313–14; and Eleanor Searle, 'Women and the Legitimization of Succession at the Norman Conquest,' *Proceedings of the Battle Conference on Anglo-Norman Studies* 2 (1979), 167–69.
144 See William of Malmesbury, *Gesta regum Anglorum*, I:570–71; I. Walker, p. 195; and Hudson, 'The Family of Harold Godwinsson,' pp. 93, 97.
145 The Norman sources claim that this was Stigand, because of the controversy of his appointment, while the English sources use Ealdred for this lack of notoriety. See Körner, pp. 131–38 and I. Walker, pp. 136–38.
146 See *Anglo-Saxon Chronicle* (C and D) 1065 (E) 1066, I:194–95, 197; *Vita Ædwardi*, pp. 122–25; John of Worcester, pp. 600–01; Symeon of Durham, *Historia regum*, II:179; *Liber Elienses*, p. 169; Eadmer, pp. 8–9; and *Waltham Chronicle*, pp. 44–45. For a discussion of this and how it fits in with English tradition see Ann Williams, 'Some Notes and Consideratios on Problems Connected with the English Royal Succession, 860–1066,' *Proceedings of the Battle Conference* 1 (1978), 165–67.
147 John of Worcester, II:600–01: ' . . . subregulus Haroldus, Goduuini ducis filius, quem rex ante suam decessionem regni successorem elegerat.' See also Freeman, *Norman Conquest*, III:576–81.

him, and everyone approved of him being there.'[148] Perhaps the *Waltham Chronicle* says it best:

> After the death of this most sainted king, therefore, Earl Harold was elected king by unanimous consent, for there was no one in the land more knowledgeable, more vigorous in arms, wiser in the laws of the land or more highly regarded for his prowess of every kind. So those who had been his chief enemies up to this time could not oppose this election, for England had not given birth to a man as distinguished as he in all respects to undertake such a task.[149]

However, to post-Conquest Norman chroniclers, Harold's occupation of a throne rightfully William the Conqueror's, and confirmed as such by Harold's oath to him, was the basest form of treason.[150] Yet even most of these sources must admit that Edward gave the throne to Harold Godwinson.[151] This seems to have presented a confusing dilemma to some of these contemporary authors. Was Edward, the saintly king who had always promised William the crown of England, thus not going against his promise by awarding the throne to Harold? Such is a fair, but somewhat condemnatory question, and to answer it some of these works were forced to 'create' a scenario which would preserve Edward's honesty and William's justification for attacking England: William of Malmesbury, for one, claims that Harold seized the crown from the dying Edward and then exhorted the English nobles to support him in this usurpation; Wace has Edward give the crown to Harold, but only under duress from the earl and with the prophecy that it would cost Harold his life; and Orderic Vitalis has Harold deceive Edward into making him heir, a tactic recognized as mendacious not only by William but also by the pope.[152]

Modern historians have confronted the granting of Edward's crown to Harold with a similar confusion. Only Tryggvi J. Oleson has chosen to deny its occurrence,[153] while others are convinced that as William of Poitiers, whose loyalty to

[148] *Anglo-Saxon Chronicle*, (E) 1066, I:197: 'Harold eorl feng to Engla landes cyne rice, swa swa se cyng hit him ge uðe. ꝺ eac men hine þær to gecuron.' See also Freeman, *Norman Conquest*, III:580–81.

[149] *Waltham Chronicle*, pp. 44–45:
Post obitum itaque sanctissimi regis, comes Haroldus unanimi omnium consensu in regem eligitur, quia non erat eo prudentior in terra, armis strenuus magis, legum terre sagatior, in omni genere probitatis cultior, ita ut huic electioni non possent contradicere qui eum summo odio persecuti fuissent usque ad tempora illa, quoniam tanto operi adeo insignem in omnibus non genuerit Anglia.

[150] William of Poitiers, pp. 110–13; William of Jumièges, II: 160–61; William of Malmesbury, *Gesta regum*, I:418–19; Henry of Huntingdon, pp. 384–85; Orderic Vitalis, II:134–39, III:92–93; Wace, II:99–103; and *The Chronicle of Battle Abbey*, ed. and trans. E. Searle (Oxford, 1980), pp. 32–34.

[151] See, for example, Orderic Vitalis, II:136–39 and Wace, II:99–103. See also Freeman, *Norman Conquest*, III:587–95.

[152] William of Malmesbury, *Gesta regum*, I:418–21; Wace, II:99–103; and Orderic Vitalis, II:136–39. See also Freeman, *Norman Conquest*, III:588–95.

[153] Oleson, *Witenagemot*, p. 85 and Oleson, 'Edward the Confessor's Promise,' p. 227.

his duke is irrefutable, even records it, such a bequest must have indeed happened.[154] Perhaps the king was 'out of his mind when he bequeathed the throne to Harold,' suggests Frank Barlow, although in saying this he must also admit that 'words spoken *in articulo mortis* were the most solemn that medieval man could imagine.'[155] While that situation certainly is a possibility, most historians studying the 1066 succession to the English throne simply accept the fact that Harold had been the designated heir to Edward for a very long time and that promises and oaths made to a foreign duke meant nothing when compared to the military might and political power held by the earl of Wessex who was, after all, also the only claimant to the throne in England at the time of the old king's death. Edward Freeman writes:

> The King was dead. The last day of his kingship had been the worthiest. After all the errors and follies of his reign, Eadward died, not only as a saint, but as an Englishman and a patriot. For the last thirteen years of his life Harold had been his guide and guardian; for the last nine years he had been the expectant successor of the Crown. And now the day had come and the word was spoken. Those faithful years of guardianship had not been without their fruit . . . England was to have an English king, the noblest man of the English people.[156]

That he was desired by the English as their chief governor is confirmed by Harold's easy election as king by the witenagemot.[157] The only other choice was Edgar Æðeling, and, despite being nephew to Edward, he had never faced an enemy such as those which the English were sure to confront.[158] As Frank Stenton notes:

> The circumstances of the moment made the choice inevitable. To the danger of invasion from Normandy and Norway was now added the certainty that Tostig would attempt a landing in the spring and the probability that the king of the Scots, his sworn brother, would cross the border to support him. There was an overwhelming case for giving the name and authority of a king to the one Englishman who had shown the ability to plan and carry out a campaign. King Edward himself realized at the end that the claim of his young kinsman Edgar, 'the Ætheling', must give way to military necessities.[159]

The names William the Conqueror, Sveinn Estriðson, and Haraldr Harðráði were never even considered.

---

154 See Freeman, *Norman Conquest*, III:587–88; Körner, p. 123; Barlow, *Edward the Confessor*, pp. 252–53; and I. Walker, pp. 118–19.
155 Barlow, *Edward the Confessor*, pp. 252–53. See also Brown, *The Normans and Norman Conquest*, pp. 116–18.
156 Freeman, *Norman Conquest*, III:17. See also Freeman, *Norman Conquest*, II:423–24, 663–65.
157 See Freeman, *Norman Conquest*, III:19–23, 597–612.
158 See Stenton, *Anglo-Saxon England*, p. 580; I. Walker, pp. 118–19; and Hooper, 'Edgar the Ætheling,' pp. 202–03.
159 Stenton, *Anglo-Saxon England*, p. 580.

We can only speculate what type of king Harold would have been had he reigned as long as Edward did because he ruled for such a short time -- nine months – during which he and the kingdom were continually beset by the threat of invasion. Yet during those nine months his governance seemed to express itself in three themes: political unity, centralized economic power, and military preparation. Political unity he achieved both by placing an increased confidence in his non-Godwinson earls, Edwin of Mercia and Morkere of Northumbria,[160] and then, shortly after being crowned, by traveling north to meet with the people in their earldoms. Taking Bishop Wulfstan of Worcester, whose renowned piety was already forecasting his later sainthood, Harold toured the north, meeting with and pacifying the leaders and citizens of these northern regions. At York, in a Northumbrian earldom which had been less than supportive of Harold's assumption of the throne, Harold and Wulfstan met with the local council and listened to their concerns while at the same time expressing his own worries about the safety of the realm. The outcome of these discussions, which the original sources do not detail, seems to have strengthened Harold's position, so that when he traveled south to London, at least for the moment, the island kingdom was largely united behind him.[161] They would have to be, Harold must have surmised, for all would have to defend it in the upcoming months: the north against the Norwegians and perhaps the Scots, the south against the Normans and perhaps the Danes.

The second theme, economic power, was achieved through the authorization of more than forty mints throughout the kingdom and the minting of an increased amount of new coinage. This in turn increased the royal revenue significantly, as the charges for bullion and new dyes brought larger sums into the state coffers.[162] All of these monies would be required to pay for the arms, supplies, and soldiers needed to defend against foreign invasions.

Finally, perhaps the most important focus of Harold's rule was his preparation for the oncoming invasions of those who also claimed the English throne.

---

[160] Part of this was undoubtedly in marrying their sister, an act which had taken place earlier, but Harold also seems to have acknowledged their leadership and sought their advice apart from that act during his reign. See Freeman, *Norman Conquest*, III:49–51.

[161] On this trip north see William of Malmesbury, *Vita Wulfstani*, pp. 22–24; Freeman, *Norman Conquest*, III:58–64; Stafford, *Unification and Conquest*, p. 99; William E. Kapelle, *The Norman Conquest of the North: The Region and Its Transformation, 1000–1135* (Chapel Hill, 1979), pp. 101–05; and I. Walker, pp. 138–39. On the opposition of Northumbria to Harold see Freeman, *Norman Conquest*, III:632–35; I. Walker, p. 138; Bertie Wilkerson, 'Northumbrian Separatism in 1065 and 1066,' *Bulletin of the John Rylands Library* 23 (1939), 504–26; and Dorothy Whitelock, 'The Dealings of the Kings of England with Northumbria in the Tenth and Eleventh Centuries,' in *The Anglo-Saxons: Studies in Some Aspects of their History and Culture Presented to Bruce Dickins*, ed. P. Clemoes (London, 1959), p. 88.

[162] See Freeman, *Norman Conquest*, III:54–55, 631–32; Stenton, *Anglo-Saxon England*, pp. 581–82; Barlow, *Edward the Confessor*, pp. 182–83; Douglas, *William the Conqueror*, p. 304; I. Walker, p. 140; and M. Dolley, *The Norman Conquest and the English Coinage* (London, 1966), pp. 11–12. Coins issued at the behest of Harold have survived from forty-five different mints.

With Harold taking the crown, four enemies could be counted on to show some amount of military force against him; three claimed the throne for themselves, William of Normandy, Haraldr Harðráði of Norway, and Sveinn Estriðson of Denmark, while one, Tostig Godwinson, could be counted on to seek revenge for his ousting as earl of Northumbria, which he blamed on his royal brother Harold. Undoubtedly, Harold knew something of the large-scale invasion plans which each of these opposing rulers were devising, as he also must have known of Tostig's movements since his exile, first to Flanders, then to Denmark, and finally to Norway, where he was certainly attempting to gain supporters for his plan to return to England. However Harold could not have known the specifics of these plans, where each might attack and in what configuration – individually or in alliance. This meant that he needed to devise a defensive strategy which could adequately confront any offensive maneuver which might be encountered. Smaller, more local armies would need to contain any assault in their region until the larger, royal force, which Harold placed on the southern shores to face his perceived greatest threat, William the Conqueror's attack from Normandy, could arrive and fight a larger, hopefully more decisive engagement. It was an enormous task, the discharge of which at least one major twentieth-century historian, Frank Stenton has criticized,[163] but Stenton's criticisms, which he bases on the results achieved, the loss of England to the Normans, are unfounded and somewhat narrow-minded. The responsibility for protecting the whole of England was simply too large for Harold to have adequately dealt with, and, as shall be seen in the following chapters, once one enemy had landed and needed to be dealt with, a second one had a far easier time performing a similar operation. In other words, the Norwegians eased the way for the Normans. As well as could be expected then, Harold's plan of defense was accomplished so that as the summer of 1066 arrived, the forces of England, 'greater naval and land forces than any king in this country had ever gathered before,' according to the *Anglo-Saxon Chronicle* (C and D), appeared ready for their opponents.[164]

All of these actions done in such a short amount of time led many contemporary sources to claim that Harold was a good ruler. Among other things, they comment on his good character. They especially report his military prowess and leadership. Henry of Huntingdon, for example, describes Harold as a 'uir bellis acerrimus.'[165] His enemies were in awe of his military acumen: according to John of Worcester the Welsh considered him to be a 'uirum fortem et bellico-

---

[163] Stenton, *Anglo-Saxon England*, pp. 582–86. Stenton does detail all of the steps that Harold must have taken, although much of this is not recorded in any contemporary sources.

[164] *Anglo-Saxon Chronicle*, (C and D) 1066, I:194–96 (the wording is nearly the same in both versions): 'þa gegadorade he swa mycele scipfyrde ⁊ eac landfyrde swa nan cinge ær her on lande ne gegaderade.' See also John of Worcester, II:600–01; I. Walker, pp. 144–45; C. Warren Hollister, *Anglo-Saxon Military Institutions on the Eve of the Norman Conquest* (Oxford, 1962), p. 122; and Nicholas Hooper, 'Some Observations on the Navy in Late Anglo-Saxon England,' in *Studies in Medieval History for R. Allen Brown*, ed. C. Harper-Bill *et al.* (Woodbridge, 1989), pp. 24–25.

[165] Henry of Huntingdon, p. 374.

sum'[166] while Orderic Vitalis describes him as 'very tall and handsome, remarkable for his physical strength, his courage and eloquence, his ready jests and acts of valour,' all traits which clearly impressed the Normans;[167] and in the *Heimskringla*, the Norwegian king, Haraldr Harðráði, is quoted saying of Harold Godwinson, 'What a little man that was; but he stood proudly in his stirrups.'[168] He was also an astute political leader, with the author of the *Vita Ædwardi* calling him 'maior sapientia Haroldus,'[169] but, above all, Harold was dedicated to his kingdom, and he loved the English people. The *Vita Ædwardi* describes this love:

> In the strength of his body and mind Harold stood forth among the people like a second Judas Maccabeus: a true friend of his race and country, he wielded his father's powers even more actively, and walked in his ways, that is, in patience and mercy, and with kindness to men of good will.[170]

Is it any wonder why John of Worcester praised his short reign with the quote which led off this chapter?

On 22 October 1066, Harold Godwinson was killed defending his throne and people against the conquest of William, duke of Normandy. Tradition has it that he was slain by being shot with an arrow in the eye, but this cannot be substantiated.[171] After the battle had ended, the canons from Waltham Abbey, so supported by Harold during his reign, sought to acquire his corpse and bury it on their grounds, but so mangled were the dead English – the *Waltham Chronicle*

---

166 John of Worcester, II:578. See also William of Malmesbury, *Gesta regum*, I:420–21.

167 Orderic Vitalis, II:136–37: 'Erat enim idem Anglus magnitudine et elegantia uiribus corporis; animique audacia et linguae facundia multisque facetiis et probitatis admirabilis.' See also Loyn, 'Harold, Son of Godwin,' pp. 312–13.

168 Snorri Sturluson, *Heimskringla*, III:187: 'Lítill maðr var þessi ok stóð steigurliga í stigreip.'

169 *Vita Ædwardi*, p. 46.

170 *Vita Ædwardi*, pp. 48–49:

> Virtute enim corporis et animi in populo ut alter Iudas Machabeus, amicusque gentis sue et patrie uices celebrat patris intentius, et eiusdem gressibus incedit, patientia scilicet et misericordia, et affabilitate cum beniuolentibus.

See also John Gillingham, 'Thegns and Knights in Eleventh-Century England: Who Was Then the Gentleman?' *Transactions of the Royal Historical Society*, 6th ser., 5 (1995), 149.

171 See William of Malmesbury, *Gesta regum Anglorum*, I:454–55 and Henry of Huntingdon, p. 204, who may be misreading the Bayeux Tapestry. Against this is David Bernstein, 'The Blinding of Harold and the Meaning of the Bayeux Tapestry,' *Anglo-Norman Studies* 5 (1982), 40–64, which, quite frankly, really stretches the evidence in an effort to prove that the blinding of Harold was nothing more than a metaphor for the falling of England to the Normans. The arguments of Freeman (*Norman Conquest*, III:497–500); I. Walker (p. 179); and N.P. Brooks and H.E. Walker ('The Authority and Interpretation of the Bayeux Tapestry,' *Proceedings of the Battle Conference* 1 (1978), 23–33) in support of the eye injury are more convincing. Most contemporary sources do not mention the method of Harold's death, except that he was killed in the battle. See *Anglo-Saxon Chronicle* (D) 1066, I:199; John of Worcester, II:604–05; Symeon of Durham, *Historia regum*, II:180–81; Eadmer, p. 9; *Carmen de hastingae proelio*, pp. 34–37; William of Poitiers, pp. 138–41; William of Jumièges, II:168–69; Orderic Vitalis, II:176–77; and the *Chronicle of Battle Abbey*, pp. 38–39.

reports that the monks 'turning them [the bodies] over on this side and that' were still 'unable to recognize the king,' something which they attribute to the fact that 'the body of a man when dead and drained of blood does not usually have the same appearance as when alive' – that they needed to bring Harold's long-time mistress, Eadgyð Swanneshals, to the battlefield to identify his body. She ably performed this very difficult task, pointing out the corpse 'among the heaps of dead,' and it was carried to Waltham and buried 'with great honour.'[172] Another tradition holds that it was Harold's mother, Gyða, who identified his body.[173] Later, William, now appropriately called 'the Conqueror' would build an abbey at the site of the battle, named equally appropriately Battle Abbey, the altar of the abbey church being placed on the spot of Harold's demise.

However, Harold's spirit and claim to the throne lived on, for in 1068, and again in 1069, his sons, Godwin, Edmund, and Magnus, attempted in vain to regain their father's realm by uprising.[174] Both times they failed, and they retreated to Ireland and then to the continent where they, together with most of their sisters and brothers, died in obscurity.

---

[172] *Waltham Chronicle*, pp. 54–57:

Gaudio igitur inestimabili fratres confortati, currunt ad cadauera, et uertentes ea huc et illuc, domini regis corpus agnoscere non ualentes, quia corpus hominis exangue non consueuit mortuum formam prioris status frequenter exprimere; unicum placuit reme-dium, ipsum Osegodum domum redire et mulierem quam ante sumptum regimen Anglorum dilexerat, Editham cognomento Swanneshals, quod gallice sonat 'collum cigni', secum adducere que, domini regis quandoque cubicularia, secretoria in eo signa nouerat ceteris amplius, ad ulteriora intima secretorum admissa, quatinus ipsius noticia certificarentur secretis inditiis qui exterioribus non poterant, quia statim letali uulnere confosso, quicquid in eo regalis erat insignii duci deportatum est, signum scilicet pros-trationis regie, quoniam consuetudinis erat antique, et adhuc credimus moderne, in regum expugnatione uel castrorum captione magnis eos donari muneribus qui primi possent regis conum deicere et regi offerre, uel primus castro expugnato regis uexil-lum, precipue ipsius castri munitioni eminentis.

Quam adduxisset Osegodus et inter strages mortuorum pluribus inditiis ipsa corpus regis Haroldi designasset, aptatum feretro, multis heroum Normmanie comitatus honorem corpori exibentibus usque ad Pontem Belli, qui nunc dicitur, ab ipsis fratribus et multa superuenientum copiositate Anglorum qui audierant eorum imminens excid-ium, quia nunquam fuit Anglis cognata Normannorum sotietas, cum magno honore corpus Waltham deductum sepelierunt, ubi usque hodie.

Perhaps his face was unrecognizable because of the facial injury caused by the arrow. See I. Walker, pp. 179–81. See also Freeman, *Norman Conquest*, IV:513–14 and Brown, *The Normans and the Norman Conquest*, pp. 151–52.

[173] See *Carmen de hastingae proelio*, pp. 36–9 and William of Poitiers, pp. 140–41. Pauline Stafford ('Women and the Norman Conquest,' *Transactions of the Royal Historical Society* 6th ser., 4 (1994), 235) agrees here with the *Carmen de hastingae proelio* and William of Poitiers. See also Freeman (*Norman Conquest*, III:511–13) who believes that both Gyða and Eadgyð could have been there to retrieve Harold's corpse.

[174] See *Anglo-Saxon Chronicle* (D) 1067, I:203; 'Florence' of Worcester, II:2–3; Freeman, *Norman Conquest*, IV:140–49, 157–59, 788–90; Stenton, *Anglo-Saxon England*, pp. 600–02; Brown, *The Normans and the Norman Conquest*, pp. 166, 169; Stafford, *Unification and Conquest*, pp. 100, 103–04; Douglas, *William the Conqueror*, pp. 213, 269; I. Walker, pp. 187–197; and Hudson, 'The Family of Harold Godwinsson,' pp. 92–100.

Harold refused to die though, at least in the hearts and stories of the English. He lived on, surviving the battle, although severally wounded. By the twelfth century, the legends of Harold's survival had grown stronger and had become more numerous. Gerald of Wales, for example, notes that the people of Chester claimed that after Hastings Harold had fled there, 'wounded many times' and having lost his left eye 'through an arrow which penetrated it.' From then on 'it is believed that he took the yoke and led the life of an anchorite, passing his days in constant attendance in one of the local churches, and so came happily to the end of his life.'[175] The legends had also traveled beyond England, as evidenced by a survival story appended to the final chapter of the Old Icelandic saga of Heming Ásláksson.[176]

By the early thirteenth century an anonymous *Vita Haroldi* had been written. It purported to tell the whole story of Harold's existence, both before and after Hastings, although the 'before' part is much shorter than the 'after.' Here Harold does not die at Hastings, saved by a woman combing the battlefield to care for the wounded. For two years he is sheltered by this woman in her home in Winchester until fully healed of all his injuries. By this time all of England is under William's control, so that even though Harold wishes to regain his throne, it becomes an impossible task. Harold even goes to Saxony and Denmark for aid against the Normans, but he is unable to gain any. Returning to England in despair, he turns to God and the church, a vocation which occupies him for the rest of his life and the majority of the pages of his *Vita*.[177]

Surely the survival of the warlord Harold Godwinson was a symbol of the survival of the English fighting spirit.

---

[175] Gerald of Wales, p. 149:
> et Haroldum regem se habere testantur: qui, ultimus de gente Saxonica rex in Anglia, publico apud Hastinges bello cum Normannis congrediens, poenas succumbendo perjurii luit; multisque, ut aiunt, confossus vulneribus, oculoque sinistro sagitta perdito ac perforato, ad partes istas victus evasit: ubi sancta conversatione cujusdam urbis ecclesiae jugis et assiduus contemplator adhaerens, vitamque tanquam anachoriticam ducens, viae ac vitae cursum, ut creditur, feliciter consumavit.

See also Freeman (*Norman Conquest*, III:758–63) for an overview of Harold's survival stories, several of which I have not included here.

[176] See Margaret Ashdown, 'An Icelandic Account of the Survival of Harold Godwinson,' in *The Anglo-Saxons: Studies in Some Aspects of their History and Culture Presented to Bruce Dickins*, ed. P. Clemoes (London, 1959), pp. 122–36.

[177] The most widely used edition of the *Vita Haroldi* is that by W.D. Birch, published in 1885 in London. It has been translated by Michael Swanton recently as *The Life of Harold Godwinson* in *Three Lives of the Last Englishmen* (New York, 1984), pp. 3–40. See also Freeman, *Norman Conquest*, III:761–63.

CHAPTER SIX

THE CONFLICT BETWEEN
HAROLD AND TOSTIG GODWINSON[1]

IN 1066 the exiled warlord earl of Northumbria, Tostig Godwinson, joined forces with the warlord king of Norway, Haraldr Harðráði, to invade England against the warlord king of England, Harold Godwinson, his brother. The brothers' personal conflict thus becomes directly important in the overall study of the Norwegian invasion of England in September of that year and indirectly important in the study of the Norman invasion of the same kingdom which followed less than a month later. Since almost the day it occurred, this conflict has been analyzed and debated. Several contemporary or near contemporary chronicles record the sibling rivalry of the then oldest Godwinsons, but even these early accounts differ in their analysis of the affair, sympathizing either with Harold or Tostig, or by introducing a third character to the conflict, as William of Malmesbury does with Saint Wulfstan in the *Vita Wulfstani*.[2] This interpretative difference has left modern historians, such as Edward August Freeman, Frank M. Stenton, and Frank Barlow, with few concrete solutions to the mysteries posed by this very important scenario in late Anglo-Saxon history.[3]

Tostig was the third son of Earl Godwin and Gyða of Denmark. As with the rest of these children, his birth date is not known, but based on information concerning the Godwin family in the *Anglo-Saxon Chronicle* and other contemporary English documents, it appears to have been 1029.[4] Little is also known about the early portion of Tostig's life, although it is probably safe to assume

---

[1] An earlier and much shorter version of this chapter appeared as 'The Conflict between Harold and Tostig Godwinson,' *Scintilla* 1 (1984), 48–62.

[2] William of Malmesbury, *Vita Wulfstani*, ed. Reginald R. Darlington (London, 1928), pp. 22–23.

[3] Edward August Freeman, *The History of the Norman Conquest* (Oxford, 1868), II:378–83, 623–28; Frank M. Stenton, *Anglo-Saxon England*, 3rd edn (London, 1971), pp. 578–80; and Frank Barlow, *Edward the Confessor* (Berkeley and Los Angeles, 1970), pp. 189, 233–39.

[4] Frank Barlow in his edition of the *Vita Ædwardi* (*Vita Ædwardi regis qui apud Westmonasterium requiescit*, ed. and trans. F. Barlow, 2nd edn (London, 1992), pp. 6–8 n. 10) bases his 1029 date on the dates of the marriage of Godwin and Gyða (1019) and the marriage of Tostig and Judith (1051). In *Edward the Confessor* (p. 163), Barlow adds that Tostig appears to have been but a young man at the time of the marriage of his sister and Edward in 1045. Henry of Huntingdon (*Historia Anglorum: The History of the English People*, ed. and trans. D. Greenway (Oxford, 1996), pp. 382–83) and Orderic Vitalis (*The Ecclesiastical History of Orderic Vitalis*, ed. and trans. M. Chibnall (Oxford, 1969), II:138–39) place the order of

that he received the same training in the arts of war and governance as his older brothers. The earliest record we have of this Godwinson comes from 1049 in the *Anglo-Saxon Chronicle* (E), which refers to Tostig's command of one of Edward the Confessor's ships sent in aid of Emperor Henry III against Count Baldwin V of Flanders: 'Then Earl Godwin turned west with two of the king's ships, one of which was captained by Earl Harold and the other by Tostig his brother.'[5] Nothing further is mentioned about the outcome of this voyage, but the reference does perhaps indicate a rather significant military responsibility that Tostig was given at but a young age, maybe as young as 20.

Tostig is not referred to again in contemporary sources for two more years until 1051, when he married Judith of Flanders. Judith's pedigree was impressive. She was the daughter of the late Baldwin IV, who had been count of Flanders until 1035, and she was the half-sister of Baldwin V, the current, very influential count of that same French county.[6] Also, she was the cousin once removed, through her mother, Eleanor of Normandy, of the king of England, Edward, and of the duke of Normandy, William.[7] Tostig's marriage into such an impressive family was, therefore, quite politically beneficial, especially for someone who was only the third son of an earl of England and not yet an earl himself,[8] although it may be assigning the marriage too much credit, as Frank Barlow does, in suggesting that it guaranteed Tostig that earldom; the idea that Tostig might not have been rewarded with an earl's position in light of the relationship of his sister, his father, and his older brother to the throne seems somewhat remote.[9]

Tostig's birth before that of Harold, but this has been successfully refuted by Freeman, *Norman Conquest*, II:552–55.

5　*Anglo-Saxon Chronicle* in *Two of the Saxon Chronicles Parallel*, ed. Charles Plummer and John Earle (Oxford, 1892), (E) 1046, I:168: 'Þa ge[wende] Godwine eorl west onbuton mid þes cynges II scipum þam anan Harold eorl ⁊ þam oðran Tostig his broðer.'

6　On Baldwin V's importance in eleventh-century northern European political history see my forthcoming article, 'Count Baldwin V of Flanders: Manipulator of Eleventh-Century European Politics.'

7　*Vita Ædwardi*, pp. 38–39; Barlow, *Edward the Confessor*, p. 195; Philip Grierson, 'The Relations between England and Flanders before the Norman Conquest,' *Transactions of the Royal Historical Society* 23 (1941), 99–100; Frank Barlow, 'Edward the Confessor's Early Life, Character and Attitudes,' in *The Norman Conquest and Beyond* (London, 1983), pp. 81–82; David C. Douglas, *William the Conqueror* (Berkeley and Los Angeles, 1964), p. 78; David G.J. Raraty, 'Earl Godwine of Wessex: The Origins of his Power and his Political Loyalties,' *History* 74 (1989), 17–18; Miles W. Campbell, 'Earl Godwin of Wessex and Edward the Confessor's Promise of the Throne to William of Normandy,' *Traditio* 28 (1972), 154–55; Miles W. Campbell, 'A Pre-Conquest Norman Occupation of England?' *Speculum* 46 (1971), 29–30; and Patrick McGurk and Jane Rosenthal, 'The Anglo-Saxon Gospelbooks of Judith, Countess of Flanders: Their Text, Make-up and Function,' *Anglo-Saxon England* 24 (1995), 251–52.

8　It was uncommon for such a noble woman to be married to a 'landless' man at this time. See the *Vita Ædwardi*, p. 38 n. 90.

9　Barlow, *Edward the Confessor*, p. 195.

These marriage celebrations were to be short, however, for it was immediately after the Godwin family returned to England from Flanders that King Edward, under the influence of Norman advisors, outlawed Godwin's family. Contemporary authors do not explain why this happened, especially when the potential relationship between Edward's wife's family and the count of Flanders could only have been beneficial to England and the king.[10] Perhaps the connection between Normandy and England was one more valued by Edward, and somehow he felt that it would be weakened by this new association with Flanders, although, with William the Conqueror espoused to Baldwin V's daughter, the marriage between Tostig and Judith would seem to have strengthened the England-Normandy bond.[11] Perhaps it was, as David D.J. Raraty surmises, that the alliance between Godwin and Baldwin V, 'a man who had repeatedly offered refuge and assistance to English exiles and against whom Eadward had just placed himself in public opposition,' could be seen as treasonous, that Godwin by doing this was, as Robert of Jumièges insisted, 'guilefully planning to attack [Edward].'[12] Or, perhaps, as Heather J. Tanner has recently written, the marriage between Tostig and Judith threatened Eustace of Boulogne's influence and power in Flanders, Normandy, and, especially, England. It was, after all, Eustace whose cruel attack on Dover provoked the refusal of Godwin to punish the townspeople and thereby led to his and his family's ousting, and it was Eustace, too, who was one of the first to flee from the island kingdom when Godwin returned.[13] Still, without more conclusive evidence from contemporary sources, none of these possibilities is convincing. Ultimately, the cause of the Godwin family's exile must still be viewed as the result of problems between Godwin and Edward: the latter was convinced by his Norman advisors that the expulsion of the earl of Wessex and his family was worth whatever hostility this might breed between England and Flanders, and the former, too busy with wedding arrangements, may have given the Normans the opportunity to get closer to the king.[14]

The result was that the family was forced to flee, with the exception of Eadgyða. Harold and Leofwine fled to Ireland; Godwin and the remainder of the family fled with Tostig and his new wife to the court of her brother where

---

[10] Barlow, *Edward the Confessor*, p. 108, and Campbell, 'Earl Godwin of Wessex and Edward the Confessor's Promise,' pp. 154–55.

[11] See Sten Körner, *The Battle of Hastings, England, and Europe, 1035–1066* (Lund, 1964), p. 188, and Miles W. Campbell, 'The Anti-Norman Reaction in England in 1052: Suggested Origins,' *Mediaeval Studies* 35 (1973), 431–32.

[12] Raraty, pp. 17–18. The latter part of Raraty's quote is from the *Vita Ædwardi*, pp. 32–33.

[13] Heather J. Tanner, 'The Expansion of the Power and Influence of the Counts of Boulogne under Eustace II,' *Anglo-Norman Studies* 14 (1991), 264–65. For Eustace's attack on Dover and the repercussions which followed see the chapter on 'Godwin and His Family' above. This theory seems to replace the influence of Robert of Jumièges with that of Eustace, or, at least, it seems to make Robert Eustace's pawn. Contemporary sources argue the opposite.

[14] See Campbell, 'A Pre-Conquest Norman Occupation,' pp. 21–31.

they were received with honor and treated well. The anonymous author of the *Vita Ædwardi* writes:

> The famous Earl Godwin was received by Count Baldwin with great honour, partly on account of their old alliance, partly in repayment of the many benefits he had received from the earl.[15]

What old alliance there was between Baldwin and Godwin is not revealed anywhere in this source, nor is it known what the 'many benefits' were which Baldwin was supposed to have received from his English ally.[16] A previous beneficial relationship between the two leaders, however, could explain the reasons behind the oddly unequal marriage of Tostig and Judith.

The flight to a wife's or daughter's land was a common practice during the late Anglo-Saxon period. A noble woman had much sway with her family, and often she would return to her father or brother at the death or exile of her husband.[17] In fact, this would not be the last time that Tostig would seek refuge with his wife's family in Flanders.

Although everything else in Tostig's life eventually disintegrated, his marriage with Judith remained solid. Young at the time of his marriage, he still may have had relationships with women before his wedding to the Flemish princess: according to tradition, he took two sons with him on his conquest of England who would have been too young had they been his children with Judith, but who the mother or mothers of these sons were is not known, nor is it known what the nature of Tostig's relationship with these women was.[18] Judith, too, may have been previously engaged to another man or meant for church service; perhaps she was being 'saved' for marriage to form a special alliance between Flanders and another land. At the very least she appears to have been older than noble women traditionally were at their first marriage, a conclusion derived because her marriage took place only one year prior to that of her niece, Baldwin V's daughter, Matilda, to Duke William of Normandy.[19] What is known is that after Tostig married Judith, he seems to have remained faithful to her, and she to him.

---

15 *Vita Ædwardi*, pp. 38–39:
Susceptus est ergo inclitus dux Godwinus ab ipso comite Balduinocum magno honore, tum pro antique federationis iure, tum pro multorum ipsius ducis beneficiorum uicissitudine.

16 Grierson ('Relations between England and Flanders,' pp. 98–100) has also attempted to discover the origins of this old alliance without success.

17 See R.I. Page, *Life in Anglo-Saxon England* (New York, 1970), p. 72.

18 Their names were Skulr and Ketill. See Snorri Sturlson, *Heimskringla*, ed. B. Aðalbjarnarson (Reykjavik, 1941–51), III:197. No other source mentions Tostig's other wives/lovers or children, and as Snorri's work is of such a late date and somewhat vague on the lineage of these boys, little credence has been placed in this assertion.

19 Stenton, *Anglo-Saxon England*, p. 585. Matilda and William's marriage was planned as early as 1049, when it was denied by Pope Leo IX on the ground of consanguinity. It was solemnized in 1053, although without papal acknowledgment until 1059 when Pope Nicholas II recognized its legitimacy after William had endowed two monasteries in Caen, St Stephen's for men and Holy Trinity for women.

The author of the *Vita Ædwardi*, who certainly knew Tostig well and always wrote favorably about him, affirms this:

> He renounced desire for all women except his wife of royal stock, and chastely, with restraint, and wisely he governed the use of his body and tongue.[20]

There is no reason found in any other source not to believe this account of Tostig's faithfulness to his spouse. The union also produced children, although it is not known how many, what their gender was, or what their names were. These children, quite young at the time according to the *Vita Ædwardi*, would travel with their father and mother to Flanders after the Northumbrian revolt of 1065.[21]

In 1052, Godwin launched his ships from Flanders against England. As mentioned, Harold and Leofwine joined him at the Isle of Wight. All sailed along the coast of Wessex gathering retainers. They then sailed up the Thames River to King Edward, who dwelt in Winchester that Easter, and made peace with their king. As no record mentions Tostig's name among those with Godwin at this meeting, he may not have accompanied his father during this return to England, remaining instead in Flanders with his wife and mother until their safety in England could be assured. On the 15 April, Godwin died in the presence of the king. Tostig was also present.[22]

In 1055, Tostig received a promotion to the position of earl over the province of Northumbria at the death of the previously very popular Earl Siward. The *Anglo-Saxon Chronicle* (E) records the event simply: 'In this year Earl Siward died, and the king gave Tostig, son of Earl Godwin, the earldom.'[23] From 1053

---

[20] *Vita Ædwardi*, pp. 50–51:
   preter eandem regie stirpis uxorem suam omnium abdicans uoluptatem, celebs moderatius corporis et oris sui prudenter regere consuetudinem.
See also Freeman, *Norman Conquest*, II:382–83; Barlow, *Edward the Confessor*, p. 132; and Pauline Stafford, *Unification and Conquest: A Political and Social History of England in the Tenth and Eleventh Centuries* (London, 1989), p. 169. Evidence of Judith's religious nature can be found in McGurk and Rosenthal.

[21] See the *Vita Ædwardi*, pp. 82–83. Although nothing further is known about them or their whereabouts, it is assumed that they were taken by Judith to the household of Welf IV of Bavaria at their marriage in 1070 or 1071.

[22] See *Anglo-Saxon Chronicle* (C) 1053, I:182. For additional references see n. 109 in the chapter 'Godwin and his Family' above.

[23] *Anglo-Saxon Chronicle* (E) 1055, I:186: 'Her on þisum geare forðferde Siward eorl . . . ʏ se cyng geaf one eorldom Tostige Godwines sunu eorles.' See also the *Anglo-Saxon Chronicle* (D) 1055, I:185; *Vita Ædwardi*, pp. 48–49; John of Worcester, pp. 576–77; Henry of Huntingdon, pp. 380–81; Geoffrey Gaimar, *Lestoire des Engles*, ed. T.D. Hardy and C.T. Martin (London, 1888), I:214–15; Freeman, *Norman Conquest*, pp. 375–78; Barlow, *Edward the Confessor*, pp. 193–94; Stafford, *Unification and Conquest*, p. 93; William E. Kapelle, *The Norman Conquest of the North: The Region and Its Transformation, 1000–1135* (Chapel Hill, 1979), pp. 86–89; Ian W. Walker, *Harold: The Last Anglo-Saxon King* (Stroud, 1997), pp. 76–77; and Tryggvi J. Oleson, *The Witenagemot in the Reign of Edward the Confessor: A Study in the Constitutional History of Eleventh-Century England* (Toronto, 1955), p. 94. Geoffrey Gaimar claims that Tostig 'had no right over York', while Henry of Huntingdon

to 1055 there had been only one member of the Godwin family who had occupied an earldom in England, that of Harold in Wessex. By the ascension of Tostig as the Northumbrian earl, Harold's power also increased, as did that of the queen, Eadgyða, Harold and Tostig's sister. Indeed, it seems that both Harold and Eadgyða used their influence with Edward the Confessor to reward Tostig with this title.[24] Otherwise, it seems difficult to reconcile the choice of Tostig, from the south, as earl of this northern, and most vulnerable, earldom. The author of the *Vita Ædwardi* concludes as much when he writes:

> And Tostig, a man of courage, and endowed with great wisdom and shrewdness of mind, with the aid of his friends, and especially, and deservedly, his brother Earl Harold, and his sister, the queen, and with no opposition from the king because of the innumerable services faithfully performed, assumed the earldom.[25]

That this earldom went to Tostig may also be the origins of the feud which develops between Ælfgar and his sons, Edwin and Morkere, and the Godwin children.[26]

Tostig would govern Northumbria for ten years. At first his rule benefitted the Northumbrians. Like Herefordshire with the Welsh, Northumbria had been a territory which frequently suffered raids from the Scots. The Romans, of course, had built Hadrian's Wall to stop such raids, but it had fallen into disrepair in the succeeding millennium, leaving later earls of the region to devise their own means of dealing with the Scottish raiders. In the late tenth and early eleventh centuries, these raids were especially prevalent.[27] Tostig's predecessor, Siward, had used a strong military presence and intimidation to keep the Scots on their side of the border.[28] In 1054, he also used a tactic shown by Swegen Godwinson to have worked effectively against the Welsh: he entered into a Scottish civil

mentions that the only reason why Tostig received this earldom is that Siward's eldest son, Osbeorn, had been killed fighting Macbeth in Scotland, and, Waltheof, his second son, was 'still a young boy.' Freeman (*Norman Conquest*, II:377–78) and R. Allen Brown (*The Normans and the Norman Conquest*, 2nd edn (Woodbridge, 1985), p. 69 n. 94) agree with Henry of Huntingdon's assertion.

24 There is obviously no indication of sibling rivalry between Harold and Tostig at this time.

25 *Vita Ædwardi*, pp. 48–49:
> Argentibus amicis, potissimum autem et pro merito hoc eius fratre Haroldo duce et eius sorore regina, et non resistente rege ob innumera ipsius fideliter acta seruitia, ducatum eius suscepit Tostinus, uir scilicet fortis, et magna preditus animi sagacitate et sollertia.

See also Freeman, *Norman Conquest*, II:375–77. Freeman believes that ultimately the decision was Edward's own and made to keep his 'personal favourite' close to him. Although Tostig is absent from the sources between 1053 and 1055, it can be assumed that he was busy at court, learning the means of rule and 'earning' his earldom. He had been witnessing charters from as early as 1049, after all. See Barlow, *Edward the Confessor*, pp. 88, 332–33.

26 See Barlow, *Edward the Confessor*, pp. 193–94 and I. Walker, pp. 76–77.

27 In 972, 994–95, 1006, and 1018, Scottish armies raided the borderlands of England, attacking as far south as Durham.

28 On the relations between Siward and the Scots, the best source is Kapelle, pp. 27–49.

war, supporting Malcolm, a rival to the Scottish king, Macbeth, who fourteen years previously, in a manner fictionalized by William Shakespeare, had gained the throne himself by usurpation, taking it from Malcolm's father, Duncan. (Malcolm had been placed in the care of Siward by King Duncan before his death, hoping perhaps that the Northumbrian earl would do exactly as he did, support the eventual placement of his son on the throne of Scotland.[29]) Macbeth fought valiantly but vainly against the Northumbrian earl's campaign, but in the end, Siward's army, a mounted force filled with Danish and English huscarls and a large fleet, was simply too much for the Scottish king, whose army was thinned of Scots, by its indecision in supporting its current king or its previous king's lawful successor, but enlarged by a detachment of Orkney Islanders, led by their earl's son, Dolfinn, and a group of Normans who had fled from England at the return of the Godwin family from exile. In one of the least well known but perhaps most bloody battles of the eleventh century, fought in an unknown place north of the Tay River, Siward's forces overwhelmed their opponents and placed Malcolm III on the throne, but victory came at a very high cost: Siward's son and heir, Osbeorn, was one of those who lost his life. Macbeth escaped death in this conflict and continued to fight for a return to his throne, but these efforts were ineffective and eventually, in 1058, at Lumfanan near Aberdeen he was defeated and finally killed.[30]

Ultimately, Tostig would choose a more diplomatic but equally successful route towards peace with Scotland. However, it did not begin that way. When Tostig became earl of Northumbria at the death of Siward, in the year following

---

[29] Siward had tried to do this in 1045 or 1046, but had failed. See Kapelle, pp. 44–46.

[30] The place of this battle is not recorded in any contemporary source and has been lost from Scottish memory. For a description of the conflict between Siward and Macbeth see *Anglo-Saxon Chronicle* (C and D) 1054, I:184–85; John of Worcester, II:574–75; Henry of Huntingdon, pp. 376–77; Geoffrey Gaimar, I:214; Symeon of Durham, *Historia regum*, ed. T. Arnold (London, 1885), II:171; Freeman, *Norman Conquest*, II:362–65, 641–47; Stenton, *Anglo-Saxon England*, p. 570; Barlow, *Edward the Confessor*, p. 202; and Kapelle, pp. 46–47. The *Anglo-Saxon Chronicle* (D), John of Worcester, and Geoffrey Gaimar are all impressed by the large number of dead on both sides, including 'all of the Normans,' while Henry of Huntingdon appends to his account an interesting anecdote concerning the death of Osbeorn which he may have taken from a lost *Siward's Saga*:

Around this time Siward, the mighty earl of Northumbria, almost a giant in stature, very strong mentally and physically, sent his son to conquer Scotland. When they came back and reported to his father that he had been killed in battle, he asked, 'Did he receive his fatal wound in the front or back of his body?' The messengers said, 'In the front'. Then he said, 'I am completely happy, for I consider no other death worthy for me or my son.' So Siward set out for Scotland, and defeated the king in battle, destroyed the whole realm, and having destroyed it, subjected it to himself.

(Circa hoc tempus Siwardus consul fortissimus Nordhymbre, pene gigas statura, manu uero et mente predura, misit filium suum in Scotiam conquirendam. Quem cum bello cesum patri renuntiassent, ait, 'Recepitne uulnus letale in anteriori uel posteriori corporis parte?' Dixerunt nuntii, 'In anteriori.' At ille, 'Gaudeo plane, non enim alio me uel filium meum digner funere.' Siwardus igitur in Scotiam proficiscens, regem nello uicit, regnum totum destruxit, destructum sibi subiugauit.)

Siward's defeat of Macbeth, King Malcolm III of Scotland used the change in leadership as an invitation to plunder the borders of the English earldom. With this invasion, at the least, Malcolm was proving that he did not feel tied to the English; at the most, he was perhaps 'testing' the new regime.[31] According to the *Vita Ædwardi*, Tostig stopped these raids without much combat and loss of life or property:

> Then, when Earl Tostig ruled the earldom, the Scots, since they had not yet tested him and consequently held him more cheaply, harassed him often with raids rather than war. But this irresolute and fickle race of men, better in woods than on the plain, and trusting more to flight than to manly boldness in battle, Tostig, sparing his own men, wore down as much by cunning schemes as by martial courage and military campaigns. And as a result they and their king preferred to serve him and King Edward than to continue fighting.[32]

It thus seems apparent that Tostig played some role in the friendship between Malcolm and Edward, his own friendship with the two monarchs bringing them together. This is confirmed by the fact that in 1059 Malcolm III traveled to London to meet with Edward under the escort of Earl Tostig. It was the first time in nearly eighty years that a Scottish king had visited the court of the king of England and an obvious symbol of the prestigious position of favor Tostig held as one of Edward's closest councilors.[33]

According to Symeon of Durham, Malcolm became Tostig's 'conjuratus frater (sworn brother),' which bound the two together in a special alliance.[34] Evidence of Tostig's friendship with and perhaps military intimidation of Malcolm III can be seen again in 1061, when Tostig went to Rome, his absence allowing Malcolm once again to attack the borders of Northumbria, which attacks stopped promptly on the return of Tostig to his earldom.[35] Finally, after Edward

---

31 Kapelle's claim (p. 47) that Malcolm was in no way Edward the Confessor's vassal in a 'feudal' sense is convincing. This claim was written against Alan O. Anderson's 'Anglo-Scottish Relations from Constantine II to William' (*Scottish Historical Review* 42 (1963), 10) which maintains that the relationship was feudal.

32 *Vita Ædwardi*, pp. 66–67:

> Secundo ducatum agent duce Tostino cum eum Scotti intemptatum haberent, et ob hoc in minori pretio habitum, latrocinio potius quam bello sepius lacesserent; incertum genus hominum et leue, siliusque potius quam campo, fuga quoque magis fidens quam audacia uirili in prelio, tam prudenti astutia quam uirtute bellica et hostili expeditione cum slaute suorum predictus dux attriuit, ut cum rege eorum delegerint ei regique Ædwardo magis seruire quam rebellare.

See also Geoffrey Gaimar, I:215–16; Freeman, *Norman Conquest*, II:645–46; and Kapelle, pp. 90–92. Frank Barlow (*Edward the Confessor*, p. 188) is frustrated that the *Vita Ædwardi* does not give more details about this campaign.

33 Symeon of Durham, *Historia regum*, II:174; Geoffrey Gaimar, I:216; Stenton, *Anglo-Saxon England*, p. 570; Barlow, *Edward the Confessor*, p. 203; and Kapelle, pp. 91–92.

34 Symeon of Durham, *Historia regum*, II:174. See also Freeman, *Norman Conquest*, II:383–84, 646–47 and Kapelle, pp. 91–92.

35 Initially attacking south towards Durham, according to Kapelle (pp. 92–94), Malcolm's target may have been the acquisition of Cumberland, the region ravaged at the end of this

outlawed Tostig in 1066, the exiled earl traveled to Malcolm's kingdom, perhaps to gain the aid of the Scottish king in the imminent invasion of himself and Haraldr Harðráði.[36]

Tostig had many other adventures in his tenure as earl of Northumbria. In 1061 he, his wife, Judith, and his younger brother, Gyrð, travelled to Saxony and then to Rome when they accompanied Ealdred, the new archbishop of York, Giso, Bishop of Wells, and Walter, Bishop of Hereford, to receive their pallia from Pope Nicholas II. This journey was not without adventurous incident, however. Not only did Nicholas refuse to give Ealdred his pallium, as he had transferred to York from his bishopric at Worcester, which was against canon law,[37] but after the travellers had begun their journey home, while still in Italy, thieves attacked and robbed them. According to the *Vita Ædwardi*, these thieves wished to gain ransom for Tostig from the English king. However, before the plan could be put into action, a young retainer of the earl, Gospatric by name, deceived the thieves into thinking that he was Tostig. Tostig and Archbishop Ealdred fled back to Rome, where they were joined shortly by Gospatric, whom the thieves had let go because they 'respected his bravery.' This action so embarrassed the pope, because Tostig was 'so famous an earl,' that he reversed his decision on Ealdred's pallium and awarded him the archbishopric.[38]

The same year after Tostig visited Rome, his brother decided to decisively defeat the Welsh king, Gruffydd ap Llywelyn. Shortly after Christmas, early in 1063, Harold began a campaign to defeat Gruffydd and put a halt to any further cross border raids from Wales. To deliver the impressive blow against Gruffydd

campaign. See also Symeon of Durham, *Historia regum*, II:174–75; Geoffrey Gaimar, I:216; Freeman, *Norman Conquest*, II:456–57; Stenton, *Anglo-Saxon England*, pp. 570–71; and Barlow, *Edward the Confessor*, p. 203.

[36] See the chapter 'The Conquest Begins' below.

[37] The complete story of Tostig's journey to Rome is found in the *Vita Ædwardi*, pp. 52–57 and William of Malmesbury, *De gestis pontificum Anglorum*, ed. N.E.S.A. Hamilton (London, 1870), pp. 251–52. See also the *Anglo-Saxon Chronicle* (D) 1061, I:189–91; William of Malmesbury, *Vita Wulfstani*, pp. 16–18; Osbert of Clare, *La vie de S. Édouard le Confesseur par Osbert de Clare*, ed. M. Bloch, in *Analecta Bollandiana* 41 (1923), 87–88; Freeman, *Norman Conquest*, II:452–56; Frank Barlow, *The English Church, 1000–1066: a Constitutional History* (London, 1963), pp. 60–61, 88, 292; Körner, pp. 211–12; and Vanessa King, 'Ealdred, Archbishop of York: The Worcester Years,' *Anglo-Norman Studies* 18 (1995), 130–31. John of Worcester (II:586–87), Symeon of Durham (*Historia regum*, II:174), and Geoffrey Gaimar (I:216–17) mention the journey to Rome of Ealdred and Tostig, but add no details of the further adventures. The canon which Nicholas used in refusing Ealdred's pallium is found in Burchard, *Decretum*, I, cc. lxxii–lxxvii: 'Ut nullo modo parochia ad aliam episcopus transeat' (That in no way should a bishop transfer from one seat to another).

[38] *Vita Ædwardi*, pp. 54–57. See also *Anglo-Saxon Chronicle* (D) 1061, I:189–91; William of Malmesbury, *De gestis pontificum*, pp. 251–52; William of Malmesbury, *Vita Wulfstani*, pp. 16–18; Freeman, *Norman Conquest*, II:454–56; Barlow, *English Church*, pp. 60–61, 292; and King, pp. 130–31. William of Malmesbury's *De gestis pontificum* (p. 252) claims that even after the robbery incident, it is not until Tostig speaks very harshly to the pope, threatening to withhold St Peter's pence from Rome, that Nicholas relents and grants Ealdred's pallium to him.

and the Welsh described in the chapter above, in the summer of that year Harold called on his brother, Tostig, to help him deliver a two-pronged attack into Wales. While Harold set sail from Bristol north to meet the Welsh army in northern Wales, Tostig marched his Northumbrian army from the north of England overland towards Gruffydd's capital city, Rhuddlan, and burned it. Wales was forced to surrender, a success that the *Anglo-Saxon Chronicle* (D) records:

> And then at Rogationtide Harold went with ships from Bristol around Wales, and that people made peace and gave hostages. And Tostig went against them over the land with his force, and they took the country.[39]

The English army, led by the earls of Wessex and Northumbria, had defeated their Welsh opponents, and the head of Gruffydd was delivered to Edward in London by Harold. Stopping attacks from both Scotland and Wales, these two warlord brothers, sons of Godwin, had protected the English borders well, and Edward now felt at ease in his kingdom. The author of the *Vita Ædwardi*, writes:

> The king . . . with them [Harold and Tostig] thus stationed in his kingdom, lived all his life free from care on either flank, for the one drove back the foe from the south and the other scared them off from the north.[40]

Through these acts and others, Tostig's influence increased with the king (William of Malmesbury claims that King Edward was 'much attached' to him[41]) and, as it did, he began to spend more time at the royal courts in the south of England and less time in Northumbria. Of all the characters written about by the anonymous author of the *Vita Ædwardi*, generally believed to have been a monastic chronicler personally attached to the court of Queen Eadgyða and hence close to her brother as well, Tostig is described the most completely.[42] Additionally, among his large land holdings, Tostig owned forty-four 'hides' of land in Wiltshire which he seemed to have especially enjoyed, and these too pulled him frequently from his northern English earldom.[43]

This absentee government began to trouble the Northumbrian people. As Dorothy Whitelock has established, such an agitation was not uncommon;

[39] *Anglo-Saxon Chronicle* (D) 1063, I:191:
þa to þam gong dagan for Harold mid scipum of Brycgstowe abutan Brytland. ꞇ þ folc griðede ꞇ gisledon; ꞇ Tostig for mid land ferde ongean. ꞇ þ land ge eoden.
For further references to this campaign see nn. 62–82 in the preceding chapter.
[40] *Vita Ædwardi*, pp. 50–51:
rex . . . eis sic in regno suo locatis omni sua rex securus utroque uixit latere, cum hic hostes repelleret a meridie, ille terreret ab aquilione.
[41] William of Malmesbury, *Gesta regum Anglorum: The History of the English Kings*, ed. R.A.B. Mynors, R.M. Thomson, and M. Winterbottom (Oxford, 1998), I:466–67.
[42] Barlow, ed., *Vita Ædwardi*, p. xlv. On Tostig's closeness to his sister see Freeman, *Norman Conquest*, II:382–83.
[43] *Vita Ædwardi*, p. lxi n. 218. In total, the *Domesday Book* records Tostig owning more than £1300 worth of land throughout the kingdom. See Barlow, *Edward the Confessor*, p. 74. It is not known what type of habitation Tostig had on his land in Wiltshire.

popular uprisings of one kind or another but usually directed against the 'southern' rulers of Northumbria had occurred several times during the tenth and eleventh centuries.[44] So perhaps it should not be seen as unusual that, although Tostig had brought peace to the province from attacks by the Scots and Welsh, it was a difficult earldom for him to govern. Tostig had no ties to the local people. As he was from the south of England, he was considered by them to be a foreigner. Moreover, he did not compare favorably with the preceding earl, Siward. Siward was Scandinavian by birth, a similarity that he had in common with many of the Northumbrians, and he had married a Northumbrian noble woman. At the same time, he spent almost all of his time in the province and not at the royal court, although part of this may have been because of his rivalry with Earl Godwin, Tostig's father and King Edward's chief advisor at the time.[45] Tostig was Danish through his mother, Gyða, but he had none of the other qualities – indeed, most of his connections were to the non-Scandinavian elements of England.[46] Added to this was a constant absenteeism mentioned above which produced factions and power-struggles among the local magnates.[47]

Tostig was also accused of burdening his subjects with heavy taxes, using the money for his own personal goods and endowments, and dealing harshly with anyone who opposed him in collecting it. In particular, his assassination of three opposing Northumbrian nobles – the thegns Gospatric, Gamel, and Ulf – brought resentment from his subjects. This act eventually led to a rebellion among the people of Northumbria. John of Worcester reports what followed:

> Then, after the feast of St. Michael the Archangel, on Monday, 3 October, the Northumbrian thegns, Gamelbearn, Dunstan, son of Æthelnoth, and Glonieorn, son of Heardwulf, came with 200 soldiers to York, and, on account of the disgraceful death of the noble Northumbrian thegns Gospatric (whom Queen Edith, on account of her brother Tostig, had ordered to be killed in the king's court on the fourth night of Christmas by treachery), Gamel, son of Orm, and Ulf, son of Dolfin (whose murders Earl Tostig had treacherously ordered the preceding year at York in his own chamber, under cover of a peace-treaty), and also of the huge tribute which Tostig unjustly levied on the whole of Northumbria, they, on that same day, slew first his Danish housecarls, Amund and Reavenswart, hauled back from the flight, beyond the city walls, and on the

---

[44] Dorothy Whitelock, 'The Dealings of the Kings of England with Northumbria in the Tenth and Eleventh Centuries,' in *The Anglo-Saxons: Studies in Some Aspects of their History and Culture Presented to Bruce Dickins*, ed. P. Clemoes (London, 1959), pp. 70–88. This article was written in part to counter Bertie Wilkinson's article, 'Northumbrian Separatism in 1065 and 1066,' *Bulletin of the John Rylands Library* 23 (1939), 504–26.

[45] See Stenton, *Anglo-Saxon England*, pp. 570–71.

[46] See Freeman, *Norman Conquest*, II:377. However, I. Walker (p. 103) does not accept the ethnic problems of Tostig's appointment as he was an Anglo-Dane. Moreover, Walker convincingly argues that he had no fewer connections with the north than had Siward when he became earl.

[47] See Freeman, *Norman Conquest*, II:376–77, 480–81; Stenton, *Anglo-Saxon England*, pp. 570–71; Barlow, *Edward the Confessor*, pp. 195–96; Barlow, *English Church*, pp. 52, 60; and Stafford, *Unification and Conquest*, pp. 94–95.

following day more than 200 men from his court, on the north side of the River Humber. They also broke open his treasury, and, having taken away all the goods, they withdrew.[48]

This was obviously a significant and violent uprising. A gathering of more than 200 people, led by lesser nobles, opposing an earl in such a bellicose manner had to be dealt with using tact and diplomacy in order not to cause a spread of the rebellion. Moreover, these rebels were serious about their intentions of removing Tostig from the governance of the earldom. Their claims that he 'encouraged injustice, because he first robbed God, and then took both the life and lands of those over whom he ruled,' to use the words of the *Anglo-Saxon Chronicle* (C), exhibited a determination which could not be crushed easily.[49] Nor was the rebels' anger quelled by the pillaging of the earl's palace and possessions in York and the slaying of several of his friends and companions.

[48] John of Worcester, II:596–99:

Dein post festiuitatem sancti Michaelis archangeli .v. non. Octobris. feria ii, Northymbrenes ministri, Gamelbearn, Dunstanus, filius Athelnethes, Glonieorn, filius Heardulfi, cum .cc. militibus Eboracum uenerunt, et pro execranda nece nobilium Northymbrensium ministrorum Gospatrici, quem regina Edgitha, germani sui Tostii causa, in curia regis .iiii. nocte dominice Natiuitatis per insidias occidi iussit, et Gamelis, filii Orm, ac Vlfi, filii Dolfini, quos anno precendti Eboraci in camera sua sub pacis federe per insidias comes Tostius occidere pracepit, necnon pro immensitate tributi quod de tota Northymbria iniuste acceperat, eodem die primitus illius Danicos huscarlas Amundum et Reavensuartum de fuga retractos extra ciuitatis muros ac die sequenti plusquam .cc. uiros ex curialibus illius in boreali parte Humbre fluminis peremerunt. Erarium quoque ipsius fregerunt ac omnibus que illius fuerant ablatis, recesserunt.

See also *Anglo-Saxon Chronicle* (C and D) 1065, (E) 1065, I:190–92; *Vita Ædwardi*, pp. 74–79; William of Malmesbury, *Gesta regum Anglorum*, I:364–65; Henry of Huntingdon, pp. 382–85; Symeon of Durham, *Historia regum*, II:178; Geoffrey Gaimar, I:217; Freeman, *Norman Conquest*, II:476–84, 686–88; Stenton, *Anglo-Saxon England*, p. 578–79; Stafford, *Unification and Conquest*, pp. 95–99; Barlow, *Edward the Confessor*, pp. 141 n. 1, 235–36; Douglas, *William the Conqueror*, p. 179; I. Walker, pp. 104–08; Kapelle, pp. 94–100; and Whitelock, pp. 83–84. William of Malmesbury notes especially the theft of horses and arms. Pauline Stafford ties this rebellion to the public display of the bones of the murdered King Oswin at Durham in the spring of 1065 'in a call to action rather than a gesture of piety.' The display of these bones is recorded in Symeon of Durham, *Historia ecclesiae Dunhelmensis*, ed. T. Arnold (London, 1882), pp. 87–89. Ian Walker (pp. 105–07) provides an alternative, unconvincing version of the murders which John of Worcester blames on Tostig. Among other problems, he sees the murdered Gospatric as the same individual who saved Tostig in Italy; there is no evidence to support this assertion. A more likely candidate is found by Barlow (*Edward the Confessor*, pp. 137 n. 2, 235 n. 3) in Gospatric, the lord of Allerdale and Dalston. Perhaps the best description of what might have been the reasons for the murders of Gospatric, Gamel, and Ulf is found in Kapelle, pp. 94–95. On Eadgyða's role see Kenneth E. Cutler, 'Edith, Queen of England,' *Mediaeval Studies* 38 (1976), 230–31.

[49] *Anglo-Saxon Chronicle* (C) 1065, I:192:

ac eall hys eorldom hyne anrædlice for sóc. ⁊ ge utlagode. ⁊ ealle þa mid hym þe unlage rærdon. for þam ðe [he] rypte God ærost. ⁊ ealle þa bestrypte þe he ofer mihte æt life.

See also Freeman, *Norman Conquest*, II:477–78; Barlow, *Edward the Confessor*, p. 235; and Kapelle, pp. 95–98.

Instead, they travelled south to Northampton to demand Tostig's deposition from the king, then residing at Oxford.[50] The story is picked up here by the *Anglo-Saxon Chronicle* (E):

> In this year the Northumbrians gathered together and outlawed Earl Tostig and slew his retainers, everyone they came across, English or Danish. And they took all of his weapons in York and his gold and silver and all of his treasures that they knew of. And they sent for Morkere, the son of Earl Ælfgar, and they named him to be their earl. They then went south with all of the people of the shire [York], and with those of Nottinghamshire, Derbyshire, and Lincolnshire. And at Northampton they were joined by his [Morkere's] brother, Edwin, with men from his earldom as well as many Welshmen who had come with him. Thereupon Earl Harold came out to meet them, and they entrusted him with a message to King Edward, and they also sent messengers with him, who asked if they might have Morkere as their earl.[51]

The fact that Tostig and King Edward were together, and that Tostig was obviously a favorite of the king's, did nothing to pacify the rebels, or to eliminate their desire to change earls. The call for removal of his favorite distressed the king – John of Worcester, William of Malmesbury, and the author of the *Vita Ædwardi* all link it to the king's death which followed shortly after Tostig's

---

[50] See *Vita Ædwardi*, pp. 74–79; *Anglo-Saxon Chronicle* (C and D) 1065 and (E) 1064, I:190–92; John of Worcester, II:598–99; William of Malmesbury, *Gesta regum*, I:364–65; Symeon of Durham, *Historia regum*, II:178; Geoffrey Gaimar, I:217; the *Annales de Waverleia*, in *Annales monastici*, ii, ed. H.R. Luard (London, 1865), p. 188; Freeman, *Norman Conquest*, II:485; Barlow, *Edward the Confessor*, pp. 236–37; and Douglas, *William the Conqueror*, pp. 179–80. At the beginning of this revolt, the king seems to have been at Britford, near Wilton. He then moved to Northampton, presumably to be close to the negotiations with the rebels, and then to Oxford, perhaps to a safer location. Tostig appears to have been with him at all three venues, but Harold seems to have joined the king only at Northampton.

[51] *Anglo-Saxon Chronicle* (E) 1064, I:190–92:

her on þisum geare fornon Norðhymbra togæder ⁊ utlagdon heora eorl Tostig ⁊ ofslogen his hiredmenn ealle þa hi mihton to cuman ægþer ge Englisce ge Dænisce. And namon ealle his wepna on Eoferwic ⁊ gol ⁊ seolkor ⁊ ealle his sceattas þe hi mihton ahwar þær geaxian. ⁊ senden æfter Morkere Ælfgares sune eorles. ⁊ gecuron hine heom to eorle. ⁊ he for suþ mid eallre þaere scire. ⁊ mid Snotinghamscire ⁊ Deorbiscire ⁊ Lincolnascire. þo he com to Hamtune ⁊ his broðer Eadwine him com togeanes mid þam mannum þe on his eorldome wæron. ⁊ eac fela Bryttas comon mid him. Ðær com Harold eorl heom togeanes ⁊ hi lægdon ærende on hine to þam cynge Edwarde. ⁊ eac ærendracan mid him sendon ⁊ bædon þ hi moston habban Morkere heom to eorle.

See also *Anglo-Saxon Chronicle* (C and D) 1065, I:191–92; *Vita Ædwardi*, pp. 76–79; Henry of Huntingdon, pp. 384–85; John of Worcester, II:598–99; William of Malmesbury, *Gesta regum*, I:364–65; Symeon of Durham, *Historia regum*, II:178; Freeman, *Norman Conquest*, II:481–86, 686–88; Stenton, *Anglo-Saxon England*, pp. 578–79; Brown, *The Normans and Norman Conquest*, pp. 71–72; Barlow, *Edward the Confessor*, pp. 236–38; I. Walker, pp. 110–11; Kapelle, pp. 99–101; and Wilkinson, 'Northumbrian Separatism,' pp. 509–11. Kapelle asserts that the desire to restore the earldom of Northumbria to 'the traditional ruling family' and Siward's son was the cause of this revolt. The presence of Welshmen among the rebel force may also to have been significant. See Freeman, *Norman Conquest*, II:485–86.

deposition[52] – and, although he recognized the grievances of the rebels and offered them justice for his earl's misdeeds, he was unwilling to dismiss Tostig. However, the rebels would have it no other way, and they refused to withdraw until Edward would meet their demands. Instead, they began to plunder the local countryside, stealing cattle and food, and killing or enslaving all who would not join their rebellion. The *Anglo-Saxon Chronicle* (E) laments: 'that shire and other nearby shires were for many years the poorer.'[53]

Hearing of this, and responsible for the situation at Northampton, Harold summoned troops to crush the rebels, but they failed to gather in numbers superior to the Northumbrian force.[54] Faced with possible civil war, and because, as William of Malmesbury writes, 'Harold . . . was a man to consider his country's tranquility in preference to his brother's personal advantage,' the earl of Wessex recalled the army and yielded to the demands of the rebels. The king then reluctantly accepted Harold's decision, and, on 1 November, Tostig, 'angered at everyone,' left England for exile in Flanders.[55] The *Vita Ædwardi* describes the scene of departure:

> But the king, the beloved of God, when he could not save his earl, graciously heaped on him many gifts and then let him depart, profoundly distressed at the powerlessness that had come upon him. And a short time after, Tostig took leave of his sorrowing mother and some friends, and with his wife and infant children and a goodly company of his thegns crossed the Channel and came to that old friend of the English people, Earl Baldwin.[56]

---

52 John of Worcester (II:598–99), William of Malmesbury (*Gesta regum Anglorum*, I:364–65), and the *Vita Ædwardi* (pp. 80–81) all attest to the sickness of the king during the Northumbrian Rebellion. They also claim that the outcome of the rebellion and the loss of his favorite was a cause of the mental anxiety which led eventually to his death. On the effect of Tostig's exile on his sister, Eadgyða, see *Vita Ædwardi*, pp. 80–81 and Barlow, *Edward the Confessor*, pp. 241–42, although it may be stretching things a bit too far to tie this to her later acceptance of William the Conqueror.

53 *Anglo-Saxon Chronicle* (E) 1064, I:192: '. . . þet seo scyre ⁊ þe oðra scyre þe þær neh sindon. wurdon fela wintra ðe wyrsan.' See also *Anglo-Saxon Chronicle* (D) 1065, I:193 and Henry of Huntingdon, pp. 384–85 who use nearly the same language. All of these sources have this pillaging and murder continuing even after Tostig's deposition had been granted. Even with this violence, Wilkinson ('Northumbrian Separatism,' p. 515) maintains that, 'the rebels were apparently fully conscious of the strong political bonds which bound them to the rest of England,' and that the rebellion was 'by no means the simple destructive movement that is frequently assumed.'

54 *Vita Ædwardi*, pp. 80–81 and William of Malmesbury, *Gesta regum Anglorum*, I:364–65. It seems that the harsh weather and storms of the English October may have prohibited the full army from gathering. See also Barlow, *Edward the Confessor*, p. 237.

55 William of Malmesbury, *Gesta regum Anglorum*, I:364–65: 'Haroldus . . . magis quietem patriae quam fratris commodum attenderet revocavit exercitum.' See also Barlow, *English Church*, p. 46 n. 1; I. Walker, pp. 111–12; and Wilkinson, 'Northumbrian Separatism,' pp. 508–09. Freeman's argument (*Norman Conquest*, II:489–91) that Edward wanted to fight for Tostig in this revolt but was hindered by Harold in doing so is unconvincing.

56 *Vita Ædwardi*, pp. 80–83:
At deo dilectus rex cum ducem suum tutare non posset, gratia sua multipliciter donatum merens nimium quod in hanc impotentiam deciderit, a se dimisit. Qui breui

Having achieved Tostig's deposition, the Northumbrians returned home.[57]

While the sad scene of departure might be touching, while the seeming sub-mission to the rebels' demands might be seen as evidence of a weak or old king, and while the role of Harold in the rebellion and finally in the deposition of his brother might arouse suspicions of collaboration, Tostig is not without a great deal of blame in inciting this rebellion. For not only do the charges of murder of two of his thegns and conspiracy with his sister in the murder of one other have numerous attestations, but all contemporary sources also accuse Tostig of being the main motivator in inciting this rebellion. William of Malmesbury, for one, uses the word 'exciter' to describe Tostig's role in causing the rebellion,[58] while the always favorable author of the *Vita Ædwardi* uses the word 'pressere' to describe the same instigation.[59] (The latter author does however add that the thegns who were murdered by Tostig and Eadgyða deserved their fate 'because of their misdeeds.'[60])

Frank Stenton notes that Edward's agreement to the Northumbrian rebels' demands was 'the last public event of the Confessor's life.'[61] On 5 January 1066, the king died. The following day, the witenagemot, supported by the people of London, elected Harold as their king. It must have been after Harold's ascension that Tostig began to plan his invasion of England. Perhaps his father's successful return to England in 1052 encouraged Tostig. Perhaps he had lost hope of returning to England peacefully so long as his brother, the same brother who had 'allowed' Tostig's exile, was now king. The reasons remain unclear to a twentieth-century perspective, but it is known that less than a year after the ascension of Harold Godwinson to the throne of England, Tostig attacked the

post tempore mernetem matrem et quosdam amicorum affectus, cum coniuge et lacen-tibus liberis plurimaque nobilium suorum manu transfretauit, et ad antiquum Anglice gentis amicum comitem Balduuinnum peruenit.
See also *Anglo-Saxon Chronicle* (C and D) 1065, (E) 1064, I:192–95; John of Worcester, II:598–99; Henry of Huntingdon, pp. 384–85; William of Malmesbury, *Gesta regum*, I:364–65; Symeon of Durham, *Historia regum*, II:178–79; Orderic Vitalis, II:138–41; Geoffrey Gaimar, I:217; Freeman, *Norman Conquest*, II:486–97; Stenton, *Anglo-Saxon Chronicle*, p. 579; Barlow, *Edward the Confessor*, pp. 237–38; Douglas, *William the Conquer-or*, pp. 179–80; I. Walker, pp. 113–14; Oleson, *Witenagemot*, p. 64; and Grierson, 'Relations between England and Flanders,' p. 103. Oleson (*Witenagemot*, pp. 29–30, 109) goes to great lengths to prove that this was not a gathering of or a decision by the witenagemot, as con-cluded by Freeman (*Norman Conquest*, II:690–91).

[57] See *Vita Ædwardi*, pp. 80–81; John of Worcester, II:598–99; Henry of Huntingdon, pp. 384–85; and William of Malmesbury, *Gesta regum Anglorum*, I:364–65.

[58] William of Malmesbury, *Gesta regum Anglorum*, I:364–65: 'quo exacto, asperitate morum Northanimbros in rebellionem excitauit.'

[59] *Vita Ædwardi*, pp. 76–77: 'Tostinus . . . presserat dominatus sui iugo.'

[60] *Vita Ædwardi*, pp. 76–79. According to this source, the people of Northumbria were also 'cruel' and 'neglected God' so that no one could travel throughout the region without 'being either killed or robbed by the multitude of robbers in wait.' Tostig, 'a son and lover of divine peace. . . reduced the number of robbers and cleared the country of them by mutilating or killing them and by sparing no one.' See also Freeman, *Norman Conquest*, II:379–82.

[61] Stenton, *Anglo-Saxon England*, p. 547.

island; he did this first on his own, and then after he had been defeated and almost all of his sailors had deserted, he turned to King Haraldr Harðráði of Norway to assist in his conquest. This would prove fatal to the once powerful earl of Northumbria. Tostig was killed at the battle of Stamford Bridge.

So ended the life of a warlord who at one time exercised great power and enjoyed position and prestige in England. He died fighting his warlord brother, the king, a brother whom he certainly might have assisted with counsel and advice had he not been outlawed less than a year before. Why did Tostig attack his brother, Harold? Had Harold betrayed Tostig at Northampton when he agreed to the Northumbrian rebels' demands and allowed the ousting and exile of his younger brother? It seems that Harold had always supported Tostig before 1065. He had undoubtedly used his influence with the king to get Tostig his promotion to earl of Northumbria.[62] Having another province, especially a northern one, controlled by another son of Godwin greatly strengthened Harold's position, as would the later elevation of Gyrð and Leofwine to earl in East Anglia and Essex/Kent respectively. By 1065 the only major province of England not controlled by the Godwin family was Mercia. The banishment of Tostig seriously weakened the power structure which Harold had so carefully put in place, especially when it is realized that Morkere, the brother of Earl Edwin of Mercia, was the desired candidate to replace Tostig. When Morkere received the earldom, the north of England was controlled by a rival family to the Godwins. This represented a very volatile situation, one which potentially could have erupted into civil war.[63] Indeed, it seems that Harold realized these potential problems, and after he ascended the throne of England, he married Edwin and Morkere's sister, Ealdyð, the widow of the Welsh king, Gruffydd ap Llywelyn, the man whom Harold had caused to be slain.[64] This certainly appeased the northern forces, but it would not have been necessary had Tostig remained in power in Northumbria; the marriage also may have appeared to Tostig in Flanders as a certain assessment of Harold's guilt in driving him from England.

Further evidence that Harold did not betray Tostig can be seen as most contemporary sources show that Harold actively fought against the rebellion. It is

---

[62] See note no.22 in the preceding chapter.

[63] Freeman, *Norman Conquest*, II:488–89, 491–94; Stenton, *Anglo-Saxon England*, p. 579; Barlow, *Edward the Confessor*, p. 238; Douglas, *William the Conqueror*, p. 180; I. Walker, pp. 112–113; and Kapelle, pp. 99–101. Wilkinson ('Northumbrian Separatism,' pp. 509–11) is adamant about this.

[64] See Orderic Vitalis, II:138; Barlow, *Edward the Confessor*, pp. 243–44; I. Walker, pp. 116–17; H.R. Loyn, 'Harold, Son of Godwin,' in *Society and Peoples: Studies in the History of England and Wales, c. 600–1200* (London, 1992), p. 320; K.L. Maund, *Ireland, Wales, and England in the Eleventh Century* (Woodbridge, 1991), p. 137; K.L. Maund, 'The Welsh Alliances of Earl Ælfgar of Mercia and his Family in the Mid-Eleventh Century,' *Anglo-Norman Studies* 9 (1988), 186–89; and Frederick C. Suppe, 'Who was Rhys Sais? Some Comments on Anglo-Welsh Relations before 1066,' *Haskins Society Journal* 7 (1995), 63.

true that he was in charge of the delegation that initially met with the rebels, and he acted as the mediator between them and the king.[65] Additionally, according to the *Anglo-Saxon Chronicle* (E), which supports the idea of Harold's neutrality in the revolt, Tostig's older brother may have only been a pawn thrust into the position of mediator between the king and the rebel party, certainly not a role he desired to fill. He tried to seek a compromise with the rebels in order somehow to allow Tostig to remain in his position as earl of Northumbria, but when Harold realized that this course of action would not be tolerated, and perhaps desiring a peaceful kingdom and not one filled with violence, he influenced the king to banish Tostig.[66] This is further verified in John of Worcester's version of Harold's role in Tostig's banishment:

> After that, almost all the men of his earldom united to meet Harold, earl of the West Saxons, and others whom the king at Tostig's request had sent them to restore peace, at Northampton. There first, and later at Oxford, on the day of the feast of the apostles Simon and Jude, while Harold and very many others wished to make peace between Earl Tostig and them, all unanimously spoke against it and they outlawed him and all who had encouraged him to establish his iniquitous rule.[67]

As can be seen in his numerous dealings with Gruffydd ap Llywelyn, Harold preferred to solve his problems without bloodshed. He was certainly not guilty of supporting the ousting of his brother, and, in fact, it was probably disadvantageous for him to lose Tostig as earl of Northumbria.

However, Tostig seems to have perceived the affair differently, and, if the sources are read as Tostig understood them, they appear to depict Harold as a royal mediator more than willing to comply with the rebels' demands when under only a little pressure to do so. This view is supported by at least three contemporary or near-contemporary chroniclers. The first, by Orderic Vitalis, bluntly, but clearly, ascribes blame for the Tostig's loss of Northumbria to his brother, Harold:

---

[65] All of the contemporary sources place Harold at Northampton as the primary mediator between the rebels and Edward. See *Anglo-Saxon Chronicle* (D) 1065 and (E) 1064, I:192–93; *Annales de Waverleia*, p. 188; John of Worcester, II:598–99; Henry of Huntingdon, pp. 384–85; William of Malmesbury, *Gesta regum Anglorum*, I:364–65; and Freeman, *Norman Conquest*, II:486–88, 688–91.

[66] *Anglo-Saxon Chronicle* (E) 1064, I:190–92. Freeman (*Norman Conquest*, II:491–94) and Douglas (*William the Conqueror*, p. 180) accept this explanation for Harold's behavior.

[67] John of Worcester, II:598–99:

> Omnis dehinc fere comitatus illius in unum congregati, Haroldo Westsaxonum duci et allis quos rex Tostii rogatu pro pace redintegranda ad eos miserat in Northamtonia occurrerunt. Vbi prius et post apud Oxnefordam, die festiuitatis apostolorum Simonis et Iude, dum Haroldus et alii quamplures comitem Tostium cum eis pacificare uellent, omnes unanimi consensu contradixerunt, ac eum cum omnibus qui legem iniquiam statuere illum incitauerunt exlegauerunt.

This account of the conflict between Harold and Tostig Godwinson influences the later chronicles of Symeon of Durham (*Historia regum*, II:178) and Geoffrey Gaimar (I:214–18). See also I. Walker, p. 112.

But Tostig, Earl Godwin's son, seeing that the wickedness of his brother Harold had prevailed, and that the kingdom was groaning under every kind of oppression, took the matter to heart, resolved to oppose him, and openly declared war on him. At this Harold in anger deprived him [Tostig] of their father's earldom which Tostig, the elder by birth, had held for a long time under King Edward, and forced him into exile.[68]

Yet, because Orderic made so many factual errors in recounting this incident, little credence is given to his indictment of Harold: Orderic dates this to after Harold's ascension to the throne; Tostig's earldom was not his father's; and Tostig was not the eldest of the two sons.

In the second chronicle, the author of the *Vita Ædwardi* describes Tostig's accusation, made to the king's council, that Harold had incited the Northumbrians to rebel. Later, Harold is personally charged by Tostig with this crime, of which the older brother clears himself with an oath. However, the anonymous author of this chronicle cynically dismisses Harold's oaths as given too quickly and too frequently:

> It was also said, if it be worthy of credence, that they had undertaken this madness against their earl at the artful persuasion of his brother, earl Harold (which heaven forbid!). But I dare not and would not believe that such a prince was guilty of this detestable wickedness against his brother. Earl Tostig, himself, publicly testifying before the king and his assembled courtiers, charged him with this; but Harold, rather too generous with oaths (alas!) cleared this charge too with oaths.[69]

Finally, a third account, the *Gesta regum Anglorum* of William of Malmesbury, also highlights Harold's role in influencing the rebels. In discussing this revolt, William uses the words *annitens* and *perstitit* to express Harold's 'insistence' and 'persistence' in banishing his brother:

> . . . and they [the Northumbrians] expelled their earl, Tostig, and with Harold's

---

68 Orderic Vitalis, II:138–39:
   Tunc Tosticus Gouini comitis filius aduertens Heraldi fratris sui preualere facinus, et regnum Angliae uariis grauari oppressionibus aegre tulit, contradixit, et aperte repugnare decreuit. Vnde Heraldus patris consulatum quem Tosticus quia maior natu erat, longo tempore sub Eduardo rege iam tenuerat; ei uiolenter abstulit, ipsumque exulare compulit.
69 *Vita Ædwardi*, pp. 78–81:
   Dicebatur quoque, si dignum esset credere, fratris sui Haroldo insidioso, quod absit, suasu hanc dementiam contra ducem suum aggressos esse; sed ego huic detestibilii nequitie a tanto principe in fratrem suum non audeo nec uellem fidem adhibere. Ipse tamen dux Tostinus, coram rege eiusque frequentibus palatinus publice testatus, hoc ille citius ad sacramenta nimis, proh dolor, prodigus, hoc obiectum sacramentis purgauit.
See also Freeman, *Norman Conquest*, II:488–90; Brown, *The Normans and Norman Conquest*, p. 68; Stafford, *Unification and Conquest*, pp. 96–97; Barlow, *Edward the Confessor*, pp. 178, 238–39; and I. Walker, p. 112.

annitens (insistence), they requested and received one of their brothers as their lord . . . Harold *perstitit* (persisted) in his resolution to banish his brother.[70]

While Orderic's narrative of what occurred can be easily dismissed, neither of the latter two authors denies that Tostig disrupted the Northumbrian people. Yet both place some blame on Harold for his brother's banishment, but if all of these authors are correct in their conjectures, why did Harold do this? What did he have to gain? Was Tostig too close to the ailing and heirless king? Perhaps Harold feared that Tostig might rule after Edward's death instead of himself. Surely in such a situation Harold's fraternal love may have become a lesser priority to his own power and the stability of his soon-to-be realm.[71] Perhaps Harold realized that he would rule shortly, and that if he did not agree with the Northumbrians in their revolt against his brother, he would later have to fight a civil war against them and perhaps also against the Mercians. Still, it is difficult not to join in the lamentation of the *Vita Ædwardi*'s poet: 'Ah vicious Discord sprung from brother's strife!'[72]

Both Tostig and Harold had many similar positive characteristics. Indeed, it is difficult to imagine that two men, brothers, so close in age and abilities, who once seemed so devoted to each other, would fight on opposite sides. In all the contemporary or near contemporary writings which chronicle their times, only superlatives are used to describe them. Even in *La Estorire de Seint Aedward le Rei*, an Old French poetic chronicle written about 1245, and extremely biased against the Godwin family, the anonymous author still uses such words as '*mut ben*,' '*pruz*,' and '*hardiz*' to describe Harold and Tostig.[73] Other texts use similar language. Perhaps the most visual picture of both Harold and Tostig can be found in the *Vita Ædwardi*:

> Both had the advantage of distinctly handsome and graceful persons, similar in strength, as we gather; and both were equally brave . . . Indeed, the fault of rashness or levity is not one that anybody could hold against him, Harold, or Tostig, or any brave son of Godwin, or anyone brought up under his rule or instruction . . . Both persevered with what they had begun; but Tostig vigorously, Harold prudently; the one in action aimed at success, the other also at

---

[70] William of Malmesbury, *Gesta regum Anglorum*, I:466–69:
. . . et Tostinum comitem suum expulerant, petierantque et acceperant unum e fratribus dominum, annitente Haroldo . . . Perstitit in incepto Haroldus ut fratrem exlegaret.
Barlow (*Edward the Confessor*, pp. 235–36) seems to accept this possibility.
[71] William of Malmesbury (*Gesta regum Anglorum*, I:364–65) obviously concludes in this manner when he writes: 'Harold . . . regarded the quiet of the country more than the contentment of his brother (Haroldus . . . magis quietem patriae quam fratris commodum attenderet).' See also Stenton, *Anglo-Saxon England*, p. 579.
[72] *Vita Ædwardi*, pp. 58–59: 'Heu discors uitium fraternis cladibus ortum!' The entire poem of lamentation, drawn in part from Horace, Seneca, and Statius, is found on pp. 58–61. See also Barlow, *English Church*, p. 61 and Barlow, *Edward the Confessor*, pp. 197–98.
[73] *La Estorire de Seint Aedward le Rei*, ed. and trans. H.R. Luard, in *Lives of Edward the Confessor* (London, 1858), p. 113.

happiness . . . And to sum up their characters for our readers, no age and no province has raised two mortals of such worth at the same time.[74]

Yet, in many ways Harold and Tostig seem to have been different. Contemporary sources record Harold as being more patient, with a mildness of temper, and more understanding of how to rule his subjects. Tostig, on the other hand, appears to have been more religious,[75] more brilliant,[76] and on the whole more charismatic.[77] At the same time, even the author of the *Vita Ædwardi* saw him as more secretive, strong willed, temperamental, inflexible, and vindictive than his brother.[78] Finally, Harold had distinct marital problems throughout his lifetime, choosing to live with a mistress, Eadgyð Swanneshals, rather than marry until late in his life.[79] Tostig remained faithful to Judith throughout his life, and although she remarried after his death, she appears to have shared a unique love with her first husband.[80]

It can also be assumed that, although most often friends and confederates – witness the joint attack on Wales in 1063 – there must have been some sibling rivalry. Harold was the oldest of the two, and although not slated to gain the familial inheritance until the death of his older brother, Swegen, the receipt of this inheritance upon their father's death gave Harold some advantage over his younger brothers. It is safe to assume that at some point Tostig became jealous

---

[74] *Vita Ædwardi*, pp. 48–49:

> Vterque satis pulchro et uenusto pollebat corpore, et, ut conicimus, non inequali robere, non disparis audacie . . . Porro de uitio precipitationis siue leuitatis, quis hunc uel illum siue quemuis de Godwino patre genitum siue eius disciplina et studio educatum arguerit? . . . Inceptum suum uterque satis constanter urguere; sed hic fortiter, ille sapienter; hic in actu suo consummationem, ille intendebat pariter et felicitatem . . . At ut legentibus de eorum moribus dicature tota summa nulla etas, nulla regio, eius pretii duos mortales eodem educauit tempore.

See also Freeman, *Norman Conquest*, II:379–80 and John Gillingham, 'Thegns and Knights in Eleventh-Century England: Who Was Then the Gentleman?' *Transactions of the Royal Historical Society*, 6th ser., 5 (1995), 149.

[75] For discussions on the religious nature of Harold, see Loyn, 'Harold, Son of Godwin,' or Walter DeGray Birch's introduction in *Vita Haroldi* (London, 1885). For Tostig's religiosity see *Vita Ædwardi*, pp. 48–51; Barlow, *English Church*, pp. 60–61; and I. Walker, pp. 104–06. Tostig and Judith were known as benefactors of Durham, especially of St Cuthbert's shrine there. This is confirmed somewhat by a story recorded in the *Historia translationum S. Cuthberti* (ed. H. Hinde (London, 1868), pp. 168–70), which tells of Tostig's release of a prisoner, Aldan-hamal, after he had repented of his sins to and received absolution from St Cuthbert.

[76] *Vita Ædwardi*, pp. 48–49 and Barlow, *English Church*, p. 60.

[77] Refer, for example, to the interaction between Tostig and Kings Malcolm of Scotland, Harald Harðráði of Norway, Baldwin V of Flanders, and Edward the Confessor of England. See also Freeman, *Norman Conquest*, II:379.

[78] *Vita Ædwardi*, pp. 48–49. See also Freeman, *Norman Conquest*, II:379–80; Barlow, *English Church*, p. 60; and Barlow, *Edward the Confessor*, pp. 195, 227.

[79] See nn. 130–134 in the preceding chapter.

[80] Judith married Welf IV of Bavaria after Tostig's death, in 1070 or 1071, a marriage which sealed an alliance between the Bavarians and her brother, Count Baldwin V of Flanders. See also Freeman, *Norman Conquest*, II:382–83.

of Harold, a jealousy which festered until Harold appeared to Tostig to have sided with those wanting to cast him from his Northumbrian earldom.

However, this jealousy may also have occurred earlier, at least that is the story given by some chroniclers. Because of the circumstances surrounding Harold and Tostig's conflict, the defeat of Tostig at Stamford Bridge and then of Harold at Hastings, and the sanctification of Edward the Confessor in the mid-twelfth century, the story of the Godwinsons' rivalry took on an added importance and was altered significantly in several later chronicles.

In the earliest Anglo-Norman sources, Harold, the enemy of and traitor to the Normans, is seen as the villain in his conflict with Tostig. The *Carmen de hastingae proelio* calls Harold 'Cain' and accuses him of personally slaying his brother at Stamford Bridge, after which he 'hewed off his brother's head' and buried it apart from the rest of his body, a canonical sin. William the Conqueror then is summoned to avenge this 'vile crime.'[81] This action, therefore, justified the Norman Conquest of England.

Henry of Huntingdon records a different story, but one that similarly paints a picture of the brothers' hatred toward each other. He alleges that the enmity between the two brothers had existed for several years. He claims that in 1064, while at the royal court in Windsor, Tostig, drunk with wine, pulled Harold's hair, to which Harold responded by throwing his brother violently to the floor. Tostig, furious at this humiliation, left the court and travelled to Hereford where Harold was preparing a banquet for the king. There Tostig beheaded his brother's servants, dismembered them, and added their body parts to the wine. He then tried to serve this concoction to the king, but Edward, made cognizant of this deception by his saintly abilities, refused to drink it and prophesied of the future conflict of these brothers:

> It happened in the same year that in the king's presence in the royal hall at Windsor, as his brother Harold was serving wine to the king, Tosti grabbed him by the hair. For Tosti nourished a burning jealously and hatred because although he was himself the first born, his brother was higher in the king's affection. So driven by a surge of rage, he was unable to check his hand from his brother's head. The king, however, foretold that their destruction was already approaching, and that the wrath of God would be delayed no longer. Such was the savagery of those brothers that when they saw anyone's vill in a flourishing state, they would take possession of the dead man's property. And these, indeed, were the justices of the realm! So Tosti, departing in anger from the king and his brother, went to Hereford, where his brother had prepared an enormous royal banquet. In which place he dismembered all his brother's servants, and put a human leg, head, or arm into each vessel of wine, mead, ale, spiced wine, morat, and cider . . . For such an immeasurable crime the king commanded him to be outlawed and exiled.[82]

---

[81] *Carmen de hastingae proelio*, ed. C. Morton and A. Muntz (Oxford, 1972), p. 10.

[82] Henry of Huntingdon, pp. 382–83:
   Contigit autem eodem anno, quod in aula regia apud Windlesores Tosti Haraldum fratrem suum, regi uina propinantem, capillis coram rege ipso arripuerit. Inuidie

Henry of Huntingdon appears to be lost in Greek mythology with a hagiographical twist. The Greek myths have several occasions of banquets where human parts are served to the gods, for example in the stories of Tantulus or Lycaon. To be able to discern the nature of a 'polluted' meal presented by an ambitious servant was in these myths a sign of divinity. In this story then, Edward the Confessor shows his sanctity by discerning that the beverages which Tostig had prepared for his banquet were defiled by the presence of human body parts, and consequently the saintly king exiled the earl of Northumbria from the kingdom.

That this scenario did not occur can almost certainly be established. None of the other contemporary accounts tell of any earlier problems between the two brothers, especially of such a gruesome nature. Furthermore, Henry is factually inaccurate in a number of places in the story. He portrays Tostig as the elder brother and King Edward loving Harold more than Tostig. From other sources the reverse is true. Also, he reports that the brothers frequently absconded with property belonging to the dead, an accusation again without foundation in other, more contemporary sources. Nevertheless, Henry's tale of sibling violence became the basis for later accounts of the conflict between Harold and Tostig. Roger of Wendover's *Chronica sive flores historiarum* and Matthew of Paris' *Chronica majora*, both written in the thirteenth century, and Ralph Higden's *Polychronicon*, Henry Knighton's *Chronicon*, and John of Brompton's *Chronicon*, all written in the fourteenth or fifteenth centuries, follow Henry of Huntingdon's tale closely.[83]

Aelred of Rielvaux's *Vita sancti Aedwardi regis*, written in the late twelfth century, and the Old French poem, *L'Estoire de seint Aedward le rei*, written c.1245, follow Henry's premise that the brothers had a long-term sibling rivalry – but they change the setting to the house of their father, Godwin and the brothers' ages to young boys. These two lives of St Edward the Confessor emphasize

---

namque et odii fomitem ministrauerat, quod cum ipse Tosti primogenitus esset, arcius a rege frater suus diligeretur. Igitur impetu furoris propulsus, non potuit cohibere manus a cesarie fratris. Rex autem pernitiem eorum iam appropinquare predixit, et iram Dei iam non differendam. Tante namque seuicie fratres illi erant, quod cum alicuius nitidam uillam conspicerent, dominatorem de nocte interfici iuberent totamque progeniem illius possessionemque defuncti optinerent. Et isti quidem iusticiarii erant regni! Tosti igitur furibunde discedens a rege et a fratre suo perrexit ad Hereforde, ubi frater suus corrodium regale maximum parauerat. Vbi ministros fratris omnes detruncans, singulis uasis, uini, medonis, ceruisie, pigmenti, morati, cisere, crus humanum, uel caput uel brachium imposuit . . . Rex ergo eum ob scelus adeo infinitum delegari et exulari precepit.
For an analysis of this text see Freeman, *Norman Conquest*, II:653–54.

[83] See page 190, below. References to these works are: Roger of Wendover, *Chronica sive flores historiarum*, ed. H.O. Coxe (London, 1841), I:507–09; Matthew Paris, *Chronica majora*, ed. H.R. Luard (London, 1872), I:533–34; Ranulph Higden, *Polychronicon*, ed. J.R. Lumby (London, 1879), VII:192–93; Henry Knighton, *Chronicon*, ed. J.R. Lumby (London, 1889), I:42–43; and John of Brompton, *Chronicon*, in *Historiae anglicanae scriptores*, X, ed. R. Twysden (London, 1652). See also Freeman, *Norman Conquest*, II:653–54.

The Diffusion of Sources Concerning the Conflict between Harold and Tostig Godwinson

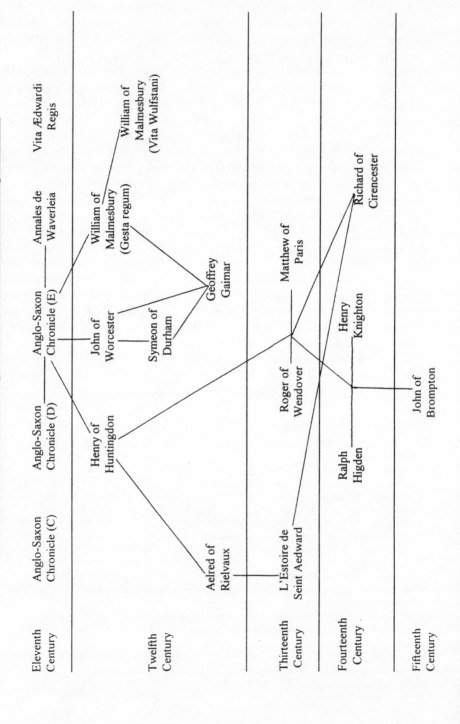

Eleventh Century — Anglo-Saxon Chronicle (C) — Anglo-Saxon Chronicle (D) — Anglo-Saxon Chronicle (E) — Annales de Waverleia — Vita Ædwardi Regis

Twelfth Century

Aelred of Rielvaux — Henry of Huntingdon — John of Worcester — Symeon of Durham — Geoffrey Gaimar — William of Malmesbury (Gesta regum) — William of Malmesbury (Vita Wulfstani)

Thirteenth Century — L'Estoire de Seint Aedward — Roger of Wendover — Matthew of Paris

Fourteenth Century — Ralph Higden — Henry Knighton — Richard of Cirencester

Fifteenth Century — John of Brompton

the brothers' fight and remove the story of the wine, but they add more of a focus on the discerning and prophetic powers of Saint Edward the Confessor. Aelred's account is as follows:

> But let us now, as God gives us the ability, set down some of those things which were revealed to him about the future and the secrets of heaven. It once happened that the blessed king sat at a table with Earl Godwin, the queen's father, of whom we spoke before, at his side. The earl's two sons, Harold and Tostig, still just boys, were playing in front of them when one of them set upon the other more harshly than the roughness of the game warranted, and they turned their game into a fight. Harold attacked his brother more fiercely and seized his hair with both hands. He threw him down and would have strangled him had not the bigger one with his strength got quickly away. The king turned to the earl and said, 'Do you see nothing else in this display than a simple game or fight between boys, Godwin?' The earl replied, 'Nothing else my lord king.' 'My mind,' the king said, 'tells me of something else that is a long way off. Through this battle it is disclosed to me what will become of these boys. For once they have passed out of boyhood and grown into men, malice will inflame their hearts against each other. At first they will seem to play a private game of cheating and plotting, but in the end the stronger will outlaw the weaker and overthrow his rebelling brother. Yet it will be only a short time before the death of the first is avenged by the destruction of the second.[84]

While this story certainly seems more possible than that found in Henry of Huntingdon's *Historia Anglorum*, the late date of Aelred of Rielvaux's *Vita* lessens its credibility. It is however interesting to note that this anecdote was not adopted by Roger of Wendover, Matthew of Paris, Ralph Higden, Henry Knighton, or John of Brompton, all of whom seemed to be more attracted to the more

---

[84] Aelred of Rielvaux, *Vita sancti Aedwardi regis*, ed. J.P. Migne, *Patrologia latina*, 195 (Rome, 1855), cols. 765–66:

> Sed jam aliqua de his quae ei sunt de futuris vel secretis coelestibus revelata, Deo nobis facultatem tribuente ponamus. Sedebat ad mensam aliquando rex beatus, et a latere ejus comes Godwinus pater reginae, de quo superius fecimus mentionem. Huius duo filii pueri adhuc Haroldus et Tostinus ludentes coram eis, cum unus ex illis amarius quam expetebat ludi suavitas insurrexisset in alterum, ludum verterunt in pugnam. Et ecce Haroldus vehementius in fratrem irruens, utramque manum capillis ejus inseruit, prostratumque nisi citius eriperetur virtute superior suffocasset. Tunc rex versus ad ducem: 'Nihilne, inquit, aliud, o Godwine, nisi simplicem in his vel ludum puerorum, vel pugna contemplaris?' Et ille: 'Nihil aliud, domine mi rex.' – Longe, ait, aliud mea mihi mens loquitur, et quid his futurum sit pueris per hoc mihi bellum revelatur. Emensis quippe puerilibus annis cum in virum uterque profecerit, utriusque pectus adversus invicem livor aduret, et primum circumventione insidiisque privatis quasi ludere videbuntur, ad ultimum fortior infirmiorem proscibet, rebellantem prosternet, et prioris mortem post modicum sequens alterius calamitas expiabit.

The anonymous *L'Estoire de seint Aedward le rei*'s version of this occurrence shows little difference from Aelred's, except that it is in vernacular verse. See *L'Estoire de seint Aedward le rei*, ed. and trans. H.R. Luard, in *Lives of Edward the Confessor* (London, 1858), p. 113. For an analysis of this text see Freeman, *Norman Conquest*, II:652–53.

dramatic and vicious Henry of Huntingdon story. That is until the late fourteenth century when Richard of Cirencester added both versions of the story of the Godwinson brothers' rivalry to his record.[85]

Overall, there exists in the story of the conflict between Harold and Tostig Godwinson a lack of understanding between the brothers and the roles they played in the Northumbrian Revolt of 1065. It seems from the sources and subsequent historical analyses of them that Harold had no part in inciting the Northumbrian Rebellion, but at the same time he seems to have accepted the exile of his brother almost too quickly and without exploring alternative solutions. Still, it is this latter part of the story which seems most confusing. Harold should have realized that the banishment of Tostig would bring future problems, and it seems only logical that the future king would not have desired those problems to be thrust upon him. Tostig, on the other hand, had lost his position over Northumbria and his favor with the king of England. Previous to the Northumbrian revolt, he may have considered the possibility of his own ascension to the throne to be made vacant by King Edward's death, but after the Northumbrian revolt that too was gone. This loss of power and prestige, both present and potential, led the exiled earl to seek a conquest of the kingdom when it later became ruled over by his brother, Harold. In 1065 all had angered Tostig, and he became desperate for revenge; it was an anger which would eventually lead to his death at Stamford Bridge at the hand of his brother.

There is an interesting postscript to Harold's and Tostig's conflict. William of Malmesbury reports that after the battle of Stamford Bridge, the body of Tostig, 'recognized by the evidence of a wart between the shoulder-blades,' was identified and allowed to be buried by Harold at York.[86] Harold obviously still had some love for his brother, despite the fact that Tostig had conspired with a foreign magnate to attack England and to take over his, the lawfully elected king's, throne.

---

[85] Richard of Cirencester, *Speculum historiale de gestiis regum angliae*, ed. J.E.B. Mayor (London, 1869), pp. 260–64.
[86] William of Malmesbury, *Gesta regum Anglorum*, I:468–69: '. . . inditio uerrucae inter duas scapulas agnitum . . .'

CHAPTER SEVEN

THE NORWEGIAN MILITARY[1]

AS A RESULT OF the romantic depictions that modern film and literature have given us about Viking military activity, we envision large, muscular Scandinavian warriors with blond, flowing hair hidden under horned helmets who carry huge battle-axes which cut easily through the shields and armor of their enemies. Needless to say, this image is not quite correct. The Scandinavian warrior was well equipped, it is true, and he seems to have fought bravely, if not entirely well, but the rest of our romantic vision falters when studying what little can be ascertained of the Norwegian army of 1066.

Because of the relatively late Christianization of much of Scandinavia – St Óláfr, Haraldr Harðráði's brother was the Christianizing force in Norway, for example – the burial of weapons with the corpses of warriors was practiced in many places well into the eleventh century.[2] This, combined with saga narratives which provide evidence of when and how these weapons were used, portrays an image of a soldier whose weapons were of absolute importance. In war, these weapons provided protection and bloodshed; in peace, they provided honor and distinction. They defined the warrior as a man of pride and honor, and it seems that most males, even those not destined for military service, were trained in their use. They were made of the finest materials, and probably because of the importance and pride placed in them, for those who could afford it, they were beautifully ornamented and sometimes even inlaid with gold, silver, or jewels. By the eleventh century, all freemen in Norway had the right to possess weapons; they usually owned a sword or axe, shield, and spear, and often also a

---

1 While this chapter is specifically given to a study of the Norwegian army of Haraldr Harðráði, in particular of the army which he used to attack England in 1066, it is almost impossible to isolate his forces from other Scandinavian armies of the time. Undoubtedly differences existed between those soldiers coming from Norway and those coming from Sweden and Denmark in the mid-eleventh century, but no scholar has to this date been able to adequately identify those differences.

2 Johannes Brønsted, *The Vikings*, trans. K. Skov (Harmondsworth, 1965), p. 119; Else Rosedahl, *The Vikings*, trans. S.M. Margeson and K. Williams (Harmondsworth, 1992), p. 140; and Bergljot Solberg, 'Weapons,' in *Medieval Scandinavia: An Encyclopedia*, ed. P. Pulsiano (New York, 1993), p. 718.

bow and two dozen arrows. As Johannes Brønsted writes: 'Any self-respecting Viking bore [the sword and axe] about him always.'[3]

Although it was indeed used and feared by the locals who were forced to face it, the battle-axe was not the primary Viking weapon, as portrayed in most cinematic, artistic, and literary depictions. (These include later medieval artistic portrayals, almost all of which distinguish a Scandinavian soldier from his similarly clad non-Scandinavian counterpart by his use of the battle-axe.) Known as the 'Danish axe,' this weapon had been used by Scandinavians since their early raids, and by the eleventh century, although used less often than the sword or spear, it had gained a vivid and violent reputation. Henry of Huntingdon even calls it the 'killer of the elect' (*cedens electa*).[4]

There were two types of battle-axes used by Scandinavian soldiers. The first was known as the *skeggǫx* or bearded axe. It received its name because the bottom of its blade was drawn down toward the haft like a beard. Archaeological specimens of this type of axe have been found dating from as early as the eighth century, when they seem to have been adapted directly from the agricultural tool-chest, and they were known to still be used into the late Middle Ages. Finally, the length of bearded axes shows that they needed two hands to be wielded in battle.[5]

The second type of battle-axe used by Viking warriors was the *breiðǫx* or broad axe. This type of axe had a splayed-out cutting edge which was much longer than the bearded axe. It also seems to have been used solely for military purposes and does not appear in grave finds with other weapons until about 1000. These axes were often ornamented or inlaid with silver. They probably were the type used mostly by both Scandinavian as well as English soldiers fighting at the battle of Stamford Bridge in 1066.[6]

Other types of Scandinavian axes appear in archaeological excavations, such as the *handǫx* (hand axe) and the "T-shaped" axes, both of which were much smaller than the bearded or broad axes, and seem capable of being wielded by only one hand or thrown. Their chief use may have been domestic, although

---

[3] Brønsted, p. 119. See also Peter G. Foote and David M. Wilson, *The Viking Achievement* (New York, 1970), p. 272.

[4] Henry of Huntingdon, pp. 386–87. See also Brønsted, p. 122; Foote and Wilson, pp. 276–77; Rosedahl, *Vikings*, pp. 142–43; Solberg, p. 719; Ian Peirce, 'Arms, Armour and Warfare in the Eleventh Century,' *Anglo-Norman Studies* 10 (1987), 245–48; Vytautas Kazakevicius, 'Some Debatable Questions Concerning the Armament of the Viking Period in Lithuania,' *Fasciculi archaeologiae historicae* 7 (1994), 37–44; and Paddy Griffith, *The Viking Art of War* (London, 1995), pp. 176–78. Jan Petersen, *De norske vikingswerd: En typologisk-kronologisk studie over vikingetidens vaaben* (Christiana (Oslo), 1919), has characterized twelve types of Viking-period axes.

[5] Brønsted, p. 122; Foote and Wilson, p. 277; Rudolf Poertner, *The Vikings: Rise and Fall of the Norse Sea Kings* (London, 1975), p. 150; and Kelly DeVries, *Medieval Military Technology* (Peterborough, 1992), pp. 16–17.

[6] Brønsted, p. 122; Foote and Wilson, p. 277; Poertner, p. 150; and DeVries, *Medieval Military Technology*, p. 17; and Peirce, 'Arms, Armour, and Warfare,' pp. 246–48.

there is some evidence that they were also used on the battlefield as missile weapons.[7]

Instead of the more frequently depicted battle-axe, the primary and most highly prized offensive weapon of the Norwegian soldiers in 1066 was the sword. The sword had existed from the earliest times among the Scandinavians, and by the eleventh century some of the finest swords in all of Europe were being forged by Scandinavian smiths.[8] These were large, double-edged, slashing weapons, on average about 95 centimeters in total length, 75 centimeters in blade length, with both cutting edges sharpened. They were strong, made of the strongest pattern-welded iron with steel edges. They were also well adorned with a guard and grip of bone or ivory and would be carried by the warrior in a sometimes ornamented wooden scabbard trimmed with leather and suspended from the belt or slung over the left shoulder by a strap over the right side. The swords, too, were often ornamented and some even carried the names of their smiths etched proudly onto their blades. The manufacture of swords was often mixed with folklore and magic, and in many instances they were named – such as *Brynjubítr* (mail-biter), *Gullinhjalti* (golden-hilt), *Fótbítr* (leg-biter), *Gramr* (fierce), *Hvati* (keen), *Langhvass* (long-and-sharp), or *Miðfáinn* (ornamented-down-the-middle). Some were even said to have been made and presented to man by the gods. Although being found as frequently or even more frequently in the graves of warriors, many swords were known to be passed down from father to son for many generations, gaining an added legacy with each new inheritance.[9]

---

[7] Foote and Wilson, p. 277; Griffith, p. 176; and DeVries, *Medieval Military Technology*, p. 17.

[8] Brønsted, pp. 119–21. Earlier Scandinavian swords appear to have been Frankish in origin. See Brønsted, pp. 121–22; Foote and Wilson, pp. 273–74; Rosedahl, *Vikings*, p. 142; and Griffith, pp. 173–74.

[9] Brønsted, pp. 119–22; Foote and Wilson, pp. 273–75; Rosedahl, *Vikings*, p. 142; Poertner, p. 150; Griffith, pp. 173–76; Solberg, pp. 718–19; Kazakevicius, pp. 40–43; DeVries, *Medieval Military Technology*, pp. 20–25; Peirce, 'Arms, Armour, and Warfare,' pp. 250–57; Ian Peirce, 'The Knight, His Arms and Armour in the Eleventh and Twelfth Centuries,' in *The Ideals and Practice of Medieval Knighthood*, ed. C. Harper-Bill and R. Harvey (Woodbridge, 1986), pp. 154–55, 162–64; Irmelin Martens, 'Norwegian Viking Age Weapons: Some Questions Concerning their Production and Distribution,' in *The Twelfth Viking Congress: Developments Around the Baltic and the North Sea in the Viking Age*, ed. B. Ambrosiani and H. Clark (Stockholm, 1994), pp. 180–82; Ian Peirce, 'The Development of the Medieval Sword, c. 850–1300,' in *The Ideals and Practice of Medieval Knighthood*, III, ed. C. Harper-Bill and R. Harvey (Woodbridge, 1990), pp. 139–50; Janet Lang and Barry Ager, 'Swords of the Anglo-Saxon and Viking Periods in the British Museum: A Radiographic Study,' in *Weapons and Warfare in Anglo-Saxon England*, ed. S.C. Hawkes (Oxford, 1989), pp. 85–122; and Holger Arbman, 'Zwei Ingelri-Schwerter aus Schweden,' *Zeitschrift für historisches Waffen-und Kostumkunde* 14 (1935–36), 146–49. Petersen has found 26 general and 20 special types of Viking-age swords. Examples of eleventh-century Scandinavian swords can be found in David C. Nicolle, *Arms and Armour of the Crusading Era, 1050–1350* (White Plains, 1988), nos. 1032, 1033, 1036, 1038, 1039, 1040, 1041. See also H.R. Ellis Davidson's excellent *The Sword in Anglo-Saxon England: Its Archaeology and Literature* (Oxford, 1962) which, despite being devoted to a study of the Anglo-Saxon sword, as its title indicates, focuses also

Another important offensive weapon used by the Norwegians in their conquest of England in 1066 was the spear (*spjót*). This weapon is the least ornamented of all Scandinavian grave finds, which may show that it had a more common use by Scandinavian soldiers; at the same time, the fact that more iron spear heads have been found in Scandinavian graves may show a commonality which precluded ornamentation or celebration.[10] Two main types of spears were used by the Scandinavian soldier: the throwing spear and the thrusting spear. The throwing spear was naturally lighter and shorter, perhaps not unlike the javelins used commonly in the classical Mediterranean world, but missing in general from continental medieval arsenals. Yet, to the Scandinavians of the early and high Middle Ages, these weapons were important, and almost every battle they fought in began with a barrage of throwing spears.[11]

The thrusting spear was of necessity much heavier, longer, and made with broader blades than the throwing spear. From extant weapons, it can be determined that these blades were also of many different shapes, although the leaf-shape was the most prominent, and on average 50 centimeters in length. Most often the spearheads were made of a single piece of metal with a sharp middle rib and a hollow conical socket, although some pattern-welded heads have also been found. (Bergljot Solberg contends that the pattern-welded spears were more than likely continental European imports.[12]) During times of peace these weapons were used in hunting, but during times of war the thrusting spear provided both an offensive and a defensive use, the latter depicted grandly in the Norwegian Kings' Sagas by the thrusting spears anchored solidly behind the Norwegian shield wall at Stamford Bridge.[13]

Bows were also used by the Scandinavians in their battles; they may have been the chief missile weapons of the eleventh-century Norwegians. Bundles of arrow heads, measuring between ten and fifteen centimeters in length with some barbed, have been found in grave sites, while at least two bows themselves have also been excavated. (The one found at Hedeby measures 192 centimeters in length.[14]) In addition, the Norwegian Kings' Sagas record the existence of

---

on Scandinavian swords found in Anglo-Saxon England and on Old Norse literary references to swords.

[10] Foote and Wilson, p. 275.

[11] Foote and Wilson, pp. 275–76; Rosedahl, *Vikings*, p. 143; Griffith, pp. 164–66; and DeVries, *Medieval Military Technology*, pp. 10–11.

[12] Solberg, p. 719. Upon what evidence such a conclusion is based is not given.

[13] *Morkinskinna: Pergamentsbog fra første halvdel af det trettende aarhundrede*, ed. C.R. Unger (Christiania (Oslo), 1867), p. 116; *Fagrskinna: Kortfattet Norsk Konge-Saga*, ed. P.A. Munch and C.R. Unger (Christiania (Oslo), 1847), p. 138; Snorri Sturluson, *Heimskringla*, ed. B. Aðalbjarnarson (Reykjavik, 1941–51). III:185–86; and *Flateyjarbók: En samling af Norske Konge-Sagaer*, ed. G. Vigfusson and C.R. Unger (Christiania (Oslo), 1860–68), III:393. On the spear see Brønsted, pp. 122–23; Foote and Wilson, pp. 275–76; Rosedahl, *Vikings*, p. 143; Griffith, pp. 178–80; Solberg, p. 719; Martens; Kazakevicius, pp. 37–40; and DeVries, *Medieval Military Technology*, pp. 9–11. Petersen has also typed these. A period Swedish spearhead with ornamented and silvered socket is found in Nicolle, no. 1043.

[14] Brønsted, p. 123; Foote and Wilson, p. 278; Rosedahl, *Vikings*, p. 143; Griffith, pp.

archers in Haraldr Harðráði's army at the battles of Fulford Gate and Stamford Bridge,[15] but much of this is speculation as the bow seems not to have been a valued weapon of most of the Scandinavian heroes depicted in the sagas. Still, when it was necessary, such as with Haraldr Harðráði at the battle of Niså, the Scandinavian hero was able to use the bow as capably as his more 'heroic' weapons.[16]

The most popular defensive armament used by the Scandinavian warrior of the eleventh century was the shield. All Norwegian males were required to possess a shield. These were large, flat, and round, constructed of wood about a meter wide and covered with hardened leather; usually they were painted with bright colors, intricate swirling designs, and animal motifs. An iron rim ran around the outside of the shield, and a large iron boss was placed in the middle of the shield's front and locked into place by an iron grip on the underside of the board.[17] As depicted in the sagas and on the excavated Gokstad ship, while traveling on the sea, Scandinavian shields would be hung along the gunwales of the ship.[18] Kite-shaped shields may also have been used by the Norwegian soldiers at Fulford Gate and Stamford Bridge, but these were not common Scandinavian armor and would have probably been acquired from the Normans or English, who preferred using them by this time.[19]

A second piece of defensive armament also worn by most of the Norwegian soldiers in their 1066 conquest of England was the helmet. Unlike the typical Hollywood portrayal of Viking helmets, with their adorning horns or feathers, most Scandinavians wore simple utilitarian helmets. Exemplars excavated in Scandinavia and England dating from the eleventh century and earlier indicate that they consisted of four parts: the cap, two hinged cheekpieces, and a section of mail protecting the back and sides of the neck. The cap was made of a wide band encircling the head, with a narrower second band attached to the first by rivets and running from back to front. The second band was linked to the wide circular band by two short bands running down towards the ears. The spaces left open by this framework were filled by plates of metal attached to the bands by rivets. Holes were sometimes cut in the front of the helmets for the eyes; at other times the helmet ended at a thick and wide brow band covering the eyebrows.

162–64; Solberg, p. 719; DeVries, *Medieval Military Technology*, pp. 33–36; Peirce, 'Arms, Armour, and Warfare,' pp. 248–29; and Jim Bradbury, *The Medieval Archer* (New York, 1985), pp. 17–23. For an example of one of the excavated bows, see Nicolle, no. 1042.

[15] *Morkinskinna*, p. 116; *Fagrskinna*, p. 138; Snorri Sturluson, *Heimskringla*, III:185; and *Flateyjarbók*, III:393.

[16] See n. 177 in the chapter 'Haraldr Harðráði' above.

[17] Brønsted, p. 123; Foote and Wilson, pp. 278–79; Rosedahl, *Vikings*, p. 143; and Griffith, pp. 166–68.

[18] See, for example, Þjóðólfr's poem in Snorri Sturluson, *Heimskringla*, III:146 (also in n. 172 in the chapter 'Haraldr Harðráði' above); Brønsted, p. 123; and Griffith, p. 68.

[19] Foote and Wilson, pp. 278–79; Griffith, pp. 166–68; DeVries, *Medieval Military Technology*, pp. 63–64; and James Mann, 'Arms and Armour,' in *The Bayeux Tapestry: A Comprehensive Survey*, ed. by Frank M. Stenton, 2nd edn (London, 1957), pp. 56–58.

Some also had a long, thin piece of metal which descended between the eyes to serve as a nose-guard. The cheek pieces, hinged onto the wide brow-band, covered both the ears and cheeks and were probably attached together under the chin by a leather or cloth strap. (Although these have not survived, the holes for such chin straps still exist.) A mail neck guard, made in a manner similar to a cuirass, was also sometimes attached to the brow-band. In addition, some ornamentation was frequently included on the helmet, such as copper eyebrows added above the eye-holes or the figure of a boar on the crown.[20]

A final, less often worn defensive armament, the mail-shirt (*hringserkr* or *hringskyrta*), was also used by some Norwegian soldiers. Although known to the Romans as the *lorica hamata*, it had first been made popular by the Carolingian forces of Charlemagne, and by the eleventh century was the most influential defensive clothing worn by warriors throughout Europe. The mail-shirt, sometimes redundantly called 'chain-mail,' was made of interlocking rings braided together over a leather jerkin. It was long, covering from the neck to the knees, with long sleeves. Additionally, as depicted in the Osberg ship tapestry, this Scandinavian armor was often painted a bright white color.[21] The epic Anglo-Saxon poem, *Beowulf*, although written at least a century earlier, gives a good description of what might have been worn by the Norwegians at Stamford Bridge:

[20] Foote and Wilson, pp. 279–80; Rosedahl, *Vikings*, pp. 143–44; Griffith, pp. 168–71; DeVries, *Medieval Military Technology*, pp. 57–58; and Peirce, 'Arms, Armour, and Warfare,' pp. 240–43. Excellent examples of this style of helmets can be found in the one excavated at Gjermundbu in southern Norway and at Lokrume in Gotland, and in the helmets found at Sutton Hoo, Benty Grange, and Coppergate. See Mann, *Bayeux Tapestry*, pp. 58–68; Peirce, 'Arms, Armour, and Warfare,' pp. 159–60; Claude Blair, *European Armour* (London, 1958), pp. 25–27; Nicholas P. Brooks, 'Arms, Status and Warfare in Late-Saxon England,' in *Ethelred the Unready: Papers from the Millenary Conference*, ed. D. Hill (Oxford, 1978), pp. 82–94; Dominic Tweddle, *The Coppergate Helmet* (York, 1984); Peter V. Addyman, Nicholas Pearson and Dominic Tweddle, 'The Coppergate Helmet,' *Antiquity* 56 (1982), 189–94; Rupert Bruce-Mitford, 'The Sutton Hoo Helmet – a New Reconstruction,' in *Aspects of Anglo-Saxon Archaeology: Sutton Hoo and Other Discoveries* (New York, 1974), pp. 198–209; Rupert Bruce-Mitford, 'The Benty Grange Helmet and Some Other Supposed Anglo-Saxon Helmets,' in *Aspects of Anglo-Saxon Archaeology: Sutton Hoo and Other Discoveries* (New York, 1974), pp. 223–52. A helmet browpiece is depicted in Nicolle, no. 1034, and a helmet carved on an elkhorn sculpture in Nicolle, no. 1037. Because of the few helmets excavated, Brønsted (p. 123) believes that only nobles wore metal helmets with other soldiers wearing leather head coverings. Griffith (pp. 168–69) agrees.

[21] Brønsted, p. 123; Foote and Wilson, p. 279; Rosedahl, *Vikings*, p. 144; Griffith, pp. 171–72; DeVries, *Medieval Military Technology*, pp. 60–66; Blair, pp. 23–24; Mann, *Bayeux Tapestry*, pp. 60–63; Peirce, 'Arms, Armour, and Warfare,' pp. 237–40; Peirce, 'The Knight, His Arms and Armour,' pp. 155–59; and James Mann, 'Arms and Armour,' in *Medieval England*, ed. Austin Lane Poole (Oxford, 1958), p. 286. A fragment of a tenth-century Russian mail shirt is depicted in Nicolle, no. 178.

His war-shirt, hand-fashioned, broad and well-worked, was to explore the mere: it knew how to cover his body-cave so that foe's grip might not harm his heart, or grasp of angry enemy his life.[22]

Sometimes these mail-shirts were named; Snorri Sturluson reports that Haraldr Harðráði wore one named 'Emma.' He goes on to describe it as an especially long armor – 'so that it reached to the middle of his leg' – made especially for the very tall Haraldr, which was very costly and strong – 'so strong that it could withstand the blows of all weapons' – certainly suitable for the king of Norway.[23]

Those not able to afford the costly mail-shirt possibly wore lamellar armor. This armor, also descended from Roman armor-smiths when known as the *lorica squamata*, was generically made of a large number of metallic scales attached to each other by wire or leather laces and affixed to a linen textile undergarment by linen cord or hooks and belts. Although not mentioned in contemporary narrative sources, grave finds have shown that this type of cloth-covered armor was used by Scandinavians during the eleventh century;[24] excavations at the site of the battle of Visby, fought in 1361, confirm that lamellar armor continued to be a favored form of Scandinavian armor throughout the rest of the Middle Ages.[25]

Scandinavian warriors might have regarded their arms and armor as the chief means of gaining military victory, but they also used other, more psychological means to ensure the defeat of an opponent. In order to motivate their men, before a battle Scandinavian generals would harangue their troops with a speech filled with heroism, honor, and incitement. The Norwegian Kings' Sagas record such a speech given by Haraldr Harðráði before the battle of Niså, and, although not similarly recorded, he also undoubtedly gave one before the battle at Fulford Gate as well.[26] (Stamford Bridge was a surprise attack by the English and thus

[22] *Beowulf*, ed. Fr. Klaeber, 3rd edn (Lexington, 1950), pp. 54–55:

    scold herebyrne   hondum gebroden,
    sid ond searofah   sund cunnian,
    seo þe bancofan   beorgan cuþe,
    þæt him hildegrap   hreðre ne mihte,
    eorres inwitfeng   aldre gesceðþan

The translation I have used is: *Beowulf*, trans. E.T. Donaldson (New York, 1966), p. 26.

[23] Snorri Sturluson, *Heimskringla*, III:188: 'Emma hét brynja hans. Hon var síð, svá at hon tók mitt bein honum, ok svá sterk, at aldri hafði vápn á fest.' See also *Fagrskinna*, p. 129; *Morkinskinna*, p. 118; and *Flateyjarbók*, III:395.

[24] DeVries, *Medieval Military Technology*, p. 54.

[25] Blair, pp. 55–56; DeVries, *Medieval Military Technology*, pp. 85–87; and Bengt Thordeman, *Armour from the Battle of Wisby, 1361* (Stockholm, 1939).

[26] *Fagrskinna*, pp. 128–29 and Snorri Sturluson, *Heimskringla*, III:145–46. See also Rosedahl, *Vikings*, p. 144. On battlefield orations in general see the numerous articles by John R.E. Bliese, 'The Courage of the Normans. A Comparative Study of Battle Rhetoric,' *Nottingham Medieval Studies* 35 (1991), 1–26; 'Leadership, Rhetoric, and Morale in the Norman Conquest of England,' *Military Affairs* 52 (1988), 23–28; 'Rhetoric and Morale: A Study of Battle Orations from the Central Middle Ages,' *Journal of Medieval History* 15 (1989), 201–26; and

there was unlikely to have been time for a Norwegian battlefield oration.) To intimidate their adversaries, the Scandinavians began an encounter with a loud trumpeting of horns which shook the earth and their enemies' courage. In many instances, upon hearing the deep-toned calls of these horns, these enemies would simply flee from the battlefield. If not, there were accompanying shouts and war cries as an attack commenced. Only the very strong-willed would not panic.[27]

As was conventional in all armies of this period, the Norwegians would also use banners and standards which doubled as symbols of organization and signalling devices on the battlefield. These banners would lead the battle charge, and only the bravest of soldiers would carry them. Most Scandinavian banners are depicted in later artistic works with animal designs and figures, and many were also named: Haraldr Harðráði's 1066 standard was called 'Land-waster' (*Landeyðuna*).[28]

Their weapons and psychological warfare were certainly important, for without them Scandinavian combat would not have been undertaken, but to emphasize them without also including the actions of the soldiers themselves, is to miss perhaps the most fundamental facet of high medieval Scandinavian warfare. Perhaps no other medieval army was as individualized as was the Scandinavian army. Based on the tales told about these warriors not only in the sagas but also on numerous rune stones, it must be concluded that individual heroism and valor were of much more importance to Scandinavian society than united military action.[29] Individual military heroism was also well rewarded. Confirmation of this can be seen in the grave goods of a Scandinavian warrior excavated at Mammen in Denmark. Not only was this soldier buried with his weapon, a silver-inlaid battle-axe, but he was also clothed in bracelets or cuffs of wool, covered in silk and sewn with gold thread. Two very well made, streamer-shaped silk ribbons, embroidered in gold, were also buried with him. It has been concluded by Johannes Brønsted and others that these were rewards for valorous military service.[30]

As such, it is easy to conclude, lacking evidence to the contrary, that the very concept of military organization might have been foreign to Scandinavian soldiers. Most historians contend that only by the eleventh century do Scandinavian military forces even begin to function like the traditional medieval army. Before this time they seem almost always to have been small gangs of fighters,

---

'When Knightly Courage May Fail: Battle Orations in Medieval Europe,' *Historian* 53 (1991), 489–504.

[27] Poertner, p. 151.

[28] Snorri Sturluson (*Heimskringla*, III:180) is the only Norwegian Kings' Saga which mentions this banner. See also Foote and Wilson, p. 283 and Rosedahl, *Vikings*, pp. 144–45.

[29] See H.R. Ellis Davidson, 'The Training of Warriors,' in *Weapons and Warfare in Anglo-Saxon England*, ed. S.C. Hawkes (Oxford, 1989), pp. 11–23.

[30] Brønsted, pp. 132, 204–07; Rosedahl, *Vikings*, pp. 145–46; and Henry R. Loyn, *The Vikings in Britain* (Oxford, 1994), p. 145.

pirates or brigands who roamed the countryside of Europe attacking poorly armed and undefended monasteries, towns, and villages. One thing that seems certain, although not without dispute, is that these 'Viking' bands appear to have consciously avoided battles with other armed forces, and when these occurred – for example, at Edington in 878, where they met a combined Anglo-Saxon army under Ælfred the Great, and at the Dyle in 891, where they faced an East Frankish force under their king, Arnulf – the Vikings almost always were soundly and decisively defeated.[31]

In the eleventh century, coupled with the rise of the more powerful central organizations of such Scandinavian kings as Sveinn Forkbeard, Knútr the Great, and Sveinn Estriðson of Denmark, and Óláfr and Haraldr Harðráði of Norway, more traditional medieval warfare (what was once called 'feudal warfare') began to be waged. For this, these kings needed larger armies, thus necessitating a more active recruitment policy, what military historians have generally called a 'levy.' This fact is accepted by almost all historians writing on the military history of eleventh-century Scandinavia; but what organizational form this levy took is hotly debated. Even the word which is to be translated as 'levy' in Old Norse is questioned. Is it *leiðangr* (*leðing* in Old Danish, *leþunger* in Old Swedish, and *leding* or *ledang* in modern English), which seems to designate almost any military expedition (indeed, Theodoricus uses the Latin term *expeditio* in its place[32]), or *lið*, which has been translated as everything from 'army,' denoting a large number of soldiers, to 'band,' denoting a much smaller number?

On the one side of the debate sit P.G. Foote and David Wilson, who believe simply that the '*leiðangr*' was a levy of ships, men, armaments and provisions,

---

[31] There has been a continuing argument throughout most of this century as to the size and brutality of the earliest Viking armies. On the issue of size, the current opinion, put forth by Peter Sawyer, among others, is that the numbers in Viking forces assailing Europe from the late eighth to the late tenth centuries were quite small and, by extension, incapable of fighting other, more traditionally sized European armies. See Peter Sawyer, *The Age of the Vikings* (New York, 1962), pp. 118–35; Peter Sawyer, *Kings and Vikings: Scandinavia and Europe, AD 700–1100* (London, 1982), p. 145; Caroll Gillmor, 'War on the Rivers: Viking Numbers and Mobility on the Seine and Loire, 841–886,' *Viator* 19 (1988), 79–109 and Neil S. Price, 'Viking Armies and Fleets in Brittany: A Case Study for Some General Problems,' *Vikingsymposium* 10 (1991), 7–24. Against this are Frank M. Stenton, *Anglo-Saxon England* (Oxford, 1971), p. 242; Christopher Dawson, *The Making of Europe* (London, 1948), pp. 190–91; and Martin Biddle and Birth Kjølbye-Biddle, 'Repton and the Vikings,' *Antiquity* 66 (1992), 36–51. At the same time, some historians have tried to lessen the brutality of these early Viking raiders. Blaming the portrayal of Vikings as 'blood-thirsty and cruel' on 'contemporary reactions to their pagan religion,' Else Rosedahl (*Vikings*, p. 192) is following in the footsteps of Albert d'Haenens (*Les invasions normandes en Belgique au IXe siècle: Le phénomène de sa répercussion dans l'historiographie médievale* (Leuven, 1967)), and others, in describing the raids of pre-eleventh-century Scandinavians as little more than 'rambunctious tourists roughing up the natives,' a contention which flies in the face of the overwhelming evidence of brutality provided not only by Christian Europeans being attacked by these forces, but also by Scandinavians, most also Christian, who also describe these brutalities, but in complimentary terms. So much evidence is extremely difficult to dismiss so simply.

[32] Theodoricus, *Monumenta historica Norvegiæ: Latinske kildeskrifter til Norges historie I middelalderen*, ed. G. Storm (Christiana (Oslo), 1880), p. 56.

called out by the king, the supreme military leader, and supplied by the population on a proportional basis,[33] and Rikke Malmros, who writes that the '*leiðangr* was a public fleet levy of the free farmers of the countries under the leadership of the king . . . [it] was the main organizing bond between the king and the farmers, who in *leiðangr* fought as his personal men.'[34] In the absence of contemporary legal documents defining the term, these authors have utilized skaldic poetry of the tenth and eleventh centuries, as well as later sagas, to contend that this particular levy, peculiar to Scandinavia, allowed for a large force: in early eleventh-century Norway, three farms joined together to support one man in military service, while later in the century, seven inhabitants of households would support one soldier.[35] It also allowed for the development of an experienced, 'professional' corps, capable of making possible the conquests of England by Sveinn Forkbeard and Knútr, and probable the conquest by Haraldr Harðráði. As Malmros writes:

> In the eleventh century, *leiðangr* was a successful military institution. Sections of the Danish and Norwegian *leiðangr* conquered England under the leadership of Knud (Cnut) the Great. Their strength lay in their discipline and in the versatility of their ships . . . The fleets fought great naval battles, where the ships were tied together, and where the crew then engaged in hand-to-hand combat. More frequently, however, they served as an organization for amphibious warfare: the ships sailed in a fast, broad formation and moored simultaneously at a shore, or sailed up a river to a suitable camping site. The surrounding area was then plundered, and the opposing force attacked by an established phalanx of infantry equipped with bows and arrows, spears, swords, or battle-axes, and large, round shields.[36]

In some instances, the *leiðangr* would also be divided, with part, usually the losing side in the choosing of lots, being left behind to protect the homeland. In Haraldr Harðráði's conquest of both Denmark and England, he left half of the *leiðangr* behind in Norway.[37] Still, the sources report, Haraldr filled from 200 to more than 500 ships for his attack on England in 1066.[38]

---

33 Foote and Wilson, p. 280.

34 Rikke Malmros, 'Leiðangr,' in *Medieval Scandinavia: An Encyclopedia*, ed. P. Pulsiano (New York, 1993), p. 389. See also Rikke Malmros, 'Leding og Skjaldekvad: Det elvte århundredes nordiske krigsflåder, deres teknologi og organisation og deres placering I samfundet, belyst gennem den samtidige fyrstedigtning,' *Aarbøger for nordisk oldkyndigheid og historie* (1985), 89–139.

35 Foote and Wilson, p. 281. See also Edv. Bull, *Leding: Militær- og finansforfatning i norge i ældre tid* (Christiana (Oslo) and Copenhagen, 1920), pp. 39–40, and A. Steinnes, 'Kor gamal er den norsk leidangsskipnaden?' *Syn of segn* (1929), pp. 49–65, who accept the reign of Harold Fairhair (c.940–960) as the origin of this system of military organization.

36 Malmros, 'Leiðangr,' p. 389.

37 See, for example, before the battle of Niså, when Haraldr sent half of his troops back to Norway (n. 156 in the chapter 'Haraldr Harðráði' above). For his attack on England, see *Fagrskinna*, p. 135; *Morkinskinna*, p. 111; Snorri Sturluson, *Heimskringla*, III:138; and *Flateyjarbók*, III:388.

38 The following totals are given for the number of ships used by Haraldr against England in

On the other side of the debate defiantly sits Neils Lund. In a series of articles and one book devoted to the question of medieval Scandinavian military organization, Lund questions the very existence of a military organizational scheme known as the *leiðangr* before the twelfth century.[39] In doing so, he completely discredits the skaldic verses as sources for what Malmros *et al.* would have them describe as a levy for any eleventh-century military adventure. Only when the word appears in more trustworthy, but significantly later legal records is it evidence of a Scandinavian military organization for Lund. Moreover, when the word *lið* is found in skaldic verses, he claims that it means only 'a naval force that any chieftain in the Viking period could gather' and that this in no way means a large number of soldiers. Lund explains further: 'The king had his own *lið* and if he was powerful enough he might be able to unite the *liðs* of all lesser chieftains in his country and compel them to fight wars but this does not imply that any particular organization was involved.'[40] By extension, it also leads Lund to the conclusion that:

> The conquests of England accomplished first by Swein Forkbeard and then by his son Cnut undoubtedly belong to the most spectacular achievements of the whole Viking age, and there can be little doubt that the armies involved were bigger and probably drawn from a wider area, indeed from most of Scandinavia, than Viking armies had previously been. This does not mean, however, that they were different in principle from those armies with which the west was already familiar.[41]

1066 (from smallest to largest): 200 (Snorri Sturluson, *Heimskringla*, III:139; 300 (Henry of Huntingdon, pp. 386–87; *Anglo-Saxon Chronicle*, in *Two of the Saxon Chronicles Parallel*, ed. Charles Plummer and John Earle (Oxford, 1892), D and E (1066), I:197; William of Malmesbury, *Gesta regum Anglorum: The History of the English Kings*, ed. and trans. R.A.B. Mynors, R,M, Thomson, and M. Winterbottom (Oxford, 1998), I:420–21); 470 (Geoffrey Gaimer, *Lestoire des Engles*, ed. T.D. Hardy and C.T. Martin (London, 1888–89), I:165); and 500 (John of Worcester, *The Chronicle of John of Worcester*, ed. R.R. Darlington and P. McGurk, trans. J. Bray and P. McGurk (Oxford, 1995), I:602–03; Symeon of Durham, *Historia regum*, ed. T. Arnold (London, 1882–85), II:180). This feat has led Per Sveaas Andersen (*Samlingen av Norge og kristningen av landet, 800–1300* (Bergen, 1977), pp. 262–73) to conclude that the *leiðangr* was Haraldr's innovation.

[39] 'The Armies of Swein Forkbeard and Cnut: *Leding* or *Lið*?' *Anglo-Saxon England* 15 (1986), 105–18; 'The Danish Perspective,' in *The Battle of Maldon, AD 991*, ed. D. Scragg (London, 1991), pp. 114–42; 'Danish Military Organisation,' in *The Battle of Maldon: Fiction and Fact*, ed. J. Cooper (London, 1993), pp. 109–26; 'If the Vikings Knew a *Leding* – What Was It Like?' in *The Twelfth Viking Congress: Developments Around the Baltic and the North Sea in the Viking Age*, ed. B. Ambrosiani and H. Clark (Stockholm, 1994), pp. 100–105; 'Is Leidang a Nordic or a European Phenomenon?' in *Military Aspects of Scandinavian Society in a European Perspective, A.D. 1–1300* (Copenhagen, 1997), pp. 195–99; and *Lið, leding og landevœrn* (Roskilde, 1996). He also refers to his thesis in *De Danske vikinger i England* (Copenhagen, 1967) and *De Hœrger og de brœnder: Danmark og England i vikingtiden* (Copenhagen, 1993).

[40] This quote comes from Lund, 'Danish Perspective,' p. 119, although all of his work contains the same sentiment. See also Brønsted, p. 200.

[41] Lund, 'Armies of Swein Forkbeard and Cnut,' p. 118.

(Undeniably, Lund would say the same about Haraldr Harðráði's invasion.) Finally, Lund does not believe that, even when it was instituted, the *leiðangr* was solely a Scandinavian military characteristic, but one which was known by other names throughout all of Europe, and probably borrowed from these other lands by the Scandinavians in the twelfth century or later.[42]

Neils Lund's arguments are quite compelling, and undoubtedly he is correct in believing that Malmros, Foote and Wilson, Edv. Bull, A. Steinnes, and Per Sveaas Andersen have too quickly accepted evidence provided by the poorly dated and often obscure-in-meaning skaldic verses and later sagas. At the same time, however, Lund himself must be questioned on his equally quick dismissal of such sources, as well as his choosing only to accept sources which have relatively few pre-twelfth-century equivalents. The fact that Sveinn Forkbeard and Knútr did conquer England with an extremely impressive and seemingly well organized army – this derived not from later Scandinavian sources, but from contemporary English ones – and that Haraldr Harðráði attempted to do the same with a navy placed by contemporary English chroniclers at no fewer than 300 ships (in this instance it is Snorri Sturluson who gives the lower tally of 200 ships), filled with soldiers whose number greatly outnumbered the levy available to Morkere and Edwin from their respective earldoms of Northumbria and Mercia, must mean that some kind of military organization existed in the Scandinavian military of the eleventh century. As a final note, it seems ludicrous to believe that someone like Haraldr Harðráði, who had served in the leadership of what was probably the most organized army in the world at the time, the Byzantine army, would abandon such a logical notion once he returned to Scandinavia. If Malmros, Foote and Wilson, Bull, Steinnes, and Andersen are incorrect in the extent to which they view the eleventh-century Scandinavian army as organized, they are still closer to what the actual levy was than is Lund, with his desire for a continuation of the loosely-knit bands of Viking raiders whose target had simply grown from an easily defeated monastery to an equally easily defeated kingdom.

Within this eleventh-century Scandinavian military organization, there appear to have been two different classes of soldiers, with titles indicating their military experience or perhaps their professional status. Principal among these were the huscarls (*húskalr*), whose special status as retainer gave them specific rights of land ownership (a house, as reflected by the name) received for this service from their chief or king. Together a group of huscarls made up the *hirð* or bodyguard of this leader and were required to provide military service whenever it was requested or wherever it was needed.[43]

Below the huscarls were the *bóndaherinn* or *bóndi*. These troops were those freemen recruited to provide temporary military service. The term bóndaherinn, meaning 'householder' or 'landowner,' but probably more accurately 'free

---

[42] Lund, 'Is Leidang a Nordic or a European Phenomenon?'
[43] Foote and Wilson, pp. 100–101. Griffith (pp. 132–34) is confused here, never equating the huscarls with the *hirð*.

farmer,' gives the impression of someone who served in the army for only a small amount of time and then returned to his otherwise everyday agricultural occupation. Less professional and experienced, the bóndaherinn operated much like the fyrd did in Anglo-Saxon England, as a troop who still could fight either an imposing offensive or defensive struggle.[44] Still, when given the opportunity to keep half of his army in Norway, the Norwegian Kings' Sagas are insistent in indicating that it was bóndaherinn which were returned to Norway and not huscarls.[45] Slaves did not fight in eleventh-century Scandianvian armies.[46]

One other type, rather than class, of Scandinavian warrior should be singled out. He was called *berserkgangr* by the Scandinavians, and his name, as 'berserker,' has come into our language to mean 'crazy and wild.'[47] In some cases, these appear to have been specific warriors, while in others, they are more conventional soldiers who 'go berserk' in the heat of battle. The latter would work themselves into a frenzy, a blood-lust which would give them incredible strength and made them seemingly indifferent to blows or pain. Because of their unconventional fighting, they were also popular among the Old Norse saga writers. For example, Snorri Sturluson's *Ynglinga Saga* uses the god, Oðinn, and his forces as examples of soldiers in the midst of a berserker rage:

> Óðinn could do such that in battle his enemies became blind, deaf, or terrified, and their weapons bit not as they were supposed to. And his own men went without armor and fought like dogs or wolves; biting on their shield-rims, they were as strong as bears or bulls. They killed men, and neither fire nor iron worked on them. That was called *berserkgangr*.[48]

More modern writers have claimed that this frenzy was induced by alcohol (Foote and Wilson),[49] or by eating 'toadstools containing muscarin, a poison and pyschotropic drug which produced effects similar to a bad LSD trip' (Poertner).[50] However there also seems to have been a belief that magic attended these warriors: that a form of lycanthropy was inborn in them. Rudolf Poertner describes this belief:

> They are evildoers who take on the shape of beasts after dark and wander through woods and moors setting fire to farms, ambushing travelers, and rav-

---

[44] Foote and Wilson, p. 81, and Griffith, pp. 137–39.
[45] *Fagrskinna*, p. 124; *Morkinskinna*, pp. 54–56; Snorri Sturluson, *Heimskringla*, III:114–15; and *Flateyjarbók*, III:338–40.
[46] Foote and Wilson, pp. 76–77.
[47] Poertner, pp. 151–52 and Foote and Wilson, p. 285.
[48] Snorri Sturluson, *Ynglingasaga*, ed. E. Wessén (Oslo, 1952):
Óðinn kunni svá gera at í orrostu urðu óvinir hans blindir eða óttafullir, en vápn þeira bitu heldr en vendir. En hans menn fóru bryniulausir ok váru galnir sem hundar eða vargar, bitu í skioldu sína, váru sterkir sem birnir eða griðungar; þeir drápu mannfólkit, en hvártki eldr né iárn orti á þá; þat er kallaðr berserksgangr.
See also Brønsted, p. 124, and Poertner, p. 151.
[49] Foote and Wilson, p. 285.
[50] Poertner, p. 151.

aging virgins until, at daybreak, they are transformed back into their harmless, good-natured daytime selves, indistinguishable from the rest of the population.[51]

It was this magic, derived from Scandinavian paganism, that made berserkers distinctive targets for missionaries trying to prove the superiority of Christianity over paganism. In *Brennu-Njáls Saga*, for example, a Christian proselytizer, named Þangbrandr, uses an unknowing, but extremely frightening berserker, named Ótryggr, in a contest of conversion. Three fires are kindled: one is consecrated by the pagans, one by the Christians, and one is left unconsecrated. The contest was to see if any of the fires would stop the berserker. 'If the berserker is frightened then of the fire I consecrate, and walks through your fire, then you should join the Christian religion,' challenges Þangbrandr. Of course, Ótryggr passes through the pagan fire without fear or damage, but he does not dare to approach Þangbrandr's fire. In anger, he begins to swing his sword, only to be disarmed by Þangbrandr's crucifix and then killed by everyone present. By this means does Iceland accept Christianity.[52]

Berserk rages, with or without actual berserker participation, seem to have occurred often in warfare. Even the most veteran of soldiers were not without their berserker rages. Snorri Sturluson reports that Haraldr Harðráði was himself overcome by such a fury at Stamford Bridge:

> And when King Haraldr Sigurðarson saw that [the charge of the English onto the Norwegian shield wall], he charged forward into the battle, where there was the most fighting [literally weapons' birth]. There was there the hardest fighting, and many men (*lið*) were killed on both sides. Then King Haraldr Sigurðarson became so enraged that he leapt in front of all of his troops, swinging his sword with both hands. Neither helmet nor armor could stop his blows.[53]

With this attack Haraldr nearly routed the English, but during it he was struck in the throat with an arrow and died.

Most Scandinavian soldiers fought as infantry. Horses, if they could be acquired from plundered sites, as there is no evidence for naval transportation of horses, would be used for military means, but almost exclusively for transportation or reconnaissance and not as combat facilitators.[54]

---

[51] Poertner, p. 151.

[52] *Brennu-Njáls Saga*, ed. E.Ó. Sveinsson (Rekjavik, 1954), pp. 267–69. The quote is on pp. 267–68: 'En ef berserkrinn hræðisk þann, er ek vígða, en vaði yðvarn eld, þá skuluð þér taka við trú.'

[53] Snorri Sturluson, *Heimskringla*, III:189:
En er Haraldr konungr Sigurðarson sá þat, gekk hann fram í orrostu, þar er mestr var vápnaburðrinn. Var þar þá in harðasta orrosta, ok fell mikit lið af hvárumtveggjum. Þá varð Haraldr konungr Sigurðarson svá óðr, at hann hljóp fram allt ór fylkingunni ok hjó báðum höndum. Helt þá hvárti við honum hjálmr né brynja.
See also *Fagrskinna*, p. 140; *Morkinskinna*, p. 118; and *Flateyjarbók*, III:395.

[54] Rosedahl, *Vikings*, p. 144; Griffith, pp. 180–81; R.H.C. Davis, *The Medieval Warhorse: Origin, Development and Redevlopment* (London, 1989), pp. 71–73; and Ann Hyland, *The*

The berserker charge was an offensive tactic, whether planned or not, and on occasions it may have won the battle, although at Stamford Bridge, once Haraldr Harðráði was slain, it failed. Other tactics included beginning a battle with a shower of arrows, firing as many in the air as possible, then following this with a volley of many thrown spears, and, finally, and only if the opposing side still stood ready to receive combat, encountering an opponent in individualized hand-to-hand melees, in other words, generally without the existence of an ordered line formation.[55] All of these tactics, including obviously the berserker charge, were designed by Scandinavians to do one thing: to force their enemies from the battlefield without, if possible, actually fighting the battle and thereby losing any of their own men. As any Scandinavian army had generally arrived on almost any battlefield from the sea, their numbers were usually limited, with few, if any, reinforcements to be expected. Almost always Scandinavian armies were outnumbered by their opposing forces, if not by those directly facing them, then certainly by the potential troops which could be raised nearby. If a battle could be won without sacrificing any of their own soldiers, the Scandinavians preferred to do so; of course, this necessitated a convincing of their opponents not to risk their own lives against the clearly more violent northerners. (If there was a persistent image of Viking bloodthirstiness and cruelty, one can be certain that no Scandinavian soldier would deny it.[56])

However, the occasions when these tactics worked for the Scandinavians were rare; indeed, there were many instances when the Scandinavians were not able to frighten an opposing force away from an engagement. In these battles, Scandinavian armies resorted to one defensive tactic which seems always to have been employed by these forces, the 'shield wall' (*skjaldborg*). At the order of their army's leader, Scandinavian warriors would order a 'fort-like' formation with their shields overlapping and their spears, unsharpened ends anchored firmly in the ground, protruding out from behind them. This formation was designed for defending against almost any charge, by infantry or cavalry, and provided a protection for those inside virtually until their opponents grew fatigued and ceased their attacks. At least that was the ideal scenario, but in some cases those inside the shield wall themselves grew weary of fighting in such a manner, and they would 'break out' from their positions of safety to try

Medieval Warhorse: From Byzantium to the Crusades (London, 1994), pp. 72–76. However, Warren Treadgold (*Byzantium and its Army, 284–1081* (Stanford, 1995), p. 115) claims that the Varangian Guard in the Byzantine army was a cavalry force, seemingly able to make a cavalry charge. Yet, on what evidence this assertion is based is not made clear.

55 See Brønsted, pp. 103–104 and Griffith, pp. 182–96.

56 That such an image existed can be seen in several articles, including: Simon Coupland, 'The Rod of God's Wrath or the People of God's Wrath? The Carolingian Theology of the Viking Invasions,' *Journal of Ecclesiastical History* 42 (1991), 535–54; Sarah Foot, 'Violence against Christians? The Vikings and the Church in Ninth-Century England,' *Medieval History* 1.3 (1991), 3–16; Roberta Frank, 'Viking Atrocity and Skaldic Verse: The Rite of the Blood-Eagle,' *English Historical Review* 99 (1984), 332–43; and Neils Lund, 'Allies of God or Man? The Viking Expansion in a Human Perspective,' *Viator* 20 (1989), 45–59.

and defeat the opposing force with their own charges. In these instances, such as what is described by the Norwegian Kings' Sagas to have happened at Stamford Bridge, the forces breaking out from the shield wall, almost always in a disorganized and weak manner, were easily and soundly defeated.[57]

Finally, a few words should be said about the ships which were used by the Norwegians in their 1066 attack of England, for although these were not directly encountered by the Anglo-Saxons, they did deliver the Norwegians to the island, and some, although only a small portion of the original number, even returned to Norway with survivors of the ill-fated conquest. There is, however, a caution which should be mentioned in dealing with the ships of Haraldr Harðráði. There is no way in which historians can be certain what the exact characteristics of these ships were. For one thing, although there have now been several ships successfully excavated throughout Scandinavia, primarily those at Skuldev, Osberg, and Gokstad, none of these vessels date as late as 1066 and none seem specifically built to transport men. Also, although it is known that King Óláfr Tryggvason of Norway built several large longships, known collectively as *drekkars* or dragon ships, which he used in 1000 at the battle of Svolder against the kings of Sweden and Denmark and the rebellious Norwegian earl, Eiríkr, and that Haraldr Harðráði had a similar ship, although perhaps only one of them, at the battle of Niså, it is not known if Haraldr also used this or any other of these large vessels in his conquest of England. Nor do the Norwegian Kings' Sagas help here, for they record no characteristics of Haraldr's 1066 fleet. Still, from saga descriptions of other ships together with excavations of earlier ships, an illustration of the vessels which transported Haraldr and his men to England might be attempted.

Scandinavian ships were not always capable of raiding the coasts of other European lands. In the early Middle Ages, these vessels had little potential for open sea sailing and were probably not unlike boats constructed elsewhere in Europe. They had a relatively shallow hull, built in a clinker style (in a manner similar to the shipbuilding techniques of the ancients), with strong ribs placed inside for added support. Loose planks were laid between these ribs to serve as a deck. They also contained no strong keel, and thus were unable to carry a mast, leaving all ships with the oar as their sole means of power. This changed in the early eighth century, when ships with stronger keels began to be built. These keels allowed deeper, flatter, and longer hulls to be constructed. They also allowed the placement of a heavy mast, perhaps as long as twelve meters. The new hull strength, depth and length made it possible for the Scandinavian ocean travel which began later in the century and continued until 1066.

Many ships took part in the Viking raids. Excavated exemplars have shown that there was no standardized design for these vessels. They varied in size and, seemingly, in purpose. Some were quite large in length and width – the Gokstad ship measures 23 meters in length and 5.2 meters in width, while the Skuldelev

---

57 Griffith, pp. 142–44, 188–91.

longship measures 28 meters long (its width cannot be estimated because of the bad state of preservation) – but shallow in depth which may indicate that they were built as warships. Others were considerably smaller in length and width, but larger in depth, perhaps denoting vessels used chiefly for transporting cargo. All Viking ships, however, may have participated in the very profitable raids, as they were only needed for transporting men to and from their raiding destination and not for naval combat. The same thing might be said also about Haraldr's 1066 fleet; without evidence to the contrary, it is unlikely that all of Haraldr's ships were 'warships.'

The Viking ship could be rowed, with most large vessels being equipped with fifteen or more oarlocks cut into both sides of the hull. (This would accommodate as many as 50–60 sailors.) However it was also equipped with a large square sail. The sail did not add to the maneuverability of the ship, but did add considerable speed. The Viking ship was steered by a single rudder attached to one side near the stern.[58]

While the Scandinavians had for many centuries proved their military skill by waging warfare continually throughout Europe, with England being perhaps their most favorite target, in 1066 at the battle of Stamford Bridge, they 'met their match.' There the Norwegians confronted and were defeated by another well-developed, well-armed, and perhaps even better led and trained army of English soldiers.

---

[58] See Brønsted, pp. 139–47; Foote and Wilson, pp. 232–56; Rosedahl, *Vikings*, pp. 83–93; Sawyer, *Age of Vikings*, pp. 79–82; Griffith, pp. 89–98; DeVries, *Medieval Military Technology*, pp. 289–92; Gwyn Jones, *A History of the Vikings* (London, 1968), pp. 182–90; A.W. Brögger and Haakon Shetelig, *The Viking Ships: Their Ancestry and Evolution* (Oslo, 1951); Ian Atkinson, *The Viking Ships* (Cambridge, 1979); Ole Crumlin-Pedersen, 'Viking Shipbuilding and Seamanship,' in *Proceedings of the Eighth Viking Congress*, ed. H. Bekker-Nielsen (Odense, 1981), pp. 271–86; Ole Crumlin-Pedersen, 'Large and Small Warships,' in *Military Aspects of Scandinavian Society in a European Perspective, AD. 1–1300* (Copenhagen, 1997), pp. 184–94; Alan Binns, 'Ships and Shipbuilding,' in *Medieval Scandinavia: An Encyclopedia*, ed. P. Pulsiano (New York, 1993), pp. 578–80; Alan Binns, 'The Ships of the Vikings, were they "Viking Ships"?' in *Proceedings of the Eighth Viking Congress*, ed. H. Bekker-Nielsen (Odense, 1981), pp. 287–94; Arne Emil Christensen, 'Viking Age Ships and Shipbuilding,' *Norwegian Archaeology Review* 15 (1982), 19–28; John R. Hale, 'The Viking Longship,' *Scientific American* 278 (February 1998), 56–63; Richard W. Unger, *The Ship in Medieval Economy, 600–1600* (Montreal, 1980), pp. 75–96; Archibald R. Lewis and Timothy J. Runyan, *European Naval and Maritime History, 300–1500* (Bloomington, 1985), pp. 92–99; and William Ledyard Rodgers, *Naval Warfare Under Oars, 4th to 16th Centuries* (Annapolis, 1940), pp. 69–87. For an analysis of Scandinavian ships closer to the time of Haraldr Harðráði, see N.A.M. Rodger, 'Cnut's Geld and the Size of Danish Ships,' *English Historical Review* 110 (1995), 392–403.

CHAPTER EIGHT

THE ENGLISH MILITARY

ACCORDING TO Henry of Huntingdon, William the Conqueror, in attempting to instill bravery in his men against their Anglo-Saxon foes, described his opponents as a 'people devoid of military knowledge.'[1] Many modern historians believe that William was correct in this description. How could an army defending its own land fail to gain victory against only a few thousand invaders? However, it was definitely not ignorance in the art of war which caused the defeat of the Anglo-Saxon army at Hastings. It was in fact one of the best armed and most highly organized military forces of the Middle Ages, a force which had been strong enough to defeat and almost completely annihilate a highly respected Norwegian force just three weeks before the Normans encountered them.

Unlike the Norwegian army, which is easier to characterize based on the weapons of its soldiers, the Anglo-Saxon armies which faced them at the battles of Fulford Gate and Stamford Bridge are easier to depict through their organization.

Until the last twenty years, most historians, following the lead of J.H. Round, Sir Charles Oman, L.M. Larson, Sir Frank M. Stenton, Michael Powicke, and C. Warren Hollister, divided the late Anglo-Saxon army into three units.[2] The first and most formidable of these was the *huscarls*. Similar to their Norwegian cousins, these were well armed and superiorly trained professional soldiers who had been brought initially from Denmark by Knútr when he ascended the throne of England in 1016. However, unlike their Norwegian counterparts, these

---

[1] Henry of Huntingdon, *Historia Anglorum: The History of the English People*, ed. and trans. D. Greenway (Oxford, 1996). pp. 392–93: 'gentem arte belli cassam.'

[2] J.H. Round, *Feudal England* (London, 1895), pp. 36–69, 116–25, 552–71; L.M. Larson, *The King's Household in England before the Norman Conquest* (Madison, 1904), pp. 97–103, 151–72; Charles Oman, *The Art of War in the Middle Ages* (London, 1924), I:67–72, 114–15; Frank M. Stenton, *The First Century of English Feudalism* (Oxford, 1932), pp. 68–69, 116–52; Frank M. Stenton, *Anglo-Saxon England*, 3rd edn (London, 1971), pp. 290–91, 582–83; Michael Powicke, *Military Obligation in Medieval England: A Study in Liberty and Duty* (Oxford, 1962), pp. 1–25; C. Warren Hollister, *Anglo-Saxon Military Institutions on the Eve of the Norman Conquest* (Oxford, 1962); C. Warren Hollister, 'The Five-Hide Unit and the Old English Military Obligation,' *Speculum* 36 (1961), 61–74; and C. Warren Hollister, 'Military Obligation in Late-Saxon and Norman England,' in *Ordinamenti militari in occidente nell'alto medioevo* (Spoleto, 1968), I:169–86.

huscarls seemed to have remained soldiers paid for their service not from land grants, but from the treasuries of their respective English employers, most notably the king. In the beginning royal huscarls were paid for by a tax levied on all of the English people; however, in the reign of Edward the Confessor this tax was removed, and the huscarls began to be paid for directly out of the royal coffers. Huscarls also served as the bodyguards for the king and his earls.[3]

By 1066, not all of the huscarls were necessarily Danish. Many English warriors desired to seek the professional status and salary of these mercenaries, and thus they also joined the ranks of huscarls. Undoubtedly, they were also trained and armed well. These new huscarls were called the *lið*. So many *lið* existed in 1066 that when Harold Godwinson marched north to Stamford Bridge, the *Anglo-Saxon Chronicle* (C) recorded that his troops were *lið* rather than huscarls.[4] However, from other sources it is known that huscarls did participate there, and at Hastings. Still, there is no way of determining from any of the contemporary or near contemporary sources how many huscarls actually participated at Stamford Bridge. There may have been as many as three thousand of these warriors there.[5]

It is likely that there was no force in Europe equal to the Anglo-Saxon huscarls. They were so well trained that they were able to use both the two-handed battle axe and the sword with equal dexterity.[6] Even the Norwegians had praise for this skilled Anglo-Saxon military unit. Snorri Sturluson writes:

> They were called the king's huscarls. They were men who were so valiant that one was a better soldier than two of the best of Harald's men.[7]

The second unit of the late Anglo-Saxon army was called the *fyrd*. The fyrd was filled by the general levied militia. In times of emergency, the king had the right to call out all able-bodied freemen. However, usually, including at most times of conflict, only a select few would be levied, and they would become the fyrd. Under these circumstances, the law of the levy called up one man for every

---

3   See Larson, pp. 152–71; Oman, I:114–15; Powicke, pp. 3–6; and Hollister, *Anglo-Saxon Military Institutions*, pp. 12–18. There are several different spellings of huscarls; I have used that which appears most frequently in the *Anglo-Saxon Chronicle*.
4   *Anglo-Saxon Chronicle*, in *Two of the Saxon Chronicles Parallel*, ed. Charles Plummer and John Earle (Oxford, 1892), (C) 1066, I:197.
5   This is the number estimated by Magnus Magnusson and Hermann Pálsson in their translation of Snorri Sturluson's *King Harald's Saga* (Harmondsworth, 1966), pp. 138 n. 1 and 149 n. 1.
6   The *Bayeux Tapestry* shows huscarls using both of these weapons at Hastings.
7   Snorri Sturluson, *Heimskringla*, ed. B. Aðalbjarnarson (Reykjavik, 1941–51), III:174–75: er kallat er þingamannalið. Þeir váru menn svá frœknir, at betra var lið eins þeira en tveggja Haralds manna inna beztu.
I have used the Magnusson and Pálsson translation of 'þingamannalið' as 'king's huscarls', as it is clearly this unit which the Icelandic historian was characterizing. See also *Morkinskinna: Pergamentsbog fra første halvdel af det trettende aarhundrede*, ed. C.R. Unger (Christiania (Oslo), 1867), p. 111 and *Flateyjarbók: En samling af Norske Konge-Sagaer*, ed. G. Vigfusson and C.R. Unger (Christiania (Oslo), 1860–68), III:388.

five 'hides' of land, and usually the same ones were summoned each time.[8] In this way they became used to war and trained by experience; there may also have been other training provided. According to C. Warren Hollister, this group should be known as the *select fyrd*, and their levy as the *trimoda necessitas*, but it should be noted that they were not professional soldiers and thus differed from the huscarls. They were also farmers and tradesmen, among other occupations, who were only required to spend two months in military service during wartime, even during an invasion, before they were sent home. Outside of wartime, they were only levied to build fortifications and repair bridges.[9]

The *great fyrd* (the combined war-experienced select fyrd and those newly called up 'rookies') was organized according to shires, and sometimes the earls would levy their own fyrd to defend their boundaries, in some instances against another earl's fyrd, although on most occasions against invading 'foreign' forces. In this way, a 'nascent feudalism' was practiced. On the other hand, there were many occasions when the fyrd accepted new members into its body; peasants rising to the ownership of five hides of land acquired the rights and title of a *thegn*, and thereby they were obligated to serve in the fyrd. This seems to have occurred several times in the late Anglo-Saxon period.[10]

Both the select and great fyrd's arms and armor were not nearly as elaborate nor as sophisticated as the huscarls'. In general they fought only with their hunting weapons, and the *Bayeux Tapestry* shows the fyrd fighting at Hastings using primarily spears. Body armor was almost entirely non-existent, although some fyrd seem to have had access to shields and helmets.

In the last twenty years, the work of Richard Abels and Nicholas Hooper has sought to correct some of what they perceived were errors among the earlier studies of late Anglo-Saxon military obligation.[11] Through more intricate and

[8] Oman, 1:67–68; Powicke, pp. 6–16; Hollister, *Anglo-Saxon Military Institutions*, pp. 25–58; Hollister, 'The Five-Hide Unit,' pp. 61–74; and Hollister, 'Military Obligation in Late-Saxon and Norman England,' pp. 174–81.

[9] See especially Hollister, *Anglo-Saxon Military Institutions*, pp. 38–102; Hollister, 'The Five-Hide Unit,' pp. 66–70; and Hollister, 'Military Obligation in Late-Saxon and Norman England,' pp. 174–78. Hollister even admits that 'the term "select fyrd" is my own invention' ('Military Obligation in Late-Saxon and Norman England,' p. 175). Most of the other historians who discuss the fyrd before 1968 do not differentiate between the two fyrds as Hollister does, although they do discuss the *trimoda necessitas* and note the possibility of different forms of obligatory recruitment. See, for example, Powicke, pp. 19–24.

[10] On the *great fyrd*, again Hollister's term, see Hollister, *Anglo-Saxon Military Institutions*, pp. 25–37; Hollister, 'The Five-Hide Unit,' pp. 66–68; and Hollister, 'Military Obligation in Late-Saxon and Norman England,' pp. 174–78.

[11] Richard Abels, 'Bookland and Fyrd Service in Late Saxon England,' *Anglo-Norman Studies* 7 (1984), 1–25; Richard Abels, *Lordship and Military Obligation in Anglo-Saxon England* (Berkeley and Los Angeles, 1988); Richard Abels, 'English Tactics, Strategy and Military Organizations in the Late Tenth Century,' in *The Battle of Maldon, AD 991*, ed. D. Scragg (London, 1991), pp. 143–55; Nicholas Hooper, 'Anglo-Saxon Warfare on the Eve of the Conquest: A Brief Survey,' *Proceedings of the Battle Conference on Anglo-Norman Studies* 1 (1978), 84–93; Nicholas Hooper, 'The Anglo-Saxons at War,' in *Weapons and Warfare in Anglo-Saxon England*, ed. S.C. Hawkes (Oxford, 1989), pp. 191–202; Nicholas

complete studies of the *Domesday Book* and other eleventh-century diplomatic evidence, they have made significant changes to our understanding of how the English armies at the battles of Fulford Gate and Stamford Bridge would have been organized.

On the force introduced by Knútr and known as huscarls, it can now be seen that within the fifty-year period between their introduction to England and the Norwegian invasion, they had become less like mercenaries paid for serving as a standing military force and more like their Norwegian cousins, 'household troops', landowners obligated to defend their *own* homelands only during times of invasion or insurrection. During peacetime, those who did not own land may also have served as bodyguards for other lords or in other 'bureaucratic' occupations, such as tax-collectors. They also received wages even as late as 1066 from the *heregeld* or Danegeld introduced by Knútr in 1016.[12] Still professional in their military training and standing, the huscarls also formed a 'law-bound guild' which served as a parliament, or perhaps even as the controlling factors in the witenagemot.[13] Knútr and Godwin saw themselves as members of this body, with Swegen Godwinson and his cousin whom he would murder, Beorn, also members.[14] They also played a role in numerous important events leading up to the Norwegian Invasion, including the protection of Knútr's widow, Emma, at the time of Harold I's usurpation of the English throne, the punishment of Worcester citizens in their rebellion against Harðaknútr, both the exile of Godwin and his family in 1051 and their return in 1052, and the Northumbrian revolt in 1065 against Tostig Godwinson.[15] (In the rebellions of Worcester and Northumbria, huscarls also became targets for the rebels in their dissatisfaction with governing authorities.) However, their primary task was to fight as soldiers, and they undoubtedly served with Harold and Tostig Godwinson in Wales, with Edwin and Morkere at the battle of Fulford Gate, and with Harold at the battles of Stamford Bridge and Hastings.

Abandoning the two fyrd thesis, Abels and Hooper tied this military organization to the ownership of land, land called *bocland* or bookland. According to Abels, 'by the reign of Cnut bookland was conceived as land for which one per-

Hooper, 'The Housecarls in England in the Eleventh Century,' *Anglo-Norman Studies* 7 (1984), 161–76; and Nicholas Hooper, 'Military Developments in the Reign of Cnut,' in *The Reign of Cnut*, ed. A.R. Rumble (London, 1994), pp. 89–100.
[12] Abels, *Lordship and Military Obligation*, pp. 160–70; Hooper, 'Military Developments in the Reign of Cnut,' 89–100; Hooper, 'Housecarls in England,' pp. 161–76; and Hooper, 'Anglo-Saxon Warfare,' pp. 85–87. See also Jim Bradbury, *The Battle of Hastings* (Thrupp, 1998), pp. 76–77.
[13] On the huscarls as the controllers of the witenagemot, see n. 17 in the chapter 'Godwin and his Family' above. Hooper ('Housecarls in England,' pp. 169–70) is not convinced of this.
[14] Hooper, 'Housecarls in England,' pp. 162–63.
[15] On the episode with Emma see n. 26 in the chapter 'Godwin and His Family' above; on the Worcester rebellion see n. 46 also in 'Godwin and His Family'; on the exile and return of Godwin and his family see nn. 70–71, 96, and 106; and on the Northumbrian rebellion see n. 48 in the chapter 'The Conflict Between Harold and Tostig Godwinson' above.

formed *fyrdfæreld.'* *Fyrdfæreld* in turn was the obligation to provide military service, to defend the 'bookland,' 'in person on the king's campaigns.' This was service owed to the lord; if a member of the fyrd deserted his lord while in military service, he stood to lose his life and his property. In national conflicts, various lords assigned their fyrd to the king or his royal agent. The muster of the late Anglo-Saxon fyrd, so imitative of traditional early medieval continental military obligation, filled out the ranks of soldiers serving at Fulford Gate, Stamford Bridge, and, later, Hastings.[16]

A final unit in the late Anglo-Saxon military, the definition of which is less disputed by modern historians, was the *butsecarls*. These appear to have been sailors who were equally adept for land and naval fighting, and they may have been paid as mercenaries for their services,[17] but, with the exception of a small group of these who joined Tostig on the southern coast of England in August 1066, some of whom stayed with him until the battle of Stamford Bridge, there is no evidence of their presence at that battle.

Judging from the chronicles which report the military activities of 1066, there seems to have been no set method of calling pre-Conquest English soldiers, whether huscarls or fyrd, to service. Some seem to have appeared when called by King Harold Godwinson, namely those who were mustered along the southern coast of England at the beginning of the summer of 1066 to meet the threat of Tostig Godwinson's raids between the Isle of Wight and Sandwich. Others responded to a call to arms from their earls, such as those who were mustered by Edwin and Morkere to defend first Lindsey, again in response to Tostig, and then York, this time in response to Tostig, Haraldr Harðráði, and the entire Norwegian army. Was there a further diffused military organization, with certain troops obligated to more local nobles, known as *thegns*? Some scholars have said yes, based on the confusing legal term, *heriot*, which is found on occasions in Anglo-Saxon legal documents, although more frequently before Knútr's 1016 conquest than after. The *heriot*, they claim, was a military obligation of a thegn to his king, although sometimes also to his earl. It generally indicated how many soldiers a thegn was required to supply his lord, although those references to the *heriots* of the upper nobility during and after the reign of Knútr indicate a payment not of soldiers but of arms.[18] Other historians have disputed this theory, claiming that there simply are not enough examples of *heriots* in Anglo-Saxon

---

[16] The quotes come from Abels, 'Bookland and Fyrd Service,' p. 2. See also pp. 1–25; Abels, *Lordship and Military Obligation*, pp. 97–132; Abels, 'English Tactics, Strategy and Military Organization,' pp. 145–47; Hooper, 'Anglo-Saxon Warfare,' pp. 87–89; and Bradbury, *Battle of Hastings*, p. 76.

[17] See Hollister, *Anglo-Saxon Military Institutions*, pp. 18, 103–26 and Nicholas Hooper, 'Some Observations of the Navy in Late Anglo-Saxon England,' in *Studies in Medieval History for R. Allen Brown*, ed. C. Harper-Bill *et al.* (Woodbridge, 1989), pp. 203–13. pp. 206–11.

[18] See, for example, Nicholas P. Brooks, 'Arms, Status and Warfare in Late-Saxon England,' in *Ethelred the Unready: Papers from the Millenary Conference*, ed. D. Hill (Oxford, 1978), pp. 81–103.

documents, especially from the eleventh century, to state positively what the term means.[19] For now, it is safest to say that there is no way to know for certain from the sources which remain how Anglo-Saxon huscarls and fyrd received their call to arms.

Also to be expected from the close ties between the two medieval areas, the weapons used by the Anglo-Saxon armies were similar to those used by their Norwegian enemies. In pre-conquest England, it was a privilege to own great weapons, and the wealthiest and most important of nobles were distinguished by their arms and those of their retainers. For example, Earl Siward of Northumbria was said by Henry of Huntingdon to have requested that he go into battle equipped with these superior but costly weapons:

> At least clothe me in my impenetrable breastplate, gird me with my sword, place my helmet on my head, my shield in my left hand, my gilded battle-axe in my right, that I, the bravest of soldiers, may die like a soldier.[20]

Similar costly armaments – mail armor, helmets, shields, swords, axes, and spears – accompanied the soldiers manning the 'skillfully made galley' given to Harðaknútr by Godwin in 1040 to appease the king whom Godwin had earlier opposed and whose half-brother he had killed.[21] Although these are obviously special cases, almost all Anglo-Saxon soldiers owned at least some offensive and defensive arms.[22]

Of all offensive weapons used by the Anglo-Saxons, none was prized as much as the sword. As Hilda R. Ellis Davidson has shown in her study *The Sword in Anglo-Saxon England*, the sword was an integral part of Anglo-Saxon military society. Relying on both literary and archaeological sources, she has determined that while the axe, spear and bow were important weapons to the pre-conquest English, 'they had none of the richness of association possessed by the sword.'[23]

---

[19] Neither Richard Abels or Nicholas Hooper accept this definition of the *heriot*. See Abels, *Lordship and Military Obligation* and Hooper, 'Anglo-Saxons at War,' pp. 191–202 and Hooper, 'Anglo-Saxon Warfare,' pp. 84–93.

[20] Henry of Huntingdon, pp. 378–81:
Induite me saltem lorica mea impenetrabili, precingite gladio. Sullimate galea. Scutum in leua. Securim auratam michi ponite in dextra, ut militum fortissimus modo militis moriar.

[21] See n. 42 in the chapter 'Godwin and his Family' above.

[22] That arms and armor were important to the social and political status of late Anglo-Saxon warriors can be seen in N. Brooks, 'Arms, Status and Warfare,' pp. 81–103; Nicholas P. Brooks, 'Weapons and Armour,' in *The Battle of Maldon, AD 991*, ed. D. Scragg (London, 1991), pp. 208–19; and Matthew Strickland, 'Military Technology and Conquest: The Anomaly of Anglo-Saxon England,' *Anglo-Norman Studies* 19 (1996), 353–82. That this was descended from earlier traditions can be found in Heinrich Härke, 'Early Saxon Weapon Burials: Frequencies, Distributions and Weapon Combinations,' in *Weapons and Warfare in Anglo-Saxon England*, ed. S.C. Hawkes (Oxford, 1989), pp. 49–61 and Heinrich Härke, ' "Warrior Graves"? The Background of the Anglo-Saxon Weapon Burial Rite,' *Past and Present* 126 (1990), 22–43.

[23] Hilda R. Ellis Davidson, *The Sword in Anglo-Saxon England: Its Archaeology and Litera-*

The sword was the weapon of leadership, an effective military tool as well as a ceremonial object. Often it would be given to a boy as a gift at birth or at his naming. The child would grow up playing with it and with other, lighter swords, until it became a weapon he could wield with strength and agility. At other times, the sword would not be presented to the boy until he had reached manhood. As such it stood as a symbol of the end of childhood and the birth of the warrior. Generally in these cases the sword would not be new, but would be a family treasure which had been passed down from one warrior to the next, a token of past wars fought and past victories won. (This need not have been a complete weapon, but could also be the shattered fragments of an ancestor's sword, although in this case the gift was obviously more symbolic than practical.) The Anglo-Saxon sword could also be won by prowess shown in military affairs: for example, Beowulf received a magnificent sword from the Danish leader, Hrothgar, to reward his defeat of Grendel and Grendel's mother. Finally, a sword might also be given to an Anglo-Saxon warrior by a lord whose army he had joined.

Once obtained, the sword became the warrior's constant companion. He carried it into the king's hall or at councils, although it could never be drawn at those venues. He used it when swearing an oath, and it was the weapon employed for a duel. Of course, it was used in battle. At night it hung above the warrior's bed, and at his death the sword would either be buried with him, or it would be passed on to his son or close relative.[24]

The Anglo-Saxon sword was a carefully and intricately made weapon. Forged of pattern-welded steel of the finest ore, its fabrication often took an extremely long time and was so cherished by its maker that he inscribed it with his name. First the smith, or an iron-worker, produced a strong bar of steel. This was accomplished in a number of ways, the difference seeming not to be the desired strength of the weapon but the personal preference of the maker: a bar of pattern-welded steel could be made by twisting a single strip of iron, by twisting a strip with filler rods, by twisting together three equal strips of iron, by twisting one main strip with two filler strips, by forging a twisted rod to close spiral grooves and then adding cutting edges, or by twisting a small central strip with larger filler strips. After this, the steel bar was heated until red hot, then reduced in thickness by hammering. At the same time, the edges and a fuller (a groove down the center of the blade which decreased its weight but not its strength)

ture (Oxford, 1962). The quote is found on p. 211. This work has since been supplemented by David M. Wilson, 'Some Neglected Late Anglo-Saxon Swords,' *Medieval Archaeology* 9 (1965), 32–54, which provides a catalogue of some Anglo-Saxon swords. Artistic and extant examples are found in David C. Nicolle, *Arms and Armour of the Crusading Era, 1050–1350* (White Plains, 1988), nos. 865–71, 875, 877–79, 1592. See also Kelly DeVries, *Medieval Military Technology* (Peterborough, 1992), pp. 21–23.

24 In addition to Davidson, *The Sword in Anglo-Saxon England*, on the sword in relation to the status of the Anglo-Saxon warrior see N. Brooks, 'Arms, Status and Warfare,' pp. 82–87, and on swords found in Anglo-Saxon gravesites see Härke, ' "Warrior Graves"? The Background of the Anglo-Saxon Burial Rite.'

were also shaped. The heating and hammering were repeated a number of times until the desired thickness was achieved. Once the fabrication was completed, the sword would be ground, first by a rough grinding stone and then by finer stones and files, until a fine sharpness had been achieved. The crossguard, grip and handle were added, and the sword polished. Modern attempts at replicating the Anglo-Saxon sword have also shown that it is extremely difficult to reproduce the high quality of this early workmanship, perhaps because the care taken in constructing the weapon is not understood by modern craftsmen.[25]

The Vikings had introduced the long sword to England, and this, with very few changes, was the type of sword used by the English in 1066.[26] It was designed to be a slashing rather than a stabbing weapon and was sharp on both edges. The blade was about two-and-a-half feet long.[27] Finally, as witnessed on the Bayeux Tapestry, both Harold Godwinson and many of his huscarls were outfitted with a long sword, probably at Stamford Bridge as well as at Hastings.[28]

Another prized instrument of war for the Anglo-Saxon soldier was the 'Danish' battle-axe. The Anglo-Saxons probably used this weapon more than either the Danes, for whom it was named, or the Norwegians. The Anglo-Saxon axe differed little from the Scandinavian *breiðǫx* or broad axe, and therein lies its probable provenance, although when used by the trained huscarls among the English armies, its effectiveness was undoubtedly increased by the training and organization that this unit required.[29] In the Bayeux Tapestry, both English

[25] On the technology and manufacture of early English swords see Davidson, *The Sword in Anglo-Saxon England*, in particular Appendix I, pp. 217–24; Robert Engstrom, Scott Michael Lankton, and Audrey Lesher-Engstrom, *A Modern Replication Based on the Pattern-Welded Sword of Sutton Hoo*, 2nd edn (Kalamazoo, 1990); Peter Bone, 'The Development of Anglo-Saxon Swords from the Fifth to the Eleventh Century,' in *Weapons and Warfare in Anglo-Saxon England*, ed. S.C. Hawkes (Oxford, 1989), pp. 63–70; Steven Walton, 'Words of Technological Virtue: *The Battle of Brunanburh* and Anglo-Saxon Sword Manufacture.' *Technology and Culture* 36 (1995), 987–999; J.-F. Fino, 'Notes sur la production du fer et la fabrication des armes en France au moyen-age,' *Gladius* 3 (1964), 47–66; Ian Peirce, 'The Knight, His Arms and Armour in the Eleventh and Twelfth Centuries,' in *The Ideals and Practice of Medieval Knighthood*, ed. C. Harper-Bill and R. Harvey (Woodbridge, 1986), pp. 152–64; and Alan R. Williams, 'Methods of Manufacture of Swords in Medieval Europe: Illustrated by the Metallography of Some Examples,' *Gladius* 13 (1977), 75–101.
[26] See Bradbury, *Battle of Hastings*, pp. 87–88; N. Brooks, 'Weapons and Armour,' pp. 212–14; James Mann, 'Arms and Armour,' in *Medieval England*, ed. A.L. Poole (Oxford, 1958), p. 315; and James Mann, 'Arms and Armour,' in *The Bayeux Tapestry: A Comprehensive Survey*, ed. by Frank M. Stenton, 2nd edn (London, 1957), pp. 65–66.
[27] An example of such a sword dating from the same period was found in September 1948 in Westminster. See G.C. Dunning, 'The Palace of Westminster Sword,' *Archaeologia* 98 (1961), 123–58.
[28] See Nicolle, no. 870.
[29] DeVries, *Medieval Military Technology*, p. 17; Mann, in *The Bayeux Tapestry*, p. 66; Bradbury, *Battle of Hastings*, pp. 90–93; and Härke, ' "Warrior Graves"? The Background of the Anglo-Saxon Weapon Burial Rite,' p. 34. Artistic and extant exemplars can be seen in Nicolle, nos. 870, 876. For a discussion of Scandinavian axes see the chapter 'The Norwegian Military', nn. 4–7 above.

huscarls and fyrd are shown using the battle-axe. However, if this was the case, and as the weapon was relatively unknown to the Normans so that the credibility of its depiction may be doubtful, the axe of the fyrd may have been but a tool used primarily for domestic purposes rather than for battle.[30] There is also some evidence that Anglo-Saxons possessed throwing axes of smaller size, although their use does not appear to be prevalent in the eleventh century.[31]

While not prized as highly as the sword or axe, the most common English weapon was the spear. There is no doubt that the spear was important, but it seems that there was in fact no consistency in these weapons among the Anglo-Saxons. M.J. Swanton's impressive study, *The Spearheads of the Anglo-Saxon Settlements*, reveals that twelve different types of spearheads have been found found in Anglo-Saxon archaeological excavations. These he has further grouped into four main categories: derivative forms of Germanic spear-types prior to the Anglo-Saxon settlement in England, leaf-shaped blades, angular blades, and corrugated blades. While certain chronological and regional differences can account for some of the variations in spearhead styles, on the whole the conclusion must be that the Anglo-Saxons saw no need for consistency. Each smith probably created his own style of spearhead without apparent official guidelines or influences.[32] From illustrations it can be determined that these spearheads were usually fitted onto the tops of seven-foot ash shafts.

The Anglo-Saxon spear was used for hunting, and in battle it could be both thrown and used as a thrusting weapon. More importantly, for this study, was the fact that when the fyrd was levied, their main weapon was the spear. As such, in 1066 the spear was quite useful, with the Bayeux Tapestry showing that Harold's bodyguards fought with spears.[33]

Finally, bows must have been used by some Anglo-Saxon soldiers. This is a disputed point, but both the Bayeux Tapestry and the Norwegian Kings' Sagas record the existence of archers in the English army. Indeed, the Norwegian Kings' Sagas even claim that King Haraldr Harðráði was killed by an English arrow at Stamford Bridge.[34] However, this artistic and literary evidence clashes with the fact that few arrowheads have been found in Anglo-Saxon grave sites –

---

[30] See Nicolle, no. 870. This might change should the Bayeux Tapestry prove to have been made by English weavers, as some scholars, primarily English historians and art historians, claim.

[31] R.I. Page, *Life in Anglo-Saxon England* (New York, 1970), p. 104.

[32] M.J. Swanton, *The Spearheads of the Anglo-Saxon Settlements* (London, 1974). Although most of Swanton's examples date from before the eleventh century, there is no indication from finds dated to the eleventh century that the design or technology of spearheads had changed. For those see Nicolle, nos. 854–64. See also DeVries, *Medieval Military Technology*, p. 10.

[33] Mann, in *The Bayeux Tapestry*, p. 66; Bradbury, *Battle of Hastings*, p. 88; and N. Brooks, 'Weapons and Armour,' pp. 210–12.

[34] References to Anglo-Saxon archery use and Haraldr's death in the Norwegian Kings' Sagas can be found in *Fagrskinna: Kortfattet Norsk Konge-Saga*, ed. P.A. Munch and C.R. Unger (Christiania (Oslo), 1847), p. 140; *Morkinskinna*, p. 119; Snorri Sturluson, *Heimskringla*, III:190; and *Flateyjarbók*, III:396. See also the later addition to *Anglo-Saxon Chronicle* c (1066), I:198 and Bradbury, *Battle of Hastings*, p. 102. For the *Bayeux Tapestry*, see Jim

only 1.1% of Anglo-Saxon warriors' graves contain arrowheads – despite the prevalence of other weapons.[35] Additionally, the author of an Anglo-Saxon riddle on the bow needed to give an internal clue for its solution, which may confirm this weapon's lack of popularity among those people. (The first word of the riddle, when read backwards, gives an earlier form of the Old English word for bow, *boga*.)[36] If used in battle, the bow may have been confined to the members of the fyrd who used it for hunting purposes as well; it was undoubtedly not used in large numbers.[37]

The only widespread defensive armament used by English soldiers in the late eleventh century was the shield. All warriors, regardless of station or rank, carried shields. The best portrayal of these shields can be found in the Bayeux Tapestry, where both the huscarls and fyrd can be seen carrying shields, with the only difference between the two being the brightly painted and ornamented shields carried by the professional huscarls in contrast to the plainer ones carried by the non-professional fyrd. According to R.I. Page, the Anglo-Saxon shield was 'of limewood, sometimes of laminated construction, usually covered with leather and having a metal central boss which masked the handgrip.'[38] Of this construction and decoration there is little doubt, although it must be determined from art and literature as there are no extant exemplars. However, there is some question as to the style of shield carried by most English soldiers fighting against the Norwegians in 1066. Were these shields round or kite-shaped? The Bayeux Tapestry shows English soldiers with both the rounded shield similar to those preferred by the Scandinavian warriors as well as the kite-shaped shield preferred by the Normans, although there is certainly more of the latter variety found among the Anglo-Saxons depicted in the Tapestry.[39] It is probably safe to assume that both shields, in fact any shields that could be found, were used by the English in 1066, or perhaps the answer is even more simple than that, such as is found in Richard Glover's statement that

Bradbury, *The Medieval Archer* (New York, 1985), pp. 19–22, 34. It should be noted that in the *Bayeux Tapestry*, however, twenty-eight of the twenty-nine archers are Norman.

[35] Härke, ' "Warrior Graves?" The Background of the Anglo-Saxon Weapon Burial Rite,' p. 34.

[36] *The Exeter Book Riddles*, ed. K. Crossley-Holland (Harmondsworth, 1979), no. 23.

[37] The most complete study of the Anglo-Saxon use of the bow is John Manley, 'The Archer and the Army in the Late Saxon Period,' *Anglo-Saxon Studies in Archaeology and History* 4 (1985), 223–35. See also DeVries, *Medieval Military Technology*, pp. 34–35; Strickland, 'Military Technology and Conquest,' pp. 355–59; Mann, in *The Bayeux Tapestry*, pp. 67–68; Bradbury, *Battle of Hastings*, p. 92; and N. Brooks, 'Weapons and Armour,' pp. 208–209.

[38] Page, *Life in Anglo-Saxon England*, p. 104. These seem not to have changed in materials or construction from earlier shields studied by Tania Dickinson, F.S.A. Härke, and Heinrich Härke, *Early Anglo-Saxon Shields* (London, 1992). See especially the chapter on 'Shield Technology' written by Heinrich Härke (pp. 31–54). See also DeVries, *Medieval Military Technology*, p. 57 and N. Brooks, 'Weapons and Armour,' pp. 214–15.

[39] See Mann, in *The Bayeux Tapestry*, pp. 63–65; Bradbury, *Battle of Hastings*, pp. 84–86; and DeVries, *Medieval Military Technology*, pp. 63–64. For the *Bayeux Tapestry* and other artistic examples see Nicolle, nos. 869–71, 874–75, 879, 1592.

none of the light-armed English spearmen shown in the *Bayeux Tapestry* carry any but the pointed shield and it would be very strange if heavy-armed professional troops voluntarily carried obsolete equipment when such equipment as the light-armed was up-to-date. Harold's housecarls, however, had just hurried south after fighting the Norse who still used the round shield and it is entirely probable that those shown with the round shield had re-equipped themselves with enemy arms picked up on the field of Stamford Bridge.[40]

Body armor was less used by Anglo-Saxon soldiers, and that in evidence in the Bayeux Tapestry and other sources seems to have been mail hauberks worn primarily by huscarls. These too were similar to those used by the Scandinavians, and again the provenance may be seen here. As with the Scandinavians, the mail hauberk was generally a coat of chain, descending to the mid-thigh or to the knee and with short sleeves. To the Exeter riddler it was an 'excellent garment'; to Beowulf it was a 'tangled war-net'; and in Aldhelm's riddles it is described as not fearing 'arrows drawn from a long quiver.' To all, it was an armament absolutely essential for the protection of a noble warrior.[41] At the battle of Stamford Bridge there appear to have been large numbers of Anglo-Saxons wearing this armor, as Snorri Sturluson writes that Haraldr Harðráði's force 'saw there a cloud of dust and under it beautiful shields and white coats of mail.'[42]

Finally, helmets were worn by the English, especially by the huscarls. (The Bayeux Tapestry shows none of the fyrd wearing helmets.) Anglo-Saxon helmets were probably similar to those worn by the Norwegians, at least that is what can be determined by three earlier prototypes, excavated at Sutton Hoo, Benty Grange and Coppergate. Also, some ornamentation was frequently included on the Anglo-Saxon helmet: copper eyebrows added above the eyeholes or the figure of a boar on the crown.[43]

Although there is nothing specifically recorded in contemporary historical sources about the training of Anglo-Saxon soldiers, early medieval Irish and

---

[40] Richard Glover, 'English Warfare in 1066,' *English Historical Review* 262 (1952), 4n.

[41] DeVries, *Medieval Military Technology*, pp. 58, 64–66; N. Brooks, 'Arms, Status and Warfare,' pp. 94–96; N. Brooks, 'Weapons and Armour,' pp. 216–18; Mann in *The Bayeux Tapestry*, pp. 60–63; Bradbury, *Battle of Hastings*, pp. 80–82; and *The Exeter Book Riddles*, no. 35. See also the artistic examples in Nicolle, nos. 870–71, 874, 1592.

[42] Snorri Sturluson, *Heimskringla*, III:184: 'Sá þeir jóreykinn ok undir fagra skjöldu ok hvítar brynjur.' See also *Fagrskinna*, p. 137; *Morkinskinna*, p. 115; and *Flateyjarbók*, III:392.

[43] DeVries, *Medieval Military Technology*, pp. 57–58, 64–65; N. Brooks, 'Arms, Status and Warfare,' pp. 93–94 Mann, in *The Bayeux Tapestry*, pp. 58–60; Bradbury, *Battle of Hastings*, pp. 79–80; Rupert Bruce-Mitford, 'The Sutton Hoo Helmet – a New Reconstruction,' in *Aspects of Anglo-Saxon Archaeology: Sutton Hoo and Other Discoveries* (New York, 1974), pp. 198–209; Rupert Bruce-Mitford, 'The Benty Grange Helmet and Some Other Supposed Anglo-Saxon Helmets,' in *Aspects of Anglo-Saxon Archaeology: Sutton Hoo and Other Discoveries* (New York, 1974), pp. 223–52; Peter V. Addyman, Nicholas Pearson and Dominic Tweddle, 'The Coppergate Helmet,' *Antiquity* 56 (1982), 189–94; and Dominic Tweddle, *The Coppergate Helmet* (York, 1984). See also *The Exeter Book Riddles*, no. 61, and the artistic examples in Nicolle, nos. 870–71, 875, 1592.

Norse literary works frequently detail the education and preparation for warfare of young warriors, those of pre-Conquest England as well as those of Ireland and Scandinavia. The impression of the Anglo-Saxon soldier given in these works is of one who was well acquainted with his weapons, in all of their numerous varieties, and accustomed to combat, both as an individual and as an army.[44] He was also well versed in the ethics of warfare.[45] More than likely this training was restricted to the more noble members of the English military, although such an assertion cannot be justified solely on this literary evidence. Certainly the more professional huscarls were well trained in military arts, but perhaps some of the fyrd were as well.

A similar lack of specific historical details on late Anglo-Saxon strategy and tactics also exists among the contemporary sources. This has given rise to the conclusions of some military historians and historians of late Anglo-Saxon/Anglo-Norman England that the armies of Harold Godwinson were, as summarized by Richard Glover:

> an unwieldy host of men who had all forgotten how to use the bow and never learnt to fight on horses; their military science rose to no higher concept than 'the stationary tactics of a phalanx of axemen'[46]

Perhaps such a conclusion is warranted, but only if the use of archery and the cavalry charge is the determining definitions of learned 'military science.' Leaving aside the possibility that nowhere in Europe was the tactical use of archery and the cavalry charge well developed,[47] and that the English of 1066 were able to use both archery, as examined above, and the cavalry charge, as discussed below, from the military actions of Harold Godwinson and other eleventh-century English military leaders, both a well developed strategy and good tactics can be seen.[48]

---

[44] Hilda R. Ellis Davidson, 'The Training of Warriors,' in *Weapons and Warfare in Anglo-Saxon England*, ed. S.C. Hawkes (Oxford, 1989), pp. 11–23.

[45] J.E. Cross, 'The Ethic of War in Old English,' in *England Before the Conquest: Studies in Primary Sources Presented to Dorothy Whitelock*, ed. P. Clemoes and K. Hughes (Cambridge, 1971), pp. 269–82.

[46] Glover, p. 1, paraphrasing Oman, I:165. Other authors who Glover targets for their beliefs in Anglo-Saxon military backwardness include F.W. Maitland (*Domesday Book and Beyond* (Cambridge, 1897), p. 156); H.C.W. Davis (*England under the Normans and Angevins* (London, 1905), pp. 1–4); and Frank M. Stenton (*Anglo-Saxon England*, p. 576). See also Hooper, 'The Anglo-Saxons at War,' pp. 198–99.

[47] On the fact that the cavalry and archery tactics used by William the Conqueror at Hastings were 'unusual' see Stephen Morillo's convincing 'Hastings: An Unusual Battle,' *Haskins Society Journal* 1 (1989), 96–103. See also Matthew Strickland, 'Slaughter, Slavery or Ransom: the Impact of the Conquest on Conduct in Warfare,' in *England in the Eleventh Century: Proceedings of the 1990 Harlaxton Symposium*, ed. C. Hicks (Stamford, 1992), pp. 41–42.

[48] Agreeing with this assertion are Hollister, *Anglo-Saxon Military Institutions*; Hooper, 'Anglo-Saxon Warfare,' pp. 84–93; Hooper, 'The Anglo-Saxons at War,' pp. 191–202; N. Brooks, 'Arms, Status and Warfare,' pp. 81–103; Abels, *Lordship and Military Obligation*; Abels, 'English Tactics, Strategy and Military Organization in the Late Tenth Century,' pp.

On strategy, for example, during the Welsh campaign in 1063, Harold, first alone and then in concert with his brother, Tostig, practiced what could only be described as good strategic generalship. During the winter, when it was least expected, Harold marched his force through the Snowdonia mountains to Gruffydd ap Llywelyn's Rhuddlan capital and sacked it. Then, later, having failed to capture Gruffydd, Harold and Tostig applied a two-prong attack to their opponent's Welsh kingdom, Harold sailing a fleet from Bristol around Wales and Tostig marching an army from Northumbria, which forced the Welsh to surrender to them and led to the assassination of Gruffydd by his war-weary subjects a short time later.[49] Leading to the battle of Stamford Bridge, Harold Godwinson also conducted one of the fastest forced marches known in history. Marching from London to the outskirts of York, a distance of more than 200 miles, with such speed (nine or ten days, an average of more than 20 miles per day), the English king completely surprised his Norwegian enemy, catching them, in the words of author of *Morkinskinna*, 'very merry,' having shed their arms and armor in the warm September sunshine.[50] Undoubtedly this surprise aided Harold and his army in their victory over the Norwegians. Other examples of good strategic practices by the Anglo-Saxons can be recognized in Harold's fortification of Hereford after Gruffydd's successful raid of the town in 1055 – according to John of Worcester, Harold 'encircled [the town] with a broad and deep ditch, and fortified it with gates and bars'[51] – and in his ability to muster a large army and navy in the summer of 1066, 'so many naval and land hosts that no king before had ever gathered so many,' and then to keep them on the southern coast of England in anticipation of an attack from Normandy for more than two months.[52]

However, it is for their tactical abilities (or, more properly, inabilities) that

---

143–55; Strickland, 'Military Technology and Conquest,' pp. 353–82; and Jennie Kiff, 'Images of War: Illustrations of Warfare in Early Eleventh-Century England,' *Anglo-Norman Studies* 7 (1984), 177–94.

[49] On this campaign see the chapter 'Harold Godwinson', nn. 64–65, above.

[50] This march and its results are discussed in the chapter 'The Battle of Stamford Bridge' below. The words used in *Morkinskinna* (p. 115) are 'catir mioc.' A similar description of the Norwegian troops can be found in *Fagrskinna*, p. 137; Snorri Sturluson, *Heimskringla*, III:184; and *Flateyjarbók*, III:392.

[51] John of Worcester, *The Chronicle of John of Worcester*, ed. R.R. Darlington and P. McGurk, trans. J. Bray and P. McGurk (Oxford, 1995), II:578–79. For a discussion of this see the chapter 'Harold Godwinson', n. 54.

[52] The quote comes from the *Anglo-Saxon Chronicle* C and D (1066), I:194–97: 'And Harold cyng his broþor gegædrade swa micelne sciphere. ꝥ eac landhere. swa nan cyng her on lande ær ne dyde.' (The quote is from (D); it differs from (C) only in spelling and word choice.) A more complete discussion of this mustering can be found in the chapter 'The Invasion' below. For a discussion of the logistical capabilities of Anglo-Saxon kings see Richard Abels, 'English Logistics and Military Administration, 871–1066: The Impact of the Viking Wars,' in *Military Aspects of Scandinavian Society in a European Perspective, AD 1–1300*, ed. A.N. Jørgensen and B. Clausen (Copenhagen, 1997), pp. 256–65. His assessment of Harold Godwinson's logistical prowess is found on pp. 257–58.

Anglo-Saxon armies have received the most criticism. Merely because they could not withstand or even imitate the tactical flourishes of William the Conqueror at Hastings, their own tactics performed on the battlefield have been seen as simple, if not actually crude. Yet simplicity should not be seen as backward; nor should a comparison with the indisputable military genius of William the Conqueror be seen as something which condemns Harold Godwinson as an uninventive general. As Nicholas Hooper writes:

> Old English battles appear to have been relatively simple affairs. The shield wall could advance slowly or quickly, but battle, when joined, consisted of a number of clashes between the opposing formations which occasionally parted to draw breath. While the armies were apart various assorted missiles were discharged – at Maldon [a battle fought in 991 and celebrated in the Old English poem, *The Battle of Maldon*] we are told of thrown spears and busy bows, and the *Bayeux Tapestry* shows thrown spears, clubs, and small axes, as well as one English archer. The battle was over when one or other force broke, and a mad rush to horse ensued, either to escape or pursue. This simplicity was not, however, a result of any lack of military skill on the behalf of Old English commanders, but rather all that could be attempted with the military instrument of the time, and in the final analysis, victory depended on numbers, fighting spirit, and morale, not on elaborate tactics.[53]

One tactic which seems to have been particularly effective when used by Anglo-Saxon armies was the shield wall. Tactically similar to the Norwegian formation of the same name, it performed the same defensive function, protecting the infantry, both huscarls and fyrd, against the attacks of either horse or foot.[54] Like the Norwegians sometimes did, as at the battle of Stamford Bridge, the English soldiers behind the shield wall, at least at the battle of Hastings, became impatient and, deceived by a Norman retreat or 'feigned retreat,' broke out from their fortified position and charged in a disordered fashion down Senlac Hill after their 'fleeing' opponents. In response, the Normans quickly turned and charged back onto the English, defeating them.[55]

Further evidence of the excellence of Anglo-Saxon soldiers on the battlefield comes from contemporary descriptions of their fighting capabilities and bravery. Knútr the Great, not one given to praise for his enemies, according to

---

[53] Hooper, 'Anglo-Saxon Warfare,' p. 93. A similar view is held by Abels, 'English Tactics, Strategy and Military Organization in the Late Tenth Century,' pp. 147–52.

[54] On the Anglo-Saxon shield wall see Abels, 'English Tactics, Strategy and Military Organization in the Late Tenth Century,' pp. 148–49, who thinks that it was an effective tactic, and Hooper, 'The Anglo-Saxons at War,' p. 200, who thinks that it was not.

[55] On whether the retreat at Hastings was 'feigned' or not see Bernard S. Bachrach, 'The Feigned Retreat at Hastings,' *Mediaeval Studies* 33 (1971), 344–47 and R. Allen Brown, 'The Battle of Hastings,' *Proceedings of the Battle Conference on Anglo-Norman Studies* 3 (1980), 14–16, who believe that the Norman retreat was 'feigned, and Morillo, pp. 96–103 and John Marshall Carter, 'The Feigned Flight at Hastings: Birth, Propagation, and the Death of a Myth,' *San Jose Studies* (Feb. 1978), 95–106, who do not. Original source references to this charge can be found in those articles.

Henry of Huntingdon, considered the English soldiers to be 'nec minori quam Dacos (not inferior to the Danes)' in their military skill,[56] and even William FitzOsbern, William the Conqueror's steward, was said to have called them 'fortissimus' (most strong).[57] A comparable respect for Harold Godwinson's soldiers can also be found in the Norwegian Kings' Sagas' description of their skill at the battles of Fulford Gate and Stamford Bridge.[58] It is perhaps fitting then that after their defeat at Hastings many of the remaining Anglo-Saxon soldiers, primarily huscarls, having fled from the battlefield or been granted their freedom on the promise of never taking up arms again against William, went south to Constantinople where they joined the Varangian Guard.[59]

As mentioned, much of the controversy surrounding the lack of tactical expertise among the Anglo-Saxons is dependent on their apparent inability to conduct cavalry charges like those used against them by William the Conqueror at the battle of Hastings. The history of this dispute stretches back at least a century and shows no sign of ending in the near future.

Until 1952, many medieval historians of the 1066 conflicts, most notably Edward A. Freeman, Sir Charles Oman, and Sir Frank M. Stenton, believed that Anglo-Saxon soldiers fought solely on foot, without the knowledge of how to fight from horseback. When horses were used militarily, as suggested in some of the original sources, they were there only as means of transportation to and from an engagement.[60] Taken by the dismounting of the Bryhtnoð's English forces in the poem, *The Battle of Maldon*,[61] by the comments of John of Worcester and Symeon of Durham that Earl Ralph of Mantes led an Anglo-Saxon army on horseback against the Welsh invaders of Herefordshire and that this was '*contra morem* (contrary to tradition),'[62] and by the assertion of the author of the *Carmen de hastingae proelio* that 'the English scorn the solace of horses and

---

[56] Henry of Huntingdon, p. 364. I have used my own translation of this passage and not Diane Greenway's.

[57] Henry of Huntingdon, pp. 386–87. FitzOsbern was quite fearful of the English and warned William against going to battle against them. For an assessment of this see Glover, pp. 2–4.

[58] This will be discussed more completely in the chapters 'The Invasion' and 'The Battle of Stamford Bridge' which follow.

[59] See John Godfrey, 'The Defeated Anglo-Saxons Take Service with the Eastern Emperor,' *Proceedings of the Battle Conference on Anglo-Norman Studies* 1 (1978), 63–74.

[60] Edward August Freeman, *The History of the Norman Conquest*, 2nd edn (Oxford, 1869–75), III:366–67, 370, 720; Oman, I:115, 150–51; and Stenton, *Anglo-Saxon England*, p. 576.

[61] 'The Battle of Maldon,' in *A Choice of Anglo Saxon Verse*, ed. and trans. R. Hamer (London, 1970), pp. 54–55.

[62] John of Worcester, II:576–79 and Symeon of Durham, *Historia regum*, ed. T. Arnold (London, 1882–85). II:171–72. Symeon of Durham uses almost the same words as John of Worcester, obviously his source for this story. Both blame the use of this tactic for the loss suffered by the Anglo-Saxons. See also *Anglo-Saxon Chronicle* (C, D, and E) 1055, I:184–87, with (C) the only version to record the use of cavalry by the English, and attributing the loss to this tactic. Other sources of this action which do not mention the use of cavalry can be found in the chapter, 'Harold Godwinson', n. 53, above.

trusting in their strength they stand fast on foot,'[63] these historians stood firm on their assertion that the soldiers of Harold Godwinson, huscarls or fyrd, were unable to make an effective cavalry charge. Yet, in making this stand, they were forced to discount the claim made in the Norwegian Kings' Sagas, or at least in Snorri Sturluson's *Heimskringla*, which is the only one of the sagas which is referred to or which is in translation, that Harold Godwinson's cavalry made several charges on the Norwegian infantry line which had formed a shield wall at Stamford Bridge.[64] (In a turn of circular logic, these historians then called on this discounting of these cavalry charges to almost completely dismiss Snorri Sturluson's account of the battle of Stamford Bridge as 'mythical' or, at least, a re-enactment of what had occurred at the battle of Hastings and not at Stamford Bridge.[65])

A new perspective to the debate was added, however, in 1952 with the publication in the *English Historical Review* of an article by Richard Glover entitled 'English Warfare in 1066.' In this work, Glover discussed the objections to Anglo-Saxon cavalry and compared these to the original source accounts of pre-Conquest English cavalry. Trusting more in Snorri Sturluson's account than his predecessors (he too used none of the other Norwegian Kings' Sagas), he concluded that Anglo-Saxon soldiers used horses not only to transport themselves to the battlefield, but into battle as well.[66] Ten years later, C. Warren Hollister, in his book, *Anglo-Saxon Military Institutions*, agreed, adding some clarifications, with Glover's assertions.[67]

Since that time the debate has continued. Using a more complete view of any sources which might add to the discussion, artistic as well as historical and literary, it can now be said with confidence that the Anglo-Saxons certainly valued horses at least as much as their continental counterparts. Even before the eleventh century, there is evidence that many different breeds of horses were bred separately for plowing and riding, and that a riding horse of good quality was a luxury which denoted wealth and status. Horses were also frequently given as gifts, prized for their show of friendship and alliance. Finally, the ownership of any horse was legally protected, with definitions of value assigned to it, should the owner need compensation.[68] Horses were prized too by Viking

---

[63] *Carmen de hastingae proelio*, ed. C. Morton and A. Muntz (Oxford, 1972), pp. 24–25: '. . . solamina spernit equorum, / Viribus et fidens, heret humo pedibus.'

[64] All of the more lengthy Norwegian Kings' Sagas mention he Anglo-Saxon use of cavalry charges: *Fagrskinna*, p. 140; *Morkinskinna*, pp. 116–17; Snorri Sturluson, *Heimskringla*, III:189; and *Flateyjarbók*, III:393–94.

[65] 'Mythical' is Freeman's word (Freeman, *Norman Conquest*, III:365–67, 720–27). See also Oman, I:150–51 and R. Allen Brown, *The Normans and the Norman Conquest*, 2nd edn (Woodbridge, 1985), p. 136.

[66] Glover, pp. 5–18.

[67] Hollister, *Anglo-Saxon Military Institutions*, pp. 18, 134–40.

[68] See R.H.C. Davis, *The Medieval Warhorse: Origin, Development and Redevlopment* (London, 1989), pp. 70–78; Ann Hyland, *The Medieval Warhorse: From Byzantium to the Crusades* (London, 1994), pp. 67–81; Sarah Larratt Keefer, 'Hwær Cwom Mearh? The Horse in Anglo-Saxon England,' *Journal of Medieval History* 22 (1996), 115–34; and Irene

raiders of the British Isles who placed them among their most cherished items of booty. Although there is no evidence that these were shipped back to their Scandinavian homelands, with their stolen mounts Vikings were able to raid much farther from their camps and landing sites than they could do on foot.[69]

Yet what of the use of horses for military purposes, in particular as cavalry mounts? There certainly seems to be enough evidence among literary sources, such as the Early Scottish poem (or poems), *Gododdin* (sixth to seventh centuries), which tells of warriors involved in mounted warfare,[70] and the late ninth-century *Vita Wilfridi*, by Eddius Stephanus, which describes King Ecgfrið 'preparing a mounted force' and then attacking the Picts,[71] as well as artistic sources such as the Aberlemno and the Repton Stones (dating c.685 and early ninth century respectively), both of which depict warriors seated on horses and involved in cavalry warfare – the Aberlemno Stone depicts two cavalry soldiers facing each other in combat,[72] while the Repton Stone portrays an armored cavalry warrior as if he was in the middle of a charge, his shield raised in his left hand and his sword brandished in his right[73] – and the Cooperate helmet, which contains four portrayals of cavalry warfare, that it must be admitted that the Anglo-Saxons were at least *capable* of cavalry charges.[74] Then there are the historical references; these seem to outnumber those mentioned above which speak against the Anglo-Saxon use of cavalry. For example, the Old English historical

Hughson, 'Pictish Horse Carvings,' *Glasgow Archaeological Journal* 17 (1991–92), 53–61. Keefer does not believe that horses were used in plowing, except in rare occasions, oxen being the preferred beast of burden for that task.

[69] R.H.C. Davis, pp. 71–73 and Hyland, pp. 72–76.

[70] For an edition and study of *Gododdin* see Kenneth Hurlstone Jackson, ed., *The Gododdin: The Oldest Scottish Poem* (Edinburgh, 1969). Its relationship to the question of Anglo-Saxon cavalry warfare can be found in Nicholas Hooper, 'The Aberlemno Stone and Cavalry in Anglo-Saxon England,' *Northern History* 29 (1993), 189–92, and Jenny Rowland, 'Warfare and Horses in the *Gododdin* and the Problem of Catraeth,' *Cambrian Medieval Celtic Studies* 30 (1995), 13–40.

[71] Eddius Stephanus, *The Life of Bishop Wilfrid*, ed. B. Colgrave (Oxford, 1927), pp. 40–43: 'rex Ecgfrithus . . . statim equitatui exercitu praeperato . . . parva manu populi Dei contra inormem et supra invisibilem hostem cum Beornheth audaci subregulo invasit.' In support of this see Hooper, 'The Aberlemno Stone,' pp. 188–89. Against this use of the text see Nicholas J. Higham, 'Cavalry in Early Bernicia?' *Northern History* 27 (1991), 236–41.

[72] A depiction of the Aberlemno Stone can be found in Strickland, 'Military Technology and Conquest,' p. 356; C. Thomas, 'The Pictish Class 1 Symbol Stones,' in *Pictish Studies: Settlement, Burial and Art in Dark Age Northern Britain*, ed. J.G.P. Friell and W.G. Watson (Oxford, 1984), pp. 169–87; and Anna Ritchie, *Picts: An Introduction to the Life of the Picts and the Carved Stones in the Care of the Secretary of State for Scotland* (Edinburgh, 1989), pp. 24–25. For a discussion on how this applies to Anglo-Saxon warfare, see Hooper, 'The Aberlemno Stone,' pp. 190–92; Strickland, 'Military Technology and Conquest,' pp. 359–60; Rowland, p. 15; and C. Cessford, 'Cavalry in Early Bernicia: A Reply,' *Northern History* 29 (1993), 185.

[73] On the Repton Stone see Martin Biddle and Birth Kjolbye-Biddle, 'The Repton Stone,' *Anglo-Saxon England* 14 (1985), 233–92.

[74] See Tweddle and Cessford, p. 185. For other artistic sources which show Anglo-Saxon cavalry warfare see Kiff.

poem, *The Battle of Brunanburh*, written c.937, reports that West Saxon troops fought on horseback 'the whole day long' against the Scots.[75] In 1016, the *Anglo-Saxon Chronicle* (E) describes how the Danish army, in encountering the forces of King Edmund Ironside, fled on horseback only to be overtaken and defeated by the English troops, also obviously on horseback.[76] In 1054, John of Worcester notes:

> Siward, the vigorous earl of the Northumbrians, at the king's command, went to Scotland with a mounted force and a powerful fleet and joined battle with Macbeth, king of the Scots, and when many thousands of Scots . . . had been killed, he put them to flight.[77]

The two expeditions carried out in 1063 against Gruffydd ap Llywelyn by Harold and Tostig Godwinson, John of Worcester again records, were made by Anglo-Saxon troops 'on horseback.'[78] John of Worcester also records Harold's gathering of a 'force of cavalry' which he mustered to oppose Tostig's attacks along the southern coast of England and which he kept there in anticipation of William's invasion across the Channel.[79] (The fact that John of Worcester made these references to cavalry warfare while at the same time writing that the Anglo-Saxons were 'unaccustomed to fighting on horseback' in 1055, does call into question what he meant when he used the term 'horseback' to describe these various instances of cavalry warfare.) Finally, in depicting Harold Godwinson fighting alongside William the Conqueror in Brittany, both William of Poitiers and The Bayeux Tapestry portray the future English king fully proficient in fighting on horseback.[80]

Still, some continue to resist the notion of a cavalry-capable Anglo-Saxon army: 'the Anglo-Saxons fought predominantly, if not exclusively, as infantry' (Matthew Strickland).[81] Others are quick to counter them: 'we must be aware of

---

[75] A copy of *The Battle of Brunanburh* is found in *The Anglo-Saxon Chronicle* A (937), I:106–10. It has been further edited in Alistair Campbell, ed., *The Battle of Brunanburh* (Cambridge, 1938). For a discussion on its relationship to cavalry warfare see Hooper, 'The Aberlemno Stone,' pp. 194–95.

[76] *Anglo-Saxon Chronicle* E (1016), I:150–51. For this as evidence of Anglo-Saxon cavalry is Glover, p. 9; against this is R.A. Brown, *Normans and Norman Conquest*, p. 82 n. 157. See also Hooper, 'The Aberlemno Stone,' p. 194.

[77] John of Worcester, II:574–75:
Strenuus dux Norðhymbrorum Siuuardus, iussu regis, et equestri exercitu et classe ualida Scotiam adiit et cum rege Scottorum Macbeotha prelium commisit ac multis milibus Scottorum . . . occisis, illum fugauit.
See also Hyland, p. 96.

[78] John of Worcester, II:592–93. See also Hyland, p. 96. On these expeditions see the chapter 'Harold Godwinson', nn. 64–65, above.

[79] John of Worcester, II:600–01. See also Symeon of Durham, II:179. The words used to describe this force are 'equestrem exercitum'.

[80] William of Poitiers, *The Gesta Guillelmi of William of Poitiers*, ed. and trans. R.H.C. Davis and M. Chibnall (Oxford, 1998), pp. 70–73. See also Hyland, p. 95. For a discussion of this incident see the chapter 'Harold Godwinson', n. 89, above.

[81] Strickand, 'Military Technology and Conquest,' p. 360. Strickland does assert, however,

the possibility that the English could be flexible in their tactics and sometimes fight on horseback' (Nicholas Hooper),[82] while yet others tend to straddle the middle ground, not ruling out the use of cavalry by the Anglo-Saxons, but not accepting the idea either: 'there simply is no reliable information on how the English fought in battle' (R.H.C. Davis).[83] The debate seems far from over.

In view of the Norwegian invasion of England taking place in 1066, two final questions concerning the Anglo-Saxon military of the time must be answered. First, why did English fortifications not stop the advance of the Norwegian army on land? And second, why did the English navy not stop the Norwegian fleet on the sea before Haraldr Harðráði and his troops could begin their invasion of the island kingdom?

While it is true that Anglo-Saxon England was covered by a large system of fortifications built by Kings Offa and Ælfred the Great, by the late eleventh century this system had fallen largely into disuse. Moreover, Offa's Dyke and other fortifications and most of Ælfred's *burhs* had been built in the southern and western parts of the kingdom, far from the territory invaded by the Norwegians in 1066.[84] The only other, more recent fortifications which had been built, the three motte-and-bailey castles made by the Normans in the late 1040s or early 1050s, were all constructed along the Welsh marches, where they had proven unable to hold off the raids of Gruffydd ap Llywelyn.[85] It thus seems easy to conclude that the late Anglo-Saxon English really had no trust in this form of military technology. This would be left up to a more defensive-minded future king of England, William the Conqueror, to change. Before his death, in 1087, castles would dot the landscape.[86]

A similar answer could be given to the question of why the Anglo-Saxon

---

that the Anglo-Saxons did this not because they were incapable of fighting on horseback, but 'out of choice' (p. 367). Also holding that the pre-conquest English armies were not capable of cavalry warfare is Higham, 'Cavalry in Early Bernica,' pp. 236–41.

[82] Hooper, 'The Aberlemno Stone,' pp. 192–93 (also p. 195 where he reiterates this claim). See also Hooper, 'Anglo-Saxons at War,' pp. 200–201; Cessford; and Rowland.

[83] R.H.C. Davis, *The Medieval Warhorse*, p. 76. See also R.H.C. Davis, 'Did Anglo-Saxons have Warhorses?' in *Weapons and Warfare in Anglo-Saxon England*, ed. S.C. Hawkes (Oxford, 1989), pp. 141–44.

[84] On these fortifications see DeVries, *Medieval Military Technology*, pp. 194–97; Abels, *Lordship and Military Obligation*, pp. 58–78; Richard Abels, *Alfred the Great: War, Kingship and Culture in Anglo-Saxon England* (London, 1998), pp. 194–207; David Hill and Alexander R. Rumble, eds., *The Defence of Wessex: The Burghal Hidage and Anglo-Saxon Fortifications* (Manchester, 1996); Edward J. Schoenfeld, 'Anglo-Saxon *Burhs* and Continental *Burgen*: Early Medieval Fortifications in Constitutional Perspective,' *Haskins Society Journal* 6 (1994), 49–66; and Bernard Bachrach and Rutherford Aris, 'Military Technology and Garrison Organization: Some Observations on Anglo-Saxon Military Thinking in Light of the Burghal Hidage,' *Technology and Culture* 31 (1990), 1–17.

[85] On these castles see the chapter 'Godwin and His Family', n. 77, above.

[86] There are many studies on these castles. For an overview of what was built and for a bibliography of the many studies devoted to these castles see DeVries, *Medieval Military Technology*, pp. 202–12.

navy did not stop the Norwegian invasion fleet of Haraldr Harðráði before it landed its cargo of warriors on the coast of Northumbria. While it is true that Harold Godwinson possessed a fleet of his own, indeed that he had mustered his ships to protect the southern coast of England in anticipation of William the Conqueror's invasion, by the time of that invasion, and even the earlier one made by the Norwegians, all of these ships had returned to their other activities – probably fishing and the carrying of cargo.[87] Even then, it is uncertain how much of a deterrent to a naval attack of the island this fleet would have been. Despite having played a significant role in Harold Godwinson's 1063 attack of Wales,[88] and although they seemed to have been able to drive Tostig Godwinson away from Lindsey earlier in 1066,[89] the late Anglo-Saxon navy simply may have been too small to cover the entire eastern coast of England and then to defeat a large number of Norwegian vessels, even if Harold had been prophetic enough to anticipate Haraldr Harðráði's attack. As it was, King Harold II Godwinson of England was forced to face King Haraldr I Sigurðarson, known as Harðráði, on land at Stamford Bridge near York. It was a battle he would win, decisively.

---

[87] On Harold Godwinson's navy see Hooper, 'Some Observations on the Navy in Late Anglo-Saxon England,' pp. 203–13, and N.A.M. Rodger, *The Safeguard of the Sea: A Naval History of Britain, 600–1649* (New York, 1997), pp. 26–32. On the possible technology of these ships see Rodger, *Safeguard of the Sea*, p. 15, and André W. Sleeswyk, 'The Ship of Harold Godwinson,' *Mariner's Mirror* 61 (1981), 87–91. A discussion of Harold's mustering of the fleet in anticipation of the Norman invasion can be found in the chapter 'The Invasion' below.

[88] On Harold's use of the navy in 1063 see the chapter 'Harold Godwinson,' n. 65, above.

[89] This too will be discussed in the chapter 'The Invasion,' to follow.

CHAPTER NINE

THE INVASION

BY THE BEGINNING OF September 1066, all the plans for the Norwegian invasion of England had been made. These plans were begun much earlier, perhaps as early as March or April of that year. Although unquestionably Haraldr Harðráði desired to make the invasion, the prime instigator of his attack in 1066 was probably Tostig Godwinson.

Tostig, the estranged brother of the king of England, may have been thinking of attacking his homeland since the time of his ousting the previous November, although there is no evidence to support such a contention. Even if that was the case, it seems clear that he did not seriously act on this thought until after his brother, Harold, ascended to King Edward's empty seat on 6 January 1066. Perhaps Tostig had anticipated that as soon as Harold became king, he would return to power in Northumbria. When this did not occur, he began to look for a benefactor, someone who could assist him in realizing his desires to return to his rightful (or perhaps even a better) English political position.

At the same time, Tostig's hatred for his now royal brother must have grown considerably, especially once he learned of Harold's marriage to Ealdyð, the sister of Edwin and Morkere, and of the king's visit to Northumbria a short time after taking the throne. Both of these moves would have confirmed to Tostig that Harold desired to make peace with the earls of the northern portion of his kingdom rather than to restore his exiled brother to that earldom. Nor if Harold was pushing for unity with Northumbria was he likely to award Wessex – which was, of course, available with Harold's assumption of the kingship – to Tostig. Therefore, at some time early in 1066, Tostig Godwinson must have realized that he was not to be returned to power. The dream of standing as chief earl in England, as his father and brother had done, with its accompanying political power, would have vanished. It even may have seemed to Tostig that Harold had desired his exile for a very long time, and that this was the reason for his brother's lack of support for him during the uprising of his Northumbrian subjects. Perhaps Harold had even incited them to rebel against Tostig. Such a conclusion may seem far fetched, but this is, after all, precisely what the *Vita Ædwardi* asserts that Tostig had accused his brother of.[1]

There is little detailed information from contemporary sources concerning

---

[1] See n. 69 in the chapter 'The Conflict Between Harold and Tostig Godwinson' above.

Tostig's movements immediately after being exiled from England. It is known that his initial destination was the county of Flanders and the care and protection of his brother-in-law, Count Baldwin V.[2] Baldwin may also have been Tostig's first benefactorial target, although the sources do not directly support this theory. If this was so, however, Baldwin seems not to have been able to support Tostig's desire to invade England. Instead, the count of Flanders' first allegiance proved to be the backing, with both men and funds, of his son-in-law, William, duke of Normandy, in a similar conquest for the island kingdom.[3]

There are several questions about Tostig's stay in Flanders left unanswered by the original sources. For one, when did Tostig begin to seek allies for his return to England? Did he do so immediately after his exile, even if they would not be needed should Harold, once king, have returned him to power? Or, did he wait until after he realized that Harold was not going to recall him to his earldom? For another, did Tostig's exile, with its apparent indication of discord among the Godwin family, signal to William the Conqueror, Haraldr Harðráði, and perhaps even Baldwin V and Sveinn Estriðson that England was ripe for invasion? Finally, there is the question of who Tostig visited, and in what order, before these invasions were launched.

Unfortunately, the answers to when Tostig began to seek allies and whether his exile somehow encouraged the later invasions cannot be determined by consulting the meagre historical sources of late 1065 and early 1066. Nor is it any easier to answer the final question posed above. Indeed, there are no fewer than

---

2   The *Vita Ædwardi regis qui apud Westmonasterium requiescit* (ed. and trans. F. Barlow, 2nd edn (London, 1992), pp. 80–83), *Anglo-Saxon Chronicle* (in *Two of the Saxon Chronicles Parallel*, Charles Plummer and John Earle (Oxford, 1892), (C and D) 1065, (E) 1064, I:192–95), John of Worcester (*The Chronicle of John of Worcester*, ed. R.R. Darlington and P. McGurk, trans. J. Bray and P. McGurk (Oxford, 1995), II:598–99), Henry of Huntingdon (*Historia Anglorum: The History of the English People*, ed. and trans. D. Greenway (Oxford, 1996). pp. 384–85), William of Malmesbury (*Gesta regum Anglorum: The History of the English Kings*, ed. and trans. R.A.B. Mynors, R.M. Thomson, and M. Winterbottom (Oxford, 1998), I:364–65), Symeon of Durham (*Historia regum*, ed. T. Arnold (London, 1882–85), II:178–79), Orderic Vitalis (*The Ecclesiastical History of Orderic Vitalis*, ed. and trans. M. Chibnall (Oxford, 1969–80), II:138–41), and Geoffrey Gaimar (*Lestoire des Engles*, ed. T.D. Hardy and C.T. Martin (London, 1888–89), I:217), all claim the county of Flanders as the destination of Tostig and Judith after his exile from England. See also Edward August Freeman, *The History of the Norman Conquest*, 2nd edn (Oxford, 1869–75), II:486–97; Frank M. Stenton, *Anglo-Saxon England*, 3rd edn (Oxford, 1971), p. 579; Frank Barlow, *Edward the Confessor* (Berkeley and Los Angeles, 1970), pp. 237–38; David C. Douglas, *William the Conqueror* (Berkeley and Los Angeles, 1964), pp. 179–80; Ian W. Walker, *Harold: The Last Anglo-Saxon King* (Stroud, 1997), pp. 113–14; Tryggvi J. Oleson, *The Witenagemot in the Reign of Edward the Confessor: A Study in the Constitutional History of Eleventh-Century England* (Toronto, 1955), p. 64; and Philip Grierson, 'The Relations between England and Flanders before the Norman Conquest,' *Transactions of the Royal Historical Society* 23 (1941), 103.

3   On the support of Baldwin V for William the Conqueror's invasion, see Robert H. George, 'The Contribution of Flanders to the Conquest of England, 1065–1086,' *Revue Belge de philologie et d'histoire* 5 (1926), 81–99.

three candidates for Tostig's visit, William, duke of Normandy, in Normandy, Sveinn Estriðson, king of Denmark, in Denmark, and Haraldr Harðráði, king of Norway, in Norway, as well as at least one journey in between the others to Flanders according to the various sources, none of which contain a visit to all three of these individuals.

It is only according to Orderic Vitalis that Tostig visited William the Conqueror early in 1066. In his *Ecclesiastical History*, as well as in a passage which he added to William of Jumièges' *Gesta Normannorum ducum*, Orderic reports that after learning of Harold's marriage to the sister of Edwin and Morkere, Tostig, 'seeing that the wickedness of his brother Harold had prevailed and that the kingdom was groaning under every kind of oppression, took the matter to heart, resolved to oppose him, and openly declared war on him.' Guided by his wife, Judith, Tostig was led first to Baldwin V in Flanders, who, although not directly given credit for this by Orderic, then sent his brother-in-law to William in Normandy. Tostig initially 'rebuked' the duke for his inaction up to this time, but then promised to 'faithfully secure the crown for him if he would cross to England with a Norman army.' William, in turn,

> greeted his comrade warmly on his arrival, thanked him for his friendly chiding, and with his encouragement called together the Norman nobles for a public discussion about what ought to be done in an affair of such moment.

However, this council was divided on whether to take on such a military adventure. Eventually, William was forced to approach the pope, who supported his claim to the English throne, and this ultimately led the Norman duke to assemble his army. Unfortunately for Tostig, this process took too much time for his liking. Impatient with the delay, the exiled earl asked for William's permission to return to England, it appears to gain a few adherents, but after his route was blocked by Harold and then his return to Normandy was impeded by bad weather, Tostig sailed north to Haraldr Harðráði in Norway and eventually to an invasion of England without the Norman duke.[4]

While William seems to have been a logical person for Tostig Godwinson to

---

4   Orderic Vitalis, II:138–45. The quotes are on pp. 138–41:
   Tunc Tosticus Goduini comitis filius aduertens Heraldi fratris sui praeualere facinus, et regnum Angliae uariis grauari oppressionibus aegre tulit, contradixit, et aperte repugnare decreuit . . . Deinde festinus Normanniam adiit, et Willelmum ducem cur periurum suum regnare sineret fortiter redarguit seque fideliter si ipse cum Normannicis uiribus in Angliam transfretaret regni decus optenturum illi spopondit. Ipsi nepe iamdudum se inuicem multum amauerant duasque sorores per quas amicicia saepe recalescebat in coniugio habebant. Willelmus autem dux aduenientem amicum cum gaudio suscepit, amicabili redargutioni eius gratias egit eiusque exhortationibus animatus Normanniae proceres conuocauit et de tanto talique negocio quid agendum esset palam consulit.
   See also William of Jumièges, *The Gesta Normanorum ducum of William of Jumièges, Orderic Vitalis, and Robert of Torigni*, ed. and trans. E.M.C. van Houts (Oxford, 1995), pp. 162–63, which is a much shorter rewriting of Orderic's narrative, although it does insist that William sent Tostig to England, not that Tostig had asked permission to go to England.

visit in his search for allies against his brother in England, especially with Harold's treachery against the duke and the duke's connection to Baldwin V, few modern historians accept Orderic Vitalis' account of the meeting.[5] This may be because there are too many errors in Orderic's narrative to give it much credibility. For example, the early twelfth-century Anglo-Norman writer claims that Tostig was the elder of the two brothers, that he was not exiled until after Harold was king and that it was Harold who forced him into exile (there is no mention at all of the Northumbrian Rebellion), that William and Tostig were both married to sisters, and that Haraldr Harðráði was Harald Fairhair. Add to these errors the problem with the time that such a visit would take, and that, although Orderic Vitalis does not have Tostig pay a visit to Sveinn Estriðson in Denmark, if the former English earl did not travel to Norway until after his attack on southern England, Haraldr Harðráði must already have had his own invasion underway. While the latter is certainly a possibility, this would mean that the detailed accounts found in the Norwegian Kings' Sagas of Tostig and Haraldr's discussions and plans for invading England did not take place. Of course, none of these sagas recount a visit of Tostig with the Norman duke, nor in fact does William of Poitiers, the most trustworthy ducal chronicler, a detail which also speaks against Orderic's credibility. Finally, there is the long-term animosity between the Normans and the Godwin family; whatever goodwill had been created with Harold's visit to Normandy had obviously been removed by his 'treasonous' assumption of the English throne. Could William trust another son of Godwin? Probably not, if we are to take as an example the duke's treatment of the last remaining Godwinson, his hostage, Wulfnoð, even after his conquest had been successful. (This could also be the reason for Baldwin V's unwillingness to send his brother-in-law to William, should the Norwegian Kings' Sagas chronology of events be believed.) On the other hand, the determination of the normally trustworthy Orderic to believe that such a visit occurred, so much so that he added it to William of Jumièges' chronicle, makes one wonder if a journey to Normandy, even a short one, was not undertaken by Tostig.

The Norwegian Kings' Sagas do not include a visit of Tostig Godwinson to Normandy, but all of the more detailed ones insist that he did travel to Denmark where he sought an audience with that land's king, Sveinn Estriðson.[6] King

---

5 Edward A. Freeman (*Norman Conquest*, III:708–12), F.W. Brooks (*The Battle of Stamford Bridge* (York, 1963), p. 6), Miles W. Campbell ('Note sur les déplacements de Tostig Godwinson en 1066,' *Annales de Normandie* 22 (1972), 4–5), William E. Kapelle (*The Norman Conquest of the North: The Region and Its Transformation, 1000–1135* (Chapel Hill, 1979), pp. 101–02), Brian Golding (*Conquest and Colonisation: The Normans in Britain, 1066–1100* (New York, 1994), pp. 28–29), and David C. Douglas (*William the Conqueror*, pp. 190–91), are the only modern historians who mention a visit by Tostig to Normandy. Only Brooks, Golding, and Douglas accept the possibility (Golding even wonders if it was not Tostig who 'alerted William to the possibilities of invasion'), with Freeman and Campbell rejecting it. Douglas claims also that 'it is probable that at least [Tostig] received some limited support from the duchy' (p. 191).

6 *Fagrskinna: Kortfattet Norsk Konge-Saga*, ed. P.A. Munch and C.R. Unger (Christiania

Sveinn had sheltered Tostig's older brother, Swegen, during his first banishment, and he had continued to remain a friend to and supporter of the Godwin
family.[7] Sveinn also had a claim to the throne of England, based on his relationship to two previous English kings, Knútr, his uncle, and Harðaknútr, his
cousin.[8] As such, these Sagas claim, he readily welcomed Tostig into his
kingdom.

At first, Sveinn and Tostig were good friends; in fact, the Norwegian King's
Sagas note that Sveinn took such pity on his deposed friend that he offered him
another earldom in Denmark to make up for the one lost in England, but Tostig
refused this gesture, for he desired nothing except to return to his homeland:

> The earl said this, 'This I desire very much, to travel back to my lands in
> England. And if I receive no support for this from you, king, then I wish rather
> to place with you all the support I can get in England if you would travel with
> a Danish army to England to conquer the land, as Knútr, your mother's
> brother, once did.'[9]

Sveinn, these sagas insist, was 'a much lesser man' than Knútr, and he would not
accompany Tostig on his venture against England and Harold.[10] Eventually, this
refusal strained relations between the two old friends, and Tostig was forced to
look elsewhere for an ally in his plans for invasion. The Norwegian Kings' Sagas
conclude: 'The earl departed thus from the Danish king, and they were both
angry.'[11]

(Oslo), 1847), p. 134; *Morkinskinna: Pergamentsbog fra første halvdel af det trettende aarhundrede*, ed. C.R. Unger (Christiania (Oslo), 1867), p. 110; Snorri Sturluson, *Heimskringla*,
ed. B. Aðalbjarnarson (Reykjavik, 1941–51), III:172–73; and *Flateyjarbók: En samling af
Norske Konge-Sagaer*, ed. G. Vigfusson and C.R. Unger (Christiania (Oslo), 1860–68),
III:387.

[7] For references to these events see the chapter 'Godwin and His Family', nn. 59–61,
120–21, above.

[8] While all of the Norwegian Kings' Sagas note the relationship of Sveinn and Knútr, as will
be seen below, it is from Adam of Bremen that the Danish king's claim is publicized (*Gesta
Hammaburgensis ecclesiae pontificum*, ed. B. Schmeidler, 3rd edn (Hanover, 1917), pp.
135–36, 151–53). For an analysis of Sveinn's claim to the English throne in general and Adam
of Bremen's account in particular see Sten Körner, *The Battle of Hastings, England, and
Europe, 1035–1066* (Lund, 1964), pp. 138–45.

[9] I have used the lines quoted by Snorri Sturluson (*Heimskringla*, III:172–73):
   Jarl segir svá: 'Þess girnir mik at fara til Englands aptr til óðala minna. En ef ek fæ
   engan styrk til þess af yðr, konungr, þá vil ek heldr þat til leggja við yðr allan styrk
   þann, er ek ákost í Englandi, ef þér vilið fara með Danaher til Englands at vinna land
   svá sem Knútr, móðurbróðir yðvarr,
but the three other, more detailed Norwegian Kings' Sagas which tell of Tostig's visit all have
a similar speech delivered by the exiled English earl. See *Fagrskinna*, p. 134; *Morkinskinna*,
p. 110; and *Flateyjarbók*, III:387.

[10] All four of the Norwegian Kings' Sagas use almost the same words to describe Sveinn
here: 'Sva miclo em ec minni maþr fire mer en varr frendi gamli Knvtr' (*Morkinskinna*, p.
110). See also *Fagrskinna*, p. 134; Snorri Sturluson, *Heimskringla*, III:173; and *Flateyjarbók*,
III:387.

[11] I have used the line from the *Fagrskinna*, p. 134: 'Skildisk jarlinn svá frá Danakonungi, at

It seems far easier for modern historians to accept Tostig's visit to Sveinn than it is for them to accept his visit to William.[12] This may be because Wace too refers to a journey which the exiled English earl made to Denmark, thus adding a non-saga source to those claiming that such a visit took place.[13] However, Wace's *Roman du Rou* is a weak text, referring only to Tostig's visit to Denmark and not also to Norway; as Tostig returns from Denmark 'with Danes and Norwegians' to invade England, Wace has obviously mistaken Denmark for Norway. Also, there seems to have been little reason for the king of Denmark not to accompany Tostig to England, and the explanation given by the obviously anti-Sveinn Norwegian Kings' Sagas (recall their animosity toward the Danish king in their narratives of his wars with Haraldr Harðráði), that he did not think that he was the man that his uncle had been, fringes on the incredible. Yet, to dismiss Tostig's journey to Denmark simply because it is not mentioned in any non-Scandinavian source seems in itself a bit foolish. Sveinn's weariness of warfare after the long struggle with Norway is certainly understandable. He might also have decided to wait until the 1066 invasions had concluded, choosing to attack the forces which were ultimately victorious, but obviously weakened by their combat. In support of this last scenario, Sveinn would in fact send a Danish army to attack the island, although not in 1066 with the others, but in 1069, when his sons and brother unsuccessfully invaded William the Conqueror's England. Sveinn himself would sail up the Humber in his own attempt at conquest in 1070, but he too failed.[14]

Despite his obvious disappointment with Sveinn Estriðson's unwillingness to assist him, Tostig continued to desire to regain his lands in England, and, according to all of the Norwegian Kings' Sagas, including the *Ágrip* and Theodoricus' *Monumenta historica Norvegiæ*, which, being much shorter, do not contain the detail that the *Fagrskinna*, *Morkinskinna*, *Flateyjarbók*, and Snorri Sturluson's *Heimskringla* do, his next target as benefactor for such an adventure was the bellicose king of Norway, Haraldr Harðráði.[15] Had Tostig remained

---

þeir váru báðir reiðir.' The *Morkinskinna* (p. 110) and *Flateyjarbók* (III:387) use similar words. Snorri Sturluson's line is a bit more muted (*Heimskringla*, III:173): 'Síðan skilðusk þeir konungr ok jarl ok ekki mjǫk sáttir (Afterwards they parted, the king and the earl, and not much at peace).'

12 Modern historians who remark on Tostig's visit to Denmark include: Freeman, *Norman Conquest*, III:330–33, 709–12; Körner, pp. 146–47; F.W. Brooks, p. 7; R. Allen Brown, *The Normans and the Norman Conquest*, 2nd edn (Woodbridge, 1985), p. 119; and Eric Linklater, *The Conquest of England: From the Viking Incursions of the Eighth Century to the Norman Victory at the Battle of Hastings* (New York, 1966), p. 192. Of these, only Körner questions its occurrence.

13 Wace, *Le Roman de Rou*, ed. A.J. Holden (Paris, 1971), II:[120].

14 See the *Anglo-Saxon Chronicle*, (D) 1068, 1071, (E) 1069–70, I:202–07 and Körner, p. 144.

15 *Ágrip af Nóregs konunga sögum*, ed. F. Jónsson (Halle, 1929), p. 41; Theodoricus, *Monumenta historica Norvegiæ: Latinske kildeskrifter til Norges historie I middelalderen*, ed. G. Storm (Christiana (Oslo), 1880), p. 56; *Fagrskinna*, pp. 134–35; *Morkinskinna*, pp. 110–11; Snorri Sturluson, *Heimskringla*, III:173–75; and *Flateyjarbók*, III:387–88.

friends with Sveinn Estriðson, whose occupation of the Danish throne was an offense to Haraldr, despite the now peaceful relations between the two, such an alliance with the Norwegian king definitely would have been impossible, but now that he and Sveinn were no longer on friendly terms, Tostig Godwinson was welcomed into Norway.[16]

Tostig, working on Haraldr Harðraði's pride, persuaded the Norwegian king to join him in a conquest of England. According to the *Ágrip* and Theodoricus, Tostig promised that if Haraldr provided the men and money for the invasion, he would provide English support. When they had defeated Harold Godwinson and expelled him, Haraldr Harðráði would reign as king over half of England, with Tostig taking the other half.[17] According to Snorri Sturluson, Tostig did not promise the Norwegian king half of England, although he did promise his support and that of 'the majority of the chieftains.'[18] Instead, after Haraldr Harðráði had cautioned Tostig 'that the Norwegians would not be willing to travel to England and make war and have an English leader over them,' adding that 'many people say . . . that there are no English who are very trustworthy,'[19] the earl reminded the king of Norway that the throne of England should actually have been his. Because Magnús, Haraldr's cousin and co-ruler of Norway, had made a treaty with Harðaknútr which made him that English king's heir, Haraldr was the rightful inheritor to the throne taken by Harold Godwinson.[20] Some discussion followed, until Tostig prodded the king with this effusive challenge:

> It is certain to everyone that no warrior had ever been born in Scandinavia equal to you; and it seems to me strange that you have fought for fifteen years against Denmark, and you will not take England which now lies free for you.[21]

---

[16] All of the sources in n. 15 above indicate the welcome response of Haraldr Harðráði for Tostig Godwinson. Other sources which also indicate a favorable response when the two met include Orderic Vitalis, II:142–43; William of Jumièges, pp. 162–63; Adam of Bremen, p. 196; William of Malmesbury, *Gesta regum Anglorum*, I:420–21; and Saxo Grammaticus, *Historia Danica*, ed. P.E. Müller and J.M. Velschow (Hannover, 1839), II:555.

[17] *Ágrip*, p. 41, and Theodoricus, p. 56. See also Körner, p. 150.

[18] *Heimskringla*, III:174: 'meiri hlutr höfðingja.' The *Fagrskinna*, *Morkinskinna*, and *Flateyjarbók* do not contain a promise of aid made by Tostig.

[19] The quote comes from Snorri Sturluson, *Heimskringla*, III:173:
Konungr segir svá, at Norðmenn munu þess ekki fýsa at fara til Englands ok herja ok hafa enskan höfðingja yfir sér. 'Mæla menn þat,' segir hann, 'at þeir inir ensku sé ekki alltrúir.'

[20] *Fagrskinna*, 134–35; *Morkinskinna*, pp. 110–11; Snorri Sturluson, *Heimskringla*, III:174; and *Flateyjarbók*, III:387–88. The *Ágrip* (p. 36), Theodoricus (pp. 46, 48), and the *Chronicon Roskildense* (in *Scriptores minores historiae Danicae medii aevi*, ed. C. Gertz (Copenhagen, 1917–18), I:22) all contain a more chronological account of this agreement; this is missing from the *Fagrskinna*, *Morkinskinna*, *Heimskringla*, and *Flateyjarbók*. On the Norwegian kings, Magnús' and Haraldr's, claim to the English throne see Körner (pp. 146–51), who does not think much of its historicity, and Brown (*The Normans and the Norman Conquest*, p. 119), who believes that at least Haraldr Harðráði thought that he had a claim to the English throne.

[21] The quote comes from Snorri Sturluson, *Heimskringla*, III:174:
Þat vitu allir menn, at engi hermaðr hefir slíkr fœðzk á Norðrlǫndum sem þú, ok þat

This was obviously not the difficult argument that Tostig Godwinson had had with Sveinn Estriðson. As Snorri Sturluson attests:

> King Haraldr considered carefully what the earl had said, and realized that he said much truth; and besides he was eager to have this kingdom.[22]

One cannot discount the fact that it was Haraldr's mental and emotional nature to fight wars. He had done it all his life. He was a 'Viking hero,' by reputation among his subjects, by fear among his opponents, by deed among historians and saga writers, and especially in his own mind. He needed to conquer lands and to raid and plunder. Perhaps he also needed to die in battle to fulfil his Viking destiny.

Moreover, Tostig was correct. England was an alluring target for conquest. Haraldr Harðráði, like William of Normandy and Sveinn Estriðson, had a claim on the English throne. He had become convinced that an agreement between Harðaknútr and Magnús had made the Norwegian kings legitimate heirs to the throne of England, certainly at Edward the Confessor's death, if not before. Furthermore and perhaps most importantly, Haraldr was the descendant of and successor to Scandinavians who always thought of attacking England. He was tired of vainly fighting the Danes, and he looked to England as a new land for conquest. He agreed to accompany the deposed earl to England.

Yet did this meeting even take place? Several prominent scholars of late Anglo-Saxon England, namely Edward A. Freeman, F.W. Brooks, William E. Kapelle, and Ian W. Walker, doubt that it did.[23] First, the lack of non-Scandinavian sources recording such a meeting being held in Norway presents somewhat of a problem. In fact, there are no Scandinavian sources beyond the Norwegian Kings' Sagas which refer to such an encounter, with Adam of Bremen and Saxo Grammaticus noting only that Tostig Godwinson met Haraldr Harðráði, and reporting Tostig's promise to provide Haraldr with soldiers and homage, but not recording where or when the meeting took place.[24] Then there is William of Malmesbury's claim that it was not until he met Haraldr in the Humber River that Tostig 'gave him his fealty'.[25] This often very trustworthy source suggests then that no earlier meeting had taken place.

Second, what benefit did Haraldr Harðráði gain from an alliance with Tostig?

þykki mér undarligt, er þú barðisk fimmtán vetr til Danmerkr, en þú vill eigi hafa England, er nú liggr laust fyrir þér.
Although not using these words, the other long Norwegian Kings' Sagas contain the same sentiment.

[22] Snorri Sturluson, *Heimskringla*, III:174:
Haraldr konungr hugsaði vandliga, hvat jarl mælti, ok skilði, at hann segir mart satt, ok í annan stað gerðisk hann fúss til at fá ríkit.

[23] Freeman, *Norman Conquest*, III:329; F.W. Brooks, pp. 7–8; Kapelle, p. 102; and I. Walker, p. 154.

[24] See nn. 15–16 above for these references.

[25] William of Malmesbury, *Gesta regum Anglorum*, I:420–21:

In the words of William E. Kapelle, 'it is hard to see how [Tostig's] recorded exploits could have helped [Haraldr Harðráði].'[26] Especially as Tostig was unable to provide the assistance which he promised, as will be seen, something which these historians affirm that the Norwegian king should have anticipated, there seems to be absolutely no reason for the two to have united for this military expedition. It is much easier to believe that the Norwegian invasion of England was Haraldr's scheme alone, and that his alliance with Tostig Godwinson was but an afterthought made only when the two met for the first time, probably in Scotland or Northumbria.

However, if these historians are correct and no Norwegian meeting was held between Haraldr Harðráði and Tostig Godwinson, what is to be done with the six Norwegian Kings' Sagas, some written in the twelfth century, which claim that he did? Simply declaring their accounts of this meeting to be fiction places a lot of belief on the accuracy of the other sources, most of which are silent to any of Tostig's movements not actually taking place in England (the *Anglo-Saxon Chronicle*, John of Worcester, Henry of Huntingdon, William of Poitiers, etc.), two of which indicate a meeting taking place with elements that are similar to those given in the Norwegian Kings' Sagas, i.e. Tostig's obeisance and promise of support, but not indicating where their meeting took place (Adam of Bremen and Saxo Grammaticus), and one which insists that the meeting took place only at the Humber River, but which has other flaws, namely not naming the correct Norwegian king (William of Malmesbury). Add to this John of Worcester's curious statement that when Tostig joined his fleet to Haraldr Harðráði's at the Tynemouth, it was 'as they had previously planned.'[27] Finally, there is the obviously troublesome account of Orderic Vitalis. Orderic, as has been seen, claimed that the deposed earl visited William of Normandy and then, unable to land in England because of the lack of forces and unable to return to Normandy because of bad weather, journeyed northeast and met with Haraldr Harðráði. He gives this account of Tostig's visit:

> As he [Tostig] was well received by the king [Haraldr Harðráði] and saw that he could not possibly fulfil the promises he had made to Duke William, he changed his plans and declared: 'Great king, I approach your throne as a suppliant, offering myself and my service in good faith to your majesty, in the hope of being restored by your aid to the honour which is mine by right of inheritance. For Harold my brother, who ought rightly to obey me as the first-born, has treacherously risen against me and presumptuously on false pre-

---

Eodem anno [1066] Tostinus, a Flandria in Humbram . . . ibi regi Noricorum Haroldo Haruagrae obuio manus dedit . . .
The *Anglo-Saxon Chronicle* (D and E) 1066, I:197) seem to agree with William on this point, except that it gives the impression that the two met initially in Scotland and not on the Humber.

26 Kapelle, p. 102.

27 John of Worcester, II:602–03: 'ut prius condixerant.' This is my translation, as I think that Bray and McGurk unnecessarily confuse the issue by translating the plural verb singularly and assigning it solely to Tostig.

tences made himself king of England. Therefore I seek help from you as your liegeman, knowing that you have a strong army and every military virtue. Destroy my brother's upstart strength in war, keep half England for yourself, and let me have the other half to hold as your faithful vassal as long as I live.' At once he ordered the army to be gathered together, weapons of war prepared, and the royal fleet fitted out for six months. The wandering exile incited the tyrant to this great task and misled him thus by using his wits to avoid being imprisoned as a spy, and further to secure the king's aid to avenge his unjust expulsion by his faithless brother.[28]

It is true that there are numerous errors in this account, also mentioned above, but as this Anglo-Norman ecclesiastical writer records the promise of Tostig as that reported exactly in the *Ágrip* and by Theodoricus and some of his speech as related in the *Fagrskinna*, *Morkinskinna*, *Heimskringla*, and *Flateyjarbók*, and as he places this meeting before Haraldr had outfitted his invasion fleet, thus taking place in Norway, his corroboration of the Norwegian Kings' Sagas cannot be ignored.

Still, this fails to adequately answer why an alliance with Tostig would have profited the Norwegian king. That the idea of an invasion did not occur to Haraldr before the advent of Tostig probably underestimates the martial desires of the 'hard-ruler,' especially if he had known before of his claim to the English throne, although the news of Edward's death might not yet have reached Norway. Nor is Tostig's promise of English support a compelling answer, although there is no reason that the king should have suspected that such support would not be forthcoming. However, there is another possibility, as pointed out by Frank M. Stenton, F.W. Brooks, Erik Linklater, R. Allen Brown, Miles W. Campbell, William W. Kapelle, Ian W. Walker, and Jim Bradbury: one of Tostig's early supporters, the only one named beyond Haraldr Harðráði, was a fellow-exile named Copsig (or Copsi). The reason for his exile is unknown, although it too took place in 1065. Copsig joined his own seventeen ships to Tostig's fleet sometime before the two attacked England. These ships, it is reported by Geoffrey Gaimar, came from the Orkney Islands, then under the

---

28 Ordericus Vitalis, II:142–45:

Cui cum ab eo honorifice susceptus fuisset, uidens quod promissa quae Willelmo duci fecerat complere non posset mutata intentione ait, 'Sullimitatem uestram magnifice rex supplex adeo, et me seruitiumque meum maiestati uestrae fideliter offero utpossim restitui per uestrum suffragium honori ex paterna successione debito. Nam Heraldus frater meus qui iure michi utpote primogenito debuisset parere, fraudulenter insurrexit contra me et regnum Angliae periuriis praesumpsit usurpare. Vnde a uobis quos uiribus et armis omnique probitate praecipue uigere cognosco uiriliter adiuuari utpote homo uester exposco. Proteruiam perfidi fratris bello proterite, medietatem Angliae uobis retinete aliamque michi qui uobis inde fideliter seruiam dum aduixero optimete.' His auditis auidus rex ualde gauisus est. Deinde iussit exercitum aggregari, bellica instrumenta praeparari et regiam classem per sex menses diligenter in omnibus aptari. Erroneus exul ad tantum laborem tirannum exciuit, eumque callida tergiuersatione taliter illexit ne ab eo quasi explorator regni sui caperetur, sed ut per eum quoquomodo iniuriam expulsionis suae de malefido fratre ulcisceretur.

control of the Norwegians and Haraldr Harðráði. As Stenton writes, '[Haraldr's] approval must have been necessary before even so small a force as this could leave the islands.'[29] Is it not possible that Copsig might have been the link between Tostig Godwinson and the king of Norway, that he could have suggested the alliance and even confirmed the possibility of Tostig's promised assistance in England? The sources do not say; but at the least it must be recognized that some interaction between Tostig and Haraldr had taken place before they both launched their separate attacks on the kingdom of Harold Godwinson, and that the likely spot for this interaction and the consequent plan for the invasion of England was Norway.

There is another question concerning the visit of Tostig Godwinson and Haraldr Harðráði curiously missing from the criticism of those who question the meeting's credibility. Did Tostig have time to travel throughout northern Europe looking for a military benefactor? It is generally assumed that Tostig began his journeys sometime after his brother ascended to the English throne, on 6 January 1066, but no other date is given in any source relating to this Godwinson or his travels until Tostig's attack of southern England 'soon after' 24–31 April when the *Anglo-Saxon Chronicle* (C and D) and John of Worcester report that the comet later known as Halley's Comet 'blazed in great splendor' across the skies of England.[30] Could Tostig have travelled from Flanders to Normandy to Denmark to Norway and then back to Flanders in time to attack the Isle of Wight sometime in May or, probably at the latest, early June? A conclusion really depends on the conjecture of how fast someone could travel on sea in the winter and spring months of the eleventh century. From sagas which detail naval voyages, such as the various Vinland Sagas, it certainly seems to have been possible.[31]

Although the Norwegian Kings' Sagas do not actually say what Haraldr and Tostig's plan for attack was, there are a couple of details that are reported: that the two spent much time together discussing what was to occur, and that ultimately they decided that the attack should take place at the end of summer.[32] After that, Tostig left the king and returned to Flanders. Snorri Sturluson reports that this was to 'meet with the troops who had followed him out of England, and

---

[29] Stenton, p. 587; F.W. Brooks, p. 9; Linklater, pp. 192–93; Kapelle, p. 103; Campbell, 'Note sur les déplacements de Tostig Godwinson,' p. 8; Brown, *The Normans and the Norman Conquest*, p. 123; I. Walker, p. 155; and Bradbury, *Battle of Hastings*, p. 125. Gaimar (I:219) is the only source which mentions this addition to Tostig's fleet, but his accuracy here has not been questioned.

[30] *Anglo-Saxon Chronicle* (C and D) 1066, I:194–95 and John of Worcester, II:600–01. This is the comet which is so prominent in the *Bayeux Tapestry*. The words 'sona þar (þer) æfter'/'non multo post' are used in each of these sources to date the attacks of Tostig on the southern coast of England in relation to the coming of the comet.

[31] *The Vinland Sagas*, ed. H. Hermannsson, Islandica, 30 (Ithaca, 1944). Other sagas detailing naval travel between Scandinavia and England also show that this journey is possible.

[32] *Fagrskinna*, p. 135; *Morkinskinna*, p. 111; Snorri Sturluson, *Heimskringla*, III:174; and *Flateyjarbók*, III:390.

others who had gathered to him both from England and there in Flanders,'[33] but it may also have been a part of his and Haraldr's plan for invasion, for Tostig's first strike was not to be in Northumbria, where he eventually would join with the Norwegian force, but on the Isle of Wight, on the southern coast of England.

Little more is known of the plan for conquest. However, from some of the sources a few details about the preparations for the invasion can be obtained. It can be determined from the Norwegian Kings' Sagas, for example, that Haraldr Harðráði mustered the customary 'half of his army,' the same number which he had taken so frequently on his invasions of Denmark.[34] It can also be seen in the same sources that there was some reluctance among the Norwegian soldiers, who feared their English opponents, especially the English huscarls.[35] From Orderic Vitalis, it is known that the whole preparation process took six months,[36] and in several sources it is recorded that when finished Haraldr Harðráði had an army so large that it filled no less than two hundred and perhaps more than five hundred ships.[37] According to analysis done by Miles W. Camp-

---

33 Snorri Sturluson, *Heimskringla*, III:175:

> Tósti jarl sigldi um várit vestr til Flæmingjalands mót liði því, er honum hafði fylgt útan af Englandi, ok því öðru, er samnaðisk til hans bæði af Englandi ok þar í Flæmingjalandi.

None of the other Norwegian Kings' Sagas report that Tostig returned to Flanders after his visit with Haraldr in Norway, although that is undoubtedly what he did, to judge from his later actions on the southern coast of England. Surely he would have returned to tell Judith what had occurred and of his future plans; it would be the last time he would see her alive. See also Linklater, pp. 193–94.

34 *Fagrskinna*, p. 135; *Morkinskinna*, p. 111; Snorri Sturluson, *Heimskringla*, III:174; and *Flateyjarbók*, III:390. On this number being mustered against Denmark see the chapter 'Haraldr Harðráði', nn. 154, 167, above.

35 *Fagrskinna*, p. 135; *Morkinskinna*, p. 111; Snorri Sturluson, *Heimskringla*, III:174–75; and *Flateyjarbók*, III:390. See also n. 7 of the chapter 'The English Military' above and Freeman, *Norman Conquest*, III:333–34.

36 Orderic Vitalis, II:144–45.

37 The following tally of ships are reported in these sources (from lowest to highest): 200 (*Morkinskinna*, p. 112; Snorri Sturluson, *Heimskringla*, III:176; and *Flateyjarbók*, III:388 – although it has been suggested that if this number were based on Old Norse numbering systems the total would actually be 240, for this see Miles W. Campbell, 'An Inquiry into the Troop Strength of King Harald Hardrada's Invasion Fleet of 1066,' *American Neptune* 44 (1984), 97); 300 (*Anglo-Saxon Chronicle* (D and E) 1066, I:197; Henry of Huntingdon, pp. 386–87; and William of Malmesbury, *Gesta regum Anglorum*, I:420–21); 470+ (Geoffrey Gaimar, I:221); and 500+ (John of Worcester, II:602–03 and Symeon of Durham, *Historia regum*, II:180). The lower number given by the Norwegian Kings' Sagas is counted before Haraldr Harðráði set sail from Norway, the higher number recorded by English and Anglo-Norman sources is from Haraldr's total after he had reached the coast of England and may reflect added vessels from the Orkney Islands and Scotland. Most modern historians attach a number of 300 to the Norwegian fleet. See Stenton, *Anglo-Saxon England*, p. 588; Linklater, p. 196; Douglas, *William the Conqueror*, p. 193; I. Walker, p. 155; Per Sveaas Andersen, *Samlingen av Norge og kristningen av landet, 800–1300* (Bergen, 1977), p. 166; and A.L. Thompson, 'The Battle of Stamford Bridge 1066,' *British Army Review* 97 (Apr. 1991), 49. Variations between 200 and 500 can be found in Freeman, *Norman Conquest*, III:340; F.W. Brooks, p. 7; R. Allen Brown, *The Normans and the Norman Conquest*, p. 134; Campbell,

bell, a fleet of 250 Norwegian ships, at between 44 and 48 soldiers per vessel, would have presented an army of 11,000 to 12,000;[38] F.W. Brooks' estimate is a larger, 18,000 troops.[39]

While Haraldr Harðráði was amassing his fleet and mustering his men, Tostig Godwinson had begun an assault on his homeland. According to the Norwegian Kings' Sagas, Tostig and Haraldr had decided to invade England at the end of summer. Their meeting spot at that time would be the coast of Tostig's old earldom, Northumbria, and, while it is not recorded in any of the sources, it is generally assumed that this had always been their targeted landfall. However, Tostig did not wait until the end of summer to set sail from Flanders; instead he set sail, as mentioned, in May or early June, and he sailed not northeast to the Northumbrian coast, but northwest across the English Channel to the Isle of Wight. Here he attacked and raided several villages and destroyed several homes. Then he followed the sea-coast northeast to Sandwich, raiding and plundering along the shore, making the people pay tribute, and pressing soldiers and sailors into his service. John of Worcester relates the story:

> Not much later, Earl Tostig, returning from Flanders, landed on the Isle of Wight, and having forced the islanders to pay tribute and maintenance, departed and raided along the sea-coast as far as Sandwich . . . [Tostig] retreated, taking some of the seamen (*butsecarls*) with him, whether they wished to go or not.[40]

'An Inquiry into the Troop Strength,' p. 97; C.R.B. Barrett, *Battles and Battlefields in England* (London, 1896), pp. 2–3; Alex. D.H. Leadman, *Proelia Eboracensia: Battles Fought in Yorkshire Treated Historically and Topographically* (London, 1891), p. 7; and Guy Schofield, 'The Third Battle of 1066,' *History Today* 16 (1966), 689.

[38] Campbell, 'An Inquiry into the Troop Strength,' pp. 96–102. While seemingly quite large, Campbell's numbers may in fact be quite conservative as he takes the lowest number of ships found in the original sources and he bases the numbers on board on the relatively small vessels which have been excavated, the Oseberg and Gokstad ships.

[39] F.W. Brooks, pp. 10–11. His tally comes from three hundred ships, at a calculation of more than 50 men per vessel. Ian Walker's count of only 7,500 is based on a too conservative estimate of 25 men on each of the 300 ships (p. 162). He bases this on no evidence that I could find.

[40] John of Worcester, II:600–601:
   Non multo post, comes Tostius de Flandria rediens, ad Vectam Insulam applicuit; et postquam insulanos sibi tributum et stipendium solvere coegerat, discessit et circa ripas maris donec ad Sandicum portum veniret, praedas exercuit . . . de butsecarlis quosdam volentes quosdam nolentes.
See also *Anglo-Saxon Chronicle* (C and D) 1066, I:194–97; Symeon of Durham, II:179; Geoffrey Gaimar, I:219; and *Carmen de hastingae proelio*, ed. C. Morton and A. Muntz (Oxford, 1972), pp. 10–11. (None of the Scandinavian sources mention these attacks.) While John of Worcester calls the men pressed into service by Tostig 'butsecarls,' the *Anglo-Saxon Chronicle* uses the term 'liðe,' a more general military term, to describe them. They were probably members of the 'fyrd,' although some might well have had the ability to perform the more specialized 'butsecarl' service. See also Freeman, *Norman Conquest*, III:324–26; Stenton, *Anglo-Saxon England*,pp. 586–87; Brown, *The Normans and the Norman Conquest*, p. 123; Kapelle, p. 103; Linklater, pp. 191–94; Douglas, *William the Conqueror*, p. 190; I.

When Harold Godwinson received news of Tostig's plundering, he levied the huscarls, fyrd, and butsecarls from his southernmost earldoms on the southern coast of England, 'so many naval and land hosts,' claims the *Anglo-Saxon Chronicle* (C and D), 'that no king before had ever gathered so many'.[41] By this time Tostig, who had heard of his brother's approach and did not wish to face him in battle with such a small force, had sailed north to rendezvous with Haraldr Harðráði. However, Harold Godwinson remained on his kingdom's south coast, for he had received intelligence reports that William of Normandy had amassed an invasion force and was ready to set sail against England. Perhaps the English king felt that the real threat to the security of his throne came from Normandy. Maybe he believed that Tostig's moves along the coast were but minor hindrances. Perhaps he also did not know of his brother's alliance with the king of Norway. Finally, if he did know of or suspected an alliance between his brother and Haraldr Harðráði, maybe he thought that Edwin and Morkere could effectively oppose them, either defeating their attacks, or at least inhibiting them until the king could march to their relief with reinforcements.

Initially, this is exactly what the two northern earls did. For once Tostig left Sandwich and the southern coast of England, he traveled to Lindsey, on the coast of Mercia, where he must have assumed that he would be able to continue his raiding and plundering. According to the sources, his fleet numbered sixty ships now, bolstered by those men and vessels which he had captured in the south and also by the arrival of Copsig and his fleet of seventeen ships from the Orkney Islands.[42] However, in Lindsey he was unable to repeat the successful raids of his southern conquests, as Edwin and Morkere were able to 'drive them from their lands.' Geoffrey Gaimar records what occurred there:

Walker, p. 144; F.W. Brooks, p. 9; Campbell, 'Note sur les déplacements de Tostig Godwinson,' p. 8; Bradbury, *Battle of Hastings*, p. 125; Pauline Stafford, *Unification and Conquest: A Political and Social History of England in the Tenth and Eleventh Centuries* (London, 1989), p. 100; and Henry R. Loyn, 'Harold, Son of Godwin,' in *Society and Peoples: Studies in the History of England and Wales, c. 600–1200* (London, 1992), p. 317.

[41] *Anglo-Saxon Chronicle* C and D (1066), I:194–97: 'þa gegadorade he swa mycele scipfyrde 7 eac landfyrde swa nan cinge ær her on lande ne gegaderade.' (The quote is from (C) which differs in (D) only in spelling and word choice.) See also John of Worcester (II:600–01) and Symeon of Durham (*Historia regum*, II:179), both of whom indicate that some of these troops were cavalry, and the *Carmen de hastingae proelio* (pp. 10–11). See also Freeman, *Norman Conquest*, III:325–26, 335–37; Stenton, *Anglo-Saxon England*, p. 587; F.W. Brooks, p. 9; Linklater, p. 194; Brown, *The Normans and Norman Conquest*, p. 123; I. Walker, p. 144; and Bradbury, *Norman Conquest*, p. 125.

[42] See *Anglo-Saxon Chronicle* (C, D, and E) 1066, I:196–97; John of Worcester, II:600–01; Symeon of Durham, *Historia regum*, II:179; Henry of Huntingdon, pp. 386–87; William of Malmesbury, *Gesta regum Anglorum*, II:420–21; Geoffrey Gaimer, I:219–20; Freeman, *Norman Conquest*, III:326–27; Stenton, *Anglo-Saxon England*, p. 587; Stafford, *Unification and Conquest*, p. 100; Linklater, p. 194; Kapelle, p. 102; Brown, *The Normans and the Norman Conquest*, p. 123; Douglas, *William the Conqueror*, p. 190; Loyn, 'Harold, Son of Godwin,' p. 317; I. Walker, p. 145; F.W. Brooks, p. 9; Campbell, 'Note sur les déplacements de Tostig Godwinson,' p. 8; Bradbury, *Battle of Hastings*, p. 125; Leadman, pp. 6–7; and Barrett, p. 2.

They went to Thanet. In that land
Copsig came to meet him,
One of his barons who was bound to him.
He came from the Orkney Islands,
Seventeen ships he had in his charge.
Then they raided in Brunemue;
That country was confounded.
Great damage and great miseries,
Were caused there and elsewhere.
Then they went into the Humber with their navy,
A great raid was made in Lindsey.
Many men were killed there,
Before they left the land.
   The Earl Edwin with a great army,
Came into Lindsey with much speed,
Then he defended that land;
But they had already done much evil.
The Earl Morkere, on the other side,
Defended his land; they were not concerned.
They were on the Humber, close to the sea,
Where he kept them from landing.
But the Flemings, when they had seen this,
Departed, failing Tostig:
Laden, they went back to their land,
With the plunder of the unfortunate English.
With those then who remained,
They turned, then they went away.[43]

---

[43] Geoffrey Gaimar, I:219–20:

> En Taneth vont; en cel pais
> Encontre lui Copsi la vint,
> Vn son baron ki de li tint.
> Il vint del isle de Orkeneie,
> Dis e seit niefs out en baillie.
> Puis corurent en Brunemue;
> Cele contre ont confundue.
> Grant damages e grant dolurs,
> Firent iloc e vnc aillurs.
> Puis vont en Humbre od lur nauire,
> Grant praie ont pris en Lindeseie.
> Plusurs homes i vnt oscis,
> Ainz kil turnasent del pais.
>   Li quens Edwine od mult grant ost,
> En Lindeseie vint mult tost,
> Puis lur defent cel pais;
> Mes mult laueient ainz malmis.
> Li quens Morkar, del altre part,

Other sources claim that it was the butsecarls who deserted from Tostig. In either case, he traveled north with his men to rendezvous with King Haraldr Harðráði in what the *Anglo-Saxon Chronicle* (D and E) described as only 'twelve small vessels.'[44] It was a far cry from the 'majority of the chieftains' he had promised to bring to his Norwegian ally.

Tostig's attack of the Isle of Wight and elsewhere along the southern and eastern coasts of England provokes one question: why do it? Why risk an attack on these coasts when in a few weeks he was to join with a large invasion force attacking the northeastern coast. There are, it seems, four possible answers.

First, if one holds entirely to the account of Orderic Vitalis, this might be the place where William the Conqueror gave permission for Tostig to go when the earl became impatient with William's delays in deciding if and when he would invade England.[45] Perhaps William saw this attack as a means to investigate what defensive forces Harold might have in southern England, although that is an assumption without the support of even Orderic, let alone any other source. If this was William's plan, however, it backfired, as Harold did not have any troops or vessels in the south until *after* Tostig made his attacks. Had the exiled English earl and his ally, Haraldr Harðráði, not attacked Northumbria before the duke of Normandy set sail, Harold Godwinson would have been much more prepared for William's onslaught than he was. Also, Orderic claims that Tostig did not return to Normandy after his lack of success in southern England, a lack of success not attested to by other sources, because of bad weather, also not attested to by any other source.[46]

A second possible solution to the question of why Tostig Godwinson attacked the southern coast of England is that he was trying to duplicate his father's return in 1052. As seen above, Godwin began his return from exile at that same spot which Tostig attacked fourteen years later. In 1052 the Isle of Wight was considered to be a base used by pirates and raiders. In 1066 it may also have had the same reputation and, although there is no evidence that Tostig was with Godwin during the earlier attack – only Harold and Leofwine are named in the contemporary narratives, and they had arrived not from Flanders with their

> Defent sa terre; nad reguat.
> Sur Humbre sunt, pres de la mer,
> Dont lur defent lariuer.
> Meis li Flemenc, quant il co virent,
> Emblerent sen, Tosti faillirent:
> Chargez sen vont en lur pais,
> De la pelfe dEngleis chaitifs.
> Od icels done ki remis sunt,
> Saturnerent, puis si sen vont.

[44] *Anglo-Saxon Chronicle* (D and E), I:197: '.xii. snaccum'.
[45] Orderic Vitalis, II:140–43.
[46] I think that this is a decisive flaw in Campbell's 'Note sur les déplacements de Tostig Godwinson,' which rejects the Norwegian Kings' Sagas' chronology of Tostig's travels in 1066 while completely accepting Orderic Vitalis' version in its place.

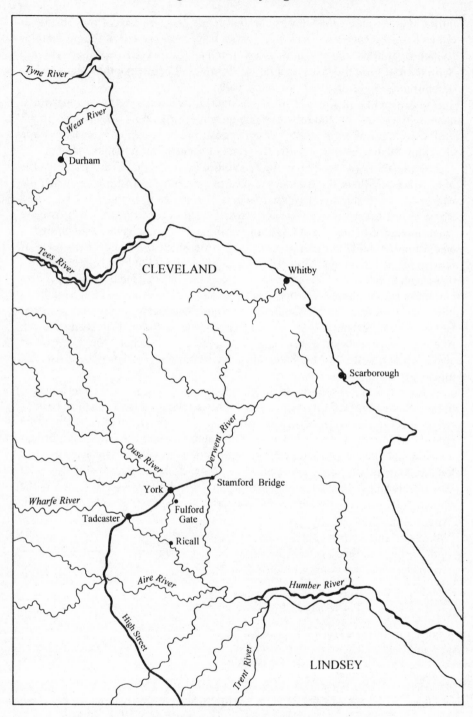

Area of Norwegian Conquest, 1066

father, but from Ireland – undoubtedly he knew the stories of how his father gained troops there and elsewhere in the south of England, and then how he sailed to Sandwich and from there up the Thames to Winchester where he met with the king and regained his former position.[47] Perhaps by repeating what his father had done, Tostig thought that he might be able to make his own way back into power without the need of either William or Haraldr. If he failed, which eventually happened, he still had his alliance with Haraldr Harðráði to fall back on.

Third, even if he was not able precisely to duplicate what his father had done, Tostig undoubtedly thought that he would be able to raise troops from his raids there, the 'majority of the chieftains' whom he had promised to Haraldr Harðráði. This, to judge from the size of his fleet when he left the region, sixty ships, was just what he did, although it is uncertain how many of these adherents were there out of fear, being pressed into service, rather than by choice. This, according to the *Anglo-Saxon Chronicle* (D and E), became a problem when Tostig faced Edwin and Morkere in Lindsay: those pressed into service simply 'deserted him.'[48]

A final solution to why Tostig attacked the southern coast of England is that this was part of the plan devised by him and Haraldr Harðráði. Not solely to acquire extra troops (if the Norwegian invasion army was as large as Miles W. Campbell or F.W. Brooks calculate, those extra soldiers which Tostig could add, especially if they were there against their will, would hardly have mattered), these attacks were diversionary measures meant to draw King Harold Godwinson and his royal army and navy away from Northumbria and the main invasion target of himself or Haraldr Harðráði. As such, their strategy was simple: the Norwegians needed to land unhindered on the English coast. Any military opposition, on sea or on the shore, would lessen their ability to successfully land. Once landed, the Norwegian army also had a much better chance of success if it could divide the English defensive force into two parts, then face first the northern troops and afterwards the larger southern army, especially if, in the meantime, Tostig might be able to add some of his old subjects, mostly Anglo-Scandinavians, to their ranks. This could be the reason why John of Worcester and Symeon of Durham claim that Tostig waited in the south only until he learned that his brother, Harold, had mustered his army and navy and was proceeding southwards against him. It could also be the reason why Tostig chanced landing at Lindsey, knowing that he would face Edwin and Morkere. Perhaps he was reconnoitering their strength and ability. In this case, the sources, such as the *Anglo-Saxon Chronicle* and Geoffrey Gaimar who see the Lindsey fight as a failure of the former earl, are in error. Certainly it was a disappointment to lose to these forces, although it seems that Tostig fled before he

---

47 See nn. 101–02 in the chapter 'Godwin and his Family' above.
48 *Anglo-Saxon Chronicle* (D and E) 1066, I:197. Both chronicles use the same words with some variant spellings: 'þa butsacarlas hine forsocan.' Identified as 'butsecarls,' these were definitely not the Flemings whom Geoffrey Gaimar claimed deserted Tostig.

encountered them; semantically this might have been a defeat, but more accurately it was not an engagement. This is, of course, all conjecture, as no plan of Haraldr's and Tostig's is recorded, but it did happen exactly this way. Thus if it was their plan, it worked very well; if it was not their plan, their strategy seems to have been incredibly flexible.

Haraldr may have been torn by his decision to invade England. On the one hand, while it appears that both the Norwegian King Magnús Olafsson and the Danish King Sveinn Estriðson may have previously desired to invade England because of their perceived inheritance claims, no one had successfully attacked the island for fifty years, since Knútr the Great came from Denmark in 1016. On the other hand, neither of those two kings had been as strong, as experienced, or as confident in military matters as was Haraldr Harðráði. He also had a member of the English royal family allying with him, with Tostig willing to commit treason against his brother, King Harold Godwinson. Surely Haraldr must have concluded that the endeavor could not fail, and in the end he would be able to add both to his land holdings and to his heroic renown.

However, in concluding this, Haraldr Harðráði was forced to ignore a number of omens which forecast failure. Three of these omens are recorded in the Norwegian Kings' Sagas. All three omens were poetically given, and all three prophesied of Haraldr's death and his army's demise. The first was given as dream to Gyrðr while the Norwegian invasion fleet was gathering at the Solund Islands off the coast of the More region of Norway. Gyrðr, whose name appears nowhere else in the Norwegian Kings' Sagas, is identified only as a man aboard Haraldr Harðráði's own ship and thus perhaps serving as one of Haraldr's own household troops. He dreamed that he was on the king's ship looking toward the island when a huge troll-woman (in Old Norse *trǫllkrona mikil*) stood in front of him holding a sword (*skálm*) in one hand and a trough (*trog*) in the other. Gyrðr could also see the entire fleet, with a bird, eagles and ravens (*ernir ok hrafner*), perched on every ship's prow. The troll-woman was singing the following song:

> Norway's warrior sea-king
> Has been enticed westward
> To fill England's graveyards;
> It's all to my advantage.
> Birds of carrion follow
> To feast on valiant seamen;
> They know there will be plenty,
> And I'll be there to help them.[49]

[49] Although this omen is contained in part in both the *Morkinskinna* (p. 112) and *Flateyjarbók* (III:389), both of which place it as the second of the three omens, it is most complete in Snorri Sturluson's *Heimskringla* (III:176), where it is listed as the first of the three omens. The troll-woman's poem is the same in each of these sagas, with only variant spellings:

> Vist es, at allvaldr austan
> eggjask vestr at leggja
> mót við marga knútu,

The second omen came in the same place also as a dream, this time to a man named Þórðr who was stationed on a ship anchored close to Haraldr's command vessel. In this dream Þórðr saw the invasion fleet sailing towards the English coast. On the shore he could see the preparations for battle, with the large armies of both sides ordered for battle and a large number of banners flying. In front of the Anglo-Saxon army stood a troll-woman riding a wolf, with the wolf carrying a dead human in its mouth and blood coursing down its jaw (*ok hǫfðu merki mǫrg á lopti, en fyrir liði landsmanna reið trǫllkrona mikill ok sat á vargi, ok hafði vargrinn manns hræ í munni, ok fell blóð um kjaptana*). When the wolf had eaten one of the dead, it grabbed another in its mouth and devoured it too, followed by another and another. Atop the wolf the troll-woman sang this:

> The troll-woman flaunts her crimson
> Shield as battle approaches;
> The troll-woman sees clearly
> The doom awaiting Haraldr.
> With greedy mouth she rends
> The flesh of fallen warriors;
> With frenzied hand she stains
> The wolf's jaws crimson –
> Wolf's jaws red with blood.[50]

The third and final omen was received by King Haraldr Harðráði himself when he was in Þrandheim visiting his brother's tomb. Again it was in the form

> minn snúðr es þat, prúðr.
> Kná valþiðurr velja,
> veit œrna sér beitu,
> steik af stillis haukum
> stafns. Fylgik því jafnan.

Fagrskinna does not contain this omen. I have used the translation of this poem found in Snorri Sturluson, *King Harald's Saga*, trans. M. Magnusson and H. Pálsson (Harmondsworth, 1966), p. 139. See also Freeman, *Norman Conquest*, III:343.

[50] This omen is found in all four of the long Norwegian King's Sagas: *Fagrskinna* (p. 136); *Morkinskinna* (p. 112); Snorri Sturluson, *Heimskringla* (III:177); and *Flateyjarbók* (III:389). In the *Morkinskinna* and *Flateyjarbók* it is the first omen, in the *Heimskringla* it is the second omen, and in the *Fagrskinna* it is the last of the two omens (the *Fagrskinna* includes only two omens). The poem is the same in all of the versions, again with variant spellings:

> Skóð lætr skína rauðan
> skjǫld, es dregr at hjaldri.
> Brúðr sér Aurnis jóða
> ófǫr konungs gǫrva.
> Sviptir sveiflannkjapta
> svanni holdi manna.
> Ulfs munn litar innan
> óðlót kona blóði –
> ok óðlót kona blóði.

I have again used the translation in Magnusson and Pálsson, p. 140. See also Freeman, *Norman Conquest*, III:343.

of a dream. There was no metaphoric message in this dream, as in the other two; instead, St Óláfr merely appeared to Haraldr and delivered this poetic message:

> The warrior King Óláfr
> Won many famous victories;
> I died a man of holiness
> Because I stayed in Norway.
> But now I fear, great Haraldr,
> That death at last awaits you,
> And wolves will rend your body;
> God is not to blame.[51]

Snorri Sturluson writes that 'many other dreams and prophesies were related there and most were foreboding,'[52] but these are the only three written by him or any of the other Norwegian King's Saga writers. They have never been studied by literary scholars, who might make something of the order, or, in the case of these sagas, the varying order. Something also might be made of the status of each of the omen recipients: one from the retinue probably not directly attached to the king, one from the king's men, and finally the king himself. Perhaps more conclusions might be reached. For historical purposes, undoubtedly these were added to the historiography later, although their legendary impact was so strong that they bore repeating in at least three of these sagas. Still, their presence might not only be the literary motif that it obviously is, but very possibly also an indication that some among the Norwegian forces were hesitant about the journey and the invasion.

None of the travels of Tostig in or around England are reported in the Norwegian Kings' Sagas. These sources tend to follow only the journeys of the main Norwegian force led by Haraldr Harðráði. From them it is learned that Haraldr left Norway in August, the time planned by him and Tostig for his departure. He sailed first to the Shetland Islands and then to the Orkney Islands. Both of these island chains, north of Scotland, were held by him, and both added soldiers to his invasion ranks. Several important lords and chieftains also joined him,

---

[51] This omen is also mentioned in all of the long Norwegian King's Sagas: *Fagrskinna* (p. 135); *Morkinskinna* (p. 112); Snorri Sturluson, *Heimskringla* (III:178); and *Flateyjarbók* (III:389). All of them, except for the *Fagrskinna*, list this as the third omen; *Fagrskinna* has it as the first omen. Again the poem is the same in all versions, with variant spellings:

> Gramr vá frægr til fremðar
> flestan sigr enn digri.
> Hlautk, þvít heima sótum,
> heilagt fall til vallar.
> Uggik enn, at, tvggi,
> yðr mani feigð of byrjuð.
> Trolls gefið fókum fyllar
> fiks. Veldra guð slíku.

The translation is from Magnusson and Pálsson, pp. 140–41. See also Freeman, *Norman Conquest*, III:343.

including Þorfinns, the earl of Orkney. In the Orkney Islands Haraldr Harðráði assembled his attack fleet and received provisions and supplies from the islanders for his conquest.[53] He may also have sent Copsig south to meet Tostig and report on the progress of the larger fleet. Haraldr also left his wife, Elizaveta, and at least one daughter, María, and perhaps a second, Ingigerðr, also in the Orkneys.[54]

From the Orkney Islands Haraldr Harðráði sailed south to Dunfermline where he met with Tostig's friend and ally, King Malcolm of Scotland. According to the *Anglo-Saxon Chronicle* (D and E) and Geoffrey Gaimar, sources which do not have Tostig meeting with Haraldr in Norway prior to the invasion, this was where the two first met, Tostig having fled to this land after his defeat in Lindsey earlier in the summer. Scotland was also where Tostig realized that Haraldr Harðráði was his best hope for returning to his former power and position; according to the *Anglo-Saxon Chronicle* (D), it was there that he 'did homage to him and became his man.'[55] The Norwegian Kings' Sagas, joined by the other sources, record nothing about this visit.

According to these sources, Tostig Godwinson was in Scotland when Haraldr Harðráði arrived there. Most other contemporary and near contemporary chronicles assert that Tostig and Haraldr met at Tynemouth on 8 September, 'as they had previously planned,' claims the anonymous author of the *Anglo-Saxon Chronicle* (C).[56] If the Norwegians were expecting Tostig to arrive with a large fleet of his own, they must have been greatly disappointed, for the exiled earl

---

52 Snorri Sturluson, *Heimskringla*, III:178: 'Margir aðir draumer váru þá sagðir ok annars konar fyrirburðir ok flestir daprligir.' None of the other sagas contain this line.

53 *Fagrskinna*, p. 136; *Morkinskinna*, pp. 112–13; Snorri Sturluson, *Heimskringla*, III: 178–79; and *Flateyjarbók*, III:389. See also Freeman, *Norman Conquest*, III:344; Kapelle, p. 103; and Douglas, *William the Conqueror*, p. 190.

54 *Fagrskinna*, p. 136; *Morkinskinna*, p. 112; Snorri Sturluson, *Heimskringla*, III:179; *Flateyjarbók*, III:389. *Fagrskinna*, *Morkinskinna*, and *Flateyjarbók* mention only the daughter, Máriá, being left behind with the queen in the Orkney Islands. Snorri Sturluson mentions both daughters.

55 *Anglo-Saxon Chronicle* (D) 1066, I:197: 'Tostig him to beah. ⁊ his man wearð.' The *Anglo-Saxon Chronicle* (E) (1066, I:197) contains only that Tostig did homage to Haraldr, while Geoffrey Gaimar (I:220) says that Tostig 'honored the king greatly and presented him many gifts'.

56 *Anglo-Saxon Chronicle* (C) 1066, I:196: 'swa hy ær gesprecen hæfdon.' Those reporting that Haraldr met Tostig in Scotland include: *Anglo-Saxon Chronicle* (D and E) 1066, I:197; William of Malmesbury, *Gesta regum Anglorum*, I:420–21; and Geoffrey Gaimar, I:220. Those indicating a later meeting are: *Anglo-Saxon Chronicle* (C) 1066, I:196; John of Worcester, II:602–03; Symeon of Durham, *Historia regum*, II:180; and Orderic Vitalis, II:142–43. Interestingly, the Norwegian Kings' Sagas do not indicate a meeting place for these two allies. Some modern authors agree with Scotland as the meeting place: Kapelle, p. 103; Brown, *Normans and the Norman Conquest*, p. 123: and F.W. Brooks, p. 10. Freeman, *Norman Conquest*, III:344–45; Linklater, p. 198; and Schofield, p. 689, all claim a Tynemouth meeting. It is possible, I suppose, that Tostig had been in Scotland, but had left before Haraldr arrived there and then the two met later at Tynemouth. There is, however, no logical reason why he would have done this.

had barely twelve ships filled with soldiers, and some of those must have been Copsig's. Still, Tostig had shown up, and he had brought some English and even perhaps a few Flemings in his small fleet.[57] Tynemouth had been the area of two rich monasteries, Wearmouth and Jarrow, famous for their role in the Northumbrian Renaissance a few centuries earlier. But in the ninth century they had both been destroyed, some of the first targets of the Viking invaders who had carried off their rich booty. The raids were well known throughout Scandinavia, and in 1066 the ruins of these monasteries must have still been impressive; they must also have stood as monuments to earlier Scandinavian success in England. Undoubtedly, a visit to this place was planned to excite the Norwegians to renewed victory against the island's inhabitants.

The combined forces now sailed south along the Cleveland coast where they disembarked. Tostig, who must have known the area well, had pre-selected a spot of disembarkation which would allow easy access to the inner Northumbria territory, but it did require an overland march, an unusual tactic for Scandinavian armies unused to land travel when there were naval options. The question ought then to be asked: why did they not sail their ships directly up the Humber and Ouse Rivers to the more populous inner Northumbrian earldom? Perhaps Haraldr and Tostig wanted to draw Morkere and Edwin's troops to the coastal region, worrying that a marine invasion would be difficult to launch, with their opponents easily able to defend the shores against a flotilla unloading its soldiers. Perhaps they also wanted to confuse their enemy; after all Edwin and Morkere surely had been tipped off to the invasion plan by Tostig's earlier plundering of the Lindsey villas or by one of his deserting sailors. Yet, in so reckoning, we may be giving the invading generals too much strategic credit. They may also have been looking for adherents, although the region had a very small population. Finally, it is possible that they launched their attack initially along the North Sea coast instead of from the rivers only to give their troops the opportunity to plunder the coastal countryside and to profit from whatever booty they might find there. After all, Haraldr Harðráði's troops had been confined to their ships without being able to take advantage of the fruits of war for several weeks now, while Tostig's troops had already plundered along both the southern and eastern coasts.

Although unknown for certain, from the sources available, Haraldr Harðráði's and Tostig Godwinson's fleet probably landed at the mouth of the Tees River, where according to the Norwegian Kings' Sagas, which are alone in the tracking of the invasion fleet from Scotland to England, the king 'took hostages and tribute from the populace.'[58] Plundering their way down the coast, the

---

[57] The *Anglo-Saxon Chronicle* (E) 1066, I:198, does mention Flemings among the dead at Stamford Bridge.

[58] The *Fagrskinna* (p. 136), *Morkinskinna* (p. 112), and *Flateyjarbók* (III:389–90) all use the same words, 'hann tók af landinu gisla ok skatta,' with Snorri Sturluson *(Heimskringla,* III:179) varying slightly: 'Þar gekk hann á land ok herjaði þegar ok lagði landit undir sik.' See also Freeman, *Norman Conquest,* III:347; Stenton, *Anglo-Saxon England,* p. 588; F.W.

Norwegians encountered their first large English settlement at Scarborough. Here they also met their first resistance. Haraldr demanded the surrender of Scarborough but was refused. This was almost totally unexpected. Scarborough had no fortifications, except for an abandoned Roman signal station (over which a monastic chapel had been built) on the cliff overlooking the sea and the town, which, it seems, the Norwegians held from the outset of the engagement. Moreover, it could not have had a sizeable militia. After all, the total population of the town was only around a thousand, and the numbers of potential warriors, let alone those experienced in war, must have been extremely small. Nevertheless, their defense against the invaders was valiant, for even though Haraldr and Tostig's armies greatly outnumbered the small defending force and eventually defeated them, the inhabitants of Scarborough fought well and kept the invaders from their town for much longer than anyone on either side must have believed possible. Eventually, according to Snorri Sturluson, Haraldr

> climbed up on the hill that was there and had a large pyre built and set alight. And they [the Norwegians] took logs from the blazing fire with forks and threw them onto the dwellings below. One house after another caught fire, until the fire went throughout the whole town.[59]

By doing this, the Norwegians killed a large number of the town's inhabitants. They also built up a reputation for violence which caused other Northumbrian towns and villages to capitulate. Snorri concludes: 'There was no other choice for the English, if they should stay alive, except to put themselves into the hands of King Haraldr. Wherever he traveled, he placed all the land under his control.'[60]

Finally, the invaders were able to continue their march south down the Holderness coast to the Humber River where they rejoined their ships which had sailed on separately. They met with only one more show of resistance in Holderness, but this proved to be an easy victory for them.[61]

Brooks, p. 10; and Bradbury, *Battle of Hastings*, p. 130. Brooks wonders what there was in Cleveland that could have been pillaged.

[59] Snorri Sturluson, *Heimskringla*, III:179:

hann gekk upp á bergit, þat sem þar verðr, ok lét þar gera bál mikit ok leggja í eld. En er bálit logaði, tóku þeir forka stóra ok skutu bálinu ofan í býinn. Tók þá at brenna hvert hús af öðru. Gekk þá upp allr staðrinn.

The other Norwegian Kings' Sagas do not go into this amount of detail on the Scarborough engagement. See also Freeman, *Norman Conquest*, III:347; Linklater, p. 198; F.W. Brooks, p. 11; and Schofield, p. 689. Although this incident is mentioned only in the Norwegian Kings' Sagas, the legend of what Haraldr Harðráði did in 1066 is still spoken of by the people of Scarborough today. See Graham Port, *Scarborough Castle* (London, 1989), pp. 5, 14.

[60] Snorri Sturluson, *Heimskringla*, III:179: 'Var enskum mönnum þá engi kostr fyrir höndum, ef þeir skyldi halda lífinu, nema ganga til handa Haraldi konungi. Lagði hann þá undir sik land allt, þar sem hann fór.' See also Stenton, *Anglo-Saxon England*, p. 588 and Bradbury, *Battle of Hastings*, p. 130.

[61] Snorri Sturluson, *Heimskringla*, III:179, is alone among the Norwegian Kings' Sagas in reporting this. The defenders in Holderness are not named or described by him. See also

Back on their ships, the invading army now sailed on what John of Worcester calls a 'swift course' down the Humber to its end, taking the Ouse branch of the river and disembarking at Ricall, ten miles downriver from York, the capital of Northumbria. King Haraldr and Earl Tostig undoubtedly felt that it would be unwise to sail directly to York as news of their invasion had certainly reached Morkere and Edwin, and the two English earls would probably be prepared for their arrival. After fighting two military engagements along the coast, although minor, not to mention Tostig's earlier assault on Lindsey, there was little chance of surprising the local forces, and thus a different tactic was needed against them. In assuming this, the invading captains were correct. It seems that Morkere had indeed received intelligence of the Norwegian raids in Cleveland and Holderness, and he had easily been able to follow the invading army's progress along the coast. In response, he had mustered the Northumbrian fyrd at York. His brother, Edwin, earl of Mercia, had also gathered forces from his province, and these too had arrived at York.[62]

Before this time, the Norwegian invasion fleet had sailed down the coast and into the interior of Northumbria without any English naval hindrance. The bulk of the Anglo-Saxon fleet, never very large, was in the south of England, recently freed from their obligations waiting for William the Conqueror's invasion across the Channel. What about the remnants of the fleet which might have stayed north? Edward A. Freeman, reading in the *Anglo-Saxon Chronicle* (C) that Harold Godwinson, in arriving at Tadcaster on the Wharfe River on his march north to oppose Haraldr Harðráði, found his *lið fylcade*, translated this as the naval force of Northumbria, which had apparently sailed up the Wharfe River either in an effort to avoid the Norwegian ships or to hopefully trap them on the Ouse River by anchoring their flotilla behind the invaders should they have ventured on the river to York.[63] Several other historians have accepted Freeman's thesis here, although at least two translators of the *Anglo-Saxon Chronicle*, G.N. Garmonsway and Dorothy Whitelock (she the principal of three translators), saw these as little more than 'household troops' which were either those brought with Harold (Garmonsway) or the remnants of the Northhmbrian and Mercian

---

Freeman, *Norman Conquest*, III:347; Stenton, *Anglo-Saxon England*, p. 588; Linklater, p. 198; F.W. Brooks, p. 11; and Bradbury, *Battle of Hastings*, p. 130.

[62] Many original sources mention this, although only John of Worcester (II:602–03) and Symeon of Durham (II:180) identify the disembarking spot as Ricall. Geoffrey Gaimar (I:221) identifies the place of landing as St Wilfrid's, although this is generally believed to be the name of a nearby church rather than a place-name (no such place-name on the Humber, Wharfe, or Ouse Rivers is known to exist). Other original sources which mention this part of the invasion are: *Anglo-Saxon Chronicle* (C, D, and E) 1066, I:196–97; Henry of Huntingdon, pp. 386–87; *Fagrskinna*, p. 136; *Morkinskinna*, p. 113; Snorri Sturluson, *Heimskringla*, III:179; and *Flateyjarbók*, III:390. Secondary sources discussing this include: Freeman, *Norman Conquest*, III:347–48; Stenton, *Anglo-Saxon England*, pp. 588–89; Linklater, p. 198; Brown, *The Normans and the Norman Conquest*, p. 134; F.W. Brooks, pp. 10–11; Bradbury, *Battle of Hastings*, p. 130; I. Walker, p. 155; and Schofield, pp. 689–91.

[63] Freeman, *Norman Conquest*, III:347–48. The reference to the *Anglo-Saxon Chronicle* (C) 1066 is found on I:197.

troops who had lost at the battle of Fulford Gate (Whitelock).[64] In support of Freeman, however, it should be pointed out that this version of the *Anglo-Saxon Chronicle* often uses *lið* in a naval context. Additionally, a naval presence at Tadcaster does give a plausible reason for the Norwegians not sailing further up the Ouse River. By stopping at Ricall, the Norwegians in essence had trapped the Northumbrian vessels on the Wharfe and rendered them inoperable for any military hindrance of their invasion.

A short time after learning of the landing of the invaders at Ricall, Morkere and Edwin, having gathered 'as great a force as they could from their earldoms,' according to the *Anglo-Saxon Chronicle* (C),[65] prepared their troops for battle and marched out of York. It was 20 September. On that day, two miles south of the town, at a place identified by Symeon of Durham as 'on the northern shore of the Ouse River at Fulford,'[66] was fought the first of the three battles which in a little more than three weeks would decide the fate of England.

Although Henry of Huntingdon reports that in his time, 'the site of the battle is still pointed out on the south side of the city,'[67] today Fulford Gate is a densely inhabited suburb of York, and so it is difficult to see what the topography was on which the two sides were fighting. Nor do the original sources assist us here, for they describe little of the terrain, except for the presence of the river on one side of the battlefield, obviously the southern side if Symeon of Durham is to be believed, with a dike and swamp possibly on the other side, according to the Norwegian Kings' Sagas.[68] Both of these features determined the tactics used by both sides in the fighting. There was also a road on which both the English and Norwegian troops traveled running somewhere through the battlefield, perhaps forming the dike mentioned in the Norwegian Kings' Sagas,[69] but except as a conduit to the battle, it did not figure in the battle.

The sources are also confusing on which army arrived first on and thus chose

---

[64] Those who agree with Freeman include: Stenton, *Anglo-Saxon England*, pp. 588–89; Brown, *The Normans and the Norman Conquest*, p. 134 n. 66; and Schofield, p. 691. Garmonsway's translation of the *Anglo-Saxon Chronicle* is *The Anglo-Saxon Chronicle*, trans. G.N. Garmonsway (London, 1953), p. 197; Whitelock's is *The Anglo-Saxon Chronicle*, trans. D. Whitelock, D.C. Douglas, and S.I. Tucker (London, 1961), p. 144. A third translator of the *Anglo-Saxon Chronicle*, Michael Swanton, agrees with Freeman's translation of this passage (*The Anglo-Saxon Chronicle*, trans. and ed. M. Swanton (New York, 1998), p. 197).

[65] *Anglo-Saxon Chronicle* (C) 1066, I:196: 'þa gegaderode Eadwine eorl ⁊ Morkere eorll of heora eorldome swa mycel werod swa hi begitan mihton.'

[66] Symeon of Durham (*Historia regum*, II:180) is the only contemporary author who identifies the battlefield to be at Fulford Gate: 'in boreali ripa Usae fluminis juxta Eboracum apud Fulford cum Norreganis praelium commisere . . .' All other sources mention only the distance from the town of York, and as these do not differ with Symeon's position, it is commonly believed that Fulford Gate (or Gate Fulford to some modern historians) is where this battle was fought.

[67] Henry of Huntingdon, pp. 386–87: 'Cuius pugne locus in australi parte urbis adhuc ostenditur.'

[68] *Fagrskinna*, p. 136; *Morkinskinna*, p. 113; Snorri Sturluson, *Heimskringla*, III:179–80; and *Flateyjarbók*, III:390.

[69] This is F.W. Brooks' conclusion (p. 11).

the battlefield and why. While it seems certain from most of the Anglo-Saxon/Anglo-Norman chronicles that the troops of Morkere and Edwin had moved out of York and then ordered their troops at Fulford Gate, a spot which they perhaps had chosen before that day as a good site for a battle to defend York, the Norwegian Kings' Sagas seem to indicate that the English were in the process of marching towards the Norwegian fleet when they were intercepted by Haraldr Harðráði's just disembarked and quickly ordered army.[70]

What is more certain is what happened on the battlefield. For this, there are not only the Norwegian Kings' Sagas whose accounts of the combat are quite detailed, but also the smaller accounts of the more contemporary English and Anglo-Norman sources which confirm what is found in the Norwegian Kings' Sagas. They describe a tactically astute Haraldr Harðráði, who in disembarking from his ships ordered his troops to stretch in a tightly packed battle line from the river on their left flank to the dike on their right flank: 'The king's standard was near the river. It was there that the flank was the thickest, but the thinnest was at the dike, and the army there was the least trustworthy.'[71] Although not naming him as such, in so identifying the soldiers on the dike side, the Norwegian Kings' Sagas obviously are referring to those troops brought to the engagement and commanded by Tostig Godwinson.

However this formation was more than simply a division of command; it was also a ploy to draw a charge from the English line. Should Morkere, who is said to have commanded the English left or dike-ward flank, and Edwin, who commanded opposite Haraldr Harðráði, have decided to hold their position, forming a defensive shield-wall, it undoubtedly would have taken the Norwegians a long time at a high casualty rate to break the English formation. There is even the possibility that the Norwegians might have broken under the strain of continually charging upon such a line, and that the battle might have been lost, despite the obvious greatly superior numbers had by the invaders. By placing the former, hated Northumbrian earl in what appeared to be a vulnerable position, Haraldr was undoubtedly trying to keep the English from forming their shield-wall by provoking them into a charge at their nemesis and his 'untrustworthy army.' Having the replacement earl, Morkere, opposite Tostig was probably not

---

[70] *Anglo-Saxon Chronicle* (C) 1066, I:196; John of Worcester, II:602–03; Symeon of Durham, *Historia regum*, II:180; Henry of Huntingdon, pp. 386–87; William of Malmesbury, *Gesta regum Anglorum*, I:420–21; Geoffrey Gaimar, I:221; *Fagrskinna*, p. 136; *Morkinskinna*, p. 113; Snorri Sturluson, *Heimskringla*, III:179–80; and *Flateyjarbók*, III:390.

[71] I have used the words of *Morkinskinna* (p. 113): 'Konvngs merkit var neer anni. var þar þyccost fylkingin. en þynnzt við díkit. oc þar liþit otravstast.' The other three detailed Norwegian Kings' Sagas use similar words. See *Fagrskinna*, p. 136; Snorri Sturluson, *Heimskringla*, III:180; and *Flateyjarbók*, III:390. The only good secondary source account of the battle of Fulford Gate is Freeman, *Norman Conquest*, III:350–52, and he mainly follows the narrative found in Snorri Sturluson's *Heimkringla*. All other modern authors merely report that the battle was won by the Norwegians. See Stenton, *Anglo-Saxon England*, p. 589; Kapelle, pp. 103–04; Linklater, p. 199; Brown, *The Normans and the Norman Conquest*, pp. 134–35; Bradbury, *Battle of Hastings*, p. 130; and I. Walker, p. 157.

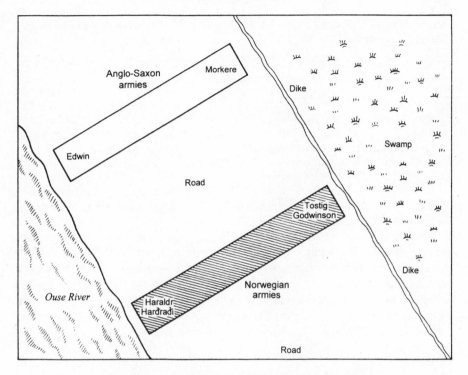

The Battle of Fulford Gate, 20 September 1066

planned by Haraldr, but it added to the effectiveness of his tactics, as the new earl seemed determined to show his superiority over his predecessor.

Morkere's charge was swift and intense. As William of Malmesbury describes it, he and his brother, Edwin, 'feared nothing' after their victory over Tostig's troops in Lindsey, and, either neglectful of or ignoring Haraldr's 'Land--waster' standard which had not earlier been present, while doing the same to the obviously increased numbers of opponents, who also had not been present at Lindsey, their left flank charged rapidly and successfully forward into the Norwegian right flank.[72] John of Worcester reports that the English attacked 'manfully in the first thrust of the battle' and that 'they laid low many.'[73] The Norwegian Kings' Sagas are more descriptive in their narrative:

> The earls charged along the dike, and then the Norwegian flank, which had been placed at the dike, broke, and the English then ran forward after them

---

[72] William of Malmesbury, *Gesta regum Anglorum*, I:420–21: 'germanos recenti uictoria feriatos, qui nichil minus quam talia latrocinia metuerunt.'
[73] John of Worcester, II:602–03: 'In primo belli impetu uiriliter pugnantes, multos prostrauere.' See also Symeon of Durham, *Historia regum*, II:180.

and thought that the Norwegian army would flee. Morkere's standard was there in the front.[74]

However, the other Norwegian flank, positioned next to the river, did not flee. Instead, as apparently he had planned, Haraldr took the initiative and attacked Edwin's force in front of him. The Sagas continue:

> When King Haraldr saw that the English flank which had charged along the dike was opposite him, he ordered his trumpets to sound and, fervently urging his troops forward, he ordered his standard, Land-Waster, to be carried in front. The violent attack was so fierce that everyone in front of it retreated. There was a slaughter of many of the earls' men. His army broke quickly into flight, some fleeing up and down the river, but most of the men leapt over the dike. The dead lay there so thick that the Norwegians could travel with dry feet over the swamp.[75]

Morkere's troops now, too, were in flight, with their leader, the young replacement earl, erroneously reported slain by the Norwegian Kings' Sagas.[76] Some of these soldiers may thus have escaped the slaughter, but Edwin's force was decimated. 'Many more of them were drowned in the river than had fallen in battle,' writes John of Worcester who insists that the English had not fled so easily in the face of the Norwegian attack, but instead fought 'for a long time' before being 'unable to withstand the Norwegian attack.'[77] The invading force

---

[74] I have chosen to use Snorri Sturluson's account (*Heimskringla*, III:180) here, although the other major Norwegian Kings' Sagas contain virtually the same words:

Þá sóttu jarlar ofan með díkinu. Veik þá fyrir fylkingararmr Norðmanna, sá er vissi at díkinu, en enskir menn sóttu þar fram eptir þeim ok hugðu, at Norðmenn mundu flýja vilja. Fór þar fram merki Morukára.

See also *Fagrskinna*, p. 136; *Morkinskinna*, p. 113; and *Flateyjarbók*, III:390.

[75] Again I have used Snorri Sturluson's more colorful description of this battle (*Heimskringla*, III:180), although the other Sagas use almost the same words:

En er Haraldr konungr sá, at fylking enskra manna var komin ofan með díkinu gegnt þeim, þá lét hann blása herblástrinn ok eggjaði herinn ákafliga, lét þá fram bera merkit Landeyðuna, snarað þá atgonguna svá harða, at allt hrökk fyrir. Gerðisk þá mannfall mikit í liði jarla. Snørisk þá liðit brátt á flótta, flýði sumt upp með ánni ok ofan, en flest fólkit hljóp út á díkit. Lá þar svá þykkt valrinn, at Norðmenn máttu ganga þurrfœtis yfir fenit.

See also *Fagrskinna*, p. 136; *Morkinskinna*, p. 113; and *Flateyjarbók*, III:390. On the slaughter of the English see also *Anglo-Saxon Chronicle* (C) 1066, I:196; John of Worcester, II:602–03; Symeon of Durham, *Historia regum*, II:180; and Geoffrey Gaimar, I:221. The slaughter in general and the number of dead in the swamp in particular are the subjects of a number of different poems contained in the various Norwegian Kings' Sagas referred to above.

[76] *Fagrskinna*, p.136; *Morkinskinna*, p. 113; Snorri Sturluson, *Heimskringla*, III:180; and *Flateyjarbók*, III:390.

[77] John of Worcester, II:602–03:

At postquam dui certatum est, Angli Norreganorum impetum non sufferentes, haud sine paruo detrimento suorum terga dedere, multoque plures ex illis in fluuio demersi fuere quam in acie cecidere.

See also Symeon of Durham, *Historia regum*, II:180.

had also undeniably received casualties, although probably not the 'slaughter' of soldiers which the *Anglo-Saxon Chronicle* (C) and Geoffrey Gaimar would have us believe.[78] More importantly, by the end of the day, as Henry of Huntingdon puts it, Haraldr Harðráði and Tostig Godwinson had taken 'the glorious prize of Mars.'[79]

Why did Morkere and Edwin come out of the protection of York and try to fight against the Norwegian invaders? Certainly they were somewhat flushed with the victory that they had won over Tostig in Lindsey, but not much should be made of William of Malmesbury's statement that this is what caused them to perform such a foolish military act. In fact, it was probably not foolish at all, just desperate. Morkere and Edwin had little recourse but to attack the Norwegians. Word had already been sent to King Harold Godwinson in the south,[80] but they probably thought that at best he would not arrive for at least a week, and the two northern English earls reckoned that York could not endure an attack for that long. Morkere and Edwin must have known how large an army Haraldr and Tostig had with them – indeed, Harold Godwinson's force was only about the size of the Norwegian army – and they must also have known that their chances against the larger and more experienced Scandinavian force were almost non-existent. Yet York was a large and prosperous town and needed to be defended.[81] Perhaps a strong show of force at Fulford Gate would keep the invaders from York. After all, had not the inhabitants of Scarborough fought better than could be expected against the Norwegians? And, perhaps when they saw what they perceived as a weakness in the Norwegian line, along the dike where Tostig was in charge of his and other men, a glimmer of hope came to them. If they could cause one flank of the opposing army to give way, perhaps the rest of the army would break and run as well. But in this instance they met their tactical match; Haraldr Harðráði must have planned the situation, and while he perhaps did not tell Tostig of his plans (or could this be called a 'feigned retreat'?), his army was prepared for Morkere's charge. Taking advantage of the disordered breaking of the English line, he swept in, and either in a short time, if the Norwegian King's Sagas' chronology is accepted, or after a long time, if John of Worcester's is believed, the battle of Fulford Gate had been won. It was to be the last Scandinavian victory on English soil.

Haraldr Harðráði and Tostig Godwinson did not pause long on the Fulford Gate battlefield to celebrate their victory. They sent part of their army back to

---

[78] *Anglo-Saxon Chronicle* (C) 1066, I:196 and Geoffrey Gaimar, I:221.

[79] Henry of Huntingdon, pp. 386–87: 'Haraldus uero rex Norwagie et Tosti cum eo Martis omine glorioso potiti sunt.'

[80] This is recorded in almost all of the contemporary or near contemporary chronicles. See, for example, *Anglo-Saxon Chronicle* (C, D, and E) 1066, I:196–97; John of Worcester, II:602–03; Henry of Huntingdon, pp. 386–87; Symeon of Durham, *Historia regum*, II:180; William of Malmesbury, *Gesta regum*, I:420–21; and Geoffrey Gaimar, I:221.

[81] This point is also supported by Ian Walker, p. 157.

protect the ships, with the remainder gathering at the crossroads of Stamford Bridge northeast of York.[82] The inhabitants of York, their defensive forces having failed, sent a message to the Norwegian leaders 'offering themselves and their town to his power,' the Norwegian Kings' Sagas claim.[83] A meeting was held four days later, on Sunday, 24 September, just outside of York.[84] Haraldr and Tostig had brought their entire army, perhaps as affirmation of their power in an effort to thwart any thoughts of defiance. Their terms of surrender were not harsh, and the town was not plundered (although Geoffrey Gaimar insists that the surrounding countryside was pillaged[85]). The Norwegian king and the exiled Northumbrian earl needed troops to make up for those lost at Fulford Gate. They also needed assistance against the main English force led by Harold Godwinson which they presumed was still in the south at the time.[86] Were they to have plundered such a well populated and respected town as York, they would certainly have received no assistance. Besides, this was to be Tostig's new capital, as it had been in the past. The victors merely requested an exchange of hostages with the town and the surrounding countryside, and no further blood was spilled. Not even Edwin, who was captured in York, was put to death. His brother, Morkere, had also survived the battle of Fulford Gate. It can be assumed that Tostig might not have been as merciful to this earl who had replaced him at that post in Northumbria. But Morkere had fled elsewhere.

All was agreed to. According to John of Worcester, 150 of the 'sons of the leading men' of the town and nearby region were to be given to Haraldr and

---

[82] This chronology is established by the Norwegian Kings' Sagas which claim that before Haraldr and Tostig marched to York that they assembled their army at Stamford Bridge. Why Stamford Bridge was chosen by Haraldr rather than Ricall, where he had beached his fleet, is not explained. There is a possibility that he had established a camp there, although this is unclear from the original sources, including but not exclusively the Norwegian Kings' Sagas. A camp at Stamford Bridge does give a reason why it would become the site of so much activity over the next few days, including the battle fought there. See *Fargrskinna*, p. 136; *Morkinskinna*, p. 114; Snorri Sturluson, *Heimskringla*, III:182; and *Flateyjarbók*, III:391.

[83] I have used the words of the *Fagrskinna* (p. 137): 'at bjóða í vald hans sjálfa sik ok svá borgina.' The other Sagas use similar words: *Morkinskinna*, p. 114; Snorri Sturluson, *Heimskringla*, III:182–83; and *Flateyjarbók*, III:391. See also Douglas, *William the Conqueror*, p. 193.

[84] This meeting is detailed only in the Norwegian Kings' Sagas. All other sources are silent as to how and where the surrender proceedings took place.

[85] Geoffrey Gaimar, I:221.

[86] This surrender provision is declared by the *Anglo-Saxon Chronicle* (C) 1066, I:197 who is alone in this assertion: 'to fullan friðe gespræcon þ hig ealle mid him suð faran woldon ⁊ þis land gegan.' Agreeing with this provision has led one historian, William E. Kapelle (pp. 104–05), to view the inhabitants of York as 'traitors,' while another, Dorothy Whitelock ('The Dealings of the Kings of England with Northumbria in the Tenth and Eleventh Centuries,' in *The Anglo-Saxons: Studies in Some Aspects of their History and Culture Presented to Bruce Dickins*, ed. P. Clemoes (London, 1959), p. 80), sees it as continued evidence of Northumbrian resistance to southern English rule.

Tostig, while they would leave 150 of their own men in exchange.[87] The *Anglo-Saxon Chronicle* (C) states that the York hostages were to be delivered the following day to the Norwegians at a predetermined place, Stamford Bridge.[88] Haraldr and Tostig returned to their ships, comforted by their achievement and confident in their continued success. The battle of Fulford Gate was fought on 20 September, and the Norwegians had received the allegiance of the York on 24 September. That night as Haraldr Harðráði and Tostig Godwinson went to sleep, they probably had no idea that the large army of Harold Godwinson was only about seven miles to the west of them.

[87] John of Worcester, II:602–03. John of Worcester and Symeon of Durham (*Historia regum*, II:180), who is using Worcester's chronicle as a source here, are the only sources which note the number of hostages to be exchanged between York and the Norwegians. They also indicate that these hostages were exchanged at the time, while the *Anglo-Saxon Chronicle* (C) (I:198) claims that these were to be delivered later.

[88] *Anglo-Saxon Chronicle* (C) 1066, I:198: 'for þam þe him wæron behaten to gewissan þ him man þær of earle þære scire ongean hy gislas bringan wolde.'

CHAPTER TEN

THE BATTLE OF STAMFORD BRIDGE

WHEN Tostig Godwinson attacked the Isle of Wight and other places along the
southern coast of England to Sandwich, the king of England, Tostig's brother,
Harold Godwinson, moved to counter his threat with the largest army that he
could muster; butsecarls, fyrd, and huscarls, navy, infantry, and cavalry, all traveled as fast as they could to defend their kingdom against the fairly minor incursions of an outlaw earl. Once there, they, and the king who commanded them,
stayed there. They stayed there throughout the summer and into the autumn.
They stayed there even though Tostig attacked Lindsey in the north. They stayed
there until they could no longer stay there, until, according to the *Anglo-Saxon
Chronicle* (C) and John of Worcester, their supplies had run out.[1] Why? Because
of the threat from across the English Channel. Because Harold Godwinson knew
that William the Conqueror had designs on his kingdom, that the duke of Normandy claimed that the English throne had been given to him by the now dead
King Edward the Confessor and that the current king had taken an oath to
support him in his assumption of the throne, an oath taken on holy relics which
had been cavalierly broken. Harold may also have had some knowledge of William's war preparations: his amassing a fleet, mustering men, and gathering
arms.

---

[1]   *Anglo-Saxon Chronicle*, in *Two of the Saxon Chronicles Parallel*, ed. Charles Plummer and
John Earle (Oxford, 1892), (C) 1066, I:196 and John of Worcester, *The Chronicle of John of
Worcester*, ed. R.R. Darlington and P. McGurk, trans. J. Bray and P. McGurk (Oxford, 1995),
II:602–03. For other original sources which mention Harold's defense of southern England in
the summer and autumn of 1066 see *Anglo-Saxon Chronicle* (D) 1066, I:195–97; Henry of
Huntingdon, *Historia Anglorum: The History of the English People*, ed. and trans. D. Green-
way (Oxford, 1996), pp. 386–87; Symeon of Durham, *Historia regum*, ed. T. Arnold
(London, 1882–85), II:179; William of Malmesbury, *Gesta regum Anglorum: The History of
the English Kings*, ed. and trans. R.A.B. Mynors, R.M. Thomson, and M. Winterbottom
(Oxford, 1998), I:420–21; and Orderic Vitalis, *The Ecclesiastical History of Orderic Vitalis*,
ed. and trans. M. Chibnall (Oxford, 1969–80), II:142–43. See also Edward August Freeman,
The History of the Norman Conquest, 2nd edn (Oxford, 1869–75), III:335–38; Frank M.
Stenton, *Anglo-Saxon England*, 3rd edn (Oxford, 1971), pp. 587–88; Eric Linklater, *The Con-
quest of England: From the Viking Incursions of the Eighth Century to the Norman Victory at
the Battle of Hastings* (New York, 1966), pp. 194–96; Brian Golding, *Conquest and Colonisa-
tion: The Normans in Britain, 1066–1100* (New York, 1994), p. 30; R. Allen Brown, *The
Normans and the Norman Conquest*, 2nd edn (Woodbridge, 1985), pp. 124–25; Jim Bradbury,
The Battle of Hastings (Thrupp, 1998), pp. 130–31; and F.W. Brooks, *The Battle of Stamford
Bridge* (York, 1963), p. 12.

Yet what of the king of Norway? Why did King Harold Godwinson not have the same concern about King Haraldr Harðráði, the man whom William of Poitiers described as he 'who passed for the strongest man living under the sun'?[2] Did Harold not fear the Norwegian king and his troops? Most historians believe that the English king must have known of Haraldr Harðráði's invasion plans, if for no other reason than that he would have kept an eye on the movements of his brother, Tostig, after the latter's attacks on the south of England, and thereby would have known of his meeting with the Norwegian king in Scotland, if he had not already heard of the alliance made between the two. However there is no evidence to support this theory, which is in fact based on an overrated eleventh-century communication network and speed of travel, elements which these same historians are not willing to grant elsewhere in their analysis of the events of 1066.[3] It is more likely that Harold knew none of this. Perhaps Harold Godwinson did not know of Haraldr Harðráði's own claims to the English throne. Perhaps he did not know of Tostig's alliance with Haraldr. Perhaps he also did not know of the Norwegians' capabilities.[4] If any or all of these were so, however, the situation changed when in early September 1066 the Norwegians began their invasion of Northumbria, and it especially changed on 20 September when the Norwegian army crushed the English force of the brother earls, Edwin of Mercia and Morkere of Northumbria. At that time, Harold Godwinson must have realized that he was on the wrong coast concerned with the wrong invasion. He must also have realized that the town of York and the earldoms of Northumbria and Mercia stood open to capture, without a defensive force to protect them. Finally, he must also have realized that in order to defend his kingdom against the potential Norman invasion, he must first take care of Haraldr Harðráði and Tostig Godwinson and their invasion. If any of these thoughts did occur to the king, however, he did not have the time to linger on

---

2 William of Poitiers, *The Gesta Guillelmi of William of Poitiers*, ed. and trans. R.H.C. Davis and M. Chibnall (Oxford, 1998), pp. 116–17: '. . . quo fortiorem sub caelo nullum uiuere opinio fuit.'

3 This criticism is directed in particular at Sten Körner. In his book, *The Battle of Hastings, England, and Europe, 1035–1066* (Lund, 1964), pp. 263–64, Körner believes that Harold Godwinson was completely in touch with his eastern coast, which he knew was going to be attacked by Haraldr Harðráði, and that he also knew of Tostig's meeting with the Norwegian king in Scotland. It is when he hears of the attacks on Cleveland, Scarborough, and Holderness, that he decides to march northward. Interestingly, Körner uses this advanced knowledge of Harold's to prove that the king marched to Tadcaster earlier than other historians, because the amount of time others have given him to reach the north is 'unrealistic'. Edward A. Freeman (*Norman Conquest*, III:357–58) also theorizes that Harold knew of the Norwegian raids on Cleveland, Scarborough, and Holderness. There is, however, no contemporary evidence to support this. Nor do either of these authors speculate on why Edwin and Morkere would have fought the battle of Fulford Gate if they knew that Harold Godwinson was on his way north with a relief army. See also David C. Douglas, *William the Conqueror* (Berkeley and Los Angeles, 1964), p. 191.

4 Orderic Vitalis (II:168–69) emphasizes that the Norwegian landing was 'unexpected'.

them, for he was busy marching an army as fast as possible north to do battle with the Norwegians.

No date is recorded in any of the sources as to when Harold received word of the Norwegian attack of northern England. It seems certain that he did not hear of it before 8 September, when the *Anglo-Saxon Chronicle* (C) says that he was forced to give permission to his troops to return home, as this chronicle also reports that after this 'the king rode up and his men sailed his ships to London . . . then after the ships had come home, King Haraldr of Norway came north into the Tyne unexpectedly,' but how much later it was than this that the king heard of the invasion into Northumbria is not mentioned, only that it was after 'King Haraldr of Norway and Earl Tostig had landed near York.'[5] This may mean that he did not hear of the Norwegian invasion until after at least 15 or 16 September, the earliest the Norwegians could have landed at Ricall.[6] This is important, for between the time Harold heard of the invasion and 24 September, when he is known to have reached Tadcaster, some fifteen miles south of York, he had re-mustered the troops which he had just returned home, gathered new provisions when he was supposed to have run out of them, and marched the from London to Tadcaster, a distance of more than 200 miles.[7]

In the end, however, the answer is only important for intellectual curiosity. If Harold had heard of the Norwegian landing only as late as 16 September, giving him but nine days to accomplish the tasks mentioned above, this military maneuver ranks as one of the greatest of any age; an earlier date for the report of invasion does not diminish the greatness of the feat. Added to this that there is no contemporary calculation of how many troops there were in Harold's army, except that Henry of Huntingdon claims that it was vastly superior in numbers than Haraldr Harðráði's force, tallied at a pre-Fulford Gate number of 15,000–

---

5   *Anglo-Saxon Chronicle* (C) 1066, I:196: 'se cynge rad up. ⁊ man draf þa scypu to Lunde[ne] . . . Þa ða scypu ham coman, þa com Harold cyning of Norwegan norð into Tinan. on unwaren . . . þ Harold cyng on Norwegan ⁊Tostig eorl wæron up cumene neh Eoferwic.' F.W. Brooks' misreading of this text (p. 12), indicating that 8 September was when Harold Godwinson learned of the Norwegian landing, caused him to dismiss this chronicle's chronology. Consequently, he comes up with a date which is probably too early (10–12 September) for Harold's hearing of the Norwegian invasion. Orderic Vitalis' claim that Harold was still with his army in Hastings and Pevensey awaiting William's conquest when he heard of the Norwegian invasion (II:168–69) is probably inaccurate.

6   This date adheres closely to the wording of the *Anglo-Saxon Chronicle* (C) and challenges the *Anglo-Saxon Chronicle* (D and E) which claim that Harold Godwinson did not hear of the Norwegian invasion until after the battle of Fulford Gate, which would have given the English army far too little time to march to the north. On the latter point, see Freeman, *Norman Conquest*, III:718–19; Körner, p. 263; and Douglas, *William the Conqueror*, pp. 193–94. Agreeing with a date of 16 September is I. Walker, p. 160. Those believing that Harold started on his march earlier than this include Freeman, *Norman Conquest*, III:357–58; Körner, pp. 263–64; Brown, *The Normans and Norman Conquest*, p. 135; and F.W. Brooks, p. 12.

7   Not to mention a later legend that Harold was sick at the beginning of the march and had to be taken for healing to the relic of the Holy Cross at Waltham Abbey. See Freeman, *Norman Conquest*, III:358–60, for an account of this illness and references to the later sources which contain it.

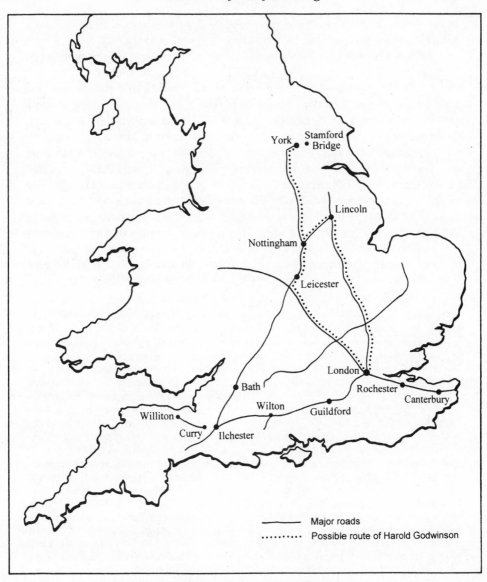

Major Roads in the Eleventh Century

18,000,[8] and that others claim 'many thousands of well-armed fighting men.'[9] Nor is it known how many of these soldiers were mounted on horses. Ian Walker believes that almost all of Harold Godwinson's troops were transported to Stamford Bridge on horseback. This would stand to reason if most of the troops were huscarls, which is the view of F.W. Brooks, who has Harold march from the south with his huscarls and muster the fyrd along the way.[10] While there undoubtedly were a large number of huscarls, there probably were not several thousands of them. Moreover, if we hold to what the *Anglo-Saxon Chronicle* (C) reports, the soldiers who joined Harold Godwinson on his march north were *fyrd*, and while some of these also probably had mounts, it is difficult to see how mounted soldiers made up even the majority of the soldiers mustered to fight against the Norwegian invaders.[11] No matter what, the troops marching north from London were forced to march at least 20–25 miles per day, an amazing task.[12] It begins to be easy to empathize with the Norwegians' surprise at their appearance at Stamford Bridge on the morning of 25 September.

King Harold Godwinson 'made all haste', to use the words of Orderic Vitalis.[13] The *Anglo-Saxon Chronicle* (C) is more detailed: 'King Harold . . .

8 Henry of Huntingdon, pp. 386–87. On the numbers in Haraldr's army see n. 38 in the chapter 'The Invasion' above.
9 This quote comes from John of Worcester, II:602–03: 'multis milibus pugnatorum armis bellicis instructorum'. I have used my own translation here as Bray and McGurk fail to do justice to John's notion that these were *experienced* troops, no doubt veterans of the Welsh campaigns. See also the *Anglo-Saxon Chronicle* (D and E) 1066, I:197–99; Symeon of Durham, *Historia regum*, II:180; *Fagrskinna: Kortfattet Norsk Konge-Saga*, ed. P.A. Munch and C.R. Unger (Christiania (Oslo), 1847), p. 137; *Morkinskinna: Pergamentsbog fra første halvdel af det trettende aarhundrede*, ed. C.R. Unger (Christiania (Oslo), 1867), pp. 114–15; Snorri Sturluson, *Heimskringla*, ed. B. Aðalbjarnarson (Reykjavik, 1941–51), III:183; *Flateyjarbók: En samling af Norske Konge-Sagaer*, ed. G. Vigfusson and C.R. Unger (Christiania (Oslo), 1860–68), III:391; Freeman, *Norman Conquest*, III:361; and Brown, *The Normans and the Norman Conquest*, pp. 135–36. William of Malmesbury (*Gesta regum Anglorum*, I:420–21) describes the army as 'all the forces in the kingdom (cunctis uiribus regni).'
10 I. Walker, p. 160, and F.W. Brooks, p. 12. Only two of Harold's soldiers are known by name. Both are thegns, from Essex and Worcestershire respectively, and both are referred to in the Domesday Book as having lost their lives during the campaign against the Norwegians. See Freeman, *Norman Conquest*, III:361 and I. Walker, pp. 158–59. While these two would have surely been mounted, they are in no way representative of the army as a whole.
11 *Anglo-Saxon Chronicle* (C) 1066, I:196.
12 I. Walker (p. 160) contends that most of these troops were mounted, because infantry troops would have been able to march only fifteen miles per day.
13 Orderic Vitalis, II:168–69. See also *Anglo-Saxon Chronicle* (D and E) 1066, I:197–98; John of Worcester, II:602–03; Symeon of Durham, *Historia regum*, II:180; William of Malmesbury, *Gesta regum Anglorum*, I:420–21; Geoffrey Gaimar, *Lestoire des Engles*, ed. T.D. Hardy and C.T. Martin (London, 1888–89), I:221; *Fagrskinna*, p. 137; *Morkinskinna*, pp. 114–15; Snorri Sturluson, *Heimskringla*, III:183; *Flateyjarbók*, III:391; Freeman, *Norman Conquest*, III:357–62, 718–19; Stenton, *Anglo-Saxon England*, p. 590; Linklater, pp. 196–97; Körner, pp. 262–66; Brown, *Tne Normans and the Norman Conquest*, pp. 135–36; I. Walker, pp. 157–60; F.W. Brooks, p. 12; William E. Kapelle, *The Norman Conquest of the North: The Region and Its Transformation, 1000–1135* (Chapel Hill, 1979), p. 104; Henry R. Loyn, 'Harold, Son of Godwin,' in *Society and Peoples: Studies in the History of England and*

marched to the north day and night as fast as he could gather his *fyrd*.'[14] The road was well known; an old and straight Roman road, designed for speed of travel, had extended from London to York for almost a millennium, and, despite its age and use, it was still in remarkable condition.[15] But, as indicated in the *Anglo-Saxon Chronicle* above, the army did not have the luxury of stopping for much of a rest, not if it wanted to surprise the Norwegians or to stop them before too much pillaging and too many deaths had occurred. Or perhaps the king feared that if he did not arrive quickly to protect the north, as he declared was his wish in his spring visit to York, that the allegiance of the inhabitants there would be transferred to their Norwegian cousins, and that he would have to contend not only with the Scandinavians but also with the Anglo-Scandinavians. (The latter especially may have been one of the factors in Harold's decision to abandon his waiting on the Channel for William the Conqueror's invasion. Otherwise, it seems rather short-sighted of the king to abandon the coast to a Norman landing.[16]) Hearing en route of Edwin and Morkere's defeat at Fulford Gate would also have quickened their pace.[17]

Harold arrived at Tadcaster, about seven miles to the west of the Norwegian fleet anchored at Ricall, on the night of 24 September, four days after the battle of Fulford Gate and the day of York's submission to the victors in that battle, Haraldr Harðráði and Tostig Godwinson.[18] There he rested his troops and was undoubtedly briefed on the recent movements of the Norwegians. He also may have added some of the English soldiers who had recently fought at Fulford Gate, including perhaps Earl Morkere, who had escaped capture there and was not present in York with his brother, Edwin,[19] and some of the butsecarls who

---

Wales, c. 600–1200 (London, 1992), p. 317; Alex. D.H. Leadman, *Proelia Eboracensia: Battles Fought in Yorkshire Treated Historically and Topographically* (London, 1891), p. 9; C.R.B. Barrett, *Battles and Battlefields in England* (London, 1896), pp. 4–5; and A.L. Thompson, 'The Battle of Stamford Bridge 1066,' *British Army Review* 97 (Apr. 1991), 49.

[14] *Anglo-Saxon Chronicle* (C) 1066, I:196: '. . . Harolde cynge . . . for he norðweard dæges ꝗ nihtes swa hraðe swa he his fyrde gegaderian michte.'

[15] Linklater, pp. 196–97.

[16] Unless you believe, as Körner does (pp. 265–66), that Harold divided his troops on 8 September, taking the huscarls north with him against the Norwegians and leaving the fyrd behind to contend with the eventual invasion of William the Conqueror. This he believes that they do by keeping William on the coast and not allowing him to proceed to London. This view, however, shows a misunderstanding of William's strategy – the Norman duke had no intention of marching on London without first building a series of motte-and-bailey castles to work out of and to protect his landing area so that he might be able to bring in reinforcements (see Kelly DeVries, *Medieval Military Technology* (Peterborough, 1992), p. 205). To my knowledge, no one else has agreed with Körner's unsupported conjecture.

[17] Leadman, p. 9.

[18] The date is recorded in *Anglo-Saxon Chronicle* (C) 1066, I:197.

[19] Where Morkere was at this moment is not mentioned anywhere, nor is it known whether he participated in the battle of Stamford Bridge or not. Neither he nor Edwin are mentioned further in the Norwegian Kings' Sagas, although as they had recorded Morkere's death at Fulford Gate, his further absence in these records should not be surprising. That said, he could as easily have been in hiding as in Tadcaster to meet Harold Godwinson.

were attending to those vessels which had taken refuge on the Wharfe River near Tadcaster.[20]

Certainly Harold was aware of the Norwegian fleet beached at Ricall and so close to his own point of rest and planning. He may have even scouted out the fleet, probably to give himself an idea of the number of troops which had been brought to England by Haraldr and Tostig and, therefore, also how many he might have to contend with in a battle.[21] However rather than risk his element of surprise by attacking the Norwegian ships, especially as it seems that the main Norwegian army had not yet returned to them, he allowed them to remain undisturbed and seemingly unaware of his presence. For this was unquestionably what the English king was hoping for, a surprise against the Norwegians which just might carry the day in his fighting what might prove to be at least a comparable if not a superior enemy army. By the time he reached Tadcaster, Harold Godwinson surely knew that such a surprise was possible.[22]

It is astounding that the Norwegians posted no scouts in or near York, but none seem to have been present.[23] Therefore, the march of Harold's army to and through that town on the morning of 25 September came as a complete surprise to the Norwegians. The appearance of Harold Godwinson's relief army as it marched through York must also have been quite surprising to the townspeople who but one day previously had given their allegiance to the invader, Haraldr Harðráði, but had they given the Norwegians any hostages yet? In reading the *Anglo-Saxon Chronicle* (C), it appears that these were still to be delivered to Haraldr at Stamford Bridge.[24] This is perhaps confirmed by the Norwegian Kings' Sagas. They claim that there was another meeting to be held between the townspeople and the Norwegian king at which he was to appoint his own governors and receive treaties and lands.[25] If this was the case, it was important for Harold not to slow his march against the Norwegians. He could save the lives of

20 On the existence of this fleet at Tadcaster see nn. 63 and 64 in the chapter 'The Invasion' above.
21 Freeman, *Norman Conquest*, III:362–63.
22 I am in agreement here with Ian Walker (p. 160) that this was the primary tactic of Harold's plan and why he pushed his soldiers so hard for so many days.
23 Other modern historians are also surprised by this. See Freeman, *Norman Conquest*, III:353–57; Stenton, *Anglo-Saxon England*, p. 590; Kapelle, p. 104; Linklater, p. 200; Brown, *The Normans and the Norman Conquest*, pp. 135–36; and Bradbury, *Battle of Hastings*, p. 132.
24 *Anglo-Saxon Chronicle* (C) 1066, I:196. On the other hand, John of Worcester (II:602–03), followed by Symeon of Durham (*Historia regum*, II:180), claims that the hostages had already been exchanged, although this source seems to indicate that they had been taken to the safety of the ships at Ricall. Freeman (*Norman Conquest*, III:353), in trying to work with John of Worcester, claims that 150 hostages *from York* were delivered to Haraldr on September 24, but, in trying to working with the *Anglo-Saxon Chronicle* (C), he writes that 150 more hostages were to be delivered to Haraldr at Stamford Bridge *from the surrounding shire*. Where he is finding this second group of hostages in the sources is not explained.
25 See Snorri Sturluson, *Heimskringla*, III:183: 'skyldi þá Haraldr konungr skipa staðinn með ríkismǫnnum ok gefa réttu ok lén.' See also *Fagrskinna*, p. 137; *Morkinskinna*, p. 114; and *Flateyjarbók*, III:391. The Norwegian Kings' Sagas claim that this meeting was to be held

potential hostages as well as encounter the invaders before they armed themselves and made their own march to the town.[26] So King Harold did not stop in York, but chose instead to march straight through the town on his way to the battlefield of Stamford Bridge. If the townspeople of York were surprised, so too would be the Norwegians.[27]

The exact location of where the battle of Stamford Bridge was fought is not known today. Original sources, even the Norwegian Kings' Sagas, are vague on the topography of the battlefield, indicating only the prominence of the Derwent River, a tributary of the Ouse River, running through the battlefield with a narrow wooden bridge crossing over it. On the western side of the river, the side approached by Harold Godwinson's army on the morning of 25 September, was a wide, slightly sloped meadow. On the eastern side of the river, where Haraldr Harðráði perhaps placed a camp, was higher ground, the slope of which rose more sharply from the riverbank. Today, the river is pretty much a narrow, sluggish stream, but its size and course have undoubtedly changed since 1066.[28] The original bridge, too, has disappeared. Now the visitor to the town crosses the river over a wide, two-lane, stone bridge. This new crossing is probably not placed over the site of the older structure, but as no archaeological remains of the earlier bridge have been found, this cannot be concluded for certain.[29]

Without knowing the 1066 course of the river or the location of the medieval bridge, it is almost impossible to know where the western part of the battle took place. The eastern part is easier to determine, but only if the name Battle Flats can be trusted, assigned as it is to an area of higher ground located to the southeast of the present town's center. This area, about fifty feet above the Derwent River, is a large, flat plain today. Farmed now, it is difficult to know if Battle Flats was always as large and flat as it is today. Could it also have accommodated as many as 15,000–18,000 soldiers, both as a possible campground and as a battlefield? Yet this is where tradition says that the main part of the battle took

in York, perhaps in addition to or in conjunction with the trading of the hostages at Stamford Bridge.

[26] Had the hostages already been exchanged, as John of Worcester and Symeon of Durham claim (see n. 23 above), but held at the Norwegian fleet, a surprise attack at Stamford Bridge could still have saved their lives.

[27] On Harold's march through York see *Anglo-Saxon Chronicle* (C) 1066, I:197; *Fagrskinna*, p. 137; *Morkinskinna*, p. 114; Snorri Sturluson, *Heimskringla*, III:182–83; *Flateyjarbók*, III:391; Freeman, *Norman Conquest*, III:362–63; and F.W. Brooks, pp. 13–14.

[28] Leadman (p. 5) measured the River Derwent at 12–14 yards in width in 1891; Barrett (p. 5) measured it at 35–40 feet in width in 1895. When visiting the site in 1995, it seemed much narrower to me.

[29] Leadman (p. 8) and Barrett (p. 5) believe that the bridge now in place stands some 500 yards below the earlier bridge. Colonel Alfred H. Burne (*More Battlefields of Britain* (London, 1952), p. 92), which is followed by P. Warner (*British Battlefields, the North* (London, 1975), p. 21) and W. Seymour (*Battles in Britain* (London, 1975), I:9), site it 250 yards from the current bridge. However, neither F.W. Brooks (pp. 19–20) or Bradbury (*Battle of Hastings*, p. 132) agree with this difference, seeing the current bridge located much closer to the medieval one.

place. It is also a tradition that during the eighteenth century skeletons and weapons were found on Battle Flats; of course, nothing of these finds survives today.[30] Haraldr Harðráði had chosen this site not only because of its large and favorable meadow, which would have serviced the soldiers, and also any horses which they might have acquired,[31] but also because its height allowed the Norwegians to observe the countryside for miles around.

Finally, it was quite a defensible location. Divided from York as it was by the Derwent River and with only a narrow bridge to this impediment – no ford is mentioned in the sources, although today it would be quite easy to ford, especially on horseback – the terrain itself protected the Norwegian army from any attack. It would seem also that the terrain, with no means of easily going around, would have protected the Norwegians from the surprise which Harold Godwinson delivered to them, but Haraldr Harðráði's strategic genius in selecting this site was matched by his over-confidence. To him, it must have seemed that there was no way that a relief army could be close to Stamford Bridge on the day of battle. York did not have the capability of providing a relief army, nor could the remnants of Edwin and Morkere's defeated forces at Fulford Gate have united for another attempt at the invaders, and Harold Godwinson was too far to the south, surely having no ability to march as far and as fast as he actually did. It was an over-confidence which would cost the Norwegian king, his ally, Tostig Godwinson, and several thousands of their soldiers their lives.

However, before trying to recreate what occurred at the battle of Stamford Bridge, two issues must be resolved. The first is relatively minor: how long did the battle of Stamford Bridge last? Drawn by comments, such as Henry of Huntingdon's that the battle was 'more arduous than any that had gone before'[32] and the *Anglo-Saxon Chronicle* (C)'s that 'such fierce fighting went on long into the day,'[33] modern historians have contended that this battle lasted a very long time, all day, a length standard for medieval battles. Yet, most medieval battles were not lengthy endeavors lasting an entire day. Instead, they were much shorter affairs, with one army usually causing the other side to flee from the battlefield in little more than an hour or two.[34] In this instance, the battle of

---

[30] On the site and topography of the battlefield see F.W. Brooks, pp. 14, 17–20; Leadman, p. 8; Barrett, pp. 5–6; Bradbury, *Battle of Hastings*, pp. 132–33; and Denis Butler, *1066: The Story of a Year* (London, 1966), p. 179. On the eighteenth-century findings see F.W. Brooks, p. 20, who awards this tradition some legitimacy.

[31] While it is not known how many horses the Norwegians had with them, both Theodoricus (*Monumenta historica Norvegiæ: Latinske kildeskrifter til Norges historie I middelalderen*, ed. G. Storm (Christiania (Oslo), 1880), p. 57) and the *Ágrip af Nóregs konunga sǫgum* (ed. F. Jónsson (Halle, 1929), p. 41) have Haraldr Harðráði mounted during the battle. Early in the battle, Haraldr also sends three mounted messengers to Ricall for reinforcements.

[32] Henry of Huntingdon, pp. 386–87: 'Pugna igitur incepta est qua grauir non fuerat.' Freeman, for one, disagrees with Henry of Huntingdon's timing of the battle (*Norman Conquest*, III:723–24).

[33] *Anglo-Saxon Chronicle* (C) 1066, I:198: 'swyðe heardlice lange on dæg feohtende wæron'. The Norwegian Kings' Sagas also seem to indicate this.

[34] Indeed, in my book, *Infantry Warfare in the Early Fourteenth Century: Discipline, Tactics,*

Hastings, which was fought for most of an entire day, does not represent an archetypal medieval battle, but an 'unusual' one, to use Stephen Morillo's word.[35] The battle of Stamford Bridge certainly lasted more than a couple of hours, but only because the fighting took place in four stages, first on the western side of the river, then with the valiant defense of the bridge, in a number of phases on the right side of the river, and finally against Norwegian reinforcements who had arrived at Stamford Bridge after most of the rest of the fighting had been completed. However, all of these stages together probably took no more than four or five hours. This is not to say that either Henry of Huntingdon or the *Anglo-Saxon Chronicle* (C) is wrong in their narratives, though. Depending on when the battle began, there is a suggestion that the conflict did not continue for more than five hours: Henry of Huntingdon claims that the fighting took place from dawn to the afternoon, with the *Anglo-Saxon Chronicle*, which appears to start the engagement later in the morning, reporting that it was fought long into the day.

The second issue is more significant. Contemporary accounts of the events of 1066 are notoriously negligent in their accounts of the battle of Stamford Bridge. Even the *Anglo-Saxon Chronicle* (C) and John of Worcester, which otherwise have solid narratives of other actions relating to the Norwegian invasion of England, have little to say about this important battle. As to be expected, the Norwegian Kings' Sagas do an admirable job of making up for this negligence. The battle of Stamford Bridge is one of the focal points of their biographies of Haraldr Harðráði, much as the battle of Hastings is a focal point of William the Conqueror's life and detailed by his chroniclers.[36] However, whereas modern historians have no difficulty accepting these accounts of the battle of Hastings,[37] no 'serious scholar' has accepted the Norwegian Kings' Sagas' accounts of the battle of Stamford Bridge.

The reason behind this disbelief is ostensibly the dates of the sources in question. The original sources of Hastings were all written (or, in the case of the *Bayeux Tapestry*, embroidered) within seventy years of the battle. The Norwegian Kings' Sagas were all written in the twelfth or thirteenth century, more than a hundred years after the battle, with the most detailed ones, *Fagrskinna*, *Morkinskinna*, and Snorri Sturluson's *Heimskringla*, written in the early thirteenth century, more than one hundred and fifty years after the battle. (The *Flateyjarbók*, which I have also been using as a source and which is also quite detailed, is a compilation of these and other sagas and was not written until the

---

and Technology (Woodbridge, 1996), which analyzes nineteen medieval battles fought between 1302 and 1347, only one, Bannockburn, lasted the entire day and into the next one. Even the very important battle of Crécy was not fought for more than a couple of hours.

35 Stephen Morillo, 'Hastings: An Unusual Battle,' *Haskins Society Journal* 1 (1989), 96–103.

36 Note for example, the number of sources which detail what occurred at that battle found in Stephen Morillo, ed., *The Battle of Hastings* (Woodbridge, 1996).

fifteenth century.) So it is not difficult to question the credibility of their battle narratives.

If these are not accounts of the battle of Stamford Bridge though, what does the Norwegian Kings' Sagas' version of what occurred, which appears with only minor variations in each of the four more detailed Sagas, then depict? Most historians think that it is the narrative of another battle which was better known to the authors of the Norwegian Kings' Sagas, either a more contemporaneous or a more famous battle.

This historiographical issue is not one which historians of the battle of Stamford Bridge alone face. It can present a problem in any military history of the Middle Ages. Indeed, J.F. Verbruggen, in his seminal work, *De krijgkunst in west-europa in de middeleeuwen (IXe tot XIVe eeuw)*, takes great pains to warn military historians against accepting contemporary battle narratives without carefully scrutinizing all of the original sources,[38] but Verbruggen's caution is assigned mostly to battle narratives written in Latin, as Latin writers, he feels, were trained in the language, not their native tongue, using classical and biblical texts, many of which contain accounts of battles. It is not uncommon, therefore, to find medieval Latin battle narratives which are wholly or in part derived from classical or biblical accounts. Vernacular authors have fewer of these kinds of problems, according to Verbruggen, because the language of composition is the writer's own. Yet is it not possible, and not considered by Verbruggen in particular, that even vernacular writers, such as the authors of the Norwegian Kings' Sagas, when faced with no previous accounts of a battle, would simply appropriate the narrative of another battle for the one which they feel should be reported? Of course, to say this, one must assume that no previous account ever existed, something which is virtually impossible to prove.

The only possible means of proof, and it is circumstantial at best, is to find something in the battle narrative which is obviously in error. The error in the Norwegians Kings' Sagas' account of the battle of Stamford Bridge is the insistence of all of the more detailed Sagas that Harold Godwinson used cavalry charges to defeat the Norwegian troops during the final stage of the battle. This, more than the problems with the late dates of the Sagas, is the principal reason given by most modern historians for dismissing their narrative of this battle. Without repeating the arguments for and against the Anglo-Saxon capability of fighting on horseback,[39] those who deny the credibility of the Norwegian Kings' Sagas' account of the battle, or more correctly, those who deny Snorri Sturluson's account of the battle of Stamford Bridge, for few know the narratives of

---

[37] See, for example, Bradbury, *Battle of Hastings*; Morillo, 'Battle of Hastings'; and R. Allen Brown, 'The Battle of Hastings,' *Proceedings of the Battle Conference on Anglo-Norman Studies* 3 (1980), 1–21, to name only three.

[38] J.F. Verbruggen, *De krijgkunst in west-europa in de middeleeuwen (IXe tot XIVe eeuw)* (Brussels, 1954). This work has been recently revised and translated into English by its author as *The Art of Warfare in Western Europe during the Middle Ages* (Woodbridge, 1996).

[39] This discussion can be found in 'The Norwegian Military' chapter above.

Fagrskinna, Morkinskinna, and *Flateyjarbók,* do so because they do not accept the English cavalry charges as described in these sagas.[40]

The most frequent battle narrative believed by these historians to have been appropriated by the authors of the Norwegian Kings' Sagas is that of the battle of Hastings.[41] Of course, there is no question of the cavalry charges used by the Normans as their primary tactic against Harold Godwinson's army, thus resolving that issue. In addition, there are several other similarities on which to build this comparative case: the stand of one army in a shield wall formation to defend against the cavalry charges of their opponents; the formation of that shield wall on high ground which forces the horses to charge uphill; the repelling of the first cavalry charge; the breaking of the shield wall to pursue the enemy 'fleeing' from the battlefield; the cavalry's turning against this disordered breakout; the remnants of the defeated force rallying around a leader; and the death of the defeated leader by an arrow shot into his head.

The case sounds pretty convincing. However, to make these similarities comparative, some manipulation of both the Stamford Bridge and Hastings narratives must be done. First, although there were two shield walls formed by what would be the losing side in these conflicts, Haraldr Harðráði's at Stamford Bridge was formed quickly, a tactic which he was forced into to face the English army's arrival which had surprised the Norwegian king, while Harold Godwinson's at Hastings was a well-planned tactic, ordered by a leader who had chosen the terrain on which to fight a battle and the shield wall as his primary tactic. (In essence, Haraldr Harðráði's shield wall was a defensive formation, while Harold Godwinson's was an offensive one.) Also, the two shield-walls were completely different in design, with Haraldr Harðráði's a circular, and Harold Godwinson's a linear formation. Second, although both battlefield narratives contain the eventual, disastrous 'breaking out' from this shield wall, that which Harold Godwinson led at Hastings was done when he saw the Norman horses in what appeared to him to be a full retreat. Either they were fleeing under the mistaken impression that their leader, William the Conqueror, had been killed, or because they were effecting a 'feigned retreat,' but in either case, Harold believed that he and his troops were pursuing a defeated opponent. At Stamford Bridge, Haraldr Harðráði was under no such impression. Although he and his soldiers had effectively repulsed the initial charge of Harold Godwinson's cavalry, the English soldiers had not broken into a retreat. Haraldr's reaction was to make a charge

---

[40] These include: Freeman, *Norman Conquest,* III:365–67, 720–27; Brown, *The Normans and the Norman Conquest,* p. 136; Charles Oman, *The Art of War in the Middle Ages* (London, 1924), I:150–51; Paddy Griffith, *The Viking Art of War* (London, 1995), pp. 191–92; Bruce E. Gelsinger, 'The Battle of Stamford Bridge and the Battle of Jaffa: A Case of Confused Identity?' *Scandinavian Studies* 60 (1988), 13–29; Shaun F.D. Hughes, 'The Battle of Stamford Bridge and the Battle of Bouvines,' *Scandinavian Studies* 60 (1988), 30–76; and Elizabeth Ashman Rowe, 'Historical Invasions/Historiographical Interventions: Snorri Sturluson and the Battle of Stamford Bridge,' *Mediaevalia* 17 (1994), 149–76.

[41] This is the view of Freeman, Brown, Oman, and Griffith.

against what he thought were 'weak' attacks by his enemy; his mistaken belief was that if he made a quick and unexpected charge out of his shield wall, he might surprise the Anglo-Saxon troops and, in their confusion, take control over the battle. Furthermore, he led this attack under no delusion that the general opposing him was dead. Third, the reordering of the shield walls by the losers in both battles was done around different leaders. At Stamford Bridge, the remnants of the Norwegian army rallied around Tostig Godwinson, their king having been killed, while at Hastings the English rallied around their king. Fourth, the repulse of a cavalry charge, especially an initial one, was customary for a medieval shield wall defense, even one which would eventually lose. Indeed, the only means of effectively defeating a shield wall was to continually attack it, suffering numerous repulses until the men forming the shield wall finally weakened and fled, surrendered, or died. Finally, leaving aside the issue of where the fatal arrows wounded the two leaders – Haraldr Harðráði in the throat and Harold Godwinson in the eye – the death or wounding of a leader in the face or head by archery was also common in medieval battles. The protective nature of the kind of armor worn both by Haraldr Harðráði at Stamford Bridge and Harold Godwinson at Hastings left only a few vulnerable spots. Of these, the face and head were the most susceptible to arrows fired by archers at a distance, and an arrow shot into this part of the body was usually fatal. One military leader who would survive from such an attack was the young Henry V whose cheek was pierced by an arrow at the battle of Shrewsbury in 1403.[42]

There are also several major differences in the Norwegian Kings' Sagas' battlefield accounts of Stamford Bridge and those others wrote of the battle of Hastings. For example, the discussions between Harold and Tostig Godwinson, and between Tostig and Haraldr Harðráði are novel, although they could be explained as literary flourishes from the more literary Saga authors. Of greater importance are the order and magnitude of the deaths of the leaders. While the Norwegian Kings' Sagas are writing about Haraldr Harðráði, his death occurs relatively early in the battle, with Tostig Godwinson's coming much later. At Hastings, the culmination of the battle was the death of King Harold Godwinson. Such an anti-climactic death of the man whom the authors of the Norwegian Kings' Sagas are focusing on cannot so easily be discarded as literary flourish. Then there is the summoning and arrival of Norwegian reinforcements from the ships beached at Ricall and, perhaps most importantly, the surprise arrival of Harold Godwinson's army to initiate the conflict. There are no equivalents in the Hastings narratives.

Ultimately, it all comes down to the cavalry charges. Those who want to see the battle of Hastings as the battle used for the narrative of the battle of Stamford Bridge by the authors of the Norwegian Kings' Sagas do so for one simple reason: cavalry charges are known to have been used at Hastings, but not at Stamford Bridge.

---

[42] See Kelly DeVries, 'Military Surgical Practice and the Advent of Gunpowder Weaponry,' *Canadian Bulletin of Medical History* 7 (1990), 134.

Such problems with the Stamford Bridge–Hastings comparison have proven too great for some recent scholars to accept it. At the same time, they have been unwilling to accept that the accounts of Stamford Bridge are about that battle. For two of these historians the Norwegian Kings' Sagas' narratives are derived from different battles. For Bruce Gelsinger, this is the battle of Jaffa, fought between Richard I (the Lion-Hearted) and Saladin in 1192 and diffused to Iceland by at least 1217, and for Shaun F.D. Hughes, it is the battle of Bouvines, fought between Philip II (Augustus) of France and an allied army of Germans, Flemings, English, Brabantese, and rebel Frenchmen, led chiefly by Emperor Otto IV and Ferrand, count of Flanders, in 1214 and known in Iceland shortly thereafter.[43] Yet neither of these battles contain even the comparative elements of the battle of Hastings, although both do have cavalry charges as their primary offensive tactic, and both have a very tenuous diffusion to where the authors of the Norwegian King's Sagas could have easily appropriated them. Consequently, they have not gained prominence or favor. Another scholar, Elizabeth Ashman Rowe, has simply dismissed the idea that these authors, in particular Snorri Sturluson, whose Saga is the only one of these works which she discusses, has appropriated any battle for their narratives of the battle of Stamford Bridge. Instead, they are 'in the largest sense fictional,' written to conform not to history but to Snorri's (and, one supposes, by extension also to the other authors') political ideology.[44] Nor has this view found favor, especially among historians who wish to believe that the authors of the Norwegian Kings' Sagas, all of whom describe what they have written as historical accounts, could have been so utterly mendacious, even though on the battle of Stamford Bridge they might have 'stretched the truth' somewhat.

What then is to be done with the Norwegian Kings' Sagas' accounts of the battle of Stamford Bridge? Should they be discarded because of the suspicions that they do not describe the battle at all? Or is there some way of considering what they report while following the recommendations of caution suggested by J.F. Verbruggen? Muddying the waters of resolution is the fact, unconsidered by most of the critics of these battle narratives, that this is not just *an* account found in *one* Saga, but slightly different accounts found in three, all of which were written about the same time in almost same place (and one compilation of the others written in the fifteenth century). Was there some collaboration between the authors of these sagas? Or did they perhaps have a single now lost source for their story? Of course, there is the problem that while there seems to be a strong connection between *Fagrskinna* and *Morkinskinna* (and later between *Morkinskinna* and *Flateyjarbók*), the connection between those two, either individually or together, with Snorri Sturluson's *Heimskringla* has never

---

[43] Gelsinger, pp. 13–29, and Hughes, pp. 30–76.
[44] Rowe, pp. 149–76. The quote is found on p. 150. For a similar view, although one which does not identify the battle of Stamford Bridge as one of its examples, see A.Ya. Gurevich, 'Saga and History: The "Historical Conception" of Snorri Sturluson,' *Mediaeval Scandinavia* 4 (1971), 42–53.

been established, neither historically nor literarily, and Snorri's account contains the most variations from the others in it. In addition, what is to be done with the two earlier Norwegian Kings' Sagas, written in the twelfth century, Theodoricus' *Monumenta historica Norvegiæ* and the *Ágrip*? Both of these briefly describe the battle of Stamford Bridge, but without the details found in the later Norwegian Kings' Sagas.[45] Are they also to be discarded, even though they were written closer to the events, or can they be regarded as credible because they do not explicitly refer to English cavalry attacks?

The purpose of the rhetorical questions in the last paragraph was not to confuse the reader, but to gain sympathy for the lack of resolution that is necessary when encountering this issue. It is impossible to accept the Norwegian Kings' Sagas' narratives of the battle of Stamford Bridge without questioning their credibility, nor is it responsible as a scholar to cursorily dismiss them. In other words, it is necessary to proceed with caution in using these accounts, as it is in using any original source, precisely as Verbruggen has recommended. The following will include the Norwegian Kings' Sagas, as it will evidence from all of the other original sources available. It will indicate clearly what is taken from the Norwegian Kings' Sagas alone, what is taken from the Norwegian Kings' Sagas but with support from non-saga sources, and what is derived from sources other than the Norwegian Kings' Sagas. As in all historical writing, it will be the reader's responsibility to determine the feasibility of the narrative and its conclusions.

The reader's responsibility must be used from the very outset of the battle. According to the Norwegian Kings' Sagas, on the morning of 25 September, after Haraldr Harðráði and the Norwegian troops had breakfasted on or near their ships in Ricall, they prepared to march to their meeting at Stamford Bridge with the citizens of York. Haraldr then met with his army, choosing which of his soldiers were to stay at the camp and which were to travel with him to the town. Apparently, although he did not fear an attack from an English army, Haraldr did feel that some of his troops should stay behind to guard the ships. Perhaps the Norwegian king did not feel it necessary to show up for his meeting with the inhabitants of York in full force; the citizens of York had, after all, already been witness to Haraldr's military might. Tostig also prepared to go to Stamford Bridge with the king. The soldiers at the ships, it is reported, were under the command of Óláfr, Haraldr's son, two earls of the Orkney Islands, Páll and Erlendr, and Eysteinn Orri, who is described in the Norwegian Kings' Sagas as 'the son of Þorberg Árnasonar, the most excellent and most noble to the king of all landed men, to whom the king had promised his daughter, Maríu.'[46]

---

[45] Theodoricus, pp. 56–57 and *Ágrip af Nóregs konunga sögum*, p. 41. Only Hughes (pp. 46–47) even mentions these texts, and then only the *Ágrip*, and he does so without judgement on their credibility.

[46] Snorri Sturluson (*Heimskringla*, III:183–84) is the only one of the Norwegian Kings' Sagas to identify all of the leaders left with the ships. *Fagrskinna* (p. 137), *Morkinskinna* (p.

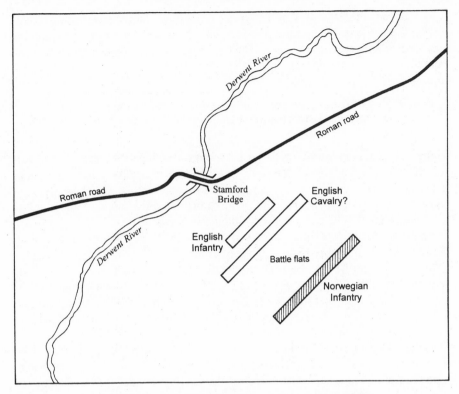

The Battle of Stamford Bridge, 25 September 1066

At this point, Haraldr Harðráði and Tostig Godwinson made what proved to be a grave error in judgement. Secure in their confidence that the day would proceed without incident, with clear weather and a warm sunshine, Haraldr and Tostig allowed the troops making what was a reasonably long march to leave their armor behind, taking only their weapons, shields, and helmets. As the anonymous author of *Morkinskinna* writes, 'they were all very cheerful.'[47]

Once at Stamford Bridge,[48] the Norwegians caught sight of what appeared to be a large force marching to meet them. Actually, the authors of the Norwegian

115), and *Flateyjarbók* (III:392) identify only Eysteinn Orri. The description of him, with minor variances, is found in each of them. I have used the quote found in *Fagrskinna*: 'sunr Þorbergs Árnasunar, er þá var ágætastr ok í mestu yfirlæti konungsins allra lendra manna; þá hafði Haraldr konungr hetit hánum Maríu, dóttur sinni.'

47 *Morkinskinna*, p. 115: 'Þeir voro catir mioc.' All of the other detailed Norwegian Kings' Sagas contain similar lines: *Fagrskinna*, p. 137; Snorri Sturluson, *Heimskringla*, III:184; and *Flateyjarbók*, III:392. See also I. Walker, p. 163.

48 None of the Norwegian Kings' Sagas initially name the place as Stamford Bridge. In fact, they say only that the action took place when they were in the proximity (*nánd*) of York. It is only later that it is revealed that they were actually fighting at Stamford Bridge. See

Kings' Sagas clearly write that the Norwegians saw a large force 'riding' (*reið*) toward them. Confused by this spectacle, King Haraldr summoned Tostig to his side and asked what army this might be, as he certainly had expected none. Snorri Sturluson describes the leaders' conversation:

> The earl said that he thought that they were probably hostile, but that he thought that it was also possible that they were some of his friends and that they sought mercy and friendship from the king in exchange for their trust and faith.[49]

Liking the latter possibility and still suspecting nothing from Harold Godwinson, Haraldr Harðráði decided to wait until he knew more about these approaching troops. The *Fagrskinna* reports what happened next: 'now the closer the men came, the more the army grew, until, with their weapons glistening, they looked like broken ice.'[50] The army was Harold Godwinson's.

The non-Norwegian Kings' Saga sources say much less on what occurred on the morning of 25 September leading up to the battle. It cannot even be ascertained for certain from these sources whether Haraldr and Tostig camped their armies at Ricall with their ships or at Stamford Bridge, although Saxo Grammaticus does report that in leaving their camp, the invaders, 'scorning danger, left off their armor' before marching off to plunder the neighborhood (no meeting with the inhabitants of York is mentioned).[51] While this seems to give the impression that the battlefield was some distance from their campsite, the place of the plundering Saxo refers to could simply have been across the bridge onto the flat meadow across the Derwent River from their campground and from the rest of the army. This conclusion might be arrived at because it appears that when Harold Godwinson showed up, unexpectedly marching with a large army from York,[52] some of the Norwegian soldiers were caught on the far side of the river from their leaders and the larger part of their army. What were they doing there? From Geoffrey Gaimar, it appears that they were rustling cattle.[53] The nature of feeding a large number was naturally a major problem for any invading

---

Fagrskinna, p. 137; *Morkinskinna*, p. 115; Snorri Sturluson, *Heimskringla*, III:184; and *Flateyjarbók*, III:392.

[49] Snorri Sturluson, *Heimskringla*, III:184:
   Jarl segir, lézk þykkja meiri ván, at ófriðr mundi vera, lét ok hitt vera mega, at þetta mundu vera frændr hans nǫkkurir ok leiti til vægðar ok vináttu, en fá í móti af konungi traust ok trúnað.
See also *Fagrskinna*, pp. 137–38; *Morkinskinna*, p. 115; and *Flateyjarbók*, III:392.

[50] *Fagrskinna*, p. 138: 'Nú sýndisk þeim þetta lið þess at meira er nálægra kom, ok var alt at sjá sem á ísmǫl, er vápnin glóðu.' See also *Morkinskinna*, p. 115; Snorri Sturluson, *Heimskringla*, III:184; and *Flateyjarbók*, III:184.

[51] Saxo Grammaticus, *Historia Danica*, ed. P.E. Müller and J.M. Velschow (Hannover, 1839), II:555: 'Quam ipsius cunctationem Norvagienses timori consentaneam rati, neglectis corporum munimentis, perinde ac securi periculorum validius praedae incubuerunt.'

[52] That Harold Godwinson's arrival was surprise can be seen in *Anglo-Saxon Chronicle* (C and D) 1066, I:197–98.

[53] Geoffrey Gaimar, I:221.

army, and if the opportunity arose to capture a herd of cattle, especially if they were peacefully feeding in a pasture only a bridge away from the assigned meeting place with the citizens of York, no one could blame Haraldr and Tostig for allowing a foraging party to acquire these cows, particularly if they had no reason to fear an attack of those men. Harold Godwinson, on the other hand, was expecting a battle and had marched from Tadcaster with that in mind.[54] He did not hesitate before rushing onto these poorly armed soldiers, cut off from their main army, and slaughtering them.[55]

Although seemingly quite different in the events they choose to recount at the start of the battle of Stamford Bridge, quite a lot of reconciliation can be made between the Norwegian Kings' Sagas and the non-Saga sources. First, the problem of where the Norwegian camp was held on the night of 24–25 September is really of little concern. (In the absence of any archaeological evidence which might assist in this matter, I am inclined to accept the Norwegian Kings' Sagas' placement of the camp at Ricall. Not only would this have been a more secure campground location, seemingly not a factor to Haraldr and Tostig, but it also meant that the transportation of foodstuffs and other necessary goods from the ships to Stamford Bridge was not necessary.) Far more important to the outcome of the battle against the Norwegians was the abandonment of their armor at the camp, wherever it was. This meant that they were completely unprepared for any battle with the English army. The abandonment of their armor may even have been the primary cause of their ultimate defeat, a reason why the mentioning of it is present in all of the Norwegian Kings' Sagas, including the smaller *Ágrip* and *Monumenta historica Norvegiæ*, as well as in the more contemporary narrative of Saxo Grammaticus' *Historia*. That it is not recorded in any of the contemporary or near-contemporary Anglo-Saxon or Anglo-Norman chronicles may only mean that the authors of those accounts either were never told about the abandoning of the armor – such an embarrassingly incautious flaw in Haraldr Harðráði's military leadership might not have been discussed by the survivors of the battle with their victors – or did not value it as a rationalization for the defeat of the Norwegian army at Stamford Bridge.[56]

The other fact about the beginning of the battle found in nearly all of the

---

54 See *Anglo-Saxon Chronicle* (C) 1066, I:197.

55 Although none of these sources is detailed enough to actually discuss the placement of Norwegian soldiers at the outset of the battle of Stamford Bridge, that there were soldiers across the river and that they were slaughtered quite easily can be concluded from Henry of Huntingdon, pp. 386–87 and Saxo Grammaticus, II:555. See also Freeman, *Norman Conquest*, III:368–69, 722; I. Walker, p. 162; F.W. Brooks, p. 20; Leadman, p. 10; Barrett, pp. 5–6, Thompson, p. 50; and Miles W. Campbell, 'Last Viking's Impact: King Harald of Norway Struck England Just Before the Norman Conquest,' *Military History* 4 (June 1988), 17.

56 The attempt to record the reasons for a defeat in battle and then their repetition in later accounts of that defeat seems to be an issue of historiographical rationalization found in many military narratives throughout the Middle Ages. See Kelly DeVries, 'Perceptions of Victory and Defeat in the Southern Low Countries during the Fourteenth Century: A Historiographical Comparison' (unpublished dissertation, University of Toronto, 1987).

sources, saga or non-saga, is Harold Godwinson's surprise of the Norwegian invaders.[57] That his arrival so completely astonished his opponents, who seem to have believed that no attack from the king of England this early in the invasion was possible, certainly gave the English army the early impetus in the battle. In addition, depending on whether they actually did catch some of the Norwegian soldiers cut off from their comrades across the river, this surprise may even have led to quite a large number of early casualties among Haraldr and Tostig's troops, casualties which they could not spare because of the larger size of Harold Godwinson's army.[58]

What about these Norwegian soldiers caught across the river? Does the fact that the Norwegian Kings' Sagas do not mention them present an irreconcilable difference between those sources and the more contemporary ones? Not really. Indeed, the Norwegian Kings' Sagas emphasize Haraldr's indecision in the wake of his initial sighting of the Anglo-Saxon army. His willingness to wait until he determined the hostility of the approaching force not only confirms the overwhelming confidence he had in believing that the main English army was still far from him to the south, but also supports the possibility that his army was not well organized that day, with some of his troops conceivably across the river in a pasture foraging for foodstuffs among a herd of cattle. This hesitation could also have delayed the return of these separated troops, inevitably leading to their deaths, especially, as they were not on the high ground that Haraldr and Tostig were, if they had failed to see the approaching English army until it was too late to again regain the opposite side of the river across the narrow bridge.

Of course, the English soldiers also needed to cross the bridge before they could engage the larger Norwegian force. This led to one of the more heroic, and more often recorded, at least among the more contemporary Anglo-Saxon/Anglo-Norman sources, incidents of the battle. The Norwegian soldiers caught by the English on the other side of the river were being slaughtered. They must have known that they were going to die, yet, rather than flee, some of these half-armed men tried to defend the bridge and thus bought, with their lives, the precious time needed by Haraldr Harðráði and Tostig Godwinson to reorder their soldiers. The story of one anonymous man in particular was retold in several early narratives. In a tale worthy of any Old Norse saga, but surprisingly absent from all of the Norwegian Kings' Sagas, it is reported that one Norwegian warrior, who had worn his armor,[59] almost single-handedly defended the bridge from constant Anglo-Saxon attack until he had killed more than forty enemy soldiers with his battle-axe. William of Malmesbury's recounting of the story is the most detailed:

---

[57] This fact is reflected also in the secondary sources: Freeman, *Norman Conquest*, III:723–24; Stenton, *Anglo-Saxon England*, p. 590; Linklater, pp. 200–01; Brown, *The Normans and the Norman Conquest*, p. 136; I. Walker, p. 162; Bradbury, *Battle of Hastings*, pp. 131, 133; and Leadman, pp. 9–10.

[58] On the 'English superiority in numbers' at Stamford Bridge see Henry of Huntingdon, pp. 386–87.

[59] That he had kept his armor can be found in *Anglo-Saxon Chronicle* (C) 1066, I:198.

The English won the day and put the Norwegians to flight; but the victory of such large and powerful forces was interrupted for many an hour (a thing posterity may hardly believe) by a single Norwegian, who is recorded to have taken his stand at the entry to the bridge called Stamford Bridge, and by killing two or three and then more of our side to have prevented them all from crossing. Called upon to surrender, that a man of such physical strength might receive generous treatment from the English, he spurned the invitation with a frown and kept taunting the enemy, saying they were a poor lot if they could not deal with a single man. So no one went near him, for it seemed unwise to attack at close quarters a desperate man who rejected all offers of safe-conduct; but one of the king's bodyguard hurled an iron javelin at him from a distance, and as he was demonstrating boastfully, rendered more incautious by justified confidence, this pierced him through and he yielded the day to the English.[60]

Henry of Huntingdon and a twelfth-century addition to the incomplete *Anglo-Saxon Chronicle* (C) relate a slightly different story, the most significant change being how the Norwegian hero died:

A single Norwegian, worthy of eternal fame, resisted on the bridge, and felling more than forty Englishmen with his trusty axe, he alone held up the entire English army until three o'clock in the afternoon. At length, someone came up in a boat and through the openings of the bridge struck him in the private parts with a spear.[61]

[60] William of Malmesbury, *Gesta regum Anglorum*, I:420–21:
Angli superiorem manum nacti Noricos in fugam egerunt, sed tantorum et tot uirorum uictoriam, quod forsitan posteritas difficile credat, unus Noricus multa hora interpolauit; siquidem in ingressu pontis qui Stanfordbrigge dicitur consistens, uno et altero et pluribus nostrae partis interemptis, omnes ab transitu arcuit. Inuitatus ad deditionem, ut tanti roboris homo largam clementiam Anglorum experiretur, inuitantes ridebat, subinde rugato uultu increpitans imbecillis animi homines esse qui nequirent uni resistere. Nemine itaque propius accedente, quod inconsultum estimarent cum illo comminus congredi qui salutis omne uiaticum desperatus effunderet, unus ex collateralibus regis iaculum ferreum in eum eminus uibrat, quo ille, dum gloriabundus proludit ipsa securitate incautior, tenebratus uictoriam Anglis concessit.

[61] This quote is from Henry of Huntingdon, pp. 386–89:
Quidam uero Norwagensis, fama dignus eterna, super pontem restitit, et plus quadraginta uiris Anglorum securi cedens electa, usque nonam diei horam omnem exercitum Anglorum detinuit solus. Vsquequo quidam nauim ingressus, per foramina pontis, in celandis eum percussit iaculo.
The account found in the *Anglo-Saxon Chronicle* (C) (1066, I:198) differs little from Henry of Huntingdon's narrative, the only notable exception being a reference to an English soldier's attempt to kill the Norwegian warrior by archery before finally slaying him by the means mentioned in Henry of Huntingdon's chronicle:
Ða wes þer an of Norwegan þe wiðstod þet Englisce folc, þet hi ne micte. þa brigge oferstigan, ne sige gerechen. Ða seite an Englisce mid anre flane ac hit nactes ne widstod ænd þa com an oþer under þere brigge end hine þurustang en under þere brunie.
The C version of the *Anglo-Saxon Chronicle* ends shortly before this passage at the bottom of a page. This was placed on a page added to the manuscript by an unknown twelfth-century scribe. See *The Anglo-Saxon Chronicle*, trans. and ed. M. Swanton (New York, 1998), p. 198,

This Norwegian alone, in the true saga-like spirit of his ancestors, withstood the entire Anglo-Saxon army giving Haraldr and Tostig ample time to regroup and order their troops on the high ground beyond the river.

As mentioned, the Norwegian Kings' Sagas contain nothing about this event or the heroic man who performed it. Instead, they record a discussion held between Haraldr Harðráði and Tostig Godwinson concerning what they should do once they realized that the oncoming force was Harold Godwinson's army. Tostig's plan was to retreat from the battlefield, return to their ships, and, with the addition of their men there, to fight Harold Godwinson. He said to the Norwegian king:

> The first thing to do is to turn back and run very quickly to the ships for the soldiers and our weapons, then to put up a defense among them, with the ships on the other side to protect us, and not let the cavalry ride over us.[62]

But Haraldr rejected this advice. Determined to face his opponent, he sent only three riders back to the ships 'on the fastest horses' to inform those left behind of the arrival of Harold Godwinson and to request that they march as fast as possible to Stamford Bridge. He told Tostig that the earl and his men could leave the battlefield, but that he and the Norwegians would stay and fight: 'the English will have an exceedingly difficult battle before we are killed.'[63] Haraldr then raised his standard, Land-waster, as a symbol to his men that they were to prepare for battle.[64]

From their description of this phase of the battle, it seems that there can be no reconciliation between the Norwegian Kings' Sagas' and the non-Saga narratives. After all, missing the story of the heroic Norwegian warrior standing alone on the bridge over the Derwent River and holding off the entire English army when so many Anglo-Norman sources were attracted to it seems to be a

---

and B. Dickins, 'The Late Addition to ASC 1066,' *Proceedings of the Leeds Philosophical and Literary Society* 5 (1940), 148–49. Secondary sources which mention the defense of the bridge include: Freeman, *Norman Conquest*, III:369–70, 721; Stenton, *Anglo-Saxon England*, p. 590; Linklater, p. 201; Brown, *The Normans and the Norman Conquest*, p. 136; I. Walker, pp. 162–63; Bradbury, *Battle of Hastings*, p. 133; Leadman, pp. 10–11; Barrett, p. 7; Thompson, pp. 50–51; and Campbell, 'Last Viking's Impact,' p. 17.

[62] I have used Snorri Sturluson's words here (*Heimskringla*, III:185), although *Fagrskinna* (p. 138), *Morkinskinna* (p. 115), and *Flateyjarbók* (III:392) also contain almost the same words for this speech:

> Þat er it fyrsta at snúa aptr sem hvatast til skipa eptir liði váru ok vápnum, veitum þá viðrtǫku eptir efnum, en at ǫðrum kosti látum skipin gæta vár, ok eigi þá riddarar ekki vald yfir oss.

[63] *Fagrskinna*, p. 138:

> Annat ráð viljum vér hafa: setjum hina skjótustu hesta undir þrjá vaska drengi, ok ríði þeir sem hvatligast ok segi sem fallit er, ok man oss þá koma lið af mǫnnum; fyrir þá sǫk at Englar skulu enn eiga snarpar hríðir, áðr en vér berim lægra hlut.

The other thirteenth-century Norwegian Kings' Sagas have a similar speech: *Morkinskinna*, p. 115; Snorri Sturluson, *Heimskringla*, III:185; and *Flateyjarbók*, III:392.

[64] *Fagrskinna*, p. 138; *Morkinskinna*, p. 116; Snorri Sturluson, *Heimskringla*, III:185; and *Flateyjarbók*, III:393.

serious historiographical flaw. Yet, even though such a scenario would seem precisely to fit the saga style, one can see that if it had not become part of the Scandinavian legend of the battle of Stamford Bridge, it would not appear in these sagas. Again, if the different perspectives of the battle are examined, this incident, viewed closely by the Anglo-Saxon troops would have made a distinct impression on them, while the confused and disheartened Norwegians, and especially their leaders, locked as they were in the planning of what to do to counter the surprising arrival of Harold Godwinson, would undoubtedly have been less aware of the defense of the bridge. As impressive as the incident was, it may well have simply gone unnoticed by those who would eventually pass along their versions of what occurred at the battle.

One thing that it did do, however, was to buy Haraldr and Tostig some valuable time, time to send riders off to Ricall for reinforcements, and time to order their troops in a shield-wall formation on the ridge of the high ground now known as Battle Flats. Only the Norwegian Kings' Sagas mention this, and their description is quite detailed:

> King Haraldr afterwards ordered his army, placing them in a long and thin formation. They bent their wings back so that they came together. They were then a wide and thick circle, equal on all sides around, shield over shield overlapping on the top, and the king's retinue of chosen soldiers was positioned inside the circle with his standard. Also placed there was Earl Tostig with his troops. He had a second standard.[65]

The shield-wall formation was ordered by Haraldr, the Norwegian Kings' Sagas claim, because he knew 'that cavalry was accustomed to charge forward and quickly to ride back.' His and Tostig's soldiers would move forward to strengthen those attacked parts of the shield-wall, and their archers would also stay in the middle of the circle to fire their arrows into the oncoming horses from whatever direction they charged. (How many archers these were is not indicated, but there were probably not that many.) He then ordered those standing in the front rank of the shield-wall that 'they should set their spear-shafts into the ground, and place the points into the breasts of the cavalry soldiers, if they charge into us,' and those standing behind them to 'set their spearheads against the breasts of their horses.'[66]

---

[65] Snorri Sturluson's is the most detailed account of this formation (*Heimskringla*, III:185):
Síðan fylkði Haraldr konungr liði sínu, lét fylkinguna langa ok ekki þykkva. Þá beygði hann armana aptr á bak, svá at saman tóku. Var þat þá víðr hringr ok þykkr ok jafn ǫllum megin útan, skjǫldr við skjǫld ok svá yfir ofan, en konungssveitin var fyrir innan hringinn ok þar merki. Þat var valit lið. Í ǫðrum stað var Tósti jarl með sína sveit. Hafði hann annat merki.
See also *Fagrskinna*, p. 138; *Morkinskinna*, pp. 115–16; and *Flateyjarbók*, III:392. Despite questioning the Norwegian Kings' Sagas' account of the battle of Stamford Bridge, F.W. Brooks (p. 21) and Paddy Griffith (pp. 191–92) both accept that this would have been the formation that Haraldr Harðráði would have chosen to use.

[66] Snorri Sturluson (*Heimskringla*, III:185–86) again provides the most detail:
Var því svá fylkt, at konungr vissi, at riddarar váru vanir at ríða á riðlum ok þegar aptr.

Nothing about the ordering of the Norwegian shield-wall is mentioned in the non-Saga sources. However, this should not be taken too seriously. Were the English soldiers so hindered by the problems of crossing the bridge against the lone Norwegian defending it, as reported in those chronicles mentioned above, they would not have had the time to notice their opponents performing this defensive maneuver. Only when they crossed the bridge would they have worried about what formation they were about to face, and, by that time, from the Norwegian Kings' Sagas' account, it seems that the shield-wall had been ordered and the soldiers in it prepared to meet the English attacks.

These attacks would follow shortly, but before they began, the English ordered their own formation, which is not detailed in any narrative, and the opposing generals rode across their lines inspecting and motivating their troops. However, as Haraldr Harðráði passed by his troops, the Sagas report, his horse, a black horse with a white mark on its forehead, stumbled and threw him to the ground. This embarrassing moment, of course, could also be perceived as ominous by the Norwegians and Anglo-Saxons who witnessed it. Haraldr understood this too, and stood up quickly, saying, 'That fall is the farewell of fortune,'[67] but Harold Godwinson, who had seen his royal opponent fall, did not see it in this light. After asking the name of that 'large man, who fell off his horse, with the blue tunic and the fair helmet,' and being told that he was King Haraldr Harðráði, the English king remarked: 'He is a large and powerful man. Here it is likely that we have come to the end of our luck.'[68]

With both armies now ordered in their lines and prepared to do battle, the Norwegian Kings' Sagas claim that twenty English horsemen, 'all clad in mail armor,' broke from their ranks and rode toward the Norwegian lines.[69] One called out to Tostig:

Nú segir konungr, at hans sveit ok jarls sveit skal þar fram ganga, sem mest þarf – 'en bogmenn várir skulu ok þar vera með oss, en þeir, er fremstir standa, skulu setja spjót-shala sína í jǫrðina, en setja oddana fyrir brjóst riddurum, ef þeir ríða at oss, en þeir, er næstir standa, seti þeir sína spjótsodda fyrir brjóst hestum þeira.'
See also *Fagrskinna*, p. 138; *Morkinskinna*, p. 116; and *Flateyjarbók*, III:393.

[67] *Fagrskinna* (p. 138), Snorri Sturluson (*Heimskringla*, II:186), and *Flateyjarbók* (III:393), the only three of the Norwegian Kings' Sagas which include this incident, have the same words coming out of Haraldr's mouth after rising from this fall: 'Fall er fararheill.' Its trans-lation seems clear, and yet the translators of Snorri Sturluson's saga, Magnus Magnusson and Herman Pálsson (Snorri Sturluson, *King Harald's Saga*, trans. M. Magnusson and H. Pálsson (Harmondsworth, 1966), p. 149) have translated the phrase, 'A fall is fortune on the way,' which is the complete opposite of its meaning, and removes its foreboding image.

[68] Again, it is only *Fagrskinna* (p. 138), Snorri Sturluson (*Heimskringla*, III:186), and *Flateyjarbók* (III:393) which include this comment. With only a slight variation, the words are the same in both. I have used those of Snorri Sturluson: 'Mikill maðr ok ríkmannligr, ok er vænna, at farinn sé at hamingju.' It is, however, possible to translate this as Harold Godwin-son believing that the luck of Haraldr Harðráði had run out, and not his own.

[69] Snorri Sturluson (*Heimskringla*, III:186) and *Flateyjarbók* (III:393) claim that their horses were also covered in mail, but *Fagrskinna* (p. 138) has only the cavalry soldiers clad in armor.

King Harold, your brother, sends you a greeting and an offer, that you should have peace and all of Northumbria. And rather than have you refuse him, he will give you one third of all of his kingdom.[70]

However, the earl had too much pride as well as too much anger to agree to this offer. He could only think of the humiliation of his exile, and the lack of support given to him by his brother then, or later when he was crowned. He responded:

This offer is somewhat different from the hostility and disgrace there was in winter. And if this would have been the first offer, then many men would still have their lives, but now do not. Then England would not be the worse country that it is now. And if we accept this offer, what will you offer to King Haraldr for all his strife?[71]

A similar offer was not to come to Haraldr Harðráði, who had after all invaded Harold Godwinson's kingdom. The rider remarked cynically: 'He has already said something of this, how much shall be his part of England: seven feet of space or more length as he is taller than other men.'[72] Tostig could do little more than refuse such an offer. Haraldr Harðráði was his ally and had shown him no treachery; Harold Godwinson was his brother and had shown him constant treachery. He replied: 'we have the same wish, either to die with honor, or to gain England with a victory.'[73]

Thus rebuked, the English riders returned to their lines. Noticing that Tostig seemed to know the main English speaker, Haraldr questioned him as to this man's identity: 'who was that eloquent man?' To which Tostig answered: 'That was King Harold Godwinson.' Haraldr was understandably angered by this

---

[70] I have used Snorri Sturluson (*Heimskringla*, III:186) here, as the *Fagrskinna* (pp. 138–39) and *Flateyjarbók* (III:394) are somewhat confusing:

Þá mælti einn riddari: 'Haraldr, bróðir þinn, sendi þér kveðju ok þau orð með, at þú skyldir hafa grið ok Norðimbraland allt, ok heldr en eigi vilir þú til hans hneigjask, þá vill hann gefa þér þriðjung ríkis alls með sér.'

Morkinskinna records none of these preliminaries to the battle.

[71] *Fagrskinna* (p. 139), Snorri Sturluson (*Heimskringla*, III:186–87), and *Flateyjarbók* (III:394) all contain the same speech with only slight variants. I am using *Fagrskinna* here:

Þá svaraði jarlinn: 'Boðit er þá nǫkkut annat en úfriðr ok svivirðingin sem í vetr, ok ef þetta væri margr maðr sá heill ok með lifi, er nú er eigi, ok þá man eigi standa verr ríki Englands; nú tǫkum vér þenna kost, en hvat vili þér nú bjóða Haraldi konungi fyrir sitt starf?'

[72] Snorri Sturluson, *Heimskringla*, III:187: 'Þá mælti riddarinn: "Sagt hefir hann þar nɔkkut frá, hvers hann mun honum unna af Englandi: sjau fóta rúm eða því lengra sem hann er hæri en aðrir menn." ' See also *Fagrskinna*, p. 139, and *Flateyjarbók*, III:394, which use slightly different words, but with the same sentiment.

[73] Snorri Sturluson, *Heimskringla*, III:187:

Þá segir jarl: 'Farið nú ok segið Haraldi konungi, at hann búisk til orrustu. Annat skal satt at segja með Norðmǫnnum en þat, at Tósti jarl fari frá Haraldi konungi Sigurðar-syni ok í óvinaflokk hans, þá er hann skyldi berjask í Englandi vestr. Heldr skulu vér allir taka eitt ráð, deyja með sœmð eða fá England með sigri.'

Fagrskinna, p. 139, and *Flateyjarbók*, III:394, contain virtually the same speech.

response and lamented not being able to kill the opposing leader, 'I wish that this had not been concealed from me, as he came right in front of our army, that this Harold would not have been able to tell of the deaths of our men.' Tostig knew this and, in a speech more reminiscent of thirteenth-century chivalry than what might have actually happened, he replied:

> It is certainly true . . . that the king acted incautiously before such a great army and what you say might have happened, but he did this because he wanted to offer his brother peace and much power. If I had told you that he was the leader, and I had caused his death, then I would be the murderer of my brother. It would be better if he was my killer than I was his.

In an effort to bolster the confidence of his men, in the face of such brotherly concern, Haraldr's only further comment was: 'That little man is like a boy, but he stood well in his stirrups.'[74]

Finally, in the waning moments before combat actually began, as is customarily found in saga battlefield narratives, a number of poems were composed. Two of those at Stamford Bridge are attributed to the king, Haraldr Harðráði, himself. In the first he seems to anticipate, if not rationalize defeat:

> We go forward
> Into battle
> Without armor
> Against blue blades.
> Helmets glitter.
> My coat of mail
> And all our armor
> Are at the ships.

This poem being a bit too despondent, Haraldr composed a second, far more proud and enthusiastic one:

> We never kneel in battle
> Before the storm of weapons
> And crouch behind our shields;

---

[74] *Fagrskinna*, p. 117:

> Þa riþo þeir aptr riddararnir. Oc eptir þat melti Haralldr konvngr Sigurþar son til iarlsins Tosta. Hverr var sia enn sniallraddaþi maþr. er viþ yþr melti. Jarllinn svarar. Þar var sialfr Haralldr konvngr Goþina son. Þa sagþi Haralldr konvngr Sigurþar son. Of lengi var ec þesso leyndr. þvi at comnir voro þeir sva fire liþ vart. at eigi mondi nafni minn kvnna at segia banorþ varra manna. Jarlinn svarar. Sam ver þat herra at ovarliga for þvilicr hofþingi. oc verþa matti þetta sem þer segit. for hann með þvi at hann villdi bioþa griþ brøþr sinom oc mikit valld. vist vera ec þa sannliga kallaðr verri hofþingi ef ec biþa sva elli. at ec vera banamaþr broþor mins. oc betra er at þiggia bana af brøþr sinom en veita honom bana. Þa melti Haralldr konvngr til sinna manna. Litill maþr var þessi sveinar. oc stoþ þo steigurliga i stigreip sin.

Snorri Sturluson (*Heimskringla*, III:187) and *Flateyjarbók* (III:394) use virtually the same words for this dialogue.

So the noble lady told me.
She told me once to carry
My head always high in battle
Where swords seek to shatter
The skulls of doomed warriors.[75]

Other poems from other poets were also composed. Almost all forecast defeat.[76]

These dialogues and poems, found in the Norwegian Kings' Sagas alone, must, of course, be dismissed as later literary flourish. However, they are certainly not more of a historiographical dilemma than any similar conversation or literary flourish which appear in more contemporary, non-saga battlefield narratives. Even the most 'trustworthy' medieval chroniclers scatter dialogues among their accounts of battles which they could in no way know the substance of. (See, for example, the contemporary accounts of the battle of Hastings which those of the battle of Stamford Bridge are invariably compared to.[77]) On the

---

[75] These poems are recorded in all four of the more detailed Norwegian Kings' Sagas. These quotes are from Snorri Sturluson's *Heimkringla*, III:187–188:

> Framm gǫngum vér
> í fylkingu
> brynjulausir
> und blár eggjar.
> Hjalmar skína.
> Hefkat ek mina.
> Nú liggr skrúð várt
> at skipum niðri.
>
> . . .
> Krjúpum vér fyr vápna,
> valteigs brǫkun eigi,
> svá bauð Hildr, at hjaldri,
> haldorð, í bug skjaldar.
> Hótt bað mik, þars mœttusk,
> menskorð bera forðum,
> hlakkar iss ok hausar,
> hjalmstofn í gný malma.

See also *Fagrskinna*, pp. 139–40; *Morkskinna*, pp. 117–18; and *Flateyjarbók*, III:394–95. I have used the translations of these poems found in Magnusson and Pálsson, pp. 150–51. Who this lady was who gave Haraldr this advice is not revealed anywhere in the Norwegian Kings' Sagas. For a discussion of these poems within the corpus of Haraldr Harðráði's poems and those by his poets see Gabriel Turville-Petre, *Haraldr the Hardruler and His Poets* (London, 1966), pp. 19–20.

[76] Most of these are not recorded in all four of these Nowegian Kings' Sagas. See the examples found in *Fagrskinna*, pp. 140–41; *Morkinskinna*, pp. 116–19; Snorri Sturluson, *Heimskringla*, III:188–89; and *Flateyjarbók*, III:393–96.

[77] All of these can be found in Morillo, ed., *The Battle of Hastings*. Even William of Poitiers and William of Jumièges, the two authors of the most widely accepted accounts of the battle of Hastings contain battlefield discourse between William the Conqueror and his fellow leaders. For other, later examples, see DeVries, 'Perceptions of Victory and Defeat in the Southern Low Countries during the Fourteenth Century'; DeVries, *Infantry Warfare in the*

other hand, that they may be dismissed as historical, does not remove their historiographical worth. For one thing, the constant repetition throughout the Norwegian Kings' Sagas of the Norwegian troops' lack of armor, even devoting one of Haraldr Harðráði's poems to it, must continue to be recognized as what the authors of these biographical tales blame for the defeat in this battle. Also, while the conversations and poems may be literary in nature, can we say the same thing about the visit between the brothers? Is it possible that these two brothers would have faced each other in battle without the one, Harold, trying to keep the other, Tostig, from death by an offer such as the one described in the Norwegian Kings' Sagas?

The battle of Stamford Bridge was still far from over. Harold Godwinson's troops had completely surprised the Norwegians, it is true, but the defense of the bridge had allowed the invading army to form a shield-wall, and a shield-wall could usually be broken only at the cost of many men. Facing an imposing shield-wall like that at Stamford Bridge had not been anticipated by troops who just minutes earlier had so surprised their foes, and the Norwegians' defensive tactic must have somewhat demoralized the attacking Anglo-Saxons. Still, it was a *defensive* tactic, and the English did greatly outnumber the Norwegian invaders, especially after defeating and killing a number of them on the other side of the river.

There were few tactical options when facing a shield-wall in the eleventh century, especially when one was formed as this one was, if the Norwegian Kings' Sagas are to be believed, in a circular fashion, thus presenting no flanks to outflank. A feigned retreat was certainly a possibility, if it was known, but it was generally unconvincing if the side using the tactic had no reason to retreat; such was the case at Stamford Bridge, with the English outnumbering the Norwegians. So, the only option was a charge, a frontal assault.

The Norwegian Kings' Sagas claim that these frontal aasaults were delivered by the Anglo-Saxon cavalry, and, as was common, that at first the Norwegian shield-wall held firmly against these charges, even harassing the attackers with a constant barrage of archery fire from within the circular formation. The *Fagrskinna* recounts what happened:

> Now the English made a cavalry charge at the Norwegians, but their defense at the impact was so strong, that they did not move. As was decided before, the

Early Fourteenth Century; and the excellent studies on the subject by John R.E. Bliese, including, 'The Courage of the Normans. A Comparative Study of Battle Rhetoric,' *Nottingham Medieval Studies* 35 (1991), 1–26; 'Leadership, Rhetoric, and Morale in the Norman Conquest of England,' *Military Affairs* 52 (1988), 23–28; Rhetoric and Morale: A Study of Battle Orations from the Central Middle Ages,' *Journal of Medieval History* 15 (1989), 201–26; and 'When Knightly Courage May Fail: Battle Orations in Medieval Europe,' *Historian* 53 (1991), 489–504.

archers fired and most of their arrows flew against the horses. Both sides fought with power, and struck down many dead men.[78]

Snorri Sturluson relates a slightly different story:

Now the battle began, and they [the English] made a cavalry charge against the Norwegians. But their defense was strong. It was difficult for the English soldiers to ride against the Norwegians because of the arrows, so they rode in a circle around them. At first it was a loose battle with the Norwegian soldiers holding their formation, and the English soldiers riding hard at them and then falling back quickly when they could not move them.[79]

Suddenly, in the midst of this fighting, the Norwegian shield-wall dissolved, as Norwegian soldiers broke out of their formation to make their own charge against the English. This was clearly a Norwegian initiative, not taken because their shield-wall was weakening, and it was wholly unsuccessful. So, why was it done? Snorri Sturluson gives the impression that it might have been a tactic designed by the English to provoke the Norwegians to charge out of their defensive formation, one which Haraldr Harðráði fell for:

[After suffering the English charges and retreats for a while,] the Norwegians saw this and thought that their attacks were weak. Then they sought to attack them. And when they had broken the shield wall, the English soldiers rode at them from all sides and attacked them with spears and arrows.[80]

Fagrskinna, *Morkinskinna*, and *Flateyjarbók* do not give this impression. Rather, they see the dissolving of the shield-wall as a counter-attack performed by the Norwegians against a particularly strong English assault:

---

[78] *Fagrskinna*, p. 140:

Nú veita Englar Norðmǫnnum áreið, ok varð á mót viðrtaka hǫrð, ok svá váru settar kesjurnar, sem fyrr var sagt, ok komsk þat mest við hestana; berjask þó hvárirtveggja með sin afli, ok réð seint mannfallit á.

Both *Morkinskinna* (p. 118) and *Flateyjarbók* (III:395) follow *Fagrskinna* in this description of the fighting.

[79] Snorri Sturluson, *Heimskringla*, III:189:

Nú hefr upp orrostu, ok veita enskir menn áreið Norðmǫnnum. Varð viðrtakan hǫrð. Varð óhœgt enskum mǫnnum at riða á Norðmenn fyrir skotum, ok riðu þeir í hring um þá. Var þat fyrst laus orrosta, meðan Norðmenn heldu vel fylkingu, en enskir menn riðu at hart ok þegar frá, er þeir fengu ekki at gǫrt.

See also Freeman, *Norman Conquest*, III:370–71; Linklater, p. 202; Bradbury, *Battle of Hastings*, p. 133; Leadman, p. 11; Barrett, pp. 7–8; Thompson, p. 51; and Campbell, 'Last Viking's Impact,' p. 17; and Guy Schofield, 'The Third Battle of 1066,' *History Today* 16 (1966), 693 (who erroneously calls the formation a square).

[80] Snorri Sturluson, *Heimskringla*, III:189:

En er Norðmenn sá þat, at þeim þótti blautliga at riðit, þá sóttu þeir at þeim ok vildu reka flóttann, en er þeir hǫfðu brugðit skjaldborginni, þá riðu enskir menn at þeim ǫllum megin ok báru á þá spjót ok skot.

Still, [despite the heavy death toll the English were suffering] there was a great difference in the numbers of men. A large number of English soldiers rode in circles around them and then charged a group of men at them. And then came the Norwegians charging back at them, losing their formation, and there was a great slaughter among both armies.[81]

Haraldr Harðráði was particularly valiant in this charge. Fighting without a shield or his long mail-shirt, Emma, which had been left with the ships, the Norwegian king swung weapons in both hands, slaying all who unluckily fell into his path. One of the 'earl's poets,' Arnórr, remembered it this way:

> Norway's king had nothing
> To shield his breast in battle;
> And yet his war-seasoned
> Heart never wavered.
> Norway's warriors were watching
> The blood-dripping sword
> Of their courageous leader
> Cutting down his enemies.[82]

Yet, despite the king's strength and bravery, this was an unwise and reckless tactic, almost pointless when the shield-wall was holding. Haraldr should also have anticipated the imminent arrival of the reinforcements from his ships which he had sent for quite a while previously; should the shield-wall have held for a bit longer, his troops' numbers would have been greatly increased. (Perhaps Harold Godwinson also knew of the possible arrival of reinforcements from the Norwegian ships, if Snorri Sturluson is to be believed, which could be the reason for directing his troops, by lack-luster charges, to draw the invaders from

---

[81] I am quoting from *Fagrskinna*, p. 140:
> ok var svá mikill liðsmunr, at mikill fjǫldi Engla gerðu hring um þá er þeir kómusk á bak þeim, þá losnaði fylkingin, ok gerði mannfall mikit í hvártveggja liðit.

Morkinskinna, p. 118, and *Flateyjarbók*, III:395, use nearly the same wording. See also Linklater, pp. 202–03 and Bradbury, *Battle of Hastings*, p. 133.

[82] All four of the detailed Norwegian Kings' Sagas record this poem. I am quoting from Snorri Sturluson, *Heimskringla*, III:189–90:
> Hafði brjóst, né bifðisk
> bǫðsnart konungs hjarta,
> í hjalmþrimu hilmir
> hlitstyggr fyr sér litit,
> þars til þengils hersa
> þat sá herr, at skatna
> blóðugr hjǫrr ens barra
> beit dǫglinga hneitis.

I have used Magnusson and Pálsson's translation (p. 152). See also *Fagrskinna*, p. 140; *Morkinskinna*, p. 118; and *Flateyjarbók*, III:395. All but Snorri Sturluson's saga also contains a similar poem written by a poet named Stufr. For Snorri Sturluson's description of the fighting of Haraldr Harðráði see the chapter 'The Norwegian Military', n. 53, above.

their protective formation.) The only conceivable reasons for the breaking out from his defensive formation were, one, if this was a *berserkgangr*, or two, if Haraldr Harðráði thought that he had a chance, by delivering an unexpected thrust at the English, of driving them from the battlefield and giving his troops victory.

This was not to be, and it was fatal for Haraldr Harðráði. The fighting spirit of the Norwegians was fierce, but ultimately the English army held its ground and in a short time had regained the advantage in battle. In the end, the charge did little for the Norwegians, with many slain by the Anglo-Saxons. Haraldr was killed himself, having been struck in the throat by an arrow. The *Fagrskinna* describes his and his men's deaths:

> Then King Haraldr was struck in the front of the neck by an arrow, so that at once blood came out of his mouth; that was his deathblow, and he fell straight to the ground. Now when these tidings were heard, the English came on so strong, that all the men who had stood near the king were killed.[83]

The 'Land-waster' had fallen and with it a powerful Norwegian warlord.

Tostig Godwinson seems not to have charged forward with Haraldr and other Norwegians, and following the death of his ally he found himself in control of the remaining forces opposing the English. He quickly called a retreat to their former secure position and attempted to re-establish a shield-wall. Once again, Harold Godwinson, approached the enemy formation and offered peace to Tostig and all the remaining Norwegians, but the invaders, too proud to resign after the honorable death of their king and so many of their comrades, and too willing to join them in a similar end, refused the English king's offer. Arnórr, the earl's poet, composed these lines:

> It was an evil moment
> When Norway's king lay fallen;
> Gold-inlaid weapons
> Brought death to Norway's leader.
> All King Haraldr's warriors
> Preferred to die beside him,

---

[83] *Fagrskinna*, pp. 140–41:

Þá var Haraldr konungr skotinn framan í óstina, svá at þegar kom út blóð at munninum; þetta var hans banasár, ok því næst féll hann til jarðar. Nú er þessi tíðendi váru orðin, þá sóttu Englar at svá fast, at þá féll alt liðit þat, er næst hafði staðit konunginum.

All of the other more detailed Norwegian Kings' Sagas relay the same story: *Morkinskinna*, 119; Snorri Sturluson, *Heimskringla*, III:190; and *Flateyjarbók*, III:396. See also Theodoricus, p. 57; *Ágrip*, p. 41; Freeman, *Norman Conquest*, III:371–72; I. Walker, p. 164; F.W. Brooks, p. 21; Leadman, p. 11; Barrett, p. 8; Thompson, p. 51; and Campbell, 'Last Viking's Impact,' p. 17. Brooks also disposes of a local tradition that Haraldr Harðráði survived the battle and lived for the rest of his life in Barrow-on-Humber in Lincolnshire.

> Sharing their brave king's fate,
> Rather than beg for mercy.[84]

The Norwegian Kings' Sagas record that Tostig and most of the remaining invaders were killed quite soon thereafter. Under the best of circumstances, they would not have lasted long. There was little else that they could do except to accept death honorably and bravely. There simply were too few defenders to plug all the gaps made in the shield-wall, and, despite fighting with as much strength as they could muster, the new formation must have collapsed quickly. Tostig himself was slain in these last attacks, shot in the face, tradition has it, by an arrow fired by one of the Anglo-Saxon fyrd, the most lowly of English soldiers.[85]

Almost as the last of the Norwegians at Stamford Bridge were fleeing or dying, their reinforcements from the ships arrived, led by Haraldr Harðráði's trusted friend and potential son-in-law, Eysteinn Orri. Most of these soldiers had run all the way from Ricall and were fatigued by the time they reached the battlefield, but when they were greeted by the corpses of their companions strewn all over the field, and on both sides of the river, they fell into their own battle fury. Eysteinn himself picked up the fallen 'Land-waster' and carried it into battle. To the English, who had now fought in intense combat for several hours, this new attack was almost too much to endure. The *Fagrskinna* reports that 'this was the most fierce part of the battle [for the English] as most of them

---

[84] All of the later Norwegian Kings' Sagas contain this poem. I am quoting from Snorri Sturluson, *Heimskringla*, III:191:

> Eigi varð ens ýgja
> auðligr konungs dauði.
> Hlífðut hlenna svæfi
> hoddum roðnir oddar.
> Heldr kuru meir ens mæra
> mildings an grið vildi
> of folksnaran fylki
> falla liðsmenn allir.

See also *Fagrskinna*, p. 140; *Morkinskinna*, p. 118; and *Flateyjarbók*, III:396. The translation of this poem is found in Magnusson and Pálsson, p. 153. See also Linklater, pp. 202–03.

[85] See *Fagrskinna*, p. 141; *Morkinskinna*, p. 119: and *Flateyjarbók*, III:396. All claim that Tostig fought bravely and skillfully until killed. They do not report how he was killed. See also Freeman, *Norman Conquest*, pp. 372–73; Linklater, pp. 202–03; I. Walker, p. 164; Leadman, p. 10; Barrett, p. 8; Thompson, p. 51; and Campbell, 'Last Viking's Impact,' p. 17. For the tradition of his death by arrow see Butler, p. 161. However, there is no evidence to support this tradition, although it could explain the damage to Tostig's face, so that his body needed to be identified by other means. Freeman, however, contends that such damage meant that he was killed with a battle axe, although there is no evidence to support this theory. Some, such as Leadman and Barrett, believe that Tostig was personally killed by his brother, Harold, which they get from a misreading of the *Carmen de hastingae proelio*, ed. C. Morton and A. Muntz (Oxford, 1972), pp. 10–11.

fell, many fighting against their own desires to flee.'[86] The Norwegian reinforcements were extremely hot and fatigued though and many threw off their
armor during their early fighting to aid in their ability to attack the English. So,
like their unarmored comrades, they were also eventually cut down. The
Fagrskinna concludes:

> Now Eysteinn and his men began to grow very weary, for they had fought long
> and hard in their coats of mail, which were made hot by the weather and the
> sun, and being nearly exhausted from running, they threw off their armor. And
> they battled so hard that they had the better of the killing. But many blows
> were received by them from English weapons, and then fell Eysteinn Orri and
> nearly all of his men. This battle was called Orri's battle, but it was the day of
> his death. It was thus said, 'they came from every direction.' For this reason, it
> was a long, ill-fated day, and few came away before the killing was ended.[87]

The slaughter continued until after dark.

Non-saga sources contain none of this. Unless the interpretation of lines such
as that from Henry of Huntingdon, 'they engaged at dawn and after fearful
assaults on both sides they continued steadfastly until midday, the English superiority in numbers forcing the Norwegians to give way but not flee,' or that from
William of Malmesbury, 'that the [English] army . . . cut down the Norwegians,
who were straying at random,' can be stretched to fit the English attacks of the
shield-wall or on the Norwegians breaking out of their shield wall, or any other
incident detailed in the Norwegian Kings' Sagas, then there is no corroboration
from non-Saga sources for that which is found in the later Scandinavian narratives.[88]

---

[86] *Fagrskinna*, p. 141: 'ok var þá orrostan miklu hǫrðust ok féllu enskir menn mest, ok var
við sjálft at þeir mundu flýja.' See also *Morkinskinna*, p. 119 and *Flateyjarbók*, III:396.
Strangely, Snorri Sturluson does not report this detail.

[87] *Fagrskinna*, pp. 141–42:
> Nú varð ok Eysteinn ok hans menn mjǫk móðir, fyrir þvi at þeir hǫfðu gengit langa
> hríð undir hringabrynjum, ok gerðisk veðrit mjǫk heitt af sólu, at þá váru þeir náliga
> úfœrir, ok steyptusk þá allir or brynjum sinum; en þessi orrosta fór sem ván var, at þeir
> hǫfðu betra hlut, er aflit hǫfðu meira ok búnað betr með vápnum; ok féll þar nú Eyste-
> inn orri ok náliga alt stórmenni, en þessi orrostu var kǫlluð Orrahríð. En þat var efra
> hlut dagsins. Var þetta sem mælt er 'æ kemr einn hvadan', ok fyrir þvi at sumum var
> auðit lengra lifdraga, ok kómusk með þvi undan.

What the internal quotation is to signify is not explained within this the context of this or any
other Norwegian Kings' Saga. See also *Morkinskinna*, pp. 119–20; Snorri Sturluson,
Heimskringla, III:191–92; and *Flateyjarbók*, III:396–97. However, none of these has the
detail that *Fagrskinna* does. Secondary sources which discuss the arrival of the reinforcements include: Bradbury, *Battle of Hastings*, p. 133; F.W. Brooks, pp. 21–22; Thompson, pp.
51–52; and Campbell, 'Last Viking's Impact,' p. 66. Brooks has developed what is a fairly
convincing route for their march from Ricall to Stamford Bridge.

[88] Henry of Huntingdon, pp. 386–87:
> Pugna igitur incepta est qua gravior non fuerat. Coeuntes namque a summo mane

Furthermore, there are a few vague details found in these more contemporary non-Saga sources which do not find their equivalent in the Norwegian Kings' Sagas, even with an extraordinary amount of interpretative manipulation. For example, Henry of Huntingdon reports that after Harold Godwinson's army crossed the bridge they 'laid low the whole Norwegian line, either with their arms or by consuming with fire those they intercepted.' The 'laying low of the whole Norwegian line with their arms' presents few problems, as this could be directed at the final English attacks of the Norwegian shield-wall, but what is to be made of the 'consuming with fire those they intercepted'?[89] Then in the *Anglo-Saxon Chronicle* (D) there is the description of a battle between the victorious English troops and the Norwegian survivors of the battle around their ships at Ricall for which there is no Saga equivalent:

> then the Norwegians who were left there [at Stamford Bridge] were put to flight, and the English fiercely attacked them from behind until some had reached their ships. Some drowned and some also burned. So many perished that there were few who still lived.[90]

Yet these and any other reports on the battle of Stamford Bridge are infrequent; other than the defense of the bridge, there is very little detail of any kind about the battle found in the more contemporary Anglo-Saxon/Anglo-Norman sources. What they do emphasize is the arduous (Henry of Huntingdon) or bitter (John of Worcester) warfare[91] and the large numbers of deaths resulting from

usque ad meridiem, cum horribiliter ruentes utrimque perseuerarent, numerus maximus Anglorum Norwagenses cedere, sed non fugere, compulit.

That Henry places this before the defense of the bridge may indicate, however, that it cannot be interpreted to mean the attacks on the shield-wall.

William of Malmesbury, *Gesta regum Anglorum*, I:420–23: '. . . exercitus triectus Noricos palantes . . . cecidit.' The words *a tergo* added between *palantes* and *cecidit* may make this a statement of the death which followed as the Norwegians who had survived the battle tried to reach the safety of their ships, rather than any reference to actual on-the-battlefield fighting.

[89] Henry of Huntingdon, pp. 388–89: 'Transientes igitur Angli . . . totam Norwagensium aciem uel armis strauerunt, uel igne deprehensos combusserunt.' Although there may be some allegorical meaning of fire here, there seems to be no way that it could refer to the archery fire of the Anglo-Saxons.

[90] *Anglo-Saxon Chronicle* (D) 1066, I:199:

> þa Normen þe þær to lafe wæron wurdon on fleame. ⁊ þa Engliscan hi hindan hetelice slogon. oð þ hig sume to scype coman. sume adrucen. ⁊ sume eac forbærnde. ⁊ swa mislice forfarene. þ þær wæs lyt to lafe.

[91] Henry of Huntingdon, pp. 386–87 and John of Worcester, II:604–05. See also *Anglo-Saxon Chronicle* (D) 1066, I:197–99; William of Malmesbury, *Gesta regum Anglorum*, I:420–21; Symeon of Durham, *Historia regum*, II:180–81; Geoffrey Gaimar, I:221–22; William of Poitiers, pp. 116–17; Orderic Vitalis, II:168–69; *Vita Ædwardi regis qui apud Westmonasterium requiescit*, ed. and trans. F. Barlow, 2nd edn (London, 1992), pp. 88–89; *The Waltham Chronicle: An Account of the Discovery of Our Holy Cross at Montacute and Its Conveyance to Waltham*, ed. and trans. L. Watkiss and M. Chibnall (Oxford, 1994), pp.

this battle – the author of the *Vita Ædwardi*, who otherwise says nothing about the battle, writes poetically 'where namesake kings had fought,/ has dyed the ocean waves for miles/ around with barbarian gore, while Heaven mourns the king' – including those of King Haraldr Harðráði and Earl Tostig Godwinson.[92]

The English had won the victory, but it was a costly victory. King Harold Godwinson had shown great military expertise mixed with some brotherly affection. He had lost many men, although no contemporary sources record just how many; but the Norwegians had lost far more than the English, including their king and his exiled English ally. For King Harold Godwinson of England, no loss was greater than the personal one suffered when his brother, Tostig, had died. He had been a brother whom Harold seemed to love, and who by a misunderstanding had found himself invading his brother's realm and opposing him on the battlefield.

Harold, sick of the bloodshed he had participated in, marched his army south to Ricall and related what had happened at Stamford Bridge to the very few Norwegians left there under the command of Óláfr, son of Haraldr Harðráði, and Páll, earl of Orkney. Not wishing for more war, after taking hostages and receiving oaths, the English king allowed the remnants of the defeated army, both those who had stayed out of the battle and those captured at Stamford Bridge, to return to Norway. What had been brought on more than three hundred ships now

---

44–45; William of Jumièges, *The Gesta Normanorum ducum of William of Jumièges, Orderic Vitalis, and Robert of Torigny*, ed. and trans. E.M.C. van Houts (Oxford, 1995), II:166–67; Freeman, *Norman Conquest*, III:373–74; Stenton, *Anglo-Saxon England*, p. 590; Loyn, 'Harold, Son of Godwin,' p. 317; and Leadman, pp. 11–12.

[92] *Vita Ædwardi regis*, pp. 88–89:

> Quis canet equoreo uastum feruore tumentem
> Humbram congressum regibus equiuocis
> sanguine barbarico per milia multa marinos
> Tinxisse fluctus   flente polo facinus?

Frank Barlow, the translator of the *Vita Ædwardi regis* translates *barbarico* as 'Viking'. I have chosen to leave the word as 'barbarian'. On the deaths at Stamford Bridge, including those of the invading leaders see *Anglo-Saxon Chronicle* (D and E) 1066, I:198–99; John of Worcester, II:602–05; Henry of Huntingdon, pp. 388–89; William of Malmesbury, *Gesta regum Anglorum*, I:422–23; Symeon of Durham, *Historia regum*, II:180–81; Geoffrey Gaimar, I:221–22; William of Poitiers, pp. 116–17; William of Jumièges, II:166–67; Orderic Vitalis, II:168–69; *Carmen de hastingae proelio*, pp. 10–11; and Adam of Bremen, *Gesta Hammaburgensis ecclesiae pontificum*, ed. B. Schmeidler, 3rd edn (Hanover, 1917), p. 196. (The *Carmen de hastingae proelio* mentions the death of Tostig Godwinson only.) The number of dead at this battle especially impresses Orderic Vitalis who claims that at the time of his writing,

> Travellers cannot fail to recognize the field, for a great mountain of dead men's bones still lies there and bears witness to the terrible slaughter on both sides.

> Locus etiam belli pertranseuntibus euidenter patet, ubi magna congeries ossuum mortuorum usque hodie iacet et indicium ruinae multiplicis utriusque gentis exhibet.

left on only twenty.[93] Harold then returned to the battlefield, identified Tostig's body, as mentioned above, by the wart between his shoulders, and commanded that it be taken back to York and buried in an unnamed church there. Finally, the English army retired from the battlefield to York. The Norwegian invasion of England had come to an end.

However, the Norman invasion, on the southern coast of England, had just begun.

[93] Several sources refer to this: *Anglo-Saxon Chronicle* (D) 1066, I:199; John of Worcester, II:604–05; William of Malmesbury, *Gesta regum Anglorum*, I:422–23; Symeon of Durham, *Historia regum*, II:181; Geoffrey Gaimar, I:222; Theodoricus, p. 57; *Ágrip*, p. 41; *Fagrskinna*, p. 142; *Morkinskinna*, p. 121; Snorri Sturluson, *Heimskringla*, III:194; and *Flateyjarbók*, III:397–98. See also Freeman, *Norman Conquest*, III:374–75; Linklater, p. 203; I. Walker, p. 164; Bradbury, *Battle of Hastings*, pp. 133–34; Leadman, p. 11; Barrett, pp. 8–9; and Campbell, 'Last Viking's Impact,' p. 66.

CHAPTER ELEVEN

AFTERMATH

KING HAROLD GODWINSON was not to live in peace for long after his victory at Stamford Bridge. According to John of Worcester:

> While these things were happening [Harold making peace with Óláfr Haraldson and sending the remnants of the Norwegian army back to Norway], and the king supposed all his enemies had been destroyed, he was informed that William, duke of the Normans, had landed his fleet at a place called Pevensey, with an innumerable multitude of knights, slingers, archers and foot-soldiers, for he had brought strong auxiliaries from the whole of Gaul with him. Whereupon the king at once moved his army to London in great haste. And although he knew that all the more powerful men from the whole of England had already fallen in two battles, and that half of his army had not yet assembled, yet he did not fear to go meet his enemies in Sussex with all possible speed, and nine miles from Hastings, where they had earlier built a fortress for themselves, before a third of his army had been drawn up on Saturday, 22 October, he joined battle with the Normans.[1]

A similar story is repeated by almost all of the contemporary or near contemporary sources.[2] Although some have Harold hearing of William's landing at York

---

[1] John of Worcester, *The Chronicle of John of Worcester*, ed. R.R. Darlington and P. McGurk, trans. J. Bray and P. McGurk (Oxford, 1995), II:604–05:
Interea dum hec agerentur et rex omnes suos inimicos autumaret detritos fuisse, nuntiatum est ei Willelmum comitem gentis Normannice cum innumera multitudine equitum, fundibalariorum, sagittariorum, peditumque aduenisse, utpote qui de tota Gallia sibi fortes auxiliarios conduxerat, et in loco qui Pefnesea dicitur suam classem, appulisse. Vnde rex statim uersus Lundoniam suum mouit exercitum magna cum festinatione, et licet de tota Anglia fortiores quosque preliis in duobus bene sciret iam cecidisse, mediamque partem sui exercitus nondum conuenisse, quam citius tamen potuit in Suthsaxonia suis hostibus occurrere non formidauit, et nouem miliariis ab Heastinga, ubi sibi castellum firmauerit priusquam tertia pars sui exercitus ordinaretur .xi. kalend. Nouembris, sabbato, sum eis prelium commisit.

[2] See Henry, Archdeacon of Huntingdon, *Historia Anglorum: The History of the English People*, ed. and trans. D. Greenway (Oxford, 1996), pp. 388–89; William of Malmesbury, *Gesta regum Anglorum: The History of the English Kings*, ed. and trans. R.A.B. Mynors, R.M. Thomson, and M. Winterbottom (Oxford, 1998), I:422–23, 450–51; Symeon of Durham, *Historia regum*, ed. T. Arnold (London, 1882–85), II:181; Orderic Vitalis, *The Ecclesiastical History of Orderic Vitalis*, ed. and trans. M. Chibnall (Oxford, 1969–80), II:168–69; William of Poitiers, *The Gesta Guillelmi of William of Poitiers*, ed. and trans.

and some at London, all reiterate the basic details: Harold was forced to march south at a pace equalling if not surpassing the speed which he used to reach Stamford Bridge and surprise the Norwegians there, and that his army was not at full strength when he faced William at the battle of Hastings.

It is not the purpose of this book to discuss the English king's defeat at Hastings, nor in fact is its purpose to agree or disagree with John of Worcester's contention that 'all the more powerful men from the whole of England had already fallen in two battles'. Of course, there is no doubt that Harold Godwinson's army had been decimated by injuries and death at the battles of Fulford Gate and Stamford Bridge. Indeed, Edwin and Morkere, their Mercian and Northumbrian armies nearly completely destroyed at Fulford Gate, did not even join the march south or the battle at Hastings. Additionally, what English troops were able to fight at Hastings must have been fatigued by their marches and fighting, and they may also have been sick of the bloodshed and warfare. How many even arrived in the south to face William is but conjecture.

Historians have often criticized Harold for not waiting at London for William to do battle there.[3] It is possible that Harold was so tired of warfare and killing that he only half-heartedly went after the Normans. It had been his command in the north that had killed many thousands of Norwegians and had sent his brother to death. Possibly this affected his judgement in this situation.

Of course, he may also have seriously feared a William securely entrenched in the south of England; after all, according to the Bayeux Tapestry and contemporary chroniclers, the Norman duke had already constructed or was in the process of constructing five motte-and-bailey castles in the estimation that he might have to fight a protracted war of invasion against the Anglo-Saxons.[4] In this scenario, it is to be understood that Harold judged that a fatigued army which surprised an unfortified invading force was better than a rested army which had to face a well fortified force.

Whatever the answer may be, on 22 October 1066, with less than half his army, weakened and fatigued, Harold stood atop Senlac Hill, attempting to halt the advance of the Norman army of conquest.[5] For a while the English held their

---

R.H.C. Davis and M. Chibnall (Oxford, 1998), pp. 116–17; William of Jumièges, *The Gesta Normanorum ducum of William of Jumièges, Orderic Vitalis, and Robert of Torigni*, ed. and trans. E.M.C. van Houts (Oxford, 1995), II:166–67; *Carmen de hastingae proelio*, ed. C. Morton and A. Muntz (Oxford, 1972), pp. 10–13; and *The Waltham Chronicle: An Account of the Discovery of Our Holy Cross at Montacute and Its Conveyance to Waltham*, ed. and trans. L. Watkiss and M. Chibnall (Oxford, 1994), pp. 44–45.

[3] See, for example, Jim Bradbury, *The Battle of Hastings* (Thrupp, 1998), pp. 165–68.

[4] Kelly DeVries, *Medieval Military Technology* (Peterborough, 1992), p. 205; R. Allen Brown, *English Castles*, 3rd edn (London, 1976), p. 50; and Derek F. Renn, *Norman Castles in Britain*, 2nd edn (London, 1973), pp. 27–28.

[5] For a description of the battle of Hastings see Bradbury, *Battle of Hastings*; Stephen Morillo, 'Hastings: An Unusual Battle,' *Haskins Society Journal* 1 (1989), 96–103; R. Allen Brown, 'The Battle of Hastings,' *Proceedings of the Battle Conference on Anglo-Norman Studies* 3 (1980), 1–21; and Bernard S. Bachrach, 'The Feigned Retreat at Hastings,' *Medi-*

own against a fresh Norman army, but as the battle went on, and after what may have been a successful 'feigned retreat' performed by the Normans, the Anglo-Saxons were defeated. Gyrð and Leofwine, brother earls of the English king, were killed. Then, finally, Harold Godwinson himself was slain. Would a 'complete,' rested, and prepared English force have changed the result at Hastings? No one can, or perhaps should, answer that question.

All that is known is that when the battlefield cleared, the warlord William, duke of Normandy, had become the king of England. He would receive the cognomen 'the Conqueror' for this victory. Dead on the field was the other Conqueror, the warlord Harold Godwinson, his recent victory but a faded memory in the history of England.

aeval Studies 33 (1971), 344–47. For the original sources of this battle see Stephen Morillo, ed., *The Battle of Hastings* (Woodbridge, 1996).

BIBLIOGRAPHY

Original Sources

Ágrip af Nóregs konunga sögum. Ed. F. Jónsson. Halle, 1929.

Anglo-Satirical Poets and Epigrammatists of the Twelfth Century, The. Ed. T. Wright. 2 vols. Rolls Series. London, 1872.

Anglo-Saxon Chronicle. In *Two of the Saxon Chronicles Parallel*, Ed. Charles Plummer and John Earle, 2 vols. Oxford, 1892.

Anglo-Saxon Chronicle, The. Trans. G.N. Garmonsway. London, 1953.

Anglo-Saxon Chronicle, The. Trans. and ed. M. Swanton. New York, 1998.

Anglo-Saxon Chronicle, The. Trans. D. Whitelock, D.C. Douglas, and S.I. Tucker. London, 1961.

Annales Cambriae. Ed. J. Williams ab Ithel. Rolls Series. London, 1860.

Annales de Waverleia. In *Annales monastici*, ii. Ed. H.R. Luard. Rolls Series. London, 1865.

Annales de Wintonia. In *Annales monastici*, ii. Ed. H.R. Luard. Rolls Series. London, 1865.

'Annals of Tigernach, The: The Fourth Fragment A.D. 973–A.D. 1088.' Ed. W. Stokes. *Revue celtique* 17 (1896).

Bayeux Tapestry, The: A Comprehensive Survey. Ed. by Frank M. Stenton. 2nd edn. London, 1957.

Beowulf. Ed. Fr. Klaeber. 3rd edn. Lexington, 1950.

Beowulf. Trans. E.T. Donaldson. New York, 1966.

Book of Advice. In *Strategicon of Cecaumenos*. Ed. V.G. Vasilievsky and V. Jernstedt. St Petersburg, 1896.

Bremen, Adam of. *Gesta Hammaburgensis ecclesiae pontificum*. Ed. B. Schmeidler. 3rd edn. Monumenta Germaniae historica. Hanover, 1917.

Bremen, Adam of. *History of the Archbishops of Hamburg–Bremen*. Trans. F.J. Tschan. New York, 1959.

Brennu-Njáls Saga. Ed. E.Ó. Sveinsson. Rekjavik, 1954.

Brompton, John of. *Chronicon*. In *Historiae anglicanae scriptores*, X. Ed. R. Twysden. London, 1652.

Brown, R. Allen, trans. *The Norman Conquest*. London, 1984.

Brenhinedd y Saesson, or The Kings of the Saxons: BM Cotton MS. Cleopatra B.v and The Black Book of Basingwerk, NLW MS.7006. Ed. and trans. T. Jones. Cardiff, 1971.

Brut y Tywysogyon, Peniarth MS. 20. Ed. T. Jones. Cardiff, 1941.

Brut y Tywysogyon, or the Chronicle of the Princes: Peniarth MS. 20 Version. Trans. T. Jones. Cardiff, 1952.

Brut y Tywysogyon, or the Chronicle of the Princes: Red Book of Hergest Version. Ed. and trans. T. Jones. 2nd edn. Cardiff, 1973.

Candidus, Hugh. *The Chronicle of Hugh Candidus, a Monk of Peterborough*. Ed. W.T. Mellows. London, 1949.

Carmen de hastingae proelio. Ed. C. Morton and A. Muntz. Oxford, 1972.

Chronicle of Battle Abbey, The. Ed. and trans. E. Searle. Oxford, 1980.

Chronicon abbatiae de Evesham. Ed. W.D. Macray. Rolls Series. London, 1863.

Chronicon abbatiae Rameseieinsis. Ed. W.D. Macray. Rolls Series. London, 1866.

Chronicon monasterii de Abingdon. Ed. J. Stevenson. 2 vols. Rolls Series. London, 1858.

Chronicon Roskildense et Chronicon Lethrense. In *Scriptores minores historiae Danicae medii aevi.* Ed. C. Gertz. 2 vols. Copenhagen, 1917–18.

Cirencester, Richard of. *Speculum historiale de gestiis regum angliae.* Ed. J.E.B. Mayor. London, 1869.

Clare, Osbert of. *La vie de S. Édouard le Confesseur par Osbert de Clare.* Ed. M. Bloch. In *Analecta Bollandiana* 41 (1923), 5–131.

Codex diplomaticus aevi saxonici. Ed. Johannis M. Kemble. 4 vols. London, 1846.

Council and Ecclesiastical Documents Relating to Great Britain and Ireland. Ed. A.W. Haddan and W. Stubbs. Oxford, 1869–78.

Domesday Book: Liber censualis Willelmi primi. Ed. A. Farley. 4 vols. London, 1783–1816.

Durham, Symeon of. *Historia ecclesiae Dunhelmensis.* Ed. T. Arnold. Rolls Series. London, 1882.

———. *Historia regum.* Ed. T. Arnold. 2 vols. Rolls Series. London, 1882–85.

Eadmer. *Historia novorum in Anglia.* Ed. M. Rule. Rolls Series. London, 1884.

Ecclesiastical Documents: A Brief History of the Bishopbrick of Somerset. Ed. J. Hunter. Camden Series. London, 1840.

Encomium Emmae Reginae. Ed. A. Campbell. Camden Series. London, 1949.

Estoire de Seint Aedward le Rei, L'. Ed. and trans. H.R. Luard. In *Lives of Edward the Confessor.* Rolls Series. London, 1858.

Exeter Book Riddles, The. Ed. K. Crossley-Holland. Harmondsworth, 1979.

Fagrskinna: Kortfattet Norsk Konge-Saga. Ed. P.A. Munch and C.R. Unger. Christiania (Oslo), 1847.

Flateyjarbók: En samling af Norske Konge-Sagaer. Ed. G. Vigfusson and C.R. Unger. 3 vols. Christiania (Oslo), 1860–68.

Gaimar, Geoffrey. *Lestoire des Engles.* Ed. T.D. Hardy and C.T. Martin. 2 vols. Rolls Series. London, 1888–89.

Gododdin, The: The Oldest Scottish Poem. Ed. K.H. Jackson. Edinburgh, 1969.

Grammaticus, Saxo. *Historia Danica.* Ed. P.E. Müller and J.M. Velschow. 2 vols. Hannover, 1839.

Hákonar Saga Ivarssonar. Ed. J. Helgason and J. Benediktsen. Copenhagen, 1952.

Harmer, F.E., ed. *Anglo-Saxon Writs.* Manchester, 1952.

Hemming. *Hemingi Chartularium ecclesiae Wignorniensis.* Ed. T. Hearne. 2 vols. Oxford, 1723.

Higden, Ranulph. *Polychronicon.* Ed. J.R. Lumby. 9 vols. Rolls Series. London, 1865–86.

Historia translationum S. Cuthberti. Ed. H. Hinde. Surtees Society. London, 1868.

Huntingdon, Henry, Archdeacon of. *Historia Anglorum: The History of the English People.* Ed. and trans. D. Greenway. Oxford, 1996.

Jumièges, William of. *The Gesta Normanorum ducum of William of Jumièges, Orderic Vitalis, and Robert of Torigni.* Ed. and trans. E.M.C. van Houts. 2 vols. Oxford, 1995.

Knighton, Henry. *Chronicon*. Ed. J.R. Lumby. 2 vols. Rolls Series. London, 1889–95.

Liber Elienses. Ed. E.O. Blake. Camden Society. London, 1962.

Liber Vitae: The Register and Martyrology of New Minister and Hyde Abbey. Ed. W. de G. Birch. London and Winchester, 1892.

Life of Bishop Wulfstan of Worcester, The. In *Three Lives of the Last Englishmen*. Trans. and ed. M. Swanton. New York, 1984.

Life of Harold Godwinson, The. In *Three Lives of the Last Englishmen*. Trans. and ed. M. Swanton. New York, 1984.

Lives of Edward the Confessor. Ed. H.R. Luard. Rolls Series. London, 1858.

Malmesbury, William of. *Gesta regum Anglorum: The History of the English Kings*. Ed. and trans. R.A.B. Mynors, R.M. Thomson, and M. Winterbottom. 2 vols. Oxford, 1998.

———. *De gestis pontificum Anglorum*. Ed. N.E.S.A. Hamilton. Rolls Series. London, 1870.

———. *Vita Wulfstani*. Ed. Reginald R. Darlington. Camden Third Series. London, 1928.

Map, Walter. *De nugis curialium*. Ed. and trans. M.R. James, revised edn. C.N.L. Brooke and R.A.B. Mynors. Oxford, 1983.

The Miracle of St. Mildred. In *Descriptive Catalogue of Materials Relating to the History of Great Britain and Ireland*. Ed. T. Hardy. Rolls Series. London, 1862–71.

Morillo, Stephen, ed. *The Battle of Hastings*. Woodbridge, 1996.

Morkinskinna: Pergamentsbog fra første halvdel af det trettende aarhundrede. Ed. C.R. Unger. Christiania (Oslo), 1867.

Njal's Saga. Trans. M. Magnusson and H. Pálsson. Harmondsworth, 1960.

Osbern. *Miracula S. Dunstani*. In *Memorials of St. Dunstan*. Ed. W. Stubbs. Rolls Series. London, 1874.

Page, R.I., ed. and trans. *Chronicles of the Vikings: Records, Memorials and Myths*. Toronto, 1995.

Paris, Matthew. *Chronica majora*. Ed. H.R. Luard. 7 vols. Rolls Series. London, 1872–83.

———. *La estoire de Seint Aedward le rei attributed to Matthew Paris*. Ed. K.Y. Wallace. London, 1983.

Poitiers, William of. *The Gesta Guillelmi of William of Poitiers*. Ed. and trans. R.H.C. Davis and M. Chibnall. Oxford, 1998.

Psellus, Michael. *Fourteen Byzantine Rulers*. Trans. E.R.A. Sewter. Harmondsworth, 1966.

Rielvaux, Aelred of. *Vita sancti Aedwardi regis*. Ed. J.P. Migne. Patriologia latina, 195. Rome, 1855.

Russian Primary Chronicle, The. Ed. S. H. Cross and O.B. Sherbowitz-Wetzor. Cambridge, 1973.

Saint-Bertin, Goscelin of. *Life of St. Edith*. In 'La légende de Ste Édith en prose et vers par le moine Goscelin,' *Analecta Bollandiana* 56 (1938), 5–307.

Salisbury, John of. *Policraticus sive nugis curialium et vestigiis philosophorum libri VIII*. Ed. C.I. Webb. Oxford, 1909.

Sturluson, Snorri. *King Harald's Saga*. Trans. M. Magnusson and H. Pálsson. Harmondsworth, 1966.

————. *Heimskringla*. Ed. B. Aðalbjarnarson. 3 vols. Islenzk Fornrit, xxvi–xxviii. Reykjavik, 1941–51.

————. *Ynglingasaga*. Ed. E. Wessén. Oslo, [n.d.]

Theodoricus. *Monumenta historica Norvegiæ: Latinske kildeskrifter til Norges historie I middelalderen*. Ed. G. Storm. Christiana (Oslo), 1880.

van Lokeren, A., ed. *Chartes et documents de l'abbaye de Saint-Pierre au Mont-Blandin*. Ghent, 1898.

Vinland Sagas, The. Ed. H. Hermannsson. Islandica, 30. Ithaca, 1944.

Vita Ædwardi regis qui apud Westmonasterium requiescit. Ed. and trans. F. Barlow. 2nd edn. Oxford, 1992.

Vita Haroldi. Ed. W.D. Birch. London, 1885.

Vitalis, Orderic. *The Ecclesiastical History of Orderic Vitalis*. Ed. and trans. M. Chibnall. 6 vols. Oxford, 1969–80.

Wace. *Le Roman de Rou*. Ed. A.J. Holden. 2 vols. Paris, 1971.

Wales, Gerald of. *Itinerarium Kambriae et descriptio Kambriae*. Ed. J.F. Dimock. Rolls Series. London, 1868.

Waltham Chronicle, The: An Account of the Discovery of Our Holy Cross at Montacute and Its Conveyance to Waltham. Ed. and trans. L. Watkiss and M. Chibnall. Oxford, 1994.

Wendover, Roger of. *Chronica sive flores historiarum*. Ed. H.O. Coxe. 4 vols. English Historical Society. London, 1841–44.

Worcester, 'Florence' of. *Chronicon ex chronicis*. Ed. B. Thorpe. 2 vols. London, 1849.

Worcester, John of. *The Chronicle of John of Worcester*. Ed. R.R. Darlington and P. McGurk. Trans. J. Bray and P. McGurk. 2 vols. Oxford, 1995.

Secondary Sources

Abels, Richard P. *Alfred the Great: War, Kingship and Culture in Anglo-Saxon England*. London, 1998.

————. 'Bookland and Fyrd Service in Late Saxon England,' *Anglo-Norman Studies* 7 (1984), 1–25.

————. 'English Logistics and Military Administration, 871–1066: The Impact of the Viking Wars.' In *Military Aspects of Scandinavian Society in a European Perspective, AD 1–1300*. Ed. A.N. Jørgensen and B. Clausen. Copenhagen, 1997, pp. 256–65.

————. 'English Tactics, Strategy and Military Organization in the Late Tenth Century.' In *The Battle of Maldon, AD 991*. Ed. D. Scragg. London, 1991, pp. 143–55.

————. *Lordship and Military Obligation in Anglo-Saxon England*. Berkeley and Los Angeles, 1988.

Addyman, Peter V., Nicholas Pearson, and Dominic Tweddle. 'The Coppergate Helmet,' *Antiquity* 56 (1982), 189–94.

Andersen, Per Sveaas. 'Harald Hardråde, Danmark og England.' In *Harald Hardråde*. Ed. A. Berg. Oslo, 1966, pp. 95–126.

————. *Samlingen av Norge og kristningen av landet, 800–1300*. Handbok I Norges historie, 2. Bergen, 1977.

Anderson, Alan O. 'Anglo-Scottish Relations from Constantine II to William,' *Scottish Historical Review* 42 (1963), 1–20.

Angold, Michael. *The Byzantine Empire, 1025–1204: A Political History.* London, 1984.

Arbman, Holger, 'Zwei Ingelri-Schwerter aus Schweden,' *Zeitschrift für historisches Waffen- und Kostumkunde* 14 (1935–36), 146–49.

Ashdown, Margaret. 'An Icelandic Account of the Survival of Harold Godwinson.' In *The Anglo-Saxons: Studies in Some Aspects of their History and Culture Presented to Bruce Dickins.* Ed. P. Clemoes. London, 1959, pp. 122–36.

Atkinson, Ian. *The Viking Ships.* Cambridge, 1979.

Bachrach, Bernard S. 'The Feigned Retreat at Hastings,' *Mediaeval Studies* 33 (1971), 344–47.

Bachrach, Bernard and Rutherford Aris. 'Military Technology and Garrison Organization: Some Observations on Anglo-Saxon Military Thinking in Light of the Burghal Hidage,' *Technology and Culture* 31 (1990), 1–17.

Barlow, Frank. 'The *Carmen de Hastingae proelio*,' in *The Norman Conquest and Beyond* (London, 1983), pp. 189–222.

———. *Edward the Confessor.* Berkeley and Los Angeles, 1970.

———. 'Edward the Confessor and the Norman Conquest.' In *The Norman Conquest and Beyond* (London, 1983), pp. 99–111.

———. 'Edward the Confessor's Early Life, Character and Attitudes.' In *The Norman Conquest and Beyond.* London, 1983, pp. 57–83; orig. *English Historical Review* 80 (1965), 225–51.

———. *The English Church, 1000–1066: A Constitutional History.* London, 1963.

———. *The Feudal Kingdom of England, 1042–1216.* London, 1955.

———. 'Two Notes: Cnut's Second Pilgrimage and Queen Emma's Disgrace in 1043.' In *The Norman Conquest and Beyond* (London, 1983), pp. 49–56; orig. *English Historical Review* 74 (1958), 649–56.

———. *William Rufus.* Berkeley and Los Angeles, 1983.

Barrett, C.R.B. *Battles and Battlefields in England.* London, 1896.

Benedikz, B.S. 'The Evolution of the Varangian Regiment in the Byzantine Army,' *Byzantinische Zeitschrift* 62 (1969), 20–25.

Berg, Knut. 'Haralds dronning Ellisiv.' In *Harald Hardråde.* Ed. A. Berg. Oslo, 1966, pp. 28–40.

Bernstein, David. 'The Blinding of Harold and the Meaning of the Bayeux Tapestry,' *Anglo-Norman Studies* 5 (1982), 40–64.

Biddle, Martin and Birth Kjølbye-Biddle. 'Repton and the Vikings,' *Antiquity* 66 (1992), 36–51.

———. 'The Repton Stone,' *Anglo-Saxon England* 14 (1985), 233–92.

Binns, Alan. 'Ships and Shipbuilding.' In *Medieval Scandinavia: An Encyclopedia.* Ed. P. Pulsiano. New York, 1993, pp. 578–80.

———. 'The Ships of the Vikings, were they "Viking Ships"?' In *Proceedings of the Eighth Viking Congress.* Ed. H. Bekker-Nielsen. Odense, 1981, pp. 287–93.

Blair, Claude. *European Armour.* London, 1958.

Bliese, John R.E. 'The Courage of the Normans. A Comparative Study of Battle Rhetoric,' *Nottingham Medieval Studies* 35 (1991), 1–26.

———. 'Leadership, Rhetoric, and Morale in the Norman Conquest of England,' *Military Affairs* 52 (1988), 23–28.

————. 'Rhetoric and Morale: A Study of Battle Orations from the Central Middle Ages.' *Journal of Medieval History* 15 (1989), 201–26.

————. 'When Knightly Courage May Fail: Battle Orations in Medieval Europe,' *Historian* 53 (1991), 489–504.

Blöndal, Sigfús. *The Varangians of Byzantium*. Trans. B.S. Benedikz. Cambridge, 1978.

Bone, Peter. 'The Development of Anglo-Saxon Swords from the Fifth to the Eleventh Century.' In *Weapons and Warfare in Anglo-Saxon England*. Ed. S.C. Hawkes. Oxford, 1989, pp. 63–70.

Bradbury, Jim. *The Battle of Hastings*. Thrupp, 1998.

————. *The Medieval Archer*. New York, 1985.

Brögger, A.W. and Haakon Shetelig, *The Viking Ships: Their Ancestry and Evolution*. Oslo, 1951.

Brønsted, Johannes. *The Vikings*. Trans. K. Skov. Harmondsworth, 1965.

Brooks, F.W. *The Battle of Stamford Bridge*. York, 1963.

Brooks, Nicholas P. 'Arms, Status and Warfare in Late-Saxon England.' In *Ethelred the Unready: Papers from the Millenary Conference*. Ed. D. Hill. BAR British Series, 59. Oxford, 1978, pp. 81–103.

————. 'Weapons and Armour.' In *The Battle of Maldon, AD 991*. Ed. D. Scragg. London, 1991, pp. 208–19.

———— and H.E. Walker. 'The Authority and Interpretation of the Bayeux Tapestry,' *Proceedings of the Battle Conference* 1 (1978), 1–34.

Brown, R. Allen. 'The Battle of Hastings,' *Proceedings of the Battle Conference on Anglo-Norman Studies* 3 (1980), 1–21.

————. 'The Norman Conquest and the Genesis of English Castles.' In *Castles, Conquest and Charters: Collected Papers*. Woodbridge, 1989, pp. 75–89.

————. *The Normans and the Norman Conquest*. 2nd edn. Woodbridge, 1985.

Brown, R. Allen, H.M. Colvin, and A.J. Taylor. *The History of the King's Works*. Vols. 1 and 2: *The Middle Ages*. London, 1963.

Brown, Shirley Ann. 'The Bayeux Tapestry: History or Propaganda?' In *The Anglo-Saxons: Synthesis and Achievement*. Ed. J.D. Woods and D.A.E. Pelteret. Waterloo, 1985, pp. 11–25, 153–54.

Bruce-Mitford, Rupert. 'The Benty Grange Helmet and Some Other Supposed Anglo-Saxon Helmets.' In *Aspects of Anglo-Saxon Archaeology: Sutton Hoo and Other Discoveries*. New York, 1974, pp. 223–52.

————. 'The Sutton Hoo Helmet – a New Reconstruction.' In *Aspects of Anglo-Saxon Archaeology: Sutton Hoo and Other Discoveries*. New York, 1974, pp. 198–209.

Bull, Edv. *Leding: Militær- og finansforfatning i norge i ældre tid*. Christiana (Oslo) and Copenhagen, 1920.

Burne, Alfred H. *More Battlefields of Britain*. London, 1952.

Butler, Denis. *1066: The Story of a Year*. London, 1966.

Campbell, Miles W. 'The Anti-Norman Reaction in England in 1052: Suggested Origins,' *Mediaeval Studies* 35 (1973), 428–41.

————. 'Earl Godwin of Wessex and Edward the Confessor's Promise of the Throne to William of Normandy,' *Traditio* 28 (1972), 141–58.

————. 'Emma, reine d'Angleterre, mère dénaturée ou femme vincidative?' *Annales de Normandie* 23 (1973), 99–114.

————. 'Hypothèses sur les causes de l'ambassade de Harold en Normandie,' *Annales Normandie* 27 (1977), 243–65.

————. 'An Inquiry into the Troop Strength of King Harald Hardrada's Invasion Fleet of 1066,' *American Neptune* 44 (1984), 96–102.

————. 'Last Viking's Impact: King Harald of Norway Struck England Just Before the Norman Conquest,' *Military History* 4 (June 1988), 12–17, 66.

————. 'Note sur les déplacements de Tostig Godwinson en 1066,' *Annales de Normandie* 22 (1972), 3–9.

————. 'A Pre-Conquest Norman Occupation of England?' *Speculum* 46 (1971), 21–31.

————. 'Queen Emma and Ælfgifu of Northampton: Canute the Great's Women,' *Mediaeval Scandinavia* 4 (1971), 66–79.

————. 'The Rise of an Anglo-Saxon 'Kingmaker': Earl Godwin of Wessex,' *Canadian Journal of History* 13 (1978), 17–33.

Carter, John Marshall. 'The Feigned Flight at Hastings: Birth, Propagation, and the Death of a Myth,' *San Jose Studies* (Feb. 1978), 95–106.

Cessford, C. 'Cavalry in Early Bernicia: A Reply,' *Northern History* 29 (1993), 185–87.

Chibnall, Marjorie. *The World of Orderic Vitalis.* Oxford, 1984.

Christensen, Arne Emil. 'Viking Age Ships and Shipbuilding,' *Norwegian Archaeology Review* 15 (1982), 19–28.

Christie, Håkon. 'Haralds Oslo.' In *Harald Hardråde.* Ed. A. Berg *et al.* Oslo, 1966, pp. 69–89.

Clarke, Peter A. *The English Nobility under Edward the Confessor.* Oxford, 1994.

Coupland, Simon. 'The Rod of God's Wrath or the People of God's Wrath? The Carolingian Theology of the Viking Invasions,' *Journal of Ecclesiastical History* 42 (1991), 535–54.

Cowdrey, H.E.J. 'Towards an Interpretation of Bayeux Tapestry,' *Anglo-Norman Studies* 10 (1987), 49–65

Cross, J.E. 'The Ethic of War in Old English.' In *England Before the Conquest: Studies in Primary Sources Presented to Dorothy Whitelock.* Ed. P. Clemoes and K. Hughes. Cambridge, 1971, pp. 269–82.

Crumlin-Pedersen, Ole. 'Large and Small Warships.' In *Military Aspects of Scandinavian Society in a European Perspective, AD. 1–1300.* Copenhagen, 1997, pp. 184–94.

————. 'Viking Shipbuilding and Seamanship.' In *Proceedings of the Eighth Viking Congress.* Ed. H. Bekker-Nielsen. Odense, 1981, pp. 271–86.

Cutler, Kenneth E. 'Edith, Queen of England,' *Mediaeval Studies* 38 (1976), 222–31.

————. 'The Godwinist Hostages: The Case for 1051,' *Annuale medievali* 12 (1971), 70–77.

Darlington, R.R. and P. McGurk. 'The "Chronicon ex chronicis" of "Florence" of Worcester and its Use of Sources for English History Before 1066,' *Anglo-Norman Studies* 5 (1982), 185–96.

Davidson, H.R. Ellis. *The Sword in Anglo-Saxon England: Its Archaeology and Literature.* Oxford, 1962.

————. 'The Training of Warriors.' In *Weapons and Warfare in Anglo-Saxon England.* Ed. S.C. Hawkes. Oxford, 1989, pp. 11–23.

————. *The Viking Road to Byzantium.* London, 1976.

Davies, R.R. *Conquest, Coexistence, and Change: Wales, 1063–1415.* Oxford, 1987.

Davies, Wendy. *Wales in the Early Middle Ages.* Leicester, 1982.

Davis, H.C.W. *England under the Normans and Angevins.* London, 1905.

Davis, R.H.C. 'The *Carmen de hastingae proelio,*' *English Historical Review* 93 (1978), 231–61.

———. 'Did Anglo-Saxons have Warhorses?' In *Weapons and Warfare in Anglo-Saxon England.* Ed. S.C. Hawkes. Oxford, 1989, pp. 141–44.

———. *The Medieval Warhorse: Origin, Development and Redevlopment.* London, 1989.

———. 'William of Poitiers and His History of William the Conqueror.' In *The Writing of History in the Middle Ages: Essays Presented to Richard William Southern.* Ed. R.H.C. Davis and J.M. Wallace-Hadrill. Oxford, 1981, pp. 71–100.

Dawson, Christopher. *The Making of Europe.* London, 1948.

DeVries, Kelly. 'The Conflict between Harold and Tostig Godwinson,' *Scintilla* 1 (1984), 48–62.

———. *Infantry Warfare in the Early Fourteenth Century: Discipline, Tactics, and Technology.* Woodbridge, 1996.

———. *Medieval Military Technology.* Peterborough, 1992.

———. 'Military Surgical Practice and the Advent of Gunpowder Weaponry,' *Canadian Bulletin of Medical History* 7 (1990), 131–46.

———. 'Perceptions of Victory and Defeat in the Southern Low Countries during the Fourteenth Century: A Historiographical Comparison.' Unpublished dissertation, University of Toronto, 1987.

Dickins, B. 'The Late Addition to ASC 1066,' *Proceedings of the Leeds Philosophical and Literary Society* 5 (1940), 148–49.

Dickinson, Tania, F.S.A. Härke, and Heinrich Härke. *Early Anglo-Saxon Shields.* London, 1992.

Dolley, M. *The Norman Conquest and the English Coinage.* London, 1966.

Douglas, David C. 'Edward the Confessor, Duke William of Normandy and the English Succession,' *English Historical Review* 68 (1953), 526–45.

———. *William the Conqueror.* Berkeley and Los Angeles, 1964.

Dunning, G.C. 'The Palace of Westminster Sword,' *Archaeologia* 98 (1961), 123–58.

Elliott, Dyan. *Spiritual Marriage.* Princeton, 1993.

Engstrom, Robert, Scott Michael Lankton, and Audrey Lesher-Engstrom. *A Modern Replication Based on the Pattern-Welded Sword of Sutton Hoo.* 2nd edn. Kalamazoo, 1990.

Fino, J.-F. 'Notes sur la production du fer et la fabrication des armes en France au moyen-age,' *Gladius* 3 (1964), 47–66.

Fisher, D.J.V. *The Anglo-Saxon England, c.400–1042.* London, 1976.

Fleming, Robin. 'Domesday Estates of the King and the Godwines: A Study in Late Saxon Politics,' *Speculum* 58 (1983), 987–1007.

———. *Kings and Lords in Conquest England.* Cambridge, 1991.

Foot, Sarah. 'Violence against Christians? The Vikings and the Church in Ninth-Century England,' *Medieval History* 1.3 (1991), 3–16.

Foote, Peter G. and David M. Wilson. *The Viking Achievement.* New York, 1970.

Forde-Johnston, J. *Castles and Fortifications of Britain and Ireland.* London, 1977.

Frank, Roberta. 'Viking Atrocity and Skaldic Verse: The Rite of the Blood-Eagle,' *English Historical Review* 99 (1984), 332–43.

Franklin, Simon and Jonathan Shepard. *The Emergence of Rus, 750–1200*. London, 1996.

Freeman, Edward August. *The History of the Norman Conquest*. 5 vols. 2nd edn. Oxford, 1869–75.

———. 'On the Life and Death of Earl Godwine,' *The Archaeological Journal* 11 (1854), 236–52, 330–44.

Gade, Kari Ellen. 'Einarr Þambarskelfir's Last Shot,' *Scandinavian Studies* 67 (1995), 153–62.

Gameson, Richard, ed. *The Study of the Bayeux Tapestry*. Woodbridge, 1997.

Gelsinger, Bruce E. 'The Battle of Stamford Bridge and the Battle of Jaffa: A Case of Confused Identity?' *Scandinavian Studies* 60 (1988), 13–29.

George, Robert H. 'The Contribution of Flanders to the Conquest of England, 1065–1086,' *Revue Belge de philologie et d'histoire* 5 (1926), 81–99.

Gillingham, John. 'Thegns and Knights in Eleventh-Century England: Who Was Then the Gentleman?' *Transactions of the Royal Historical Society*, 6th ser., 5 (1995), 129–53.

Gillmor, Caroll. 'War on the Rivers: Viking Numbers and Mobility on the Seine and Loire, 841–886,' *Viator* 19 (1988), 79–109.

Glover, Richard. 'English Warfare in 1066,' *English Historical Review* 262 (1952), 1–18.

Godfrey, John. 'The Defeated Anglo-Saxons Take Service with the Eastern Emperor,' *Proceedings of the Battle Conference on Anglo-Norman Studies* 1 (1978), 63–74.

Golding, Brian. *Conquest and Colonisation: The Normans in Britain, 1066–1100*. New York, 1994.

Gransden, Antonia. *Historical Writing in England, c.550 to c.1307*. Ithaca, 1974.

Green, J.R. *The Conquest of England*. 3rd edn. 3 vols. London, 1899.

Grekov, B. *Kiev Rus*. Trans. Y. Sdobnikov. Ed. D. Ogden. Moscow, 1959.

Grierson, Philip. 'The Relations between England and Flanders before the Norman Conquest,' *Transactions of the Royal Historical Society* 23 (1941), 71–112.

———. 'A Visit of Earl Harold to Flanders in 1056,' *English Historical Review* 51 (1936), 90–97.

Griffith, Paddy. *The Viking Art of War*. London, 1995.

Gurevich, A.Ya. 'Saga and History: The "Historical Conception" of Snorri Sturluson,' *Mediaeval Scandinavia* 4 (1971), 42–53.

Hadley, Dawn M. ' "And They Proceeded to Plough and to Support Themselves": The Scandinavian Settlement of England,' *Anglo-Norman Studies* 19 (1996), 69–96.

Haenens, Albert d'. *Les invasions normandes en Belgique au IXe siècle: Le phénomène de sa répercussion dans l'historiographie médievale*. Leuven, 1967.

Hale, John R. 'The Viking Longship,' *Scientific American* 278 (Feb 1998), 56–63.

Hanawalt, Emily Albu. 'Scandinavians in Byzantium and Normandy.' In *Peace and War in Byzantium. Essays in Honor of George T. Dennis, S.J.*. Ed. T.S. Miller and J. Nesbitt. Washington, 1995, pp. 114–22.

Härke, Heinrich. 'Early Saxon Weapon Burials: Frequencies, Distributions and Weapon Combinations.' In *Weapons and Warfare in Anglo-Saxon England*. Ed. S.C. Hawkes. Oxford, 1989, pp. 49–61.

———. ' "Warrior Graves"? The Background of the Anglo-Saxon Weapon Burial Rite,' *Past and Present* 126 (1990), 22–43.

Hey, David. *Yorkshire from AD 1000*. London, 1986.

Higham, Nicholas J. 'Cavalry in Early Bernicia?' *Northern History* 27 (1991), 236–41.

Hill, David. *An Atlas of Anglo-Saxon England*. London, 1981.

––––––. ed., *Ethelred the Unready: Papers from the Millenary Conference*. BAR British Series, 59. Oxford, 1978.

Hill, David and Alexander R. Rumble, eds. *The Defence of Wessex: The Burghal Hidage and Anglo-Saxon Fortifications*. Manchester, 1996.

Hollister, C. Warren. *Anglo-Saxon Military Institutions on the Eve of the Norman Conquest*. Oxford, 1962.

––––––. 'The Five-Hide Unit and the Old English Military Obligation,' *Speculum* 36 (1961), 61–74.

––––––. 'Military Obligation in Late-Saxon and Norman England.' In *Ordinamenti militari in occidente nell'alto medioevo*. Spoleto, 1968, I:169–86.

Hooper, Nicholas. 'The Aberlemno Stone and Cavalry in Anglo-Saxon England,' *Northern History* 29 (1993), 188–96.

––––––. 'Anglo-Saxon Warfare on the Eve of the Conquest: A Brief Survey,' *Proceedings of the Battle Conference on Anglo-Norman Studies* 1 (1978), 84–93.

––––––. 'The Anglo-Saxons at War.' In *Weapons and Warfare in Anglo-Saxon England*. Ed. S.C. Hawkes. Oxford, 1989, pp. 191–202.

––––––. 'The Housecarls in England in the Eleventh Century,' *Anglo-Norman Studies* 7 (1984), 161–76.

––––––. 'Military Developments in the Reign of Cnut.' In *The Reign of Cnut*. Ed. A.R. Rumble. London, 1994, pp. 89–100.

––––––. 'Some Observations on the Navy in Late Anglo-Saxon England.' In *Studies in Medieval History for R. Allen Brown*. Ed. C. Harper-Bill *et al*. Woodbridge, 1989, pp. 203–13.

Houts, Elisabeth M.C. van. 'Latin Poetry and the Anglo-Norman Court, 1066–1135: The *Carmen de Hastingae proelio*,' *Journal of Medieval History* 15 (1989), 39–62.

Hudson, Benjamin T. 'The Destruction of Gruffudd ap Llywelyn,' *Welsh Historical Review* 19 (1991), 331–50.

––––––. 'The Family of Harold Godwinsson and the Irish Sea Province,' *Journal of the Royal Society of Antiquaries of Ireland* 109 (1979), 92–100.

Hughes, Shaun F.D. 'The Battle of Stamford Bridge and the Battle of Bouvines,' *Scandinavian Studies* 60 (1988), 30–76.

Hughson, Irene. 'Pictish Horse Carvings,' *Glasgow Archaeological Journal* 17 (1991–92), 53–61.

Hyland, Ann. *The Medieval Warhorse: From Byzantium to the Crusades*. London, 1994.

James, J.W. 'Fresh Light on the Death of Gruffudd ap Llywelyn,' *Bulletin of the Board of Celtic Studies* 30 (1982–83), 147.

Jenkins, Romilly. *Byzantium: The Imperial Centuries, AD 610–1071*. 1966; rpt. Toronto, 1987.

John, Eric. 'Edward the Confessor and the Celibate Life,' *Analecta Bollandiana* 97 (1979), 171–78.

––––––. 'Edward the Confessor and the Norman Succession,' *English Historical Review* 94 (1979), 241–67.

————. 'War and Society in the Tenth Century: The Maldon Campaign,' *Transactions of the Royal Historical Society* (5) 27 (1977), 173–91.

Jones, Gwyn. *A History of the Vikings*. London, 1968.

Kapelle, William E. *The Norman Conquest of the North: The Region and its Transformation, 1000–1135*. Chapel Hill, 1979.

Kazakevicius, Vytautas. 'Some Debatable Questions Concerning the Armament of the Viking Period in Lithuania,' *Fasciculi archaeologiae historicae* 7 (1994), 37–44.

Keefer, Sarah Larratt. 'Hwær Cwom Mearh? The Horse in Anglo-Saxon England,' *Journal of Medieval History* 22 (1996), 115–34.

Kendrick, T.D. *A History of the Vikings*. New York, 1930.

Keynes, Simon. 'The Æthelings in Normandy,' *Anglo-Norman Studies* 13 (1990), 173–205.

————. 'Cnut's Earls.' In *The Reign of Cnut: King of England, Denmark and Norway*. Ed. A.R. Ramble. London, 1994, 43–88.

————. 'Giso, Bishop of Wells (1061–88),' *Anglo-Norman Studies* 19 (1996), 203–71.

Kiff, Jennie. 'Images of War: Illustrations of Warfare in Early Eleventh-Century England,' *Anglo-Norman Studies* 7 (1984), 177–94.

King, Vanessa. 'Ealdred, Archbishop of York: The Worcester Years,' *Anglo-Norman Studies* 18 (1995), 123–37.

Körner, Sten. *The Battle of Hastings, England, and Europe, 1035–1066*. Lund, 1964.

Lang, Janet and Barry Ager. 'Swords of the Anglo-Saxon and Viking Periods in the British Museum: A Radiographic Study.' In *Weapons and Warfare in Anglo-Saxon England*. Ed. S.C. Hawkes. Oxford, 1989, pp. 85–122.

Larson, L.M. *The King's Household in England before the Norman Conquest*. Madison, 1904.

Lawson, M.K. *Cnut: The Danes in England in the Early Eleventh Century*. London, 1993.

Leadman, Alex. D.H. *Proelia Eboracensia: Battles Fought in Yorkshire Treated Historically and Topographically*. London, 1891.

Lewis, Archibald R. and Timothy J. Runyan. *European Naval and Maritime History, 300–1500*. Bloomington, 1985.

Lewis, C.P. 'The French in England before the Norman Conquest,' *Anglo-Norman Studies* 17 (1994), 123–44.

Linklater, Eric. *The Conquest of England: From the Viking Incursions of the Eighth Century to the Norman Victory at the Battle of Hastings*. New York, 1966.

Lloyd, J.E. *A History of Wales*. 3rd edn. 2 vols. London, 1939.

Logan, F. Donald. *The Vikings in History*. 2nd edn. London, 1991.

Loyn, Henry R. 'Harold, Son of Godwin.' In *Society and Peoples: Studies in the History of England and Wales, c. 600–1200*. London, 1992, pp. 299–321.

————. *The Vikings in Britain*. Oxford, 1994.

Lund, Niels. 'Allies of God or Man? The Viking Expansion in a Human Perspective,' *Viator* 20 (1989), 45–59.

————. 'The Armies of Swein Forkbeard and Cnut: *Leding* or *Lið*?' *Anglo-Saxon England* 15 (1986), 105–18.

————. 'Danish Military Organisation.' In *The Battle of Maldon: Fiction and Fact*. Ed. J. Cooper. London, 1993, pp. 109–26.

————. 'The Danish Perspective.' In *The Battle of Maldon, AD 991.* Ed. D. Scragg. London, 1991, pp. 114–42.

————. *De Danske vikinger i England.* Copenhagen, 1967.

————. *De Hærger og de brænder: Danmark og England i vikingtiden.* Copenhagen, 1993.

————. 'If the Vikings Knew a *Leding* – What Was It Like?' In *The Twelfth Viking Congress: Developments Around the Baltic and the North Sea in the Viking Age.* Ed. B. Ambrosiani and H. Clark. Stockholm, 1994, pp. 100–105.

————. 'Is Leidang a Nordic or a European Phenomenon?' In *Military Aspects of Scandinavian Society in a European Perspective, AD. 1–1300.* Copenhagen, 1997, pp. 195–99.

————. *Lið, leding og landeværn.* Roskilde, 1996.

Magnusson, Magnus and Hermann Pálsson. 'Introduction,' in Snorri Sturluson. *King Harald's Saga.* Trans. M. Magnusson and H. Pálsson. Harmondsworth, 1966.

Mahaney, Christine, and David Roffe, 'Stamford: The Development of an Anglo-Scandinavian Borough,' *Anglo-Norman Studies* 5 (1982), 197–219.

Maitland, F.W. *Domesday Book and Beyond.* Cambridge, 1897.

Malmros, Rikke. 'Leding og Skjaldekvad: Det elvte århundredes nordiske krigs-flåder, deres teknologi og organisation og deres placering I samfundet, belyst gennem den samtidige fyrstedigtning,' *Aarbøger for nordisk oldkyndigheid og historie* (1985), 89–139.

————. 'Leiðangr.' In *Medieval Scandinavia: An Encyclopedia.* Ed. P. Pulsiano. New York, 1993, pp. 389–90.

Manley, John. 'The Archer and the Army in the Late Saxon Period,' *Anglo-Saxon Studies in Archaeology and History* 4 (1985), 223–35.

Mann, James. 'Arms and Armour.' In *The Bayeux Tapestry: A Comprehensive Survey.* Ed. by Frank M. Stenton. 2nd edn. London, 1957, pp. 56–69.

————. 'Arms and Armour.' In *Medieval England.* Ed. Austin Lane Poole. Oxford, 1958.

Martens, Irmelin. 'Norwegian Viking Age Weapons: Some Questions Concerning their Production and Distribution.' In *The Twelfth Viking Congress: Developments Around the Baltic and the North Sea in the Viking Age.* Ed. B. Ambrosiani and H. Clark. Stockholm, 1994, pp. 180–82.

Martin, Janet. *Medieval Russia, 980–1584.* Cambridge, 1995.

Matthew, D.J.A. *The Norman Conquest.* London, 1966.

Maund, K.L. 'Cynan ab Iago and the Killing of Gruffudd ap Llywelyn,' *Cambridge Medieval Celtic Studies* 10 (1985), 57–65.

————. *Ireland, Wales, and England in the Eleventh Century.* Woodbridge, 1991.

————. 'The Welsh Alliances of Earl Ælfgar of Mercia and his Family in the Mid-Eleventh Century,' *Anglo-Norman Studies* 9 (1988), 181–90.

McGurk, Patrick and Jane Rosenthal. 'The Anglo-Saxon Gospelbooks of Judith, Countess of Flanders: Their Text, Make-up and Function,' *Anglo-Saxon England* 24 (1995), 251–311.

Meyer, Marc A. 'The Queen's 'Demesne' in Later Anglo-Saxon England.' In *The Culture of Christendom: Essays in Medieval History in Commemoration of Denis L.T. Bethell.* Ed. M.A. Meyer. London, 1993, pp. 75–113.

————. 'Women's Estates in Later Anglo-Saxon England: The Politics of Pos-session,' *Haskins Society Journal* 3 (1991), 111–29.

Morillo, Stephen. 'Hastings: An Unusual Battle,' *Haskins Society Journal* 1 (1989), 96–103.

Nicolle, David C. *Arms and Armour of the Crusading Era, 1050–1350.* 2 vols. White Plains, 1988.

Nordhagen, Jonas. 'Harald og Bysants.' In *Harald Hardråde.* Ed. A. Berg. Oslo, 1966, pp. 7–27.

Obolensky, Dimitri. *The Byzantine Commonwealth: Eastern Europe, 500–1453.* London, 1971.

Oleson, Tryggvi J. 'Edward the Confessor's Promise of the Throne to Duke William of Normandy,' *English Historical Review* 72 (1957), 221–28.

———. *The Witenagemot in the Reign of Edward the Confessor: A Study in the Constitutional History of Eleventh-Century England.* Toronto, 1955.

Oman, Charles. *The Art of War in the Middle Ages.* 2 vols. London, 1924.

Ortenberg, Veronica. *The English Church and the Continent in the Tenth and Eleventh Centuries.* Oxford, 1992.

Page, R.I. *Life in Anglo-Saxon England.* New York, 1970.

Palmer, J.J.N. 'The Conqueror's Footprints in Domesday Book.' In *The Medieval Military Revolution: State, Society and Military Change in Medieval and Early Modern Europe.* Ed. A. Ayton and J.L. Price. London, 1995, pp. 23–44.

Peirce, Ian. 'Arms, Armour and Warfare in the Eleventh Century,' *Anglo-Norman Studies* 10 (1987), 237–57.

———. 'The Development of the Medieval Sword, c. 850–1300.' In *The Ideals and Practice of Medieval Knighthood,* III. Ed. C. Harper-Bill and R. Harvey. Woodbridge, 1990, pp. 139–58.

———. 'The Knight, His Arms and Armour in the Eleventh and Twelfth Centuries.' In *The Ideals and Practice of Medieval Knighthood.* Ed. C. Harper-Bill and R. Harvey. Woodbridge, 1986, pp. 152–64.

Petersen, Jan. *De norske vikingsverd: En typologisk-kronologisk studie over vikingetidens vaaben.* Christiana (Oslo), 1919.

Pettifer, Adrian. *English Castles: A Guide by Counties.* Woodbridge, 1995.

Poertner, Rudolf. *The Vikings: Rise and Fall of the Norse Sea Kings.* London, 1975.

Poole, R.G. *Viking Poems on War and Peace: A Study in Skaldic Narrative.* Toronto, 1991.

Port, Graham. *Scarborough Castle.* English Heritage. London, 1989.

Powicke, Michael. *Military Obligation in Medieval England: A Study in Liberty and Duty.* Oxford, 1962.

Price, Neil S. 'Viking Armies and Fleets in Brittany: A Case Study for Some General Problems,' *Vikingsymposium* 10 (1991), 7–24.

Purser, Toby Scott. 'Castles of Herefordshire, 1066–1135,' *Medieval History* 4 (1994), 72–90.

Raraty, David G.J. 'Earl Godwine of Wessex: The Origins of his Power and his Political Loyalties,' *History* 74 (1989), 3–19.

Rigg, A.G. *A History of Anglo-Latin Literature 1066–1422.* Cambridge, 1992.

Ritchie, R.L. Graeme. *The Normans in England before Edward the Confessor.* London, 1948.

Rodger, N.A.M. 'Cnut's Geld and the Size of Danish Ships,' *English Historical Review* 110 (1995), 392–403.

———. *The Safeguard of the Sea: A Naval History of Britain, 600–1649.* New York, 1997.

Rogers, Nicholas. 'The Waltham Abbey Relic-List.' In *England in the Eleventh Century: Proceedings of the 1990 Harlaxton Symposium*. Ed. C. Hicks. Stamford, 1992, pp. 157–81.

Rodgers, William Ledyard. *Naval Warfare Under Oars, 4th to 16th Centuries*. Annapolis, 1940.

Rosedahl, Else. *The Vikings*. Trans. S.M. Margeson and K. Williams. Harmondsworth, 1992.

———. *Viking Age Denmark*. Trans. S. Margeson and K. Williams. London, 1982.

Rosenthal, Joel T. 'Edward the Confessor and Robert the Pious: 11th Century Kingship and Biography,' *Mediaeval Studies* 33 (1971), 7–20.

Round, J.H. *Feudal England*. London, 1895.

Rowe, Elizabeth Ashman. 'Historical Invasions/Historiographical Interventions: Snorri Sturluson and the Battle of Stamford Bridge,' *Mediaevalia* 17 (1994), 149–76.

Rowland, Jenny. 'Warfare and Horses in the *Gododdin* and the Problem of Catraeth,' *Cambrian Medieval Celtic Studies* 30 (1995), 13–40.

Rumble, Alexander R., ed. *The Reign of Cnut*. London, 1994.

Sawyer, Birgit and Peter Sawyer. *Medieval Scandinavia: From Conversion to Reformation, circa 800–1500*. Minneapolis, 1993.

Sawyer, Peter. *The Age of the Vikings*. New York, 1962.

———. 'Cnut's Scandinavian Empire.' In *The Reign of Cnut: King of England, Denmark and Norway*. Ed. A.R. Rumble. London, 1994, pp. 10–22.

———. *Kings and Vikings: Scandinavia and Europe, AD 700–1100*. London, 1982.

Schoenfeld, Edward J. 'Anglo-Saxon *Burhs* and Continental *Burgen*: Early Medieval Fortifications in Constitutional Perspective,' *Haskins Society Journal* 6 (1994), 49–66.

Schofield, Guy. 'The Third Battle of 1066,' *History Today* 16 (1966), 688–93.

Scragg, D., ed. *The Battle of Maldon, AD 991*. London, 1991.

Searle, Eleanor. 'Emma the Conqueror.' In *Studies in Medieval History Presented to R. Allen Brown*. Ed. C. Harper-Bill *et al.* Woodbridge, 1989, pp. 281–88.

———. 'Women and the Legitimization of Succession at the Norman Conquest,' *Proceedings of the Battle Conference on Anglo-Norman Studies* 2 (1979), 159–70.

Seymour, W. *Battles in Britain*. 2 vols. London, 1975.

Skaare, Kolbjørn. 'Harald Hardråde som myntherre.' In *Harald Hardråde*. Ed. A. Berg *et al.* Oslo, 1966, pp. 41–67.

Skovgaard-Petersen, Inge. 'Vikingerne I den nyere forskning,' *Historisk tidsskrift* (Copenhagen) (12) 5 (1971), 651–721.

Sleeswyk, André W. 'The Ship of Harold Godwinson,' *Mariner's Mirror* 61 (1981), 87–91.

Solberg, Bergljot. 'Weapons.' In *Medieval Scandinavia: An Encyclopedia*. Ed. P. Pulsiano. New York, 1993, pp. 718–20.

Southern, Richard W. 'The First Life of Edward the Confessor,' *English Historical Review* 58 (1943), 385–400.

Southern, Richard W. *Saint Anselm and his Biographer*. Cambridge, 1963.

Spear, David S. 'Recent Scholarship on the Bayeux Tapestry,' *Annales de Normandie* 42 (1992), 221–26.

Stafford, Pauline. *Queen Emma and Queen Edith: Queenship and Women's Power in Eleventh-Century England*. Oxford, 1997.

————. *Unification and Conquest: A Political and Social History of England in the Tenth and Eleventh Centuries.* London, 1989.

————. 'Women and the Norman Conquest,' *Transactions of the Royal Historical Society*, 6th ser., 4 (1994), 221–49.

Steinnes, A. 'Kor gamal er den norsk leidangsskipnaden?' *Syn of segn* (1929), 49–65.

Stenton, Frank M. *Anglo-Saxon England.* 3rd edn. Oxford History of England. London, 1971.

————. *The First Century of English Feudalism.* Oxford, 1932.

————. *William the Conqueror and the Rule of the Normans.* London, 1928.

Strickland, Matthew. 'Military Technology and Conquest: The Anomaly of Anglo-Saxon England,' *Anglo-Norman Studies* 19 (1996), 353–82.

————. 'Slaughter, Slavery or Ransom: the Impact of the Conquest on Conduct in Warfare.' In *England in the Eleventh Century: Proceedings of the 1990 Harlaxton Symposium.* Ed. C. Hicks. Stamford, 1992, pp. 41–59.

Suppe, Frederick C. 'Who was Rhys Sais? Some Comments on Anglo-Welsh Relations before 1066,' *Haskins Society Journal* 7 (1995), 63–73.

Swanton, M.J. *The Spearheads of the Anglo-Saxon Settlements.* London, 1974.

Tait, James. 'Large Hides and Small Hides,' *English Historical Review* 17 (1902), 280–82.

Tanner, Heather J. 'The Expansion of the Power and Influence of the Counts of Boulogne under Eustace II,' *Anglo-Norman Studies* 14 (1991), 251–86.

Thomas, C. 'The Pictish Class 1 Symbol Stones.' In *Pictish Studies: Settlement, Burial and Art in Dark Age Northern Britain.* Ed. J.G.P. Friell and W.G. Watson. Oxford, 1984, pp. 169–87.

Thompson, A.L. 'The Battle of Stamford Bridge 1066,' *British Army Review* 97 (Apr. 1991), 49–52.

Thomson, Rodney. *William of Malmesbury.* Woodbridge, 1992.

Thordeman, Bengt. *Armour from the Battle of Wisby, 1361.* 2 vols. Stockholm, 1939.

Treadgold, Warren. *Byzantium and Its Army, 284–1081.* Stanford, 1995.

————. *A History of the Byzantine State and Society.* Stanford, 1997.

Turville-Petre, Gabriel. *Haraldr the Hardruler and His Poets.* Dorothea Coke Memorial Lecture in Northern Studies. London, 1966.

Tweddle, Dominic. *The Coppergate Helmet.* York, 1984.

Unger, Richard W. *The Ship in Medieval Economy, 600–1600.* Montreal, 1980.

Vasiliev, A.A. *The History of the Byzantine Empire, 324–1453.* 2nd edn. 2 vols. Madison, 1964.

Verbruggen, J.F. *De krijgkunst in west-europa in de middeleeuwen (IXe tot XIVe eeuw).* Brussels, 1954. English translation: *The Art of Warfare in Western Europe during the Middle Ages.* Woodbridge, 1996.

Vernadsky, G. *Kievan Rus.* New Haven, 1942.

————. *The Origins of Russia.* Oxford, 1959.

Walker, David. 'A Note on Gruffydd ap Llywelyn (1039–63),' *Welsh Historical Review* 1 (1960–63), 83–94.

Walker, Ian W. *Harold: The Last Anglo-Saxon King.* Thrupp, 1997.

Walton, Steven. 'Words of Technological Virtue: *The Battle of Brunanburh* and Anglo-Saxon Sword Manufacture,' *Technology and Culture* 36 (1995), 987–99.

Warner, P. *British Battlefields, the North.* London, 1975.

Whitelock, Dorothy. 'The Dealings of the Kings of England with Northumbria in the Tenth and Eleventh Centuries.' In *The Anglo-Saxons: Studies in Some Aspects of their History and Culture Presented to Bruce Dickins*. Ed. P. Clemoes. London, 1959, pp. 70–88.

Wilkerson, Bertie. 'Freeman and the Crisis of 1051,' *Bulletin of the John Rylands Library* 22 (1938), 3–22.

———. 'Northumbrian Separatism in 1065 and 1066,' *Bulletin of the John Rylands Library* 23 (1939), 504–26.

Williams, Alan R. 'Methods of Manufacture of Swords in Medieval Europe: Illustrated by the Metallography of Some Examples,' *Gladius* 13 (1977), 75–101.

Williams, Ann. ' "Cockles Amongst the Wheat": Danes and English in the Western Midlands in the First Half of the Eleventh Century,' *Midland History* 11 (1986), 1–22.

———. 'The King's Nephew: The Family and Career of Ralph, Earl of Hereford.' In *Studies in Medieval History Presented to R. Allen Brown*. Ed. C. Harper-Bill, C.J. Holdsworth, and J. Nelson. Woodbridge, 1989, pp. 327–43.

———. 'Land and Power in the Eleventh-Century: the Estates of Harold Godwinson,' *Proceedings of the Battle Conference on Anglo-Norman Studies* 3 (1980), 171–87.

———. 'Some Notes and Consideratios on Problems Connected with the English Royal Succession, 860–1066,' *Proceedings of the Battle Conference* 1 (1978), 144–66, 225–33.

Wilson, David M. 'Some Neglected Late Anglo-Saxon Swords,' *Medieval Archaeology* 9 (1965), 32–54.

INDEX